FREEDOM TO HARM

FREEDOM TO HARM

The Lasting Legacy of the Laissez Faire Revival

Thomas O. McGarity

Yale

UNIVERSITY

PRESS

New Haven & London

Published with assistance from the foundation established in memory of
Calvin Chapin of the Class of 1788, Yale College.

Yale University Press books may be purchased in quantity for educational,
business, or promotional use. For information, please e-mail sales.press@yale.edu
(U.S. office) or sales@yaleup.co.uk (U.K. office).

Set in Electra and Trajan types by Newgen North America.
Printed in the United States of America.

Library of Congress Cataloging-in-Publication Data

McGarity, Thomas O.
Freedom to harm : the lasting legacy of the laissez faire revival / Thomas O. McGarity.
pages cm
Includes bibliographical references and index.
ISBN 978-0-300-14124-5 (cloth)
1. Deregulation–United States.   2. Consumer protection–United States.
3. Environmental law—United States.   I. Title.
KF1600.M395 2013
338.973—dc23
2012043155

A catalogue record for this book is available from the British Library.

This paper meets the requirements of ANSI/NISO Z39.48–1992 (Permanence of Paper).

10 9 8 7 6 5 4 3 2 1

CONTENTS

PREFACE

In a very real sense, I began writing this book when I began my career as a professor of torts and environmental law in the autumn of 1977. Far from the Washington, D.C., action in Lawrence, Kansas, I paid a premium to have the Washington Post mailed to me so that when the papers arrived several days after they were printed, I could extract clippings for files that I was building on various topics of relevance to my teaching and research interests. I labeled one of those files "Assault on Regulation," and I included in that file clippings from the Washington Post and copies of various articles from the trade press and magazines on the activities of the Chamber of Commerce, the American Enterprise Institute, the Heritage Foundation, and other institutions that were attacking recently created regulatory agencies attempting to implement the progressive legislation that Congress had enacted in the late 1960s and early 1970s.

At the time, I viewed the assault as more than the predictable response of an industry to a burdensome regulatory program because it seemed to come from multiple institutions and had a strong ideological component. As I listened to radio commentator (and likely presidential candidate) Ronald Reagan complain about federal regulation in the mornings over breakfast, I realized that there must be more to the assaults than just resistance to change. Though it seemed unlikely to me at the time that federal regulation could become a serious political issue that might affect the votes of ordinary people, Governor Reagan apparently thought that it had political salience.

By the time I had moved to Austin, Texas, in the fall of 1980, the single file folder had grown into a set of files labeled "Assault on EPA," "Assault on OSHA," and so on. Then, as it became clear after the 1980 election that the assaults were coming from the White House and from within the agencies as well as from the regulated industries and the think tanks, I decided to devote at least part of my scholarly efforts to studying this phenomenon.

I did not realize at the time that I was observing the first of several assaults on regulation and that the assaults would expand to include my other teaching interest—the law of torts. As the years passed, the single file grew to several overflowing file cabinets and much more information stored in electronic files on my computer. On numerous occasions, I would dip into the files for sources as I wrote books on regulatory impact analysis and OSHA and articles on various aspects of the regulatory reform movement. Finally, it appeared that the assaults had run their course in the wake of a series of crises involving unsafe toys, unsafe food, global warming, and a catastrophic financial meltdown. I thought the time was ripe to tell the remarkable story of the business community's concerted efforts to free itself from the restraints of federal regulation and the threat of tort liability. At the same time, I wanted to show how the great expansion of economic freedom that resulted from these efforts had weakened the regulatory and common law protections that most citizens take for granted.

This book is the product of that project. It tells the story of how the business community and its allies in the conservative funding community, conservative think tanks, and conservative public interest groups seized the mantle of "reform" in a bold and sustained attempt to roll back the regulatory programs and civil justice reforms of the 1960s and 1970s with the ultimate goal of returning to the laissez faire benchmark of the late nineteenth century. It highlights the impacts of the regulatory "reforms" on the beneficiaries of federal regulatory programs in the areas of worker safety, environmental protection, drug and device safety, food safety and nutrition, transportation safety, consumer protection, and systemic financial protection. And it examines the impacts of changes in the civil justice system on the victims of irresponsible corporate behavior. My overall thesis is that thirty years of regulatory and tort reform have disturbed the necessary balance among economic freedom, corporate responsibility, and corporate accountability to such an extent that companies have acquired more freedom to harm consumers, workers, and the environment than at any time since the New Deal and perhaps since the late nineteenth century.

As I was preparing the prospectus for this book, there were unmistakable signs of change in the air. The 2006 elections had delivered both houses of Congress to the Democratic Party, and many of the prevailing candidates had run against the George W. Bush Administration's deregulatory agenda. In addition, Congress passed two new laws—the Credit Rating Agency Reform Act of 2006 and the Consumer Product Safety Improvement Act of 2008—that for the first time in two decades expanded the protections afforded by federal regulatory agencies. As I was preparing the manuscript, the 2008 elections increased the Democratic majorities in both houses and produced an exciting young president who had run a campaign based on the theme of hope. In addition, an ongoing confluence of crises had increased public awareness of the extent to which individuals were vulnerable to unconstrained market forces. The stars seemed to be aligned for another "transformative moment" when Congress enacts comprehensive laws designed to change the incentives of the companies that threaten public health and welfare.

That moment has apparently passed without comprehensive legislation, but Congress did enact some important "patch-and-repair" statutes that will offer greater protections in the future, if the agencies can effectively implement them. Still, I approached writing the "solutions" chapter with a sense of disappointment that so few of the changes that thoughtful scholars had suggested for restoring the balance among freedom, responsibility, and accountability had been accomplished and a sense of foreboding that a fourth assault on federal regulation and the civil justice system seemed to be underway.

As always, I am indebted to many people and institutions for making this book possible. The Joe R. and Teresa Lozano Long Endowed Chair in Administrative Law at the University of Texas School of Law freed up my summers for research and writing. My assistant, Dottie Lee, provided administrative support, and my library liaison, Barbara Bridges, made the superb resources of the Tarlton Law Library easily accessible to me. The scholars and policy analysts that make up the Center for Progressive Reform were a continuing source of ideas, inspiration, and feedback. In addition to providing a constant flow of information for my expanding files, my wife, Cathy, served as an insightful sounding board and a continuing source of inspiration.

INTRODUCTION: TWO TRAGEDIES

On December 6, 1907, a train of fourteen three-ton cars hauling coal from the interior of the Consolidation Coal Company's number 6 mine in Monongah, West Virginia, broke free and descended 1,500 feet into the darkness below. The company had anticipated this sort of accident and had installed a "derailing switch" at the mine entrance. The young man in charge of the derailing switch, however, was also responsible for keeping the mine's ventilation fans oiled, and he was oiling a fan when the runaway train sped by. When it reached the bottom of the mine, a huge explosion lit up the early morning sky. Within minutes, the accident had taken the lives of 361 mostly immigrant miners who were working below. It was and remains the worst industrial disaster in U.S. history.[1]

At the time of the accident, Consolidation Coal was struggling to meet the "nearly insatiable appetite" of the country's railroad, steel, and steamship companies for coal. During the boom years of the early twentieth century, the coal industry was highly profitable, but wages remained pitifully low in West Virginia, where the economic power of the large coal companies and their financiers combined with a corrupt political culture to keep unions at bay. Monongah, West Virginia, was a classic company town in which miners and their families lived in company-owned houses and purchased their food and supplies from the company store with company-issued "script." Dust from the coal operations and emissions from the company's 320 coke ovens bathed the town in a cloudy soup of toxic air pollution.

No federal agency was responsible for regulating coal mining in 1907, but the Commerce Department maintained a small staff to investigate mine accidents. The state of West Virginia had one of the weakest regulatory programs in the country. The "fire boss" on duty at the Monongah mine was an uncertified

22-year-old with less than one year's experience. The state mine safety inspector had allowed this deviation from the otherwise applicable certification and
three-year experience requirements because the company had convinced the
agency that the mine was not "gassy," despite the fact that a methane explosion
had killed 34 miners in a nearby mine the previous week.

Teams of investigators from West Virginia, Ohio, Pennsylvania, and the
Commerce Department reached different conclusions as to the precise cause
of the disaster, but they agreed that government needed to play a stronger role
in protecting miners from the risky mining practices. The Commerce Department's Clarence Hall, one of the nation's preeminent experts on coal mine
safety, concluded that the country needed "more intelligent legislation, more
rigid regulations and better practice connected with all mining operation."[2]
The Ohio investigators opined that "the sacrifice of over six hundred lives by
mine explosions in [three states] during the present month ought to . . . prompt
every possible precaution against such calamities."[3] The West Virginia state legislature called for additional studies but took no further action. A local grand
jury ultimately exonerated the company of all criminal responsibility for the
disaster.

After several families of victims sued Consolidation, the company's president
asked its lead attorney whether it would "not be cheaper and safer to keep a stiff
upper lip and fight it out—than to do anything more than charity requires."[4]
Consolidation paid for the dead miners' funeral expenses and provided compensation of $150 for each widow and $75 for every child of a dead miner under
the age of 16. Since the state and federal courts of the era did not award compensation for accidents attributable to the negligence of the plaintiff or any
of his fellow workers, that was essentially the end of the matter. The lawsuits
were either dismissed or settled for small sums. Within two months, the mine
was back in operation and the victims' families were *persona non grata* in the
company town.[5]

Almost exactly a century later, on August 6, 2007, instruments at the University of Utah recorded what appeared to be a modest 3.9 magnitude earthquake
in the vicinity of Crandall Canyon, Utah, where the Murray Energy Corporation was operating a small coal mine. One of the seismologists on duty called
the 911 emergency unit in Huntington, Utah, to report the strong likelihood
that a mine in the vicinity had just suffered a major cave-in. Because the Crandall Canyon mine was among the deepest in the country, the tremendous pressures generated by the overburden required miners to leave very large "pillars"
of coal in place to hold up the roofs of the chambers. The seismologists knew
that when the forces proved too much for one of those pillars the collapse could

generate earthquake-like seismic activity, and accompanying aftershocks could go on for days.[6]

Within minutes of the seismic shock, four of the ten miners who were working in a remote section of the Murray Energy mine reported that the roof had collapsed and that six of their fellow miners were missing. Rescue efforts were greatly hampered by the fact that the miners' location was unknown because the collapse had severed existing communications lines. After ten fruitless days of intense rescue efforts, the situation changed, in the words of Utah Governor Jon Huntsman, "from a tragedy to a catastrophe" when one of the many seismic jolts (called "bumps") that followed the original collapse caused a wall to explode in a chamber in which the rescuers were working. A second rescue mission successfully located the rescuers, three of whom later died and six of whom were badly injured. At that point, the federal Mine Safety and Health Administration (MSHA) suspended rescue activities. The company later closed the mine permanently.[7]

Prior to the collapse, the company had been employing an especially risky technique, called "retreat" or "cut and gut" mining, in which the machinery removes the large support pillars and the chamber then collapses as the miners and equipment retreat toward the entrance. Because the operator encounters no expense in reaching the coal in the pillars and little additional expense in extracting it, the industry refers to it as "free coal" or "pure profit." The National Institute of Occupational Safety and Health, however, characterizes retreat mining as "one of the most hazardous activities in underground mining." Although the previous operator concluded that removing the pillars would be too dangerous, MSHA had approved Murray Energy's retreat mining plan. Some observers suggested that MSHA officials had not objected to retreat mining at the Crandall Canyon mine because they did not want to tangle with its volatile owner.[8]

Robert Murray was a committed advocate of the American free enterprise system and an outspoken opponent of governmental regulation of business activity, especially insofar as it affected his businesses. He blamed Congress, bureaucrats, and environmentalists for many of society's problems, and he vigorously opposed as "extremely misguided" the congressional efforts to strengthen the mine safety statute. As with many small and medium-sized mining companies, Murray's mines had a lengthy history of violations of MSHA regulations. Between early 2004 and the August 2007 accident, MSHA inspectors had issued 324 citations to the Crandall Canyon mine, 107 of which were for "significant and substantial" violations, a category that included only hazards that could "result in an injury or illness of a reasonably serious nature." In 2003, a Murray

Energy subsidiary in Kentucky and four of its officials were convicted of know-ingly violating MSHA ventilation regulations for four years and for lying to federal investigators about the practice.[9]

At the first press conference following the Crandall Canyon collapse, Mur-ray's laissez faire ideology was on full display. Before addressing the pressing question of the status of the rescue operations, he reminded the national audi-ence that the coal industry was vital to the national economy. He complained that "every one of these global warming bills that has been introduced in Con-gress [will] eliminate the coal industry and will increase your electric rates four- to five-fold." When he finally turned his attention to the accident, he assured the reporters that the disaster "was caused by an earthquake, not some-thing that Murray Energy . . . did or our employees did or our management did" and that the operations at the mine were "in compliance with all laws and in ac-cordance with all mining plans that were approved by the regulatory agencies." Public relations experts later characterized Murray's extraordinary performance as "callous," "damaging," and "unhelpful," but to the local *Salt Lake Tribune*, it was just "Murray being Murray."[10]

When Murray finally allowed the district manager of MSHA to say a few words at the end of the press conference, the diminutive federal official de-clined to defend the agency from Murray's attacks. His deferential posture was characteristic of an agency that had, by 2007, become a shadow of the institu-tion that Congress created in 1977 to prevent mining accidents from happen-ing. The head of the agency, Richard Stickler, had been a mining company executive for thirty years prior to directing the Pennsylvania Bureau of Deep Mine Safety from 1997 through 2003, a period that, according to the president of the United Mineworkers union, had been "marked by repeated attempts to limit regulations and reduce health and safety for miners."[11] Unable to secure Senate confirmation for Stickler, President George W. Bush had awarded him a "recess appointment" that was good until the end of the congressional session. During the Bush Administration, the agency had shifted its enforcement strat-egy from one of assessing fines for every significant violation to one of "com-pliance assistance," under which inspectors (renamed "compliance assistance specialists") worked cooperatively with mine operators to come up with ways to avoid future violations.[12]

The Monongah disaster came at the end of a thirty-year period of American history in which the nation experimented with a radically noninterventionist approach to the relationship between government and a relatively new eco-nomic entity called the private corporation. During this period, which Mark Twain aptly labeled the "Gilded Age," corporations were free to pursue their economic ends with little or no governmental interference. Under the "laissez faire minimalist" ideology that dominated the political economy, the proper role of government was to protect private property, enforce private contracts, and ensure domestic tranquility through clear and transparent rules of civil and criminal liability. The catchword was "economic freedom." Extending from the post–Civil War Reconstruction until the first decade of the twentieth century, the Gilded Age spawned tremendous economic growth and huge disparities in wealth, culturally diverse cities and widespread environmental degradation, peaceful interstate commerce and government-sanctioned violence by private armies against unruly workers.

The Huntington disaster came after a similar thirty-year period in which advocates for the nation's business community had, with some success, pressed policymakers to resurrect many of the Gilded Age's laissez faire minimalist policies. This book will refer to this later period as the "Laissez Faire Revival." The revival followed a chaotic period extending from the mid-1960s through the mid-1970s during which Congress had enacted dozens of statutes protecting workers from irresponsible employers, the environment from irresponsible polluters, and consumers from irresponsible product manufacturers, bankers, and salespersons. At the same time, the common law courts had reworked deeply encrusted tort doctrines to impose greater liability on companies whose products and activities caused damage to their consumers, their workers, their neighbors, and the environment. The legal and institutional infrastructure in place at the end of this activist period (referred to here as the *"protective governmental infrastructure"*) placed far more constraints on the economic freedom of corporate America than any legal regime that preceded it.

Adopting a strategy of "divert and delay," the business community lobbied against the new statutes and resisted the efforts of newly empowered regulatory agencies and common law plaintiffs to implement the changes. The Laissez Faire Revival, however, required more than resistance to change. It also took the determined efforts of a small number of far-sighted philanthropists and academics to create an *idea infrastructure* capable of reviving the ideology of laissez faire minimalism, and it took a sophisticated *influence infrastructure* capable of popularizing that ideology and of persuading Congress, the executive branch, and the courts to scale back constraints that those institutions had been putting into place since the end of the Gilded Age. During the Laissez Faire Revival, the business community's idea and influence infrastructures launched three vigorous assaults on the protective governmental infrastructure. In the interregnums between the assaults, the business community continued to resist the enactment of new interventionist legislation and additional expansions of legal doctrines, yielding ground only in the wake of crises of sufficient magnitude to generate strong public demand for additional protections. This strategy proved remarkably successful. By the mid-point of the George W. Bush Administration, governmental interference with economic freedom was at the lowest level since the years prior to the New Deal, and arguably since the Gilded Age. Although the foundational statutes and common law principles of the Public Interest Era that had brought about much improvement in public health, environmental protection, and consumer welfare remained in place, the protective governmental infrastructure was timid and severely debilitated.

This book tells the story of how the business community's idea and influence infrastructures gained the political advantage and forced a renegotiation of an ongoing social bargain between the business community and the people. Part I will describe the evolution of the social bargain from the Gilded Age to the Laissez Faire Revival and explore the tension among the concepts of freedom, responsibility, and accountability that informed the bargaining process. It will highlight the crisis, response, and reaction pattern that characterized the Progressive Era (a period roughly extending from 1905 to 1925), the New Deal Era (a period spanning the years 1932 through 1946), and the Public Interest Era (the decade extending from 1965 through 1975) through which Congress and the common law courts created and maintained a protective governmental infrastructure with the power to define new rules of responsibility for the business community and to hold them accountable for violating those rules. Part II will describe how the business community and a handful of conservative foundations seized the offensive by creating the idea and influence infrastructures needed for a sustained attack on the protective governmental infrastructure.

Part III will describe the three vigorous assaults that the business community launched against the protective governmental infrastructure during the first years of the Reagan Administration, the 104th (Gingrich) Congress, and the first George W. Bush Administration. Chapters 8–14 will explore the impact of the assaults on seven broad areas of government regulation—occupational safety and health, environmental protection, drug and device safety, food safety, transportation safety, financial protection, and consumer protection. Chapter 15 will examine the related attacks on the civil justice system at both the state and federal levels.

Part IV will explore the institutional legacy of the Laissez Faire Revival and the prospects for a major renegotiation of the social bargain to rebuild and extend the protective governmental infrastructure. Chapter 16 will assess the damaged state of the institutions of responsibility and accountability that make up the protective governmental infrastructure. A confluence of crises during the first decade of the twenty-first century presented an ideal opportunity to re-negotiate the social bargain. Chapter 17 will describe the efforts of proponents of greater governmental protections to shift the balance during the first three years of the Obama Administration, highlighting efforts to enact more protective laws and to implement the existing laws more aggressively. Congress and the Obama Administration brought about some much-needed patches and repairs to the protective governmental infrastructure prior to the Republican takeover of the House of Representatives in 2011, but they accomplished very little by way of renegotiating the bargain. Chapter 18 will offer some ideas for bolder proactive changes that can begin moving the American political economy away from the laissez faire benchmark and toward a better balance among freedom, responsibility, and accountability.

The question remains whether the Laissez Faire Revival has run its course. At this writing, a fourth assault is well underway as the idea and influence infrastructures of the business community gear up for what they hope will be a takeover of both houses of Congress by a Republican Party that has become even more favorably disposed ideologically to removing the statutory edifices of the protective governmental infrastructure than in the past. The future of the protections that government affords its citizens from the risks to their physical and economic well-being posed by powerful economic actors in the marketplace hangs in the balance.

Part One

THE EVOLVING SOCIAL BARGAIN

With the same trowel that President George Washington used to lay the cornerstone of the United States Capitol, President Franklin Delano Roosevelt in 1936 set the cornerstone for the long-awaited headquarters of the Federal Trade Commission at the apex of the Federal Triangle in Washington, D.C. Soon thereafter, the New Deal "Public Works of Art Project" commissioned sculptor Michael Lantz to create an appropriate landmark for the building that would house the powerful federal agency. The resulting Art Deco statue portrays a muscular male clothed only in bell-bottom trousers struggling with both sinewy hands to restrain a powerful stallion. Entitled "Man Restraining Trade," the statue symbolized the ongoing struggle between the powerful forces of the free market and the governmental agencies responsible for reining in those forces to protect vulnerable citizens from harm.[1]

The impressive monument is an apt symbol for a vision of American society that emerged during the New Deal in response to the unrestrained free enterprise economy that yielded the Great Depression. It represents an evolving social bargain between the powerful economic actors driving the American economy and the citizens who benefit from that economy and, through their elected representatives, determine how it shall be governed. It reflects a general understanding on both sides of the bargain that while the business community should be free to innovate and compete, that freedom does not extend to products and practices that pose significant risks to the public. The ever-changing outcome of the bargain is the web of legislation, regulations, and common law rules that govern the marketplace and determine when injured citizens may hold companies liable for losses they have sustained.

The evolving social bargain represents a continuing adjustment and readjustment of business and social institutions to three compelling but competing

9

ideals—freedom, responsibility, and accountability. First, it recognizes that in order to reap the material benefits of a growing economy, society must give productive business entities the freedom to operate without unwarranted governmental interference. Even in the times of greatest economic and social turmoil, the vast majority of Americans have recognized (or at least reluctantly acknowledged) that the United States economy is a capitalist economy in which business entities must have the freedom to attract investors, contract for labor, and provide goods and services to citizens who are willing and able to pay for them.

Second, while business entities are generally free to carry out their activities on their own terms, they also have certain moral and legal responsibilities to their workers, their customers, and their neighbors. In their legitimate pursuit of bottom-line profitability, they must adhere to standards and norms established by the common law courts and the governmental entities that regulate industrial activity and commerce in the public interest. The government in turn has a correlative responsibility to protect potentially affected citizens. The system works best when the relevant governmental actors clearly articulate private sector responsibilities in advance through fair and open procedures in rules, regulations, or permit conditions. But the absence of a bright line rule does not diminish a company's obligation to adhere to general norms as articulated and enforced by common law courts.

Third, when companies violate the relevant rules of responsibility, they must be held accountable for their actions. Government must vigorously enforce the relevant rules, regulations, and permits, and injured citizens should have access to the common law courts to seek compensation from irresponsible companies and thereby hold them accountable for the damage they caused.

At different periods in our history, economic and political conditions have emphasized one or another of these three ideals, but both sides to the bargain have always recognized, or at least paid lip service to, the legitimacy of all three. The disagreements arise out of the unavoidable tension between freedom on the one hand and responsibility and accountability on the other. The essence of the bargain at any given time lies in the details of the evolving legal requirements and institutional arrangements that are worked out in the executive, legislative, and judicial branches of government.

The social bargain is always in a constant state of renegotiation as the political climate changes in ways that advantage one side or the other. The negotiation goes on almost imperceptibly over long periods of prosperity as the economy grows, people perceive their situations to be improving, and the protections of the past gradually erode under constant pressure from the business community for greater freedom. The terms of the bargain can, however, shift dramatically during periods of economic or social crisis in which an aroused public insists that the government do something to protect it from the widely apparent consequences of unconstrained economic activity. Sometimes referred to as "transformative moments," these short bursts of legislative and judicial activity are inevitably followed by much longer periods of initial implementation, grudging acceptance, and gradual erosion as powerful economic actors reluctantly change their ways (at least for a time) but continue to press for greater economic freedom.[2] The pattern then repeats itself over subsequent periods of social ferment and quiescence.

This book examines the negotiation of the social bargain that occurred during the last quarter of the twentieth century and the first decade of the twenty-first century. In many ways that renegotiation resembled past periods of prosperity during which a satisfied citizenry demanded little of the economic actors who were perceived to be creating a general prosperity. In other important ways, however, it represented a dramatic departure from past periods of erosion during which the terms of the bargain were gradually readjusted in ways that generally expanded the freedom of previously constrained economic actors.

This time, the "business community," the men and women who had benefited most from the American free enterprise system as the owners and managers of the corporations that dominated the economy, recognized that the cumulative outcome of past negotiations had been a burdensome protective governmental infrastructure. This time, it was not content with merely resisting the general trend toward increased governmental intrusions. Instead, it seized the "reform" mantle and launched a vigorous counter-offensive aimed at changing the existing institutional arrangements dramatically in much the same way that the reformers of the past had erected the protective governmental infrastructure during previous periods of social crisis. This time, the target of the reforms would be "big government," rather than "big business." And this time, the goal would be a return to a political economy that more closely resembled the laissez faire benchmark of the Gilded Age. This remarkably successful 30-year project ushered in a Laissez Faire Revival that continues to dominate the American political economy.

The Laissez Faire Benchmark

The American economy of the antebellum years was dominated by farmers, traders, and small shops and factories owned by single proprietors or a few partners. The corporate form was reserved for financing large-scale public projects (roads, dams, canals, and the like) operating under state-issued charters that subjected the underlying business entities to extensive oversight and control. Under the forceful prodding of advocates for economic growth, however, state legislatures in the years leading up to the Civil War began to enact general incorporation statutes that permitted private business entities to incorporate under charters drafted by their lawyers and approved by state agencies. Because it allowed a single company to draw on the resources of thousands of investors, this new legal entity swept the nation in the postwar years.[1]

The emergence of the corporate form blended nicely with the laissez faire ideology of an expanding class of economic elites in the growing industrial economy. For the laissez faire gurus of the Gilded Age, the ultimate repository of virtue was the marketplace. Social Darwinism's assurance of the "survival of the fittest" provided a "scientific" underpinning for the values of hard work and self-reliance, while providing an objective rationale for public policies that tolerated large disparities in wealth. As state and local Chambers of Commerce promoted laissez faire ideology as the only respectable civic virtue, free market values were championed in media, the classrooms, and the churches.[2]

The laissez faire ideology that dominated the Gilded Age, referred to in this book as "laissez faire minimalism," featured four fundamental tenets.[3] The first—*ensuring economic liberty*—shielded consensual private economic arrangements from governmental interference except for very limited purposes like protecting individuals and their property from force and fraud. The second tenet—*protecting private property*—was necessary to maintain the incentive to

accumulate wealth, which was in turn the primary stimulant for effort and innovation. The third tenet—*enforcing private contracts*—was critical to a smoothly
functioning capitalist economy under which private wealth increased through
investment in socially useful goods and services. The fourth tenet—*ensuring industrial peace and economic growth*—recognized an affirmative role for the government in stimulating economic activity by sponsoring public works projects,
making commonly held resources available for development and exploitation,
preventing inflation of the currency, and ensuring that companies could pursue legitimate trade without fear of disruption from striking laborers, picketing
boycotters and other disgruntled disturbers of the peace.[4]

For Gilded Age elites who believed that "economic liberty" and "individual
liberty" were inextricably linked, the logical next step was to afford corporations the status of "personhood." State courts abandoned the theory that the
corporation was a mere legal construct allowed to exist as a "concession" of the
state legislature, and the Supreme Court then bestowed on it the constitutional
status of personhood without even entertaining legal argument on the matter.
The final step in the legal evolution of the corporation was to weave "economic
freedom" for corporations into the texture of the Bill of Rights. Since state law
permitted corporate persons to hold title to property, they could claim the protections of both the due process clause and the "takings" clause, under which
government could not "take" private property for public use without paying
just compensation. The Court held that governmental intervention was justified only when an entire industry was "affected with the public interest," and
it narrowly construed legislation that met this test to constrict governmental
authority.[5]

At the same time, courts expanded traditional land-based notions of "property" to include virtually anything of value in the marketplace, thus rendering
suspect any government action that reduced a private entity's profits. Labor was
merely a form of property that workers could freely sell to employers, and legislative attempts to regulate the terms and conditions of such contracts (through
minimum wage, minimum hour, or child labor laws) unconstitutionally deprived laborers of property without due process of law. That the arrangement
was imposed upon an economically weaker party by a powerful corporation
wielding the collective resources of its shareholders on a "take it or leave it
basis" was irrelevant to the law.[6]

If the courts were inclined to restrain governmental attempts to set high standards of corporate responsibility, they were even more willing to limit corporate
accountability by fashioning business-friendly common law rules. First, a manufacturer of a defective product other than food could be held liable to direct

consumers and others in the chain of title, but not to third parties who were injured by the product because they lacked "privity of contract." Second, the common law adopted a fault-based "negligence" standard that forced the plaintiff to prove that the risk to others posed by the defendant's conduct outweighed its benefits. Third, the courts adopted an "unholy trinity" of defenses that made it exceedingly difficult for injured workers to receive compensation from their employers for injuries due to unreasonably dangerous workplace conditions. The doctrine of *contributory negligence* precluded recovery by a worker whose own negligence contributed in the slightest to the injury; the *fellow servant rule* precluded recovery if another worker's negligence caused the injury, even if the employer was negligent in supervising the workers; and the *assumption of the risk* defense allowed employers to argue that the employee should not recover because he accepted the job with full knowledge of the risks involved. Fourth, to reduce the threat of ruinous liability to fledgling industries, the courts also restricted the scope of compensable damage to the clearly proven economic consequences of obvious physical injury.[7]

With economic power came political power as the industrialists and bankers behind the largest corporations were able to determine the makeup of many state legislatures, state courts, and to some degree even Congress. Corporate entities had the power to "bend laws and regulations to [their] own purposes," but that power was incomplete. Crises caused by abuses of corporate power could stimulate state legislatures and Congress into action. Nearly every state created a commission to regulate railroad rates and shipping practices, and about half of the states enacted antitrust legislation and/or created agencies to regulate banks and insurance companies. Twenty-five states enacted pure food and drug laws, and twenty-one states created agencies to conduct workplace inspections to protect worker health and safety.[8]

Laissez faire minimalism yielded undeniable benefits for society. By almost every conceivable measure, the United States economy grew during the last quarter of the nineteenth century. The unconstrained growth, however, came at a terrible social cost as the large corporations that dominated the economy stubbornly resisted even weak regulatory constraints and avoided being held accountable for much socially destructive behavior. Many of the state laws were only sporadically enforced, and others were declared unconstitutional by state and federal courts.[9]

Because the easy availability of unskilled immigrant labor severely limited the negotiating power of any individual worker, employers determined the rules of the workplace. Most workers labored for ten hours a day six days a week, often in dangerous conditions. Mining companies could demand huge sacrifices from employees, and they easily replaced those who could not bear the strain or were injured or killed in the effort. The Monongah explosion was merely the worst of an ongoing series of major mining disasters that injured or killed thousands of workers. Railroad workers, too, were killed and maimed by the thousands in the push to extend commerce into the nation's interior. By the end of the century, approximately 2,000,000 injuries and 35,000 deaths per year were attributable to job-related accidents. Most of the 4,500 annual railroad grade crossing accidents resulted in fatalities. Flimsy rail construction combined with poor scheduling and increased length, weight, and speed of trains to cause hundreds of devastating derailments.[10]

Companies paid little attention to the adverse environmental consequences of the by-products of mass production. Coal combustion, the primary source of energy for homes, offices, and industrial facilities, generated thousands of tons of particulate emissions that contributed to lung disease and cloaked urban areas in soot. Sulfur dioxide emissions from railroad locomotives, industrial boilers, foundries, and mills often overpowered nearby neighbors. Although most cities paid some attention to municipal garbage and sewage disposal, they rarely regulated activities within the gates of industrial facilities. The modest municipal pollution control ordinances of the day were generally toothless and seldom enforced. When they were enforced, the courts were as likely to set them aside as unconstitutional impediments to interstate commerce as to issue injunctive relief. And common law nuisance lawsuits did not fare much better.[11]

Another important Gilded Age commercial development was the use of advertising for mass marketing of consumer products. Although consumers had been sickened and defrauded by purveyors of adulterated food for centuries, the advent of large-scale advertising and impersonal multi-state markets made massive consumer fraud a commonplace occurrence.[12]

Not everyone approved of the blatant corruption of the marketplace and the political system. An assemblage of Eastern establishment professionals known as Liberal Republicans and later called "Mugwumps" were generally suspicious of the machinations of the large banking and manufacturing concerns of the day. They were, nevertheless, strong proponents of laissez faire, especially at the federal level, and they generally opposed government intervention into "properly conducted" private economic arrangements. Believers in the power of careful deliberation among educated elites, they supported programs for solving social problems that drew upon professional expertise.[13] The populist movement that emerged from the human suffering during the economic depression brought on by a bank failure of 1873 presented a far more serious threat to the Gilded Age laissez faire regime. Like the equally unruly urban labor movement, the populists wanted not just to clean up the government, but to use it proactively to protect farmers from corporate abuse. Despite much commonality of interest, however, the three movements found it difficult to forge an effective political alliance.[14]

The business community forcefully rejected the claims of all three movements and resisted all of their efforts to regulate economic behavior. Railroads successfully opposed state legislation requiring automatic airbrakes and automatic couplers. The American Mining Congress came up with its own standards for mine safety, and it persuaded Congress to establish a mine safety program in the Bureau of Mines to adopt those standards and preempt more stringent state standards. The newspapers of the time were nearly always hostile to both organized labor and organized farmers. With vastly superior resources at its disposal, the business community ultimately prevailed. William Jennings Bryan's stunning defeat at the hands of William McKinley in the 1896 elections, to which the business community contributed unprecedented sums, eliminated the only serious political threat to the lengthy reign of laissez faire minimalism.[15]

FREEDOM REINED: THE PROGRESSIVE ERA THROUGH THE PUBLIC INTEREST ERA

During three critical periods of American history, a confluence of crises revealed the consequences of unconstrained economic freedom in vivid tragedies that were too stark to ignore. At these junctures, the terms of the social bargain were readjusted to reflect a more protective balance among the values of freedom, responsibility, and accountability. During the Progressive Era of the early twentieth century, the New Deal Era of the 1930s, and the Public Interest Era of the late 1960s and early 1970s, Congress enacted bold legislation designed to bring about fundamental change in the relationship between the business community and its consumers, workers, neighbors, and environment. During each of these periods of large-scale crisis and reform, the business community adopted a strategy of "diversion and delay," but to little avail as Congress enacted powerful new laws and created new implementing institutions to provide a more protective governmental infrastructure.

With each wave of protective legislation, the newly empowered agencies initially wrote stringent rules and held private sector actors accountable for violating them. As the crises faded from public attention, however, the agencies settled into routines, and the regulated companies challenged the rules in court, demanded exemptions and variances, and pressed the envelope of compliance. Corporate targets of personal injury, nuisance, and consumer fraud claims adopted scorched earth strategies designed to force plaintiffs' attorneys to spend so much time and money on the litigation that their contingency fees were unlikely to cover their costs. The business community gradually freed itself of many of the restraints until the next confluence of crises yielded public demands for more comprehensive change, and the cycle of reform, reaction, and erosion repeated itself.

THE PROGRESSIVE ERA

As the twentieth century dawned, a growing middle class of shopkeepers, managers, professionals, clergymen, and skilled laborers created a variety of civic associations to demand laws protecting workers, consumers, and the environment from dangerous business practices. An invigorated mainstream press joined in their calls for reform. Unlike their populist predecessors, twentieth-century progressives adopted a "scientific" approach to solving social problems that emphasized expertise over empowerment. Their efforts received a jump start when President William McKinley was assassinated on September 6, 1901, and Theodore Roosevelt assumed the presidency. Although Roosevelt began his political career as a laissez faire minimalist, his views underwent a radical transformation when he witnessed economic freedom in action during a personal tour of New York City tenements. The Progressive Era reached its zenith during the first decade of the twentieth century when a series of crises, beginning with the Monongah disaster and extending through the Triangle Shirtwaist fire of March 25, 1911 (in which gross violations of local safety codes resulted in the deaths of 146 mostly immigrant women), generated public outcries for action that could no longer be ignored.[1]

Although the progressives had many ideas for reforming American business, the legislative output at the federal level was surprisingly thin. The most significant reform came as a congressional response to a crisis of public confidence in the nation's food supply brought on by Upton Sinclair's novel *The Jungle* and a series of related articles in *Ladies Home Journal* and *Colliers*. The Meat Inspection Act of 1906 required a government inspector from the United States Department of Agriculture (USDA) to be on the premises at all times that cattle were being slaughtered and processed in a meat packing plant. The Pure Food and Drug Act of 1906 prevented the sale in interstate commerce of "adulterated" or mislabeled drugs and foods other than meat. Congress assigned implementation responsibilities to the Bureau of Chemistry in the USDA.[2]

Following the Monongah disaster, the coal industry realized that some form of federal legislation was inevitable, and it worked to secure the enactment of a 1910 statute that created a Bureau of Mines in the Department of Interior and authorized it to conduct investigations into the causes and prevention of mining accidents. But the law explicitly declined to grant any power to act on the information it gathered. Congress reacted to the carnage among railroad workers (4,534 job-related deaths and 87,644 injuries in 1907 alone) by creating a new federal cause of action for damages attributable to negligent workplace conditions, and it substituted a comparative negligence regime for the harsh "unholy trinity" of common law defenses that had effectively prevented railway workers from obtaining compensation from their employers during the Gilded Age. After the Triangle Shirtwaist fire, several states enacted rudimentary worker protection laws.[3]

In 1913, President Woodrow Wilson's trusted economic advisor, Louis Brandeis, penned a series of influential articles in *Harper's Weekly* (later turned into a popular book entitled *Other People's Money*) in which he recommended strong regulatory constraints on banking institutions. Soon thereafter, Congress enacted the Federal Reserve Act of 1913, which created the Federal Reserve Board (the Fed) and gave it limited powers to regulate the banking industry. Wilson began a long tradition of deference to Wall Street, however, when he appointed J. P. Morgan's chief lieutenant to be the first chairman.[4] With Wilson's strong support, Congress also enacted the Federal Trade Commission Act of 1914, which created the Federal Trade Commission (FTC) and gave it a broad and flexible mandate to issue orders prohibiting "unfair methods of competition" and unlawful restraints on trade.[5]

Progressive reformers also persuaded state legislatures to enact no-fault workers compensation regimes under which injured workers received prompt compensation for medical expenses and disabilities attributable to injuries "arising out of" the employment relationship without regard to fault on the part of either the employer or the worker. As a quid pro quo, workers received no compensation for non-economic loss, such as pain and suffering. The compensation regimes were administered by state courts or, more typically, state agencies and were paid from privately financed, but heavily regulated insurance pools. The statutes, however, usually excluded domestic and agricultural workers and employees of small businesses, and they ignored most occupational diseases.[6]

Guided by the insights of Progressive Era legal realists, state supreme courts abandoned many Laissez Faire Era legal doctrines that limited corporate liability. In a 1916 case, Judge Benjamin Cardozo established the sensible principle that "[i]f the nature of a thing is such that it is reasonably certain to place life and limb in peril when negligently made, it is then a thing of danger," and the manufacturer has a legal duty to those who might foreseeably be injured whether or not they had a contractual relationship with the manufacturer. Spurred on by that path-breaking opinion, Progressive Era courts greatly expanded the range of potential plaintiffs in products liability lawsuits by allowing recovery for any foreseeable plaintiffs who could prove that the manufacturer was negligent in the manufacture or design of the product.[7]

With a few exceptions, the business community resisted Progressive Era reform legislation and did what it could to narrow its scope at the implementation stage. By the "return to normalcy" following World War I, the impetus for reform had faded, and the familiar themes of economic freedom and personal responsibility echoed once again from the Chambers of Commerce and civic booster clubs of the booming 1920s. Trade associations hired "public relations counselors" to burnish their industries' images, and companies made effective use of charitable contributions to encourage universities to hire more business-friendly academics. Gradually, the public image of the businessperson shifted from robber baron to community benefactor.[8]

THE NEW DEAL

The stock market crash of 1929 and the subsequent economic depression of the early 1930s focused public attention once again on irresponsible business practices. The recurring crises of the Great Depression provided fertile soil for social reformers and ushered in the ambitious reforms of Franklin Roosevelt's New Deal. Congress created powerful federal agencies like the Securities and Exchange Commission (SEC) to protect investors from stock market fraud and manipulation, and it increased the power of existing agencies to protect citizens from dangerous and unscrupulous business practices. The Wheeler-Lea Act of 1938 for the first time empowered FTC to regulate "unfair and deceptive" trade practices without regard to whether they resulted in injury to competition. The Glass-Steagall Act prohibited federally chartered banks from engaging in the business of investment banking (for example, underwriting and marketing securities) or selling insurance. A crisis over the drug sulfanilamide motivated Congress to amend the Pure Food and Drug Act in 1938 to require manufacturers to obtain FDA approval before marketing new drugs. Existing drugs, however, were grandfathered into the system if the manufacturer determined that they were "generally recognized as safe." After six major disasters and several minor accidents during 1940 took the lives of 1,388 miners, Congress finally gave the Bureau of Mines the authority to inspect mines. It did not, however, give the Bureau any authority to write safety standards.[9]

The business community attempted to harness the New Deal agencies procedurally by persuading Congress to enact the Administrative Procedure Act of 1946, a law that gave businesses and other affected parties the presumptive right to judicial review of agency action under a broad "arbitrary and capricious" standard of review. As later interpreted by the Supreme Court, this vague standard empowered a court to set aside an agency rule if "the agency has relied on factors which Congress has not intended it to consider, entirely failed to consider an important aspect of the problem, offered an explanation for its decision that runs counter to the evidence before the agency, or is so implausible that it could not be ascribed to a difference in view or the product of agency expertise." The statute thus allowed regulated entities to threaten to tie up regulatory action in resource-intensive litigation, the outcome of which was always uncertain.[10]

The country experienced another "return to normalcy" following the Second World War as the New Deal regulatory agencies, headed by businessmen during the Eisenhower years, grew docile. Congress continued, however, to respond to particular crises with protective legislation. In response to a December 21, 1951 explosion that killed 119 miners in West Frankfort, Illinois, it enacted the Federal Coal Mine Safety Act of 1952, which for the first time gave federal inspectors limited authority to issue notices of violation and orders of withdrawal when they encountered dangerous conditions in the nation's underground coal mines. Congress also enacted the Food Additives Amendment of 1958, which required FDA approval for all food additives that were not "generally recognized as safe." If the additive contained a human or animal carcinogen, the "Delaney clause" provided that the manufacturer could not add it in any amount.[11]

THE PUBLIC INTEREST ERA

In 1964 and 1965, millions of Americans made the pilgrimage to Queens for the New York World's Fair, a Disney-crafted Technicolor celebration of corporate America, replete with a "Hall of Free Enterprise." The business community basked in a renewed public respect generated by economic prosperity and the "great big, beautiful tomorrow" that one exhibit's theme song promised to all Americans.[12] But the early sixties was also a period of "rising public expectations about the capacity of government to improve the quality of life" for which the business community was ill prepared.[13] During the late 1960s and early 1970s, the forces for change that had been building domestically from the first decade of the twentieth century overwhelmed the political culture as students, teachers, workers, radical critics, and liberal reformers demanded that government do more to protect the public from irresponsible corporate conduct. From their offices in freshly renovated DuPont Circle townhouses, aggressive political entrepreneurs working for newly created "public interest" groups funded by progressive foundations forced their issues onto the public agenda. Suspicious of glossy, but largely ineffectual voluntary initiatives by so-called socially responsible business interests, these activists demanded "corporate accountability" for the adverse social consequences of business decisions.[14]

Investigative journalists who shared young activists' suspicion of powerful corporations and weak regulatory agencies became willing accomplices in the efforts of consumer and environmental activists to use litigation and street drama to highlight unremedied corporate abuses. News clips of oil-drenched birds and billowing smokestacks were visually compelling and had a common-sense appeal to readers and viewers. The Santa Barbara Oil Spill of 1969, the images of the Cuyahoga River on fire, and news reports of denuded mountains and dead Appalachian streams created a crisis atmosphere. Congress was receptive to the lobbying efforts of the new environmental groups, whose bright young staffers prepared detailed analyses of environmental problems and of the apparent incapacity of the existing legal institutions to address those problems. For a time, the new groups were able to hold their own, despite the huge financial advantage of the polluting industries.[15]

Congress responded to these demands with an unprecedented outpouring of legislation. The first indication of the new wave of legislation came in response to a crisis of confidence in the Food and Drug Administration (FDA) growing out of press accounts of the horrible side effects caused by the anti-cholesterol drug MER-29 and the morning sickness drug thalidomide. The bill that President Kennedy signed in October 1962 required drug companies to demonstrate that their products were both safe *and* effective before receiving FDA approval. A November 1968 explosion that killed 78 miners at a Farmington, West Virginia, mine motivated Congress to enact the Coal Mine Health and Safety Act of 1969 and the Occupational Safety and Health Act of 1970. Another tragedy in March 1976 that killed 15 miners, 11 rescuers, and 2 federal inspectors in Oventork, Kentucky, prompted Congress to enact the Mine Safety and Health Amendments of 1977.[16] A National Commission on Product Safety appointed by President Nixon published an influential report in 1970 concluding that consumers had little access to objective information on the risks posed by consumer products and market forces alone could not adequately protect them.[17] Between 1966 and 1977, Congress enacted more than 20 comprehensive statutes creating new agencies, reorganizing existing agencies, and empowering all of them to protect consumers, workers, neighbors, and the environment from irresponsible products and practices of corporate America.[18]

During the Public Interest Era, Congress was also willing to appropriate large sums of money, sometimes over the strong objections of the White House, to ensure that the agencies effectively implemented the new legislation. The resulting regulatory activity during the 1970s created a wide variety of new legal responsibilities for American businesses, and compliance was rarely cheap. Many of the statutes also authorized individual citizens to sue companies that violated federal regulations and permit requirements for injunctive relief and/ or fines to be paid to the federal treasury.[19]

A thumbnail sketch of the relevant federal programs and state common law protections put into place during the Public Interest Era follows:

Environmental Protection. The Clean Air Act of 1970 required the newly created Environmental Protection Agency (EPA) to write national ambient air quality standards (NAAQS), performance standards for new sources, and national emission standards for hazardous air pollutants, and to oversee state efforts to ensure the attainment of the NAAQS by specific statutory deadlines. The Clean Water Act of 1972 established a similar program under which states achieved EPA-approved state water quality standards through EPA-approved state implementation plans, and it further required that a company (or public sewage treatment plant) that discharged pollution directly into rivers and lakes obtain a state-issued, EPA-approved permit containing "effluent limitations" reflecting EPA-promulgated pollution reduction standards for new and existing sources of both conventional and toxic pollutants. Companies desiring to deposit fill into the nation's wetlands were required to obtain a permit from the U.S. Army Corps of Engineers, subject to an EPA veto. Under the Surface Mine Control and Reclamation Act of 1977, the Office of Surface Mining (OSM) in the Department of Interior administered a regulatory program under which OSM or a state agency (in states with approved programs) issued permits for new and existing surface mines and ensured that the operators complied with OSM-promulgated regulations and adequately reclaimed the mines after completing their operations.

Occupational Safety and Health. The Occupational Safety and Health Act of 1970 created the Occupational Safety and Health Administration (OSHA) and authorized it to write occupational safety and health standards. The statute also imposed upon every employer the "general duty" to maintain a safe and healthful place of employment, and it empowered OSHA inspectors to conduct unannounced inspections for violations of OSHA standards or the general duty clause. The Federal Mine Safety and Health Act of 1977 greatly enhanced the regulatory powers of the Mine Safety and Health Administration (MSHA) by empowering it to prescribe mine safety standards and requiring it to conduct unannounced inspections at mines of all sizes at least four times per year.

Device Safety. The Medical Device Amendments of 1976 required manufacturers of medical devices to obtain FDA approval of their devices by demonstrating that they would be safe and effective for their designated uses. An abbreviated approval process allowed a manufacturer to avoid the requirements for full approval if FDA concluded that its device was "substantially equivalent" to an existing device that was either FDA-approved or in existence prior to 1976.

Transportation Safety. The National Traffic and Motor Vehicle Safety Act of 1966 created the National Highway Traffic Safety Administration (NHTSA) and authorized it to promulgate and enforce motor vehicle safety standards and to order recalls of unsafe motor vehicles. Two earlier enacted transportation safety statutes empowered the Federal Aviation Administration to regulate airline safety and the Federal Railroad Administration to regulate railroad safety.

Consumer Protection. The Consumer Product Safety Act of 1972 created the Consumer Product Safety Commission (CPSC) and charged it with promulgating and enforcing standards and labeling requirements for consumer products in general and children's toys in particular. Under several pre-existing statutes, CPSC was also responsible for promulgating standards for consumer products containing hazardous substances, standards for labeling packages containing poisonous substances, and standards for children's toys and games. The Magnuson-Moss Warranty and Federal Trade Commission Improvement Act of 1975 greatly expanded federal consumer warranty protections by prescribing particular provisions for such warranties and authorizing FTC to promulgate regulations governing the content of most other consumer warranties. The statute also empowered FTC to write "trade regulation rules" governing "unfair and deceptive trade practices."

Financial Protection. The Truth in Lending Act of 1968 required creditors to disclose information for consumers to use in comparing loan offers and information related to the full cost of the credit. It also authorized consumers to bring lawsuits against lenders for statutory damages and attorneys' fees.

Civil Justice Reform. The Public Interest Era spirit of reform also overtook the civil justice system and the legal institutions that provided its theoretical underpinnings. Inspired by a new wave of legal scholarship and the second edition of the *Restatement of Torts*, courts throughout the country began to drop ancient procedural and substantive constraints on the rights of injured citizens to seek compensation for their injuries. A major expansion in legally protected interests included nonpurchasers of defective products who were foreseeably injured and persons suffering mental distress but not otherwise injured. The courts also changed the substantive law of torts in ways that generally expanded the liability of companies for the adverse consequences of their products and practices. The expansive theory of "enterprise liability," under which courts held companies responsible for all physical losses caused by their products, flourished during this period of intense intellectual ferment in the courts. And the courts relaxed procedural requirements in ways that facilitated broad "class action" lawsuits involving hundreds or even thousands of plaintiffs in a single legal proceeding.

Finally, several states responded to the 1972 report by the bipartisan National Commission on State Workmen's Compensation Laws by increasing benefits for injured workers.

CONCLUSIONS

The statutory changes of the Progressive, New Deal, and Public Interest Eras came in response to perceived crises in the political economy as manifested in media reports of widespread corporate abuses. Cumulatively, the statutes imposed broad obligations on companies to pay far more attention to the impact of their products and activities on their consumers, workers, neighbors, and the environment than they had in the past. The stallion was fully harnessed and pressed into the service of society. Although the changes mandated by the new statutes rarely demanded more than what was already technologically feasible, they greatly improved the lives of most Americans. As we shall see in Chapters 8–15, workplaces are much safer, the environment is much cleaner, the food we eat is safer and more nutritious, the drugs and devices that doctors prescribe for us are safer and more effective than they would have been in the absence of the fundamental changes in our nation's governmental infrastructure that those statutes brought about. We also travel in safer cars, trains, and planes than the unimpeded market would have provided, and we do not have to worry as much about whether toys will maim our children or whether our nest eggs will be drained by a fraudulent scam artist or a run on the bank. The primary impact of these laws on the business community was to force companies to devote a higher proportion of their resources to protecting others than they had in the past.[20] That modest burden, however, was too much to bear for a business community that never fully accepted governmental constraints on its economic freedom.

3

FREEDOM, RESPONSIBILITY, AND ACCOUNTABILITY

At the outset of the 1970s, some respected scholars believed that "the ideological clash between the advocates of laissez faire and the advocates of the general welfare state [had] been resolved in theory, in practice, and in public esteem in favor of the general welfare state."[1] What was good for American workers and consumers, not General Motors, was good for America. Most conservative intellectuals agreed that liberalism was ascendant, but they did not agree with the historians who concluded that the debate was over.[2] Indeed, the business community would soon launch a fierce counterattack against the protective governmental infrastructure that emerged from the Public Interest Era.

Before continuing with that story, however, this chapter will briefly describe the institutions that make up the protective governmental infrastructure. These are the institutions that government has created to craft rules of responsibility for business entities and to ensure that violators are held accountable for the adverse social consequences that result from violating those rules. It will then probe the tension among freedom, responsibility, and accountability that any capitalist society must resolve in determining the degree to which it is willing to tolerate private sector arrangements that have the potential to cause public harm. In the process, it will highlight some of the arguments that free market advocates and government intervention advocates have made in the ongoing debates over the terms of the social bargain.

THE INSTITUTIONS OF RESPONSIBILITY

The institutions charged with articulating legally binding rules defining responsible business practices function in different, but complementary ways.

Legislatures can establish them directly in statutes, or they can delegate rule-making authority to regulatory agencies. Agencies promulgate rules through "notice-and-comment" procedures in which interested persons are able to comment on proposed rules, and agencies are obliged to respond to material comments in the preambles to the final rules. Both forms of rulemaking are subject to judicial review. Statutes must pass constitutional muster, and administrative agencies must compile a rulemaking record and provide a reasoned explanation demonstrating that their rules are authorized by statute and are not arbitrary and capricious. Companies that violate the rules are subject to formal enforcement actions that may result in fines or criminal sanctions.[3]

The common law plays a complementary regulatory role by virtue of the incentives that it provides to prospective defendants to comply with the common law standards of care. The standard of care in negligence actions is that of the reasonable person in the same or similar circumstances. If the defendant violated a statute or regulation, the plaintiff may introduce evidence of the violation to prove that the defendant was negligent, and in most states the burden will shift to the defendant to show that the violation was excused. For example, it is ordinarily negligent to cross a yellow stripe into the left lane of a two-lane highway, but that conduct may be excused if a pedestrian suddenly appears in the right lane and no vehicles are approaching in the left lane. A defendant may introduce evidence of compliance with an applicable statute or regulation, but that evidence ordinarily has no impact on the burden of proof. Courts typically invite juries to consider the risks posed by the defendant's conduct and the burden of avoiding harm to the plaintiff in applying the reasonable person standard.[4]

A plaintiff bringing a products liability action need not prove that the manufacturer was guilty of any specific act of negligence. In the case of a defectively manufactured product, the essence of the plaintiff's claim is that some flaw in the manufacturing process resulted in a dangerous product. Subjecting a company to liability will provide an incentive to manufacturers to monitor that production process more carefully to prevent such flaws in the future. In the case of a defectively designed product, the courts employ either a risk-utility test for liability that is, for all practical purposes, identical to applying a negligence test to the product itself or a "consumer expectation" test under which a product is defective if it fails to meet a reasonable consumer's expectations concerning its safety. Holding a company liable for harm caused by its defectively designed products encourages all similarly situated companies to design safer products.[5]

THE INSTITUTIONS OF ACCOUNTABILITY

Most regulatory statutes prescribe civil fines and criminal penalties for violations of regulations that the agency detects and elects to prosecute. Some statutes go further to allow the government to seek the equitable remedy of "disgorgement" through which the court forces the company to pay not a predetermined fine, but the amount that the company saved or profited by violating the law.[6] Recognizing that government enforcers have limited resources at their disposal and are not always willing to antagonize politically powerful companies, Congress has on relatively rare occasions empowered affected citizens to maintain their own enforcement actions in court and to collect reasonable attorney's fees when they substantially prevail. Beyond serving as a prod to federal and state enforcers, deputizing ordinary citizens increases the resources available to hold scofflaws accountable.[7]

In providing corrective justice to injured plaintiffs, the common law ensures that companies are held accountable for violating the relevant rules of responsibility. The common law is the only legal institution capable of holding companies accountable for the adverse effects of unregulated products and activities.[8] Over time, common law courts replaced unjust doctrines like contributory negligence (which precluded recovery by a plaintiff who was in the slightest degree negligent) with doctrines like comparative negligence (which allowed a plaintiff to recover for his or her loss discounted by the plaintiff's percentage of the overall negligence). Similarly, the doctrine of "joint and several liability," under which any one of multiple defendants that contributed to an indivisible harm may be held liable for all of the damage and must seek "contribution" from the remaining defendants for their respective shares, ensured that innocent plaintiffs did not bear the risk of insolvent or otherwise unreachable defendants.[9]

Class action lawsuits increase the likelihood that a company will be held accountable for the consequences of its irresponsible conduct when it harms each of many plaintiffs by a small amount. A representative of the class pursues the litigation in the name of all members of the class, and any damage awards are allocated among the class members pursuant to a judicially approved formula.[10] Courts in most states allow juries to assess "punitive" or "exemplary" damages when defendants have egregiously violated the relevant standard of care. Punitive damages are designed to punish socially unacceptable conduct, to provide victims a degree of retribution, and to deter companies from engaging in egregious misconduct in the future. The district courts have complete discretion over whether juries may assess punitive damages over the amount of compensatory awards.[11]

RESOLVING THE TENSION

Even the most doctrinaire of libertarians agree that the business community must accept some measure of responsibility for protecting consumers, workers, and neighbors from fraud and risks to their health and well-being.[12] Yet disagreement soon erupts over how society should resolve the tension among freedom, responsibility, and accountability in determining the content of the rules of responsibility and the degree to which companies should be held accountable for violating those rules. Free market proponents argue that the rules of responsibility must not be so stringent that they unduly interfere with the economic freedom of businesses to sell their products, provide their services, and foster innovation in smoothly functioning markets.[13] Proponents of government intervention advocate highly precautionary rules of responsibility. If society must tolerate risks in order to reap the benefits of economic activity, the government should err on the side of protecting innocent victims. Companies should do the best that they can to protect workers, neighbors, and the environment by using the best available protective technologies. The costs of compliance are relevant, but should not be determinative.[14]

Free market proponents argue that consumers should be free to choose products they enjoy (be they Big Macs or variable rate mortgages) without the officious intervention of government bureaucrats. Likewise, workers should be free to bargain for less safety and higher wages. Stringent rules of responsibility take away this freedom and lead to "moral hazard," an insurance industry term for the concern that the beneficiaries of government protections will not pay sufficient attention to their own well-being because they know they will be compensated for any losses by the government or others.[15] Proponents of stringent rules find such arguments surprisingly naive. The argument that workers can bid up wages in return for accepting greater risk, for example, erroneously assumes that they are fully informed about those risks, ignores the limited options available to low-wage workers, and ultimately shifts the burden of medical treatment for injured workers to government-provided social security disability programs. Likewise, the argument that consumers should be completely free to choose risky products assumes that they are fully informed about their risks and the benefits when that information is either unavailable or easily lost in the blizzard of seller-provided information that they encounter in advertising or the fine print of incomprehensible adhesion contracts. Preferences are not inherent in the genes of consumers, but are shaped in powerful ways by "exogenous" influences like schools, churches, the mass media, and advertising.[16]

Laissez faire minimalists argue that any governmental intervention should be limited to the minimum intrusion necessary to approximate the outcomes of perfectly functioning markets. Ordinarily, that degree of intervention is best determined by assessing the costs and benefits of the intervention to society. The same test (risk-utility) should govern common law negligence and products liability actions. In both contexts, the proponent of intervention should bear a heavy burden of demonstrating with scientific data and quantitative analysis that the intervention passes the cost-benefit test.[17] Recognizing the virtues of economic efficiency, proponents of stringent rules of responsibility argue that it is not a "meta-value" that trumps other values like fairness, equality, and concern for future generations. In particular, quantitative cost-benefit analysis should not be the decision criterion for determining the rules of responsibility. In addition to ignoring huge uncertainties in available scientific and economic information, cost-benefit analysis falsely assumes that economists can assign dollar values to priceless benefits, like human life, pristine views, and the existence of endangered species.[18]

Critics of strict rules believe that regulation and common law litigation can hamper innovation. The prospect of undergoing a lengthy and expensive regulatory approval process or vexatious tort litigation may dissuade companies from developing life-saving drugs and other useful products.[19] Proponents of strict rules find this contention wholly lacking in empirical support. The resources that companies devote to research on new drugs, for example, are dwarfed by the industry's prodigious investment in promoting and marketing existing drugs. Stringent rules of responsibility do not hamper innovation so much as they channel the incentive to innovate toward safer products and away from superficially attractive bells and whistles.[20]

Proponents of governmental intervention believe that the rules of responsibility are of very little value if companies that violate those rules are not held accountable for their misconduct. Common sense teaches that violations that go unpunished will be repeated. Holding violators accountable by forcing them to pay fines, compensate victims, or spend time in jail thus serves the dual goals of retribution and deterrence.[21] Free market advocates recognize the need for strict accountability when it comes to enforcing contracts and punishing fraud and theft, but violations of regulatory laws require softer approaches designed to achieve "compliance," rather than retribution. Excessive fines, they warn, will result in "overdeterrence" as companies invest too much in safety and too little in innovative new products and practices.[22] Governmental intervention advocates respond that voluntary approaches are too easily manipulated by companies willing to "game the system." Furthermore, deference to promises to do better in the future "delegitimizes" the rules of responsibility, while strict enforcement shores up the moral authority of the rules and enhances public trust in government.[23]

Free market advocates acknowledge a legitimate role for the civil justice system in forcing negligent parties to compensate their victims, but they would limit that compensation to what the victim would have received from a hypothetical insurance policy purchased prior to the accident. Compensatory damage awards larger than this "optimal compensation" award and all punitive damage awards will, like excessive civil and criminal penalties, result in innovation-killing overdeterrence.[24] Proponents of government intervention respond that the hypothetical insurance policy test for optimal compensation has all the earmarks of a makeweight argument and none of the moral force of corrective justice, a concept with a lineage dating at least as far back as Aristotle. Overdeterrence is not likely to be a serious problem, they argue, because the high costs of litigation and the difficulty of proving that a plaintiff's harm was caused by a particular defendant's product or activity ensure that a large number of injuries will go uncompensated.[25]

CONCLUSIONS

The great debates highlighted in this chapter reflect the tension between freedom, accountability, and responsibility that is at the heart of the ongoing bargain over the role that government plays in American life. Although the two sides occasionally reach a temporary accommodation, often as the result of a crisis demonstrating the failure of the regulatory or civil justice systems, the debate will never end. Since the proper balance depends on cultural, ideological, economic, political, and technological factors that change over time, this is as it should be.

Part Two

PREPARING FOR THE LAISSEZ FAIRE REVIVAL

The Laissez Faire Revival did not spontaneously erupt from the void that was American conservatism following Barry Goldwater's defeat in 1964. It grew slowly from seeds planted during the 1940s by businessmen who were repelled by communism and an intrusive governmental infrastructure that the New Deal had erected, which, they were convinced, was not far removed from communism. Chapter 4 describes the "Wilderness Years" during which small enclaves of free market thinkers at the London School of Economics and the University of Chicago, supported by one or two conservative foundations, formed the Mont Pelerin Society to advance a laissez faire minimalist intellectual agenda. It will also describe how five conservative foundations carried out a plan outlined by soon-to-be Justice Lewis Powell and former Treasury Secretary William Simon to build an intellectual infrastructure capable of articulating and disseminating bold new ideas to capture the attention of the American public.

Chapter 5 will provide thumbnail sketches of several of the most important think tanks and academic organizations that proved highly influential in bringing the Laissez Faire Revival to fruition. In addition to this "idea infrastructure," the founding funders and the business community also created an influence infrastructure to provide public support (or at least the appearance of public support) for the ideas and to press policymakers to implement them. The influence infrastructure consisted of a wide variety of organizations, ranging from "astroturf" grass-roots organizations to traditional lobbying firms and various ad hoc alliances. Unlike the business community's previous reactions to progressive reforms, its broad and sustained support for the idea and influence infrastructures was not limited to resistance. These new institutions were fully prepared to launch an all-out assault on the institutions of responsibility and accountability in a way that would force a renegotiation of the social bargain.

4

The Intellectual and Financial Foundations

In the aftermath of the successful efforts of the Roosevelt Administration to steer the nation out of the Great Depression, the business community could not credibly advocate a return to a laissez faire economy. It was in fact busily accommodating itself to the New Deal as the country entered the "great compression" of the 1950s. Conservative thinkers, however, had not come to terms with the New Deal, nor were they pleased by developments around the world as the Soviet Union's power grew and many Western nations adopted moderately socialist domestic programs. During these "wilderness years," the keepers of the laissez faire flame were tucked away in academia where they quietly poured the intellectual foundation for a resurgence of laissez faire minimalism.[1]

THE WILDERNESS YEARS

The clearest voice crying in the wilderness was that of Friedrich von Hayek, whose 1944 book *The Road to Serfdom* became the sacred text of true believers in laissez faire minimalism.[2] Soon after he took his law degree, Hayek became a member of an elite invitation-only seminar convened by the libertarian economist Ludwig von Mises in his office at the Austrian Chamber of Commerce. Mises believed that any attempt to regulate markets would inevitably erode individual freedom. Although Hayek believed that the state could play a significant humanitarian role by aiding the poor and disabled, he was persuaded that any government intervention into the affairs of the business community would always result in more harm than good. Hayek also drew a curious distinction between government, which should stay away from private economic arrangements, and a judicially administered "rule of law," which was the primary protector of the individual (and his property) from intrusive government and from other individuals who threatened his legally protectable interests through force, fraud, or theft.[3]

Hayek first made a name for himself with a wide-ranging critique of John Maynard Keynes's famous *Treatise on Money,* which was published just as Hayek took a position at the London School of Economics in September 1931. His colleagues at the London School included several intellectual forebears of modern laissez faire minimalist economics. If his attack on Keynes made Hayek a notable among British conservative intellectuals, the 1944 publication of *The Road to Serfdom* made him a celebrity throughout the United States. It was, as Hayek later acknowledged, a "political book . . . derived from certain ultimate values."[4] As the *Reader's Digest* condensation of the book hit the best-seller lists, Hayek traveled to the United States in the spring of 1945 for a triumphal author tour. Critics suspected that the book's commercial success was attributable to the strong promotional efforts of the National Association of Manufacturers and the Chamber of Commerce.

Anxious to expose as many Americans as possible to Hayek's ideas, the Volker Fund, a foundation established in 1944 to promote "free-market economics," agreed in advance to pay Hayek's salary at any university in the United States that would add him to its faculty. After the Institute for Advanced Studies at Princeton University declined, Hayek accepted an invitation to teach at the University of Chicago. He did not, however, become a member of Chicago's prestigious economics department, which at that time had little use for a moral philosopher. Instead, he joined the Committee for Social Thought, a novel cross-disciplinary program established by Professor John Nef with funding from his wealthy wife, as a "Professor of Social and Moral Science." The courses that Hayek taught during his decade-long stay at Chicago were devoted almost exclusively to political philosophy.[5]

Since Hayek's ideas were not rooted in scientific theory or empirical observation, they were eminently contestable. And defenders of the New Deal Era programs Hayek attacked vigorously resisted his call for a return to laissez faire principles of governance. Hayek's message, however, was music to the ears of the American business community. When he returned to Europe in 1961, he left behind several devoted colleagues and protégés, including Milton Friedman and Frank Knight, to carry the flag for laissez faire minimalism at the University of Chicago.[6]

Hayek was inspired by his like-minded colleagues at the University of Chicago to write a paper entitled "On Being an Economist," in which he proposed a gathering of scholars dedicated to reviving laissez faire minimalism in postwar economics. With generous support from the Volker Fund and a Swiss businessman, Hayek's suggestion became a reality at a gathering of thirty-nine European and American economists in April 1947 at Mont Pelerin in the Swiss Alps. Among the American participants were Milton Friedman, Frank Knight (the founder of the Chicago School of economics), George Stigler, and Aaron Director (the founder of the law and economics program at the University of Chicago School of Law).[7]

A "Statement of Aims" delivered to the press at the end of the meeting announced in ominous tones that "[t]he central values of civilization are in danger," because "the essential conditions of human dignity and freedom have already disappeared" over "large stretches of the earth's surface." This worrisome condition was "fostered by the growth of a view of history which denies all absolute moral standards" and "a decline of belief in private property and the competitive market." It warned that "without the diffused power and initiative associated with these institutions it is difficult to imagine a society in which freedom may be effectively preserved."[8]

Concluding that further fully funded meetings of this sort were highly desirable, the participants created a permanent "Mont Pelerin Society" and elected Hayek president. The Society met again in Switzerland two years later and annually thereafter. Although differences developed among the Society's strong personalities over the years, it continued to add to its membership and to meet annually for more than sixty years.[9]

THE FOUNDING FUNDERS

Barry Goldwater's stunning defeat in 1964 signaled to many prominent members of the business community that it was time to reach an accommodation with Public Interest Era activists. Not all business leaders, however, shared this accommodationist view. They were deeply troubled by the onslaught of new regulatory programs with their burdensome rules and nettlesome inspectors and by the rapidly expanding threat of liability in the common law courts. In their view, the proper response to these frightening developments was not accommodation, but resistance, and they were prepared to invest substantial sums of money to create a new idea infrastructure capable of challenging the dominant "liberal" paradigm.[10]

One of the earliest financial backers of the Laissez Faire Revival, the Volker Fund, was established in 1947 upon the death of the owner of a successful Kansas City dry goods business. It was administered by his nephew, an ardent

free-market libertarian named Harold W. Luhnow. In addition to funding
Friedrich von Hayek's chair at the University of Chicago and the initial meeting of the Mont Pelerin Society, the Volker Fund supported the work of Milton
Friedman and his brother-in-law, Aaron Director. The small fund spent down
its capital over a decade and went out of business in 1965. By then, several
larger foundations had taken up the cause of laissez faire minimalism, and they
continued to support it for decades. Once the phalanx of institutions that these
founding funders put into place began to have a discernable impact on government policy, affected business entities were easily persuaded to pitch in, especially on projects that had direct relevance to their business activities.[11]

The Olin Foundation. Perhaps the most dedicated and consistent supporter
of the Laissez Faire Revival was John M. Olin, the long-time CEO of one of
the country's largest manufacturers of ammunition and small arms and a major government contractor. Established in December 1953, the John M. Olin
Foundation initially supported local charities, hospitals, and museums. In the
late 1950s, it quietly served as a money-laundering operation for the Central
Intelligence Agency (CIA), steering almost two million CIA dollars to the Ver-
non Fund and the American Enterprise Institute as part of a covert effort to
"combat the influence of communism upon artists, writers, and intellectuals in
the western democracies." Repelled by the willingness of elite private colleges
to tolerate the social upheavals of the sixties, Olin resolved to steer the foundation's giving exclusively toward alternative institutions charged with mounting
a vigorous defense of economic freedom. The foundation made its first non-
covert grant to the American Enterprise Institute in 1973.[12]

Olin's East Hampton neighbor, a wealthy financier and former Treasury Secretary named William Simon, was just beginning his own crusade to persuade
the business community to channel substantial resources in precisely the same
direction. Olin persuaded Simon to become president of the foundation in
early 1977. Another early influence on the foundation was Irving Kristol, a New
York University professor who later became the "godfather" of neoconservatism.
Olin was taken with Kristol's trademark assertion that a "new class" of liberal
professionals had taken over the most prominent positions in academia, the media, and the government with the primary aim of expanding government's role
in the American economy. Kristol eagerly assisted Simon's efforts to persuade
conservative foundations and the business community to devote substantially
greater resources to funding a laissez faire minimalist ideological infrastructure.
By the end of 1977, the Olin Foundation was giving away more than $1 million a
year to support Washington, D.C., think tanks and carefully selected academics
at elite universities.[13] By design, the foundation spent down its capital during
the first decade of the twenty-first century and quietly went out of business.[14]

The Lynde and Harry Bradley Foundation. The Lynde and Harry Bradley Foundation was established by two brothers who had made their fortunes in the electronics industry. Harry Bradley was a member of the John Birch Society, a strong supporter of Robert Taft's campaign for president in 1952, and one of the original funders of William F. Buckley's *National Review*. The foundation began as a relatively small funder of specialty conservative causes, but vaulted to the top of the heap when the Bradleys' company was sold to Rockwell International in 1985 and the foundation's treasury swelled to $300 million. It then hired Michael Joyce away from the Olin Foundation, and he launched a similar program of funding laissez faire minimalists at elite universities and conservative think tanks.[15]

The Scaife Foundations. Richard Mellon Scaife inherited a fortune in excess of one billion dollars from his mother, who was a niece of the Gilded Age financier and railroad magnate Andrew Mellon. By the time he was 22, Scaife had been expelled from Yale, and he soon acquired a reputation as a bully who bore grudges. After his mother's death, he wrested control of a trio of family foundations from his sister and steered their grants away from liberal causes to organizations that advanced a laissez faire minimalist agenda. The impact of Scaife's targeted philanthropy was broad and immediate. It achieved a degree of notoriety in 1998 when investigators discovered that Scaife had contributed $2 million to an effort to dig up dirt on Bill and Hillary Clinton called the "Arkansas Project." By 2005, the Scaife foundations had contributed more than half a billion dollars, mostly in general support grants with few strings attached, to a wide variety of conservative institutions devoted to creating and maintaining the Laissez Faire Revival.[16]

Joseph Coors and the Sunbelt Entrepreneurs. Beginning in the 1970s, a new breed of "sunbelt entrepreneurs" played a powerful role in bringing about the resurgence in laissez faire minimalism. Deriving their wealth from the beer and ceramics dynasty created by Adolph Coors, his descendants Joseph, Holly, William, and Jeffrey, became strong supporters of institutions promoting free enterprise. Joseph Coors wrote a $250,000 check in 1973 to pay for the first year's operating expenses of the Heritage Foundation. Other beneficiaries over the years included the Institute for Educational Affairs (funding conservative student newspapers), the Center for the Defense of Free Enterprise (free market advocacy), and Accuracy in Media (mainstream media criticism).[17]

Koch Family Foundations. The Koch Family Foundations were established by David and Charles Koch, sons of a wealthy Kansas oil man who was also one of the founders of the John Birch Society. The second-largest privately held company in the United States, Koch Industries currently controls a large number of companies associated with the oil and gas industry, the paper industry, and real estate development. The foundations were prominent patrons of conservative causes generally, but they specialized in supporting libertarian institutions advocating a return to laissez faire minimalism. This orientation may have reflected Koch Industries' status as a frequent violator of environmental laws. Primary beneficiaries were the libertarian Cato Institute, a small anti-regulatory think tank called the Mercatus Institute, and the "astroturf" grass-roots organization Citizens for a Sound Economy (CSE). After a breakup at CSE produced two institutions, FreedomWorks and Americans for Prosperity, both of which provided training and technical support to the Tea Party movement, the Kochs supported Tea Party political candidates through the latter organization.[18]

This handful of foundations "helped turn a collection of outposts and tendencies into a full-fledged movement." They accomplished this remarkable feat by devoting well over one billion dollars' worth of critical "seed" and "general support" grants to support the work of laissez faire minimalist academics, to jump-start a wide variety of think tanks, to launch the law and economics movement, to fund conservative student organizations and publications, to create a new breed of laissez faire-oriented grass-roots groups, to launch a massive "tort reform" movement aimed at shielding corporate defendants from lawsuits, and to finance attacks on and alternatives to the "liberal media."[19]

5

THE IDEA INFRASTRUCTURE

As the business community began to feel the cumulative impact of Public Interest Era regulatory programs and common law expansion, a prominent Richmond, Virginia, attorney named Lewis Powell captured the alarming implications of these developments in a lengthy memorandum to his good friend and neighbor Eugene B. Sydnor, Jr., who was at the time the Chairman of the Education Committee of the U.S. Chamber of Commerce. Widely circulated among business leaders, the memo contained a powerful call to arms. Powell ventured that "no thoughtful person can question that the American economic system [was] under [a] broad attack." At the forefront of the attack was consumer activist Ralph Nader, who had "become a legend in his own time and an idol of millions of Americans." While "much of the media . . . voluntarily accord[ed] unique publicity to these 'attackers,'" the leaders of the business community had "shown little stomach for hard-nosed contests with their critics, and little skill in effective intellectual and philosophical debate." At stake was nothing less than the "survival of what we call the free enterprise system."

Powell offered several prescriptions for fighting back. First, the business community needed to exert greater influence on the nation's campuses, which were producing students that "end up in regulatory agencies or governmental departments with large authority over the business system they do not believe in." He urged the Chamber of Commerce to establish "a staff of highly qualified scholars in the social sciences who do believe in the system," to create a "staff of speakers of the highest competency" to give lectures on college campuses, and to "exert whatever degree of pressure" was necessary "to assure opportunities" for these free enterprise advocates to speak. It was "especially important" that the scholars publish their views in books, academic journals, pamphlets, and popular magazines. To ensure that they were heard by the general public, "[e]qual time should be demanded" of the media, and complaints should be filed with television companies and the Federal Communications Commission when programs appeared to be "unfair or inaccurate."[1]

Two months after Powell penned this memorandum, President Nixon appointed him to the Supreme Court of the United States.[2] Five years after that, former Treasury Secretary and "Energy Czar" William Simon wrote a best-selling polemic entitled *A Time for Truth* containing a similar call to action in less restrained language. Like Hayek, Simon drew a stark contrast between free enterprise "which creates a powerful and inventive economic system and produces wealth" and "totalitarian-collectivist planning" which "destroys both the political and the economic freedom of the individual and produces collective poverty and starvation." Simon believed that "most existing regulation is so irrational that it should be wiped out by law, along with the bureaucracies that have spawned it." He harshly criticized the business community for indirectly "financing the destruction of both free enterprise and political freedom" by providing unrestricted contributions to universities. Instead, it should be creating and supporting "intellectual refuges for the non-egalitarian scholars and writers in our society." These scholars "must be given grants, grants, and more grants in exchange for books, books, and more books." Simon urged the business community to join him in "building up the influence of the counterintelligentcia [sic], whose views, if known, would command a respectful hearing in the marketplace of ideas."[3]

The founding funders who responded to the Powell and Simon manifestos envisioned a radical restructuring of the American political economy that would return it to the laissez faire benchmark of the late nineteenth century. And they were prepared to finance a new conservative idea infrastructure to lay the intellectual foundation necessary to accomplish that ambitious goal. Wealthy individuals and corporations joined the conservative foundations in writing large checks to fund the work of scholars who would be more than objective academics and technocrats of the sort that inhabited existing academic centers and think tanks. The recipients of their largess would be policy entrepreneurs capable of conceiving and, more important, promoting laissez faire minimalist prescriptions for the pressing policy issues of the day.[4]

THE CHICAGO SCHOOL

The singular exception to the grim Powell/Simon assessment of academia was the University of Chicago, where laissez faire minimalism was tolerated in the economics department, respected in the law school, and afforded gospel-like status in the Committee for Social Thought where Hayek spent the 1950s. When Hayek returned to Europe in 1961, he left behind several fellow travelers who formed the nucleus for the "Chicago School" of Economics that in turn became the cornerstone of the business community's idea infrastructure.[5]

The founder of the Chicago School was Frank Knight, an accomplished economist who, like Hayek, was a fierce advocate of economic freedom at a time when government restrictions were in vogue. No fan of the empirical research that policymakers were then demanding, Knight was confident that economists could deduce practical solutions to social problems from fundamental economic assumptions. And the Chicago School's bedrock assumption was that the marketplace itself would ordinarily establish clear rules of responsibility and hold companies accountable, through lost profits, for deviations from those rules. Knight therefore opposed any governmental intervention into private economic arrangements absent a strong demonstration that the market had failed and that the intervention would do more good than harm. For example, he opposed occupational safety and health regulation, because it interfered with the worker's right to accept risky jobs for higher wages. What distinguished workers from financiers, in his mind, was only a matter of preference: financiers preferred to risk their capital while laborers preferred to risk their bodies.[6]

One of Knight's many influential students, Henry Simons, was one of the first genuine policy entrepreneurs of the Laissez Faire Revival. His Depression-era pamphlet, "A Positive Program for Laissez Faire," offered an accessible blueprint for a return to a Gilded Age political economy. Later, Simons played an important role in arranging for the University of Chicago Press to publish the United States edition of Friedrich Hayek's *Road to Serfdom* in 1944. When Simons did not receive a tenure track appointment in the economics department, Knight arranged for him to become the first economist to join the faculty of the University of Chicago's School of Law in 1939. From there, he was instrumental in launching the "law and economics" movement discussed below.[7]

With Simons's untimely death in 1946, Milton Friedman assumed the role of the Chicago School's resident policy entrepreneur. Like Simons, Friedman excelled at building networks of similar thinkers. He became one of the first "fellows" at the American Enterprise Institute. From his tenured sinecure in the economics department, Friedman led the academic assault on Public Interest Era regulatory programs in weekly *Newsweek* columns and easily digested books written for general audiences. He was an economic advisor to the Barry Goldwater campaign of 1964 and the Ronald Reagan campaign of 1980. By the mid-1970s, Milton Friedman's thinking dominated the Chicago School, and he had become the preeminent public spokesperson for laissez faire minimalism.[8]

Friedman's best-selling book *Capitalism and Freedom* laid out the case for a laissez faire revival with an intensity bordering on religious commitment and provided a convenient accounting of market-oriented solutions to social problems. Impressed by the book's popular success, the Scaife Foundation committed $500,000 to an Erie, Pennsylvania, public television station to underwrite a television series based on the book. In the series and a companion book, Friedman and his wife Rose held forth on the virtues of laissez faire capitalism and the evils of government regulation. Proclaiming the Gilded Age to be a "golden age in both Great Britain and the United States," Friedman called for such radical changes as the abolition of the Food and Drug Administration and most other regulatory agencies.[9]

Reflecting Frank Knight's aversion to empirical studies, the Chicago School stressed theory over empiricism. Its favored theory, the "efficient market hypothesis," posited that "decision makers so allocate the resources under their control that there is no alternative allocation such that any one decision maker could have his expected utility increased without a reduction occurring in the expected utility of at least one other decision maker."[10] Any inconsistencies between actual economic data and the efficient market theory were either wrong or anomalous. Therefore, no amount of empirical analysis could justify governmental intervention absent a theoretical explanation for how the efficient hypothesis had failed. Not all economists were as committed to the efficient market hypothesis as the Chicago School, but by the mid-1990s, it had become so dominant in academia that many young economists who were willing to allow facts to trump the theory found themselves shut out of the best economics departments and the mainstream economics journals.[11] As we shall see, the efficient market hypothesis came to dominate thinking on Wall Street and in Washington, D.C., as well.

THE LAISSEZ FAIRE LEGAL SCHOLARS

The common law is constantly evolving with changing cultural norms, changing ideas of the role that law should play in society, and the changing composition of the judiciary. Yet changes in the common law rules of responsibility are difficult to accomplish without solid doctrinal underpinnings formulated by the judges in crafting their opinions, by practitioners through intermediary institutions like the American Law Institute and the American Bar Association, and by legal scholars in the nation's law schools. Although federal administrative law is largely statutory, the broad language of the Administrative Procedure Act and the often malleable language of regulatory statutes usually permit a similar evolution of legal understandings over time. The ideas that drive legal change come from a variety of sources, but legal scholarship is an especially prominent one.[12]

Fully aware of the important role of legal scholarship in determining public policy, the founding funders devoted substantial resources to supporting scholars in the budding field of "law and economics" at elite American law schools and to a migrating center on law and economics associated with Professor Henry Manne. Their hope was that a well-endowed contingent of "intellectual entrepreneurs" in the law schools would provide the intellectual foundation for their efforts to persuade Congress, agencies, and judges to rewrite regulatory and common law rules of responsibility in ways that moved the law closer to the laissez faire benchmark.[13] They were not disappointed.

The Olin Foundation was the most generous investor in the law and economics movement. In the early 1980s, Olin began to fund law and economics programs at several elite law schools, beginning with the University of Chicago. The programs included a wide variety of activities, including faculty research, symposia and workshops, law journals, and student writing. Many of the Olin-funded articles were published in the Olin-funded *Journal of Legal Studies*. Looking toward the future, some programs established research internships akin to graduate postdoctoral programs in which prospective law and economics professors could spend a year or two writing law review articles, thereby making them more attractive to law schools looking to hire entry-level professors. As the programs began to flourish, other founding funders and individual corporations joined the effort.[14]

CHICAGO SCHOOL LAW AND ECONOMICS

The field of law and economics was never single-minded in scope or approach, and it has over the years blossomed into a wide variety of sub-disciplines and specialties. The "normative" branch of law and economics that is of primary interest here purported to derive objective rules of responsibility from the simple bedrock principles of Chicago School economics. The starting point was the fundamental assumption that consumers were "rational actors" who were maximizing their own utility in accordance with an underlying set of ordered preferences. Since the outcomes reached by freely functioning markets reflected the combined preferences of the individuals participating in those markets, those outcomes were the best measure of overall consumer welfare. Consequently, government's proper role was the limited one of defining and protecting the property and contractual rights required for a smoothly functioning marketplace. Beyond that, government action had to be justified as necessary to address a specific market failure, and it had to be designed to steer the rational actors in the marketplace toward outcomes that the markets would have reached but for the market imperfection.[15]

Friedrich Hayek and Henry Simons persuaded the Volker Fund to create a position at the law school from which Aaron Director launched the nation's first formal program in law and economics. After the Volker Fund went out of existence, the Olin Foundation became the program's primary funder. Director's courses had a profound impact on a small but dedicated core of law students, many of whom became evangelists for the law and economics movement. The program published the first issue of the *Journal of Law and Economics* in 1958. Director's successor, Ronald Coase, wrote what became one of the most widely cited articles in law and economics, an essay entitled "The Problem of Social Cost."[16]

The "pied piper" of the law and economics movement was Richard Posner. A gifted writer, Posner turned the movement into an "academic phenomenon of the first rank" through the sheer force and clarity of his prodigious output. The first edition of Posner's classic treatise *Economic Analysis of Law* showed how economic analysis could illuminate the direct and indirect consequences of legal rules governing property, contracts, torts, business regulation, and income redistribution.[17] Another prolific member of the Chicago faculty, Richard Epstein, was an uncompromising libertarian for whom the institution of private property was the wellspring of social well-being. His first major salvo, a densely written book entitled *Takings: Private Property and the Power Of Eminent Domain*, became the *Das Kapital* of the populist "property rights" movement. Epstein argued that all property rights were pre-political and therefore immune to redefinition by elected officials. To the obvious question of what entity was responsible for the original pre-political definitions of property rights, Epstein had a simple answer—the common law courts of the Laissez Faire Era.[18]

Convinced that it could get more bang for the buck by focusing on elite law schools, Olin awarded a substantial grant to Yale Law School to establish the John M. Olin Center for Studies in Law, Economics, and Public Policy, and it contributed more than $11 million to the Yale program over the years. The founding funders created similar programs at several other prominent law schools. The fact that law and economics scholars at these schools were sometimes less doctrinaire than their Chicago School counterparts only enhanced the credibility of the discipline in the profession. When a program strayed too far from the ideological boundaries defined by the watchful founding funders, however, it was quickly "defunded."[19]

REFOCUSING TORT LAW

A bookshelf in Judge Richard Posner's office features a scale given to him by his Chicago colleague George Stigler when Posner was appointed to the federal bench. A small block labeled "justice" sits on one pan of the scale, but the other pan holds a much larger block labeled "efficiency." The scale aptly symbolizes the priorities of the founders of Chicago School of law and economics and the conservative foundations that funded its rapid dissemination throughout legal academia. For them, tort law was less about corrective justice and more about efficiency. In *Economic Analysis of Law*, Posner referred to the "erroneous impression" that tort law was "intended solely as a device for compensation." The law's "economic function," he argued, was "to deter uneconomical conduct," and it could achieve the "right amount of deterrence" by forcing "negligent injurers to make good the victim's losses," when "negligence" incorporated a risk-benefit standard for responsible conduct. Since uneducated juries were in no position to determine the degree to which businesses should be deterred from engaging in risky conduct, Posner's more subtle message was that judges should exercise more control over juries in tort litigation. Both messages represented substantial departures from the highly pragmatic common law tradition, which had until the late 1970s rather successfully eschewed dogmatic formulas.[20]

The first major undertaking of the Olin Center at Yale was a September 1984 conference devoted to "Critical Issues in Tort Law Reform: A Search for Principles" that attracted more than 120 prominent torts scholars, state and federal judges, policymakers, practicing attorneys, and corporate officials. In addition to the Olin Foundation, the conference's sponsors included 42 companies, nearly all of which were frequent defendants in products liability lawsuits. The commissioned papers, all of which were published in the *Journal of Legal Studies*, ranged from Professor Alan Schwartz's highly theoretical expositions on the relationship between products liability, corporate structure, and bankruptcy to Professor Richard Epstein's polemic against the Progressive Era's move away from nineteenth-century privity requirements in products liability law. The conference host, George Priest, contributed a lengthy paper critiquing the Public Interest Era doctrine of "enterprise liability," which, he argued, was created out of whole cloth by activist legal academics and was therefore quite illegitimate.[21] The overall message of the conference was that tort law was badly in need of reform and that judges and legislators should move expeditiously to realign tort doctrine with the Chicago School law and economics model.[22] The conference performed its intended function of validating a budding "tort reform" movement that, as we shall see in Chapter 15, flourished into a full-scale attack on the post–Public Interest Era civil justice system.

EDUCATING LAW PROFESSORS AND JUDGES

Once they had gained a foothold in the elite law schools, the next step for the founding funders was to ensure that law professors at other institutions employed insights derived from law and economics in their teaching and writing. And the final step was to ensure that state and federal judges were exposed to law and economics through seminars, retreats, and the like. The most successful programs for educating law professors and judges on the virtues of law and economics were run by Professor Henry Manne at the four institutions to which he migrated over the years. With support from the Liberty Fund, Manne conducted the first Economics Institute for Law Professors at the University of Rochester in 1971. The Institute paid the twenty-five participants a generous stipend to study economic theory for three-and-a-half weeks under a distinguished group of law professors and economists that, in the early years, included Milton Friedman. With ample support from the Olin Foundation, which regarded the Institute as "one of its premier projects," the center grew into a major training ground for law students, law professors, and judges.[23]

THE FEDERALIST SOCIETY

Another major project of the founding funders was a student group called the Federalist Society. The organization had its origins in conversations among three friends, Lee Liberman, David McIntosh, and Stephen Calabresi, during their undergraduate years at Yale. During their second year of law school, they created a student organization for conservative law students at the University of Chicago, where McIntosh and Liberman had relocated, and Yale, where Calabresi remained. They were soon joined by Spencer Abraham, a Harvard Law student who had obtained funding from the Olin Foundation to launch a conservative legal periodical called the *Harvard Journal of Law and Public Policy*. The journal became the Federalist Society's official publication. The organization's first faculty advisor was Chicago law professor Antonin Scalia. Well connected in conservative legal circles, Scalia helped the original leaders to connect with students and faculty at other schools and to secure office space at the American Enterprise Institute for its national headquarters.[24]

Within two years of its founding in 1982, student chapters of the Federalist Society existed at most major law schools, and lawyer chapters were in place in most major cities. In short order, the Federalist Society became a pipeline to judicial clerkships with conservative judges and to mid-level jobs in Republican administrations. During the George H. W. Bush Administration, Federalist Society members were at the center of power as Liberman became the White House point person on judicial appointments and McIntosh served as the executive director of Vice President Dan Quayle's Competitiveness Council. During the Clinton Administration, Abraham was elected to the Senate and McIntosh served in the House, where Newt Gingrich appointed him to head a new Regulatory Reform subcommittee in his freshman year. Federalist Society members served as the "elves" who ensured that the revealing tapes of Linda Tripp's conversations with Monica Lewinsky wound up in the hands of Special Prosecutor Kenneth Starr (also a Federalist Society member).[25]

Over a brief span of twenty years, the Federalist Society grew to an organization with more than 40,000 members at more than 150 U.S. law schools and an annual budget exceeding $4 million. The organization ultimately provided the "network entrepreneurs" necessary for building a coalition of like-minded law professors, law students, and lawyers to carry out the assaults on the protective legal infrastructure. Its members dominated the White House Counsel's office during the George W. Bush Administration, and prominent members served as Solicitor General and Secretary of Energy. At a black-tie twenty-fifth anniversary celebration in 2007, 1,800 members packed into Union Station's great hall to hear President Bush and four sitting Supreme Court Justices sing the Federalist Society's praises. The founding funders could not have been more pleased.[26]

THE THINK TANKS

One Progressive Era innovation with considerable staying power was the Washington, D.C., "think tank," a private institution unconnected with academia that served as a source of social science expertise for policymakers. The Brookings Institution, established in 1906, was the paradigm. Its highly trained specialists offered "objective" advice backed by "scientific" analysis to government officials. While the professed neutrality of think tanks was always questionable, it was abandoned entirely in the mid-1970s when the founding funders and many large corporations responded to the Powell and Simon calls to action by pouring money into a wide variety of think tanks that were specifically designed to convey laissez faire minimalist policy prescriptions to policymakers and the public. During the Laissez Faire Revival, think tanks became policy entrepreneurs par excellence, producing hundreds of anecdote-laden books, white papers, and reports supporting predetermined positions on policy issues.[27]

THE AMERICAN ENTERPRISE INSTITUTE

The American Enterprise Association was created in 1943 by Louis Brown, the Chairman of the Johns-Mansville Corporation (the nation's premier purveyor of asbestos products) to oppose New Deal regulatory programs. When General Electric CEO A. D. Marshall assumed AEI's presidency in 1951, he raided the U.S. Chamber of Commerce to hire William Baroody, Sr., as its Executive Director. After changing the Association's name to the American Enterprise Institute (AEI) to avoid the common impression that it was merely a trade association, Baroody began to recruit laissez faire minimalist scholars like Milton Friedman to become AEI "associates." The associates remained at their universities, but received generous annual stipends and impressive academic-sounding titles from AEI for lending their names to the Institute's masthead, showing up at conferences and briefings, and writing occasional white papers and op-eds.[28]

AEI did not shy away from the political fray. Baroody was a major player in Barry Goldwater's 1964 presidential campaign, and President Nixon appointed a number of AEI associates to senior positions in his administration. When Jimmy Carter replaced President Ford in 1977, AEI recruited a number of Ford Administration officials, including Robert Bork, Antonin Scalia, and President Ford himself to serve in various capacities, thereby acquiring the reputation as a government in exile. As the Carter Administration's aggressive regulators began to implement the Public Interest Era statutes, AEI staff and associates critiqued the new regulatory programs and touted the virtues of free enterprise. AEI became the institutional home for "supply side" economics, which preached the virtues of cutting tax rates for the wealthy. In 1977, AEI launched a slick newsstand magazine, aptly named *Regulation*, to serve as a forum for easy-to-read articles advocating a wide range of business-friendly regulatory reforms. That year AEI also released more than 50 studies, organized more than 20 conferences, published 7 journals and newsletters, facilitated the publication of more than 100 op-eds, and produced a television show that was aired on more than 300 local stations.[29]

Fortune smiled on the AEI in the early 1980s. Many AEI employees accepted senior positions in the Reagan Administration. William Baroody, Jr., who inherited the executive directorship from his father in 1978, expanded the corporate donor base from 200 companies in 1977 to more than 500 in 1982. As the business community basked in the deregulatory policies of the Reagan Administration, however, AEI's fortunes shifted. Corporations eased back on their contributions, and some funders grew dissatisfied with AEI's apparent willingness to tolerate the continued existence of the federal bureaucracy. After AEI's budget suffered a 50 percent reduction over a three-year period, Baroody, Jr., was forced to resign. His replacement, Christopher DeMuth, a committed laissez faire minimalist, quickly steered AEI in a strongly deregulatory direction.[30] As we shall see in Chapter 13, it was an especially strong advocate of deregulating the banking industry during the 1980s and 1990s, lending intellectual firepower to the banking industry's successful efforts to free itself from New Deal restrictions. On the eve of the financial collapse in May 2008, AEI "scholar" Peter J. Wallison strongly opposed any new controls on the banking industry. And after the collapse, Wallison blamed the government-sponsored entities Fannie Mae and Freddie Mac for the meltdown.[31]

DeMuth headed AEI for 21 years until 2008 when he was replaced by Arthur C. Brooks, a professor of business and government policy at Syracuse University.[32] During the DeMuth years, AEI created a new Liability Project to "conduct and publicize research on the ever-expanding liability litigation crisis in the United States and abroad." The project became a major player in the ongoing "tort reform" debates by publishing a bimonthly newsletter, hosting frequent conferences on liability and insurance issues, and publishing short books on consumer class action lawsuits, securities law reform, and lawsuit reform.[33]

HERITAGE FOUNDATION

In the early 1970s, a group of conservative activists assembled by direct mail guru Paul Weyrich asked the founding funders to support a new think tank that would emphasize both economic freedom and conservative positions on "social" issues like abortion and gun control. The timing was perfect, because Joseph Coors had just read the Powell memo and was highly motivated to launch a new weapon in the culture wars that were just getting underway. With Coors's agreement to provide $200,000 per year for two years, the Heritage Foundation was born. More money soon began to flow from Coors, the Scaife and Olin foundations, and several Sunbelt entrepreneurs. The foundation also developed a direct mail solicitation program that would in time account for more than half of its budget. Making no pretense of objectivity, Heritage specialized in providing timely advice to policymakers in easily digested "briefing papers" that it circulated during the one-to-two-day news cycle of most action-forcing events.[34]

The Reagan years were very good to Heritage. At Board member William Simon's suggestion, it prepared a 3,000-page sourcebook, entitled *Mandate for Leadership*, for the incoming administration in late 1980. Among other things, it recommended that Congress replace EPA with effluent and emissions taxes and that the federal government's auto and railroad safety programs be eliminated. Heritage also provided a convenient "hit list" of mid-level holdovers that the Reagan-appointed agency heads should either fire or transfer to meaningless positions. Its Leadership Institute served as a "farm club" for prospective upper- and mid-level administration officials, and an internship program provided housing and jobs for bright young college students. Its "Resource Academic Bank" contained more than 1,000 reliably conservative academics to serve as consultants or members of federal advisory committees. At an April 1986 banquet celebrating its successful completion of a $30 million fund-raising campaign, President Reagan paid the Heritage Foundation the ultimate compliment when he credited it with breeding a "revolution in ideas occurring throughout the world."[35]

Heritage initially assumed a government in exile role during the Clinton Administration, but it came back into its own with the ascension of Newt Gingrich to the pinnacle of power in the Republican Party. Heritage advisors played a major role in drafting the "Contract with America," around which Republican candidates for the House of Representatives rallied during the 1994 election cycle. Instead of attending the traditional orientation provided by Harvard's Kennedy School, the new class of Republican freshmen attended the orientation put on by the Heritage Foundation.[36] The foundation reprised its role of purveyor of policy prescriptions and source of political appointees during the George W. Bush Administration. With an endowment of $105 million and an annual budget exceeding $25 million, Heritage helped set the Bush Administration's domestic agenda and provided unflagging support for the administration's free-market regulatory policies. Its proposed solution to the human misery following Hurricane Katrina, for example, was to create an "Emergency Regulatory Relief Board" to repeal "federal, state, and local regulations that unnecessarily impede redevelopment."[37]

CATO INSTITUTE

The Cato Institute was founded in 1977 by libertarian activists Edward Crane and Murray Rothbard with support from the Koch foundations, Sunbelt entrepreneurs, conservative foundations, and various corporations. Its strictly libertarian agenda of severely limited government and maximum individual freedom was attractive to the business community, but it occasionally conflicted with the moral agendas of social conservatives. When the Republican Party gained control of Congress in 1995, Cato urged it to repeal a long list of legislation that included most of the modern environmental statutes. Cato continued to deny that greenhouse gas emissions caused global warming long after most other conservative think tanks had switched to opposing climate change legislation on economic grounds. At the height of the Laissez Faire Revival, Cato had a budget of more than $15 million, a staff of more than 100 full-time employees, and a stable of 41 resident scholars. Every two years, it bestowed its $500,000 Milton Friedman Prize for Advancing Liberty on some deserving libertarian.[38]

MANHATTAN INSTITUTE

The Manhattan Institute was the most prominent think tank participant in the business community's efforts to reshape the civil justice system. Its initial executive director was William Hammett, "a brilliant but mercurial libertarian" whose forte was "raising money from Wall Street bankers." The Institute also received substantial sums from the founding funders and the tobacco industry, a perennial litigation defendant. It put most of its resources behind the books and articles written by its two in-house "gurus," project director Walter Olson and "Civil Justice Fellow" Peter Huber. Among other things, their books featured stories of purported abuses of the civil justice system that bore little resemblance to the actual facts. Factual accuracy was of modest importance to Hammett, who wrote that "journalists need copy, and it's an established fact that over time they'll 'bend' in the direction in which it flows." The Institute regularly invited reporters from prominent newspapers and magazines to luncheons at the Harvard Club to "mingle over cocktails with conservative elites" and the Institute's staff.[39]

THE BROOKINGS INSTITUTION

As the newer think tanks began to receive greater attention from the media and policymakers, the Brookings Institution adopted a more laissez faire-oriented approach to regulation and litigation. It supported greater use of economic incentives to induce companies to act responsibly, and it generally opposed any expansion of strict tort liability.[40] Both positions were so closely aligned with AEI's views that the two institutions in 1998 formed the Joint Center for Regulatory Studies. Generously funded by the founding funders and the business community, the Joint Center produced studies, analyses, and essays on regulatory policy, the vast majority of which suggested that federal regulation was overly burdensome and inefficient. In one of its monographs, for example, University of Chicago economist Sam Peltzman argued that "the actual effect of [automobile] safety regulation on the death rate [was] substantially less than it would be if real people behaved like crash dummies," because drivers engage in "offsetting" behaviors (like driving less carefully) that neutralize the life-saving effects of the regulations.[41]

MERCATUS CENTER

A comparatively small organization with an annual budget of around $7 million and a staff of about 30, the Mercatus Center specialized in detailed analyses of federal consumer and environmental regulations. For example, in the late 1990s, it urged EPA not to make the air quality standard for photochemical oxidants more stringent on the dubious ground that clearing the air would allow the sun's rays to cause more skin cancer. In addition to support from the founding funders, Mercatus received contributions from individual companies and donors, each of which ponied up at least $1,000 for a membership. A $10 million five-year grant from the Charles C. Koch Foundation in 1997 established the Regulatory Studies Program at the Center's headquarters at George Mason University. Its first director was Wendy Lee Gramm, a former Texas A&M economics professor who, in addition to being the wife of Senator Phil Gramm, held a number of regulation-oriented positions during the Reagan Administration. The Center regularly invited congressional staffers to catered lunchtime lectures on a variety of regulatory topics at its Capitol Hill office.[42]

THINK TANK "SCHOLARSHIP"

Although the think tanks were created to be fountainheads of "new ideas," they produced very few ideas that were really new. For the most part, they merely reframed the tenets of laissez faire minimalism for use in various regulatory and litigation settings. Few of their in-house "scholars" had been subjected to the rigorous standards that topflight academic institutions employ to promote independence and diversity, and their writings were not typically vetted by independent peers. The holder of an endowed "chair" at a think thank was far more likely to be a departing Republican political appointee than a respected academic with a graduate degree and a long list of publications. The "scholars" did not need an advanced degree in their area of claimed expertise; they did not have to meet prescribed tenure standards; they did not have the independence that tenure provides; and they bore none of the academic's responsibilities for teaching classes, serving on committees, and engaging in public service.[43]

According to long-time AEI executive director Christopher DeMuth, this freedom from academic expectations was a great virtue, because it allowed think tank scholars to "focus on what they do best."[44] And what they did best was: (1) produce thinly documented and easy-to-read books, pamphlets, congressional briefing papers, and op-ed opinion pieces, and (2) make themselves available to the press and morning talk shows for instant commentary, to congressional committees for testimony, and to political candidates for expert advice. Unlike that of academic scholarship, the purpose of think tank writing was not to expand knowledge but to create plausible justifications for laissez faire minimalist policy prescriptions. For busy policymakers, their easily digested reports were just as "authoritative" as less accessible academic work written and peer reviewed by academics. Because they were prepared to meet journalists' demands for sound bites and titillating anecdotes in a timely fashion, think tanks were an especially attractive source of expert commentary for reporters under increased pressure to do more with less.[45]

CONCLUSIONS

By any conceivable measure, the founding funders' efforts to steer the policy-making process in a business-friendly direction by supporting policy-oriented scholarship and analysis in academia and think tanks was a huge success. The Chicago School proved remarkably successful at disseminating the gospel of economic freedom to students, policymakers, politicians, and the public. Not all of those scholars and policymakers who wanted to roll back or modify Public Interest Era statutes and common law were laissez faire minimalists. Many merely wanted to fine-tune them to cure specifically identified market failures or to redirect market forces in socially desirable directions. In the pages that follow, however, we will focus on the ideas and activities of the laissez faire minimalists who were committed to changing the protective governmental infrastructure in fundamental ways to bring it closer to the laissez faire benchmark of the late nineteenth century.

With substantial financial support from conservative foundations ($68 million from the Olin Foundation alone), law and economics became an effective vehicle for incorporating a business-friendly approach to legal analysis into American legal education. Most law schools now offer multiple courses in law and economics, and few law professors feel free to ignore law and economics altogether. The Federalist Society's meetings and conferences provided a "shelter" where conservative scholars and students could network, share ideas, and critique mainstream legal scholarship in a supportive atmosphere. The think tanks were remarkably successful at what they set out to accomplish, and they now appear to be a permanent fixture in our deeply divided political culture. These institutions provided powerful critiques and bold policy prescriptions in the ideological "air war" over the power and size of the protective governmental infrastructure that took place during the Laissez Faire Revival.[46]

We should not be misled into thinking that all free enterprise advocates in the business community were motivated by or even familiar with the principled arguments of its academic proponents. It was, for example, highly unlikely that Robert Murray, the owner of the Crandall Canyon coal mine described in the Introduction, was familiar with the work of Friedrich von Hayek, Milton Friedman, or Richard Epstein, even as he mimicked their positions on the importance of private property in a capitalist economy. Most free market advocates in the business community drew on their own experiences with what they regarded to be oppressive governmental interference with their freedom to run their companies. For them, the argument was not about freedom in the abstract, but about freedom on the ground where they were struggling with the day-to-day trials of running a business. They and the lobbyists they hired provided the troops in the political "ground war" that took place in the media, the regulatory agencies, the Congress, and state legislatures. We now turn to the "influence infrastructure" that they created and continue to maintain.

6

The Influence Infrastructure

The Powell memorandum recognized that business-friendly academics and think tanks would need an influence infrastructure to place their ideas on the policy agenda and ensure that their policy prescriptions became the law of the land. Think tanks were sufficiently adaptable that they could fill that need with the help of traditional lobbying organizations like the Chamber of Commerce, the Business Roundtable, and the National Association of Manufacturers. To supplement those efforts, the founding funders created a network of pro-business activist groups to promote business-friendly solutions to social problems at the grass-roots level. The business community also established an extensive communications network to take the message to the people and to attack the messages coming from progressive advocates of stronger regulation and a more robust civil justice system.

THE GROUND TROOPS

Regulatory legislation usually requires a crisis and a resulting groundswell of public opinion. For the business community, crises of over-regulation were difficult to come by, but crises in litigation arose periodically when insurance premiums spiked and companies discovered that they could not purchase liability insurance at rates they deemed affordable. To generate the necessary groundswell of public opinion, the founding funders created organizations that were adept at fitting the laissez faire minimalist message to a populist frame, two of the most effective of which were Americans for Tax Reform (ATR) and Citizens for a Sound Economy (CSE). To coordinate the message at the state level, it created the American Legislative Exchange Council (ALEC).

AMERICANS FOR TAX REFORM

ATR was the institutional home of the anti-government firebrand Grover Norquist, an unabashed libertarian who was both a supremely confident spokesperson and an effective organizer. Although he was raised in an upper middle-class family and graduated from Harvard University, Norquist carefully projected a public image of himself as a gun-toting, venom-spitting populist. Soon after he became the executive director of ATR in 1985, Norquist conceived of an anti-tax pledge through which activists demanded that Republican politicians promise never to raise tax rates for incomes or businesses or reduce tax deductions and credits. The purpose of the pledge (which continues to stymie negotiations over budget deficits) was not so much to ensure fiscal responsibility as it was to reduce the federal government "to the size where I can drag it into the bathroom and drown it in the bathtub."[1]

Norquist skillfully turned the wonkish ATR into the premier networking vehicle for conservatives in the Washington, D.C. area. The legendary invitation-only Wednesday morning meetings that he convened and carefully micromanaged were attended by representatives of more than eighty conservative think tanks, litigation groups, and grass-roots organizations, reporters, and commentators from the business-friendly media, conservative congressional staffers, and (during conservative Republican administrations) White House officials. The meetings provided an opportunity for conservative activists to gather support for particular initiatives, coordinate messaging, and strategize. Norquist referred to the agglomeration of interests represented at these meetings as the "Leave Us Alone Coalition" because it consisted of "groups that wanted lower taxes and less government in almost every sense."[2]

CITIZENS FOR A SOUND ECONOMY

Established in 1984 by George Mason University economics professor Richard Fink with funding from the David H. Koch Foundation, Citizens for a Sound Economy (CSE) was both a think tank and a sophisticated "astroturf" lobbying operation. The chairman of its board for many years was C. Boyden Gray, the scion of a wealthy North Carolina family who had been President George H. W. Bush's White House Counsel. CSE's analysts prepared hundreds of policy papers for distribution to Congress, state legislatures, and executive branch policymakers. Its grass-roots strategies included state, local, and national advertising campaigns and public rallies targeting specific issues relevant to its overall program of regulatory and civil justice reform. Sometimes CSE initiatives followed quickly on the heels of large contributions from companies that stood to benefit directly from the policies CSE advocated. The CSE staff was also adept at generating telephone calls and personalized letters from individuals to the offices of elected officials.[3] In 2004, CSE merged with Empower America to form a new group called FreedomWorks. The Koch Industry money, however, followed a second spin-off organization called Americans for Prosperity. Both organizations played prominent roles in launching the populist "Tea Party" movement.[4]

AMERICAN LEGISLATIVE EXCHANGE COUNCIL

Conservative activist Paul Weyrich founded the American Legislative Exchange Council (ALEC) in 1973 (the same year that he co-founded the Heritage Foundation) to provide information and assistance to sympathetic state legislators. The $50 dues that each of ALEC's 3,000 legislative members paid every two years made up less than one percent of its $6 million annual budget, the remainder of which came from conservative foundations and corporations. ALEC operated through "task forces" established to address selected topics. A "national board" of elected officials and a "private enterprise board" of business leaders defined the organization's policy agenda. ALEC hosted frequent gatherings at commodious locales to provide opportunities for its public and private sector members to interact informally out of the public spotlight. For legislators who could not obtain state funding to attend, ALEC's corporate members offered generous "scholarships." Its primary products were business-friendly policy prescriptions and model state legislation. Its "disorder in the court" project worked with the defendant-oriented American Tort Reform Association and the U.S. Chamber of Commerce to press the business community's tort reform agenda at the state level.[5]

THE PINSTRIPED WARRIORS

To ensure that their voices were heard with sufficient clarity, many companies during the 1970s opened their own Washington, D.C. offices to join the lobbying shops that lined the K Street corridor. In time "K Street" became synonymous with "corporate influence" as the trade associations and "Washington reps" for individual companies filled the corridors of the Capitol and the regulatory agencies with pinstriped pleaders for particular economic interests. The Powell memo pointed out, however, that few of these corporate lobbyists purported to speak for the business community generally, and even fewer pursued a broader ideological agenda. The business community responded by creating new entities, like the Business Roundtable (BR), and revamping existing entities, like the U.S. Chamber of Commerce (CoC), the National Association of Manufacturers (NAM), and the National Federation of Independent Business (NFIB), to press a broader laissez faire minimalist agenda on behalf of all of corporate America. With resources that dwarfed those of the major think tanks, these entities extolled the virtues of free enterprise and attacked those who were not sufficiently committed to that ideal in a wide variety of forums ranging from "issue advertising" to amicus briefs in the Supreme Court. These "pinstriped warriors" became powerful political forces in the assaults on regulation and the civil justice system.[6]

CHAMBER OF COMMERCE

The CoC has been "the voice of business" and a powerful advocate of free enterprise in Washington, D.C. since 1912. As the impact of Public Interest Era legislation became painfully apparent to its members, CoC transformed itself into a fierce opponent of consumer, worker protection, and environmental regulation and a strong proponent of changes to the civil justice system. In the late 1990s, it beefed up its Washington, D.C. lobbying operation and created an in-house law firm, called the National Chamber Litigation Center, to challenge regulations and file amicus briefs in appellate cases on behalf of the business community. With a budget of around $4 million per week, the Chamber was a major player in the assaults on regulation and the civil justice system. It hosted more than 2,500 programs, meetings, seminars, and forums annually at which business leaders rubbed shoulders with members of Congress, the heads of regulatory agencies, and upper-level White House officials. The Chamber proved especially adept at channeling large contributions from its corporate members into local "issue ads" targeting candidates that they wanted to defeat. This service allowed individual companies to avoid antagonizing the targets of the ads when the attacks proved unsuccessful. Thomas Donohue, the Chamber's president for more than a decade, boasted that when the Chamber of Commerce "bites you in the butt, you bleed."[7]

NATIONAL ASSOCIATION OF MANUFACTURERS

Sometimes referred to as the "mother of business organizations," the National Association of Manufacturers (NAM) is a large agglomeration of more than 14,000 companies and 350 trade associations from the manufacturing sector of the U.S. economy. Founded in 1895, it was a prominent opponent of Pro-

MCGARITY, THOMAS O.

FREEDOM TO HARM: THE LASTING LEGACY OF THE
LAISSEZ FAIRE REVIVAL.
                                    Cloth   394 P.
NEW HAVEN: YALE UNIVERSITY PRESS, 2013

AUTH: UT/AUSTIN SCHOOL OF LAW. EXAMINES POWERFUL
BUSINESS ASSAULTS ON FEDERAL REGULATORY SYSTEM.
   LCCN 2012-43155
   ISBN 0300141246   **Library PO#** FIRM ORDERS

		List	45.00	USD
8395 NATIONAL UNIVERSITY LIBRAR	**Disc**	14.0%		
App. Date 2/12/14 SOC-SCI 8214-08	**Net**	38.70	USD	

SUBJ: 1. DEREGULATION--U.S. 2. CONSUMER PROTECTION
--U.S.
AWD/REV: 2014 CHOS
CLASS KF1600   DEWEY# 338.973   LEVEL ADV-AC

YBP Library Services

MCGARITY, THOMAS O.

FREEDOM TO HARM: THE LASTING LEGACY OF THE
LAISSEZ FAIRE REVIVAL.
                                    Cloth   394 P.
NEW HAVEN: YALE UNIVERSITY PRESS, 2013

AUTH: UT/AUSTIN SCHOOL OF LAW. EXAMINES POWERFUL
BUSINESS ASSAULTS ON FEDERAL REGULATORY SYSTEM.
   LCCN 2012-43155
   ISBN 0300141246   **Library PO#** FIRM ORDERS

		List	45.00	USD
8395 NATIONAL UNIVERSITY LIBRAR	**Disc**	14.0%		
App. Date 2/12/14 SOC-SCI 8214-08	**Net**	38.70	USD	

SUBJ: 1. DEREGULATION--U.S. 2. CONSUMER PROTECTION
--U.S.
AWD/REV: 2014 CHOS
CLASS KF1600   DEWEY# 338.973   LEVEL ADV-AC

gressive Era, New Deal Era, and Public Interest Era regulatory interventions. During the early years of the Clinton Administration, NAM created a nonprofit Manufacturing Institute to conduct studies, hold conferences, and issue reports supporting its policy goals. In the early 2000s, NAM began to file amicus briefs in litigation and to lobby for products liability reform and class action limits at the national level. Its Fair Litigation Action Group promoted changes in the civil justice system at the state level. With the shuttering of many plants and the migration of thousands of manufacturing facilities overseas, however, NAM's influence in Washington diminished in the late 2000s. To make matters worse, the deep divisions among its members on many issues of importance to its mission prevented it from speaking with a unified voice in some major policy debates.[8]

THE BUSINESS ROUNDTABLE

In 1972 Exxon CEO Clifton Garvin and Alcoa CEO John Harper created the Business Roundtable, an organization composed entirely of corporate CEOs with the sole mission of representing big business in Congress and the regulatory agencies. The group soon grew to an organization of more than 200 CEOs of corporations with nearly 10 million employees and annual revenues totaling about $4.5 trillion. The key to its success in commanding the attention of influential policymakers has been the willingness of its members to participate personally in its lobbying activities. As one congressional aide explained, the CEO of General Motors or DuPont had "a hell of a lot more impact than some lobbyist."[9]

NATIONAL FEDERATION OF INDEPENDENT BUSINESS

The National Federation of Independent Business (NFIB) was founded in 1943 by a former CoC official who was distressed at the way that the Chamber neglected its small business members. Although it agreed with the Chamber's general opposition to government regulation, NFIB argued that small businesses deserved special treatment in regulatory programs because large companies could more easily spread regulatory costs across larger production volumes. Because no politician could safely ignore the complaints of the owners of the cafes, auto dealerships, pharmacies, and other small businesses that made up most local economies, NFIB carried a great deal of political clout. In early 2000, it created the NFIB Legal Foundation to challenge federal agency regulations, assist small businesses in regulatory enforcement actions, and file amicus briefs on behalf of small business in tort litigation and challenges to agency regulations.[10]

THE COMMUNICATIONS NETWORK

During the Public Interest Era, the United States news media consisted of three major television networks broadcasting through local affiliates, several national news magazines, one or more newspapers in most major cities, hundreds of local newspapers, AM and FM radio stations (some of which were affiliated with the major television broadcasters), and the Public Broadcasting Corporation. Newsrooms were populated by professional journalists, most of whom had majored in journalism and felt an obligation to adhere to professional norms of objectivity. Except for the public broadcasting stations, they all depended on advertising for a substantial portion of their revenues. Yet the budgets of the television networks and the major newspapers were large enough to support in-depth investigative reporting on important social issues. The Federal Communications Commission enforced media ownership rules to ensure that no single broadcast company had a monopoly on the news in any region, and its "Fairness Doctrine" required television and radio stations to give equal time to opposing editorial views.[11]

The founding funders and the business community employed three broad strategies to reduce what they believed to be a "liberal bias" in the mainstream media. First, they funded media monitoring organizations and tasked them with identifying examples of liberal bias and registering bitter complaints with the press, public officials, and anyone else who would listen. Second, conservative think tanks co-opted the mainstream media by providing easily accessible sources of expertise for reporters attempting to avoid such criticism by seeking "balance" in their stories. Finally, they hoped to alter the very nature of news reporting and political commentary in the United States by creating a business-friendly media of their own. They were greatly assisted in this regard by technological changes, including the emergence of cable television, and by the rapid consolidation of media ownership during the 1980s and 1990s. Their efforts received a significant boost from the Federal Communications Commission during the Reagan Administration when it repealed the Fairness Doctrine. By the 1990s, an identifiable segment of the American media, much of it owned by Rupert Murdoch, had become a powerful conveyor belt for conservative commentary, storylines, jargon, and spin.[12]

ATTACKING THE MAINSTREAM MEDIA

The founding funders and the business community created two "media cops" to validate their conviction that the mainstream media were generally biased against business. The Coors and Scaife foundations and several large corporations created Accuracy in Media in the early 1970s in direct response to the Powell memo. The Media Research Center was founded in the early 1990s by L. Brent Bozell, III, a nephew of William F. Buckley.[13] The poorly documented "liberal bias" claim provided conservative commentators with several important tactical advantages. First, the threat of being accused of liberal bias could have a chilling effect on editors deciding whether to run controversial investigative reports into corporate malfeasance. Second, it allowed the corporate targets of published investigative reports to parry their thrust. Third, it motivated reporters to seek out "both sides" of significant public policy disputes, thereby giving conservative commentators access to the mainstream media. Finally, readers and listeners who were already persuaded looked to the conservative media for the bulk of their diet of reinforcing news and commentary.[14]

CO-OPTING THE MAINSTREAM MEDIA

As cost-conscious editors drove journalists to present the news in standardized formats that required little digging into the details of the underlying subject matter, a subtle change in journalistic emphasis occurred through which "objectivity" in reporting (a goal that required the journalist to ferret out the truth of factual claims) was transformed into "balance" (a criterion that could easily be met by airing both "sides" of any purported dispute). Conservative think tanks made their experts instantly available to reporters to convey the business community's take on the issues of the day and to defend it against criticisms from academics and progressive activists. Astroturf organizations like Citizens for a Sound Economy and FreedomWorks generated crowds of protestors that attracted mainstream news outlets hungry for controversy. These vehicles for moving conservative viewpoints into the mainstream media were far less expensive than paid advertising, and the patina of objectivity that think tank "experts" carried made them far more effective than corporate flacks for communicating a laissez faire minimalist message.[15]

CREATING A BUSINESS-FRIENDLY MEDIA

At the heart of the business community's strategy for determining the content of news and political commentary was a sustained effort to coordinate a single message on any given issue across many media outlets owned or managed by people who would adopt a business-friendly perspective. By the early 1990s, it had created a conservative "echo chamber," a term that Professors Jamieson and Cappella define as "a bounded, enclosed media space that has the potential to both magnify the messages delivered within it and insulate them from rebuttal." Much of the content of the echo chamber's message was determined by conservative think tanks, like-minded academics, corporate public relations experts, and Republican political strategists. A singular exception was the *Wall Street Journal,* which had a laissez faire minimalist editorial page but allowed professional journalists to determine the content of the news it reported. After Rupert Murdoch purchased the paper's holding company in 2008, however, the news coverage began to demonstrate an unmistakable anti-government, pro-business slant.[16]

Soon after the repeal of the Fairness Doctrine in 1987, a new medium dubbed "talk radio" allowed conservative hosts like Rush Limbaugh to preach laissez faire minimalism to millions of listeners. Limbaugh's three-hour weekday attacks on liberals and the federal government attracted such large audiences that he could command an eight-year contract with Clear Channel Communications worth $400 million.[17] The television equivalent of talk radio was Fox News. Its owner, Rupert Murdoch, was a committed laissez faire minimalist whose views were reflected in both the editorial and substantive content of Fox News broadcasts. Fox programming featured far more political commentary than the major networks, and its regular commentators included Limbaugh, Glen Beck. and other conservative entertainers as well as a stable of Republican politicians and conservative think tank scholars.[18] Although Clear Channel, Fox News, and other major news outlets that made up the echo chamber were profit-making entities, most of the opinion magazines and many of the smaller news outlets that reverberated with laissez faire minimalist prescriptions were subsidized by the founding funders and the business community.[19]

CONCLUSIONS

As the business community's influence infrastructure grew and matured, it had a profound impact on public policy. Pro-business activist groups demonstrated that consumer and environmental groups did not have a monopoly on defining the public good. A pro-business echo chamber gave think tank pundits and conservative academics easy access to op-ed pages, political talk shows, and news programming that other academic scholars lacked. Through the transubstantiating power of repetition in multiple media outlets, speculative conclusions became unassailable facts and marginal theories became conventional wisdom, not just within the echo chamber itself but also in the public consciousness.[20]

Part Three

The Laissez Faire Revival

The founding funders and the business community created the idea and influence infrastructures with a single broad goal in mind—a return to the laissez faire benchmark of the Gilded Age. They were committed to replacing the government that emerged from the Public Interest Era with a government that provided a great deal more freedom to companies to invent, manufacture, and deliver their products and services without the restrictions of regulations and without the threat of crushing liability. To accomplish this Laissez Faire Revival, they would have to "reform" the existing institutions of responsibility and accountability in radical ways. Since those who benefited from the existing regulatory and civil justice systems were not likely to accept radical change without a fight, free enterprise proponents were prepared to carry out a sustained effort over a long period of time.

The attack came in three waves. The first assault stretched from the last two years of the Carter Administration through 1983, when the Reagan Administration beat a hasty retreat in anticipation of the 1984 elections. There followed an interregnum during which the business community focused its energies on impeding the efforts of resource-strapped agencies to implement the Public Interest Era statutes and the protective statutes that Congress enacted in reaction to the deregulatory excesses of the Reagan Administration. This interregnum lasted through the first two years of the Clinton Administration with a brief resurgence of the assault from within the George H. W. Bush Administration during the 1992 election year. The second assault was launched by Newt Gingrich and the Republican congresspersons who signed the Contract with America in 1994 and lasted until just after a face-off between President Clinton and Gingrich resulted in a disastrous government shutdown at the end of 1995.

There followed a second interregnum during which Congress passed some mildly progressive legislation, the agencies became more aggressive, and the business community concentrated on impeding the Clinton Administration's implementation of the Public Interest Era statutes, all of which had survived the second assault. The third assault came with the election of George W. Bush and a Republican-controlled Congress in 2001.

Chapter 7 will provide a broad overview of the three assaults on regulation, highlighting the efforts in the executive branch to rein in the regulatory agencies and in Congress to pass "omnibus" regulatory reform legislation. Chapters 8 through 14 will highlight the Laissez Faire Revival in the regulatory agencies charged with implementing and enforcing the Public Interest Era statutes in the substantive areas of worker safety, environmental protection, drug and device safety, food safety, transportation safety, financial protection, and consumer protection. Chapter 15 will describe the three assaults on the civil justice system, which differed slightly in timing from the assaults on the regulatory system and also focused on state legislatures and judicial elections.

THE ASSAULTS ON REGULATION

Toward the end of the Public Interest Era in the mid-1970s, the business community found itself in an uncomfortable world in which the scope and depth of its responsibilities had expanded, its accountability to plaintiffs and the beneficiaries of regulatory programs had grown, and its freedom to pursue profits had correspondingly diminished. Having lost the critical legislative battles, it sought to cushion the impact of the new statutes by delaying their implementation, demanding exemptions, and pressing for industry-friendly interpretations. It also went to great lengths to persuade the White House and Congress to impose constraints on the rulemaking process that regulatees could employ to impede agency rulemaking initiatives. As memories of the crises faded, it petitioned agencies to amend the rules in light of their "unintended consequences" and tested their boundaries in individual enforcement actions.

The business community's reaction to the Public Interest Era legislation, however, differed from the typical crisis, reform, and erosion pattern that characterized the periods of retrenchment following the Progressive and New Deal Eras. The goal this time was not merely to forestall the advance of regulatory programs. It was to reverse the gains of all three eras and return to the laissez faire benchmark of the last quarter of the nineteenth century. With assistance from its new idea infrastructure, the business community launched a continuous "air war" on protective governmental programs, the goal of which was to change public attitudes about the role of government in society. Beginning with Ronald Reagan's first inaugural address, the message that big government, not big business, was the problem resonated in the conservative media echo chamber for thirty years. In every available forum, think tank "scholars" blamed government for every conceivable social ill. As people's views began to change, the business community's influence infrastructure launched three full-scale assaults on the protective governmental infrastructure in a take-no-prisoners "ground war" waged in Congress, the regulatory agencies, state legislatures, and the courts.

The ground-level assaults were sporadically interrupted by crises that focused public attention on the failures of one or another regulatory program. Congressional committees would hold hearings, the industry would disclaim responsibility, the agency would promise to do better, and Congress occasionally amended the statute to address the particular failure that gave rise to the crisis. As time passed and memories of the crisis faded, however, the industry would reassert itself, the agency would get bogged down in the details of implementation and judicial review, and the program would make little progress. In the meantime, the idea infrastructure continued the air attacks, the media dutifully reported their regulatory horror stories, and public attitudes toward government continued to sour as it appeared less and less capable of protecting workers, consumers, neighbors, and the environment.

As the assaults grew in intensity and public support for the agencies dwindled, the business community chipped away at the protective governmental infrastructure. The business community's efforts to resist regulation were frequently aided by unrelated developments like a weakening economy or an energy crisis. It also took advantage of a resurgence of social conservatism as many middle-class Americans rebelled against attempts by civil rights advocates to use government institutions to advance racial and economic justice. At times the interests of the business community and those of social conservatives were perfectly aligned, as in the case of employment discrimination laws, and at other times they diverged, as in the case of stem cell research to develop new blockbuster drugs. But Grover Norquist's goal of shrinking government resonated with both social conservatives and regulatory reformers.

Over time, Congress flat-lined or reduced agency budgets and erected procedural and analytical barriers to promulgating regulations, thereby rendering the task of protective rulemaking far more difficult. Headed by political appointees who were unsympathetic to their statutory missions, the agencies abandoned the proactive approaches that they employed during the Public Interest Era and assumed a reactive posture. They promulgated fewer protective regulations, and when they did impose new requirements, they usually lacked the resources (and often the inclination) to enforce them. As the hand of restraint weakened, the powerful stallion of corporate America gained greater freedom to benefit or harm society.

RESISTANCE AND EROSION IN THE NIXON/
FORD ADMINISTRATIONS

Beginning in the early 1970s, presidents of both political parties required agencies to prepare detailed analyses of the costs and benefits of major regulations. These and other requirements that the courts added to the simple "notice-and-comment" model of informal rulemaking had the effect of "ossifying" the rulemaking process to such a degree that it became extremely difficult for the agencies to promulgate the regulations their statutes demanded. Every president since President Nixon has also created a process for inter-agency review of regulations issued by executive branch agencies. Since 1980, the agency responsible for managing the review process has been the Office of Information and Regulatory Affairs (OIRA) in the Office of Management and Budget. The reviews provided opportunities for the business community's allies within the administration to pressure the rulemaking agency to weaken the rules. Occasionally, regulated companies gained direct access to the internal review process and presented their arguments directly to administration policymakers before others had a chance to comment on agency proposals.[1]

As the nation entered the 1976 election cycle, newly minted and refurbished think tanks weighed in for the first time with studies purporting to demonstrate that the costs of federal consumer, health, and environmental regulations outweighed the benefits. The American Enterprise Institute (AEI) sponsored its first conference on "regulatory reform" in September 1975 featuring a debate on federal regulation between California Governor Ronald Reagan and consumer activist Ralph Nader in which Reagan regaled the audience with the regulatory "horror stories" that he would feature in his morning radio broadsides for the next four years.[2]

THE FIRST ASSAULT IN THE CARTER ADMINISTRATION

President Jimmy Carter rewarded the consumer and environmental activists who helped elect him by appointing more than 60 of them to high-level positions in the regulatory agencies. For expertise, he turned not to the regulated industries, but to academics and the legislative aides who had been responsible for steering strong legislation through Congress. Instead of rewarding loyal campaign workers with patronage jobs, he crossed party lines to appoint experienced bureaucrats.[3] As the administration struggled to revive the flagging spirit of the Public Interest Era, it faced an array of think tanks that focused public discontent over steadily increasing energy prices and a deteriorating economy on the cost of protective regulations. With far greater credibility than corporate public relations exercises, their polished reports moved public opinion while providing cover for wavering politicians.[4] Environmental destruction, workplace fatalities, and consumer fraud became yesterday's news as the mainstream media began to pay closer attention to horror stories featuring abusive bureaucrats and senseless regulations.[5]

With the U.S. Chamber of Commerce (CoC) leading the charge, the business community's influence infrastructure launched the first ground-level assault on federal regulation in the late 1970s. The Chamber assembled a massive grass-roots lobbying network that was capable of generating 12,000 phone calls a day. The National Federation of Independent Business appealed to its 600,000 members to generate similar grass-roots pressure on targeted members of Congress. The Business Roundtable flew in CEOs of Fortune 500 companies for one-on-one meetings with influential senators and representatives. The business community brilliantly seized the reform mantle as it pressed Congress and the White House to scale back federal regulation.[6]

The Carter Administration not only failed to present a coherent defense of government regulation, but it also appeared to ratify the business community's critique as it began to scale back regulatory protections. In response to a souring economy during the winter of 1977–78, President Carter signed an executive order that for the first time required agencies to review existing regulations and rescind those that were no longer cost-beneficial. Later that year, the president created a new reviewing entity called the Regulatory Analysis Review Group (RARG) to counterbalance the regulators. Chaired by White House economic advisor Charles Schultze, the committee selected 10–20 of the most contentious new regulations per year for detailed review. The RARG process made the agencies more sensitive to economic considerations and stimulated them to experiment with more flexible incentive-based approaches toward regulation. But when the agency heads elevated disputes to the Oval Office, they usually prevailed. Because Congress continued to increase agency budgets, regulatory output remained high.[7]

Since the Democratic Party controlled both houses of Congress after the 1976 elections, public interest advocates anticipated another round of legislation to build on past Public Interest Era victories. That expectation, however, went largely unfulfilled as a severe inflation combined with an economic downturn to command Congress's attention. The business community seized the offensive with a regulatory reform agenda and a public relations campaign that focused on fighting inflation and increasing employment. Consequently, things moved in a decidedly deregulatory direction during the last three years of the Carter Administration. Consumer activists supported Carter Administration initiatives to eliminate "economic" regulation in the transportation and energy sectors because such regulation often protected the regulated industries from healthy competition and kept prices artificially high. The generally accepted critiques of economic regulation, however, blended with the business community's far more controversial critiques of consumer, worker safety, and environmental regulation to precipitate a growing public skepticism of government intervention of all kinds.[8]

Legislation providing for greater regulatory intervention like the Carter Administration's proposal to create a new Consumer Protection Agency died on the vine, while deregulatory legislation passed easily. Amendments to the Federal Trade Commission Act made it far more difficult for FTC to protect consumers from unfair trade practices and effectively repealed some ongoing rulemaking initiatives. Mid-course corrections to the environmental statutes extended compliance deadlines and relaxed some standards while imposing constraints that ensured that EPA's rules would be even more controversial. The Regulatory Flexibility Act of 1980 required agencies to prepare a separate analysis detailing the impact of proposed rules on small business entities. Referring to the surprisingly rapid shift in congressional sentiment, Ralph Nader explained that "[t]he consumer movement hasn't gotten weaker, the opposition has gotten stronger." The business community's careful attention to the Powell/Simon message was beginning to pay off.[9]

THE FIRST ASSAULT IN THE REAGAN ADMINISTRATION

Ronald Reagan was the charismatic champion that the business community needed to change the political culture. A steady dose of Hayek and the *National Review* during the years that he sold progress as the General Electric Company's most important product had turned Reagan into a supremely effective spokesperson for laissez faire minimalism. In 1975, Reagan became one of the Laissez Faire Revival's first media stars as a syndicated radio commentator, newspaper columnist, and speaker on the lecture circuit. Although he was not the business community's first choice for president in 1980, it quickly warmed to him as he made his free enterprise narrative a major theme in his successful campaign.

On December 9, 1980, the American Enterprise Institute (AEI) hosted a breakfast for the incoming president and high-level White House staff at which AEI scholars presented a laundry list of regulatory reforms for the administration to implement forthwith. Since five of those scholars were currently serving on the transition team, they could have some confidence that the suggestions would be taken seriously. The Heritage Foundation went AEI one better by serving up a 3,000-page *Mandate for Leadership* offering hundreds of suggestions for reducing the size and power of regulatory programs. In addition to influencing the new administration's thinking on federal regulation, think tanks also played a critical role in matching reliable young conservative activists with recently appointed officials looking for mid-level staff. The Federalist Society played a similar role as a supplier of conservative young law graduates to the Justice Department and the general counsel offices of the regulatory agencies.[10]

The influence infrastructure was also prepared for an all-out assault on regulation. The CoC hit the ground running with a "hit list" of federal regulations that it targeted for repeal or revision. It spearheaded a "Coalition on Regulatory Reform" that assembled more than sixty "strategy groups" from many different industries to coordinate lobbying strategy. And the Chamber's national headquarters hosted an "Insiders' Breakfast" every other Thursday morning at which representatives from dozens of trade associations gathered to get updates and plan upcoming activities.[11]

President Reagan delivered an enormous boost to the business community's air war when he proclaimed in his first inaugural address that in the "present crisis, government is not the solution to our problems, government *is* the problem." And he supported the ground war by making "regulatory relief" one of the four cornerstones of his "economic recovery program."[12] To emphasize the importance of that goal, he created a special "Task Force on Regulatory Relief" chaired by Vice-President George H. W. Bush. Drawing on recommendations solicited from regulated companies, the Task Force prepared a series of "hit lists" that it sent to the agencies with instructions to repeal or revise listed regulations to the extent allowed by their statutes. The president wasted no time in replacing Carter Administration holdovers in the regulatory agencies with devoted deregulators, most of whom had worked for either the regulated industry or one of the many think tanks and pro-business activist groups that the founding funders had recently established. The president appointed James Miller, the co-director of AEI's Center for the Study of Government Regulation, to head OIRA. When Miller left to chair the FTC, his replacement was Christopher DeMuth, a lecturer at Harvard's Kennedy School and a committed deregulator.[13]

During his first week in office, President Reagan signed an executive order greatly expanding OIRA's oversight powers and directing any agency appeals to the Task Force. It also prescribed in more detail the requirements for the "regulatory impact assessments" that had to accompany major rules. When not explicitly prohibited by statute, agencies had to choose the alternative with the largest benefit-to-cost ratio. Subsequent executive orders requiring agencies to submit biannual regulatory agendas and to analyze "takings," "trade," "federalism," and "family" impacts of regulations only added to the disincentive to promulgate rules.[14]

An early OMB briefing package to the president advised that "fewer regulators will necessarily result in fewer regulations and less harassment of the regulated." Accordingly, the budgets of the regulatory agencies, which had nearly quadrupled between 1970 and 1980, stayed flat in 1981 and decreased by 9 percent in 1982. As predicted, rulemaking at several agencies came to a halt. And the agencies took care to craft the regulations that they did propose in a more business-friendly fashion to enhance the likelihood that they would survive OIRA review. Especially severe cuts to agency enforcement budgets produced dramatic declines in inspections, citations, and prosecutions.[15]

The business community was initially quite pleased with the Reagan Administration's regulatory relief program, but by 1983 the Heritage Foundation was worrying that its accomplishments would be "transitory." Controlled by Democrats, congressional committees were shining a harsh light on agency failures to enforce their laws and other improprieties. Committee staffers discovered that an EPA assistant administrator for hazardous wastes had accepted a number of lavish meals from industry lobbyists and had ordered her staff to shred documents relevant to the committee's inquiry. Another dispute arose over OIRA's secret meetings with industry representatives to discuss pending agency rulemaking proposals. After the House voted 302–118 to "zero-out" OIRA's appropriation, OIRA Administrator Wendy Gramm negotiated a compromise under which all documents exchanged between OIRA and the agencies were made public. The heavily publicized EPA and OMB confrontations allowed public interest advocates to characterize the administration as a den of corrupt zealots bent on subsidizing the business community at the expense of the environment. The degree of public outrage that attended the scandals caught the administration off guard, and it never regained the high ground in the debate over regulation.[16]

The administration's efforts to undo the protective governmental infrastructure met with only limited success. Congress did not roll back a single substantive statutory protection, and in 1984 and 1986 it expanded the protections afforded by two hazardous waste control and cleanup statutes. An attempt to enact "omnibus" regulatory reform legislation likewise failed. Administration insiders later admitted that they had failed to lay the necessary foundation of public support for legislative reform. Attempts to repeal the rules identified by the Vice-President's Task Force failed in large part because reviewing courts demanded the same degree of analysis and explanation for rule rescission as for rule promulgation. The Task Force quietly went out of business in August 1983, and deregulation went into "cold storage."[17]

Although the first assault did not succeed in dismantling the protective governmental infrastructure, it did make considerable headway. Repeated cuts to their budgets caused agencies to delay or abandon proactive rulemaking except for a few deregulatory initiatives and proactive rules implementing specific statutory mandates. In the hands of the "great communicator," Ronald Reagan, the administration's laissez faire minimalist message became deeply imbedded in media coverage of regulatory developments. And the scandals ironically contributed to a growing public distrust of government that over time proved quite corrosive to the protective governmental infrastructure. Finally, the Reagan Administration served as a training ground for the next generation of conservative activists.[18]

THE FIRST INTERREGNUM

To the chagrin of the CoC, candidate George H. W. Bush announced that he would be an "environmental president." Rejecting for the most part the think tanks' long lists of possible appointees, President Bush stressed pragmatism and administrative competence over ideology in selecting agency heads.[19] The president, however, relied more heavily on laissez faire minimalists in filling important White House positions. His long-time aide C. Boyden Gray became Counselor to the President with a wide portfolio. Gray was a strong proponent of market-based approaches to regulation and of radical reforms to the civil justice system. To staff his office, Gray drew on a group of highly ideological lawyers, including Federalist Society founder Lee S. Liberman. A practitioner at a prominent D.C. law firm prior to joining the government, Gray always had his door open to his former clients from the Business Roundtable. After leaving government, he became the chairman of Citizens for a Sound Economy.[20]

Reacting to reports that the agencies were increasing regulatory burdens, President Bush in March 1989 created a "Council on Competitiveness" under Vice-President Dan Quayle to perform the same function that his Regulatory Relief Task Force had played during the Reagan Administration. Federalist Society founder David M. McIntosh, the Council's Deputy Executive Director, positioned himself at the center of the most important interagency regulatory battles. Centralized review returned to the shadows as the Council eschewed

written records and resisted all requests to appear before congressional committees.[21] For the administration's first three years, however, the agencies went
about their business without much interference from the Competitiveness
Council. Agency budgets rose slightly, though most did not regain Carter Administration levels. The administration's crowning domestic policy achieve-
ment was the Clean Air Act amendments of 1990, which created several major
regulatory programs.[22]

As the 1992 election season drew near, the business community was in a state
of rebellion. The *National Journal* ran a cover story entitled "The Regulatory
President" reporting that the president's "first term has witnessed the broadest
expansions of government's regulatory reach since the early 1970's."[23] Reacting to the criticism, the Competitiveness Council became far more aggressive
in reining in the agencies, but took care to leave "no fingerprints." A Competitiveness Council working group issued a report containing 50 far-reaching
recommendations for deregulatory legislation. In January 1992, President Bush
imposed a "moratorium" on all new regulations (except those designed to foster
economic growth) and ordered the agencies to rescind or rewrite all existing
rules that failed a cost-benefit test. Vice-President Quayle urged the business
community to suggest rules for revision or repeal, and appreciative regulatees
scrambled to take advantage of the overture. The most assertive agency leaders, however, were not cowed by the Council's rather ham-handed attempt at
deregulation, and very few substantive changes ensued.[24]

At first blush, President Clinton's victory in the 1992 elections appeared to
signal a significant setback for the business community's regulatory reform efforts, but it turned out that Clinton was not as interested in expanding the protective governmental infrastructure as he was in "reinventing" government to
make it more effective and less intrusive. His initial appointees to important
regulatory positions tended to be moderate pragmatists with experience in either business or state government. His choice of Sally Katzen, a prominent
Washington, D.C. attorney, to head OIRA drew rave reviews from C. Boyden
Gray and James C. Miller III.[25]

President Clinton disbanded the Council on Competitiveness, reassigned
the interagency review process to OIRA, and made Vice-President Gore the
final arbiter of interagency disputes. A new executive order continued to require agencies to prepare regulatory analyses of major rules, but it was not as
demanding as the Reagan executive order in requiring agencies to maximize
net benefits. OIRA Administrator Katzen regarded herself as a "process person,"
and OIRA reviews became less intrusive than they were during the Reagan and
Bush Administrations. She also took steps to make the review process more

transparent. The number of rules that OIRA reviewed dropped dramatically from more than 2,200 per year during the Reagan Administration to less than 750 per year. Moreover, the percentage of the rules for which OIRA suggested changes dwindled from over 27 percent in 1991 to just under 20 percent in 1993. In general, OIRA had a much better relationship with consumer and environmental activists than at any other time in its history. Substantively, the Clinton Administration's regulatory policies during its first two years did not vary greatly from those of the early Bush Administration.[26]

THE SECOND ASSAULT — THE GINGRICH CONGRESS

As the economy blossomed under the centrist Clinton Administration, the business community did not quietly pursue modest retrenchment as it had during the great compression of the fifties. Instead, it launched a second and even more vigorous assault on government regulation, focusing this time on Congress. The unlikely leader of the second assault was Newt Gingrich, the strategically brilliant, but highly abrasive leader of the conservative wing of the Republican Party. His persistent attacks on the federal government and prodigious fund-raising efforts during the 1994 off-year elections had paved the way for the election of a militantly anti-government freshman class in the House. With the help of political consultant Frank Luntz, Gingrich drafted a proposed renegotiation of the social bargain called the "Contract with America" and persuaded most Republican House candidates to pledge to uphold it if elected. Among other things, the Contract promised to pass during the first 100 days of the 104th Congress: (1) a Job Creation and Wage Enhancement Act that would subject all federal regulation to new risk assessment and cost-benefit analysis requirements and provide small business entities more opportunities to block federal regulations; and (2) a Common Sense Legal Reform Act that would force plaintiffs to pay the litigation costs incurred by successful defendants, place "reasonable" limits on punitive damage awards, and reform product liability laws.[27]

After Gingrich was elected Speaker of the House, he assigned the task of running its day-to-day affairs to the new majority leader, Richard K. Armey (R-Texas), as pure a laissez faire minimalist as existed in national politics. If Gingrich and Armey deeply distrusted the federal government, Republican whip Tom DeLay positively despised it. The fiercely partisan freshman members were even more confident of their mandate to dismantle the protective governmental infrastructure than the leadership. Although great admirers of Gingrich, they were constantly pressing him to advance a deregulatory agenda that went considerably beyond the Contract's promises.[28]

At the outset of the 104th Congress, the think tanks reinvigorated the air war with a flood of studies, white papers, and pamphlets urging Congress to repeal or substantially rewrite the Public Interest Era statutes and revamp products liability law. At a special AEI seminar on regulatory reform, one of the sessions was entitled "What to Kill First: Agencies to Dismantle, Programs to Eliminate, and Regulations to Stop." The Cato Institute urged Congress to "jettison the entire foundation of modern environmental law." Harvard's Kennedy School was forced to cancel its long-running orientation for congressional newcomers, because the Republican freshmen decided to attend a three-day Heritage Foundation training session instead.[29]

The influence infrastructure was fully engaged in the ground war. In early February, the CoC presented a wish list of legislative proposals, called the "National Business Agenda," to Gingrich at a staged "town meeting" and conducted a national educational effort, called the "Campaign for Regulatory Efficiency," to build grass-roots support for the agenda. NAM created an umbrella group of more than 2,600 companies called the Alliance for Reasonable Regulation (ARR) to lobby for changes to the Public Interest Era statutes. The Business Round Table published a document entitled "Towards Smarter Regulation" containing twelve tenets of rational regulation. Citizens for a Sound Economy commissioned the pollsters and media strategists who had marketed the Contract with America to assist it in "combat message development."[30]

Having contributed heavily to the Republican victory, the business community received unprecedented access to the House leadership. House Republican Conference chairman John Boehner met with corporate lobbyists and representatives of selected think tanks and conservative activist groups every Thursday morning in the Speaker's office, where they matched their lobbying initiatives to the Republican agenda. The Republican leadership and the business community coordinated regulatory reform strategy through an umbrella organization called "Project Relief." The brainchild of Majority Whip Tom DeLay, the group consisted of more than 300 companies, trade associations, and lobbyists who committed their time and resources to drafting and lobbying for the leadership's regulatory reform bills. At the same time that they were drafting industry-friendly legislation for the Republicans, the lobbyists were also actively soliciting funds for their campaign coffers. DeLay explained that "[i]f you're going to play in our revolution, you've got to live by our rules."[31]

The second assault in Congress proceeded along three major fronts. First, the Republican leadership introduced "omnibus" regulatory reform legislation that, among other things, would have imposed numerous procedural and analytical requirements on agency rulemaking and required agencies to base their regulations on formal cost-benefit analysis. Second, it attempted to repeal or substantially rewrite many of the Public Interest Era statutes. We will take up these substantive bills in the chapters that follow. Third, they launched piecemeal attacks on the federal bureaucracy through funding cuts and riders to "must pass" bills that were aimed at preventing the agencies from carrying out their statutory responsibilities.

The leaders of most of the regulatory agencies vigorously defended their programs in congressional testimony and public appearances and with "truth squads" they assembled to arm congressional allies with responses to the often wildly inaccurate accusations and apocryphal horror stories that appeared daily in congressional testimony and think tank pamphlets. President Clinton attempted to co-opt the regulatory reformers by offering his own reforms. While Congress was debating regulatory reform legislation, the administration was announcing a stream of deregulatory initiatives. For example, a "page-by-page" review of existing agency regulations yielded proposals to eliminate 20 percent and modify 35 percent of them. With barely a nod to the role that regulation had played in improving American lives, the president in his January 1996 State of the Union message declared that "the era of big government is over."[32]

The House passed omnibus regulatory reform legislation within the promised hundred days. The even more restrictive Senate bill, introduced by Senate Majority Leader Bob Dole, got off to a bad start when the press reported that attorneys for a law firm representing some of the country's biggest polluters had conducted a briefing for Senate staffers to explain the bill's complex provisions, many of which they had drafted. Seizing the initiative, President Clinton warned that he would not hesitate to veto bills that weakened federal health and environmental protections. The Senate debates during the summer of 1995 were filled with tales of abusive government inspectors and pointless regulations. Consumer groups responded by flying in victims of corporate abuse to demonstrate the carnage that could result if Congress dismantled existing regulatory protections. After three cloture votes to stop a threatened filibuster barely failed, however, the Senate Republican leadership put omnibus regulatory reform legislation on the back burner.[33]

Congress later passed two modest regulatory reform bills that added to the agencies' rulemaking burden. The Unfunded Mandates Reform Act required agencies to prepare an impact statement prior to publishing a proposed rule containing a federal mandate that could result in an annual expenditure of $100 million by public or private sector entities. The "Small Business Regulatory Enforcement Fairness Act" (SBREFA) allowed small businesses to seek judicial review of the content of the impact statements that agencies were obliged to prepare under the Regulatory Flexibility Act of 1980. In addition, the law required EPA and OSHA (but not other agencies) to convene a "review panel" of government officials and small business representatives and consider their views prior to publishing major regulations.[34]

The stealth strategy of starving the agencies and attaching substantive riders to appropriations bills met with surprising resistance from the Clinton White House, and the battle over the FY 1996 budget marked the turning point in the second assault on regulation. As the House Appropriations subcommittees proposed draconian cuts to the FY 1996 agency budgets, Majority Whip Tom DeLay insisted upon adding 17 deregulatory riders to EPA's appropriation bill. The day after the House bill passed, President Clinton promised to veto the "polluter's protection act." After the Senate passed a bill that did not vary greatly from the House bill, the president vetoed a continuing resolution to keep the government running on an interim basis. On November 14, all nonessential federal agencies ceased doing business. As public sentiment coalesced against the Republicans, Gingrich made matters worse by complaining that he would have been more willing to make concessions if Clinton had not made him exit from the rear of Air Force One on a trip to attend the funeral of Israel's assassinated president. After a brief return to activity, the government shut down again for three weeks in mid-December. A holiday season's worth of bad press put Gingrich in a less petulant mood. In April 1996, the president signed a FY 1996 appropriations bill that cut agency budgets far less than the original House bill, dropped some of the environmental riders, and weakened others.[35]

By late fall 1996, it had become clear from multiple polls that the public strongly opposed radical surgery on the Public Interest Era protective statutes. The economy was booming, the regulatory agencies were busily reinventing themselves, and the second assault was effectively over. An uncharacteristically subdued Gingrich acknowledged that "we mishandled the environment all spring and summer." The second assault, however, had a profound *in terrorem* effect on the regulatory agencies. The modest trend toward increasing regulatory activity during the first interregnum reversed itself as the agencies shifted into defensive mode. Budget cutbacks resulted in reduced regulatory output as well as less stringent enforcement of existing requirements.[36]

THE SECOND INTERREGNUM

With the White House in the hands of a president who had demonstrated his willingness to veto radical legislation, the business community refocused the ground war on preventing the agencies from writing additional restrictions. At the same time, the air war continued in the media where, in the view of many in the business community, the think tanks had done a poor job of "marketing and explaining" their ideas to the public. In the much less visible debates over health and environmental regulation during the 105th Congress, the think tanks appeared to concede the virtue of governmental protections while attacking the bureaucrats that administered them. Instead of "command-and-control" regulation through which agencies attempted to specify appropriate conduct, they recommended market-oriented approaches aimed at stimulating companies to behave responsibly by making it more expensive for them to behave irresponsibly.[37]

With President Clinton's convincing re-election in 1996, some regulatory agencies began to ease out of their defensive postures while others remained hunkered down. Those agencies, like EPA, that seized the offensive adopted moderate "reinventionist" approaches to regulation that yielded few controversial regulations. After the poor Republican showing in the 1998 off-year elections, Gingrich stepped down as Speaker of the House, and House Majority Leader Tom DeLay assumed effective control. Rather than reviving the second assault, DeLay adopted a twofold strategy of destroying Bill Clinton personally and raising as much money as possible to finance a third assault after George W. Bush (the Republican presidential frontrunner) became president. The first strategy failed miserably in the Senate, which resoundingly rejected the House's impeachment of the president.[38]

The second strategy yielded the highly successful "K Street Project." The brainchild of Grover Norquist, the project's goal was to turn Washington, D.C. lobbyists (a critical component of the business community's influence infrastructure) into a bottomless well of campaign contributions channeled exclusively to Republican candidates. In return, the Republican Party would richly reward their clients with government contracts, tax breaks, and regulatory relief. The K Street Project became the vehicle through which the influence infrastructure gained direct access to the congressional leadership during the third assault.[39]

THE THIRD ASSAULT—
THE GEORGE W. BUSH ADMINISTRATION

Tom DeLay's vision of a Republican political hegemony became a reality in December 2000 when five Supreme Court justices called a halt to a controversial recount of the Florida ballots and George W. Bush became President of the United States. With Republican majorities in both houses of Congress and much of the federal judiciary appointed by Republican presidents, the stars were finally aligned for a major renegotiation of the social bargain. The business community's think tanks and lobbyists went into overdrive to ensure that regulatory reform was high on the policymaking agenda. The Federalist Society devoted its annual conference in March 2001 to "Rolling Back the New Deal." The Heritage Foundation urged Congress to cut agency budgets and resurrect the regulatory reform legislation that had been on the back burner since 1996. The Business Roundtable produced a set of principles to govern future environmental regulation.[40]

The business community's legislative agenda was briefly waylaid when its aggressive efforts to roll back environmental protections so alienated a moderate senator from Vermont that he abandoned the Republican Party and the Democrats regained control of the Senate for a year. That, too, changed when the Republican Party regained control of both houses of Congress in the 2002 elections. By then, however, the distractions of a series of business scandals (Enron, WorldCom, and others) prevented Congress from revamping statutory underpinnings of the protective governmental infrastructure. Nevertheless, the administration, operating without significant congressional oversight, was able to achieve many of the business community's goals by weakening existing regulations, slicing regulatory agency budgets, and cutting back on enforcement.[41]

With the assistance of the Heritage Foundation, President Bush filled a large number of sub-Cabinet-level positions with laissez faire minimalists from conservative think tanks and law firms that represented corporate interests.[42] The new head of OIRA, John D. Graham, had directed the Harvard Center for Risk Analysis, an industry-sponsored adjunct of the Harvard School of Public Health that prepared controversial studies on the costs and benefits of regulation for regulated companies to use in their attacks on the regulatory agencies. After Graham left in late 2006, Bush gave a "recess" appointment to Susan Dudley, the director of the regulatory studies program at the Mercatus Center and an even more aggressive laissez faire minimalist than Graham.[43]

Both the Heritage Foundation and the CoC urged OIRA to reprise the "gatekeeper" role that it had played early in the Reagan Administration, and John Graham was happy to oblige. He avoided controversy at the outset by leaving the Clinton Administration regulatory review executive order in place and working within its broad confines to ensure that the estimated benefits of agency rules outweighed the predicted costs. Consumer and environmental groups applauded Graham's efforts to make its input more transparent by expanding its use of the internet to post notices of meetings with outsiders and the content of its comments on regulations under review. The interchanges between OIRA and agency staff prior to the agencies' formal submissions, however, remained clouded in secrecy. This was a matter of some importance, because OIRA began to interject itself into the process of formulating rules much earlier and more actively than in the past.[44]

Although Graham spoke of "smarter" regulation, the OIRA position on most issues reprised its Reagan-era campaign for "regulatory relief." During the first eight months that Graham was in charge, OMB returned 21 draft rules to the agencies for more work.[45] Two Government Accountability Office reports concluded that OIRA's comments had significantly affected the content of most of the rules that it returned to agencies.[46] OIRA also generated a number of "hit lists" of existing regulations that the agencies had to consider for revision or repeal. Consumer and environmental groups complained that it was inappropriate for the administration to cut agency budgets while at the same time demanding that they respond to industry-generated demands to revisit existing regulations.[47] By early 2005, however, the business community was complaining that the effort had yielded no tangible results, noting that the agencies had acted on only 135 of OIRA's 576 referrals.

Pursuant to an obscure appropriations rider called the "Data Quality Act," OIRA issued guidelines requiring agencies to develop "information resource management procedures" for "reviewing and substantiating" the quality of risk-related information before disseminating it to the public. The agencies also had to develop procedures for allowing affected persons to "seek and obtain, where appropriate, timely correction of information" that failed to comply with the guidelines. The business community quickly seized on the new statute to demand that agencies cease disseminating a wide variety of documents ranging from the federal government's 2002 report on global warming to the National Heart, Lung and Blood Institute's warning that salt could lead to higher blood pressure.[48]

Long-time conservative activist Paul Weyrich concluded that the George W. Bush Administration was "far superior" to the Reagan Administration when it came to understanding and addressing the concerns of the business community. As we shall see in the following chapters, the administration attempted to achieve its policy objectives through the rulemaking process when it encountered resistance to its legislative initiatives, even if that involved a considerable stretching of statutory language. The regulatory agencies stressed voluntary approaches and accommodation over rulemaking and strict enforcement. Although the George W. Bush Administration touted the need for "sound science" in regulatory decisionmaking, the agencies tended to disregard scientific studies and analysis that pointed in the direction of greater regulation.[49]

The White House was defiant in the wake of the 2006 elections, in which the Democrats gained control over both houses of Congress. In January 2007, President Bush signed an executive order that added to the regulatory analysis and review requirements established by the Clinton Administration order and extended them to "significant" guidance documents.[50] The return of both houses of Congress to Democratic control, however, ensured that the Bush Administration's deregulatory activities received vigorous oversight.[51] Deregulation was no longer on the agenda as Congress began the slow process of rebuilding the institutions of responsibility and accountability. Several decimated agencies received larger appropriations increases than they had seen since the Public Interest Era. And Congress reacted to several highly visible crises with legislation that expanded the powers of FDA to regulate food and drugs and of CPSC to regulate dangerous toys.

CONCLUSIONS

Over the span of three decades from 1975 through 2005, advocates of regulatory reform launched three broad assaults on the protective governmental infrastructure erected by the Progressive Era, New Deal, and Public Interest Era statutes. The assaults proceeded along many dimensions as the business community's influence infrastructure pressed Congress to repeal or substantially rewrite protective statutes and, failing that, to enact legislation designed to slow down or hamstring the regulatory agencies as they promulgated the regulations needed to implement those statutes. At the same time, they pressed the White House to impose cumbersome procedural and analytical restrictions on executive branch agencies.

In the next eight chapters, we will examine the three assaults on regulation and corresponding assaults on the civil justice system in the context of the institutions of responsibility and accountability that were responsible for making the protections provided by the regulatory statutes and the common law a reality in the day-to-day lives of ordinary people. In each of these chapters we will see how the protective governmental infrastructure that emerged from the Public Interest Era had great potential to shield consumers, workers, neighbors, and the environment from harm and how the business community's assaults on the institutions of responsibility and accountability severely reduced their capacity to accomplish protective goals.

WORKER SAFETY

Many workplaces and all underground mines pose significant risks to the health and safety of the workers who labor there. The Occupational Safety and Health Administration (OSHA) is responsible for the safety and health of employees in nearly every private sector workplace in the United States. The Mine Safety and Health Administration (MSHA) is responsible for protecting miners at all the nation's more than 14,600 mines. According to the Bureau of Labor Statistics, U.S. private sector employers in 2009 reported 3.1 million injuries and at least 166,000 workplace illnesses. The actual numbers are likely much higher because some employers underreport workplace injuries, and doctors frequently fail to inquire into the likelihood that particular diseases, like cancer, have a workplace origin. A total of 4,551 workers died on the job, which represents a fatality rate of about 3.5 per 100,000 full-time employees.[1] Mine operators reported just over 3,000 lost workday injuries to miners in 2009. The number of mine fatalities varies greatly from year to year. An average of 23 workers per year were killed in mines during 2005–09.[2]

THE POTENTIAL

The laws that Congress enacted during the Public Interest Era had a genuine potential to improve workplace safety. The 1977 mine safety statute prescribed specific mine safety and health standards to protect miners from accidents and diseases, and it empowered MSHA to increase their stringency as the agency identified new hazards and safety technologies. MSHA inspectors were required to conduct an unannounced inspection of every underground mine at least four times annually. The agency could issue civil fines of up to $10,000 per violation and initiate criminal proceedings in the case of "knowing and willful" violations. Since the statute did not *require* it to levy extra penalties in any particular case, however, the agency retained significant discretion to go easy on chronic offenders.[3]

The Occupational Safety and Health Act of 1970 empowered OSHA to write safety and health standards designed "to assure so far as possible every working man and woman in the Nation safe and healthful working conditions." The standards were to be based on the recommendations of a research agency called the National Institute for Occupational Safety and Health (NIOSH) and on the record of a resource-intensive quasi-adjudicatory hearing. Safety standards were supposed to require conditions and practices "reasonably necessary or appropriate" to provide safe employment. Health standards were to be set at a level that assured "to the extent feasible" that no employee would "suffer material impairment of health or functional capacity" when exposed to a hazard throughout his working life. A separate "general duty clause" required every employer to provide a workplace that was "free from recognized hazards" that were likely to cause "death or serious physical harm." OSHA inspectors were authorized to make unannounced inspections. Violators were subject to civil and criminal penalties.[4]

During the Public Interest Era and at times during the interregnums between the assaults on regulation, the agencies charged with implementing these statutes demonstrated their power to protect workers. During its first ten years, OSHA promulgated 21 safety standards and 13 health standards (one of which addressed 14 carcinogens). Its 1982 hazard communication standard contributed greatly to workers' awareness of occupational health hazards and gave them vital information to use in bargaining for safer workplaces and higher wages. The 1987 fieldworker protection standard made sanitary facilities available to thousands of migrant workers for the first time. Its 1991 bloodborne pathogen rule protected hospital workers from the risks of contracting AIDS and Hepatitis B. The agency estimated that its 1996 butadiene standard would prevent around 60 cancer deaths among workers over their working lives.[5]

MSHA usually had to be prodded by Congress to exercise its rulemaking authority. But the regulations that it did promulgate offered critical protections to miners who spent their days in a dirty environment that could cause black lung, deprive them of life-sustaining oxygen, or crush them to death. In 1978, MSHA promulgated regulations requiring operators to provide each miner a "self-contained self-rescue" (SCSR) device capable of providing sufficient oxygen for the miner to survive at least one hour while awaiting rescue. That rule has saved dozens of lives, including that of Kyle Medley who survived the three explosions that rocked the Willow Creek Mine near Castle Gate, Utah. He was able to don his 10-minute SCSR and escape to a cache of 60-minute SCSRs which provided enough oxygen for him to exit the mine.[6] And in 2000, MSHA promulgated a standard protecting miners from a variety of health risks posed by emissions from diesel-burning heavy equipment. It estimated that the standard would prevent between 68 and 620 out of every 1000 lung cancers suffered by miners.[7]

As MSHA's enforcement budget steadily grew during the Nixon/Ford and Carter Administrations, the number of annual inspections increased dramatically. The number of mine fatalities dropped 47 percent between 1970 and 1977. An 89-count indictment against the Clinchfield Coal Company for flagrantly violating a requirement that miners wear coal dust monitors resulted in a fine of $100,000. In 1991, 33 companies, 41 executives, and two consultants pleaded guilty to conspiring with a testing laboratory to produce false black lung monitoring reports.[8] When OSHA was motivated to enforce the law, it likewise had ample authority do so. During the George H. W. Bush Administration, for example, the agency proposed $66.6 million in total fines and referred 24 criminal cases to the Justice Department.[9]

THE REALITY

Both OSHA and MSHA were prominent targets of the business community's assaults on federal regulation. Saddled with shrinking budgets and leaders who were at times unsympathetic to their missions, both agencies gradually shrank in size and became less aggressive. Not surprisingly, neither agency lived up to its potential.

WRITING THE RULES

OSHA got off on the wrong foot in 1971 when it promulgated "consensus standards" that, according to the statute, could be based on existing standards for federal contractors or voluntary standards promulgated by various private sector standard-setting bodies. Although the agency had two years to accomplish this daunting task, Assistant Secretary George Guenther, a Nixon appointee, instructed the staff to finish the job in six months. Rather than carefully culling the often-outdated standards as Congress intended, the staff rushed 400 pages of unexamined standards into print. Incredulous employers soon found themselves subject to thousands of petty and sometimes plainly ridiculous federal requirements that OSHA inspectors felt duty-bound to enforce. By the time that the agency removed hundreds of inappropriate standards during the Carter

Administration, the damage to OSHA's fragile reputation had been done, and it had become the poster child for senseless regulation.[10]

OSHA reached the peak of its productivity in the Carter Administration under Assistant Secretary Eula Bingham, a former occupational hygiene professor. During her 4-year tenure, the agency promulgated stringent occupational health standards for such economically important, but highly toxic substances as lead, benzene, acrylonitrile, and cotton dust. The onslaught of new rules, however, drew harsh criticism from industry trade associations, think tanks, and conservative academics.[11] Bingham's *piece de resistance* was an ambitious "generic carcinogen policy" that would have resolved in a single proceeding many of the most contentious issues that came up in every rulemaking addressing carcinogens. A Supreme Court opinion in the petroleum industry's challenge to the benzene standard, however, severely undermined the legal basis for that ambitious project. A year later, the Reagan Administration unceremoniously dumped it, and the agency returned to its ponderous chemical-by-chemical approach.[12]

MSHA promulgated very few rules during the Carter Administration, and the mining industry strongly opposed nearly all of them. It argued that MSHA regulations had caused a 25 percent drop in labor productivity, increased the cost of coal, and contributed to the overall economic stagflation of the late 1970s. As the administration broadened its commitment to coal in response to higher oil prices in the wake of the Iranian hostage crisis, mine safety took a back seat.[13]

The first assault on worker safety regulation began in earnest in 1981 when President Reagan appointed Thorne Auchter, a former building contractor, to head OSHA. Auchter announced that he would be turning OSHA into a "cooperative regulator." True to his word, the agency spent much of his tenure ignoring or terminating pending Carter Administration projects and rewriting existing rules to make them less stringent. Auchter's hostility to regulation and a steadily declining budget had a devastating impact on staff morale. The only significant standard that OSHA promulgated during Auchter's term—a regulation requiring employers to inform employees of workplace chemical hazards—came in response to demands from large companies for a uniform standard to preempt more stringent state "worker right-to-know" statutes. MSHA Administrator Ford B. Ford likewise brought the proactive days of the Carter Administration to a rapid end. MSHA's budget fared even more poorly than OSHA's during the early 1980s, staff morale sank to an all-time low, and the agency promulgated no significant standards.[14]

With the first assault on the wane in mid-1986, John A. Pendergrass, another industrial hygienist, took over the helm at OSHA. During the first interregnum, the agency promulgated several more regulations, the most important of which was a generic update of 400 of the national consensus standards for chemicals commonly encountered in the workplace. That massive effort came to naught, however, when a court of appeals set aside the rule in an opinion that made it clear that the agency's statute was not hospitable to a generic approach.[15]

President George H. W. Bush appointed Gerard F. Scannell, a safety officer at Johnson & Johnson Co., to head OSHA. Scannell was not as aggressive at standard-setting as Pendergrass, and he was greatly hampered by shrinking budgets, the burdensome analytical requirements of Reagan-era executive orders, and intrusive oversight by the Vice-President's Competitiveness Council (discussed in chapter 7). Under William T. Tattersall, a former coal-industry lobbyist, MSHA kept a low profile by promulgating no regulations of any consequence.[16]

Clinton appointee Joseph Dear pledged that a "revitalized OSHA" would issue 20 proposed rules and 24 final rules during 1994 and 1995. The second assault on federal regulation, however, soon overtook that ambitious undertaking as OSHA became a prime target for the deregulators of the Gingrich Congress. Citing a raft of mostly apocryphal OSHA horror stories, conservative commentators and think tanks called for Congress to abolish OSHA altogether. MSHA likewise spent the second assault in defensive mode.[17] The greatest threat to both agencies was a regulatory reform bill in the House of Representatives that would have drastically changed how OSHA promulgated regulations, folded MSHA into OSHA, and taken away some of MSHA's enforcement authorities. Although the radical bill petered out in the face of a promised presidential veto (which had considerable credibility after the appropriations act vetoes described in Chapter 7), the legislative activity had a profound *in terrorem* effect on the agencies' rulemaking activities.[18]

Attempting to co-opt the radical reformers, President Clinton promised that a "new OSHA" would "change its fundamental operating paradigm" to emphasize "interaction with business and labor in the development of rules." Dear reassigned 100 employees to a new "standards improvement project," which conducted an extensive search through the agency's 3,000 pages of existing rules for obsolete or otherwise ineffectual rules.[19] The one regulation of any consequence that MSHA managed to complete was a "midnight regulation" issued at the very end of the Clinton Administration to protect miners from the health risks posed by diesel emissions in mines.[20]

President George W. Bush's Secretary of Labor, Elaine Chao, was the wife of Kentucky Senator Mitch McConnell, the chairperson of the Republican Senatorial Campaign Committee and a tireless critic of OSHA and MSHA. At the time of her appointment, Chao was working as a "fellow" at the Heritage Foundation. Soon after she assumed office, she created a high-level "management review board" to oversee budgetary and management issues at MSHA and OSHA.[21] Bush's pick to head MSHA was David Lauriski, a Utah consultant who had worked for the coal industry for most of his career. Lauriski promptly withdrew 17 proposed Clinton Administration regulations, and he told an industry group that the agency would henceforth promulgate only rules that "all parties can accept as necessary and practical."[22]

The new Assistant Secretary for OSHA was John Henshaw, an industrial hygienist who wanted to make the agency more "employer-friendly." Henshaw reorganized the agency to assign a higher priority to cooperative initiatives with the business community. He also added an extra step to the standard-setting process for considering voluntary approaches as an alternative to mandatory rules. The agency leadership removed more than twenty items from a longstanding list of high priority rulemaking projects, many of which had already received a great deal of attention from the agency staff, and it consistently rejected staff recommendations for new rulemaking initiatives. The only significant rule that OSHA promulgated during the George W. Bush Administration was a long-delayed occupational health standard for the carcinogen hexavalent chromium, and that came in response to a direct order from a federal court.[23]

A series of mining disasters in 2006 that claimed the lives of 21 miners (see Box 8.1) shook the public conscience with such ferocity that the business community's idea and influence infrastructures were incapable of resisting the demands of the families of the dead miners for more protection. Congress responded with the first significant occupational safety legislation since the onset of the Laissez Faire Revival.[24] Among other things, the Mine Improvement and New Emergency Response Act (MINER Act) of 2006 required operators to prepare and "periodically update" written accident response plans providing for the evacuation of all miners in an emergency and for the maintenance of miners trapped underground. For the first time, MSHA was empowered to seek injunctive relief, including closure, against mines that failed to pay assessed fines on a timely basis. With strict statutory deadlines for rulemaking in place and vigorous oversight from a Democrat-controlled Congress, MSHA acted with great dispatch to implement the new statute. Assisted by volunteers from OSHA, MSHA's small rulemaking staff promulgated rules at an unprecedented pace.[25]

Two disasters in 2008 generated similar pressures on OSHA to kick its moribund rulemaking process into gear, but to less effect. On February 8, 2008, the Dixie Crystal sugar refinery in Port Wentworth, Georgia, exploded in a fireball that killed 14 workers and severely burned 10 more. The House of Representatives unanimously passed a bill requiring OSHA to write a standard for combustible dusts, but President Bush threatened to veto any resulting legislation. Two unions then petitioned OSHA to promulgate an emergency temporary standard for combustible dust, but OSHA took no action on the petition.[26] The collapse of two construction cranes in New York City, killing a total of nine people, generated pressure on OSHA to revive a negotiated standard for cranes that had been delayed for three years while a panel of small businesspersons reviewed it pursuant to a Gingrich-era regulatory reform statute. The rule remained moribund during the George W. Bush Administration but was finally promulgated in August 2010.[27]

FOREGONE PROTECTION

From the outset of the Laissez Faire Revival, efforts by workplace safety advocates to induce OSHA and MSHA to promulgate protective rules of responsibility encountered stiff resistance from the regulated industries and serious roadblocks created by unsympathetic officials within the executive branch. Consequently, neither agency promulgated as many standards as Congress envisioned when it enacted their statutes, and the standards they did promulgate often did not measure up to protective policies embedded in those laws. OSHA's marathon attempts to promulgate standards for silicon dust, hexavalent chromium, and ergonomics are illustrative.

Silicon Dust. In the early 1970s, NIOSH recommended that OSHA promulgate a standard for silicon dust, which in high concentrations can cause a debilitating disease called silicosis. Industry lobbyists, however, persuaded the agency to put silicosis on the back burner, where it remained for twenty years until the Clinton Administration identified it as a high priority for rulemaking in 1994. At that time, the permissible exposure level for silicon dust was twice as high as the NIOSH recommendation. Nevertheless, after another intensive industry lobbying campaign, silicon returned to the back burner. The agency terminated the rulemaking in the summer of 2008 as part of the Bush Administration's coordinated effort to accomplish as many deregulatory initiatives as possible before the election. By that time, more than two million workers were being exposed to crystalline silica, and between 3,600 and 7,300 people (most of whom were workers) were contracting silicosis annually.[28]

Hexavalent Chromium. After concluding that hexavalent chromium at existing exposure levels posed a high lung cancer risk to workers, NIOSH in 1975 recommended that OSHA set a permissible exposure level (PEL) of 1 microgram per cubic meter ($\mu g/m^3$). Because the existing "national consensus standard" of 52 µg/m³ was based on 1943 data, OSHA head Morton Corn in 1976 agreed that a standard was "urgently needed." When the agency failed to propose a rule by the late 1980s, Public Citizen petitioned it to promulgate an emergency temporary standard. OSHA rejected the petition soon after President Clinton was inaugurated, but promised to promulgate a standard by March 1995. By that point, the second assault was underway, and the agency decided to let sleeping dogs lie. Public Citizen returned to court, and OSHA agreed to a new deadline of September 1998. After the agency missed that deadline by four years, the court finally ordered it to decide whether to issue a standard by October 2004. OSHA then published a proposal to reduce the PEL to 1µg/m³, the level recommended by NIOSH in 1975. At this point, the affected industries weighed in with reams of data and lengthy briefs arguing that hexavalent chromium was not danger-ous at low exposure levels and that it would be impossible to comply with the proposed PEL. Agreeing with the industry, OSHA promulgated a lax standard of 5 µg/m³ for most affected industries in February 2006, more than three decades after the original NIOSH recommendation. According to OSHA's own calcula-tions, 4–19 percent of workers with long term exposure to hexavalent chromium were contracting cancer during all of those years, and the new standard still al-lowed 0.4–2.2 percent of exposed workers to contract cancer.[29]

Ergonomics. Workers in large poultry plants throughout rural America suf-fered an "epidemic" of musculoskeletal diseases as they stood shoulder-to-shoulder in near-freezing temperatures on assembly lines operating at rates of 91 birds per minute, pulling knives through raw meat 20,000 times a day. Mus-culoskeletal diseases, like carpal tunnel syndrome, tendonitis, and lower back disorders, were the bane of the poultry processing industry and many other modern workplaces ranging from Wall Street offices to overnight delivery ser-vices. By the early 1990s, they accounted for 60 percent of newly reported oc-cupational injuries.

Early in the Clinton Administration, OSHA assembled a special team of er-gonomics experts to draft a proposed rule. The National Association of Manu-facturers responded by forming a "Coalition on Ergonomics" made up of nearly 500 companies and trade associations to fight the rulemaking initiative. The coalition persuaded the Gingrich Congress to pass an appropriations rider pre-venting OSHA from developing the standard during FY 1997, but the agency revived it again after the 1998 elections. After scaling back the proposal to mol-lify small business groups and OIRA, OSHA published a notice of proposed rulemaking on November 23, 1999. President Clinton vetoed another appro-priations rider aimed at shutting down the rulemaking just days before the hotly contested 2000 election.

The agency published the final rule on November 14, 2000, and it went into effect on January 8, 2001. Although a number of companies challenged the standard in court, the business community decided that the quickest way to rid itself of the standard was to ask the Republican-controlled Congress to pass a joint resolution of disapproval under the Congressional Review Act (CRAct). That statute provided an expedited procedure for Congress to review every major rule prior to its effective date. If both houses of Congress passed a joint resolution disapproving the rule and if it was signed by the president, the regulation would be rendered null and void. House Majority Leader Tom DeLay met with business lobbyists every day for a week at 6:00 AM to plot strategy, and he provided an office for them to use as a war room. In March 2001 Congress enacted a joint resolution repealing the standard, and President George W. Bush signed the resolution on March 20. With that, a ten-year effort that cost OSHA $1.5 million and consumed thousands of person-hours came to an ignominious end. Under the terms of the CRAct, OSHA could not promulgate a new ergonomics standard for another ten years. In the meantime, musculoskeletal disorders accounted for about 335,000 annual workplace injuries involving days away from work.[30]

LIMITED ACCOUNTABILITY

Both OSHA and MSHA faced formidable enforcement challenges. OSHA's small inspectorate focused on responding to worker complaints and on spot-checking bad actors in the most hazardous industries. With a larger inspectorate and far fewer workplaces to inspect, MSHA was supposed to conduct extended inspections at every underground mine at least four times per year. These in-depth investigations typically yielded multiple citations. Because citations issued by both agencies were appealable to a three-person review commission, inspectors had to document violations very carefully, and they tended to assess small fines to avoid resource-intensive appeals. For example, the more than 700,000 notices of violation that MSHA issued between 1970 and 1977 resulted in an average penalty of just under $100. OSHA issued far fewer citations, but identified many more serious violations, for which it demanded stiffer penalties. The intensity of both agencies' enforcement efforts peaked during the Carter Administration due in large part to substantial increases in their enforcement budgets.[31]

The momentum rapidly dissipated during the Reagan Administration as both agencies suffered deep budget cuts and the new leadership told inspectors to change their image from "tough cop" to "trusted advisor." OSHA exempted from routine inspections companies that established safety and health management plans and kept good records, and it dramatically reduced fines in return for employer promises to do better in the future.[32] MSHA head Ford B. Ford encouraged mine operators to meet privately with MSHA supervisors to protest violation notices issued by lower-level inspectors. Inspectors who failed to get Ford's conciliatory message were routinely overruled. Instead of conducting follow-up inspections, MSHA allowed operators to "self-certify" that they had taken proper corrective action. Not surprisingly, the number of inspections and assessed fines both dropped dramatically during the first assault.[33]

Toward the end of the Reagan Administration, OSHA Assistant Secretary John Pendergrass took more aggressive actions against an increasing number of scofflaws who engaged in serious, willful, and repeat violations. The agency also began to impose dramatic "mega-fines" on companies guilty of egregious misconduct. The agency maintained Pendergrass's tough stance during the George H. W. Bush Administration, but it frequently reduced fines by up to one-half when the employer agreed to abate the hazard expeditiously.[34] At the outset of the Clinton Administration, OSHA increased inspections by more than 7 percent from the previous year, and it assessed fines of more than $100,000 in 10 percent more cases. With the second assault in 1995, however, both agencies became considerably less aggressive. For example, the number of OSHA inspections fell 43 percent between 1994 and 1996 to a record low. Enforcement picked up somewhat during the last two years of the Clinton Administration when, for example, MSHA-assessed fines more than doubled.[35]

As the third assault got underway in 2001, OSHA head John Henshaw put into place two voluntary compliance programs. First, the agency agreed to forgo imposing any fines at all on small companies that agreed to undergo a comprehensive site visit by OSHA inspectors and to correct any detected violations. Second, it agreed to forgo routine inspections at facilities operated by more than 450 companies with exemplary safety records that agreed to work with OSHA inspectors to improve safety and health. When OSHA inspectors did enforce the law, the penalties were insignificant. In 2006, fines for serious violations involving a substantial probability of death or serious harm averaged less than $900.[36]

Although the number of mines subject to MSHA inspection increased in the early 2000s, the Bush Administration was sufficiently confident in the industry's ability to police itself that it cut MSHA's budget by about 25 percent. Even though MSHA failed to complete the four annual inspections required by law at 107 of the country's 731 coal mines during 2006, President Bush vetoed a bill adding $10 million to the agency's appropriation for enforcement. Assistant Administrator David Lauriski shifted MSHA's emphasis away from enforcement and toward compliance assistance. Upper-level management instructed compliance officers to bring disputes to quick resolution through informal conferences, rather than formal litigation. The number of citations and the amount of fines assessed declined steeply. When MSHA enforcers did decide to levy substantial penalties, they invariably reduced them on appeal.[37]

The criminal enforcement record of both agencies was unimpressive throughout the entire Laissez Faire Revival. Criminal prosecutions for willful violations of OSHA standards were exceedingly rare, even in cases in which multiple workers were killed. From 1982 to 2002, the Department of Labor referred only 7 percent of OSHA's 1,242 criminal investigations to the Justice Department for prosecution. Between 2003 and 2007, MSHA referred a total of 16 violations to the Justice Department. In stark contrast, a single Kentucky U.S. Attorney's office on its own secured 112 convictions against mining companies between 1992 and 2002.[38]

THE CONSEQUENCES

On March 23, 2005, the worst industrial accident in 15 years killed 15 workers and injured more than 180 others as flammable liquids from a distillation tower ignited into a massive fireball at the BP Corporation's Texas City refinery. A two-year investigation by the Chemical Safety and Hazard Investigation Board (CSHIB) concluded that the explosion was caused by "organizational and safety deficiencies at all levels of the BP Corporation." The CSHIB also found that OSHA had failed to protect the plant's workers from the easily avoided catastrophe. The plant was subject to OSHA's 1992 process safety management standard, but it had failed to comply with many of its requirements for more than a decade. The violations had escaped OSHA's attention because it had never conducted a comprehensive process safety inspection at the facility. Indeed, between 1995 and 2005, the agency had undertaken only nine process safety inspections in the entire country.[39] Similar explosions had killed or seriously injured workers at five other facilities during the preceding seven years, but OSHA had taken no action to step up enforcement. The standard itself was out of date, but instead of updating it, the agency substituted guidance documents and outreach programs.[40]

The Texas City explosion is but one of many examples of dramatic workplace accidents that engulfed the country during the later stages of the Laissez Faire Revival, a few of which are described in Box 8.1. In addition to the dramatic loss of life and limb that attended catastrophic accidents, the workplace extracted a less dramatic daily toll on workers who were maimed by repetitive stress injuries and poisoned by toxic dusts and chemicals as related in Box 8.2.

Box 8.1

Workplace Disasters

Buckhannon, West Virginia (January 2006). Twelve miners were killed in the International Coal Corporation's Sago Mine when lightning ignited methane gas that had accumulated in an area that had recently been sealed off with inexpensive "Omega blocks" instead of the more expensive solid concrete blocks that the company had previously used for seals.[a]

Logan County, West Virginia (January 2006). Two miners were killed in a conveyor belt fire at Massey Energy Company's Alma No. 1 mine soon after the operator received a waiver from MSHA's prohibition on using conveyor belts to convey fresh air to underground operations. An MSHA inspector had recommended that portions of the mine be closed to address the fire hazard several days before the fire, but his superiors told him to "back off and let them run coal."[b]

Holmes Mill, Kentucky (May 2006). Five miners died when cheap Omega block seals failed to contain a methane gas explosion at the Darby Mine No. 1. In the five years that its current owner had operated the mine, it had received 257 MSHA citations, 99 of which were for "serious and substantial" violations, but it had been fined a total of only $27,651.[c]

Port Wentworth, Georgia (February 2008). Fourteen workers were killed and 10 were severely burned when the Dixie Crystal sugar refinery exploded as a result of easily preventable accumulations of highly combustible sugar dust. The plant had experienced a smaller explosion several weeks before the blast, but had done nothing to address the problem.[d]

Institute, West Virginia (August 2008). An explosion at a Bayer CropScience chemical plant that killed two employees and almost set off a catastrophic release of methylisocyanate (the chemical that killed thousands of people in Bhopal, India, in December 1984) was, according to CSHIB, attributable to poor management and human error.[e]

Charleston, West Virginia (April 2010). Twenty-nine miners were killed when methane gas and improperly managed coal dust ignited in the Massey Energy Company's Upper Big Branch mine. The company had previously been cited 17 times for failure to maintain methane monitors in proper working order at the mine. Investigators also discovered that it had kept two sets of books—one set for MSHA inspectors that deleted critical information contained in another set prepared for company executives.[f]

Anacortes, Washington (April 2010). Five workers were killed at a Tesoro refinery when a sudden release of hydrocarbons produced a fireball that obliterated an area half the size of a football field. The state OSHA had just a year prior to the explosion cited the facility for 17 serious violations of OSHA's process safety standard.[g]

NOTES

a. J. Davitt McAteer & Associates, The Sago Mine Disaster: A Preliminary Report to Governor Joe Manchin III 11 (July, 2006); West Virginia Office of Miners' Health, Safety, and Training, Report of Investigation into the Sago Mine Explosion 1–2 (December, 2006).

b. George Miller, Review of Federal Mine Safety and Health Administration's Performance from 2001 to 2005 Reveals Consistent Abdication of Regulatory and Enforcement Responsibilities 3 (House Committee on Education and the Workforce Democratic Staff, January 21, 2006); Dennis B. Roddy, *Mine Fire Warnings Thwarted*, Pittsburgh Post-Gazette, April 23, 2006, at A1 (quote).

c. James R. Carroll, *Owners Abandon Mine Where 5 Died*, Louisville Courier-Journal, November 30, 2006, at A1; James R. Carroll, *Mine Operator's Record*, Louisville Courier-Journal, May 21, 2006, at A4.

d. Chemical Safety and Hazard Investigation Board, Sugar Dust Explosion and Fire 2 (2009).

e. *Lapses in Process Safety Management Likely Led to Bayer Explosion, Board Says*, 39 BNA OSHR 344 (2009).

f. MSHA Officials Say Massey Kept Two Sets of Safety Records for Upper Big Branch Mine, 41 BNA OSHR 587 (2011); Kris Maher, *Methane Monitors at Center of Mine-Explosion Probe*, WSJ, August 6, 2010, at A1; Steven Mufson, Kimberly Kindy & Ed O'Keefe, *W. Va. Mine Has Years of Serious Violations, Officials Say*, WP, April 9, 2010, at A1.

g. *Five Workers Killed After Fireball Ignites Inside Tesoro Refinery, Safety Board Says*, 40 BNA OSHR 294 (2010).

Box 8.2

Quiet Workplace Killers

Black Lung. Between 1997 and 2007, the rate of black lung disease among miners with 25 or more years' experience in the mines had increased from 4 percent to 9 percent, and the rate among those with 20–24 years' experience had jumped from 2.5 percent to 6 percent.[a]

Diacetyl. In May 2000, a Kansas City occupational health specialist uncovered a mini-epidemic at a local microwave popcorn manufacturing facility among workers who were suffering from *bronchiolitis obliterans*, an exceedingly rare and irreversible lung disease that clogs the lungs of its victims and eventually kills them. Federal investigators concluded that the mini-epidemic had been caused by a butter flavoring agent called diacetyl.[b]

Slaughterhouses. On the cutting floor of a slaughterhouse, workers slice cattle carcasses on mechanical assembly lines that move at a rate of up to 400 carcasses per hour. In addition to causing deep cuts and dismemberment, the repetitive motions can cause carpal tunnel syndrome and other repetitive stress diseases. The animal slaughtering and processing industry reported almost 27,000 lost workday injuries in 2008.[c]

NOTES

a. *After Rising Black Lung Rates Reported, Mine Union Calls for Stronger Dust Controls,* 37 BNA OSHR 823 (September 20, 2007); Ken Ward, Jr., *NIOSH Reports Black Lung Rates Double Since '97,* Charleston Gazette, September 14, 2007, at A1.

b. Stephen Labaton, *OSHA Leaves Worker Safety in Hands of Industry,* NYT, April 25, 2007, at A1; Stephanie Armour, *Is Butter Flavoring Ruining Popcorn Workers' Lungs,* USA Today, June 20, 2002, at A1; Jim Morris, *Slow Motion,* 39 National Journal 32 (May 5, 2007), at 32.

c. U.S. Government Accountability Office, Workplace Safety & Health: Safety in the Meat and Poultry Industry, While Improving, Could be Further Strengthened 8, 21 (2005); Nivedita L. Bhushan, *Injuries, Illnesses, and Fatalities in Food Manufacturing,* 2008, table 2 (2009); Karen Olsson, *On the Line at IBP,* Texas Observer, May 22, 1998, at 8.

CONCLUSIONS

Both OSHA and MSHA have had a discernable impact on workplace safety and health. The frequency of mine disasters and overall mine-related fatalities declined during much of the Laissez Faire Revival, but they began to creep upward during the George W. Bush Administration, and they shot up dramatically in 2006. Workplace fatalities declined throughout the 2000s as well, reaching all-time lows in 2008 and 2009, due in large part to a severe economic recession brought on by the financial meltdown of 2008, but they were on the rise again in 2010 with the economic recovery. Workplace illness rates declined as well, but not as dramatically. The fact remains that an average of 15 workers die each day from work-related injuries, and an unknown number suffer from work-related diseases, some of which may not manifest themselves for 20–40 years.[41] An effective regulatory system would not have reduced those numbers to zero, but it would have avoided many needless tragedies.

ENVIRONMENTAL PROTECTION

Many federal agencies bear some responsibility for protecting the nation's natural resources and environment. In this chapter, we will focus on four of those agencies—the Environmental Protection Agency (EPA), the Army Corps of Engineers (CoE) in the Department of Defense, and the Office of Surface Mining (OSM) and Minerals Management Service (MMS) in the Department of Interior. EPA oversees programs that are responsible for controlling air and water pollution from thousands of industrial facilities that discharge tens of millions of tons of pollutants into the air and water every day. EPA and CoE are responsible for protecting the nation's 107 million acres of wetlands. OSM oversees permits for the nation's 812 surface mines. And MMS is responsible for overseeing oil and gas leasing on federal lands, including the outer continental shelf, where it is responsible for more than 7,400 active leases.[1]

THE POTENTIAL

The Clean Air Act of 1970 (CAAct) created the first truly national pollution control regime in which the newly created EPA promulgated binding national ambient air quality standards to protect public health, and the states administered EPA-approved "state implementation plans" capable of achieving the air quality standards by stated deadlines. At the same time, EPA had to promulgate nationally uniform technology-based standards applicable to new stationary sources and modifications of existing stationary sources. Emitters of hazardous air pollutants had to comply with even more stringent emissions standards. Finally, the statute provided for both federal and citizen enforcement of the national standards and the requirements in EPA-approved state plans.[2]

The Clean Water Act of 1972 (CWAct) required EPA to promulgate national technology-based standards for point sources of water pollution with the goal of making all waters of the United States fishable and swimmable by 1983 and the (far more drastic) goal of eliminating the discharge of pollutants by 1985. The states had the initial responsibility for promulgating water quality standards for every river and lake within their borders, subject to EPA approval. The states then issued permits for point sources that implemented the national technology-based standards and ensured the attainment of the water quality standards.[3]

Under the Surface Mine Control and Reclamation Act of 1977 (SMCRAct), OSM established a federal permit program for strip mining. OSM was required to write implementing regulations, and the states were responsible for implementing the federal regulations through state-administered permit programs. The Act empowered OSM to conduct inspections and levy civil and criminal penalties for violations of permit requirements. Like the CAAct and the CWAct, it provided for extensive public participation in both rulemaking and enforcement.[4]

The Outer Continental Shelf Lands Act of 1953 as amended in 1978 (OCSLAct) required MMS to take environmental considerations into account in awarding and overseeing leases for oil and gas development on the outer continental shelf. The statute instructed MMS to select "the timing and location of minerals leasing, to the maximum extent practicable, so as to obtain a proper balance between the potential for environmental damage, the potential for discovery of oil and gas, and the potential for adverse impact on the coastal zone." It further authorized MMS to promulgate regulations to ensure that federal oil and gas lessees took steps to protect the marine environment and the coastal zone, but it provided no explicit criteria for those regulations. MMS therefore had a great deal of discretion to write very stringent or very lenient regulations for operators to follow under the leases that they obtained from the Department.[5] MMS did not begin to regulate offshore oil and gas operations until the early 1980s, after the first assault was well underway.

The enormous potential that these laws had to protect human health and the environment was much in evidence during the early years and sporadically apparent in the interregnums between the three assaults described in Chapter 7. EPA got off to an aggressive start under its first Administrator, William Ruckelshaus, and his immediate successor, Russell Train, both of whom were moderate Republicans appointed by President Nixon. With an energized staff, the new agency promulgated stringent emissions standards for automobiles, ambient air quality standards for the primary pollutants, technology-based standards for 27 categories of water polluters, and a number of other foundational rules of the road for companies that discharged pollutants into the environment. Between 1972 and 1982, discharges of suspended solids, biological oxygen demand, phosphates, and heavy metals from industrial sources declined by 70–80 percent.[6]

With strong public support, Administrator Train beat back early attempts to weaken the Clean Air Act in response to an "energy crisis" brought on by Arab oil boycotts in the mid-1970s. EPA's impressive rulemaking output continued into the first two years of the Carter Administration as EPA promulgated new source performance standards for coal-fired power plants, established two major programs to prevent the significant deterioration of air quality in pristine areas and to improve air quality in areas that failed to achieve the national ambient air quality standards, and issued another round of technology-based effluent limitations under the CWAct to address discharges of toxic pollutants.[7] EPA demonstrated the statute's power to protect public health in the late 1970s and mid-1980s when its regulations requiring the petroleum industry to remove tetraethyl lead from gasoline resulted in dramatic decreases in the levels of lead, a powerful neurotoxicant, in the blood of urban children.[8]

Ruckelshaus adopted a "fair but firm" approach to enforcement that considered mitigating circumstances and gave the "benefit of the doubt" to companies making good faith efforts to comply. But he also insisted on compliance within a reasonable time, and he was determined to punish foot draggers. The agency continued to stress strict enforcement during the Train years, despite growing White House opposition, and it hammered out stringent settlements with several major polluters.[9] At the outset of the Carter Administration, EPA initiated a "file first/negotiate later" enforcement policy and a tough new "civil penalty policy" under which enforcement officials were to insist on a monetary penalty that was high enough to match the amount of money that the source saved by failing to comply with the law.[10]

The George H. W. Bush Administration pressed Congress to enact much-needed amendments to the CAAct, and it wrote dozens of stringent regulations to implement the new law. Environmental enforcement picked up as an aggressive assistant administrator placed greater emphasis than any of his predecessors on criminal penalties.[11] The Clinton Administration EPA aggressively implemented the 1990 CAAct amendments until it shifted to a defensive posture in 1995 to deflect the second assault from the Gingrich Congress. It continued to emphasize enforcement, filing record numbers of enforcement actions in 1993 and 1994, before backing off somewhat during the second assault.[12] During the second interregnum EPA undertook a massive revision of the national ambient air quality standards for ozone and particulate matter to increase the degree to which they protected human health.

OSM got off to a good start in the Carter Administration. Among other things, it promulgated regulations implementing the statutory requirement that operators restore disturbed surface areas to "the approximate original contour." The stringent regulations, however, allowed operators to apply to the relevant state or federal permitting authority for variances from this requirement. Another regulation, which lacked a variance possibility, prohibited operators from placing spoil from mining operations within a 100-foot "buffer zone" on either side of a valley stream.[13] The former rules had the potential to render surface mining far less intrusive (at least in the long run), and the latter rules protected sensitive headwaters of rivers and streams from pollution by heavy metals and silt. Despite dire warnings from the Heritage Foundation that the regulations would "remove a significant portion of our coal reserves from potential production," coal production increased by 50 percent between 1978 and 1988 as the rules went into effect. OSM was also an aggressive enforcer during the Carter Administration. During 1979 alone, it conducted more than 20,000 inspections, issued more than 4,000 notices of violation, assessed almost $8 million in fines, and closed almost 1,000 outlaw surface mining operations.[14]

THE REALITY

During the Laissez Faire Revival, the level of regulatory and enforcement activity of all three agencies rarely matched the levels of the early years. EPA was by far the most prolific of the environmental agencies, but it often had to be prodded by "agency-forcing" lawsuits to fulfill its regulatory responsibilities. OSM promulgated far fewer regulations than EPA, but its regulation of mountaintop removal mining in Appalachia generated as much consternation in the business community as EPA's most controversial rules. MMS promulgated the fewest rules of all, and they rarely raised industry hackles because the agency relied heavily on the industry for its standards. It did receive criticism, however, for failing to open more federal lands to oil and gas development.[15]

WRITING THE RULES

Under a constant barrage of criticism from think tanks, radio commentators, and unsympathetic members of Congress in the late 1970s, EPA and OSM grew more receptive to industry demands for "flexible" regulation and academic prescriptions for more "efficient" regulatory approaches to pollution control. EPA's "bubble policy," under which an existing source could increase emissions from one unit without a permit so long as it offset those emissions with reductions from another unit within the same facility, survived a challenge by environmental groups in the Supreme Court.[16]

Reflecting a dramatic break with the immediate past, President Reagan's first EPA Administrator, Anne Gorsuch, told an American Enterprise Institute (AEI) symposium that she was not so much interested in *better* regulation as in *less* regulation. Gorsuch and her carefully selected associates adopted three strategies to change the agency's culture. First, they removed career civil servants from mid-level management positions and replaced them with ideologues, many of whom were wholly unqualified. Second, they initiated a series of reorganizations aimed primarily at enhancing their control over career employees, most of whom they neither respected nor trusted. Third, they negotiated directly with the regulated industries, thereby undercutting professional staffers who were struggling to withstand industry pressure to reduce the stringency of regulatory requirements and the severity of enforcement sanctions. The three strategies had a severely negative impact on staff morale, and many highly qualified employees simply left the agency.[17]

Gorsuch's clear disdain for the laws that she was charged with administering and her poor choice of upper-level leadership soon put her at odds with House Democrats, many of whom had been actively involved in writing the original Public Interest Era statutes. After several confrontations with congressional committees investigating EPA's crude attempts to provide regulatory relief and an embarrassing document-shredding incident, Gorsuch resigned. The Heritage Foundation provided a refuge for nineteen high-level EPA officials who departed soon thereafter.[18]

Returning for a second stint as Administrator, William Ruckelshaus appointed competent professionals to high-level positions. His obvious concern for improving EPA's public image and his pep talks to the agency staff helped restore morale and smooth relations with Congress. Having steered the agency back on course, Ruckelshaus departed in February 1985 to be replaced by Lee Thomas, a career civil servant who was careful to maintain the agency on the even keel that Ruckelshaus had set as the agency entered the second interregnum.[19]

Secretary of Interior James Watt, the former director of a conservative litigation group, created MMS in 1982 to manage mineral leases on federal lands. Although Watt made it clear that its primary obligation was to ensure that lessees developed the resources efficiently and paid appropriate royalties to the government, MMS also functioned as a regulatory agency for the purpose of protecting workers and the marine environment in offshore areas beyond the jurisdiction of OSHA and EPA.[20] The agency, however, lacked the expertise and the resources to keep up with the risks posed by new deepwater drilling technologies that the industry developed in the 1990s and 2000s. Most of the regulations that it promulgated were drawn from voluntary standards developed by the American Petroleum Institute. The impact of even those mild standards was softened by provisions allowing companies to employ "alternative compliance" technologies that, in their judgment, would function just as effectively as those upon which the agency modeled its standards.[21]

Secretary Watt was convinced that strip-mined coal would become an increasingly significant source of the nation's electrical energy, and he made regulatory relief at OSM his top priority. He picked James Harris, a coal industry consultant, to head the agency, and Harris picked Steven J. Griles, a Virginia environmental official, to be his deputy. During the first year of the Reagan Administration, OSM's budget declined by 37 percent and the staff fell to about half its pre-Reagan size. Following the Heritage Foundation's recommendations, Watt assigned four top priorities to OSM—reorganizing the agency to give political appointees more control over day-to-day decisions, delegating OSM's regulatory powers to the states, rewriting the Carter Administration's stringent regulations, and changing the agency's enforcement approach from tough cop to helpful partner. Harris and Griles moved aggressively to implement all four of these priorities. Some of the changes were either overturned by courts or abandoned after Secretary Watt resigned in disgrace in October 1983, but many survived into the twenty-first century. Watt's replacement, Donald Hodel, made several concessions to environmental groups, including slight increases in the agency's budget, as the agency entered the first interregnum.[22]

President George H. W. Bush's pragmatism was on display during the first major crisis of his administration, the breakup of a huge Exxon oil tanker in the pristine Prince William Sound near Valdez, Alaska. With the president's support, Congress responded with the Oil Pollution Act of 1990. The new law put the United States in the forefront of environmental spill control by requiring tankers using U.S. ports to be fitted with double hulls and increasing ship owner liability for response costs.[23]

William Reilly, a moderate Republican with strong conservationist credentials, was President Bush's choice to head EPA. Reilly adopted a low-key approach to rulemaking that served EPA well when the agency came under attack toward the end of the Bush Administration from laissez faire minimalists in Vice-President Dan Quayle's Council on Competitiveness. Reilly's main accomplishment was to steer comprehensive amendments to the Clean Air Act through a contentious Bush Administration and an even more divided Congress. Reilly had a powerful White House ally in C. Boyden Gray, the President's Counsel and a long-time advocate of alternative fuels and market-based approaches to pollution problems. The agency's progress in implementing the new law, however, suffered a significant setback in 1992 when President Bush imposed a moratorium on new regulations for the remainder of his term.[24]

In July 1991, MMS took a rare step toward promulgating a regulation when it solicited public comments on a proposed requirement that offshore lessees develop and implement "safety and environmental management programs" to identify and control the risks of blowouts and spills. The industry balked at the idea and suggested instead that the agency work with the American Petroleum Institute to come up with a voluntary standard. The agency dithered over the matter until 2009, when it published an advance notice of proposed rulemaking that contained only four of the twelve generally accepted elements of a process safety standard.[25]

Carol Browner, a former head of the Florida Department of Environmental Protection, served as EPA Administrator for the entire Clinton Administration. Browner's confidence that economic growth could proceed hand-in-hand with environmental protection was reflected in the agency's emphasis on "collaborative" approaches to regulation in which the agency brought together "stakeholders" to negotiate the details of regulatory requirements with the (rarely achieved) goal of avoiding political grandstanding and contentious litigation.[26]

The agency's equilibrium was upset once again when the "revolutionaries" who took over the House of Representatives during the second assault singled out EPA for special opprobrium and threatened to amend its foundational statutes. As with the attacks on OSHA, the Clinton Administration tried to co-opt these legislative initiatives by demonstrating that it was already busily engaged in reforming environmental regulation from within. In language that could have been written by AEI economists, its March 16, 1995, report *Reinventing Environmental Regulation* criticized "command and control" regulation and urged EPA to adopt "performance standards" and pollutant trading regimes. EPA reported in June 1995 that its "line-by-line" review of 12,766 pages of regulations had identified almost 1,500 pages that it would be deleting.[27]

EPA created a new "Office of Reinvention" to oversee a rapidly growing number of initiatives designed to provide greater flexibility for regulatees. The most ambitious program, Project XL, assembled groups of state and local officials and company-selected stakeholders to consider proposals for replacing existing regulatory requirements with more discretionary environmental management strategies at particular facilities. Since violations of the voluntary agreements were not necessarily unlawful, the consequences were usually limited to further negotiations over corrective action. The process soon devolved into a "regulatory free-for-all," of limited effectiveness and dubious legality.[28]

OSM head Robert Uram devoted much of his attention to protecting the agency's budget and to defeating several extreme "property rights" bills that posed a serious threat to the agency's viability. He was wholly unsuccessful on the first front, where a 25 percent budget cut forced the agency to lay off many seasoned inspectors. But Congress failed to enact property rights legislation, and it did not even take up deregulatory surface mine legislation.[29]

The most significant environmental law on the Gingrich Congress's agenda was the CWAct. That statute's past emphasis on technology-based standards made it a favorite target for criticism from industrial dischargers, and its wetlands protections were anathema to private real estate developers and property rights activists. The House easily passed industry-drafted amendments to the CWAct that would have rewritten all of the core pollution control provisions of the 25-year-old statute to reflect a far more industry-friendly approach to water pollution. The bill would also have redefined the critical term "wetland" to include far fewer areas, eliminated EPA's role in the wetlands permit process, and made it much easier for surface mines in mountainous areas to get permits. After President Clinton promised to veto the bill, however, the moderate Republican chairman of the Senate environmental committee decided not to schedule it for a markup.[30]

The mining industry gained unprecedented access to the White House as the business community launched the third assault on federal regulation during George W. Bush's first term. Vice-President Cheney's Energy Task Force recommended that the nation commit to building 1,900 new coal-fired power plants in twenty years. The new Deputy Secretary of the Interior, Steven Griles, had been working for coal companies since he left the government at the end of the Reagan Administration. As Griles took over many of the Department's day-to-day management functions, he focused especially carefully on OSM.[31]

The Bush Administration EPA continued the Clinton Administration's emphasis on market-based regulation and voluntary programs, but it terminated or significantly revised several protective Clinton Administration initiatives. Administrator Christine Todd Whitman drew most of her upper-level managers from the regulated industries, and she supported the administration's efforts to reduce the agency's enforcement budget. But she spent most of her time in conflicts with the White House Office of Information and Regulatory Affairs (OIRA) and political operatives in the Office of the Vice-President who demanded even greater regulatory relief for the energy industry. As staff morale sank to Reagan Administration lows, environmental activists criticized Whitman's reluctance to support agency scientists in disputes with the White House over global warming, wetlands, and power plant mercury emissions.[32]

Whitman resigned in frustration in May 2003 after it became painfully apparent that the White House would not allow her to set administration policy on any environmental issue that mattered to the business community. Her two successors, Governor Mike Leavitt of Utah and Stephen Johnson, a career EPA employee, were more comfortable as advocates for the White House's deregulatory policies. During their tenures, EPA lost a surprising number of judicial challenges brought by environmental groups in which the courts held that its deregulatory actions were prohibited by the plain language of the relevant statutes.[33] There were, it seems, limits to the extent to which the agency could advance a laissez faire minimalist agenda in the absence of amendments to the relevant statutes.

From its inception in 1982, MMS viewed itself as a "partner" with the industry in extracting as much oil as possible from federal leases. Agency officials overseeing the Gulf Coast offshore leases usually lived in the same communities as the employees who worked on the rigs, and they were steeped in the same oilpatch culture. The agency's enthusiasm for drilling in the Gulf of Mexico grew to unprecedented levels after President George W. Bush issued an executive order requiring all energy agencies to "expedite their review of permits" and "accelerate the completion of" energy development projects. Indeed, the partnership got out of hand as MMS officials freely accepted gifts, trips, tickets, and invitations to wild parties from oil company executives. All the while, deepwater drilling technology was rapidly outrunning MMS's capacity to promulgate up-to-date safety requirements.[34]

FOREGONE PROTECTION

The preceding pages described in general terms how attacks on EPA, OSM, and MMS during the Laissez Faire Revival had a powerful impact on their willingness and ability to fulfill the potential of the Public Interest Era statutes. The following pages explore how the attacks affected agency implementation of five particular regulatory initiatives, each of which, if properly implemented, would have provided much-needed environmental protections that Congress envisioned in enacting the agencies' statutes.

Global Warming. With the exception of a small group of skeptics, most of whom were funded by the energy industry, the scientific community had come to a consensus by 1990 at the latest that human activities were at least partially responsible for increasing global temperatures and associated climate change. The energy industry and the Chamber of Commerce, however, conducted a decade-long $100 million campaign to sow doubt in the minds of policymakers about the scientific basis for that conclusion. The strategy worked. The United States declined to commit itself to any target for reducing greenhouse gas emissions at a June 1992 United Nations conference in Rio de Janeiro.[35]

Despite Vice-President Al Gore's declaration that the United States was committed to "reducing our emissions of greenhouse gases to their 1990 levels by the year 2000," the Clinton Administration's legislative efforts to address climate change went nowhere. The climate skeptics had their day in the limelight during the second assault in a series of congressional hearings featuring prominent climate change skeptics and commentators from conservative think tanks. Congress then passed a number of appropriations riders halting any agency efforts to regulate greenhouse gas emissions. The business community launched an even more vigorous lobbying and public relations blitz in anticipation of a major conference on climate change held in Kyoto, Japan, in December 1997. Its efforts were rewarded when the Clinton Administration declined to submit the Kyoto Treaty to the Senate for ratification.[36]

Candidate George W. Bush promised to take strong action to reduce emissions of greenhouse gases, but President George W. Bush in March 2001 announced that the administration would disavow the Kyoto Treaty and decline to regulate carbon dioxide emissions from power plants. The moving force behind this dramatic reversal was Vice-President Dick Cheney, whose Energy Task Force was regularly meeting with energy and electric utility lobbyists to craft the administration's energy bill and associated "Clear Skies" amendments to the Clean Air Act, both of which called for "voluntary" reductions in greenhouse gas emissions.[37]

The Bush Administration also did very little to address the problem administratively. The Department of Transportation's anemic corporate fuel economy standards did little to reduce fuel consumption in a growing fleet of new automobiles, half of which by 2003 was composed of gas-guzzling SUVs and Hummers. EPA concluded that it lacked authority under the Clean Air Act to limit greenhouse gas emissions from automobiles because greenhouse gases were not "pollutants." The Supreme Court overturned that clearly erroneous interpretation in 2007 and remanded the case to EPA to decide whether greenhouse gases "endangered" public health and the environment. Not content with its own refusal to regulate, the administration for the first time in 40 years denied a request by California to promulgate more stringent auto emissions standards for vehicles in that state. In the meantime, carbon dioxide levels in the air reached record highs.[38]

Mercury. In early December 2003, EPA and the Food and Drug Administration issued a warning to women of childbearing age and parents of young children to limit their consumption of tuna and certain other fish to avoid the risks posed by mercury in the tissues of the fish. The warnings were based on risk assessments concluding that the offspring of mothers who consume high levels of mercury in their food are at risk for a number of devastating diseases, including mental retardation, cerebral palsy, deafness, and blindness. Even relatively low levels of mercury can produce adverse neurological effects that can affect childhood development. EPA estimated that around 630,000 children and 8 percent of women of childbearing age already had unsafe levels of mercury in their blood. More than one-half of the fish in the nation's lakes and reservoirs contained concentrations of mercury in excess of government standards, and one of the largest contributors of mercury in domestic fish was mercury emissions from coal-fired power plants.[39]

The 1990 CAAct amendments required EPA to prepare a report on the health effects of hazardous air pollutants emitted by power plants and to regulate those emissions under the statute's stringent requirements for hazardous air pollutants if it determined that such regulation was "appropriate and necessary." EPA did not complete the required report until 1997, and it took three more years for the agency to make the required finding that a standard was "appropriate and necessary." As the agency proceeded ahead, it issued drafts of reports indicating that the technologies it had in mind were capable of reducing power plant mercury emissions by at least 90 percent from the current 48 tons per year (tpy) in the U.S. to as low as 5 tpy.[40]

Mercury regulation was high on the list of utility industry concerns when its representatives met with members of the Cheney Energy Task Force in 2001, and the Bush Administration was anxious to help. In December 2003, EPA issued a proposal to withdraw the Clinton Administration finding and substitute a cap-and-trade program that would reduce mercury emissions by only 61 percent by 2018.[41] The radical shift in direction was the handiwork of Assistant Administrator Jeffrey Holmstead, an attorney whose former clients had included several major utility companies. After instructing the staff to tailor their analyses to support his predetermined outcome, Holmstead forced the proposal through the EPA review process over the strong objections of attorneys in the Office of General Counsel, who concluded that the CAAct did not authorize the radical new approach. Holmstead then inserted legal language into the proposal's preamble that tracked almost word-for-word the memos that Holmstead's old law firm had submitted to the agency on behalf of the electric utility industry. The EPA attorneys were vindicated, however, when the D.C. Circuit, in an opinion that found EPA's logic comparable to that of the Queen of Hearts in Lewis Carroll's *Alice's Adventures in Wonderland*, vacated the regulations in December 2008.

More than 18 years after Congress instructed EPA to address mercury emissions from power plants, the agency was back to square zero. In the meantime, mercury emissions continued to increase, and at least five mercury "hot spots" were identified in New England and Canada.[42]

Wetlands. Wetlands perform several valuable natural functions, including water storage, nutrient transformation, and habitat for fish, wildlife, and other organisms. Many of these functions are of direct benefit to human beings beyond their obvious recreational value. In addition, about one-third of North American bird species rely on wetlands for food, water, shelter, or breeding.[43]

Federal law protecting the nation's wetlands dates back to the Refuse Act of 1899, which made any discharge of "refuse matter" into navigable waters illegal without a permit. The permit program was historically administered by CoE, but the CWAct expanded the definition of "navigable waters" to include wetlands and assigned to EPA the role of promulgating the criteria that CoE used in issuing permits. In addition, EPA could veto a site upon a determination that filling the wetland would have an unacceptable adverse effect on drinking water supplies, fish and wildlife, or recreational values.[44] In 1985, the Supreme Court upheld CoE's broad definition of "waters" to include wetlands that were not constantly inundated or even frequently flooded by navigable water. As CoE began to implement this expansive new test, many more real estate and agricultural developments had to obtain permits. Still, almost 300,000 acres per year of wetlands were being lost to development during the housing boom of the late 1980s.[45]

To fulfill President George H. W. Bush's campaign promise that there would be "no net loss of wetlands" during his tenure, EPA and CoE circulated a draft manual containing an even broader definition of "wetlands" based on recent scientific research into aquatic ecosystems. Congress halted that effort with an appropriations rider preventing CoE from applying the new definition during fiscal year 1992. White House Competitiveness Council executive director David McIntosh, a strong property rights advocate, then ordered the agencies to narrow the definition. When EPA Administrator Reilly refused, McIntosh backed off to avoid giving President Bush's opponents an easy target in the upcoming election. After the 1992 elections, however, Vice-President Dan Quayle tried to force EPA to push through McIntosh's narrower definition before the Clinton Administration took over. Reilly once again demurred, but he dropped his broader definition, thereby leaving things where they stood in 1987. The Clinton Administration likewise adhered to the 1987 definition.[46]

In 2001, the Supreme Court roiled the waters with a controversial holding that a "wetland" had to have a "significant nexus" to waters that were in fact navigable or could reasonably be made navigable through dredging. The George W. Bush Administration followed with a January 2003 policy directive that excluded "isolated waters," including headwaters and seasonal streams. Environmental activists noted that in addition to excluding most mountaintop removal mining (discussed below) from the CoE permit requirement, the guidelines put 20 million acres of wetlands at risk. CoE and EPA then issued a new set of guidelines that limited protected waters to those directly connected to navigable streams. At the same time, EPA enforcers refrained from filing more than 400 enforcement actions involving wetlands that were not clearly connected to navigable waters.[47] By the end of the third assault, the protections afforded wetlands in the United States had shrunk as rapidly as the wetlands themselves.

Mountaintop Removal Mining. An especially efficient form of surface mining called "mountaintop removal" mining became popular in Appalachia during the 1990s. Employing that technique, operators gained access to an underground coal seam by scraping the trees and topsoil off the mountainous terrain overlying the seam, flattening the peak by removing rock with explosives and huge bulldozers, and taking out the exposed coal with giant cranes. Much of the "spoil" material remained as "valley fill," leaching heavy metals and silt into the streams that naturally flowed along the valley floors and rendering them incapable of supporting aquatic life. Valley fills could be more than a mile long and hundreds of feet deep, and they were especially destructive of the environmentally sensitive headwaters of Appalachian streams and rivers.[48] Hills that had been familiar landmarks for generations of Appalachian families became barren plateaus as their tops disappeared into the streams below.[49] Although the ultimate impact on the downstream waters was not easy to predict, a government scientist observed that "nothing on this scale has ever happened before."[50]

Although the SMCRAct required operators to restore mined lands to their original contours, it allowed OSM and the states to grant variances from that requirement in exceptional cases. Because it was impossible to rebuild a mountain once its top had been turned into valley fill, every mountaintop removal permit needed a variance, and industry-dominated state agencies routinely granted them. In theory, OSM was responsible for ensuring that the state programs implemented the law properly, but limited resources and a laissez faire minimalist mentality within OSM ensured that it rarely intervened.[51]

Since valley fill invariably wound up in the streams that ran along valley floors, mountaintop removal operations also needed a "dredge and fill" permit from CoE. In 1991, CoE issued a "nationwide" permit that allowed mountaintop removal activities with "minimal" environmental impact to proceed with only cursory review. Under its very liberal interpretation of the word "minimal," CoE required only about 7 percent of almost 1,000 removals per year to obtain full-fledged permits.[52]

As mountains began to disappear and pristine streams filled with heavy metals, two environmental groups in October 1999 persuaded a conservative Republican federal judge to issue an injunction against all discharges of material from mining operations into navigable streams without a full-fledged CoE permit. Although the Fourth Circuit Court of Appeals reversed the district court on technical grounds, the mining industry felt sufficiently threatened by the litigation to launch a lobbying campaign to change the EPA and CoE regulations defining "fill." It found a receptive audience in Deputy Interior Secretary Steven Griles, who persuaded his counterparts at EPA and CoE to rewrite their regulations to state that residual material from mountaintop removal operations was beneficial "fill" material subject to CoE's lenient nationwide permit and not "waste" material subject to EPA's far more stringent discharge permit requirements. The regulations were finalized in record time, and the threat was over by the end of May 2002.[53]

Griles was also determined to rewrite OSM's "buffer zone" rule that required a permit for any material deposited within 100 feet of a navigable stream. To accomplish this, the agency had to prepare an environmental impact statement (EIS). The draft EIS that the Department published in May 2003 detailed the severe adverse effects resulting from the permanent loss of 1,200 miles of mountain streams. In December 2008, OSM promulgated a final rule allowing operators to disturb the 100-foot buffer zone so long as they took steps "to the extent possible" to "minimize" damage to streams. Delighted with the new regulation, the mining industry ramped up production.[54]

LIMITED ACCOUNTABILITY

The aggressiveness with which the environmental agencies and the Justice Department attempted to hold companies accountable for violating the nation's environmental laws varied during the Laissez Faire Revival. The uneven performance was largely attributable to the willingness of different administrations to devote resources to enforcement, but it also reflected differences in attitudes concerning the relative desirability of strict enforcement versus compliance assistance.

The first assault on regulation during the Reagan Administration brought about radical changes in direction at both EPA and OSM that paralleled similar changes at OSHA discussed in Chapter 8. EPA's enforcement budget declined 39 percent between 1980 and 1983. EPA Administrator Anne Gorsuch firmly believed in encouraging voluntary compliance, and she preferred to settle civil cases for modest fines. As the word got out that too many referrals of cases for prosecution would result in "black marks" on an enforcement attorney's performance evaluation, referrals declined 84 percent during Gorsuch's first year. Civil and criminal referrals from EPA to the Justice Department fell by the same amount. After Gorsuch departed in 1983, however, Administrator Bill Ruckelshaus adopted a much more vigorous enforcement policy (as had Pendergrass at OSHA), and referrals increased substantially.[55]

OSM also adopted a cooperative approach to enforcement. In late 1980, it issued regulations capping the penalty for a single violation at $750 per day. Headquarters officials routinely vetoed recommendations from the field offices to prosecute new cases and to appeal adverse rulings. Occasionally, they even directed local officials to drop ongoing investigations and to reduce or eliminate penalties. Inspectors who insisted on taking tough enforcement stances were transferred to headquarters where they could be more easily supervised. Notices of violation declined 70 percent during the first year of the Reagan Administration, and appeals of dismissals dropped by 50 percent.[56]

EPA filed a record number of enforcement actions during the first two years of the Clinton Administration. In response to the second assault from the Gingrich Congress, however, it shifted gears and placed more emphasis on "compliance assistance." Enforcement actions fell by 18 percent in 1995 and by another 35 percent in 1996.[57] OSM followed a similar pattern of reinvigorated enforcement during the first two years of the Clinton Administration and dramatically reduced efforts as the agency absorbed severe budget cuts imposed by the 104th Congress. The number of inspections dropped by almost 50 percent in many regions.[58]

During the George W. Bush Administration, EPA returned to the Gorsuch-era emphasis on compliance assistance over vigorous prosecution. The crown jewel of the agency's 75 voluntary programs was the "Performance Track" initiative under which about 550 "exemplary" companies agreed to improve their environmental performance in return for reduced reporting obligations, fewer inspections, and more flexible permit requirements. A confidential 2006 analysis prepared by EPA enforcement officials, however, concluded that there was "considerable noncompliance" among Performance Track companies. In March 2007, the agency's Inspector General found that only two of the thirty facilities that it examined were in fact meeting their obligations under the program.[59]

Almost 90 percent of EPA's enforcement activity during the George W. Bush Administration consisted of administrative enforcement actions brought pursuant to a low visibility "sue-and-settle" strategy that resulted in penalties far too low to deter future violations. The Justice Department filed only 93 civil enforcement actions during the first six years of the Bush Administration compared to 157 during the last three years of the Clinton Administration. At the same time, judicial and administrative penalties declined almost 25 percent from Clinton Administration levels. Among other things, EPA sharply scaled back a major Clinton Administration enforcement initiative aimed at eliminating thousands of tons of unlawful emissions of hazardous air pollutants from the country's 145 petroleum refineries. Criminal enforcement investigations dropped by 50 percent and criminal penalties declined 38 percent.[60]

Under the watchful eyes of a Democrat-controlled Congress, EPA's enforcement efforts picked up significantly during the last two years of the Bush Administration. For example, the American Electric Power Corporation agreed to pay a $15 million fine, spend $60 million restoring parks and waterways that had been damaged by acid rain, and devote up to $4.6 billion to reducing emissions. The agency began to police the refinery consent decrees more vigorously, and it even filed a few criminal enforcement actions against egregious violators.[61]

THE CONSEQUENCES

On April 20, 2010, the BP Corporation's Mississippi Canyon Block 252 exploratory well, located in the Gulf of Mexico about 50 miles southeast of Venice, Louisiana, suffered a massive blowout as a floating offshore drilling rig named *Deepwater Horizon* was in the process of completing the well. The resulting explosion killed eleven workers and sank the rig. As the oil flowed at a rate of more than 40,000 barrels per day into the Gulf, BP and the federal government undertook a massive campaign to contain the spill. Long before BP finally sealed off the well in mid-September 2010, it had become the largest oil spill in U.S. history. Subsequent investigations revealed that BP had taken a number of shortcuts to bring the over-budget project to completion as rapidly as possible, many with the tacit approval of MMS.[62]

A national commission empaneled by President Obama to investigate the causes of the spill concluded that BP's upper-level management had created a "culture of complacency" that elevated short-term profits over long-term investments in safety, and a lengthy review of BP's record by the *New York Times* concluded that it was "chronically unable or unwilling to learn from its mistakes." The Transocean Corporation, the owner of the *Deepwater Horizon*, was known for its tendency to "push the envelope" of both deepwater technology and the law. A report detailing the "safety culture" on the *Deepwater Horizon* prepared for the company by Lloyd's Register Group noted that workers "often saw unsafe behaviors on the rig" and that "drilling priorities [had taken] precedence over planned maintenance." An "equipment assessment" prepared by the same company concluded that many key safety components had not been fully inspected for ten years.[63]

The full impact of the massive release on the Gulf of Mexico will probably remain an open question for years to come. For a time, business at BP filling stations dropped, but within four months it had rebounded in response to a $5 million per week BP advertising campaign. BP also invested more than $20 million between January 2009 and May 2010 in lobbying MMS and Congress not to adopt measures that would unduly restrict future drilling activities. In the meantime, more than 4,000 wells continued to produce oil and gas in the Gulf of Mexico.[64]

The *Deepwater Horizon* crisis was unique only in the stark visibility of its impact on the marine and coastal environments. Most of the adverse environmental effects of reduced regulatory protections during the Laissez Faire Revival were hidden in far less visible statistics documenting steady or declining air and water quality, in rising atmospheric temperatures, in vanishing wetlands, and in isolated valleys below decapitated Appalachian mountains. Box 9.1 details some of these consequences.

Box 9.1

Environmental Degradation

Wasted Wetlands. Reacting to dramatic declines in the nation's wetlands due to agricultural "reclamation," rapid suburban growth, and poor land management, President George H. W. Bush declared a national policy of no net loss of wetlands. However, a Supreme Court opinion restricting the legal definition of "wetlands," a congressional failure to clarify the law, and a general reluctance in the executive branch to enforce the law have resulted in a continued loss of wetlands at a rate of about 58,000 acres per year.[a]

Polluted Streams. Fully 44 percent of the nation's rivers, 64 percent of its lakes, and 30 percent of its estuaries fail to meet the applicable water quality standards, in part because almost 25 percent of the 6,600 major industrial facilities and municipal treatment plants discharging into those waters are in "significant noncompliance" with permits at any given time.[b]

Decapitated Mountains. Between 1992 and 2002, mountaintop removal mining destroyed around 400,000 acres of old forest and buried about 1,200 miles of Appalachian streams under the rocks and soil. According to independent scientists, the practice had a "pervasive and irreversible" impact on the Appalachian environment and local communities.[c]

Unhealthy Air. As of September 2010, almost 120 million people lived in areas of the United States that had not attained the ambient air quality standard for photochemical oxidants (smog), and over 88 million people lived in areas that failed to attain the standard for fine particulate matter.[d]

Global Warming. The years 2005 and 2010 tied for the warmest years on record. A 2007 update of the Intergovernmental Panel on Climate Change (IPCC) report concluded that in the absence of dramatic reductions in greenhouse gas emissions, the earth will experience more drought, rising sea levels, increasingly severe hurricanes, increases in tropical disease rates, and massive population dislocation.[e]

NOTES

a. National Academies of Sciences, Compensating for Wetland Losses Under the Clean Water Act 17, table 1–1 (2001).

b. Environmental Protection Agency, National Water Quality Inventory: Report to Congress, 2004 Reporting Cycle: Findings (Jan 2009); Guy Gugliotta & Eric Pianin, *EPA: Few Fined for Polluting Water*, WP, June 6, 2003, at A1.

c. Michael Shnayerson, Coal River (2008); Erik Reece, Lost Mountain (2006); M. A. Palmer, et al., *Mountaintop Mining Consequences*, 327 Science 148 (2010) (pervasive quote); *Proposed Buffer Zone Rule Seeks Protection for Existing Valley Fill Practices, Groups Say*, 38 BNA Env. Rept. 1888 (2007) (statistics).

d. Environmental Protection Agency, 8-Hour Ozone Nonattainment Areas, available at http://www.epa.gov/oar/oaqps/greenbk/gntc.html (smog statistics); Environmental Protection Agency, Particulate Matter (PM 2.5) 1997 Standard Nonattainment Area Summary, available at http://www.epa.gov/oar/oaqps/greenbk/qnsum.html(particulate statistics).

e. National Oceanic & Atmospheric Administration, NOAA: 2010 Tied for Warmest Year on Record, January 12, 2011, available at http://www.noaanews.noaa.gov/stories2011/20110112_globalstats.html; Intergovernmental Panel on Climate Change, Climate Change 2007: The Physical Science Basis, Summary for Policymakers 9, 16 (2007).

CONCLUSIONS

Flush with resources and backed by strong public opinion, the environmental agencies initially generated a healthy flow of proactive implementing regulations that they vigorously enforced against some of the most powerful corporations in the country. The first assault on environmental regulation, however, derailed many of those early efforts and slowed down future initiatives. Yet public support remained strong for a federal role in protecting the environment. Attempts to gut the Public Interest Era statutes during the second and third assaults failed, and those laws continue to provide vital protections for human health and the environment. By the end of the third assault, however, the statutes were aging and the implementing agencies were showing the effects of years of budget cuts, dozens of restrictions on the rulemaking process, and a constant stream of criticism from the business community's idea infrastructure. Congress no longer appeared capable of enacting legislation to address emerging environmental problems. The last two significant environmental statutes were the Clean Air Act amendments of 1990 and the Oil Pollution Act of 1990. The former statute was enacted before global warming became a pressing social problem, and the latter only obliquely addressed the threat to the marine environment posed by deepwater drilling for oil and gas.

DRUG AND DEVICE SAFETY

The Food and Drug Administration (FDA) regulates a huge variety of products that account for about 25 percent of overall consumer spending, and about 25 percent of that amount is devoted to pharmaceutical products and medical devices. As of 2004, Americans were spending about $200 billion annually on prescription drugs, and the pharmaceutical industry was the most profitable industry other than Wall Street finance. The next year, however, congressional hearings and testimony in civil litigation revealed that a disturbing number of widely used drugs and devices had not been properly tested for adverse side effects and that manufacturers had failed to reveal to FDA or the public information in their possession about the adverse side effects of their products.[1]

THE POTENTIAL

Under authorities dating back to the Pure Food and Drug Act of 1906 and consolidated in the Food, Drug, and Cosmetic Act of 1938 (FDCAct), FDA administers a comprehensive permitting regime under which manufacturers must obtain FDA approval of new drugs and devices by demonstrating with objective scientific studies that they are both safe and effective. A drug manufacturer can avoid the process by showing that its product is "generally recognized as safe and effective," and a device manufacturer can obtain expedited approval if its product is "substantially equivalent" to a device already on the market. Drug and device manufacturers have historically chafed under these regulatory restrictions, which unquestionably limited their freedom to market innovative new products. But the process has protected patients from devastating side effects of drugs, from quack medications that do not perform as claimed, and from defective devices that could easily kill or maim when they malfunction.[2]

The best-known example of the regulatory regime's potential to protect patients involved a drug that was heavily used in Europe to treat morning sickness in pregnant women. In 1953, the Richardson-Merrell Company (a source of the substantial endowment that the Smith-Richardson Foundation later devoted to supporting anti-regulatory think tanks) petitioned FDA to approve its new drug thalidomide. An alert FDA medical officer named Frances Oldham Kelsey reviewed the company's application and did not like what she saw. Noting that many of the supporting "studies" were little more than unsupported testimonials, she urged her superiors to reject the application. The company responded with a fierce personal attack on Dr. Kelsey. Unintimidated, she held her own until reports started coming in from Germany that the drug was causing severe birth defects in the babies of women who had taken it. Although thalidomide was never approved in the U.S., thanks to Dr. Kelsey's timely intervention, it caused much human tragedy in Europe.[3]

THE REALITY

We cannot know how many similar tragedies have been avoided by FDA's premarket approval process, but the examples recounted in Box 10.1 provide a clear demonstration of the potential for harm when the protective federal drug and device regulatory regime is not functioning properly. In this chapter, we shall explore how the regime that prevented a thalidomide crisis became the regime that brought us the Vioxx crisis fifty years later. For much of the Laissez Faire Revival, FDA's leaders were committed to the agency's protective mission, but low budgets, lack of White House support, occasional leadership lapses, and a constant barrage of complaints from drug industry lobbyists, think tanks, and the conservative media echo chamber prevented the agency from protecting patients from unnecessary risks posed by drugs and devices.

WRITING THE RULES

With the thalidomide near-disaster a fading memory, the first assault on FDA began in earnest in the mid-1970s, roughly the same time as similar assaults on OSHA, MSHA, and EPA. The drug industry seized on an academic paper published in 1971 by pharmacologist William Wardell to argue that an FDA-caused "drug lag" was depriving Americans of pharmaceutical products that were easily available in Europe. Another academic paper, authored by University of Chicago business school professor Sam Peltzman, concluded that the benefits of the FDCAct's efficacy requirement were outweighed by a "substantial decline in drug innovation."[4] The American Enterprise Institute's (AEI) industry-funded Center for Health Policy Research, with the assistance of "adjunct scholars" Wardell and Peltzman, sponsored conferences, published reports, and republished reprints featuring the "drug lag" claim.[5] Several academics and a prestigious Review Panel on New Drug Regulation appointed by the Secretary of Health, Education, and Welfare systematically refuted both studies, pointing out that the recent decline in drug approvals was more likely attributable to the fact that drug companies had shifted resources from research on new products to promoting existing products. Yet the sheer volume of mutually reinforcing publications sounding the drug lag theme resonated in the mainstream press and drowned out the rebuttals.[6]

To tackle the swirling controversy, President Carter appointed an articulate Stanford University biologist named Donald Kennedy to head FDA. When Kennedy departed in the summer of 1979 to become the provost of Stanford University, President Carter appointed Jere Goyan, the Dean of the Pharmacy School at the University of California at San Francisco, to replace him. Both appointees stressed "science-based" approaches to regulation and resisted drug company pressures to approve their products on the basis of flawed or incomplete studies. But neither appointee was able to dampen the criticism coming from the industry and the think tanks. By the end of the Carter Administration, the drug lag claim had become conventional wisdom in business and political circles.[7]

Candidate Ronald Reagan made much of the drug lag, which he pledged to eliminate by persuading Congress to repeal the FDCAct's efficacy requirement as Peltzman had suggested. Although his legislative initiative failed, the White House pressured FDA to speed up drug approvals by relaxing the standards for approving new drug applications. FDA Administrator Arthur Hull Hayes, a former consultant to drug companies, dutifully jettisoned the science-based approach of his two predecessors in favor of a "cooperative" approach that gave the pharmaceutical industry a much greater say in how their drugs were tested, marketed, and advertised. After Hayes resigned in July 1983, his replacement, Frank E. Young, adopted the same cooperative approach.[8]

Unlike OSHA and EPA, FDA did not resume a more vigorous regulatory role during President Reagan's second term, in part because the drug lag debate took on a whole new dimension in the late 1980s with the discovery of a new disease called acquired immune deficiency syndrome (AIDS). Complaining bitterly about the absence of proven therapies for this devastating illness, AIDS activists pressed FDA and Congress to do something quickly. The agency responded with a program to speed up approvals of experimental drugs aimed at treating deadly diseases, and it quickly approved AZT, the first drug that seemed to slow the progression of AIDS.[9]

President George H. W. Bush found a remarkably qualified replacement for Young in Dr. David Kessler, a multi-tasking overachiever with an M.D. degree from Harvard and a law degree from the University of Chicago. When he arrived at the agency in November 1990, Kessler discovered that it was "under-funded, under-staffed, and demoralized." Within six months, Kessler had reinstated the science-based approach and restored staff morale. He jousted with the medical device industry over the safety of silicone breast implants and demanded that manufacturers of more than 100 other grandfathered devices conduct thorough safety studies.[10]

In the meantime, the drug industry's drug lag complaints continued un-abated. This time, however, the industry was joined by AIDS activists and patients' groups advocating easier approvals for drugs capable of treating rare diseases. Kessler was committed to reducing FDA approval times for life-saving drugs, but the agency faced resource shortages that made rapid approvals very difficult. After an intense series of negotiations, FDA and the drug industry struck a deal that Congress adopted in the Prescription Drug User Fee Act of 1992 (PDUFAct). The statute required new drug applicants to pay "user fees" to FDA to be used exclusively for new drug reviews. A side deal under which the agency agreed to adhere to specific deadlines in approving drugs was incorporated into the legislative history. To ensure that Congress did not place the entire burden of the new drug review program on the user fees, the side deal provided that if Congress did not continue to fund the Office of New Drugs at 1992 inflation-adjusted levels, the user fees would cease. Finally, Congress created an abbreviated "fast track" approval process for new drugs that would "address unmet medical needs" for "serious or life-threatening condition[s]."[11]

Reappointed by President Clinton in 1993, Kessler was the target of vicious attacks from the congressional leadership during the second assault in 1995. House Speaker Newt Gingrich called Kessler "a bully and a thug," and he described FDA as "the leading job killer in America." Sensing a unique opportunity to push through radical deregulatory drug legislation, industry lobbyists trotted out the decade-old Wardell and Peltzman drug lag studies for another tour of duty. Conservative critics in Congress and the think tanks accused the agency of killing thousands of Americans by delaying approval of valuable drugs and medical devices.[12]

The agency responded with an up-to-date analysis showing that the average new drug review time had decreased from 30 months in 1992 to 20 months in 1994, a rate that compared favorably with those in other developed countries.[13] Deftly shifting ground, critics complained of a recently discovered "device lag." New device applications were coming into the agency at an unprecedented rate, and the number of devices to which FDA had granted full approval had declined from 47 in 1990 to 12 in 1992. Moreover, the average time required for full approval had risen from 12 months in 1989 to 22 months in 1991. Acknowledging that the pace of device approval was too slow, FDA in 1993 modified its procedures to establish a "fast track" for innovative devices, speed up approvals of low-risk devices, and require more complete applications at the front end. During 1994, the backlog declined dramatically from more than two thousand applications to about five hundred. But it began to grow again after the Gingrich Congress slashed the agency's budget.[14]

Drug companies hired an army of lobbyists, many of whom had at one time worked for FDA, to push their legislative agenda in the Gingrich Congress. But the industry's reforms were no match in either breadth or intensity for the radical restructuring that several prominent think tanks had in mind. The Competitive Enterprise Institute, for example, urged Congress to replace the drug approval process with one in which FDA merely ensured that drug and device labels were not misleading. Surprisingly, such radical proposals encountered opposition from drug companies worried that they would undermine public confidence in their products. Realizing that they did not have the votes to override a certain veto by President Clinton, Republican leaders pulled the radical bills in late 1996.[15] With that threat no longer hanging over the agency, Kessler left to become the Dean of the Yale Medical School. As the agency was completing 95 percent of its new drug reviews within the statutory deadlines, he announced that it was "time to stop fighting the battles of the past."[16]

To prevent the user fee authorization from expiring, Congress enacted the FDA Modernization Act of 1997 (FDAMAct). Under the new law, FDA was obliged to approve 90 percent of new drug applications within 10 months (down from the 12 month deadline of the 1992 statute) and 90 percent of "priority" new drug applications within 6 months. The statute also loosened the standard for determining drug efficacy, "streamlined" the agency's good manufacturing procedures, and allowed manufacturers to circulate peer-reviewed articles from medical journals to promote drugs for unapproved uses. In addition, it required FDA to use the "least burdensome" procedures for approving medical devices, and it eliminated mandatory postmarket surveillance requirements for device manufacturers. Although the drug and device industries were quite pleased with the outcome, the radical deregulators in the think tanks viewed the statute as a "profound disappointment."[17]

President George W. Bush chose Mark McClellan, another overachiever with degrees in medicine and economics, to head FDA. By the time that McClellan took over, the pace of drug approvals was slowing, and the pharmaceutical industry and think tanks were complaining once again about the "drug lag." With the industry's acquiescence, the 2002 renewal of the PDUFAct increased the user fees once again, and this time the statute allowed FDA to spend a small proportion of the fees on monitoring existing drugs. In return, FDA agreed to adhere to strict timelines in responding to drug company requests for meetings.[18]

When McClellan left the agency in February 2004, President Bush appointed Andrew von Eschenbach, the head of the National Cancer Institute and a strong advocate of loosening the approval criteria for cutting-edge cancer therapies, to the position. By the time that Eschenbach took over in September 2005, morale at the agency was at an all-time low. The agency came under intense congressional scrutiny as several popular drugs to which it had granted "fast track" approval in the late 1990s (the most notorious of which was the pain killer Vioxx) produced deadly side effects that should have been detected much sooner. Hoping to enhance the agency's fading public image, Eschenbach announced a plan to monitor new drugs for 18 months after approval. The Vioxx crisis, in which the manufacturer discovered that the drug was causing high incidences of cardiovascular problems that resulted in as many as 139,000 heart attacks and strokes (an FDA scientist's estimate), had little effect on the White House or the Republican-controlled Congress.[19] The chairman of the House committee with jurisdiction over FDA drug regulation, Joe Barton (R-Texas), suggested that safety concerns about Vioxx and similar painkillers were "being blown out of proportion," and he found "nothing wrong with the [FDA] approval process."[20]

At the same time that Eschenbach was expressing an openness to dissent, he was overruling agency scientists who objected to abbreviated approval of a medical device for repairing knees that the agency had earlier rejected during the more extensive full-approval process. The manufacturer's lobbyists (two of whom were former FDA employees) had persuaded lawmakers from its home state of New Jersey (all of whom received substantial campaign contributions from the company) to demand that Eschenbach personally involve himself in the decisionmaking process. Eschenbach assigned the matter to the head of the device division, who then overruled the scientists.[21]

By 2007, drug companies had withdrawn or heavily restricted sales of more than a dozen drugs that FDA had approved since 1992. As in previous years when the user fee program came up for renewal, FDA and the industry negotiated over the content of the expected 2007 amendments. It soon became clear, however, that concerned members of Congress and several consumer groups were not going to accept the outcome of the closed-door negotiations this time. With a Democrat-controlled Congress and the most knowledgeable

Republican, Senator Charles Grassley (R-Iowa), backing stronger regulation, the drug and device industries understood that compromise was in order.[22]

The Food and Drug Administration Amendments Act of 2007 (FDAAAct) raised user fees for both drug and device manufacturers by modest amounts, and it allowed the agency to allocate more of the funds they generated to post-market surveillance of approved drugs and devices. It further empowered FDA to require companies to conduct and complete post-approval clinical studies, and it allowed FDA to impose specific label changes. For the first time, Congress required manufacturers to submit advertisements to FDA before running them, but, in a curious compromise, it did not give the agency authority to disapprove such ads. The burden remained on FDA to prove in court that an ad was false or misleading after-the-fact. The statute also required FDA to set up a publicly available database containing data from clinical trials for drugs and medical devices. Finally, the new law required drug manufacturers to obtain FDA approval of "risk evaluation and mitigation strategies" (REMS) for new and existing products. As part of its REMS approval authority, the agency could require companies to disseminate information about their products to doctors, restrict distribution of those products to certain institutions (e.g., hospitals), and require manufacturers to employ specific risk minimization tools. The new law, however, contained few substantive requirements for device manufacturers.[23]

FOREGONE PROTECTION

Although the drug lag claim continued to resonate in conservative think tanks and media outlets, any supporting evidence had evaporated by 2001 when the U.S. was approving drugs faster than any other country. In 2004, the average time for approval had shrunk to 11.9 months. By then, it was clear that the relentless pressure from the pharmaceutical industry and its allies in Congress to approve more new drugs had resulted in a dangerous "drug rush." The agency's overly solicitous response extended to its responsibilities to regulate medical devices, drug and device imports, and promotion of drugs and devices to doctors and the public.[24]

The Drug Rush. After almost a decade of frenetic activity aimed at increasing the approval rates for new drugs and devices, FDA drug reviewers were complaining of a "sweatshop" atmosphere in which deadlines were strictly enforced without regard to the complexity of the scientific issues. They could audit only about one percent of the scientific studies that the drug companies submitted, and they did virtually nothing to enforce conflicts of interest restrictions on the investigators who conducted the studies. Their underlying inquiry had shifted from whether applications were supported by sound scientific data to how the agency could justify approving drugs that were supported by questionable data. Reviewers who held up the process by requiring applicants to respond to legitimate questions had to answer to their superiors. In a 2002 survey of almost 400 medical reviewers, nearly 20 percent said that they had felt pressure to recommend approval over their own reservations, and 21 percent reported discomfort with expressing a scientific opinion that differed from the outcome the agency leadership expected. Many simply left the agency for more lucrative positions in the industry or less stressful positions in academia.[25] A great many of the drugs that FDA rushed onto the market in the late 1990s and early 2000s had to be withdrawn in subsequent years because they caused serious (sometimes catastrophic) side effects in unsuspecting patients.[26]

FDA's approval of the diabetes drug Rezulin in 1997 provides a good example. The Warner-Lambert Company applied for FDA approval in July 1996 under the "fast track" procedures reserved for drugs capable of preventing death or serious diseases. Pointing to "worrisome" indications in the clinical studies that Rezulin caused liver and heart damage, FDA's reviewer questioned both its efficacy and its safety. Upper-level managers purged his review from the files and assigned the application to another medical officer. Within a year after the agency approved Rezulin in January 1997, it had received several reports of sudden liver failure caused by the drug. Instead of withdrawing its approval, the agency negotiated a series of label changes. By April 1999, the agency had received reports of dozens of deaths and hundreds of serious adverse reactions. Nevertheless, the product remained on the market until March 2000, when the agency announced that Warner-Lambert was voluntarily withdrawing it. By then, Rezulin had caused thousands of liver injuries, 90 cases of liver failure, and at least 60 confirmed deaths.[27] Box 10.1 indicates that the Rezulin fiasco was just one of many rapid approval disasters.

Post-Market Drug Surveillance. At the same time that it was rapidly approving potentially dangerous new drugs, FDA was slow to pull bad actors off the market and to require better warnings when products began to cause serious adverse reactions. The short-term clinical studies upon which the medical officers in the Office of New Drugs (OND) evaluated the safety and efficacy of new drugs were quite incapable of detecting adverse effects on vulnerable subpopulations or hazards with long latency periods. FDA lacked authority to require further testing after it had approved a drug for a particular use, and it had little power to force companies to complete "Phase IV" studies that they promised during the drug approval process. Consequently, many of the most disturbing side effects did not become apparent until the drugs were already on the market and the Office of Drug Safety (ODS), which conducted post-market surveillance, had collected enough "adverse event" reports from manufacturers, doctors, and hospitals to support regulatory action.[28] For most of the Laissez Faire Revival, the FDA leadership did not care to hear what ODS had to say. When the head of ODS approved a staff recommendation to require a "black box" warning on the label of the diabetes drug Avandia, for example, upper-level agency officials reprimanded her, ordered her to retract the recommendation, and rescinded her authority to approve warnings in the future.[29]

Medical Device Approvals and Surveillance. FDA's evaluation of medical devices during the Laissez Faire Revival paralleled its experience with drugs. About 98 percent of FDA-approved medical devices were approved under an abbreviated "notification" procedure through which the manufacturer only had to demonstrate that its device was "substantially equivalent" to a previously approved device. Since all devices marketed prior to 1976 were automatically approved under the statute's "grandfather" clause, this meant that nearly all FDA device approvals were based on very little information at all. The notification process had the virtue of getting devices to the market rapidly, but it was far less reliable than the full approval process and far more subject to abuse by manufacturers willing to press the conceptual boundaries of "substantial equivalence."[30]

The full approval process gave FDA a much better opportunity to prevent bad devices from entering the market, but the medical officers responsible for new device approval were under the same pressure from superiors to speed up approvals as their colleagues in OND. As it subtly relaxed the approval criteria, the agency began to receive hundreds of reports of injuries attributable to bad devices. Between 2001 and 2006, manufacturers withdrew almost 80 devices from the market because of potentially fatal side effects and initiated more than 2,300 recalls. For example, within months after FDA's 1999 full approval of Medtronic's AneuRX stent, the company informed FDA that five patients had suffered aortic ruptures during ongoing clinical trials. Although FDA sent the company a letter complaining of "violations of FDA regulations," it took no action until August 2002, when it finally withdrew the device. By then, FDA had received reports of 58 deaths and 361 injuries due to failed AneuRX stents.[31]

FDA's post-market surveillance of medical devices also left much to be desired. Device manufacturers were required by statute to file annual reports with FDA containing detailed data on product performance, and they were obliged to forward immediately any reports that devices had caused death or serious injury. If the companies concluded that their devices were not responsible for adverse events (because, for example, they had been improperly installed by surgeons), they did not have to report them to FDA. Not surprisingly, many device manufacturers gave themselves the benefit of the doubt in deciding whether to report. Physicians were under no legal obligation to report adverse outcomes directly to FDA, and the agency conducted very few studies of its own on how devices performed in patients over the long haul.[32]

Imports. In the early 1990s, drug companies began to import large quantities of finished drugs and the active pharmaceutical ingredients (APIs) from which they fashioned finished products. By 2010, 40 percent of the drugs consumed in the U.S. were imported, and 80 percent contained APIs that were manufactured in other countries. Competitive pressures, however, induced manufacturers in exporting countries to cut corners in their manufacturing practices and to substitute inferior or even counterfeit substances.[33] FDA's tiny force of fewer than 500 inspectors was responsible for spot-checking about 18 million shipments through 300 U.S. ports of entry and inspecting hundreds of overseas manufacturing facilities for compliance with the agency's good manufacturing practices regulations. FDA inspectors were able to inspect foreign manufacturers of high-risk medical devices once every seven years and foreign drug manufacturing plants only once per decade. Inspectors sent to investigate foreign sources of contaminated drugs sometimes found the suspect facilities closed down with no hint of where to locate the responsible parties.[34]

Promotion and Advertising. Drug and device manufacturers traditionally promoted prescription drugs to doctors through advertisements in medical journals and displays at medical conventions. FDA monitored those activities to ensure that they were not misleading and that companies did not unlawfully promote drugs and devices for unapproved uses. During the Laissez Faire Revival, however, FDA's oversight became much less restrictive, and manufacturers used the resulting freedom to engage in questionable promotional practices, some of which bordered on outright bribery. In addition to free meals and coffee mugs, they treated heavy prescribers of their drugs to expenses-paid trips to exotic places to attend medical education programs. To no one's surprise, studies of prescription practices concluded that physicians were in fact influenced by these promotional goodies.[35] In 2009, forty drug companies agreed to adhere to voluntary guidelines issued by their trade association prohibiting companies from giving branded gifts like pens and coffee mugs to doctors. All of this, however, was undertaken voluntarily, and there were no vehicles for enforcing the agreements or even for determining the extent of compliance.[36]

As the major pharmaceutical companies' profit margins narrowed during the late 1990s, they concluded that "direct to consumer" (DTC) advertising was the best way to ensure widespread dissemination of important new medications. FDA had greatly limited the attractiveness of DTC advertising for prescription drugs by requiring the advertisements to contain a "brief summary" of the drug's risks and benefits. Although print advertising could include that information in the fine print at the bottom of the ad, the requirement effectively banned DTC on television and radio as companies concluded that viewers would be turned off by such ads.[37] In 1997, FDA issued new guidelines that loosened the prior restrictions, and the United States became one of the few industrialized countries to experience multi-million dollar advertising campaigns featuring sports figures and movie stars attempting to persuade patients to lobby their doctors to prescribe specific prescription drugs. Between 1997 and 2007 spending on DTC advertisements increased 300 percent to $4.8 billion. The new wave of DTC advertising often subtly minimized the health risks and exaggerated the efficacy of the advertised drugs. Noting that FDA did not require pre-approval of drug advertisements, consumer advocates worried about FDA's ability to police millions of ads to ensure that they would not mislead consumers.[38]

LIMITED ACCOUNTABILITY

Of all of FDA's manifold responsibilities, none suffered more during the Laissez Faire Revival than its duty to enforce the protections provided by the drug and device safety laws. The Reagan Administration budget reductions were so severe that inspectors had to use their own vehicles, and attorneys were forced to purchase their own office supplies. As the total number of FDA inspections declined by 40 percent, morbid tales circulated of deaths and injuries resulting from discontinued or delayed enforcement actions.[39] David Kessler, the hard-charging FDA head during the George H. W. Bush and early Clinton Administrations, emphasized enforcement, pursuing several high-profile drug and device cases. But when he circulated proposed legislation to grant the agency subpoena power, the White House rejected it after meeting with industry lobbyists.[40]

Things began to deteriorate again during the second assault. For example, inspections of medical device firms dropped from 3,602 in 1995 to 1,841 in 2000, even though the number of device manufacturers grew steadily. FDA's enforcement presence declined even more dramatically during the first term of the George W. Bush Administration. FDA's oversight of misleading advertisements suffered under Chief Counsel Dan Troy, an attorney who had previously represented drug companies in challenges to the constitutionality of FDA's advertising restrictions. The number of warning letters dropped from 1,032 in 2001 to 471 in 2007. Ignoring a statutory requirement that it inspect intermediate-risk medical device manufacturing facilities once every two years, the agency proceeded at a rate that would have taken twenty-seven years to inspect every facility once. The agency's new policy of informing manufacturers in advance of inspections provided ample opportunity for them to put on their best faces for the inspectors. And the punishments that FDA did administer were usually so light that the companies had little incentive to comply with the law. Criminal arrests and convictions declined by 20 percent between 2000 and 2006.[41]

A crisis involving the anti-coagulant Heparin in early 2008 focused public attention on FDA's weak enforcement of import restrictions. Heparin came from the intestines of pigs harvested by unregulated Chinese villagers and sold to Chinese companies that manufactured "crude Heparin" for export. A U.S. company refined the crude Heparin and sold it to Baxter Healthcare for incorporation into a blood thinner. At some point during the manufacturing process in China, someone had deliberately substituted a substance that mimicked Heparin in chemical tests for the real thing. After the substitute caused severe allergenic reactions in some people, Baxter Healthcare recalled its entire production of certain forms of Heparin. By that time, 81 people had died and hundreds of patients had suffered severe allergic reactions.[42]

After the Heparin crisis, the Chinese government vowed to step up its enforcement efforts. To demonstrate its commitment to reform, it executed the head of its food and drug agency for taking bribes from pharmaceutical companies. A massive sweep of Chinese manufacturing centers involving 30,000 inspectors discovered that nearly 20 percent of the examined products were either substandard or contaminated. The country was, however, struggling with a culture of counterfeiting, corruption, and no-holds-barred capitalism that extended back to the beginnings of its economic boom in the early 1980s.[43] FDA could do very little on its own to address the problem, because it lacked sufficient resources to establish an effective regulatory presence in China or any other country. A Government Accountability Office report concluded that FDA needed at least $70 million in additional resources to do an adequate job, but the George W. Bush Administration resisted congressional efforts to increase the agency's $11 million foreign inspection budget. The administration also opposed demands from congressional Democrats for FDA to promulgate more stringent import regulations. Instead, the agency established a voluntary pilot program for 100 companies that agreed to improve quality control over imported drugs.[44]

THE CONSEQUENCES

In June 2001, FDA approved Sanofi-Aventis's new antibiotic Ketek to treat pneumonia after finding that it was effective against a virulent antibiotic-resistant bacterium. However, the agency put off approving Ketek for the far less serious diseases of acute bacterial sinusitis (common sinus infections) and acute bacterial exacerbation of chronic bronchitis pending further safety and efficacy studies. Thanks to Sanofi-Aventis's aggressive marketing campaign, Ketek soon became popular with doctors for treating pneumonia as well as many other "off-label" uses, including sinusitis and chronic bronchitis. By 2006, U.S. doctors were prescribing Ketek at a rate of about one prescription every five seconds.[45]

Anxious to promote Ketek for other uses, Sanofi-Aventis sponsored a large clinical trial that was specifically designed to investigate its potential to cause adverse liver, heart, and visual effects. That study, however, was plagued with numerous irregularities, including gross violations of FDA's "Good Laboratory Practices" regulations that ultimately resulted in the criminal conviction of one of the principal investigators. Although FDA investigators concluded that the integrity of the data produced at all the sites was questionable, Commissioner Andrew von Eschenbach warned FDA reviewers that if they disclosed the problems with that study to outsiders, they would be "traded from the team." The agency then approved Ketek for sinusitis and chronic bronchitis on April 1, 2004.

Less than two years later, a peer-reviewed study found that Ketek had caused three cases of serious liver toxicity, one of which had resulted in the patient's death. On February 12, 2007, the agency announced that it was withdrawing Ketek's approval for sinusitis and bronchitis and requiring a "black box" warning about liver toxicity on the label for the pneumonia use. By that time, doctors had written over five million prescriptions for Ketek, and it had been linked to twenty-three cases of liver damage and twelve cases of acute liver failure, four of which were fatalities. Doctors were still free to prescribe Ketek for any unapproved use, including sinus infections and bronchitis, and the company escaped with a single warning letter.

The Ketek story was only one of many highly publicized instances of drug company malfeasance on display in the late 2000s as the country learned that many companies had manipulated scientific data, hired ghostwriters to prepare scientific articles, promoted prescription drugs with lavish gifts to doctors, and failed to take action when they learned of serious adverse side effects. By then, many of the drugs and devices that had received fast track and abbreviated approval during the previous decade were being recalled. Some of the more egregious cases are described in Box 10.1. Given the dramatic increase in drug and device usage between the early 1970s and the mid-2000s, this irresponsible conduct affected millions of people. By one estimate, prescription drugs were killing about 270 Americans every day, more than double the rate of highway fatalities.[46]

Box 10.1

Bad Drugs and Devices

Vioxx. When two large clinical trials that Merck conducted after FDA granted "fast track" approval to its painkiller Vioxx yielded high incidences of cardiovascular problems, the company withdrew it from the market. By one estimate, 88,000 to 139,000 of the 80 million patients who had taken it may have suffered heart attacks or strokes, and 26,000 to 55,600 of them may have died as a result.[a]

Propulsid. Soon after FDA approved the anti-reflux drug Propulsid for adults suffering from nighttime heartburn, it started receiving reports that infants and children given the cherry-flavored medication had died. By the time the company withdrew the drug, it had caused more than 80 deaths and 300 injuries.[b]

Avandia. Not long after GlaxoSmithKline released its popular diabetes drug Avandia, FDA began to receive reports that it caused symptoms indicative of congestive heart failure. After a May 2007 article in the *New England Journal of Medicine* concluded that patients using Avandia had a 43 percent higher risk of heart attack, FDA required a "black box" warning but otherwise allowed the drug to remain on the market.[c]

Sulzer Hip Joints. At the machine shop where the Sulzer Company manufactured hip replacement devices, lubricating oil leaked from the machinery into many of the artificial hip sockets, thereby preventing them from adhering to the pelvic bones of the patients into which they were inserted. After receiving many reports of malfunctioning devices, the company recalled 17,500 devices, about 350 of which had to be removed at great pain and expense to the patients.[d]

NOTES

a. Eric J. Topol, *Failing the Public Health—Refocoxib, Merck, and the FDA*, 351 New Eng. J. Med. 1707 (2004); Mark Kaufman, *FDA Officer Suggests Strict Curbs on 5 Drugs*, WP, November 19, 2004, at A1 (estimates).

b. Gardiner Harris & Eric Koli, *Lucrative Drug, Danger Signals and the F.D.A.*, NYT, June 10, 2005, at A1; *How a New Policy Lead to Seven Deadly Drugs*, LAT, December 20, 2000, at A1.

c. Gardiner Harris, *Diabetes Drug Maker Hid Test Data, Files Indicate*, NYT, July 12, 2010, at A1 (failure to report); Gardiner Harris, *Caustic Government Report Deals Blow to Diabetes Drug*, NYT, July 9, 2010, at A1 (FDA reevaluation);

Alicia Mundy, *Doctors Claim Glaxo Dismissed Worries on Avandia*, WSJ, November 19, 2008, at A1; Rob Stein, *Doctor Says Avandia Maker Intimidated Him*, WP, June 7, 2007, at A6; Gardiner Harris, *After Debate, F.D.A. Backs Sale of Diabetes Medicine*, NYT, November 15, 2007, at A24 (black box warning); Anna Wilde Mathews, *Sequel for Vioxx Critic: Attack on Diabetes Pill*, WSJ, May 22, 2007, at A1 (NEJM article).

  d. Robert Cohen & J. Scott Orr, *A Hip Makers Billion-Dollar Mistake*, Newark Star-Ledger, August 13, 2002, at A1; Sharon Bernstein, *Lawsuits Filed over Hip Implants that Failed to Attach to Bone*, LAT, February 14, 2001, at A3.

CONCLUSIONS

The drug and device industries have always had the freedom to become a diverse and technologically dynamic industry capable of designing and manufacturing a broad array of lifesaving products. But they also had the obligation to refrain from foisting inefficacious and dangerous medicines and devices on unsuspecting patients. For more than a century, FDA was the governmental institution with the power to draw the proper balance between freedom to innovate and freedom to harm. During the Laissez Faire Revival, however, Congress severely limited FDA's capacity to perform this vital role by reducing the resources available to its surveillance and enforcement functions, while adding to its responsibilities and demanding that it approve new products and technologies at an impossible pace. Although the agency's leadership during much of the period was committed to the agency's protective role (an unusual posture for the agencies portrayed in this book), it was often hamstrung by White House officials in both Democratic and Republican administrations who did not want to irritate the politically powerful pharmaceutical industry. The result was a severely debilitated agency with a limited capacity to protect the public and a decline in public confidence in FDA from around 80 percent at the end of the Public Interest Era to 36 percent at the peak of the Laissez Faire Revival.[47]

FOOD SAFETY

In the early 1990s, scientists discovered that more than half of the poultry that Americans consumed was contaminated by *Salmonella Enteriditis,* a virulent bacterium that causes diarrhea, fever, intestinal cramping, and more serious complications in immune compromised patients. Worse, as modern egg production facilities forced huge flocks of hens into close quarters, their ovaries became infected with *Salmonella.* As a result, the bacterium became an invisible contaminant of millions of eggs. Scientists estimated that one in ten thousand eggs was infected. Health experts estimated that 2–4 million cases of *Salmonella* poisoning occurred annually, resulting in around 2,000 deaths.[1]

The *Salmonella* bacterium that continues to sicken tens of thousands of Americans every year is but one of many pathogens that infect the food that we consume. One especially virulent pathogen, *E. coli* O157:H7, can contaminate red meat and vegetables grown in the vicinity of cattle. In vulnerable populations (e.g., children and elderly persons) that bacterium can cause a vicious disease called hemolytic uremic syndrome (HUS) that can result in renal failure and a cascade of other life-threatening afflictions. *Listeria monocytogenes,* a pathogen that can contaminate a variety of raw foods, can cause Listeriosis, a relatively mild sickness in healthy adults, but a deadly disease in fetuses and in persons with compromised immune systems.[2]

Food safety regulation falls under the jurisdiction of the Food Safety and Inspection Service (FSIS) in the United States Department of Agriculture (USDA) and the Food and Drug Administration (FDA) in the Department of Health and Human Services. FSIS is responsible for ensuring the safety of meat and poultry, and it maintains an inspector at every one of the nation's 934 slaughterhouses and 175 poultry processing plants. These inspectors are responsible for the safety of the 25 billion pounds of beef and 33.5 billion pounds of broiler meat that U.S. companies produce annually.[3] FDA has regulatory responsibility for more that $450 billion worth of food each year that is manufactured, prepared, and sold at more than 156,000 establishments throughout the country.[4]

THE POTENTIAL

The Meat Inspection Act of 1906 established a comprehensive regulatory regime under which a meat packing facility could not operate without an inspector from USDA on the premises. The inspectors were required to examine all animals before slaughter for evidence of disease and all carcasses after slaughter to see if they were "filthy, decomposed, or putrid." The statute, however, had several significant weaknesses. Among other things, it did not authorize USDA to levy fines, seek criminal penalties, or initiate recalls for violations. The exclusive remedy was the "atom bomb" of withdrawing the inspector and thereby prohibiting the company from selling meat slaughtered there in interstate commerce.[5]

The Pure Food and Drug Act of 1906 prevented the sale in interstate commerce of "adulterated" or mislabeled foods other than meat. The Act authorized federal inspectors to initiate judicial action to seize adulterated or mislabeled items at any point in the manufacturing or marketing process. As a practical matter a company could be held accountable only if the agency detected an outbreak of food poisoning and could trace the source of the outbreak to that company's product. The amended statute required FDA approval for all substances deliberately added to food (food additives) that were not "generally recognized as safe" (GRAS). FDA also regulated animal feed to ensure that dangerous chemicals did not contaminate meat derived from animals consuming the feed.[6]

These statutes have unquestionably made the nation's food supply much safer than it would have been in their absence. Manufacturers may not add chemicals to foods to enhance flavor, change color, or modify other characteristics unless they can demonstrate that they present a "reasonable certainty of no harm."[7] Most food manufacturing facilities must comply with regulations establishing "good manufacturing practices" designed to ensure that their products do not become contaminated with pathogens, toxic chemicals, or other undesirable constituents. During the Clinton Administration, USDA and FDA promulgated regulations requiring slaughterhouses and manufacturers of fruit juices and processed seafood to establish procedures to identify food hazards at critical points in the manufacturing process and control those hazards. FDA estimated that the juice regulation would prevent more than 6,000 cases of food poisoning per year and the seafood regulation would prevent between 58,000 and 113,000 cases per year. A retrospective study of juice-related disease outbreaks by the Centers for Disease Control concluded that fewer outbreaks occurred after the regulations became effective. As anyone who has ever suffered through a painful bout of foodborne disease knows, these are not trivial benefits.[8]

Labels on packaged food products provide much more information about the nutritional content, caloric intake, and the presence of potential allergens than was available to consumers in the 1950s. Packaged meat and poultry must contain instructions for refrigeration, handling, and cooking to help consumers to avoid contracting foodborne diseases. Packages of fresh eggs must inform consumers to keep them refrigerated and to cook them until the yolks are hard. Meat packagers may no longer load up ground beef with inexpensive fillers, and marketers of "fresh" juice can no longer make their products out of stored concentrates. And manufacturers cannot lawfully make bogus health claims for their foods in the absence of scientific proof that the claims are warranted.[9]

THE REALITY

At the outset of the Laissez Faire Revival, the food industry was undergoing massive change. Pressed by large retailers to keep prices low, food manufacturers searched for efficiency at every stage of the increasingly complex process of bringing food from the farm gate to the dinner plate. Giant centralized production facilities were far more efficient than local slaughterhouses, canneries, and butcher shops, but they were also ideal breeding grounds for pathogens. In a large meat grinding establishment, a single contaminated carcass could contaminate sixteen tons of ground beef. Chickens were bred to come in two uniform sizes to make them more compatible with the production lines on which they were slaughtered, de-feathered, eviscerated, and cut up into identical pieces. But the same production lines allowed microorganisms to spread from feces to the wings, thighs, and breasts that were machine packaged for sale to grocery stores and restaurants.[10]

The same competitive forces affected the production and marketing of fruits and vegetables. Large corporate growers planted fields of lettuce in central California with little regard for the cattle grazing nearby. Pre-washed and packaged salads were the order of the day for busy consumers, but the process of mixing leafy greens from many fields for packaging allowed contaminants to spread to thousands of packages. Improved rapid transportation technologies and a global economy facilitated massive imports of produce and processed foods from countries with questionable sanitation standards. These rapid technological developments surged far ahead of the government's capacity to address the new risks they created.[11]

The food industry was economically diverse and politically powerful. It consisted of small family farmers, huge industrial growers, meat producers, specialized food manufacturers, grocery store chains and mom-and-pop shops, huge fast food franchisers and local diners, and a number of highly diversified intermediary institutions. Although their economic interests diverged on many issues, the companies and trade associations that made up the food industry had one thing in common—they were generally opposed to stringent food safety regulation. With their allies in conservative think tanks, the food industry constantly reiterated the themes of economic freedom, personal responsibility, and limited government.[12]

WRITING THE RULES

The Laissez Faire Revival in food regulation began early in the Carter Administration when FDA in April 1977 published a notice of proposed rulemaking to ban the sweetener saccharin because it caused bladder cancer in male rats. The action drew anguished protests from dieters and ridicule from conservative commentators. The food and beverage industries launched an intense advertising campaign condemning the agency and touting the benefits of saccharin for persons suffering from diabetes and obesity. Congress reacted by enacting a statute that prevented FDA from banning saccharin so long as the package contained a prescribed warning.[13]

The deregulatory pressures continued into the Reagan Administration. To implement the mandates of President Reagan's Task Force on Regulatory Relief, FDA withdrew Carter Administration proposals for nutrition labeling and infant formula safety, and it took steps to reduce the stringency of existing regulations governing health claims. Although the FDA process for approving food additives was just as burdensome as the drug approval process, the American Enterprise Institute did not devote conferences to a "food additive lag," because the food industry had solved the problem through liberal use of the "generally recognized as safe" exemption. The food industry's primary concern was that consumer groups would persuade FDA to use its recall authority more liberally. Since FDA Commissioner Arthur Hull Hayes was a strong proponent of voluntary programs and since FDA lacked authority to order mandatory recalls without a court order, even this was not a serious concern.[14]

As related in Chapter 10, President George H. W. Bush chose a strong safety advocate, David Kessler, to head FDA, and Kessler remained in office through much of the Clinton Administration. Nevertheless, the agency made very little progress on the food safety front during the Bush Administration, because it had to overcome heavy opposition by both the industry and Vice-President Quayle's Competitiveness Council. Given much broader discretion by the Clinton White House to write protective rules, Kessler put into place a program requiring seafood processors to test for microorganisms. But the agency yielded to industry desires in regulating dairy company use of genetically engineered growth hormone to increase milk production.[15]

President Bush did not replace Lester Crawford, a Reagan appointee, as head of the Food Safety and Inspection Service (FSIS). When Crawford resigned in August 1991 to work for the National Food Processors Association, he was replaced by H. Russell Cross, a professor of animal sciences at Texas A&M University. President Clinton allowed Cross to remain as head of FSIS, in part because the Department was in the midst of a crisis (discussed in more detail below) involving a new pathogen called *E. coli* O157:H7 in hamburgers sold at Jack-in-the-Box restaurants in the Seattle area.[16]

With the *E. coli* outbreak still fresh on the public's mind, the regulatory re-formers in the Gingrich Congress were not anxious to put radical food safety de-regulation on the table. During the second interregnum, USDA promulgated an important consumer protection regulation establishing standards for organic foods and a path-breaking program (discussed in detail below) requiring meat and poultry production facilities to come up with plans to control safety hazards at "critical control points" in the meat preparation process. FDA promulgated similar rules for manufacturers of fruit and vegetable juice and eggs.[17]

The discovery of a mad cow in Mabton, Washington, dominated the George W. Bush Administration's efforts to address meat safety during his first term. When President Bush's first FSIS director, Elsa A. Murano, returned to Texas A&M University in late 2004, she was replaced by Richard Raymond, the meat regulator for the State of Nebraska. The first physician to head FSIS, Raymond adopted a protective approach to food safety that delighted consumer groups and angered the food industry.[18] The situation was very different at FDA, where the head of the food safety program was told by his superiors that "more regulation is not something we want to do." As we shall see below, the agency dealt so ineptly with a series of outbreaks of contaminated produce that public confidence in its ability to protect the food supply sank to a new low.[19]

Things began to unravel for the industry in the late 2000s as a series of food crises focused public attention squarely on the absence of effective regulatory controls. Congressional investigations focused the spotlight on how the industry manipulated the science and the regulatory process to avoid accountability for irresponsible manufacturing and marketing practices. Still, the politically savvy industry managed to stave off regulation by adopting unenforceable voluntary measures, accepting modest (and easily reversible) regulatory constraints, and continually stressing the theme of the consumers' personal responsibility for their own safety. In the meantime, foodborne diseases continued to sicken 48 million people, hospitalize 128,000, and kill 3,000 annually.[20]

FOREGONE PROTECTION

During the Laissez Faire Revival, food safety regulation consisted mainly of lax regulation interrupted by spurts of activity in response to crises. Very little legislation emerged from Congress in response to the crises, and the agencies tended to adopt the least intrusive responses that they could identify to address the particular problems that gave rise to the crises. The protections that these limited, ad hoc responses afforded were generally quite modest.

Poultry and Eggs. Carter Administration FSIS head Carol Tucker Foreman later recalled that her worst decision was to yield to pressure from poultry producers during the first assault to allow them to avoid the agency's "zero tolerance" rule for fecal matter on meat by rinsing carcasses in a 5 percent chlorine water bath. The industry much preferred this alternative to the prior practice of cutting feces-laden tissue from the birds because the carcasses gained additional weight during the washing process that was reflected in the price of the final product. As the day wore on, however, the bath became a "fecal soup" that contaminated all of the carcasses contained in the large vat. In July 1994, FSIS issued a formal notice of proposed rulemaking to reinstate the "zero tolerance" policy, but it died during the Gingrich Congress. In the meantime, raw poultry became so contaminated with *Salmonella* and *Listeria* that it had to be treated as a biohazard in the kitchen.[21]

FDA was also very slow in responding to the problem of *Salmonella*-contaminated eggs. In 1999, FDA announced an "Egg Safety Action Plan," and it spent the next five years drafting proposed regulations. After FDA completed the final rule in July 2008, OIRA held it up for the remainder of the Bush Administration. One consequence of the unwarranted delay was a massive *Salmonella* outbreak in August 2010 that sickened more than 1,200 people and resulted in a recall of more than one-half billion eggs.[22]

HACCP. A May 1987 National Academy of Sciences report urged USDA to shift from its traditional "poke and sniff" inspection method to a "science-based" approach, called "hazard analysis at critical control points" (HACCP), under which operators develop objective tests for contamination risk at various "critical control points" of the manufacturing process and adopt measures to ensure that those risk levels are not exceeded. After jousting with the industry for almost a decade, FSIS promulgated a final rule in July 1996 that required meatpackers to develop and implement FSIS-approved HACCP plans capable of reducing the prevalence of *Salmonella* contamination in the end product to a level below a national baseline. A facility that failed the *Salmonella* test had to reassess the plan and modify it as necessary. A third failure was supposed to result in a shutdown of the plant until it demonstrated that it had fixed the problem. The Fifth Circuit Court of Appeals, however, held that the agency could not lawfully apply the "three-strike" rule to meat grinding facilities because the agency could not prove that the *Salmonella* contamination occurred during the grinding process. USDA did not appeal the ruling, nor did it ask Congress to overrule it.[23]

The agency continued to require HACCP plans, but it no longer attempted to shut companies down when their products flunked the *Salmonella* test. Not surprisingly, the program's effectiveness suffered. Operators started "gaming the system" by specifying critical control points at locations where contamination was unlikely. A 2003 USDA audit of HACCP programs at the nation's 35 largest plants concluded that 60 percent of the plans did not meet the rule's requirements.[24] For example, at a poultry plant that was responsible for a *Listeria* outbreak that killed 8 people and sickened 54 others in the summer of 2002, the company had filed reports documenting a sharp rise in the occurrence of *Listeria* at several critical control points for two straight months in a drawer labeled "USDA," but the FSIS inspectors had failed to open the drawer.[25]

E. coli Policy. In early 1993, investigators concluded that burgers prepared at a Seattle Jack-in-the-Box restaurant contained a virulent new pathogen called *E. coli* O157:H7 that had sickened 732 people, 55 of whom were hospitalized and four of whom had died. The Centers for Disease Control estimated that 250–500 deaths per year were attributable to *E. coli* O157:H7 alone. In August 1994, FSIS shocked the industry with an announcement that it would henceforth apply the same "zero-tolerance" policy to *E. coli* O157:H7 that it applied to visible fecal matter on meat.[26] However, neither the new policy nor the HACCP regulations required manufacturers to test for *E. coli*, and few did. Although USDA inspectors occasionally tested for *E. coli* in ground beef, they seldom tested meat for *E. coli* at slaughterhouses on the assumption that the meat would be washed and cooked prior to eating. When inspectors detected *E. coli* O157:H7 in the output of meat grinding facilities or in packaged products, they rarely could trace the bacteria to its source because grinders typically used "trimmings" from a wide variety of sources. The grinders could of course test incoming meat, but all of the largest suppliers of trimmings strictly prohibited such testing. In October 2007, USDA proposed to require beef processors to test incoming products several times a year, but it withdrew the proposal in the face of intense industry opposition. In the meantime, the zero-tolerance policy went largely unenforced, and *E. coli* continued to contaminate beef products.[27]

Antibiotics in Animal Feed. Scientists have known for decades that the arsenal of antibiotics that doctors use to fight serious human and animal infections is at risk as pathogens become resistant to those powerful drugs. Since the unnatural setting of a concentrated animal feeding operation (CAFO) was a perfect breeding ground for animal diseases, operators routinely supplemented cattle, pork, and poultry feed with antibiotics, whether or not they had identified any sick animals. An added bonus was the fact that antibiotic-laced feed enhanced weight gain. By 2000, CAFOs used more than 26 million pounds of antibiotics annually, only 2 million of which were used to treat sick animals. This compared to about 3 million pounds of antibiotics used in humans. And scientists were uncovering troubling evidence that antibiotic use in animals was contributing to resistance in human pathogens.[28]

FDA proposed to ban nontherapeutic use of antibiotics in animal feeds in 1977, but Congress suspended the action at the behest of meat and drug industry lobbyists. After that, FDA's approach to the building crisis of antibiotic-resistant bacteria was to approve even more human antibiotics for use in animals as it studied the matter. Finally, in October 2005, FDA banned two critical human antibiotics for use in poultry. In July 2008, the agency proposed to ban the use of cephalosporin antibiotics in all animal feed. A strong negative reaction from the industry, however, convinced the agency to withdraw the proposal in November 2008. Meanwhile, the evidence that animal use was contributing to antibiotic resistance in humans continued to mount.[29]

Produce. FDA's good manufacturing practice regulations did not apply to raw agricultural commodities like whole fruits, nuts, and vegetables, because the agency believed that the risk of contamination was small in the fields where they were grown, harvested, and sometimes packaged. Food safety experts, however, knew that produce could become contaminated by feces from animals in nearby fields, poor quality rinse water, poor worker sanitation practices, and mixing of fresh-cut products. The risk grew when companies began to sell "prewashed" leafy vegetables in plastic bags for easy use, because it was very difficult to remove microorganisms from the folds and crevices of leafy vegetables prior to packaging. In September 2006, an outbreak of *E. coli* O157:H7 that was traced to bagged spinach sickened more than 200 people in 26 states and killed two children and an elderly woman. It was the ninth *E. coli* outbreak in a decade due to contaminated produce from the Salinas Valley, in which virtually every waterway was contaminated with *E. coli* from cattle and wildlife. Nevertheless, upper-level George W. Bush Administration officials scotched an ambitious FDA plan to write mandatory risk-based regulations for produce packagers.[30]

Imported Food. As modern transportation technologies facilitated a tidal wave of food imports into the United States during the late 1990s and early 2000s, dozens of foodborne disease outbreaks were attributed to imported produce from Central and South America. Nevertheless, by 2010 the U.S. was importing 15 percent of its food supply, 50 percent of its fresh fruit, 20 percent of its fresh vegetables, and 80 percent of its seafood. The rapid growth in food imports presented unique challenges to a food safety protection system that had traditionally depended heavily on foreign governments and the importing companies to ensure the safety of imported food.[31]

The Meat Safety Inspection Act required a meat exporting country to have a system in place for inspecting meat that was "equivalent" to the U.S. system. The reports of USDA's annual audits of selected individual facilities, however, were not always comforting. For example, in a May 1991 inspection of a packing plant in Hermosillo, Mexico, USDA auditors discovered rampant filth and insect infestation and a condemned carcass being prepared for further processing into food. After USDA withdrew the plant's approval, Mexican officials quickly re-approved the facility under new owners and a changed name. Trusting the Mexican agency to do the right thing, USDA approved the "new" plant without a subsequent inspection. USDA also conducted cursory checks of import shipments at 150 facilities during which only 10–15 percent of the containers were opened for further inspection.[32]

The import safety program was in even worse shape at FDA, where a small group of inspectors at some, but not all, of the nation's 350 ports of entry conducted cursory spot checks of less than one percent of imported items subject to its jurisdiction and tested only a tiny fraction of those for dangerous pathogens. The Bioterrorism Act of 2002 authorized FDA to establish an electronic food tracking system to monitor imports, but the George W. Bush Administration declined to exercise that authority because of strong objections from the domestic food industry. FDA audited an average of about 150 out of almost 190,000 registered foreign food production facilities per year. In 2002, FDA visited only 13 out of 160 seafood exporting countries and inspected 108 out of 13,000 processors.[33]

Ineffectual Recalls. One perennial impediment to effective protection of the public health from foodborne disease was the absence of any authority on the part of either FDA or FSIS to order mandatory recalls of adulterated food. A company could minimize the adverse economic impact of a voluntary recall by negotiating with the agency for several days as the product became so thoroughly integrated into the supply lines that the recall was not likely to produce a very high yield. The recovery rate for recalled products steadily declined between 1988 and 2004. In the 73 meat recalls that occurred during 2007, for example, the recovery rate was only 44 percent.[34] Such low recovery rates meant that most of the potentially contaminated products were being eaten by consumers who reasonably, but mistakenly believed that they were fit for human consumption.

LIMITED ACCOUNTABILITY

As the food industry grew and foodborne disease outbreaks multiplied during the Laissez Faire Revival, the resources that USDA and FDA devoted to food safety enforcement dwindled. Between 1981 and 2007, the number of full-time USDA inspectors fell 7.5 percent from 9,932 to 9,184. Chronic staffing problems resulted in 30 percent vacancy rates in some areas, leaving each of the remaining inspectors to do the jobs of two or three. FDA delegated much of its responsibility for inspecting food manufacturing facilities and all of its responsibility for inspecting retail establishments to state agencies that were suffering under similar budgetary constraints. And its tiny imports inspectorate was not nearly up to the task of protecting the food supply from a rapidly growing stream of imports from Mexico, South America, and China.[35]

Both agencies worked within the confines of ancient Progressive Era statutes that provided inadequate authority to operate effective deterrence-based enforcement programs. FDA's primary enforcement tool was a court action to seize adulterated products, for which it had the burden of proving that the particular items seized were probably contaminated. USDA's only weapon was the "atom bomb" of closing down the production facility. Neither agency had authority to assess civil penalties tailored to fit particular violations. FDA even concluded that it lacked authority to require repeat violators to take corrective action.[36]

FDA enforcement actions declined more than 60 percent during the first two years of the Reagan Administration. Immediately upon assuming office at the outset of the George H. W. Bush Administration, however, FDA Commissioner David Kessler ordered the staff to impound 24,000 cartons of Procter & Gamble's "Citrus Hill's Fresh Choice" reprocessed orange juice because its label misleadingly suggested that it was fresh-squeezed. The agency then initiated a series of similar actions against other companies that employed deceptive labeling to make unsupported health claims.[37] Kessler's aggressive approach to enforcement continued into the Clinton Administration, but cooled down during the Gingrich Congress.

Food safety enforcement was not a high priority for the George W. Bush Administration. FSIS inspectors faced constant pressure from their superiors to keep production lines moving. Formal instructions to inspectors stated that they were authorized to stop a line only if "a product that is going into the food supply has been directly contaminated and you can justify the production loss." A May 2002 memorandum told Kansas City inspectors that they could be held accountable for lost production if they slowed the lines to check for feces or to wash their hands, because small smears of feces on meat were tolerable.[38]

FDA suffered a loss of more than 400 inspectors between 2003 and 2007 as the number of domestic facilities requiring inspection increased by 7,200. Inspectors' workloads doubled and sometimes tripled. By the end of 2006, food safety inspections had dropped to 20 percent of 1972 levels. The number of enforcement actions resulting from inspections dropped from 614 in 2004 to 283 in 2008.[39] Despite the fact that an FSIS inspector remained in every major meat production facility, the agency's enforcement efforts were also spotty. For example, FSIS in late 2002 threatened to close down a Nebraska Beef Corporation facility after citing it for numerous violations of the agency's HACCP regulations over a three-year period. After the company took the agency to court, however, the agency settled for a promise from the company to do a better job in the future. Then, in August 2008, Whole Foods Market recalled all fresh ground meat from all of its stores after learning that more than 30 people in Massachusetts had been infected by *E. coli* O157:H7 from prime cuts of beef that Whole Foods had turned into ground beef at its stores. Although Whole Foods had avoided doing business with Nebraska Beef because of its poor reputation, its supplier had processed the prime cuts at Nebraska Beef. The outbreak occurred even though USDA inspectors were supposed to be keeping an especially watchful eye on the belligerent company's facility.[40]

THE CONSEQUENCES

When the Peanut Corporation of America (PCA) bought a Blakely, Georgia, peanut processing plant in 2001, the company headquarters was a converted garage behind the CEO's Lynchburg, Virginia, home. PCA turned the sleepy Georgia facility into a model of cost-cutting efficiency as it negotiated contracts with large retailers anxious to minimize costs. While employees struggled to meet aggressive new production targets, safety concerns took a back seat. The plant undertook full-scale sanitation procedures only in anticipation of visits from state inspectors (who always provided advance notice) and private inspectors hired by the company at the behest of large retailers. As annual sales jumped from $15 million in 2005 to $25 million in 2008, the company knowingly shipped *Salmonella*-contaminated peanuts to customers on 12 separate occasions.

In early November 2008, the Centers for Disease Control detected two clusters of food poisoning victims in 14 states that shared a common strain of pathogenic *Salmonella* bacteria that was ultimately traced back to PCA's Blakely plant. After FDA discovered evidence of unsanitary conditions at the plant, PCA ceased production and conducted a voluntary recall of all peanut products produced at the plant over a two-year period. The agency then discovered that the company also operated a facility in Plainview, Texas, that lacked a Texas license and had not been inspected since it opened in March 2005. When inspectors discovered peanuts contaminated with the same strain of *Salmonella*, that plant also ceased production. Before the outbreak was over, contaminated peanuts had sickened at least 700 people (estimates ran as high as 19,000) and killed nine.[41]

The Peanut Corporation outbreak focused public attention on private auditing companies that food suppliers hired to conduct periodic inspections of their facilities at the behest of large retailers demanding assurance that the products were manufactured under sanitary conditions. The auditing company that missed the *Salmonella* contamination at the Peanut Corporation plant had inspected more than 10,000 facilities in 80 countries in 2008. The highly competitive auditing firms had a strong incentive not to alienate their clients. Among other things, they usually announced their inspections in advance, giving the facilities ample time to prepare. Even when auditors uncovered serious problems, the companies were under no obligation to take corrective action, and they sometimes simply ignored the reports, often with disastrous consequences.[42]

The incidence of foodborne diseases and food-related allergies grew at an alarming rate during the Laissez Faire Era. At the same time that foodborne pathogens were getting heartier and more virulent, globalization facilitated the rapid spread of newly evolved pathogens. A changing culture that put more emphasis on work and less on food preparation rendered consumers less attentive to proper food safety practices. And a heavier reliance on fast food put consumers at risk of infections spread by a poorly trained, low-wage work force with a high turnover rate.[43] More than ever, consumers needed strong protections from the federal government. As the sampling of recent outbreaks of foodborne illness in Box 11.1 reveals, the needed protections were not forthcoming during the Laissez Faire Revival.

Box 11.1

Contaminated Food

Pathogens in Meat. In September 2007 Topps Meat Company recalled 21.7 million pounds of hamburger patties after 40 people in eight states became infected with *E. coli* O157:H7.[a] In August 2008, Nebraska Beef, Ltd., recalled 1.36 million pounds of beef after more than 30 people were sickened by *E. coli*-contaminated ground beef they had purchased at Whole Foods Market.[b]

Pathogens and Toxins in Fish. FDA estimates that contaminated shellfish cause over 100,000 illnesses and cost the country around $200 million annually. In addition, several species of fish at the top of the food chain accumulated mercury to such high levels that they posed a hazard to pregnant women and small children.[c]

Pathogens in Eggs. In August 2010, a large outbreak of *Salmonella*-induced disease sickened more than 1,200 people and resulted in a recall of more that one-half billion eggs by two large Iowa producers, neither of which had ever been inspected by FDA.[d]

Pathogens in Produce. Almost 100 outbreaks of illnesses attributable to fresh produce between 1996 and 2006 caused over 10,000 illnesses and 14 deaths.[e]

Pathogens in Processed Foods. Between July 2009 and March 2010, FDA oversaw recalls of 300,000 cases of Nestle cookie dough that had sickened more than 65 people, 1.2 million pounds of "ready to eat" sausage containing *Salmonella*-contaminated black pepper that sickened more that 225 people, and all existing supplies of processed foods containing a *Salmonella*-contaminated flavor enhancer.[f]

Imports. In August 2011, one person died and 135 people in 34 states were sickened by a strain of antibiotic-resistant *Salmonella* in ground turkey, and in December ground beef containing another antibiotic-resistant strain of *Salmonella* sickened fourteen people, seven of whom were hospitalized. Sixty-one persons (mostly toddlers) in 19 states were sickened by "Veggie Booty" snack foods containing spices from China that had become contaminated with *Salmonella*. An outbreak of *Salmonella* poisoning caused by imported Serrano peppers from Mexico caused more than 1,400 illnesses, 280 hospitalizations, and two deaths.[g]

NOTES

a. Annys Shin, *Beef Recalled by Whole Foods Fell into Regulatory Gray Area*, WP, August 12, 2008, at D1 (Nebraska Beef recall); Christopher Drew & Andrew Martin, *Many Red Flags Preceded a Recall*, NYT, October 23, 2007, at C1 (Topps recall); Bud Hazelkorn, *Poultry Plant Slow to Report Sharp Increase in Bacteria*, NYT, December 21, 2002, at A14 (Pilgrims Pride recall); Elizabeth Becker, *19 Million Pounds of Meat Recalled After 19 Fall Ill*, NYT, July 20, 2002, at A1 (ConAgra recall).

b. USDA *Expands its Recall of Beef*, WSJ, August 15, 2008, at A3; Shin, *Beef Recalled by Whole Foods*.

c. Lisa Heinzerling & Rena Steinzor, "*A Perfect Storm" Mercury and the Bush Administration*, 34 Env. L. Rept. 10,297, 10,299 (2004); General Accounting Office, Food Safety: FDA's Imported Seafood Safety Program Shows Some Progress, but Further Improvements are Needed 9 (2004).

d. David Brown, *Salmonella-Tainted Eggs From Big Producer in Iowa Have Sickened at Least 1,200*, WP, August 20, 2010, at A3.

e. Government Accountability Office, Food Safety: Improvements Needed in FDA Oversight of Fresh Produce 10 (2008).

f. Lyndsey Layton, *Salmonella Prompts Processed-Food Recall*, WP, March 5, 2010, at A2; Lyndsey Layton, *Salmonella Blamed as Hundreds Fall Ill after Eating Italian Sausages*, WP, February 15, 2010, at A12; Jane Zhang, *Nestle Cookie-Dough Probe Ends*, WSJ, July 9, 2009, at A12.

g. Jennifer Brown, *Concerns Grow Over Salmonella that Survives Antibiotics*, Denver Post, December 26, 2011, at A1 (antibiotic-resistant *Salmonella*); Helena Bottemiller, *Recall Prompts More Calls for Action on Ag Antibiotics*, Food Safety News, December 20, 2011, available at http://www.foodsafetynews.com/2011/12/recall-prompts-more-calls-for-action-on-antibiotics-in-ag/ (same); Stephen J. Hedges, *Food Safety Lacks Teeth, Critics Say*, Chicago Tribune, July 16, 2007, at C1 (Veggie Booty); Annys Shin, *FDA Officials Narrow Salmonella Warning to Mexican Peppers*, WP, July 26, 2008, at D1 (Serrano peppers).

CONCLUSIONS

By the end of the third assault, the nation's food safety programs were clearly dysfunctional. A 2009 report prepared for the Trust for America's Health concluded that the food safety laws had "not kept pace with scientific advancements . . . and changes in consumer culture."[44] The report echoed a November 2007 report prepared by a subcommittee of FDA's Science Advisory Board, which concluded that the nation's food supply was "at risk," because the agency's "ability to provide its basic food system inspection, enforcement and rule-making functions" had been "severely eroded."[45]

TRANSPORTATION SAFETY

In 2010, Americans drove more than three trillion miles on U.S. roads and highways, airlines flew more than 700 million passengers from U.S. airports, and trains carried more than 24 million passengers on U.S. rails.[1] Virtually every mode of transportation poses risks to the people and property being transported and to people and property in the vicinity of the transportation corridors. Railroad collisions and derailments were killing hundreds of people annually during the 1890s, and they continue to kill hundreds and injure thousands in the twenty-first century. In 2010, 1,873 train accidents caused 8 fatalities and 1,682 grade crossing collisions resulted in 261 fatalities. Around 40,000 people are killed in motor vehicle collisions every year. Fortunately, commercial airline crashes are much rarer. There were no fatalities in 2010, but in 2009, 49 people were killed in a single crash.[2]

Congress has over the years empowered regulatory agencies to regulate various sectors of the transportation industry, and these agencies have promulgated hundreds of regulations aimed at protecting lives and property from transportation risks. In this chapter we will focus on four agencies, all of which are located in the Department of Transportation—the National Highway Traffic Safety Administration (NHTSA), the Federal Motor Carrier Safety Administration (FMCSA), the Federal Railroad Administration (FRA), and the Federal Aviation Administration (FAA). All of these agencies can take advantage of recommendations from the independent National Transportation Safety Board (NTSB), which Congress created for the purpose of investigating transportation-related accidents and recommending changes to prevent future accidents.[3]

THE POTENTIAL

By the end of the Public Interest Era, the federal government was well positioned to regulate the safety of transportation. The National Traffic and Motor Vehicle Safety Act of 1966 authorized the NHTSA to promulgate motor vehicle safety standards that were both "objective" and "practicable" but also were capable of "meet[ing] the need for motor vehicle safety." Truck safety regulation extended back to the New Deal Era, where it played a minor role in the Interstate Commerce Commission's broader regulatory responsibilities. When that agency was abolished in the late 1970s, its modest truck safety responsibilities were assigned to a small agency in the Department of Transportation called the Office of Motor Carriers (OMC), which Congress later renamed FMCSA.[4] The FAA was empowered by statutes dating back to the New Deal Era to ensure the airworthiness of aircraft and to write and enforce regulations and directives governing maintenance and operation of commercial aircraft.[5] Similarly, the FRA could prescribe "appropriate rules, regulations, orders and standards for all areas of railroad safety."[6]

The transportation agencies have unquestionably rendered the forms of transportation that they regulate much safer than they would have been in the absence of federal regulation. Highway traffic deaths in 2010 were at a 60-year low, having decreased 25 percent from 2005 levels, due in large measure to NHTSA-required technologies and the incentives provided by state tort litigation.[7] The recalls, regulations, and other fixes that they implemented prevented many accidents and saved thousands of lives. For example, although the auto industry fought tooth and nail over three decades against NHTSA's on-again-off-again attempts to require airbags in automobiles, the technology (with some adjustments to accommodate children) ultimately proved cheaper and more effective than even its proponents predicted in the mid-1970s, when NHTSA initially proposed to require them. By the time that the agency promulgated final regulations in August 2006 requiring side-impact airbags, auto manufacturers were engaged in an "arms race" to install airbags to meet the demands of safety-conscious consumers. NHTSA has estimated that the passive restraint standard saved over 15,000 lives in 2009 alone.[8]

THE REALITY

As the population and the economy of the United States grew during the Laissez Faire Revival, the reality of safety regulation in the rapidly evolving transportation sector did not match its great potential. The political appointees who headed the transportation agencies were not inclined to exercise their powers proactively. Unlike EPA and OSHA, each of the four agencies discussed here oversaw a single industry. Over time, agency officials and industry managers became quite familiar with one another, because they interacted on a daily basis. Agency leaders were often drawn from the industry, and agency officials at all levels frequently migrated through the "revolving door" to more lucrative industry positions after a few years of government service. It was not an atmosphere conducive to stringent regulation except in times of crisis when the public spotlight highlighted their past failures.

Even if agency leaders had been more inclined to promulgate and enforce protective regulations, the intrusive analytical and oversight requirements and the deep budget cuts that the Reagan Administration initiated and succeeding presidents retained made rulemaking an extremely burdensome undertaking. Instead of binding industry discretion in advance with rules, the agencies tended to react to particular accidents and NTSB recommendations with recalls (in the case of NHTSA) or discrete directives (in the case of the other agencies). After the first rush of rulemaking activity during the Public Interest Era, rulemaking initiatives were by and large limited to those specifically required by statute.

WRITING THE RULES

President Carter's appointment of Joan Claybrook, the head of Ralph Nader's auto safety group, to head NHTSA triggered the business community's first assault on transportation regulation. Under Claybrook, the agency proposed several important rules, including a "passive restraints" standard that pressed automakers to install airbags and a standard requiring air brakes in tractor trailers to prevent them from jackknifing. Both were fiercely resisted by manufacturers and challenged in court, and neither standard went into effect as written.[9]

The first order of business for the transportation safety agencies at the outset of the Reagan Administration was to withdraw all pending Carter Administration rulemaking proposals and to purge their internal rulemaking agendas of Carter Administration initiatives. Because NHTSA had achieved a high public profile during Joan Claybrook's tenure, the new administration singled it out for especially severe budget cuts. An August 1982 purge removed thirty-two professionals from the rulemaking and research staffs, and a second purge at the beginning of President Reagan's second term replaced long-time civil servants with Reagan loyalists to ensure that the deregulatory policies would continue into the next administration. NHTSA spent most of the Reagan Administration rescinding and weakening existing regulations on a hit list prepared by the Vice-President's Task Force on Regulatory Relief.[10]

OMC likewise did very little during the Reagan Administration to enhance truck safety. As reports came in that much higher truck traffic on the nation's highways was contributing to a larger number of highway fatalities, however, Congress enacted the Commercial Motor Vehicle Safety Act of 1986, which established a nationwide system of testing and licensing for truck and bus drivers. The agency promulgated the mandated testing standards, but it denied a consumer group's petition to promulgate regulations requiring trucks to install "black box" data recorders to aid investigators in probing the causes of collisions.[11]

At the FRA, headed by Robert Blanchette, a former attorney for the railroad industry, the only significant safety initiative during the Reagan Administration was to begin the process of proposing a drug testing rule for railway workers, a policy that was highly unpopular with both the railroads and the railroad workers' union. A January 1987 collision between an Amtrak passenger train and a Conrail freight train near Baltimore, however, inspired Congress to enact the Rail Safety Improvement Act of 1988, which required FRA to promulgate regulations for improving train braking systems.[12]

As an unusually large number of airline crashes in 1984–85 yielded the highest fatality rate in the FAA's history, safety advocates complained that the agency was too cozy with the airline industry and took far too long to promulgate safety regulations. Blaming pilots and other airline personnel for the increase in accidents, Administrator Donald D. Engen, a former Piper Aircraft Corporation executive, inaugurated a "Back to Basics" training program emphasizing the fundamentals of airline safety. But the agency did not promulgate any regulations to address either pilot fatigue or improper maintenance, two other factors that had contributed to the carnage.[13]

The transportation agencies' regulatory output picked up a bit during the first two years of the George H. W. Bush Administration before declining once again under the watchful eye of Vice-President Quayle's Competitiveness Council.[14] The undistinguished heads of the transportation agencies were not as willing to stand up to the Council as EPA Administrator Reilly and FDA head David Kessler. The transportation agencies spent much of the first term of the Clinton Administration conducting "zero-based reviews" of their existing regulations and exploring voluntary approaches to regulation pursuant to the president's "reinvention" policies.[15]

Three months after President Clinton's belated appointment of Ricardo Martinez, an injury specialist from Emory University, to head NHTSA, the Gingrich Congress began to lob bombs at his agency. University of Chicago economist Sam Peltzman's much-criticized theory that vehicle safety regulations caused drivers to behave recklessly (because they did not worry so much about their own safety) provided ammunition to the auto industry as it went on the offensive. Hoping to avoid controversy, the agency adopted a conciliatory approach to rulemaking. The only regulation of any consequence issued during Martinez's five-year tenure required manufacturers of passenger vans to strengthen the rear door latches at a cost of about $1 per vehicle.[16]

A series of charter bus accidents culminating in a dramatic May 1999 New Orleans crash put the obscure OMC in the public spotlight. Congress responded with the Federal Motor Carrier Safety Amendments of 1999, which created FMCSA, assigned it all of OMC's employees and responsibilities, and provided some additional regulatory authorities, including the power to require operators to install "black box" event recorders to monitor vehicle speeds and hours of operation.[17]

Another highly publicized outbreak of accidents toward the end of the Clinton Administration involving Ford Explorers and Bridgestone/Firestone ATX tires led to the first serious oversight hearings that NHTSA had experienced since the Reagan Administration. The public learned that the agency's ancient tire tread standard predated the industry's universal adoption of steel-belted radial tires and the advent of the sport utility vehicle (SUV). After a Senate committee reported a bill instructing NHTSA to promulgate stringent regulations governing vehicle rollovers and tire safety, the Chamber of Commerce and an armada of industry lobbyists persuaded the House to pass a much less protective bill.[18] President Clinton signed the pared-down Transportation Recall Enhancement, Accountability and Documentation Act of 2000 (TREAD Act) in November 2000. The new law required NHTSA to promulgate more than a dozen new regulations within 2–3 years. It also broadened NHTSA's powers to order and enforce recalls and established modest civil and criminal penalties for noncompliance. But it authorized only $9 million in additional appropriations to accomplish those massive undertakings.[19]

President George W. Bush's choice to head NHTSA, Jeffrey W. Runge, was an emergency room doctor from North Carolina, and he entered office committed to advancing the agency's safety mission.[20] Runge pressed the agency staff to meet the TREAD Act deadlines. He also steered the agency toward proposing a standard for side-impact crashes to protect occupants of small cars from right-angle collisions with SUVs. The agency approached this ambitious agenda, however, with a severely depleted rulemaking staff that continued to suffer from budget shortages throughout the administration. Not surprisingly, the rulemaking initiatives soon fell far behind schedule. Adding to NHTSA's workload, the Safe, Accountable, Flexible, Efficient Transportation Equity Act

of 2006 required the agency to promulgate additional protections against rollovers, crushed roofs, side-impact collisions, power window injuries to children,
and several other matters by specific deadlines. The agency accomplished none
of the required rulemakings before the end of the Bush Administration.[21]

To head the recently created FMCSA, President Bush appointed Joseph M.
Clapp, the retired CEO of one of the country's largest trucking companies.[22]
Under Clapp, FMCSA retained its predecessor's close relationship with the
regulated industry. Among other things, it formed "alliances" with industry
trade associations under which the agency offered companies assistance in interpreting and applying agency rules. Its primary accomplishment was to *reduce*
the stringency of the "hours of service" rule regulating the number of hours that
drivers could be on the road between breaks for sleep.[23]

The railroad industry thrived during the 2000s as increased global trade and
fuel prices gave it a competitive advantage over the trucking industry. FRA
head Allan Rutter, President Bush's Transportation Policy Director when he
was governor of Texas, hoped to promulgate fewer standards but to make them
more effective. On the first front, at least, he was quite successful. When Rutter
left in the fall of 2004, his deputy became the acting head of the agency for a
few months before resigning in disgrace over revelations that she and the chief
lobbyist for the Union Pacific Railroad had routinely vacationed together on
Nantucket Island while the agency was negotiating with the company over a
large fine that it had assessed for safety violations. Rutter's permanent replacement, Joseph H. Boardman, announced that two of his top priorities would be
rail safety and enhancing railway security systems, but he devoted far more attention to the latter than to the former.[24]

FAA Administrator Marion C. Blakey had been a partner in a public relations
firm that served the transportation industry, and she left the agency to become
the head of the Aerospace Industries Association. The absence of any major
airline disasters allowed her to deflect criticism as the White House reduced
resources to the agency and OIRA slowed down the regulatory process. During her tenure, the agency delegated major regulatory and inspection responsibilities to the airlines. Yet, while airline fatalities were down by 60 percent,
a continuing stream of less visible crashes of small airliners, mostly at regional
airports, suggested that all was not well with the industry.[25]

FOREGONE PROTECTION

The three assaults on regulation during the Laissez Faire Revival had a noticeable impact on the pace at which the transportation safety agencies promulgated protective regulations and on the content of those regulations. The agen-

cies only very rarely attempted to update regulations as technologies changed. The most significant protections came not on the agency's initiative, but as a result of legislation enacted in the wake of crises.[26] The following rulemaking exercises addressed serious transportation safety problems, but they all took much longer than necessary, and none of them achieved the level of protection envisioned by the authorizing legislation.

Regulating SUVs. When NHTSA promulgated its first round of safety standards during the Public Interest Era, it put pickup trucks, jeeps, vans, and other "multi-purpose" vehicles in a separate category called "light duty trucks" for which many of the auto safety standards did not apply. During the Reagan Administration, NHTSA slotted SUVs into the light duty truck category because they were originally built on pickup chassis. Yet SUVs were so much heavier and so much higher from the road than sedans that they posed a serious risk to sedan passengers during collisions. Moreover, their height and narrow wheel bases posed a much higher risk of rolling over during sharp turns or upon encountering low objects like guardrails. By the late 1980s families had purchased more than 3 million "mini-vans" and SUVs, and the rationale for regulating them less stringently was no longer viable.[27]

During the 1990s, NHTSA promulgated several regulations aimed at bringing the safety standards for SUVs up to the level of the standards for passenger sedans, but it did not address rollover risks until a crisis in early 2000 involving Ford Explorer SUVs and Firestone ATX tires forced it into action. Six years later, the agency promulgated a rule requiring all 2011 model year SUVs to come equipped with "electronic stability control" (ESC) systems employing sophisticated computer technologies to adjust vehicle speeds during possible rollovers. Two studies published in 2011 found that the fatality rate due to rollovers in SUVs with ESC was far less that the rate in SUVs without it.[28]

NHTSA also took up its 1971 roof-crush standard, which employed a "static" test developed by the automobile industry long before SUVs even existed. Although U.S. automakers strongly opposed "dynamic" testing for roof strength that simulated an actual rollover, their European subsidiaries had been employing dynamic tests for years. In the meantime, collapsing roofs had caused about 6,900 deaths and serious injuries. The final standard, which was published in May 2009, retained the static test but slightly increased the pressure applied to the roof. The auto industry was quite comfortable with both the ESC and the roof-crush standards.[29]

Side-impact collisions between SUVs and sedans were among the deadliest of all traffic accidents. Passenger-side airbags did not solve the problem, because the high frames of the much heavier SUVs could come crashing through the windows of the much lower sedans. U.S. auto manufacturers, however, dismissed the mismatch issue as an inevitable consequence of diversity on the roadway. After NHTSA Administrator Ricardo Martinez told auto executives that the industry's engineers should "design this issue away," they began to consider changes to the profiles of most SUVs to make them somewhat less deadly to passengers of other vehicles during collisions. Yet, despite studies demonstrating that lowering bumper heights had a significant impact on side impact fatalities, NHTSA did not attempt to impose mandatory standards. In mid-July 2008 the automakers abandoned the voluntary compatibility initiative. Side-impact collisions continue to account for 27 percent of all vehicle occupant deaths.[30]

Fatigue. By the mid-1990s, a booming internet-assisted economy combined with "just-in-time" inventory systems to create a huge demand for interstate trucking services, and large commercial trucks crowded the nation's highways. By the late 2000s, 711,000 commercial carriers were transporting more than 11 billion tons of goods annually. Although the drivers of these massive vehicles had to remain constantly alert to highway risks, the economic realities of this highly competitive industry generated strong pressures for drivers to stay on the road for as long as possible. FMCSA's predecessor agency had promulgated "hours of service" regulations in 1962 under which drivers could not be on duty for more than 15 hours or undertake more than 10 hours of actual driving time without spending at least 8 hours "off-duty." Drivers could, however, take the eight-hour "sleep break" in the truck cab in two separate periods totaling less than eight hours, so long as each break was at least two hours long. Weekly limits allowed a driver to be on duty for a maximum of sixty hours in seven consecutive days or seventy hours in eight consecutive days.[31]

Truck drivers routinely ignored the rules. It was easy enough for drivers and maintenance personnel to doctor the required records, because the OMC's miniscule inspectorate of 500 could not possibly oversee 3.6 million trucks and state inspectors were notoriously lax. Safety advocates noted that the agency could substantially improve the enforcement picture if it promulgated regulations requiring operators to install electronic on-board recorders that automatically monitored truck speeds and hours of operation. Both operators and drivers, however, strongly opposed any such requirement as an unnecessary restriction on driver freedom. During the Reagan and George H. W. Bush Administrations, agency officials agreed with the industry that the cost of installing recorders would outweigh the benefits.[32]

Toward the end of the Clinton Administration, FMCSA proposed more stringent regulations that would have, among other things, limited the number of driving hours in any given 24-hour period to 12, eliminated the "sleeper-berth" option for solo drivers, imposed a "mandatory weekend" requirement, and required manufacturers of the most dangerous class of trucks to include on-board recorders. The final rule published by the George W. Bush Administration in April 2003, however, was far less stringent than the proposal. The regulations allowed drivers who performed no other work to drive for 11 hours, rest for 10 hours, and drive for another 11 hours in a suboptimal 21-hour cycle that the agency recognized was not "ideal from a scientific viewpoint." It also rejected the mandatory "weekend" proposal, retained the "sleeper berth" option for solo drivers, and abandoned the on-board recorder requirement. The D.C. Circuit Court of Appeals found the rule to be arbitrary and capricious because the agency neglected to factor driver health into its analysis.[33]

Undeterred, FMCSA responded to the remand with an interim-final "midnight" rule in the waning days of the George W. Bush Administration that simply reinstated the requirements of the April 2003 rule and supplemented its analysis with an additional consideration of driver health. Safety advocates returned to court once more, but this time the Obama Administration entered into a settlement under which it agreed to start the rulemaking exercise over again from scratch. In the meantime, the ancient 1962 regulations remained on the books, and large truck and bus crashes cause around 3,600 deaths and 93,000 injuries annually, approximately 13 percent of which are caused by driver fatigue.[34]

Hazardous Rail Cargo. In July 1991, a 97-car freight train traveling through a winding valley in Northern California derailed on a bridge, causing a tank car filled with the pesticide metam sodium to break apart on the rocks below and spill its contents into the Sacramento River as it flowed toward Lake Shasta. The pesticide instantly destroyed virtually all aquatic life on many miles of the pristine river and ultimately contaminated portions of the lake. Subsequent investigations revealed that the ruptured tank car should have been upgraded or replaced with a sturdier version. Since FRA's regulations did not classify agricultural chemicals as "hazardous materials," the tank car contained no warnings, and the rescue crews had no way of knowing the chemical composition of the liquid that they were struggling to contain. Although FRA Administrator Gilbert Carmichael endorsed legislation to fill serious gaps in the agency's authority, the Gingrich Congress preferred industry self-regulation.[35]

Hazardous materials transportation became a major issue again in late 2000 following three major derailments in Louisiana, Nebraska, and Maryland. In 2005, NTSB found that half of the more than 60,000 aging tank cars did not meet current standards and were susceptible to rupture during accidents. FRA, however, refrained from taking any action that would have required the railroad industry to upgrade its fleet. It did not even require railroads to inform cities through which they traveled of the nature of the hazardous materials they were transporting at speeds of up to 60 miles per hour. When some cities began to enact local ordinances imposing their own speed limits and routing requirements, the George W. Bush Administration convinced a federal court that they were preempted by FRA's far less stringent regulations.[36]

A dramatic January 2005 derailment in Graniteville, South Carolina, in which chlorine gas killed nine and injured hundreds of other local residents inspired Congress to enact the Hazardous Materials Transportation Safety and Security Reauthorization Act of 2005. That statute empowered the agency to issue emergency directives to correct unsafe conditions and practices that presented an "imminent hazard" to the public. It did not, however, require FRA to upgrade tank car standards or promulgate regulations requiring trains containing hazardous materials to slow down in urban areas.[37] The agency finally reacted to public demands for more protective regulation in April 2008 when it published an "interim final" regulation requiring railroads to consider 27 separate criteria in selecting routes for transporting hazardous materials with the goal of finding the route "posing the least overall safety and security risk." Since the regulations placed no practical limits on the railroads' discretion in balancing the conflicting factors, safety advocates characterized the regulations as an "abdication of government responsibility."[38]

INEFFECTIVE RECALLS

As the transportation safety agencies migrated away from promulgating proactive regulations during the Laissez Faire Revival, they made more extensive use of vehicle recalls (in the case of NHTSA) and directives (in the case of the other agencies) when they were willing to take any action at all to address emerging safety risks.[39] From a purely political perspective, forcing a single company to recall a "defective" vehicle or directing a single airline to fix a particular maintenance problem was considerably more attractive than attempting to promulgate broad proactive regulations over the strong opposition of an entire industry. From a practical perspective, recalls and directives were easier to accomplish and far more likely to survive judicial review than proactive safety standards. From the public's perspective, however, the move to recalls and directives was protective only to the extent that they were effectively implemented and enforced. During the Laissez Faire Revival, recalls were often quite ineffective, and, as we shall see in the next section, the agency inspectorates did not always follow up on important safety directives.

The Reagan Administration botched the one significant recall that it attempted, a forced recall of 1.1 million General Motors (GM) "X-cars," when the D.C. Circuit Court of Appeals held that NHTSA had failed to prove that the vehicle presented an unreasonable risk.[40] NHTSA's most important recall effort during President Clinton's first term, involving General Motors pickup trucks with "side-mounted" fuel tanks that were more vulnerable to breach during collisions, was also a failure. GM rejected NHTSA's request that it recall 4.7 million trucks, arguing that the agency could not order a recall of a vehicle that fully complied with its outdated fuel system integrity standard. As its lawyers sued NHTSA, GM's lobbyists generated an outpouring of complaints from congressional allies. The agency then backed off and entered into a face-saving settlement that did not take any of the dangerous pickups off the road.[41] The agency had run up against its own failure to update its ancient standards.

As NHTSA continued to emphasize recalls over regulations during the George W. Bush Administration, the Department of Transportation's Inspector General concluded that the recall program was a "seriously flawed system" that suffered from incomplete and often inaccurate information, did not pay sufficiently close attention to consumer complaints, and failed to take timely action to require manufacturers to repair defective vehicles. When the agency did take action, it often allowed manufacturers to implement a "service campaign" under which the manufacturer quietly offered to replace defective components, rather than a noisy recall under which the agency issued a public warning and companies were under a legal obligation to fix defects. Even when NHTSA resorted to a full-fledged recall, manufacturers often found ways to avoid compliance. More than a quarter of all recalled vehicles never got repaired.[42]

LIMITED ACCOUNTABILITY

During the Laissez Faire Revival, the transportation agencies were less than aggressive enforcers as severe cutbacks in enforcement staffs forced them to rely heavily on the regulatees to self-report and self-correct violations. FAA was probably the least effective enforcer of all the transportation agencies. The Reagan Administration's budget cuts reduced FAA's inspectorate by 23 percent just as airline deregulation yielded a number of inexperienced new airlines and caused all commercial carriers to cut corners. The agency did not regain its lost inspectors during the George H. W. Bush and Clinton Administrations. NTSB accident investigations frequently uncovered problems that FAA inspectors should have discovered before the crashes. For example, the May 1996 crash of a Valu-Jet airliner (killing 110 persons) was caused by an explosion of one of several oxygen generators that the plane was transporting from one company facility to another in violation of FAA regulations. When inspectors did cite airlines, upper-level officials frequently settled the cases for a fraction of the fines originally assessed. Some inspectors reported that they had been reassigned after airline officials complained to their superiors about aggressive inspections. Although agency leaders maintained that corrective action, not punishment, was the goal of the inspection process, follow-up inspections were infrequent.[43]

As pressures mounted on airlines to reduce costs in the wake of a precipitous decline in air travel following the 2001 terrorist attacks, they faced new pressures to "outsource" maintenance responsibilities to companies (frequently in foreign countries) that could avoid the higher cost of a unionized workforce by hiring local (sometimes unlicensed) mechanics. Between 1996 and 2008, the proportion of maintenance activities that major airlines outsourced rose from 37 to 70 percent. These developments placed a tremendous burden on a shrinking FAA inspectorate to ensure that required maintenance was taking place. More than 4,300 domestic and 680 foreign repair and maintenance facilities were overseen by fewer than 3,200 FAA inspectors, only 103 of whom were responsible for international facilities. Foreign countries generally prohibited FAA inspectors from making unannounced inspections, leaving them to rely on company reports that were often "incomplete and incomprehensible."[44]

FAA increasingly relied on private inspectors hired by the airlines to oversee the repair and maintenance activities of their outside contractors. This arrangement came into question in March 2008 when FAA announced that it would seek $10.2 million in penalties from Southwest Airlines for operating nearly 60,000 flights over a two-year period with 46 planes that had not been inspected for fatigue-related cracks on their fuselages. More than 1,400 of those flights took place after the company had "self-disclosed" to FAA that it had not conducted the required inspections. Worse, the FAA supervisor overseeing Southwest's repair and maintenance operations gave the airline verbal approval to continue flying the planes until the inspections could be completed. Agency whistleblowers later revealed that the supervisor had repeatedly undermined attempts by on-site inspectors to discipline Southwest for numerous violations of FAA requirements and that supervisors in several other regions had forced inspectors to change entries in FAA enforcement databases to clear the way for the companies to disclose violations without penalty. Critics concluded that the Southwest Airlines fiasco was not an isolated incident, but a symptom of a regulatory culture of collaboration in which such abuses were inevitable.[45]

The FRA inspection and enforcement program ran a close second behind FAA. In 2006, FRA had only 400 field inspectors to ensure that an industry with 235,000 employees, 219,000 miles of track, 158,000 signals and switches, and over 1.6 million locomotives and cars complied with FRA regulations. The agency relied heavily upon the railroads themselves to inspect rolling stock and track, even though the companies were also cutting inspectors to meet competitive pressures resulting from economic deregulation. FRA investigated fewer than 15 percent of the worst grade crossing accidents. When inspectors discovered violations, the agency's policy was to work with the railroads to correct them voluntarily, rather than to levy large fines for past transgressions. Having assessed a civil penalty, agency officials typically negotiated a settlement under which the penalty was reduced, sometimes substantially, in return for promises to do better in the future.[46]

FMCSA's primary enforcement tool was the "compliance review" under which the inspector conducted an in-depth examination of a company's records. Companies falling into the "unsatisfactory" category had to address the problems identified in the inspector's report or risk being taken out of service, a penalty that, like USDA's "atom bomb" threat to shut down an entire slaughterhouse, the agency was very reluctant to administer. With little aid from state transportation agencies, the agency's tiny inspectorate of fewer than 100 inspectors was incapable of conducting compliance reviews for more than a tiny fraction of the nation's 711,000 carriers in any given year. FMCSA inspectors were also responsible for conducting random roadside checks of individual trucks for compliance with FMCSA safety equipment regulations and recordkeeping requirements. During the Laissez Faire Revival, however, agency inspectors conducted very few inspections of vehicles on the road, and they administered low fines when they detected violations. Even the few egregious violators that the agency grounded easily figured out ways to get back on the road.[47]

Since NHTSA only regulated vehicle manufacturers and since violations of its standards would be apparent in tests of vehicles before a model went on the market, its primary enforcement function was to police recalls of vehicles in which problems were detected after they had been on the market. In 1980, when 146 million vehicles were on the road, NHTSA employed 119 enforcement personnel to enforce recalls. By 2010, when there were 256 million vehicles on the road, NHTSA employed 57 enforcers. During the last half of the George W. Bush Administration, NHTSA stopped assessing fines altogether against companies that failed to undertake timely recalls of defective tires, vehicles, and vehicle parts. Even an aggressive inspectorate, however, would have had difficulty holding true scofflaws accountable, because the agency's statutes did not provide for criminal sanctions.[48]

THE CONSEQUENCES

On February 12, 2009, at 10:17 PM, a Continental Connections Bombardier turboprop plane crashed near the Buffalo Niagara Airport, killing 50 people. The plane's pilot had never received hands-on training with its safety system, and he had previously failed five tests conducted in airplane cockpits and flight simulators. He had flown to his home base in Newark from his Florida residence the previous evening, sleeping briefly in the crew lounge at the airport. The co-pilot had taken an evening flight from Seattle to Memphis and transferred in the middle of the night to a plane to Newark, arriving at 6:30 AM. She lived with her parents in Seattle and had to supplement her $16,254 salary by taking a second job as a waitress. When the wings of the aircraft began to ice up as the plane approached the airport, the plane's "stick shaker" provided an automatic warning that it was stalling, but the pilot took no action. He then overrode the "stick pusher," which had automatically assumed control of the plane to bring it out of the stall, thereby ensuring that the plane would not regain altitude. The NTSB later concluded that "pilot error" played a significant role in causing the crash.[49]

By 2009, regional airlines were handling half of all domestic flights as economically hard-pressed major airlines farmed out less lucrative regional service from their primary hubs. The investigations into the Buffalo crash revealed how much cost cutting had undermined safety on those airlines. Most regional airlines had lowered their requirements for new pilots, scrimped on training costs, and paid pitifully low salaries compared to the unionized major airlines. Many companies used the threat of bankruptcy to press pilots to work longer hours. Consequently, the serious accident rate per 100,000 departures was 10 times higher for regional airlines than for the majors.[50]

FAA's "propeller age" hours of service regulations were designed for pilots who typically flew one or two legs per day. They did not take into account the added strain of taking off and landing five or six times per day that regional airline pilots often endured, nor did they account for the long commutes that typified the regional airline industry. Regional airline pilots often had to fly many legs over several days with only a few hours of intervening sleep in makeshift "crew rooms" or "crash pads." FAA had proposed revisions to its hours of service regulations in 1995, but they encountered strong resistance from the airlines and powerful members of the Gingrich Congress. Instead of pressing forward, the agency assembled an 18-member rulemaking advisory committee composed of representatives of the airline industry and the pilots' unions to negotiate a compromise on crew scheduling. The negotiations continued on-

and-off until the agency withdrew the proposal near the end of the George W. Bush Administration.[51]

Dramatic plane crashes and train wrecks during the Laissez Faire Revival, some of which are described in Box 12.1, attracted public attention, but they were only part of a broader transportation safety crisis that was captured in statistics on transportation-related deaths and injuries. Highway crash fatalities varied from year to year, but always exceeded 30,000. Although commercial trucks were involved in only 3 percent of highway accidents, they caused 10 percent of highway fatalities, killing nine people per day on average. According to some estimates, 2,000 occupants of smaller vehicles were killed every year in collisions with the larger and higher SUVs. Accidents between motor vehicles and trains at railroad grade crossings accounted for about one fatality per day and 1,000 injuries per year. Almost 450 people were injured and 14 killed every year in train derailments and collisions with other trains.[52]

CONCLUSIONS

A safe and efficient transportation system is essential to a healthy modern economy. The governmental infrastructure that Congress established during the Progressive, New Deal, and Public Interest Eras for regulating transportation safety could not eliminate all transportation accidents or even all transportation-related disasters, but it had the potential, if effectively implemented, to reduce the frequency of accidents and the extent of the resulting human carnage. The federal regulatory regime did not live up to its potential for several reasons. First, the laissez faire minimalist political appointees who headed the agencies for much of the Laissez Faire Revival were disinclined to regulate. Second, at the lower levels where industry engineers and supervisors interacted with professionals from the single-industry agencies, there developed over the years a degree of familiarity and even camaraderie that rendered even committed civil servants sympathetic to the needs of the industries they were regulating. Third, even in those rare moments when the agencies were headed by aggressive regulators, analytical and procedural requirements imposed by Congress, the White House, and the courts combined with shrinking budgets and determined resistance from the industry to make it almost impossible to implement their statutes through informal rulemaking. The agencies therefore found it much easier to advance their safety agendas by reacting to specific identifiable failures with recalls and directives, neither of which were especially effective. Finally, the limited legislative responses to particular crises did not get to the root of the problems of captive agencies, severely limited resources,

Box 12.1

Transportation Tragedies

Unsafe Cars. More than 160 people burned to death in GM pickups with side-mounted fuel tanks that fully complied with NHTSA standards. The popular Ford Explorer equipped with Bridgestone ATX tires caused more than 200 deaths and 700 injuries due to separating tires and subsequent rollovers.[a]

Train Collisions. In June 2004, a tank car released a cloud of chlorine gas that killed 5 people and injured 30 others in Macdonna, Texas, when the fatigued conductor allowed the train to plow into another train. A head-on collision between a Los Angeles Metrolink commuter train and an oncoming freight train in September 2008 killed 25 persons and badly injured 135 others. In June 2009, a Washington, D.C. Metro train crashed into the back of a stopped train, killing 9 and injuring at least 70, when its outdated computerized signal system failed to stop its forward progress.[b]

Train Derailments. In January 2002, a Canadian Pacific freight train derailed near the small town of Minot, North Dakota, rupturing five tank cars full of anhydrous ammonia and sending a plume of toxic gas into the surrounding neighborhoods that killed one resident and injured 333 others, because the company had failed to inspect and maintain the track running through the town. An improperly aligned switch caused a Norfolk Southern freight train traveling at almost 50 mph through Graniteville, South Carolina, to derail, releasing a cloud of chlorine gas that killed the engineer and eight local residents, injured around 250 people, and caused more than 5,000 residents to flee their homes in the middle of the night.[c]

NOTES

a. Keith Bradsher, High and Mighty 320 (2002) (Explorer/ATX statistics); Myron Levin, *Upgrades on Auto Safety Standards Languish*, LAT, September 18, 2000, at A1 (GM trucks).

b. Christopher Conkey & Cam Simpson, *Washington Metro Crash Kills Nine*, WSJ, June 23, 2009, at A1 (Metro crash); Randal C. Archibold, *Investigators Say Train Engineer Sent Text Messages Seconds Before Crash*, NYT, October 2, 2008, at A19 (Metrolink); Dan Weikel, *Over the Long Haul, Fatigue Kills*, LAT, April 24, 2005, at A1 (Macdonna).

c. National Transportation Safety Board, Collision of Norfolk Southern Freight Train 192 With Standing Norfolk Southern Local Train P22 With Subsequent Hazardous Materials Release at Graniteville, South Carolina, January 6, 2005 v (2005); *Minot Residents Count Blessings After Derailment*, Minneapolis Star-Tribune, January 20, 2002, at A20.

and a general unwillingness of the single-industry agencies to antagonize their "partners" in the transportation industry. The consequences of these failures were apparent in a series of transportation tragedies highlighted in Box 12.1 that sent a strong message to the White House and Congress that the agencies had strayed a long way from their original protective missions.

FINANCIAL PROTECTION

The banking system of the United States has changed dramatically since the major regulatory overhaul of the New Deal Era, during which time some but not all sectors were regulated by federal agencies. The Office of the Comptroller of the Currency (OCC) is currently responsible for the safety and soundness of the nation's 1,500 federally chartered commercial banks. It is also responsible for 800 federally chartered savings and loan institutions (S&Ls), which prior to 2010 were regulated by the Office of Thrift Supervision (OTS) and, before that, by the Federal Home Loan Bank Board (FHLBB). The Federal Reserve Board (the Fed) is responsible for supervising and regulating the 5,400 bank holding companies that own or control banks and other kinds of financial institutions. The Federal Deposit Insurance Corporation (FDIC), which insures deposits in national banks and S&Ls up to prescribed maximum amounts is responsible for "resolving" failed banks and ensuring that depositors do not lose more than the maximum amounts as a result of bank failures.[1]

THE POTENTIAL

The savings and loan industry flourished in the early twentieth century under the simple George Bailey model of returning money deposited by local citizens to the community in the form of home mortgage and commercial loans. Like the S&Ls, commercial banks flourished as local depository institutions, paid interest on deposits, and loaned them back to local businesses or placed them in safe investments. After both industries survived the Great Depression (with substantial help from the government), New Deal legislation turned them into heavily regulated financial institutions. OCC and FHLBB ensured the "safety and soundness" of covered lending institutions by promulgating regulations that, among other things, required them to maintain capital reserves sufficient to cover specified percentages of outstanding obligations. Typically expressed as "debt-to-equity" ratios, these requirements limited the amount of "leverage" a bank could exercise in investing its customers' deposits by requiring the bank to maintain a certain percentage of its outstanding obligations in cash or other very liquid assets to provide a cushion against unexpectedly high withdrawal rates by depositors. Agency "examiners" audited the books of the lending institutions to ensure that they complied with the regulations. The banking industry did very well for itself under this strict regulatory regime, without any of the meltdowns that had previously plagued the financial system. When crises erupted, the agencies normally had adequate authority to take protective action.[2]

Nondepository financial institutions called "investment banks," most of which were located on Wall Street, borrowed money from banks and large investors and invested that money in new business enterprises, stocks and bonds, real estate, corporate mergers and acquisitions, and other investments that generally put the funds at higher risk than those deposited in federally insured and regulated banking institutions. Although they were not insured by the federal government and were not subject to the "safety and soundness" requirements of the federal banking agencies, they typically offered higher rates of return than the interest rates available at regulated banks. They were subject to antifraud laws administered by the Federal Trade Commission (FTC) and (if they were publicly traded corporations) to modest minimum capital requirements promulgated by the Securities and Exchange Commission (SEC). To ensure that federally insured banks did not engage in overly risky investments, the Glass-Steagall Act prohibited them from functioning as investment banks, securities dealers, or insurance companies.[3]

Congress enacted the Truth in Lending Act of 1968 (TILAct) to curb "predatory lending," a generic term for deceptive, manipulative, and overly aggressive lending practices that are especially prevalent in markets where borrowers are less educated, have limited access to mainstream banks, and lack the tools necessary to engage in comparison shopping. The statute required lenders to disclose in a standardized format using comprehensible language specific aspects of covered loan agreements, including the annual percentage interest rate and the total finance charge. In addition, lenders had to inform consumers of late fees, security interests, and other loan characteristics that would facilitate loan comparisons. Finally, the consumer had a right to rescind the agreement within three days if the creditor received a security interest in the consumer's home.[4]

These statutes provided significant protections to consumers on both ends of transactions with banks. Consumers depositing modest sums of money in a bank could be confident that it would invest them wisely and pay the promised interest, without having to worry about the possibility of a run on the bank. Borrowers could rest assured that the relevant terms and conditions of loans were apparent in the lending documents and that they could back out of agreements if deeper reflection revealed that the terms were unacceptable or unaffordable. Finally, the regulatory regime provided a great deal of assurance that risky lending or investment practices by federal depository institutions would not place the financial system as a whole at risk of a systemic meltdown. For forty years following World War II, this complex regulatory regime functioned quite effectively to make capital available to homeowners and businesses while protecting depositors from loss and providing them a respectable rate of return on their savings.

THE REALITY

By the late 1970s, memories of the Great Depression had faded, and enthusiasm for economic deregulation was growing among both liberals and conservatives. New financial institutions entered the picture, existing financial institutions grew more sophisticated, investment opportunities for middle-class consumers grew more plentiful, and pressures mounted for the federal banking agencies to allow regulated financial institutions greater freedom to manage other people's money. During the Laissez Faire Revival, Congress and the regulatory agencies relied on the "efficient market hypothesis" (the laissez faire minimalist notion that the financial markets would police themselves to eliminate fraud and abuse) to justify broad deregulation of the banking industry. By the mid-2000s, the regulatory agencies and the common law courts were incapable of reining in the powerful forces that laissez faire minimalism had loosed upon global capital markets.

WRITING THE RULES

The comfortable postwar economic environment for banks and S&Ls changed rapidly during the late 1970s. Modern computer and communications technologies revolutionized the banking business, and a host of new financial instruments allowed middle-class consumers to reap much higher returns on their investments than the banks and S&Ls could provide by paying interest at fixed rates. Rapidly growing pension funds, mutual funds, and insurance companies were also on the lookout for the higher yields that were generally associated with the more sophisticated but riskier investments. Competitive pressures stemming from these new developments generated powerful political constituencies for freeing national banks and S&Ls from the constraints of the New Deal legislation. As banks and S&Ls began to offer a wider variety of options to a broader range of borrowers, the predatory lending practices that the TILAct was intended to curb grew more prevalent. Activist attorneys became a thorn in the side of the lending industry as they filed class action lawsuits against abusive lenders on behalf of low-income and middle-class borrowers seeking millions of dollars in compensation plus attorney's fees.[5]

The first assault on banking regulation began midway through the Carter Administration, when the president's economic advisors persuaded him that banking deregulation belonged in the category of "economic" regulatory reform that could only benefit consumers by increasing competition. Lost in their enthusiasm for deregulation was the risk to consumers and the financial system that could result from carving away New Deal and Public Interest Era protections. The Truth in Lending Simplification Act of 1980 (TILSAct) severely limited the TILAct's disclosure requirements and provided considerable room for creditors to avoid liability for making misleading statements to consumers. The Depository Institutions Deregulation and Monetary Control Act of 1980 (DIDMCAct) eliminated all state and federal caps on interest rates paid for deposits in national banks and S&Ls. In one fell swoop, the banks were freed from the restrictions of usury laws that had governed banking practices for millennia.[6]

Risky Lending. The DIDMCAct freed lenders to make high-interest, high-risk loans while at the same time collecting hefty fees at the front end out of the loaned monies. These loans could be profitable even if the borrower went into default, so long as the equity in the mortgaged property exceeded the amount of the loan plus anticipated foreclosure costs.[7] With the strong support of the Reagan Administration, the Garn-St. Germain Depository Institutions Act of 1982 allowed S&Ls to transform the tightly regulated short-term, fixed-rate "second mortgages" that they had traditionally offered for financing home improvements into long-term, variable rate "home equity loans" that borrowers could use for any conceivable purpose. In making both original and home equity loans, lending institutions began to rely on computer programs that spat out credit scores based on lightly documented and weakly validated loan applications.[8]

The Reagan years witnessed the arrival on the lending scene of "mortgage companies" that were not subject to the regulatory restrictions that applied to federally insured banks and S&Ls because they did not take deposits. To fund the loans, they relied exclusively on monies provided by the big Wall Street banks. They specialized in "subprime" loans, so labeled because the borrower did not meet the lending standards for conventional loans insured by the Federal Housing Administration. To cover the added risk, mortgage companies charged higher interest rates and extracted larger fees at closing. Accurately sensing that they were losing out on a lucrative opportunity, federally regulated banks and S&Ls followed the mortgage companies into the subprime lending market. By the mid-1990s, subprime lending had been transformed from a backwater practice engaged in by a few marginal companies into a widely used strategy for funneling billions of dollars into inner cities, aging suburbs, and shiny new exurbs.[9]

The engine driving these aggressive lending practices was a financial innovation that allowed Wall Street investment banks to diversify mortgage loan risks by turning large pools of mortgages into "mortgage-backed securities" that could be sold to a wide variety of investors. Securitization made vast pools of cash available to loan to borrowers looking to finance new homes or refinance existing ones. It allowed lending institutions to collect hefty up-front fees while retaining very little of the risk of default, which was spread out among the purchasers of the securities. The investment banks that securitized the loans likewise charged hefty fees to investors while avoiding any legal responsibility for the predatory tactics of the loan originators. With securitization came a proliferation of specialized entities that originated loans, appraised real estate, evaluated default risks, funded loans, serviced loans, and produced and marketed securities, none of which believed that it could be held accountable if the loans went into default.[10]

As investors from around the world became enamored of mortgage-backed securities, investment banks demanded more mortgages to securitize, and opportunistic lenders pushed their loan officers to beat the bushes for borrowers. Independent "mortgage brokers" signed up prospective borrowers, collected their fees from lenders, and moved on in search of new borrowers with no concern for whether any borrower could make the monthly payments. Neither the banks nor the brokers had the interests of borrowers in mind as they cajoled them into high-interest subprime loans that they probably could not afford. The Clinton Administration strongly encouraged these developments as a vehicle for making the dream of home ownership a reality for low-income Americans.[11]

By the mid-1990s, the conditions were ripe for abuse as the modest disclosure requirements of the TILSAct proved unequal to the task of protecting consumers from highly motivated predatory lenders. Subprime loans set thousands of unsophisticated borrowers on a course of borrowing and refinancing that ultimately ended in foreclosure, humiliation, and bankruptcy.[12] Congress partially addressed the problem with the Home Ownership and Equity Protection Act of

1994 (HOEPAct), which allowed the Fed to promulgate regulations protecting owners of existing homes from unfair and deceptive practices in the marketing of all home equity loans with interest rates that exceeded the rate for treasury securities by more than a prescribed percent. The new law also ensured a degree of accountability by holding subsequent purchasers of covered mortgages liable for the predatory lending practices of loan originators if they failed to exercise "reasonable due diligence" in selecting and purchasing covered mortgages. And it gave borrowers the right to rescind loan agreements if the lender engaged in prohibited predatory practices.[13]

Soon after the HOEPAct was enacted, attorneys for thousands of financially distressed homeowners filed more than 50 class action lawsuits against lenders asserting their new statutory right to rescission.[14] This was too much for the newly arrived Gingrich Congress. With no serious opposition from the Clinton Administration, it enacted the Truth in Lending Amendments of 1995, which eviscerated the HOEPAct by making it more difficult for borrowers to raise their rescission rights in response to foreclosure actions. Fed chairman Alan Greenspan was convinced that intervention into the consumer lending market was unnecessary, and the Fed did not promulgate a single protective regulation during his tenure.[15] The Clinton Administration also came to the aid of the lending industry by urging federal courts to hold that lawsuits filed by aggressive state attorneys under state predatory lending laws were preempted by the seriously weakened federal banking laws.[16]

Like President Clinton, President George W. Bush pressed the banking agencies to encourage banks to make more loans to low-income borrowers as part of his promise to turn the nation into an "ownership society." This policy combined with the Fed's efforts to stimulate the economy in the wake of the September 11 terrorist attacks to produce the unprecedented housing boom of the early 2000s. The volume of subprime loans increased from $145 billion in 2001 to $625 billion in 2005.[17]

National Bank and S&L Regulation. President Reagan's first Comptroller of the Currency, a committed deregulator named C. T. Conover, eased requirements for obtaining new national bank charters, reduced restrictions on "brokered deposits" (large investments that brokers subdivided into federally insurable increments and spread across many banks), resisted the efforts of FDIC and the Fed to increase capital reserve requirements, and looked the other way as banks and appraisers relaxed real estate appraisal standards. At the same time, the Reagan Administration's budget cuts severely reduced OCC's capacity to uncover risky lending practices. When delinquency rates predictably increased during the 1982 recession, many banks became highly stressed.[18]

As the Fed staved off a possible financial meltdown by injecting huge amounts of money into the banking system, OCC in 1982 promulgated regulations requiring banks to disclose more information about bad loans. It then dealt consumers a blow by preempting state regulation of fees that national banks charged for consumer services. Meanwhile, the commercial banking industry was unraveling. In May 1984, the country's sixth largest commercial bank, Continental Illinois, encountered a self-made crisis as borrowers defaulted on risky loans and depositors staged a run on the bank. Deciding that Continental Illinois was simply too big to fail, the government agreed to be responsible for making all of the bank's creditors and depositors whole without regard to the $100,000 ceiling ordinarily applicable to FDIC-insured deposits.[19]

President Reagan appointed Richard Pratt, a laissez faire minimalist finance professor, to chair the FHLBB. By the time he was confirmed, 85 percent of all S&Ls were suffering serious losses. Pratt's solution to the industry's serious structural problems was to relieve it of regulatory burdens. Among other things, the FHLBB allowed S&Ls to make no-down-payment loans and to purchase risky futures contracts as investments. At the same time, severe budget cuts forced the Board to reduce the number of individual S&L examinations. The Reagan Administration supported the Garn-St. Germain Act of 1982, which jettisoned what remained of the FHLBB's authority to establish interest rate ceilings for deposits, allowed S&Ls to invest up to 40 percent of their assets in nonresidential loans, eliminated existing loan-to-asset-value limits, and freed up S&Ls to market risky home mortgage loans with adjustable interest rates and balloon payments.[20]

All this regulatory relief allowed the S&L industry to experience one last spectacular hurrah. Between 1982 and 1985, the industry grew by leaps and bounds when, by any standards of responsible banking, it should have been slowly contracting. With FHLBB's blessing, Wall Street investment banks placed billions of dollars' worth of brokered deposits in thinly capitalized S&Ls and purchased thousands of mortgages from them for securitizing. The S&Ls used this huge influx of discretionary capital to invest in speculative real estate deals, corporate takeovers, and junk bonds. With the depositors protected by federal insurance and S&L operators protected from personal liability by the corporate shield, no one other than the overworked FHLBB examiners had any incentive to limit the risk that S&L operators took on in pursuit of the highest possible profit. Freed of any effective federal oversight, a whole new cast of high-flying financiers purchased small S&Ls and then systematically looted them to finance lavish lifestyles for themselves and their friends.[21]

Pratt left the agency in May 1983 to become the president of the branch of Merrill Lynch that brokered and securitized mortgages. President Reagan filled the vacant position with Edwin Gray, a former reporter who saw an S&L crisis looming over the horizon. Gray became the proverbial skunk at the picnic as he struggled in vain to "reregulate" some of the more risky aspects of the S&L industry in an administration that was committed to deregulation. Frustrated at every turn, he resigned in June 1987 and was replaced by Danny Wall, a former congressional aide who assured Congress that FHLBB had matters firmly under control. By 1988, however, the house of cards began to collapse as the Federal Savings and Loan Insurance Corporation (now part of FDIC) bailed out dozens of S&Ls and FBI agents began to uncover massive fraud throughout the industry. Ultimately, more than 700 S&Ls had to be rescued at a cost to taxpayers of around $150 billion.[22]

Drawing the obvious conclusion that many of the largest S&Ls had abused the freedom granted by financial deregulation, Congress enacted the Financial Institutions Reform, Recovery, and Enforcement Act of 1989 (FIRREA). That statute created the Resolution Trust Corporation to liquidate insolvent S&Ls and turn their assets into mortgage-backed securities. It also abolished the FHLBB and replaced it with a new Office of Thrift Supervision (OTS) in the Treasury Department. Finally, the new law imposed stringent minimum capital requirements on S&Ls, restricted the kinds of activities in which S&Ls could invest, and gave OTS broad new authorities to regulate the industry.[23] The newly created OTS, however, spent much of the George H. W. Bush Administration struggling to find "flexibility" in the tight new law for the industry. OCC spent much of its time revisiting existing regulations with the goal of eliminating those that were obsolete or overly stringent.[24]

By the time that President Clinton was inaugurated, the S&L crisis was a distant memory, and the new president announced to the Chamber of Commerce that he was determined to remove unnecessary regulatory impediments to lending to low-income borrowers. The administration then launched a series of deregulatory changes that allowed banks to accept property as collateral without first undertaking an appraisal of its value and permitted them to rely upon the "reputation and good character" of potential borrowers, rather than on objective measures of their ability to pay. With the Gingrich Congress looking on approvingly, OTS announced that it would be rescinding 8 percent of its regulations and carefully examining an additional 60 percent for possible revision or repeal.[25]

As the 1998 off-year elections elevated laissez faire minimalist Senator Phil Gramm (R-Texas) to the chairmanship of the Senate Banking Committee, the economy was booming and credit was easy. With the strong support of Fed Chairman Alan Greenspan, Treasury Secretary Robert Rubin, and the

Heritage Foundation, Congress enacted the Financial Services Modernization Act of 1999 (the Gramm-Leach-Bliley Act). That statute fulfilled the financial sector's longstanding desire to be rid of the Glass-Steagall Act's restrictions on commercial banks acting as investment banks, securities dealers, and insurance companies. The statute allowed federally insured national banks to form holding companies that could in turn create separate subsidiaries called structured investment vehicles (SIVs) (often located "offshore" in the Cayman Islands) to house investment banking operations and sell insurance. The beauty of the holding company arrangement for a bank subject to the federal minimum capital requirements was that the SIV's assets and liabilities did not have to be reflected on the regulated bank's balance sheets.[26]

Things got even better for the banking industry with the election of George W. Bush. The heads of OTS, OCC, FDIC, and the Fed staged a press conference in the summer of 2003 where they posed behind a huge stack of papers wrapped in red tape brandishing garden shears and, in the case of the OTS Director James E. Gilleran, a chainsaw. A passionate deregulator, Gilleran reduced the agency's staff by 25 percent at the same time that the value of the loans and assets that it regulated increased by half. To stimulate more loans to homeowners, OTS reduced the capital reserve requirements for S&Ls to historic lows. Demonstrating a similar commitment to deregulation, OCC issued a fateful rule allowing national banks to reduce capital reserves by purchasing risky derivatives to hedge against losses.[27] The stage was set for another major crash.

Derivatives and Hedge Funds. Mortgage-backed securities were part of a larger class of "collateralized debt obligations" (CDOs) that investment banks created by "slicing and dicing" the expected principal and interest payments from legally enforceable income streams. CDOs were in turn a subset of a larger universe of financial instruments called "derivatives," so named because they derived their value from other financial assets or financial conditions. The contracts for derivatives were often standardized, and they were usually traded privately in nontransparent "over-the-counter" exchanges managed by Wall Street investment banks for hefty fees.[28]

An investment bank could package a large pool of CDOs by subdividing them into tiers called "tranches," each of which contained a group of securities that, in turn, received a rating ranging from AAA to BBB by a separate (and supposedly independent) entity hired by the bank called a "credit rating agency" (CRA). Because their AAA ratings allowed risk-averse institutions like pensions, university endowments, and mutual funds to purchase the upper tranches of derivative offerings that were so complex that virtually no one understood them, the CRAs were critical to the extraordinary success of CDOs. Rather than attempting to second-guess the lenders' evaluation of the creditworthiness of the borrowers, the CRAs based their ratings on historical analyses of similar loan obligations. For an additional fee, the CRA would provide advice to the investment bank on where to draw the lines between tranches in order to maximize the number of securities that went into the higher rated groups. The top tranche had the first claim on future cash flows and therefore received the highest rating, but it also paid the lowest yields. The securities in the bottom tranche (the residuals or "toxic waste") received the highest yields, but they received the lowest ratings because they were the first to suffer if the borrowers missed their payments. Borrowers sent their monthly payment to the "servicers" of their loans, which in turned transferred the money (minus the servicing fee) to an investment bank SIV that held the mortgages in trust for the purchasers of the securities. The SIV then transferred the income flows to the holders of the CDOs in accordance with the tranching arrangement.[29]

As demand for high-yield investments grew, investment banks began spinning out CDO offerings with dozens of tranches and creating "synthetic CDOs" by converting groups of CDOs into securities. These "CDOs-squared" were far more sensitive to downswings in the economy, but they could be hedged against with another form of derivative called the "credit default swap" (CDS). A CDS was simply a contract under which one party provided cash or some other valuable consideration for a promise by the other party to pay a specific sum if a debtor defaulted on a specified obligation. Banks could use swaps to meet a portion of their capital reserve requirements by arranging with an investment bank or insurance company to guarantee its loan portfolio against all losses above an agreed-upon level. The insuring institution accomplished this by using sophisticated computer models developed by physicists-turned-investment bankers (euphemistically called "quants") to purchase a portfolio of derivatives designed to hedge against the risk of default in the bank's loan portfolio. Because anyone could buy or sell CDSs for any purpose, including speculative bets against companies, they soon became one of the fastest growing products in the financial markets.[30]

Another investment entity that came into its own during the 1990s was the "hedge fund." Originally designed to allow large investors to hedge against the risk of loss due to fluctuating interest and currency rates, hedge funds evolved into unregulated vehicles for implementing a variety of investment strategies. Hedge funds were often managed by individuals, but they were also run by SIV subsidiaries of bank holding companies where their activities did not affect the balance sheets of the parent corporations. They borrowed very heavily from banks and from each other to purchase the securities with which they made their bets for or against various market outcomes. When their bets failed, however, they had to come up with money to pay back their debts. This constant status of high leverage made them very profitable but inherently unstable. Just as derivatives were beyond SEC's broad jurisdiction over stocks traded on the national stock exchanges, hedge funds were likewise exempt from that agency's registration and disclosure requirements. Since they were not depository institutions, hedge funds were also beyond the jurisdiction of OCC, OTS, and the Fed.[31]

Derivatives bore a close resemblance to contracts for future deliveries of commodities, which had since 1974 been regulated by a small five-member federal agency called the Commodity Futures Trading Commission (CFTC). Concerned about the "systemic risk" that a large unregulated market in financial derivatives posed to the stability of the overall financial system, Congress in the late 1980s instructed CFTC to decide whether it should regulate derivatives. The chairperson of CFTC at the time was Wendy L. Gramm, a committed laissez faire minimalist and wife of Senator Phil Gramm. During the last week of the George H. W. Bush Administration, CFTC concluded that although it had jurisdiction over derivatives, it saw no need for government regulation of derivatives markets. Weeks later, Gramm resigned from CFTC and joined the board of the Enron Corporation, a prominent derivatives trader.[32]

Toward the end of the Clinton Administration, CFTC, now chaired by Washington, D.C. lawyer Brooksley Born, decided to revisit the issue of regulating complex financial derivatives. In addition to the obvious potential for derivatives to deceive unsophisticated investors, she worried that large financial institutions were purchasing credit default swaps to hedge against unexpected eventualities instead of putting aside cash reserves. If the "counterparties" to the swaps failed to cover any unexpected losses, then the entire financial system could come unglued. Federal Reserve Board Chairman Alan Greenspan, Treasury Secretary Robert Rubin, and Deputy Treasury Secretary Lawrence Summers, however, quashed every move by CFTC to regulate derivatives.[33]

Born's fears were borne out in 1998 when a well-connected hedge fund called Long Term Capital Management (LTCM) suffered heavy losses after Russia announced that it was defaulting on its bonds. The sophisticated model that Nobel Prize–winning economists Myron Scholes and Robert Merton had designed for LTCM failed to take into account the risk of such a major default. The Fed staved off a financial meltdown by cajoling LTCM's lenders to bail out the failing company. Instead of seeing the LTCM crisis as a wake-up call, however, Congress enacted a bill authored by Phil Gramm called the Commodity Futures Modernization Act of 2000 (CFMAct), which prohibited CFTC, SEC and state agencies from regulating derivatives.[34]

FOREGONE PROTECTION

The real estate bubble began to deflate in the spring of 2006 as housing prices for the first time in many years moved downward. As monthly payments on adjustable rate mortgages rapidly increased, default rates and foreclosures accelerated. The worsening economic conditions caused the credit rating agencies to be more cautious, and institutional investors purchased fewer CDOs and began to unload them from their portfolios.[35] As the flow of money from Wall Street slowed, housing prices declined in a vicious spiral that led to the financial system meltdown of September 2008.

None of this was inevitable. Federal agencies had ample authority to prevent the predatory loans and risky lending practices, but failed to use it. At the same time, Congress divested the banking agencies of effective power to regulate the investment banks and hedge funds that converted worthless mortgages into incomprehensibly complex derivatives and traded them in highly leveraged transactions that placed the entire financial system at great risk.

Predatory Lending. The regulatory protections against predatory lending that Congress had enacted during the Public Interest Era seriously eroded during the Laissez Faire Revival. First, the DIDMCAct freed lenders to make loans for any purpose at usurious rates. Second, the federal statutes contained critical gaps in coverage that left nondepository mortgage companies and mortgage brokers beyond the reach of federal regulatory protections. Third, the primary regulatory tool—disclosure—had, after the enactment of the TILSAct, proved inadequate to the task of protecting unsophisticated borrowers from predatory lenders. Fourth, the agencies responsible for implementing the federal laws against predatory lending were either unwilling or unable to keep up with the rapid innovations in loan instruments of the late 1990s. Finally, the private remedies provided by the TILAct—rescission and class action lawsuits—were scaled back greatly by Congress and the courts.[36]

Freed from regulatory constraints, banks and mortgage companies came up with an assortment of lending vehicles to entice new and existing homeowners into borrowing beyond their means. Adjustable rate mortgages (ARMs) with low "teaser" rates for five-to-ten years and "balloon" payments of the remaining principal and interest made new home purchases appear affordable to borrowers who were persuaded by aggressive brokers that increasing housing values and declining interest rates would permit easy refinancing during the balloon year. "Option ARMs" gave optimistic borrowers the option to pay less for a fixed-rate mortgage in the early years and defer the difference to later years when they would hopefully have higher incomes. At the same time large prepayment penalties often limited the options of borrowers who realized that they had been hoodwinked. Existing homeowners were bombarded with advertising, telephone solicitations, and personal visits from mortgage companies eager to show them how to use their home's equity to finance new appliances, vacations, or "debt consolidation" loans. Mortgage brokers operated below the radar of the federal consumer protection laws and could easily avoid state regulators. Some engaged in outright fraud as they persuaded unsophisticated borrowers to take on unaffordable loans by misrepresenting their assets.[37]

The lending industry and its allies in academia and the think tanks generally blamed borrowers for taking on loans that they could not afford, a practice that the Heritage Foundation dubbed "predatory borrowing." To be sure, many subprime borrowers were affluent families who wanted second homes or residences that were simply beyond their means. And others took advantage of increasing housing prices and declining interest rates to take out speculative loans on dwellings that they never intended to occupy. Even cautious and sophisticated borrowers, however, had difficulty digesting the "reams of paper" that lenders "thrust" at them just prior to closing when it was normally too late to make a well-informed choice.[38]

As the industry consolidated, the Fed had a unique opportunity under the TILAct to ban "unfair and deceptive" lending practices of the growing number of banks and mortgage companies that were subsidiaries of bank holding companies, and the HOEPAct offered it a similar opportunity to protect elderly homeowners from predatory home equity loans. Fed Chairman Alan Greenspan, however, steadfastly refused to promulgate rules under either statute until long after the bubble had burst. The Fed even announced in January 1998 that it would discontinue consumer compliance examinations and consumer complaint investigations at the nonbank subsidiaries of bank holding companies. When aggressive state agencies attempted to fill the gap, the federal agencies stepped in to protect the industry by preempting more stringent state laws.[39]

Banks and S&Ls. Banks and mortgage companies had little incentive during the Laissez Faire Revival to avoid risky lending arrangements, because they retained very little of the risk of default on mortgages that they immediately sold to investment banks for securitization. Since they could charge higher fees and interest rates for high-risk subprime loans, they had every incentive to generate as many as they could. A "race-to-the-bottom" ensued as they lowered lending standards, pressured real estate appraisers into inflating underlying property values, and enticed low- and moderate-income borrowers into signing loans they could neither understand nor afford. Between 2004 and 2006, more than 2,500 lending institutions made high-interest, high-risk loans worth more than $1.5 trillion.[40]

The federal banking agencies took no affirmative steps to dampen the enthusiasm of lenders for pouring money into risky loans. To the contrary, they reduced capital reserve requirements and allowed banks to hedge against losses by purchasing risky derivatives. When they did react to clear patterns of abuse, they issued unenforceable guidelines. The Fed lacked the authority to gather critical information on the "shadow banking" operations that holding company subsidiaries conducted off-the-books in SIVs. Worst of all, the Gramm-Leach-Bliley Act of 1999 allowed large holding companies to shop among the relevant agencies for the one with the fewest regulatory restrictions by locating the bulk of their operations in the least regulated subsidiary.[41]

Systemic Risk. Financial derivatives are tools for managing financial risk and, as such, are not inherently good or evil. In the deregulated environment of the Laissez Faire Revival, however, these tools turned out to be, in the words of investor Warren E. Buffet, "weapons of mass destruction." By 2008, the global market in derivatives had reached the staggering sum of $683 trillion, the vast bulk of which was on either side of hedges and therefore did not, in theory, pose a risk to the financial system. The volume of subprime mortgage-backed securities, which clearly did pose high systemic risk, ballooned from $87 billion in 2001 to $450 billion in 2006. Since the investment banks were earning their fees at the front end, they had little incentive to worry about the downside risks, even when they retained some of the "toxic waste" in their offshore SIVs. Trusting the mathematical models of their brilliant quants, they did very little "due diligence" on their own to assess the underlying risk of default. Since the models were incapable of addressing large deviations from historical patterns, however, the entire edifice predictably collapsed when housing prices dropped dramatically and borrowers began to default on their loans in unprecedented numbers in 2006.[42]

Much of this activity took place out of public view in the closed and largely unregulated world of hedge funds and investment banks.[43] The investment banks were subject to modest debt-to-equity requirements that SEC promulgated to protect shareholders from fraud. At the urging of the "big five" investment banks, however, SEC in April 2004 relaxed the requirements to allow investment banks to use their models to set their own minimum capital reserves. As the banks poured more and more resources into mortgage-backed securities, leverage rose dramatically from debt-to-equity ratios of 12:1 to ratios of 30–40:1. With capital reserves at historic lows, the investment banks were in no position to survive the crisis of confidence that hit the industry in the late summer of 2008.[44]

The credit rating agencies (CRAs) were also subject to SEC's light regulatory oversight. Because the CRAs were paid by the investment banks whose securities they rated, they were vulnerable to pressure to keep their ratings high. The investment banks took full advantage of the situation by pitting company against company in another race-to-the-bottom for the millions of dollars in fees that came with being selected to rate an investment bank's securities. The SEC had no problem with this obvious conflict of interest. Although the purchasers of highly rated mortgage-backed securities assumed that the rating agencies were combing through the investment banks' due diligence reports and the mortgage companies' loan documentation to assess default risks, they too relied on mathematical models that assumed that home prices would continually increase and default rates would remain at the very low rates of the 1990s.[45]

Long after the cows were out of the barn, Congress enacted the Credit Rating Agency Reform Act of 2006. This toothless statute required the rating agencies to allow SEC to examine their models and to disclose conflicts of interest and the histories of their ratings to investors. A provision strictly prohibiting SEC from regulating in any way the "substance of the credit ratings or the procedures and methodologies" that the credit rating agencies employed, however, deprived the new law of any substantive bite. SEC did very little to implement its new authority, and the agencies were back to their old tricks within two years.[46]

After Congress enacted the CFMAct of 2000, no federal agency regulated over-the-counter trading in complex derivatives. Banks hedged against risky CDO acquisitions by purchasing insurance or credit default swaps. Charging large premiums for what their models assured them were miniscule risks, insurance companies covered a large percentage of potential claims with credit default swaps. Missing from this rosy scenario, however, was the uncomfortable fact that many of the hedge funds that flourished during the early 2000s as counterparties to credit default swaps were in no position to deliver on the promised payouts if the underlying debt obligations did turn sour. Although these arrangements posed a serious risk to the global financial system, they did not have to be disclosed to government officials charged with protecting against systemic risk.[47]

The person in the best position to spotlight the connection between lax regulation and the impending financial meltdown and to do something about it was Timothy Geithner. A protégé of Clinton Administration Treasury Secretaries Robert Rubin and Lawrence H. Summers, both of whom were laissez faire minimalists when it came to regulating the financial markets, Geithner became the governor of the Federal Reserve Bank of New York in the midst of the boom market for over-the-counter derivatives. As Fed Chairman Alan Greenspan sang the praises of derivatives, Geithner forged unusually tight social alliances with many of Wall Street's most prominent movers and shakers. His light regulatory touch aligned nicely with their economic interests. Even after an internal Fed review of the capacity of bank holding companies to withstand the stresses of an economic downturn sent a clear warning, Geithner did not urge Greenspan to raise minimum capital requirements for bank holding companies.[48] The predictable outcome was the worst systemic banking crisis since the Great Depression.

LIMITED ACCOUNTABILITY

Although the TILAct and HOEPAct empowered both the Fed and the Federal Trade Commission (FTC) to bring civil and criminal enforcement actions against violators of the Fed's predatory lending regulations, enforcement was quite spotty during the Laissez Faire Revival. For much of that time, FTC devoted the bulk of its dwindling enforcement resources to voluntary compliance agreements. During the 1990s, FTC and the Justice Department conducted two major enforcement initiatives aimed at curbing predatory lending practices by mortgage companies, most of which resulted in settlements in which the companies paid small fines and promised to do better in the future.[49] As the abuses continued into the 2000s, FTC began to take on much larger companies. In March 2002, for example, First Alliance Mortgage Co. entered into a settlement agreement with FTC, six states, and several groups of private litigants under which it agreed to pay up to $60 million in restitution, $20 million of which was to come from the personal assets of its founder and CEO. Even these more potent actions, however, had little overall effect on irresponsible practices in the highly lucrative home equity lending business.[50]

Federal prosecutors were very reluctant to indict large lending institutions and investment banks because it was extremely difficult to prove criminal intent on the part of a corporation. Investment banks were one step removed from the overt fraud of mortgage banks and brokers and could plausibly claim to be ignorant of their illegal activities. Such cases also involved complex accounting and business judgment decisions that required expert testimony and massive document reviews. In August 2008, the Justice Department instructed prosecutors to consider the economic health of corporations in deciding whether to indict out of concern for the interests of innocent employees who could lose their jobs if an indictment caused the company to go bankrupt. Consequently, less than a handful of scofflaws were indicted for the blatant criminal activity that brought on the financial crisis, and none were convicted.[51]

THE CONSEQUENCES

When Jennifer and Eric Hinz exchanged the fixed-rate 30-year mortgage on their home for an adjustable rate mortgage with initial monthly payments that were about half the previous amounts, the mortgage broker convinced them that they were getting a very good deal. He failed to tell them that the bank would be adding interest payments of about $600 per month to the loan principal and that the one percent teaser rate would soon balloon to 7.68 percent. But the extra cash was a welcome addition to the family's income flow. A year later, however, Jennifer and Eric were facing a very different situation. Their mortgage payments were much higher than they could afford, and they faced the prospect of steadily increasing monthly payments for the foreseeable future. Refinancing the new loan was out of the question, because they could not pay the required $15,000 in up-front fees. Jennifer was convinced that the couple "got totally screwed," but the law did not provide a remedy.[52]

Over the next two years, the consequences of the steady erosion of legal protections from predatory lending during the Laissez Faire Revival became painfully apparent. A vast financial network that was based to a remarkable degree on loans like the one that "screwed" the Hinz family began to collapse of its own weight as thousands of similarly situated families failed to make their monthly payments. Before long, foreclosures outnumbered new home loans in some parts of the country. Elderly borrowers who were persuaded to take out home equity loans faced eviction from homes their families had owned for generations. Predatory lending crippled entire communities as abandoned homes fell into disrepair and became havens for vagrants and drug dealers.[53] The losses extended to the pension funds and municipalities that relied on the credit rating agencies when they purchased mortgage-backed securities for their portfolios. All of this unnecessary suffering was a direct consequence of the deregulatory policies that federal policymakers implemented during the Laissez Faire Revival, a point that even prominent Chicago law and economics scholar Richard A. Posner later acknowledged.[54]

It would take an unprecedented infusion of cash and subsidized loans by the United States government to stave off a complete financial meltdown and begin the process of purging the financial circulatory system of the toxins that it had absorbed from years of irresponsible conduct by lenders, mortgage brokers, appraisal companies, investment banks, credit rating agencies, and hedge funds. In the meantime, the financial meltdown of 2008 had a devastating impact on the U.S. economy, which contracted by around 4 percent. On paper, financial institutions lost more than a trillion dollars. Yet, even as the federal government shoveled billions of dollars into the coffers of failing Wall Street banks, the banks were paying their executives over $18 billion in bonuses for work done during what was clearly a very bad year for those institutions. For example, Goldman Sachs paid out almost $11 billion in compensation in 2008 while the company was benefiting from $8.1 billion of federal bailout money that AIG channeled to Goldman to cover 100 percent of its credit default swap obligations. AIG itself paid huge bonuses to its executives and feted favored employees at a weeklong retreat at a resort that cost $442,000.[55]

CONCLUSIONS

The mortgage market collapse of the mid-2000s should have come as a surprise to no one. The savings and loan and Continental Bank crises of the 1980s had already demonstrated that reducing the stringency of the rules and minimizing oversight and enforcement of financial institutions inevitably leads to meltdowns. If history alone was insufficient to put Congress and the agencies on notice of the coming crisis, they received repeated warnings from knowledgeable public servants. In seventeen separate appearances before congressional committees between 1996 and 1999, CFTC chairwoman Brooksley Born warned that unregulated derivatives posed a serious threat to the entire economic system. She was pooh-poohed by Alan Greenspan, Larry Summers, and a Republican-dominated Congress. Later, FDIC chairperson Sheila C. Bair's calls for greater transparency of the over-the-counter markets in CDOs also fell on deaf ears as Wall Street bankers plowed on full-speed-ahead.[56]

The financial meltdown was a bipartisan meltdown. The DIDMCAct was enacted during the Carter Administration, and the Glass-Steagall Act was repealed during the Clinton Administration. The leadership of both parties accepted the efficient market hypothesis and allowed Wall Street to develop ever more complex financial products on the foolish assumption that they were freeing up capital for productive uses. In fact, the Wall Street banks were simply enriching themselves at the expense of investors from around the world who, like the government regulators, could not comprehend the impenetrable algorithms that the investment banks' quants (with the help of the credit rating agencies) created to spin the dross of subprime mortgages into the gold of AAA-rated bonds.[57]

None of the executives who made billions of dollars during the run-up had the grace to apologize for the mess they left when the bubble burst. Indeed, many of the key players could not think of anything that they would have done differently. Instead, they denied responsibility and pointed the finger at other companies, unanticipated market forces, and even the press as causes of the meltdown. The meltdown did not, however, signal the end of Wall Street as we know it. The laissez faire minimalist ethos still pervades the firms that survived the meltdown, and they have only gotten larger and more dominant, secure in the knowledge that the government will bail them out again the next time.[58]

14

———————•◆•———————

CONSUMER PROTECTION

As modern mass production technologies and the "great compression" of the postwar period enabled average Americans to purchase more automobiles, appliances, and other consumer products, it became readily apparent that defectively designed and manufactured products could kill and maim innocent people. Although reputational considerations gave manufacturers a natural incentive to produce safe products, safety often played second fiddle to style and price considerations. The Consumer Product Safety Commission (CPSC) is responsible for protecting consumers from dangerous consumer products ranging from children's toys to all-terrain vehicles. The FTC has broad-ranging jurisdiction to protect consumers' pocketbooks from unfair and deceptive trade practices. Its writ runs to a huge universe of topics ranging from used cars to funeral homes and a wide variety of practices ranging from telemarketing to bogus loan modifications.

THE POTENTIAL

The Consumer Product Safety Act of 1972 created an independent 5-member Consumer Product Safety Commission and empowered it to promulgate standards and labeling requirements "reasonably necessary" to protect consumers from "unreasonable" risks posed by the products subject to its jurisdiction. The statute contained a novel procedural device, called the "offeror process," under which consumer groups or companies could offer to draft standards to address particular product hazards and the agency could then use the draft as the basis for a rulemaking. It further empowered CPSC to ban dangerous products when standards would not adequately protect the public and to order recalls of products that presented a "substantial product hazard."[1]

183

In addition to its new statutory authority, CPSC also assumed responsibility for implementing several older product safety statutes that empowered it to prescribe labels for products containing listed hazardous substances, establish flammability standards for clothing and other fabrics used around the home, require special packaging material for household products containing hazardous substances, and prescribe warning labels for toys and games used by young children.[2] The combination of authorities put CPSC in a good position to be the public's primary protector from the hazards posed by modern consumer products. For example, in 1992, the Commission promulgated a standard requiring new automatic garage door openers to employ one of three fail-safe technologies to prevent them from crushing children. And in 1998, it negotiated a voluntary standard under which manufacturers of baby strollers incorporated a new technology that prevented hundreds of injuries to young children by preventing occupied baby strollers from descending staircases.[3]

Reacting to consumer group demands for greater protection from worthless warranties, Congress enacted the Magnuson-Moss Warranty–Federal Trade Commission Improvement Act of 1975 (Magnuson-Moss Act). The statute authorized the Federal Trade Commission (FTC) to write regulations governing the disclosure and content of warranties for consumer products, and it specified with some particularity the factors that the agency had to consider in writing the new rules. But it also empowered the agency to promulgate "trade regulation rules" governing "unfair and deceptive trade practices."[4] The new law turned the moribund FTC into a powerful agency with the authority to protect consumers from a wide variety of unfair and deceitful trade practices that posed significant risks to their bank accounts. For example, the Commission reacted to scam artists preying on consumer demand for environmentally friendly products with "Green Guides" for advertising such products. In October 2010, the agency updated the guidelines to address an emerging "carbon offset" market that had a huge potential for consumer fraud.[5]

THE REALITY

Neither agency met the expectations of the drafters of their Public Interest Era statutes. Before they even got a good start on implementing their new authorities, a strong attack on both agencies from the business community's lobbyists and the conservative media echo chamber aided by constant pummeling from conservative think tanks persuaded Congress to amend the laws to make it more difficult for them to take protective action. As the Laissez Faire Revival continued apace, new agency leaders reined in their staffs and switched from enforceable regulations to voluntary approaches. CPSC moved away from proactive rulemaking and focused more on retroactive recalls of products that had already caused harm. FTC returned to its familiar case-by-case approach of filing individual complaints against especially egregious business practices.

WRITING THE RULES

Writing the Rules at FTC. In the years immediately following the Magnuson-Moss Act's enactment, Congress consistently increased the agency's budget. In an extraordinary surge of activity, FTC during the Ford Administration proposed fifteen major trade regulation rules on a broad range of topics, including hearing aids, funeral practices, and used cars.[6] When Michael Pertschuk took over the FTC chairmanship at the outset of the Carter Administration, the agency's aggressive young staffers recognized that they had a kindred spirit at the helm. As a powerful aide to the Senate Commerce Committee, Pertschuk had played a major role in enacting the statute, and he was chomping at the bit to put its new powers to effective use. By the mid-point of the Carter Administration, FTC was managing several high-profile rulemaking hearings that provided ideal forums for the affected industries, some of which were tightly woven into the fabric of local communities, to complain about burdensome FTC regulations.[7]

By far the most controversial FTC initiative was the so-called kid-vid rulemaking that it conducted in response to demands from consumer groups for a regulation preventing food and candy manufacturers from targeting young children in television advertising. Finding that the average child was exposed to 21,000 commercials a year, more than a third of which hawked food and soft drink products, the Commission concluded that regulation was necessary to protect the dental health of children from the effects of sugary foods. It therefore proposed to ban all advertising targeting children and most advertising for sugared foods aimed at audiences containing a "significant proportion" of children. Because it directly affected broadcasters, advertisers, food manufacturers, retailers, and any other industry that might find itself subject to an FTC "unfairness" determination, the kid-vid proposal "woke the sleeping giant." The business community spent millions of dollars on advertising campaigns attacking the proposal as "regulatory overkill." The *Washington Post*, which owned several radio and television stations, dealt the agency a severe blow with an editorial entitled "The FTC as National Nanny" in which it called the proposed regulation a "preposterous intervention." The steady drumbeat of criticism rapidly undermined public support for all of the agency's consumer protection efforts.[8]

In mid-1979, the U.S. Chamber of Commerce headed an intense lobbying campaign to persuade Congress to take away some of FTC's recently acquired rulemaking powers. No member of Congress could ignore the shrill Chamber-generated complaints from business owners in their districts about the intrusiveness of the federal bureaucracy. The agency was powerless to launch a counterattack, because FTC staffers were prohibited by statute from lobbying, and consumer activists were no match for the well-financed industry effort.[9] The Federal Trade Commission Improvement Act of 1980 (FTCIAct) left FTC's authority to regulate unfair and deceptive trade practices intact, but subjected all FTC rules to a formal cost-benefit analysis. It also prohibited the agency from promulgating any rules for commercial advertising under its authority to regulate "unfair" trade practices for three years.[10]

The Commission got the message. It terminated the kid-vid rulemaking and narrowed or terminated several other pending rulemaking initiatives. The only proposal that survived into the 1980s was a rule regulating egregious practices by funeral homes, and it was significantly watered down. The agency was especially reluctant to launch new rulemaking initiatives that might subject it to further congressional scrutiny. Instead of issuing generally applicable rules to address emerging problems, the agency returned to case-by-case enforcement against individual companies.[11]

President Reagan appointed James C. Miller III, a long-time advocate of regulatory reform, to chair the Commission. During the Carter Administration, Miller had been the co-director of the American Enterprise Institute's Center for the Study of Government Regulation. To direct the Bureau of Consumer Protection, Miller appointed Timothy Muris, a brash young attorney who, like Miller, believed in eliminating "needlessly adversarial relations with the business community."[12] Miller and Muris quickly terminated many pending rulemaking initiatives, revised the remaining proposals to be less burdensome, and raised the bar for issuing new rules. The agency initiated only two significant new rulemakings during the Reagan years, both of which were deregulatory in nature. Instead of rulemaking, the agency throughout the Reagan and George H. W. Bush years continued to rely on its highly discretionary "case-by-case" approach to correcting specific egregious abuses. To the consternation of consumer activists, the agency's approach to consumer protection did not change significantly during the Clinton Administration.[13]

President George W. Bush's choice for FTC Chairman was none other than Timothy Muris. Although Muris assured the business community that FTC would avoid "cumbersome rule making designed to transform entire industries," he launched a successful legislative initiative to limit abuse by telemarketing companies. When Muris resigned in May 2004 to return to teaching, President Bush appointed a Washington, D.C. antitrust attorney, Deborah P. Majoris, to replace him. At the end of an undistinguished four years, Majoris resigned to become Vice-President and General Counsel of Proctor & Gamble Co. The agency failed to promulgate any regulations of any significance under Muris and Majoris.[14]

Writing the Rules at CPSC. The CPSC's first chairman, Richard O. Simpson, was a consumer advocate who believed that the agency could make a substantial dent in the 15–25 percent of consumer accidents that were caused by unnecessary product hazards. He did not anticipate, however, that his new agency would be seriously underfunded or that it would run into judicial roadblocks. During its first three years, the Commission received more than 200 petitions for rulemaking, many from the regulated industries. Lacking adequate staff to separate the serious from the trivial petitions, the Commission soon amassed a considerable backlog of unanswered petitions that in turn generated criticism from consumer groups and their allies in Congress. The agency's most significant early rulemaking, a regulation setting safety standards for lawn mowers, generated such a powerful outcry from the industry that Congress passed an appropriations rider requiring the agency to weaken the standard.[15]

After a series of congressional hearings at which angry representatives of the business community pummeled the struggling agency, Congress enacted the Consumer Product Safety Commission Improvement Act of 1976 (CPSCIAct), which required CPSC to give the industry at least 150 days to "offer" a voluntary alternative to a rulemaking proposal before publishing it in the *Federal Register* and to terminate the rulemaking if the industry plan was acceptable. The amendments also prohibited CPSC from disclosing information about a product's dangers before giving the manufacturer an opportunity to argue that the information would mislead consumers or would reveal protected trade secrets.[16] These debilitating changes hobbled the agency's rulemaking power and made it more difficult for the agency to justify protective interventions.

At the outset of the Carter Administration, the *Washington Post* accurately described CPSC as "an agency tied up in knots." It had spent a large proportion of its very limited resources addressing trivial risks like pool slides in response to industry petitions while ignoring serious hazards like carcinogenic insulation and flammable furniture fabrics.[17] President Carter appointed two strong consumer advocates to empty seats on the Commission and elevated one of them to the chairmanship. The new chairperson, Susan B. King, a former congressional aide, restored staff morale, narrowed the agency's priority list to 24 initiatives, and began to shift its focus to product recalls and outright bans on especially hazardous products. As the agency assumed a more activist role, however, the business community launched another counterattack. The Chamber of Commerce complained that a spate of product recalls was increasing consumer prices and contributing to inflation. Although King dismissed the inflation argument as a "bogus issue," she modified her previous opposition to voluntary standards, pointing out that the starving agency lacked "the manpower for doing anything else." By the end of the Carter Administration, regulatory initiatives had slowed to a trickle.[18]

The Reagan Administration initially supported the Heritage Foundation's recommendation that Congress simply abolish CPSC, but it soon joined the Chamber of Commerce's more realistic efforts to eliminate the agency's independent status and subject it to White House control.[19] In late 1981, Congress enacted amendments to the Consumer Product Safety Act that made it even more difficult for the agency to promulgate product safety rules. Among other things, the amendments provided that a product safety standard could be issued only if its benefits bore "a reasonable relationship to its costs" and it imposed the "least burdensome" requirement necessary to address the relevant risk. The combined effect of the 1981 amendments and severe budget cuts during the first term of the Reagan Administration was to reduce CPSC's regulatory output to zero. The agency also reduced its data collection system by half, thereby depriving it of the information it needed to identify candidates for future rulemaking initiatives.[20]

President Reagan's first pick to chair CPSC was Nancy H. Steorts, a public relations consultant who listed hosting two candlelight dinners during the inauguration as her "government experience." She soon joined Carter Administration holdovers to initiate several rulemakings, including a controversial ban on urea formaldehyde insulation. While consumer groups were pleasantly surprised by Steorts's commitment to the agency's statutory mission, this was not the sort of regulatory relief that the business community had in mind.[21] Steorts resigned in December 1984 after the White House signaled she would not be reappointed, and President Reagan elevated Terrence Scanlon, a conservative Democrat, to the chairmanship. Scanlon fiercely resisted the other members' efforts to steer the agency in a slightly more activist direction.[22]

Things only got worse in 1986 when Congress defunded two of the agency's five positions, thereby turning it into a three-member body that required all three members for a quorum. The dysfunctional agency did not issue a single product safety standard between 1983 and the end of the Reagan Administration. The one rulemaking that it initiated, a ban on a deadly foot-long, metal-tipped toy dart, was brought to completion by Congress after the Commission failed to respond to the highly publicized pleas of the anguished father of a 7-year-old who was killed by a stray dart as she played with her dolls. Scanlon resigned the chairmanship soon after the 1988 election to become the vice-president and treasurer of the Heritage Foundation, the institution from which he took his cues while serving on the Commission.[23] During the George H. W. Bush Administration, the "emasculated" agency suffered additional budget cuts and was forced to move to an apartment building overlooking a grocery store and a bowling alley. Lacking a quorum for much of the time, it went into a state of suspended animation.[24]

President Clinton appointed Ann Brown, a former vice-chairperson of Consumers Union, to head CPSC. A strong critic of CPSC during the Reagan-Bush years, she was determined to "jump start" the agency. She was severely hampered, however, by a dearth of resources, a problem that President Clinton only exacerbated by cutting the agency's budget request by 10 percent in FY1994. Further constrained by two conservative holdover commissioners, Brown decided to take the case for product safety directly to the people. She made herself available to the media as often as possible to educate the public about the often hidden risks of ordinary products. At the same time, the agency initiated four new rulemakings, three of which were designed to protect infants and children from hazards that had become painfully apparent. Although the struggling agency was not a direct target of the regulatory reformers during the Gingrich Congress, Brown spent much of her time responding to dubious "horror stories" like the erroneous assertion that CPSC would soon be promulgating a regulation requiring five-gallon buckets to have holes in them to prevent infants from drowning.[25]

With Brown's departure soon after the 2000 election, President George W. Bush appointed former New Mexico Attorney General Harold Stratton to the chairmanship. A committed laissez faire minimalist, Stratton had recently created a conservative public interest law group. He spent much of his time at CPSC taking expenses-paid trips to exotic locations to speak to industry groups. When he resigned in 2006 to join a Washington law firm, the two remaining commissioners once again lacked a quorum and were therefore powerless to promulgate rules or order recalls. The low point for the agency came when its only full-time toy tester retired after 25 years, leaving no heir apparent to analyze toy hazards in the agency's rat-infested testing laboratory.[26]

Nancy Nord, who became acting chairperson when Stratton resigned, had worked for Eastman Kodak and the Chamber of Commerce before becoming a commissioner in May 2005. She continued Stratton's practice of traveling at industry expense, and she resisted attempts by the Democrat-controlled Congress to double the agency's budget. By late 2006, the agency was engaging in seven voluntary standard-setting negotiations for every mandatory standard that it initiated.[27] In response to a constant stream of headlines about lead-contaminated imported toys, however, the Bush Administration in 2008 reluctantly accepted a $17 million increase in CPSC's budget, the largest in 20 years. Still, the budget remained at only half its Carter Administration level.[28]

FOREGONE PROTECTION

Massive changes in the means of production and techniques for marketing consumer products would have posed major challenges to a fully funded CPSC and FTC headed by committed regulators. In the 1970s, 90 percent of the toys sold in the U.S. were manufactured domestically, and mass marketing consisted mainly of television advertising and catalogue sales. By 2007, only 13 percent of the toys sold in the U.S. were made in this country, and the internet had revolutionized the way consumers considered and made new purchases. Yet despite these challenges, CPSC and FTC remained reluctant regulators. Both agencies tended to wait until the evidence was overwhelming and outside pressures had grown intolerable before taking proactive regulatory action. When they did act on their own, it was often to ease the burdens on the regulated industries.[29]

Childhood Obesity. Between 1980 and 2008, obesity rates among children between 6 and 11 rose from 6.8 to 19.6 percent. Many studies and expert reports published during the mid-2000s concluded that aggressive marketing by food manufacturers on television, on the internet, and in video games had played a powerful role in children's food preferences and, consequently, in the childhood obesity crisis. Of the 40,000 television ads that the average child saw every year, fully half were for food, and most of those were for high-calorie sweetened cereals, snack foods, and beverages. "Product placement" advertising (in which sponsored products are subtly featured in the programming itself), sponsorships at sporting events, and celebrity endorsements interfered with the ability of children to process the proffered information and view it skeptically. Food companies even used "educational" children's books and teaching materials as vehicles for pushing their products.[30]

The food industry borrowed a page from the tobacco industry's playbook to fund research raising doubts about the incidence of obesity, the connection between obesity and disease, the relative roles of consumption and exercise in causing obesity, and the connection between food marketing and obesity. It also contributed millions of dollars to professional nutrition associations to ensure that it had a seat at the table as they developed nutrition guidelines. Conservative academics and think tanks provided "independent" confirmation for the industry's message that obesity was solely a matter of personal and parental responsibility. At an AEI-sponsored conference titled "Obesity, Individual Responsibility, and Public Policy," University of Chicago law professor Richard Epstein argued that the solution to the obesity problem was to permit employers, schools, and insurance companies to "viciously discriminate against any person who is obese."[31]

Despite the growing consensus in the scientific community, neither Congress nor the FTC acted to curb the food industry's contributions to the mounting childhood obesity crisis. FTC's limited authority to regulate advertising did not clearly extend to regulating marketing that was not deceptive. Furthermore, neither Congress nor the FTC could regulate advertising too aggressively without running afoul the Supreme Court's recent holdings on the First Amendment rights of corporations to engage in commercial speech. The George W. Bush Administration joined the industry in framing the obesity issue as one of personal responsibility and leapt to the industry's defense when it came under attack from consumer groups.[32]

Internet Privacy. An inadvertent release of a large number of Social Security numbers in 1996 shined a light on a tiny industry of "look up" companies that gathered information on consumers' purchasing preferences from commercial websites and sold it to subscribers who used that information to target individuals with advertisements as they used the internet. In December 1997, FTC formally endorsed voluntary industry guidelines on such "behavioral targeting" that made companies who sold information on their viewers' preferences to other companies responsible for ensuring that the purchasers were legitimate.[33] By May 2000, FTC had concluded that the voluntary approach was simply not working, and it asked Congress for legislation empowering it to promulgate and enforce "fair information principles" for internet companies and to regulate how information gathered on the internet was sold to third parties. With Microsoft and EBay taking the lead, the industry launched a major lobbying offensive against the threatened legislation. AEI published a study predicting that it would cost the industry at least $30 billion to comply with the proposed statute. When the Clinton Administration weighed in on the side of the industry, any hope for legislation to address behavioral targeting vanished. In October 2001, incoming FTC Chairman Muris formally withdrew the agency's request for legislation.[34] In the meantime, behavioral targeting continued unabated.

Flammable Fabrics. One of Chairperson Susan King's early initiatives was a November 1978 proposal for a flammability standard for furniture fabrics to prevent sofas and chairs from igniting when exposed to smoldering cigarettes. The agency estimated that 800 people per year died from such fires. The agency

noted that half of the fabric used on furniture already complied with the proposed standard, and the industry could bring most of the remaining fabrics into
compliance at a modest cost of less than $10 per unit. Nevertheless, the agency
failed to finalize the proposal during the Reagan and George H. W. Bush Administrations. Early in the Clinton Administration, CPSC initiated another
round of comment on the proposal, but it slowed the process once again to
wait out the Gingrich Congress. The Commission revived the project in 1999,
only to be forced by an appropriations rider to put the initiative on hold once
again pending further study of the health risks of fire-retardant chemicals.[35]
Based on the staff's conclusion that "[n]umerous new technologies, products
and modern equipment" had been developed in the 50 years since the original
standard went into place, CPSC in May 2002 solicited still another round of
public comment. In March 2008, the Commission published a standard based
on more recent fire repellant technologies. While the agency tarried, fires attributable to upholstered furniture had killed more than 3,600 people, injured
around 6,500, and caused more than $1.5 billion in damage between 1994 and
2008.[36]

   Chinese Imports. During the late 1990s global competition induced American toy manufacturers to "outsource" most production to facilities in countries
that paid low wages and were not subject to strong worker safety and environmental laws. CPSC's miniscule import inspectorate of 11 full-time employees
could not inspect more than a tiny fraction of the tens of millions of imported
products subject to its jurisdiction that entered through the nation's 300 ports
of entry every year. The agency devoted a single inspector to Los Angeles area
ports, and another inspector showed up at the busy New York City harbor only
two or three times a year. Although it had the authority to require foreign manufacturers to consent to inspections of their plants, CPSC maintained no inspectors at overseas facilities.[37]

   In 2007, the nation suffered a major "Chinese import" crisis as one after
another of the nation's major toy manufacturers recalled millions of defective
products that had been manufactured by Chinese companies under their supervision. The massive recalls included 17.6 million toys containing excessive lead,
9.5 million toys containing dislodgeable magnets, and 4.2 million packages of
"Aqua Dots" laced with a powerful hallucinogen. Press coverage of the crisis
highlighted weak Chinese consumer protection laws, poor enforcement, government corruption, and a general lack of accountability on the part of Chinese
manufacturers.[38] China responded by summarily rescinding the export licenses
of around 750 toymakers. CPSC initially took little action to stem the tide of
defective imported toys, and it actually contributed to the problem by covering

up the information that it received about defective foreign imports. The agency ultimately adopted a vague "four-point" plan to increase import safety and entered into an agreement with Chinese officials under which they agreed to ban the use of lead in toys. At the same time, the George W. Bush Administration insisted that CPSC needed no additional resources to police the rising tide of imports.[39]

Ineffectual Recalls. By the mid-1980s, CPSC had virtually abandoned rulemaking to devote its dwindling resources to recalls of clearly dangerous products like arsenic-coated candy Easter chicks. Even those modest but essential undertakings gradually declined during the first few years of the Reagan Administration. The emphasis on recalls continued through the George H. W. Bush and early Clinton years. After Chairwoman Ann Brown revamped the recall process in 1994, the number of recalls picked up substantially, but recalls declined again during the George W. Bush Administration before increasing slightly in 2006.[40] The "overwhelming majority" of recalls were voluntary because the agency lacked the staff to support mandatory recalls. This gave manufacturers the upper hand in negotiations with the agency over the terms and conditions of the recalls. Many recalls were so vaguely worded that they were confusing to consumers and retailers alike. Some were so watered down that they did not convince consumers of the importance of returning the recalled item. Others subtly placed most of the burden of fixing the problem on the consumer.[41]

LIMITED ACCOUNTABILITY

Accountability at CPSC. CPSC's enforcement presence declined significantly with the heavy budget cuts of the early Reagan years. Between 1981 and 1983, CPSC inspections dropped by 45 percent, recalls declined by 66 percent, and injury investigations fell by 28 percent. The agency's ability to enforce recalls also received a significant setback when a court of appeals held that it lacked the power to impose civil penalties administratively. Reagan-appointed commissioners delivered a body blow to the agency's enforcement efforts when they turned a cold shoulder on a request from its Compliance Director for more authority to seek court orders granting inspectors access to establishments suspected of violating voluntary standards.[42]

With CPSC lacking any credible enforcement presence, manufacturers had little incentive to comply with its regulations and recalls. Although CPSC estimated that 120 children per year were being killed in accidents involving all-terrain vehicles, for example, its tiny enforcement staff was powerless to punish retailers who routinely ignored its rule prohibiting their sale for use by children under 16. An October 2004 investigation by *Consumer Reports* discovered retail shelves filled with products that violated product safety standards or had been recalled but not removed. One company imported more than 111,000 unsafe toys between 1994 and 2002 and received 16 "letters of advice" from CPSC requesting corrective action without suffering a single penalty.[43]

Accountability at FTC. Soon after taking over as FTC chairman at the outset of the Reagan Administration, Jim Miller told the staff to stop enforcing the agency's truth-in-advertising requirements. Convinced that consumers might desire to purchase defective products if the price were right, Miller also questioned the utility of requiring sellers of products to investigate and disclose defects. Not surprisingly, deceptive trade practice enforcement declined precipitously.[44] Enforcement picked up slightly during the George H. W. Bush Administration as the agency took an aggressive approach to ill-defined or bogus "environmental" claims. During the first term of the Clinton Administration, FTC attempted to head off criticism from the Gingrich Congress by stepping up its efforts to negotiate voluntary compliance agreements with violators, rather than suing them for civil penalties and injunctive relief.[45] When the threat from Congress diminished in the late 1990s, the agency filed actions against dozens of violators of its recently promulgated telemarketing regulations. But the fines it collected were small change for the burgeoning telemarketing industry.[46]

During the George W. Bush Administration, FTC responded to strong public demand for government to protect personal privacy with a number of politically popular enforcement actions. It continued to crack down on violators of the highly popular telemarketing regulations. In August 2004, it conducted a major crackdown on known email "spammers" that resulted in more than 100 arrests and the seizure of dozens of computers. And in July 2005, the agency entered into a $1.2 million settlement with eight companies that hired spammers to send pornographic emails. None of these actions involved major corporate actors, but they did help rid the internet of some of its most flagrant bottom dwellers.[47]

THE CONSEQUENCES

After scientific advances made powerful "rare earth" magnets widely available at low cost, toy manufacturers used them in a variety of popular toys. The toy designers gave little thought to what might happen if the magnets became dislodged from their casings and were swallowed by small children. Family physicians soon learned that the magnetic attraction could cause two or more swallowed magnets to adhere to each other through a child's intestines with forces strong enough to tear through the intestinal walls, thereby exposing the internal organs to intestinal bacteria. This "magnet disease" was especially difficult to diagnose, because its symptoms mimicked those of any intestinal disorder.

As sales of magnetic toys skyrocketed during the early 2000s, CPSC and toy manufacturers received a steady stream of reports of emergency surgeries needed to remove rare earth magnets from the intestines of children. When a 20-month-old boy who swallowed several magnets from a MEGA Brands "Magnetix" building set died of the resulting injuries, CPSC determined that a recall was appropriate. Rather than order a mandatory recall, the agency took three months to persuade the company to conduct a voluntary recall. In the meantime, as required by its amended statute, the agency made no mention of the risks posed by other magnet-containing toys, and four more children were hospitalized for magnet-induced injuries. The "recall" consisted of little more than a promise to replace any returned sets with sets containing more secure magnets and instructions to retailers to attach a sticker to the existing products containing a new CPSC-approved warning. During the first four months of the recall, the company received replacement requests for only 12,000 of the 3.8 million recalled sets. After another year's worth of prodding, MEGA Brands reluctantly expanded the recall, but it made no effort to contact individual retailers. By then, rare earth magnets had caused at least one death and 33 serious injuries.[48]

Every year around 33 million Americans are injured by consumer products and approximately 27,000 people die from those injuries. Far too often, the victims are children. The number of toy-related injuries jumped from around 130,000 in 1996 to over 220,000 in 2006.[49] The Magnetix recall is just one example of many instances in which CPSC has not identified a product risk until it was too late, allowed manufacturers to engage in ineffectual voluntary recalls, and taken weak regulatory action that was unlikely to prevent future deaths and injuries. In November 2007, for example, CPSC announced a recall of more than 4 million packages of a popular Chinese-made arts-and-crafts product called "Aqua Dots," because they contained a chemical that mimicked the effects of a well-known date-rape drug when ingested. By the time that the recall was announced, two children had already slipped into temporary comas.[50] And despite CPSC's modest efforts to regulate all-terrain vehicles, they caused more than 136,000 injuries requiring emergency room treatment and around 870 fatalities in 2005 alone. This represented a 24 percent increase in injuries in just four years.[51]

Manufacturers and retailers of consumer products have perfected techniques for appealing to consumers with catchy advertisements in the mainstream media. Doctors, professional nutritionists, and health agencies cannot compete with the billions of dollars per year that the food industry pays for advertisements aimed at persuading children to eat more calorie-laden food. Consequently, obesity rates in children 6–19 years old tripled from 5 to 16 percent between the late 1960s and the early 2000s. Since childhood obesity is a risk factor for adult obesity and heart disease, today's children may for the first time in two centuries have a shorter life expectancy than their parents. Despite FTC's modest efforts to protect internet privacy, the internet remains a huge and largely unregulated marketplace where deceptive advertising, bogus products, overcharging, and many other scams abound. So long as companies maintain a relatively low profile, they can dupe consumers with little risk of prosecution by FTC's tiny enforcement staff.[52]

CONCLUSIONS

As the primary protectors of consumers from deceptive and dangerous products, FTC and CPSC were responsible for defining the rules of responsibility for product manufacturers and retailers and for holding them accountable when they violated those rules. With the rapid globalization of the world economy, their rulemaking role assumed even greater importance. Yet the agencies grew leaner and less protective during the Laissez Faire Revival as they relied on the marketplace to police itself, rather than rising to the challenges of a global economy with innovative approaches to making the marketplace a safer place for consumers and their children.

CIVIL JUSTICE

As a lawful form of self-help, state tort law is the vehicle through which individual citizens protect their persons and property from invasion by private sector actors. The possibility that a jury composed of twelve representatives of the community will hold powerful corporations accountable for violating standards of conduct articulated by common law courts provides a strong incentive to act responsibly and some assurance to victims that their wrongs will be redressed.[1]

State common law serves as an institutional counterweight to a regulatory system that is too easily controlled by the very interests it is supposed to be controlling. Common law juries cannot be lobbied or captured by well-endowed special interests, and there are no "revolving doors" to the jury box. Regulatory agencies are supposed to be politically accountable to the president and to congressional committees. Judges and juries, by contrast, are supposed to be neutral decisionmakers in an institutional setting that was designed to be politically unaccountable. The wide disparity in resources available to corporations and individual citizens does not affect decisionmaking outcomes as heavily in the civil justice system as in the regulatory system. Box 15.1 provides a few representative examples of the hundreds of instances in which the civil justice system has held federally regulated companies accountable to the people they harmed, often with verdicts and settlements that far exceeded any fine that the regulatory agencies could have imposed.

During the Public Interest Era, the American Law Institute (ALI), a 3,000-member self-perpetuating body of judges, lawyers, and law professors, recommended a strict products liability regime in its influential *Restatement (Second) of Torts*, under which manufactures of "defective products" that were "unreasonably dangerous" would be held strictly liable without regard to fault. By 1976, the courts in 41 states had adopted some form of strict products liability,

Box 15.1

Civil Justice Remedies

Diacetyl. Attorneys for disabled workers discovered that the synthetic butter flavoring agent diacetyl caused a rare affliction (named "popcorn lung") in many of the workers exposed to it long before OSHA initiated the standard-setting process for that chemical. By December 2007, the company had paid more than $145 million in verdicts and settlements. OSHA has yet to promulgate a rule protecting workers from diacetyl.[a]

Zyprexa. Eli Lilly agreed to pay $1.2 billion to settle more than 28,500 cases brought by patients claiming that it knew that its antipsychotic drug Zyprexa could cause obesity and diabetes, but failed to warn doctors of that fact as they prescribed it for treating many forms of dementia. The drug remains on the market.[b]

Marquis Defibrillators. Medtronic Inc. paid $114.1 million to settle most of the 2,682 consolidated federal claims in which the plaintiffs alleged that it knew that its Marquis line of implantable cardiac defibrillators were capable of shorting out instead of delivering a life-preserving shock to the heart. The company recalled the defective defibrillators, but continues to market a newer version, and many of the older products remain in the bodies of patients.[c]

Metrolink Crash. The Los Angeles commuter railroad Metrolink entered into a $200 million settlement with victims of a collision between a freight train and a commuter train that occurred while the engineer was busily texting messages to admirers. At the time, FRA did not prohibit such texting.[d]

Magnetic Toys. Not long after a botched CPSC recall of toys containing small but powerful magnets, MEGA Brands settled with the families of 14 children damaged by the magnets for $13.5 million.[e]

Predatory Lenders. In March 2005, Ameriquest Mortgage Co. agreed to pay up to $50 million to settle a private class action lawsuit alleging that it had defrauded thousands of borrowers in four states. At the time, the Fed insisted that there was no need to regulate mortgage company lending practices.[f]

Food Fraud. In September 2009, Dannon paid $35 million to settle a class action lawsuit alleging that it had deceived consumers with an advertising campaign claiming that its Activa and DanActive yogurts, enhanced with a bacterium that it named "bifidus regularis," were "clinically proven" to improve digestion and enhance immunity. This and many other instances of deceptive marketing of foods escaped the attention of FDA and FTC.[g]

NOTES

a. Andrew Schneider, *Additive Found in More than 6,000 Products*, Seattle Post-Intelligencer, December 20, 2007, at A19; Stephen Labaton, *OSHA Leaves Worker Safety in Hands of Industry*, NYT, April 25, 2007, at A1.

b. *Lilly, Plaintiffs Agree to Settlement in 18,000 Claims Over Schizophrenia Drug*, 35 BNA PSLR 34 (2007); Gardiner Harris & Alex Berenson, *Settlement Called Near on Zyprexa*, NYT, January 15, 2009, at B1.

c. Kathy Shwiff, *Medtronic to Pay $114 Million in Settling Heart-Device Suits*, WSJ, December 21, 2007, at A3.

d. *New Rule Would Bar Railroad Crew Members from Using Handheld Electronic Devices*, WP, May 18, 2010, at A3; Rich Connell, *Metrolink Proposes Cash Payout*, LAT, August 26, 2010, at A1.

e. Nicholas Sasey & Nicholas Zamiska, *Mattel Does Damage Control After New Recall*, WSJ, August 15, 2007, at B1; Gretchen Morgenson, *Toy Magnets Attract Sales, and Suits*, NYT, July 15, 2007, at B1.

f. Binyamin Appelbaum, *As Subprime Lending Crisis Unfolded, Watchdog Fed Didn't Bother Barking*, WP, September 27, 2009, at A1; E. Scott Reckard & Josh Friedman, *States Follow Long Trail of Complaints Against Lender*, LAT, March 15, 2005, at A1.

g. *Dannon Settles Lawsuit Over Activa, DanActive Yogurt*, LAT, September 19, 2009, at B2.

and most had adopted the *Restatement* language. During the same period, the courts and state legislatures restricted or eliminated many defenses that companies had used since the late nineteenth century to defeat claims. The courts also extended the traditional law of trespass and nuisance to create a new body of "toxic tort" law available to neighbors of industrial facilities who suffered property loss or health-related damages due to pollution. To a far more limited extent, state legislatures rewrote the workers compensation laws that had been on the books since the Progressive Era to reflect the realities of the modern workplace and to increase benefits to offset the effects of inflation.[2]

The potential for the "class action" lawsuit to bring about social change was greatly enhanced by amendments to the Federal Rules of Civil Procedure in 1966 making it easier to structure class-based claims. As discussed in Chapter 3, class action lawsuits allow courts to hold irresponsible companies accountable when their products or activities injure a large number of people, but do not cause enough damage to any individual to justify the cost of a lawsuit. Within a decade, consumer class actions seeking to hold corporate defendants accountable for harm caused by defective products, environmental pollution, and deceptive sales practices were commonplace. Plaintiffs' attorneys used the expanded procedural tool to press novel legal claims seeking huge damage awards and "institutional" relief aimed at reducing the likelihood of future abuses.[3]

All of these changes posed a serious threat to the freedom of American companies, and they were determined to push back in every conceivable forum. In a clever turnaround, the business community framed its attempt to reverse the recent expansions of common law protections as "tort reform." It devoted hundreds of millions of dollars to a massive public relations campaign aimed at changing public attitudes toward the civil justice system with the ultimate goal of returning the common law of torts to the laissez faire benchmark of the late nineteenth century. And it opportunistically seized upon cyclical downturns in the insurance industry to generate the sense of crisis that is often necessary to support statutory change.[4]

SHAPING PUBLIC ATTITUDES

At the outset of the Laissez Faire Revival, there was not the slightest indication that ordinary citizens were dissatisfied with the American civil justice system. The first task for the business community's idea and influence infrastructures was therefore to shape public attitudes in ways that would create at least the appearance of dissatisfaction so that industry lobbyists could credibly claim that the public was demanding civil justice reform. The campaign advanced its interests in several ways. First, changed public attitudes about juries and courts enhanced the prospects for legislation at both the state and federal levels. Second, the steady drumbeat of criticism in the media sent a not-so-subtle message to elected judges that Public Interest Era reforms should be reversed. Finally, changing public attitudes could produce a jury pool that was generally more sympathetic to arguments of defense counsel in individual trials.[5]

CREATING A LITIGATION MYTHOLOGY

The bread and butter of the business community's public relations campaign was an appeal to common sense through constant repetition of well-rehearsed anecdotes that, if true, cast serious doubt on the rationality of the civil justice system. An analysis of a large sample of these "tort tales" by two political scientists noted that the stories: (1) rarely took more than three to five sentences to tell; (2) characterized plaintiffs as "morally if not legally blameworthy individuals" and defendants as "blameless, responsible, or hard working individuals or entities"; (3) featured greedy lawyers; (4) emphasized the price that such lawsuits exacted from society; and (5) suggested that the listener was probably aware of similar outrageous tales. Nearly all of the anecdotes, however, either stretched the truth or omitted critical details indicating that the lawsuits were far from frivolous.[6]

Perhaps the most widely circulated myth was the story of Stella Liebeck, the 79-year-old New Mexico sales clerk who in August 1994 won a $2.9 million judgment against McDonalds. Liebeck was in the passenger seat of her grandson's parked automobile when she put her recently purchased cup of coffee between her legs to remove the lid. As she struggled with the uncooperative lid, the coffee spilled onto her lap, was rapidly soaked up by her sweatpants, and severely burned her legs and genital area. At that time McDonald's policy was to brew coffee at between 195 and 205 degrees Fahrenheit, which was hot enough to cause disfiguring third-degree burns in seven seconds. Liebeck had to undergo several surgeries that left her permanently disfigured. At trial, the jurors were initially quite skeptical of her claim until they learned that McDonalds had received at least 700 complaints of similar instances of severe burning. It ultimately awarded Liebeck $200,000 in actual damages, but it reduced that by $40,000 after finding that her own negligence had contributed to the damage. It then award $2.7 million in punitive damages, which the judge reduced to $480,000 Liebeck eventually settled the case for less than that.[7]

The headlines following the original verdict proclaimed that Liebeck had won $3 million, and the case was featured on Jay Leno and David Letterman. Few mainstream news outlets and none of the commentators or comedians reported the virtually automatic reduction in Liebeck's punitive damages award. The Chamber of Commerce ran advertisements for weeks parodying Liebeck's "ridiculous" lawsuit, and citing it as a fine example of a civil justice system gone awry. The story was both simplified and amplified until it bore only the faintest resemblance to the actual facts. Several editorials, for example, falsely stated that Liebeck was "fumbling" for her coffee in a moving vehicle.

Hard-pressed by dwindling budgets, the mainstream media was on the lookout for easily digested capsules of information that did not require much independent verification. The tort reformers' facile portrayals of the civil justice system were specifically crafted to meet this need.[8]

The Stella Liebeck story and similar carefully crafted myths were quite effective in conveying the message that the civil justice system was badly broken. Prominent law and economics scholars who should have known better lent their credentials to the propagation of the myths. Professor Victor Schwartz, co-author of the most popular torts casebook of the 1980s, became so enthusiastic about the enterprise that he left academia to assume leadership positions in several industry-sponsored tort reform organizations. Non-academics wrote popular anecdote-filled books that nicely complemented the business community's advertising campaigns. Setting the record straight, by contrast, lacked the pizzazz of the original telling, and defending the Public Interest Era tort regime did not lend itself to thirty-second sound bites.[9]

REPEATED THEMES

The campaign to change the common law featured several constantly repeated themes, all of which were carefully designed by public relations firms to appeal to bedrock American values. At the top of the list was the core value of *personal responsibility*. Too often, they argued, people blamed others for their own misfortune.[10] A second prominent theme stressed the *freedom* of consumers to pay less for a product in exchange for accepting greater risks and of workers to accept riskier working conditions for higher pay. Allowing consumers and workers to recover damages for known risks created "moral hazard," an insurance industry term for the tendency of insured individuals to go to less effort to minimize accident costs.[11]

The corporate critics vilified *"greedy trial lawyers"* whose only goal was to enrich themselves at the expense of their clients and the corporations they sued. A special target of the tort reformers was the traditional contingency fee compensation arrangement through which attorneys agreed to represent plaintiffs, advance most of the upfront costs of litigation, and remain uncompensated in the event of loss in return for a specified percentage (typically 25–33 percent) of any resulting award. Since most injured individuals lack the resources to bear the expenses of litigation in advance, the contingency fee arrangement provided access to an otherwise inaccessible civil justice system. Since it also subjected more companies to lawsuits, the business community had no use for the arrangement.[12] A corollary was the theme of *corporate victimhood* according to which undeserving plaintiffs and their rapacious lawyers were stealing resources from innocent companies and discouraging them from developing socially useful products.[13] Thus, litigation and the threat of litigation constituted a serious *drag on the economy* as litigation wasted resources that could otherwise have been devoted to productive endeavors.[14]

Two other related themes complained of *activist judges* who had changed the rules of responsibility and *incompetent juries* who were not qualified to determine whether companies had violated those rules and to determine how much victims should be compensated for such violations. As framed by the public relations specialists, the "litigation lottery" of the civil justice "casino" yielded "jackpot justice" for a few lucky plaintiffs at the expense of all consumers. Headlines featuring multi-million-dollar punitive damages awards against well-known companies lent credibility to the claim that "runaway juries" in "judicial hellholes" were arbitrarily raiding corporate treasuries to reward undeserving plaintiffs.[15]

The tort reformers blended all of the foregoing themes into a general warning that the nation faced a "litigation crisis" that was discouraging innovation, contributing to higher prices for consumer goods, killing jobs, and leading to a general decline in American competitiveness. Because the civil justice system was all but invisible to most citizens, the idea that the nation faced a litigation crisis was a hard sell for the business community's talented image shapers, but with the help of think tanks like the Manhattan Institute, conservative talk show hosts like Rush Limbaugh, and media outlets like Fox News their message slowly penetrated the public consciousness.[16]

THE LACK OF AN EFFECTIVE RESPONSE

Defenders of the civil justice system had persuasive responses to all of these themes, many of which were firmly grounded in empirical studies. The personal responsibility argument ignored the undeniable fact that tort doctrine did demand individual responsibility through comparative negligence, product misuse, and similar doctrines that reduced or eliminated the plaintiff's award to the extent that the plaintiff's own irresponsible conduct contributed to the injury. In response to the greedy lawyer claim, defenders of the civil justice system cited empirical studies demonstrating that plaintiffs' attorneys received about the same hourly rate on average as corporate lawyers. As for the alleged drag on the economy, torts scholars pointed out that only about 10 percent of injured citizens actually filed lawsuits, and only a tiny fraction of the lawsuits resulted in trials. A far larger volume of business-versus-business lawsuits claimed a much larger share of the nation's resources.[17] Defenders of the civil justice system cited numerous empirical studies concluding that juries were not unduly sympathetic to plaintiffs and were usually quite parsimonious in award-ing punitive damages in the 10 percent of the cases in which the presiding judges allowed punitive damages at all. Finally, the activist judges theme took on a hollow ring as judges appointed by Republican presidents began to domi-nate the federal bench and the business community's candidates prevailed in state judicial elections.[18]

Once implanted in the public mind, however, the themes proved quite im-pervious to correction by empirical data and scholarly analysis. The studies de-bunking the myths were published in academic books and journals. Unlike the think tank fellows who were rewarded for connecting with the media, academic scholars lacked the time and resources necessary to rebut the tort reform themes in forums that attracted the attention of the general public. Their concern for the academic integrity of their studies precluded resort to anecdote-laden po-lemics of the sort that poured out of the think tanks. Consequently, they failed to replicate the tort reformers' moralistic appeals to shared public values.[19]

With the exception of Public Citizen, consumer and environmental groups expressed little interest in tort reform. The plaintiffs' bar had sufficient re-sources to fight back, but it devoted nearly all of them to lobbying efforts and to litigation challenging the constitutionality of tort reforms. Such forays as the American Trial Lawyers Association (ATLA) and its supporters in academia made into the public arena tended to be quite defensive in nature. They failed to make the affirmative case that a robust civil justice system was necessary to protect the public at the same time that it offered damaged victims their only ef-fective recourse against irresponsible companies. Defenders of the civil justice system were unable to create a compelling moral narrative in which corporate responsibility and accountability were at least as important to a good society as personal responsibility.[20]

CHANGING THE LAW

Like the assaults on federal regulation, the assaults on the civil justice sys-tem came in three great waves, but unlike the regulatory wars, the civil justice battles were waged at both the state and federal levels. The state campaigns were timed to correspond to the business cycles of the insurance industry where they could be characterized as responses to "insurance crises" of the late 1970s, the mid-1980s, and the early 2000s. While the ultimate goal was to return the common law to the laissez faire benchmark, the immediate aim was to discour-age lawsuits by increasing the cost of bringing them and rolling back expansive Public Interest Era tort doctrines. Thus, early tort reform initiatives targeted class action procedures, joint and several liability, contingency fees, strict products liability, liberal workers compensation awards, "noneconomic damages" for pain and suffering, and punitive damages.[21]

THE WARNING SHOTS

The initial salvo came during the last two years of the Carter Administration with the business community's loud complaints about an "explosion" in products liability litigation and the American Enterprise Institute's call for a major overhaul of workers compensation statutes to place more of the onus of accidents on workers. The Department of Commerce responded with a business-friendly "Model Uniform Product Liability Act" drafted by Professor Victor Schwartz for use at the state level.[22] But state legislatures proceeded in an ad hoc fashion. Twenty states limited contingency fees, fourteen enacted caps on noneconomic damages, and sixteen overturned recent decisions by state courts. Several states also enacted administrative changes in workers compensation law to make it more difficult for injured employees to claim benefits. A few extreme state laws even allowed defendants to beg off liability by showing that they had complied with prevailing custom in the relevant industry.[23]

THE FIRST ASSAULT

The election of Ronald Reagan provided an ideal opportunity for the business community to launch a full-scale assault on the civil justice system. The tort reformers' civil justice myths were tailor-made for the inveterate storyteller, and he relished the role. The necessary precipitating "crisis" came in the mid-1980s in the form of a rapid increase in liability insurance rates. During the early 1980s, the insurance industry had offset growing losses in investment income by increasing rates and refusing to issue or renew risky policies. It then mounted a multi-million-dollar advertising campaign to convince the public that the resulting crisis was attributable to uncertainties in the litigation climate, rather than to the industry's own foolish investment strategies. A credulous mainstream media accepted this analysis without examining whether the dramatic increases in rates were in fact matched by increased payouts on claims.[24]

The American Tort Reform Association (ATRA), an umbrella group heavily funded by the tobacco industry, coordinated the business community's lobbying efforts at the federal level and provided resources to more than forty affiliated state organizations. A separate entity, called the Product Liability Coordinating Committee (PLCC), purported to represent more than 700,000 companies and small business organizations, but its primary supporters were the U.S. Chamber of Commerce, the Business Roundtable, and the National Association of Manufacturers. An affiliated organization called the Product Liability Advisory Council (PLAC) filed amicus curiae briefs in state and federal courts. The moving force behind all three organizations was Victor Schwartz, who now worked for a major law firm representing products liability and toxic tort defendants.[25]

After his re-election in 1984, President Reagan added the bully pulpit of the presidency to the business community's efforts to reorient the civil justice system. An Interagency Tort Policy Working Group (chaired by Attorney General Ed Meese) recommended radical legislation that would have eliminated strict products liability, imposed a higher burden of proof for toxic tort plaintiffs, limited joint and several liability, capped noneconomic and punitive damages, and reduced contingency fees. Although President Reagan endorsed the bill in his 1987 State of the Union Address, it went nowhere in a Democrat-controlled Congress.[26]

In 1986, the Manhattan Institute launched its Project on Civil Justice Reform with a conference on the "liability crisis" that, it maintained, was engulfing the nation. The conference was hosted by the project leader, Walter Olson, and invited participants included University of Chicago Law School professor Richard Epstein and Peter Huber, a prominent critic of products liability law who was also an Institute fellow. Huber's 1988 book, *Liability*, made the thinly supported but heavily publicized claim that Americans paid a $300 billion annual "tort tax" on specious lawsuits. His 1991 book *Galileo's Revenge* coined the politically salient term "junk science" that became a staple of the business community's attacks on products liability and toxic tort litigation. Olsen's book, *The Litigation Explosion*, was an anecdote-laden polemic against the civil justice system in general and trial lawyers in particular. The Institute sent complimentary copies of all three books to all state and federal judges. Over the next four years, the Institute sponsored more than 20 additional meetings to develop suggestions for making the civil justice system more business-friendly, and it prepared dozens of reports, pamphlets, videos and op-eds promoting tort reform.[27]

An industry-funded organization called the American Legislative Exchange Council (ALEC) served as a national coordinator for the state initiatives. The initial battleground was Texas, where the Supreme Court had been especially aggressive in expanding liability for manufacturers of defective products. The tobacco industry spared no expense in hiring local lobbyists and political strategists like Karl Rove to influence the Texas legislature. It also financed several local astroturf organizations to lend the impression that tort reform mattered to ordinary Texas citizens. More than thirty states joined Texas in enacting legislation modifying some aspect of the civil justice system in defendant-friendly ways. Several states enacted industry-demanded reforms, only to watch industry profits skyrocket as insurance rates remained high.[28]

State tort reform efforts also responded to employer complaints that courts and workers compensation boards were recognizing too many new industrial diseases and new forms of damage that were not necessarily "work related." Many states enacted legislation reducing the range of compensable claims for cumulative stress injuries and occupational diseases, limiting recovery for mental stress and other noneconomic damages, restricting compensation for medical examinations and treatment, reducing procedural protections for workers, or some combination of those reductions in coverage.[29]

The first assault on the civil justice system experienced a brief revival at the federal level near the end of the George H. W. Bush Administration when a "Working Group on Legal Reform" chaired by Solicitor General Kenneth Starr made 50 far-reaching recommendations for civil justice reform. As ATRA coordinated a massive publicity campaign to air the report's conclusions and recommendations, Vice-President Dan Quayle embarked on a multi-state speaking tour to tout its virtues. Quayle then threw down the gauntlet at the American Bar Association's annual convention in a widely publicized diatribe against the American legal system featuring many of the Manhattan Institute's claims. Although federal legislation was not forthcoming, the public response to Quayle's attacks was so positive that President Bush made them a cornerstone of his 1992 re-election campaign.[30]

THE SECOND ASSAULT

At the urging of prominent Republican strategists Frank Luntz, Grover Norquist, and Karl Rove, tort reform moved to the top of the Republican Party agenda in 1994. A "lawsuit crisis" largely manufactured by the Chamber of Commerce, conservative think tanks, and commentators working for Fox News gave renewed impetus to the initiative. Working closely with Luntz, Newt Gingrich decided to feature tort reform as one of the ten promises in the "Contract with America." The business community vigorously supported the Contract's promise to pass a "Common Sense Legal Reform" bill containing punitive damage limitations, "loser pays" requirements, and products liability reforms.[31]

The Second Assault in Congress. Stella Liebeck's lawsuit against McDonalds came just in time to serve as the poster child for the second assault on the civil justice system. In early 1995, business groups created the Civil Justice Reform Group (CJRG), and it joined PLCC, ATRA, and Americans for Lawsuit Reform in a new umbrella group called the Legal Reform Coalition. Flush with tobacco industry money, Citizens for a Sound Economy (CSE) played a prominent role in the business community's astroturf grass-roots campaign.[32] The House passed the promised legislation in early March, but the House sponsors ultimately agreed to a more modest Senate version of the bill, which passed both houses. President Clinton vetoed the bill anyway on the ground that it would have intruded too greatly on state prerogatives.[33]

The Second Assault in the States. When attorneys general from 39 states reached a precedent-setting $350 billion settlement with the tobacco industry, Republicans denounced the huge contingency fees that the companies agreed to pay to the attorneys who had financed the litigation, pored through millions of documents, taken hundreds of depositions, and worked with dozens of expert witnesses to bring the powerful industry to the settlement table. With the assistance of Frank Luntz, the Chamber of Commerce launched a multi-million-dollar advertising campaign focusing on the "avaricious trial lawyers" who were lining up to receive the huge fees. Political consultant Karl Rove saw tort reform as the perfect issue for advancing the interests of large Republican campaign contributors through a populist appeal to the party's conservative base while at the same time inflicting great pain on plaintiffs' attorneys who traditionally supported the Democratic Party. While Rove was being paid $3,000 per month as a tobacco industry lobbyist, he recruited political novice George W. Bush to run for governor of Texas.[34]

In 1993, several prominent corporate players in the Texas tort reform battles created Texans for Lawsuit Reform (TLR), which instantaneously became the state's largest political action committee. The tobacco industry funded a new astroturf organization called Citizens Against Lawsuit Abuse (CALA). As other industries joined in the effort, the Texas CALA filled billboards, newspaper ads, and television and radio spots with carefully crafted "bumper sticker" slogans attacking plaintiffs' attorneys and targeted "activist" state judges.[35] Soon after his inauguration, Governor Bush declared the need for civil justice reform to be a state "emergency," and the Texas legislature responded by passing a number of tort reform bills. As the new laws became effective, personal injury filings fell 40 percent between 1993 and 2002.[36] Between 1995 and 1999, more than 30 additional states enacted some kind of tort reform legislation. A much quieter assault by small business interests resulted in legislation in several states cutting back on longstanding state workers compensation benefits, especially for mental disabilities.

Having failed to prevent the wave of tort reform legislation, plaintiffs' attorneys challenged the statutes in court. By the mid-1990s, several state Supreme Courts had declared many of the most aggressive measures to be unconstitutional.[37] Unwilling to accept the judgment of the courts, the business community decided to throw out judges in the 39 states in which judges must stand for re-election. What in the past had been low-key, often uncontested elections suddenly became heated battlegrounds featuring political consultants, attack ads, and injudicious promises to overturn prior precedent.[38] Once again, the campaign began in Texas, where Karl Rove channeled $10 million from the business community to carefully selected candidates in a highly successful effort to pack the state Supreme Court. The effort was well worth the investment as major donors to the judicial campaigns later won nearly four-fifths of their cases in that court.[39]

Revising the Restatement. During the second assault, the business community also targeted the *Restatement (Second) of Torts* for "reform." When the powers that be at the American Law Institute selected the two most prominent critics of its strict liability approach to products liability, Professors James Henderson and Aaron Twerski, to be the Reporters for a separate volume of a third edition of the *Restatement* devoted exclusively to products liability, they appeared to have a particular agenda in mind. Any doubts on that score were dispelled when Henderson and Twerski stated at the outset that their aim was not simply to restate the law, but to improve it along the lines that they had long advocated.[40]

As the insurance industry lobbied behind the scenes for major changes, the delegates apparently ignored the informal ALI rule that members "check their clients at the door."[41] To no one's surprise, the *Restatement Third of Products Liability* that emerged in mid-1997 could have been drafted by the Products Liability Advisory Council. It avoided any mention of "strict liability" and replaced the Public Interest Era "consumer expectation" test for product defects with the "risk-utility" test favored by the business community. It also required plaintiffs to present expert testimony that safer designs were reasonably available, a subtle change that enhanced the role of experts and limited the role of juries.[42]

The new test for products liability retained the well-accepted common law rules that a manufacturer's unexcused failure to comply with an applicable safety regulation automatically rendered the product defective and that compliance did not necessarily shield the manufacturer from liability. A special rule for drugs and devices, however, deferred to FDA approval and adopted a "reasonable health-care provider" test that required plaintiffs to secure expert testimony. The new test also precluded recovery if the benefits of the drug or device outweighed the risks for any class of patients, even if the plaintiff was in a class of patients for which the opposite was true. Although the business community was thrilled with the changes, the reaction in academia and the state courts was decidedly mixed.[43]

With George W. Bush in the White House and the Republican Party controlling both houses of Congress in 2001, the business community believed that the time was ripe for another attempt to shape state common law through federal legislation. The Institute for Legal Reform (ILR), which the Chamber of Commerce created in 1998, poured more than $120 million over a seven-year period into the business community's tort reform efforts. At the same time, the business community's allies in academia and think tanks repeated the by-now familiar tort reform mantras, generated a new round of tort myths, and dressed up available data to lend the appearance of authenticity to the third assault on the civil justice system.[44]

The Third Assault in the Bush Administration. President Bush made tort reform a high legislative priority for his first administration, but the terrorist attacks of September 11, 2001 diverted the attention of both Congress and the administration to other matters. When the Democratic Party made plaintiffs' attorney John Edwards its vice presidential candidate, tort reform rose to the top of the agenda once again. Soon after winning the 2004 election, President Bush announced that he "expect[ed] the House and the Senate to pass meaningful liability reform." The case for federalizing the civil justice system was, however, more difficult to make in 2005 than in 1995. The number of civil trials in the nation's largest counties had declined by 50 percent between 1992 and 2001, and the success rate for plaintiffs was at an all-time low with a median award of only $37,000.[45]

As plaintiffs' attorneys began to file more class action lawsuits in state courts in response to unfavorable procedural precedent in federal courts, the business community assigned top priority to legislation designed to reverse that trend. The result was the Class Action Fairness Act of 2005 (CAFAct). With some modest exceptions, the statute allowed defendants in state class action lawsuits claiming more than $5 million in damages to remove them to federal court.[46] Having achieved only that rather modest legislative success, the Bush Administration proceeded to implement a "stealth tort reform" agenda in the regulatory agencies. FDA, CPSC, and NHTSA inserted language in preambles to regulations declaring that all state common law claims against manufacturers of products that complied with the regulations were preempted.[47]

The Third Assault in the States. The National Association of Manufacturers entered the fray at the state level for the first time in the early 2000s, joining other tort reform organizations in spending a combined $100 million on tort-related ballot initiatives during the 2003–2004 election cycle. The Chamber of Commerce crossed the line between news reporting and advocacy when it purchased several local newspapers in locales that it deemed to be especially plaintiff-friendly. Circulated free of charge, the newspapers featured accounts of outrageous jury verdicts and recycled editorials from the Chamber and other tort reform groups. The papers did not disclose the Chamber's ownership, a failing that academic critics called "deceitful and imbalanced." Local plaintiffs' attorneys saw the enterprise as a transparent ploy to spread pro-defendant propaganda to prospective members of local juries.[48]

After the 2002 elections gave the Republican Party substantial majorities in both houses of the Texas legislature, business community lobbyists set up shop in a corner of the House of Representatives gallery dubbed the "Owners' Box." In 2003, the legislature enacted the most thoroughgoing changes to the civil justice system in the state's history. Among other things, the new law limited class action lawsuits, shielded manufacturers of FDA-approved drugs and devices from liability, and required plaintiffs to pay the defendant's litigation costs in some cases. Fearing that the courts would hold the statutes unconstitutional, the tort reformers persuaded voters to pass a constitutional amendment permitting the state legislature to impose damage caps.[49]

Several other states followed suit. The Mississippi legislature attempted to shed the Chamber of Commerce's "hellhole" label by enacting comprehensive tort reform legislation. Illinois enacted a "cheeseburger liability" bill to shield restaurants from liability to persons claiming that their heavily advertised high-calorie servings caused obesity. In states where the 2006 election returned the Democratic Party to power, however, the tort reformers found themselves in the unfamiliar position of defending the status quo against efforts to roll back recently enacted tort reform legislation and to create new private causes of action.[50]

Remaking the State Judiciary. The Chamber of Commerce poured tens of millions of dollars into state judicial races, flooding local television stations with advertisements attacking justices who had voted to overturn recently enacted tort reform legislation. Because the Chamber refused to disclose the identities of the companies that contributed to the campaign, it provided ideal cover for local businesses wanting to finance attacks on judges who had previously ruled against them. Between 2000 and 2003, the Chamber's candidates won 23 of the 24 races in which it participated. Having placed its people on the courts, the Chamber then worked hard to keep them there. In the 2008 elections, all of the Republican Supreme Court incumbents retained their positions.[51]

The potential for money-driven judicial politics to undermine public respect for the legal system was on full display in West Virginia. After Massey Energy

Company was hit with a $50 million verdict in 2002 at the hands of a small coal operator it had forced out of business, its CEO, Don Blankenship, assured a reporter that he had "the willingness to spend enough money to make the changes that need to be made" in the state judiciary. In 2004, Blankenship spent $3.5 million to finance vicious attack ads in a campaign to replace long-time justice Warren McGraw with a little-known attorney named Brent Benjamin. While the company's case was pending before the court, Blankenship and another Supreme Court justice, Elliott E. Maynard, dined together several times as they vacationed in Monte Carlo. The court later decided the case in Massey's favor by a 3–2 margin with both Benjamin and Maynard joining the slim majority. The Supreme Court of the United States, however, held that Benjamin should have recused himself because of the serious risk of bias that Blankenship's large contributions had created.[52]

The organized bar and most legal academics viewed these sordid developments with horror. A coalition of more than 30 state and national organizations, including the American Bar Association, launched a campaign called "Justice at Stake" to educate the public about judicial elections and clean up the worst abuses. Neither the Supreme Court opinion nor the criticism, however, had a noticeable impact on the Chamber and the local businesses that joined its campaigns to repopulate state courts with business-friendly judges.[53]

THE CONSEQUENCES

Thirty years of defendant-friendly civil justice reforms undermined public confidence in the fairness of the system and reduced the incentives that the threat of liability provided to businesses to behave responsibly. Between 1985 and 2003, the number of jury trials in federal personal injury cases declined by 80 percent. The number of jury verdicts exceeding $100 million fell from 27 in 2000 to 2 in 2007.[54] After the enactment of the Class Action Fairness Act, the number of class action lawsuits filed in state courts decreased dramatically, while the number of class actions filed in federal courts increased by 72 percent.[55] In Texas, personal injury lawsuits declined from 63,000 to around 55,000 between 1995 and 2000 while other types of filings increased.[56] Yet instead of falling, as predicted by the tort reformers, insurance rates stabilized or increased slightly after legislatures enacted tort reform legislation, while insurance profits soared.[57]

Several of the most frequently enacted reforms had devastating impacts on low- and middle-income Americans who were the most vulnerable to the consequences of corporate malfeasance. Caps on damages for pain and suffering limited the ability of plaintiffs' attorneys to take on elderly and low-income clients with clearly meritorious cases because quantifiable economic loss (usually limited to expected income loss attributable to the defendant's conduct) did not warrant the expense of conducting discovery, hiring experts, and preparing for trial.[58] Changes to workers compensation laws had a similar impact on injured workers. For example, successful claims dropped from 75 percent of all claims filed to 42 percent after the West Virginia legislature changed its workers compensation law.[59]

The business community's massive investment in judicial elections through the Chamber of Commerce and related organizations had an impact on judicial behavior. A study of the votes of Supreme Court justices elected in Texas between 1994 and 1998 concluded that the justices were four times as likely to hear appeals from their campaign contributors and ten times more likely to hear appeals from substantial contributors. An analysis of the Ohio Supreme Court concluded that justices receiving contributions from parties involved in cases before their courts voted in favor of their contributors 70 percent of the time. And in a 2002 poll of 894 elected judges, only 36 percent said that campaign contributions had "no influence at all" on their decisions.[60]

CONCLUSIONS

At a June 2008 dinner honoring the tenth anniversary of its Institute for Legal Reform, Chamber of Commerce CEO Thomas J. Donohue boasted that the Chamber's efforts to create a business-friendly civil justice system had "succeeded beyond our expectations." Supporting that assessment was a *Business Week* cover story explaining "How Business Trounced the Trial Lawyers." Yet while the tort reformers had successfully reshaped the public's opinion of the civil justice system, their efforts had little lasting impact at the federal level. None of the far-reaching products liability reform bills that the business community pushed for more than a decade became law. Except for major restrictions on state class action litigation, federal tort reform legislation was modest in nature and limited to specific industries.[61]

At the state level, however, Donohue's assessment was much closer to the mark. Legislatures in several critical states dramatically changed longstanding rules governing class actions and joint and several liability, and nearly all states passed tort reform legislation limiting awards for noneconomic and punitive damages. Only a few states, however, adopted "loser pays" legislation, and limitations on contingency fees were likewise uncommon. Except for a few statutes providing a defense to manufacturers of products that complied with state and

federal regulations, state tort reform legislation did little to change the substance of state tort law. State legislatures enacted no restrictions on "frivolous
litigation," probably because it was impossible to articulate a concrete definition for an epithet. Instead of targeting *unwarranted* litigation, state legislatures
attempted to reduce *all* litigation through brute force restrictions on the rights
of plaintiffs to bring certain kinds of lawsuits and the discretion of jurors to
award damages. Ultimately, the assaults on the civil justice system were not so
much about reforming the common law of torts as they were about freeing the
business community from the threat of future liability.[62] And on that score, the
tort "reforms" accomplished a great deal.

Part Four

RENEGOTIATING THE
SOCIAL BARGAIN

During the late 2000s, the nation experienced a confluence of crises that seriously undermined both the bedrock assumptions of laissez faire minimalism and the faith of American people in the capacity of government to protect them from corporate malfeasance. The financial sector meltdown, the Texas City refinery explosion, the Upper Big Branch mine catastrophe, the *Deepwater Horizon* oil spill, the Peanut Corporation scare, and the Chinese toy recalls were just a few of the more visible consequences of the laissez faire mentality that had pervaded the American political economy for a generation. But the legacy of the Laissez Faire Revival was also manifested in hundreds of heart attacks caused by poorly regulated painkillers, the quiet desperation of homeowners with overdue payments on their adjustable rate mortgages, and the subtle increase in global temperatures that signaled irreversible climate change. Many of these consequences were directly attributable to the debilitated state of the protective governmental infrastructure that had only barely survived the three assaults detailed in Chapters 7–15. The laissez faire culture that prevailed in both government and the private sector so deeply discounted the risks to workers, neighbors, consumers, the financial system, and the environment that the crises and their consequences were inevitable.

By the 2006 off-year elections, that legacy had affected the lives of a sufficient number of Americans that they were ready for significant change, and they placed the Democratic Party in control of both houses of Congress. The bellwether 2008 elections, which gave the Democrats the White House and a filibuster-proof 60-vote majority in the Senate, could have signaled the beginning of a new era in which the American public and the business community engaged in a fundamental renegotiation of the social bargain of the sort that took place during the Progressive, New Deal, and Public Interest Eras. Instead, they ushered in a period of continued crisis in which Congress reacted to some, but not all crises with patch-and-repair solutions to the immediate problems but very little comprehensive legislation aimed at changing the underlying incentives of the private sector actors who brought on the crises.

DISABLED GOVERNMENT

If the business community did not succeed in repealing the bedrock regulatory statutes and common law innovations of the Progressive, New Deal, and Public Interest Eras, it was remarkably successful in disabling the institutions of responsibility and accountability that were basic to their implementation. Responding to an ongoing ideological air war and three powerful ground assaults, Congress, the agencies, and the courts gradually chipped away at the protective governmental infrastructure. Protective governmental action nearly always came in response to particular crises and was usually limited to the minimum required to address the specific causes of the crises. By the mid-2000s, the protective governmental infrastructure was in a bad state of disrepair.[1]

The forgone protections highlighted in the previous seven chapters were not attributable to any inherent limitations on the ability of government to protect its citizens. They were the predictable consequences of the regulatory and tort "reforms" put into place during the Laissez Faire Revival. This chapter highlights the institutional impact of the three assaults on the protective governmental infrastructure.

RELUCTANT REGULATORS

Throughout much of the Laissez Faire Revival, the White House and the executive branch agencies were controlled by men and women who strongly believed in the power of private markets to enhance public welfare. These leaders instructed their underlings to view themselves as "partners" with the regulated industries, rather than as advocates for the beneficiaries of the programs they were administering. Because agency leaders were generally unsympathetic to the protective statutes they were charged with implementing, the regulations that emerged were often far less protective than they could have been.

The paragons of reluctant regulation were the financial regulatory agencies. The Fed had ample authority to prevent much of the predatory lending that inflated the real estate bubble of 2005–06, but it issued unenforceable guidance documents instead. After Congress in 1980 divested both state and federal agencies of any power to set maximum interest rates or regulate loan products, the banking agencies quietly oversaw a gradual loosening of lending standards and capital reserve requirements and a rapid escalation of highly risky mortgage lending practices. The fact that lenders could pick and choose among regulators by manipulating their corporate form encouraged further regulatory laxity.[2]

Few investors could even remotely comprehend the risks that Wall Street investment banks bundled into sophisticated derivatives that were traded in unregulated "over-the-counter" markets. The credit rating agencies could have protected investors from risky mortgage-backed securities by digging deeper into the underlying loans, but they were heavily conflicted by a fee system that discouraged serious inquiry into the bona fides of the underlying loans and encouraged rosy assessments. All of this took place in a regulatory vacuum with the active encouragement of conservative think tanks and laissez faire minimalist government officials. After Congress summarily divested CFTC of jurisdiction over financial derivatives, the markets for collateralized debt obligations and credit default swaps ballooned into an unregulated multi-trillion dollar business. Likewise, following the repeal of the Glass-Steagall Act, a series of mergers of investment banks, insurance companies, and commercial banks produced a handful of mega-banks that dominated the financial sector. The Fed was in a position to prevent financial institutions from becoming too big to fail, but it was not remotely interested in slowing down the consolidation. As the government struggled to keep the financial system afloat in the fall of 2008, both SEC and the Fed acknowledged that they had utterly failed to exercise their oversight responsibilities.[3] But by then it was too late.

The regulatory agencies missed many other opportunities during the Laissez Faire Revival to promulgate regulations that could have saved lives, reduced fraud, and protected the environment. For example, as a huge increase in rail traffic on an aging rail system became a recipe for disaster, FRA could have reduced the risks of major derailments and collisions by requiring the railroads to outfit trains with available accident prevention technologies, construct tank cars with thicker steel, and route hazardous materials more carefully to avoid major urban areas. But the FRA leadership was disinclined to force the railroads to implement expensive safety technologies that might increase shipping costs. Similarly, the leadership at MMS had no interest in requiring the petroleum industry to install available technologies to reduce risks to the environment posed by deepwater drilling.

STARVED AGENCIES

When agency leaders did support protective intervention, the agencies they headed were usually so starved for resources that they could not possibility perform the tasks that Congress assigned to them. For example, FTC's staff declined from a high of 1,746 work years in 1979 to slightly above 1,000 during the George W. Bush Administration, and CPSC's staff dropped from a high of 978 at the end of the Carter Administration to just 401 in 2006.[4] In 1975, an OSHA staff of 2,405 was responsible for protecting 67.8 million workers at almost 4 million workplaces. Thirty years later, a reduced staff of 2,208 was responsible for 131.5 million workers at 8.5 million establishments. By the end of the George W. Bush Administration, NHTSA had only 635 full-time employees, down from 800 in 1980.[5] As the corps of civil servants who entered government during the Public Interest Era neared retirement, low starting salaries made government service unattractive to young professionals who might otherwise have been inclined to fill their shoes.[6] Only the few "portal" agencies that could assess "user fees" for the privilege of awarding permits or licenses could keep their budgets up to tolerable levels, and those resources often came with strings attached.

CAPTIVE AGENCIES

The tendency of agencies to become captured by regulated interests and the related "revolving door" between agency and industry employment are longstanding problems that predate the Laissez Faire Revival. Those weaknesses were especially pronounced during that period, however, as the leaders in virtually every agency studied here were at one time or another drawn from the regulated industries and/or accepted jobs in those industries upon departure. The prospect of a future job can temper the enthusiasm with which government employees implement the protective goals of their statutes, and the knowledge that the regulated industry is prepared to challenge every aspect of their activities in Congress, the courts, and the media can steer even the most committed public servants toward compromise.[7]

CONFLICTED GOVERNMENT

Many of the agencies examined here labored under longstanding institutional conflicts of interest. Because revenue generation from oil and gas lessees was "the dominant objective" of MMS, it was quite reluctant to impose environmental restrictions on oil and gas leasing. The Department of Agriculture's obligation to promote the agricultural sector could conflict with its responsibility to protect consumers from adulterated meat and poultry. And the statutes creating FAA and FRA charged them with both promoting and regulating the aviation and railroad industries. Too often the agencies resolved the tension between promotion and regulation in favor of the former.[8]

HAMSTRUNG GOVERNMENT

What began as a modest attempt to facilitate interagency comment on important regulations during the Nixon Administration blossomed into a formal review exercise in which the obscure Office of Information and Regulatory Affairs (OIRA) became a powerful institutional bottleneck restricting the flow of protective regulations in both Republican and Democratic administrations.[9] The Small Business Regulatory Enforcement Fairness Act of 1996 and the Information Quality Act of 2001 added steps to the regulatory process, required special analyses of the impacts of rules on small businesses, and empowered companies to demand that agencies review disseminated information that was allegedly based on unsound science. In 2000, Professor Mark Seidenfeld identified more than 120 procedural and analytical hurdles that regulatory agencies had to negotiate in promulgating a major rule.[10] Some agencies simply stopped promulgating regulations absent the impetus of a statutory deadline or a court order. Those agencies that could avoid rulemaking by issuing recalls or directives did so.

REGULATORY GAPS

As companies found ways around existing regulatory restrictions during the Laissez Faire Revival, serious gaps in the protective governmental infrastructure became apparent. Sometimes deregulatory legislation intentionally created regulatory gaps. For example, a signal event in bringing on the financial crisis of 2008 was the enactment of the Gramm-Leach-Bliley Act, which repealed the Glass-Steagall Act's separation of federally insured commercial banking from risky investment banking and facilitated a rapid consolidation of the banking industry.[11] Sometimes the gap was of the agency's own making. For example, FDA devoted little attention to the risks that produce would become contaminated with *E. coli* O157:H7 and *Salmonella* until it began to receive dozens of reports in the 1990s of produce contaminated by both bacteria.[12] During the first decade of the twenty-first century "black lung" disease rates soared while MSHA refused to acknowledge the need to update its 1969 coal dust standard.[13] As institutions, technologies, and scientific understandings changed, gaps frequently appeared in regulatory coverage. Many NHTSA and CPSC standards, for example, remained static as vehicle and product designs changed and safety engineers developed more protective technologies.[14]

LOOSE PORTALS

Several of the statutes that created the protective governmental infrastructure require companies to obtain a permit or license from a regulatory agency before marketing certain products or engaging in certain activities. In such regulatory regimes, the agency serves as a portal through which companies gain access to the marketplace. The statutes typically place the burden of proof on the applicant to demonstrate that its product or activity will not cause more harm than good, and they authorize the agency to write regulations prescribing the kinds of information that applicants must provide to meet this burden. Examples of portal statutes include FDA's drug, device, and food additive approval programs, EPA's air and water permit requirements, the Corps of Engineers' dredge and fill permit program, and OSM's permit program for surface mines. During the Laissez Faire Revival, these programs frequently behaved more like open gates than narrow portals as hard-pressed agency staffers reacted to pressures from the regulated industries and their superiors to allow more products on the market and to permit more economically useful activity to proceed.

One favored technique for removing regulatory restraints while retaining the appearance of a protective portal regime was the "abbreviated review" under which an agency allowed permit applicants to avoid the full permit application process if they could show that their products or activities were sufficiently well understood generically that there was no need to examine them individually. These shortcuts were frequently abused during the Laissez Faire Revival. Companies made a mockery of FDA's abbreviated device approval process by stretching the malleable concept of "substantial equivalence" to absurd lengths, and drug companies similarly abused the "fast track" approval process that Congress created in 1992 for getting life-saving drugs rapidly to market. The Corps of Engineers sidestepped the requirement that mountaintop removal mines obtain a "dredge and fill" permit to discharge "valley fill" into mountain streams by issuing a "nationwide" permit that allowed activities with "minimal" environmental impact to proceed with only cursory review and interpreting the term "minimal" very liberally to include 93 percent of the permit applications.

During the Laissez Faire Revival, even the full-fledged permit reviews undertaken by agencies administering portal programs were often quite cursory. For example, the statute under which MMS approved offshore oil and gas leases required the agency to decide within 30 days of receiving the application, a deadline that did not allow for a serious review of the lengthy environmental documents that the applicants generated. With the agency's acquiescence, the environmental assessments tended to rely upon boilerplate descriptions and conclusions prepared by consultants who did not even go to the trouble of adapting the language to the particular projects. MMS waived its environmental review requirements altogether for more than 400 projects per year, one of which was BP's ill-fated *Deepwater Horizon* project.[15]

WEAK IMPORT RESTRICTIONS

The weakest portals of all were the 300 ports of entry through which the United States imported 40 percent of its drugs, 80 percent of its active pharmaceutical ingredients, 80 percent of its seafood, and nearly 100 percent of its children's toys. Most observers agreed that the government could not rely on regulatory agencies in the exporting countries to ensure that their companies complied with U.S. standards. The tiny corps of inspectors that FDA, USDA, and CPSC devoted to spot-checking imports at the ports and the even tinier staff that inspected foreign manufacturing facilities were wholly incapable of ensuring the safety of those imported products. When agencies did send inspectors to visit foreign plants, it was often difficult to distinguish the foreign officials from the company managers or to know who had the most authority. For example, Chinese drywall manufacturers and government officials collaborated to deny basic information to a team of CPSC inspectors attempting to locate the origins of contaminated drywall that had been installed in thousands of U.S. homes. FDA inspectors encountered similar resistance when they attempted to identify the Chinese source of contaminated Heparin that wound up in U.S. drugs.[16]

REACTIVE GOVERNMENT

The original informal rulemaking model of the 1946 Administrative Procedure Act (APAct) was designed to provide an efficient vehicle for agencies to promulgate regulations. During the Laissez Faire Revival, however, the model became so laden with analytical and procedural accretia that agencies that were inclined to take protective action tended to choose alternative tools for accomplishing their goals. OSHA effectively abandoned rulemaking and focused instead on issuing guidance documents that could sometimes be enforced under the "general duty clause" of its statute. FTC returned to case-by-case enforcement against individual companies after issuing informal guidelines defining particular unfair and deceptive trade practices. FAA and FRA issued directives that were carefully tailored to fix discrete problems. Product regulators like NHTSA and CPSC shifted from rulemaking to recalls.[17]

These alternatives tended to be less protective than regulating in advance. They also tended to be less transparent, because they usually involved behind-the-scenes negotiations between agency officials and company representatives during which companies typically "bargained the agency down" from its initial position. The vast majority of recalls were voluntary and therefore unenforceable, and participation rates in recalls were universally low.[18] Recalls of some medical devices forced patients to decide whether to have the devices removed from their bodies or leave them intact and bear the risk that they would fail. Directives usually came too late to prevent tragedies from happening. Thus, FAA issued an order requiring airlines to strengthen cargo door locks only after nine passengers were sucked out of a United Airlines 747 jet when an unsecured cargo door opened during flight.

POOR SURVEILLANCE

Agencies need information to support regulation, and the best source of risk-related information is usually data on how regulated products and activities function in practice. During the Laissez Faire Revival, this critical "surveillance" function was often lacking in the agencies that needed it most. For example, the resources that FDA devoted to its offices that authorized new drugs and devices to enter the marketplace far exceeded those devoted to its offices that monitored how they functioned in the real world. FDA also lacked an effective program for collecting and managing data on food contamination. NHTSA's 57-person Office of Defects Investigation was incapable of managing the huge amount of information that flowed into its early warning system from auto manufacturers, insurance companies, state agencies, and other sources. CPSC devoted a single staff employee to testing existing toys for safety hazards, and he worked in a tiny rat-infested laboratory with very few tools.[19]

GOVERNMENT INCOMPETENCE AND CORRUPTION

The vast majority of the civil service employees who labor in the lower echelons of the agencies are conscientious and competent public servants who accomplish a great deal with very limited resources. When the leadership of government agencies placed laissez faire ideology over professionalism, however, the result was often incompetent government. The rampant incompetence of

EPA's leadership during the Reagan Administration resulted in the resignation of Administrator Ann Gorsuch and a felony conviction for one of her assistant administrators. Sometimes the malfeasance of government employees went beyond incompetence to corruption. In the early 1990s, FDA suffered the huge embarrassment of discovering that three scientists in its generic drug approval division were being bribed to give high priority to particular generic drugs. Far more common were stories of high-level political appointees accepting trips to resorts or negotiating for a lucrative position in a company while overseeing its products or activities.[20] In the past, reports of government corruption and incompetence inspired efforts to drive out the corruption and make the system work more effectively. During the Laissez Faire Revival, however, they merely ratified the conservative critique of government programs and provided a rationale for attempts to roll back regulation.

PRIVATIZING OVERSIGHT

As an alternative to incompetent government bureaucrats, the regulatory reformers of the Laissez Faire Revival offered private sector auditors charged with evaluating safety-related aspects of a company's products and activities on a continuing basis. For example, USDA relied on private auditors to "certify" that agricultural establishments complied with its regulations defining "organic" agricultural practices, and SEC effectively delegated its oversight of the securitizing and marketing of complex derivatives to credit rating agencies.[21] Experience teaches, however, that private auditors cannot resist competitive pressures to shade their reports in ways that make them acceptable to their clients. One food industry consultant called private auditors hired by food manufacturing companies to certify compliance with good manufacturing practices the "diploma mills" of food manufacturing.[22]

BANKRUPT VOLUNTARY PROGRAMS

During the Laissez Faire Revival, regulatory agencies in both Democratic and Republican administrations vigorously promoted voluntary approaches as alternatives to regulation and enforcement. Such approaches typically involved a quid pro quo under which the agency agreed to forgo inspections or some other regulatory requirements if the regulatees met the program's broad conditions. Many voluntary programs were very effective in allowing regulatees to avoid regulatory requirements, but not so successful in changing their overall conduct. Some, like EPA's Project XL, were of dubious legality. OSHA's Voluntary Protection Program for facilities with exemplary safety records rarely expelled a company, even when its injury rates crept upward past the national average. The banking agencies routinely ignored the predatory lending practices of banks enrolled in voluntary programs during the housing boom of the early 2000s. As the financial system melted down in September 2008, SEC Chairman Christopher Cox admitted that it was "abundantly clear that voluntary regulation does not work."[23]

MORAL HAZARD

Extensive deregulation in areas in which the regulatees were effectively insured against risk by the explicit or implicit promise of a federal bailout created a serious "moral hazard" problem. As Congress and the banking agencies deregulated financial institutions during the 1990s and 2000s, several bank holding companies and insurance companies became so systemically important that they were deemed "too big to fail." These big investment banks and insurance companies had every incentive to take overly risky positions because they knew that if they ever were at serious risk of declaring bankruptcy, the federal government would find a way to bail them out. They therefore threw caution to the wind, overleveraged their assets, and reaped gargantuan profits until the collapse of late 2008, at which point they gratefully accepted the expected government bailouts.[24]

INADEQUATE ENFORCEMENT

In virtually all of the agencies studied here, enforcement resources diminished dramatically during the first three years of the Reagan Administration, and they remained woefully thin at the end of the George W. Bush Administration. OSHA's inspectorate shrank from one inspector per 30,000 workplaces in the late 1970s to one per 60,000 workplaces in 2010.[25] In the late 1970s, FDA inspected about half of the country's food manufacturing facilities every year, but by 2008 it inspected only about 5 percent of them.[26] The FSIS inspection presence fell from 190 to 88 inspectors per billion pounds of inspected meat between 1981 and 2007.[27] NHTSA employed 119 enforcement personnel in 1980 when 146 million vehicles were on the road, but only 57 in 2010 when there were twice as many vehicles.[28] MMS devoted 62 inspectors to the 3,000 facilities that were operating in the Gulf of Mexico.[29] Around 3,200 FAA inspectors oversaw more than 4,300 domestic and 680 foreign repair and maintenance facilities.[30]

The Laissez Faire Revival was characterized by weak enforcement as agencies emphasized "compliance assistance" instead of strict enforcement. Not surprisingly, the number of citations fell and the size of the fines declined as compliance assistance evolved into a tolerance for noncompliance.[31] OSHA frequently reduced penalties for companies that had a history of serious violations and had shown little evidence of improvement.[32] NHTSA ceased assessing any fines at all against companies that failed to undertake timely recalls of defective tires and vehicles.[33] And USDA's meat sanitation regulations were so rarely enforced that they were essentially voluntary standards.[34]

When hard-pressed agency inspectors identified clear violations, they were often undermined by their supervisors. In 2006, OSHA supervisors downgraded about one-fifth of all citations for "willful" violations.[35] Officials at OSM headquarters routinely ordered field offices to drop ongoing investigations and vetoed their recommendations to prosecute new cases.[36] After FDA amended its enforcement policy in 2002 to require that all warning letters be cleared by the Office of the Chief Counsel, the number dropped from 1,032 in 2001 to 471 in 2007.[37] When FAA's inspectors cited airlines for violations of safety regulations, upper-level officials frequently settled for a fraction of the amounts originally assessed.[38] In failing to hold violators accountable, the agencies breached their obligation to the beneficiaries of the regulatory programs and undermined the integrity of the regulatory process by giving scofflaws a competitive advantage over their compliant competitors.

INEFFECTIVE PUNISHMENT

In January 2003, a dramatic series of articles in the *New York Times* detailed the hellish conditions in several pipe foundries owned by McWane, Inc., a Birmingham-based pipe manufacturer that became hugely profitable by cutting costs at every conceivable opportunity. Between 1995 and the end of 2002, at least 4,600 workers were injured and nine were killed at McWane foundries. Widely regarded by OSHA investigators as a "renegade" company, McWane calculated to the penny the cost of OSHA fines in deciding how much to invest in workplace safety. In virtually every instance, it was far cheaper for the company to pay the fines than it was to comply with OSHA's standards.[39]

Dozens of similar tragedies in which workers were needlessly killed in workplaces that were in chronic violation of OSHA and MSHA standards suggest that the McWane experience was not unique. The punishment that corporate wrongdoers received during the Laissez Faire Revival frequently amounted to little more than a slap on the wrist. The maximum penalty allowed by law for a willful violation of an occupational safety standard was only $70,000. But fines rarely came close to that amount; as of 2009, the median fine in cases involving worker fatalities was $3,675.[40] Prior to late 2006, the minimum penalty for a non-serious violation of an MSHA standard was $60, and fines in that amount were the norm.[41]

Perhaps the most remarkable legacy of the Laissez Faire Revival is the fact that not one of the scofflaws that foisted predatory loans off on families who could ill afford them, sliced and diced the resulting mortgages into incomprehensible derivatives, assigned AAA ratings to worthless mortgage-backed securities, and induced unsuspecting investors to purchase those securities while betting against them spent a day in jail (though the Justice Department continues to investigate possible crimes).[42] The reluctance of federal prosecutors to file criminal actions was not limited to the banking agencies. The Justice Department brought only 82 criminal actions for violations of OSHA regulations during the agency's first forty years. In many cases, companies that caused enormous harm had not clearly violated any law, because the relevant regulations were built on the laissez faire minimalist assumption that a self-correcting marketplace would eliminate predatory practices and fraud. Even in cases of clear violations, however, federal prosecutors were reluctant to indict because it was so difficult to prove criminal intent.[43]

NEUTERED COMMON LAW

For the most part, the civil justice system performs its essential functions out of public view. Most people do not recognize its value until they or people they know become victims of irresponsible conduct. Even less visible is the protective role that tort law plays in discouraging corporate malfeasance. The business community's often misleading complaints about a "litigation explosion" and "frivolous lawsuits," by contrast, attained a high degree of visibility in both the mainstream media and the conservative echo chamber. By 2008, 45 states had enacted reforms advocated by the American Tort Reform Association. Once those changes were in place, potential plaintiffs discovered that the tort system no longer offered them recourse against corporate wrongdoers.[44]

SUBSTANTIVE CHANGES IN TORT LAW

The business community's efforts to roll back Public Interest Era products liability doctrines had a noticeable impact on the substance of tort law. The notion that the primary function of tort law was to increase the efficiency of product markets was foreign to legal scholars prior to the advent of the law and economics movement that the founding funders vigorously nourished. The impact of that movement was greatly amplified as Republican presidents appointed members of the Federalist Society to the federal judiciary and Chamber of Commerce–sponsored candidates prevailed over incumbents in state judicial elections.

The *Restatement (Third) of Products Liability* was the product of a flawed process in which the primary drafters did not pretend to restate the principles that the majority of state supreme courts had articulated in judicial opinions. In defining a product defect, it abandoned any suggestion of strict liability and adopted the cost-benefit balancing test preferred by conservative law and economics scholars. It also placed a heavy burden on plaintiffs to prove that a specific alternative design would have been safer and just as effective as the design employed by the manufacturer.[45] In those states that have adopted the *Third Restatement*, fewer victims of defectively designed products will be compensated, and manufacturers will have less incentive to design safer products.

After the financial meltdown of 2008, municipalities, pension funds, and other institutional investors that had purchased AAA-rated securities filed dozens of lawsuits against credit rating agencies, alleging that they had relied to their detriment on the agencies' negligently prepared ratings. The courts were reluctant, however, to impose liability on the credit rating agencies because of the absence of any direct contractual relationship between them and the investor plaintiffs. State common law suits against credit rating agencies were even less likely to succeed after the enactment of the Credit Rating Agency Reform Act of 2006, which contained a clause preempting any state or local law regulating "the substance of credit ratings or the procedures and methodologies" employed by credit rating agencies.[46]

PROCEDURAL CHANGES IN TORT LITIGATION

Tort reform legislation usually included procedural restrictions designed to discourage lawsuits. States that enacted "loser pays" legislation requiring plaintiffs who did not substantially prevail to reimburse the defendants' litigation expenses created a powerful disincentive to bring meritorious cases.[47] The doctrine of "joint and several" liability was a modest attempt to ensure that innocent plaintiffs did not bear the risk of insolvent or otherwise unreachable defendants, but it attracted strong criticism from "deep pocket" corporate defendants that did not want to bear that risk. With the abolition of joint and several liability, defendants found it easier to avoid accountability by pointing the finger at other companies. But it also left purchasers of houses containing contaminated imported drywall with no remedy when builders and retailers pointed the finger at the unreachable Chinese manufacturers.[48]

The class action lawsuit is the only effective way for consumers to challenge predatory lending practices and consumer fraud in court. The same is true for food safety litigation in which defendants cause transitory illnesses in thousands of people, few of whom suffer sufficient damage to warrant bearing the expense of a lawsuit. The drafters of the Class Action Fairness Act of 2005 meant to discourage class actions by giving defendants the option of transferring them from state courts to federal courts where it was generally more difficult to certify class actions. Thus, after a large February 2007 recall of *Salmonella*-contaminated peanut butter generated a number of class action lawsuits in state courts around the country, a federal court consolidated all of the state cases into a single federal action and then refused to certify them. This forced individual plaintiffs to file separate actions for their often modest damages and thereby reduced the likelihood that most of their lawsuits would go forward.[49]

DAMAGE CAPS

The business community and its allies in academia believed that juries could not be trusted to award damages for pain and suffering and other noneconomic losses that were not easily quantified. Punitive damage awards, in their view, were especially arbitrary. Caps on "noneconomic" and punitive damages could reduce uncertainty in business decisions and in calculating liability insurance premiums.[50] But damage caps also had the potential for grave injustice. By reducing the likelihood that plaintiffs' attorneys would represent plaintiffs who did not incur large medical expenses or severe disabilities, they deprived millions of plaintiffs of corrective justice. Because actions for consumer fraud and violations of privacy rights often involved "noneconomic" damages, the civil justice system lost much of its capacity to discourage cyberspace outlaws. Caps on punitive damages reduced the most powerful remaining incentive for large companies that had little to fear from the criminal justice system.[51]

ERODING WORKERS COMPENSATION

Under the social bargain reflected in the Progressive Era workers compensation laws, workers gave up their right to demand full compensation for workplace injuries in return for the promise of rapid reimbursement of medical expenses and adequate compensation for disabling injuries. Under the constant pressure of employer resistance, however, these protections gradually eroded. Companies saved money by contesting claims interminably, and they discouraged future claims by assigning claimants to meaningless or unpleasant jobs. Because most workers compensation statutes capped compensation for permanent disabilities, the allowable awards diminished as the currency inflated over time. The business community hastened the erosion of workers compensation

protections during the Laissez Faire Revival by successfully lobbying state legislatures for various "reforms" precluding awards for soft tissue injuries, cumulative stress injuries, and mental disabilities.[52]

STEALTH TORT REFORM IN THE FEDERAL AGENCIES

The greatest threat to the civil justice system at the federal level came indirectly through the determination of several regulatory agencies that their lax
regulatory requirements preempted state common law. Although the federal
courts did not always go along with this "stealth attack" on state tort law, it
proved devastating to many plaintiffs. The Supreme Court held that federal law
preempted all products liability claims against manufacturers of medical devices that had undergone FDA's full approval process and complied with FDA
requirements. Since the Supreme Court had also held that a plaintiff injured
by a medical device could not bring a claim based on the defendant's successful
attempt to defraud the FDA, this left victims of devices that FDA had approved
on the basis of fraudulent information without a remedy.[53] The banking agencies also persuaded the courts to hold that lawsuits brought under stringent state
predatory lending laws were preempted by the weak federal regulations that
they had put into effect during the Laissez Faire Revival.[54]

PUBLIC PERCEPTIONS

The most profound consequence of the business community's efforts to escape common law accountability was its negative impact on public perceptions
of the civil justice system. A constant barrage of misleading advertisements over
the years convinced citizens who rarely encountered the civil justice system
that it was administered by activist judges and incompetent jurors who were
easily manipulated by wily trial lawyers. At the same time that attacks on the
civil justice system reduced public respect for the common law, tort reform
legislation rendered it less potent as a source of countervailing power. Citizens
who perceive that the courts no longer dispense justice will seek justice on their
own through boycotts, direct action, and even violence.

TRUNCATED INCENTIVES

During the Laissez Faire Revival, many companies externalized the social
costs of their products and activities to workers, consumers, and ultimately the
taxpayers. This happened because the law failed to provide adequate incentives,
either *ex ante* through regulations or *ex post* through tort liability, for companies to provide adequate protections. Perhaps the starkest example of misplaced

incentives yielding irresponsible conduct was the common practice on Wall Street of paying huge bonuses to employees at the end of the year based on profits brought in during that year without regard to potential losses that might be incurred in future years. But misplaced incentives also pervaded other sectors of the banking industry. The mortgage companies that sold mortgages to Wall Street securitizers realized the value of the loan immediately and therefore had a strong incentive to write as many loans as possible without regard to the risk of default. Mortgage brokers operating under the same formula had no incentive to educate borrowers about the risks they were incurring and every incentive to belittle those risks.[55]

The Chemical Safety and Hazard Investigation Board (CSHIB) report on the March 2005 explosion at BP's Texas City refinery that killed 15 workers and injured 180 noted that the company had emphasized reductions in lost-time injury rates that contributed immediately to the company's bottom line while virtually ignoring long-term risks of catastrophic events. The CSHIB's plea for OSHA to "pay increased attention to preventing less frequent, but catastrophic" accidents could have applied equally well to insurance companies that speculated in credit default swaps, utility companies that continued to burn fossil fuels, auto manufacturers that continued to design gas-guzzling SUVs, railroad companies that resisted implementing positive separation control technologies, and BP's deepwater drilling activities in the Gulf of Mexico.[56]

CONCLUSIONS

The business community's sustained assaults on the protective governmental infrastructure during the Laissez Faire Revival resulted in a hamstrung federal regulatory regime run by resource-starved agencies that were more solicitous of the needs of the business community than they were attentive to the risks faced by the citizens that they were created to protect. A conciliatory federal enforcement apparatus stressed accommodation over vigorous prosecution, and an emasculated civil justice system was far less inclined to hold companies accountable for the harmful consequences of their products and activities than it had been during the Public Interest Era. Private sector actors acquired greater freedom to pursue their economic goals without regard to the risks that their products and activities posed to their consumers, their workers, their neighbors, and the environment. No longer guided by powerful human hands, the splendid stallion of free enterprise was free to serve human society or to trample anything in its path.

PATCH-AND-REPAIR

Pressed by Congressman Henry Waxman (D-California) to explain the ongoing financial meltdown, former Fed Chairman Alan Greenspan admitted that the "entire intellectual edifice" that housed the financial establishment during the Laissez Faire Revival "collapsed in the summer of" 2008. That edifice was designed by Chicago School academics in the 1960s and erected by laissez faire minimalists like Greenspan, Senator Phil Gramm (R-Texas) and his wife Wendy, and Treasury Secretaries Robert Rubin, Lawrence Summers, and Henry Paulson. Dubbed the "efficient market hypothesis," it held that the collective wisdom of the sophisticated rational actors participating in the financial markets would prevent irrational bubbles and subsequent collapses. A necessary corollary was laissez faire minimalism—the belief that government intervention into markets was highly undesirable.[1]

Greenspan had been one of the strongest advocates of the efficient market hypothesis, and his bias against regulation was strikingly apparent in the way he administered the Fed's regulatory responsibilities during his tenure. Over the years, he filled the staff of the Fed with like-minded laissez faire minimalists. Confident that the market would "self-correct" for any tendency to create asset bubbles, he rejected a proposal by Fed governor Edward Gramlich to conduct a comprehensive examination of the lending practices of banks and their mortgage company affiliates at precisely the time when those practices were most abusive. He likewise rejected requests by consumer activists to exercise the Fed's authorities to prevent the same unfair and deceptive lending practices.[2]

Greenspan was joined on this road to Damascus by Richard Posner, the guru of the law and economics movement, who subsequently recognized that "the movement to deregulate the financial industry went too far by exaggerating the resilience—the self-healing powers—of laissez faire capitalism."[3] A commission appointed by Congress to examine the causes of the 2008 crisis concluded that "markets cannot be counted upon to regulate themselves or to function efficiently in the absence of regulation."[4] These were wrenching revelations to the political elites in Washington, D.C., where the notion that "unregulated financial markets were good for America and the world" had become "the consensus position . . . on both sides of the political aisle."[5]

As Greenspan tacitly acknowledged, the financial meltdown of 2008 was a direct consequence of the failure of Congress and the regulatory agencies to articulate and enforce rules of responsibility capable of holding the destructive forces of free markets in check. Chapter 16 demonstrated that laissez faire minimalism and its adverse consequences were not limited to the financial sector. The debilitated protective governmental infrastructure that survived the business community's three assaults on regulation and the civil justice system was incapable of protecting Americans from a wide variety of threats to their health, safety, and economic welfare posed by companies that had acquired too much freedom to harm.

REACTING TO THE CRISES

History teaches that crises provide the catalysts for change in the legal system. It usually takes widely publicized tragedies or abuses to raise public consciousness to levels sufficient to overcome the inertial forces that otherwise overwhelm policymaking institutions. The cost of complying with rules of responsibility are directly (and often intensely) felt by the companies subject to those rules, but the benefits of their protections are usually spread across so many beneficiaries that few individuals are likely to be motivated to expend time and resources demanding stronger protections in the absence of some consciousness-raising crisis.[6] Ordinarily, the changes that crises inspire are incremental in nature, consisting primarily of "patches and repairs" to the existing legal system that proponents can characterize as reasonable compromises or "win-win" solutions. These patch-and-repair fixes are easily eroded as the crises fade from public memory and the affected industry challenges new requirements in court, insists on narrow interpretations of the requirements that survive judicial review, demands broad exemptions, and probes the boundaries of the rules once they are in place.[7]

On a few rare occasions, a confluence of crises has generated strong public demand for a major renegotiation of the social bargain to correct systematic flaws in the legal system. During these periods of intense crisis and re-examination, Congress has considered comprehensive reforms aimed at changing underlying incentives and readjusting the balance of freedom, responsibility, and account-ability. During the Progressive, New Deal, and Public Interest Eras, Congress responded to public demands for systemic change with bold statutes creating new administrative agencies and empowering new and existing regulators to protect the public. The common law courts likewise changed substantive legal doctrines and modified procedural rules to allow injured individuals to hold irresponsible companies liable for the damages they caused. Comprehensive changes, however, are far more difficult to accomplish than patch-and-repair re-forms because the business community always pours its considerable resources into "divert and delay" strategies that concede as little power and preserve as many avoidance options as possible.

The confluence of crises that occurred between 2005 and 2010 (detailed in Chapters 8–14) generated sufficient anxiety on the part of ordinary Americans about the risks that the unruly economic forces set loose by the Laissez Faire Revival posed to their physical health and economic well-being that compre-hensive legal change was a politically realistic governmental response.[8] The 2006 elections, which put the Democratic Party in control of both houses of Congress, signaled a clear public rejection of laissez faire policies. After the dramatic 2008 elections placed a charismatic president in the bully pulpit of the White House, bright young progressives brimming with fresh ideas for com-prehensive reforms and the energy to move them forward were eagerly awaiting calls inviting them to serve in the new administration.

The calls never came. Candidate Barack Obama had campaigned as an agent of change, but President Obama was not committed to bringing about fundamental change in the relationship between government and business. Al-though he filled many high-level positions in the federal agencies with exceed-ingly competent professionals, surprisingly few came with strong progressive credentials.[9] The top policymakers in the White House who determined the administration's overall direction were mostly experienced returnees from the Clinton Administration, many of whom had played prominent roles in bringing about the deregulation that had caused the crises that the new administration was struggling to address.[10]

Even if the president had been a strong proponent of comprehensive reform, he would have encountered impediments that Presidents Theodore Roosevelt, Franklin Roosevelt, Lyndon Johnson, and Richard Nixon did not have to over-come. As a confluence of crises engulfed the nation, the business community's idea and influence infrastructures were firmly in place, and they worked over-time to forestall change. The conservative media echo chamber and industry lobbyists effectively channeled public outrage at corporate malfeasance into legislation narrowly tailored to the specific abuses that gave rise to crises and containing ample room for evasion and erosion. After two years, the Obama Administration and the Democrat-controlled Congress accomplished some notable "patch-and-repair" reforms that helped shore up a sagging protective governmental infrastructure, but they achieved no comprehensive reforms of the sort that characterized the Progressive, New Deal, and Public Interest Eras.

PRAGMATIC ADMINISTRATION BY WISE MEN

More than any president since Jimmy Carter, President Obama reached beyond the regulated industries for qualified professionals to head the regulatory agencies. OSHA head David Michaels had taught at the George Washington University School of Public Health, and MSHA head Joseph A. Main had worked for the United Mineworkers of America.[11] EPA Administrator Lisa Jackson had served as the Commissioner of New Jersey's Department of Environmental Protection, and FDA head Margaret A. Hamburg had been the Public Health Commissioner for New York City.[12] Joe Szabo, the United Transportation Union's Illinois legislative director, headed FRA, and Randy Babbitt, a former president of the Airline Pilots Association directed FAA.[13]

In the area of financial regulation, however, President Obama relied almost exclusively on former industry executives and individuals with strong ties to the banking industry until he appointed Elizabeth Warren, a Harvard law professor, to a position he created in the White House to oversee the implementation of her brainchild, the new Consumer Financial Protection Bureau. Gary Gensler, President Obama's pick to chair CFTC, and Mark Patterson, the Treasury Department's Chief of Staff, had been investment bankers at Goldman Sachs. The SEC chairperson, Mary Schapiro, was a long-time regulator, having served on the SEC and the CFTC in the Clinton Administration. And the president re-appointed Ben Bernanke, a Bush appointee, to be Chairman of the Federal Reserve Board.[14]

REGULATORY OVERSIGHT

At the outset of the administration, President Obama defended strong federal regulation. In early 2009, he revoked the Bush Administration's last-minute addendum to the regulatory review executive order, and he issued a memorandum strongly discouraging regulatory agencies from preempting state common law.[15] The business community was pleasantly surprised, however, when the president appointed his former University of Chicago Law School colleague Cass

Sunstein to head the Office of Information and Regulatory Affairs (OIRA). Sunstein was not a laissez faire minimalist, but he was a strong proponent of cost-benefit-based regulatory decisionmaking, and he believed that OIRA should exercise its review powers aggressively.[16] Sunstein retained most of the Bush Administration's personnel and review policies, and he even recruited a former American Enterprise Institute fellow and long-time critic of federal regulation to join the team. A surprisingly aggressive OIRA changed 76 percent of the rules submitted to it for review during the Obama Administration compared to only 64 percent during the George W. Bush Administration and 20 percent during the Clinton Administration. The substance of OIRA's input remained largely deregulatory in nature.[17] For example, OIRA objected to EPA's efforts to update the ambient air quality standards for sulfur dioxide on the patently unlawful ground that compliance would be too expensive.[18]

After the 2010 elections, in which the Republican Party regained control of the House and narrowed the Democratic majority in the Senate, the administration hit the emergency brake and slammed the regulatory engine into reverse. President Obama signed a new executive order on regulation that left the Clinton executive order in place, but amended it to require agencies to re-examine existing regulations and provide more transparency in the review process.[19] To emphasize his intention to mollify the business community, the president himself wrote an op-ed in the *Wall Street Journal* to announce the changes. Proclaiming that the "free market" was "the greatest force for prosperity the world has ever known," he promised in the future to "strike the right balance" by "remov[ing] outdated regulations that stifle job creation and make our economy less competitive."[20] One progressive advocate complained that the president had "swallowed the GOP's frame for the debate hook, line, and sinker." Observers on both sides agreed that the message of the executive order was that OIRA would be reviewing future regulations more skeptically than in the past.[21]

The impetus behind the new approach to regulation came from Sunstein and newly appointed White House Chief of Staff Bill Daley, a former executive at JPMorgan Chase and co-chairman of the Chamber of Commerce's committee on financial regulation.[22] It soon became clear that the administration planned to use the regulatory "look-back" as an opportunity to demonstrate that it was committed to easing regulatory requirements. In February, Sunstein authored a blog entitled "Smarter Regulation" in which he boasted that OIRA had already blocked five regulations, and he penned a memo to the independent agencies requesting that they re-examine their existing regulations as well.[23]

In May, Sunstein announced the preliminary results of the agencies' look-back efforts in a speech to the American Enterprise Institute and an op-ed in the *Wall Street Journal*. Thirty agencies had submitted proposed plans for how they would repeal or rewrite hundreds of existing regulations that were imposing millions of dollars of compliance costs every year. Sunstein estimated that the look-back would result in a total of $1 billion in savings to industry. A spokesperson for the U.S. Chamber of Commerce, however, characterized the project as "tinkering around the edges."[24] In August, the administration released the final version of the agency plans containing 500 proposed reforms that would, according to the administration, save industry $10 billion over a five-year period, but the business community remained underwhelmed. Advocates of greater governmental protection were just "disappointed at the whole exercise."[25]

The White House demonstrated its commitment to reducing the cost of regulation in September 2011 when it reviewed EPA's proposal to tighten the George W. Bush Administration's standard for photochemical oxidants (smog). The petroleum, chemical, and electric utility industries and their Republican allies in Congress strongly opposed the proposal.[26] Representatives of the affected industries expressed their concerns about the high cost of achieving the proposed standard to high-level OMB and OIRA officials in a series of meetings that culminated in a meeting attended by Sunstein and newly appointed Chief of Staff William Daley.[27] The industry officials warned that the rule was a key test of the administration's seriousness about reducing unemployment during the ongoing recession.[28] The head of the American Petroleum Institute impressed Daley with a color-coded map of the economically affected areas, most of which were in traditionally Republican states that President Obama had won in 2008.[29] In a September 1, 2011 meeting attended by Jackson and Daley in the Oval Office, President Obama ordered Jackson to withdraw the proposal and revisit it in 2013.[30] Although Jackson was stunned by the public rebuke, she decided that a resignation would be a futile gesture.[31]

President Obama's rapid turnaround on federal regulations after the 2010 elections resembled that of President George H. W. Bush during the last year of his administration, discussed in Chapter 7. And the results were similar. The moves failed to appease the business community, and they infuriated proponents of stronger regulation who had hoped that the administration would bring on a new era of greater health, safety, and environmental protection.[32]

BRIEF FIXES TO AGENCY BUDGETS

For the first time in years, many agency budgets received major increases during the first year of the Obama Administration. Both OSHA and MSHA received an infusion of resources from the economic stimulus bill that President

Obama signed in February 2009 and the continuing appropriations resolution that he signed a month later. EPA received an eye-popping 36 percent increase for FY 2010.[33] The administration's budget for FY 2011, however, froze overall federal spending, with modest decreases for EPA and NHTSA, but it suggested a large increase for FDA and small increases for MSHA, OSHA, FSIS, and CPSC.[34] The administration requested a 30 percent cut in EPA's FY 2012 budget, but it sought a slight increase in OSHA's budget for that year.[35]

MODEST CHANGES IN THE RULES

The president devoted his first 100 days to a frantic effort to stabilize the collapsing financial markets that he had inherited from the Clinton and Bush Administrations. Rather than pressing ahead with comprehensive financial reform legislation as a quid pro quo for the government bailout of Wall Street, however, he decided to make health care reform his top domestic priority. Throughout the remainder of the year, the new administration steadily lost momentum as it engaged in a quixotic attempt to forge bipartisan agreements with Republican legislators who were under strict orders from their leadership not to cooperate. The Republicans adopted a strategy of inserting the words "job killing" before any regulatory initiative that came before Congress.[36] On the regulatory front, the regulatory agencies during the first two years of the Obama Administration promulgated fewer major rules than the George W. Bush Administration during the same period.

FINANCIAL PROTECTION

In a move that was designed specifically to reassure the financial markets, President Obama appointed Timothy Geithner, the head of the New York Fed, to be Secretary of the Treasury. Former Treasury Secretary Lawrence Summers, a strong advocate of banking deregulation during the Clinton Administration, assumed command of the administration's economic policies as Director of the National Economic Council. During the 2008 election season, Summers had attended a tribute to Milton Friedman at which he proclaimed that "we are all Friedmanites."[37]

Days after the 2008 election, Rahm Emanuel, President Obama's intensely pragmatic chief of staff, remarked that "Rule Number One" for the new administration would be "never allow a crisis to go to waste." Soon thereafter, President Obama announced that one of his administration's top priorities would be financial reform legislation.[38] Many highly regarded economists were convinced that nothing short of comprehensive reform of the financial sector could adequately address the badly misplaced incentives that had brought on the 2008 meltdown. For starters, the massive conglomerates that had come to dominate Wall Street as a result of the Gramm-Leach-Bliley Act had to be broken up into much smaller institutions, no one of which was so vital to the financial system that it was too big to fail. Otherwise, competitive pressures to consolidate and take on greater risk would combine with the implicit guarantee of a federal bailout to produce another speculative bubble. Proponents of comprehensive reform ranged across the entire spectrum of economists from Nobel Prize winners Paul Krugman and Joseph Stiglitz to former Fed chairpersons Paul Volcker and Alan Greenspan.[39]

The Heritage Foundation, however, advised against any new government initiatives, because the private sector had already responded to the crisis with "market improvements" that made the markets much more "transparent, efficient and stable." The new administration took the path advocated by the Heritage Foundation in early 2009 when it refused to channel public outrage over huge Wall Street bonuses into support for comprehensive financial reform legislation. Both Geithner and Summers adamantly opposed breaking up large financial institutions, and contrary views were not welcome at the White House so long as the strong-willed Summers was in control of economic policy. President Obama thus effectively ceded the competition for the ears of angry Americans to a nascent "Tea Party" movement.[40]

If comprehensive reforms were not to be on the agenda, many economists from both ends of the political spectrum favored legislation that would expand the power of the federal government to regulate derivatives, credit rating agencies, and hedge funds. They urged Congress to lodge that power in fresh New Deal–like agencies that were not, like the Fed, so deeply steeped in laissez faire minimalism that they were institutionally incapable of strong regulation.[41] Stiglitz proposed a new "Financial Markets Stability Commission" with authority over the entire financial system, and Harvard Law School Professor Elizabeth Warren suggested an independent Consumer Financial Protection Agency to administer the consumer protection laws applicable to the financial sector. Volcker urged Congress to restore the Glass-Steagall Act's prohibitions on commercial depository institutions engaging in investment banking.[42]

It took until June 2009 for the administration to produce an anemic "blueprint" for legislation prescribing "technical solutions" to identified problems. The proposal left the badly misaligned incentive structure of Wall Street banks largely intact, failed to regulate credit rating agencies, and lodged most regulatory authority in the Fed as the industry had hoped. The administration's only proposal for fundamental change was a new Consumer Financial Protection

Agency (CFPA) to curb predatory lending practices and to ensure that banks did not make unaffordable loans to uninformed borrowers.[43]

The banking, securities, and insurance industries spent more than $220 million in 2009 on an army of more than 2,500 lobbyists to push back against any major reforms and to ensure that the resulting legislation contained plenty of loopholes, exceptions, and roadblocks to hinder agency implementation efforts. In addition, a "Coalition of Derivatives End Users" consisting of the Chamber of Commerce, the National Association of Manufacturers, the Business Round-table, and a number of large nonfinancial corporations weighed in against derivatives regulation.[44] On the other side of the debate, a coalition of consumer, labor, and civil rights groups called Americans for Financial Reform operated out of a borrowed office with a tiny staff and a limited budget.[45]

By the time that financial reform legislation rose to the top of the legislative agenda, memories of the meltdown were fading, and the banking industry was back on its feet. The industry was not pressed to make serious concessions by a White House negotiating team that largely shared its regulatory philosophy. The two primary sources of disagreement were the administration's proposal to create a new Consumer Financial Protection Agency and its belated insistence on an amendment, suggested by Volcker, that prohibited banks from trading with their own monies (proprietary trading). President Obama signed a modest financial reform bill dubbed the Dodd-Frank Wall Street Reform and Consumer Protection Act of 2010 in July.[46]

The Dodd-Frank Act created a quasi-independent Consumer Financial Protection Bureau (CFPB) within the Fed to implement and enforce the consumer financial protection laws including new authority to prohibit unfair, deceptive, or abusive practices in the provision of consumer financial products and services.[47] Those regulations, however, were subject to a veto by a two-thirds vote of a new Financial Stability Oversight Council (FSOC) that included the Treasury Secretary, the Fed chairman, the CFTC chairman, and an "independent" member with expertise in insurance. Lenders were required to verify a borrower's ability to repay, and borrowers were allowed to raise violations of CFPB regulations as a defense to foreclosure actions. The law also prohibited banks from paying mortgage brokers more for higher-priced loans, thereby reducing the incentive of brokers to steer borrowers to costlier loans.

The statute eliminated the Office of Thrift Supervision and merged its powers into the Office of the Comptroller of the Currency (OCC). It also enlarged the authority of OCC and the Fed to regulate insured banks, S&Ls, and bank holding companies. Hedge funds were required for the first time to register with SEC and make themselves available for periodic inspections. Although it did not break up existing banks, the law allowed the Fed by rule to limit the extent to which large financial entities could merge with or acquire stock in other financial institutions in the future. It also required the banking agencies to establish larger capital reserve requirements for "systemically important" financial institutions, a term that included all bank holding companies with at least $50 billion in assets and any other companies identified by the FSOC as posing a systemic risk to the financial system.

The so-called Volcker Rule prohibited bank holding companies from trading for their own accounts and from owning more than 3 percent of any private equity or hedge fund. Nondepository financial institutions that engaged in such activities were subject to additional capital reserve requirements and such limitations on trading as the Fed required by rule. Since large investment banks like Goldman Sachs made a great deal of money on proprietary trades, the sponsors hoped that this would result in a renewed separation between investment banks and depository institutions.

The new law repealed the Gramm-Leach-Bliley Act and for the first time created a regulatory regime for "over the counter" derivatives trading. Among other things, it required that all derivatives be traded on public exchanges or through private clearinghouses that assumed responsibility for the promised payments and met agency-established margin requirements. CFTC and SEC could subject swap dealers (but not end users) to capital reserve requirements and require public reporting of all swap transactions. Securitizers were required to retain at least 5 percent of the credit risk and to disclose sufficient data on the underlying loans to allow investors to perform due diligence. Credit rating agencies had to establish internal controls and take specific steps to prevent marketing considerations from interfering with objective ratings. Credit rating agencies that "knowingly or recklessly" failed to conduct reasonable due diligence were subject to liability to the investors who purchased the rated securities.

The statute required companies to disclose more information about executive compensation to shareholders and to give shareholders an opportunity to hold non-binding votes on compensation for top executives. The banking agencies could prohibit covered financial institutions from entering into any incentive-based compensation arrangements that encouraged inappropriate risk-taking by providing "excessive compensation." And companies trading on the national stock exchanges had to adopt "clawback" policies to recoup incentive compensation based on information that turned out to be erroneous.

Wall Street breathed a collective sigh of relief when the president signed the bill. The statute left intact most of the banking industry's perverse incentives to maximize short-term gain at the expense of long-term risks. Too-big-to-fail financial institutions were still able to make high-risk bets with the expectation that the federal government would bail them out again in the next financial crisis. Credit rating agencies were still paid by the issuers of the securities they rated. The legislation thus did little to prevent the race-to-the-bottom as the three big credit rating agencies competed with one another for business by providing higher ratings. By subjecting CFPB regulations to veto by a two-thirds majority of a board composed of the heads of easily captured agencies, the statute may have ensured that CFPB will promulgate few regulations that the lending industry strongly opposes.[48] The Fed emerged with all its powers intact and with new authorities that greatly enhanced its discretion to regulate financial institutions or leave them to their own devices.[49] With the exception of the newly empowered CFPB, the governing philosophy underlying the statute was one of limited intervention into freely functioning markets.[50]

The ink was barely dry on the statute when the banking industry began to complain that it went too far. According to the U.S. Chamber of Commerce, the new law would generate a "regulatory tsunami" that would "hobble" the American economy.[51] Recognizing that the full impact of the Dodd-Frank legislation would not be felt until the agencies promulgated hundreds of required implementing regulations, the financial services industry redeployed its army of lobbyists to the agency battlefields. On the first anniversary of the statute's enactment, Professor James Cox concluded that the industry had "thrown a lot of wrenches into the rule-making process, thanks to very aggressive lobbying."[52]

The CFPB. The new Consumer Financial Protection Bureau (CFPB) got off to what can charitably be characterized as a very slow start. The obvious choice to head the CFPB was Elizabeth Warren, the Harvard law professor who had conceived of the agency and who had worked tirelessly to see it created. Consumer groups strongly supported her for the post, but the business community was adamantly opposed to the idea. Unwilling to take on a lengthy confirmation battle and anxious to get the new agency up and running, President Obama made Professor Warren an assistant to the President and a special advisor to Treasury Secretary Timothy Geithner, and he charged her with overall responsibility for the agency until a director was confirmed. Professor Warren recruited an all-star team to staff important positions at the new agency. She also met dozens of times with bankers to reassure them that the agency would not radically alter how they did business. Nevertheless, she was viciously attacked by Republicans on Capitol Hill.[53]

The president's failure to appoint Professor Warren to head the agency was ultimately of little consequence, because Senator Richard Shelby (R-Alabama) and 44 other Republican senators announced that they would filibuster *any* nominee until the president and Senate Democrats agreed to amend the Dodd-Frank Act to replace the single director of the agency with a 5-member board composed of Republicans and Democrats. The banking industry supported this unprecedented move. President Obama's belated appointment of Richard Cordray, a former Ohio Attorney General, to direct the office almost a year after the statute was enacted did not change the Republican position. Backed by the business community, Senate Republicans delivered on Senator Shelby's threat by defeating a cloture motion on the nomination in December 2011.[54]

Since the new agency did not have legal authority to promulgate any rules under the new powers granted by the Dodd-Frank Act until a director was in place, it was effectively out of business for its first two years of existence. President Obama responded with a "recess" appointment of Cordray in January 2012 that put him in charge of the agency for the remainder of that year. Arguing that the Senate had not technically been in recess when the president made the appointment, the Chamber of Commerce issued a thinly veiled threat to challenge the lawfulness of any rules signed by Cordray.[55] Although the agency proceeded as if it were fully empowered after the recess appointment, uncertainty remained over the validity of its regulations.[56]

The Volcker Rule. Even before President Obama signed the Dodd-Frank Act, Goldman Sachs, Citigroup, and other large financial institutions were lobbying the Fed to exclude some of their most lucrative transactions from the Volcker Rule's proprietary trading limits.[57] The efficacy of the rule will depend on how the implementing agencies interpret several statutory exclusions. One exempts from the ban on proprietary trading any bank engaged in "market making" (agreeing to purchase or sell securities when asked to do so by an entity seeking to be on the other side of the transaction).[58] Citigroup got ahead in the game by moving personnel who formerly traded for the company's own accounts to a new division that would engage in the same kinds of trades when "requested" to do so by its clients. One investment banker boasted that he could "find a way to say that virtually any trade we make is somehow related to serving one of our clients."[59]

The five agencies responsible for promulgating the implementing regulations had difficulty reaching a consensus on many issues. For the most part, the agencies resolved their differences by deciding not to decide. The proposal that the banking agencies released in late September 2011 raised more than 1,300 questions on 400 topics.[60] It satisfied no one. Adopting the familiar divert and delay approach to implementation, the large banks formed "Volcker Rule Task Forces" to lobby the agencies, file thousands of pages of comments, and make the case for delaying implementation until after the 2012 election.

Referring to the length of the preamble and its 381 footnotes, they complained that the proposal was far too expensive and complicated. Like the statute itself, the regulations would "discourage investment, limit credit availability and increase the cost of capital for companies." Paul Volcker blamed banking lobbyists for the complexity of the rules, suggesting that they may have "want[ed] to disrupt the whole process." Consumer advocates complained that the vague terms used in crafting exemptions and exceptions gave the banking institutions too much leeway to avoid compliance. They pointed out that no law of nature decreed that too-big-to-fail banks were the only institutions capable of making markets in opaque financial instruments.[61]

The proposed rule repeated the statutory requirements, but crafted a number of exceptions and definitional qualifications that gave the banking industry a great deal of leeway in determining how to comply. For example, one exception that had the potential to swallow the rule would have allowed investment banks to purchase derivatives for the purpose of hedging risks on a "portfolio" basis. According to sophisticated observers, this gave the banks an opportunity to make bets on various markets as in the old days by characterizing them as hedges against vaguely defined risks. One former Clinton Administration official concluded that the exception would give the banks "a license to do pretty much anything." The exception was regarded as a major victory for the investment banks, whose lobbyists had met with the banking agencies 350 times before the proposed rule was published.[62]

One of the strongest proponents of the portfolio exemption was Jamie Dimon, the CEO of JPMorgan Chase, the nation's largest bank. Arguing that Paul Volcker (and presumably other proponents of the Volcker rule) did not understand modern capital markets, Dimon met behind closed doors on many occasions with sympathetic Fed and Treasury Department officials to make his case for a broad exemption. Dimon received a comeuppance in May 2012, however, when the bank suffered a loss of more than $2 billion on a complex array of derivatives that constituted a hedge against a hedge that a trader nicknamed the "London whale" had made against a large portfolio of corporate bonds. JPMorgan's comments on the proposed rule had stressed the need to preserve just this sort of trade within the portfolio exemption. Yet, even after the JPMorgan fiasco, officials at the Office of the Comptroller of the Currency were still insisting on a broad portfolio exemption.[63]

Derivatives Regulation. Banking industry lobbyists brought their influence to bear especially forcefully on the once-sleepy Commodity Futures Trading Commission as it assumed its new obligation to regulate credit default swaps and other derivatives. To the consternation of the banking industry, Gary Gensler, the former Goldman Sachs investment banker, proved to be a fierce regulator.[63] But he was also willing to listen to the banking industry, meeting more than 600 times with various groups in less than a year.[64]

Two of the greatest threats that the Dodd-Frank reforms posed to Wall Street's profits were the mandate that derivatives markets be more transparent and the margin requirements that it imposed on "swap dealers" and "major swap participants."[65] Since the statute excluded "end users" from both requirements, CFTC had to address early on the critical definitional question of what entities constituted "end users." The agency published a proposed rule defining that term in early December 2010 and received more than 1,000 comments on it.[66] A Business Roundtable–sponsored survey of end users predicted that the requirements CFTC was proposing would put 130,000 jobs at risk. Despite Chairman Gensler's protests that the survey preceded the agency's proposal, which clearly exempted nearly all end users from the transparency and margin requirements, the 130,000 figure played a prominent role in the attempts by the Business Roundtable, the U.S. Chamber of Commerce, and others to delay and weaken the regulation. Responding to a lobbying blitz from energy companies, hedge funds, and banking institutions, the agency broadened the exemption considerably to exempt any firm that arranged less than $8 billion worth of swaps for the first three years and $3 billion thereafter.[67]

In the midst of CFTC's efforts to promulgate dozens of rules required by the Dodd-Frank Act, a mid-sized trading firm named MS Global, which was headed by former senator and New Jersey governor Jon Corzine, went bankrupt. It soon became apparent that the company had used its client's money to pay debts that it had incurred on its own proprietary accounts, and up to $1.2 billion in client funds were nowhere to be found. The agency had in fact begun crafting regulations to tighten restrictions on how brokerage firms like MS Global could use their clients' funds, but the industry strongly opposed any further regulation. Corzine and his staff had in fact met with CFTC chairman Gary Gensler on a conference call to urge him not to go forward with the rulemaking. Soon after the MS Global scandal broke, however, the agency promulgated regulations that required brokerage firms to segregate customers' swaps funds from the firm's proprietary accounts, but it allowed a firm to pool all of its customer money into a single account to reduce administrative costs. [68]

Too-Big-to-Fail. The Fed and the Financial Stability Oversight Council (FSOC) got off to an unambitious start in promulgating regulations for identifying the financial institutions with fewer than $50 billion in assets that would be subject to the additional capital and oversight requirements for "systemically important" banks. The FSOC proposed regulations in January 2011 that crafted an exceedingly vague test for identifying systemically important financial institutions on a case-by-case basis at some point in the future. After being deluged with comments from a wide variety of companies, all claiming that they were too insignificant to be considered systemically important, the Council issued another proposal in October 2011. The final rule, which came out in early April 2012, adopted a complex three-tiered process for designating nonbanks as "systemically important financial institutions." It subjected all financial firms with more than $50 billion in assets and met one of five quantitative thresholds to an individualized examination of its potential threat to the financial system.[69]

In the meantime, the Fed in January 2012 proposed regulations for the banks that passed the $50 billion threshold and those banks that would be deemed systemically important in the future that, among other things, established debt-to-equity limits, risk-based capital requirements and leverage limits, liquidity requirements, and single-party counterparty limits for those institutions. Although many of the provisions contained little more than additional paperwork burdens and the capital limits were no more stringent than the international standards to which the banks were already subject, the counterparty exposure limits raised a howl from the large banks, because the 10 percent limit that was imposed on the total credit exposure that the largest bank holding companies could have to a single counterparty was considerably more stringent than the 25 percent default cap that the statute imposed.[70]

As the agencies struggled with the implementation regulations, a handful of very large financial institutions, like Citibank, JPMorgan Chase, and Goldman Sachs, grew even larger and, for a time, were bringing in higher profits than ever. The largest financial institutions earned more in the first 30 months of the Obama Administration than they made during the entire George W. Bush Administration. Yet, despite the modest Dodd-Frank limitations, they remained too big to fail.[71]

ENVIRONMENTAL PROTECTION

EPA Administrator Lisa Jackson and her activist staff moved forward aggressively with more than 25 major rulemaking initiatives during her first year. At the same time, the agency reviewed many of the Bush Administration regulations with an eye toward revising or withdrawing them. Jackson elevated science to a more prominent role in agency decisionmaking, and she assigned a less prominent role to cost-benefit analysis by placing a prominent critic at the head of the policy office.[72] She eliminated the Performance Track program (under which the agency had rewarded companies undertaking voluntary compliance initiatives with fewer inspections) as "one of those window dressing programs that has little value." The business community raised such a furor, however, that the agency allowed several other equally ineffective voluntary programs to remain in effect.[73]

Greenhouse Gas Legislation. President Obama got off to a good start toward fulfilling his campaign promise to secure enactment of climate change legislation by appointing former EPA head Carol Browner to be the administration's "energy czar" and putting her in charge of the administration's legislative efforts. The chances for enacting protective climate change legislation had never been better than in early 2009. A coalition of 32 environmental groups and large corporate greenhouse gas emitters, called the U.S. Climate Action Partnership (USCAP), agreed to support comprehensive legislation creating a "cap and trade" regime for greenhouse gases aimed at achieving a 42 percent reduction in emissions from 2005 levels by 2030 and an 80 percent reduction by 2050. To gain industry support, however, the environmental groups agreed to soften the economic impact by bestowing a substantial proportion of the original emissions allocations on current emitters at no cost, thereby providing an economic windfall for large emitters.[74]

In February 2009, the Obama Administration proposed a slightly more ambitious cap and trade regime that would have allocated the initial credits through an auction and used the proceeds to fund research and assist low-income citizens with increases in energy costs.[75] The House passed its own 1,300-page cap and trade bill in May over the unanimous opposition of House Republicans. That bill would have reduced emissions by 17 percent by 2020 and 83 percent by 2050, and it would have awarded 85 percent of the initial credits to current emitters. To attract the votes of oil patch and Midwestern Democrats, however, the bill also included a number of malodorous pork barrel subsidies to a few favored industries.[76]

The Chamber of Commerce and many coal and oil companies joined the Competitive Enterprise Institute and the Heritage Foundation in adamantly opposing all climate change legislation. Americans for Prosperity, a Koch-funded offshoot of Citizens for a Sound Economy, hosted eighty "grass-roots" events at which speakers asserted (erroneously) that backyard barbeques would be taxed if Congress enacted the House bill.[77] Discredited climate change skeptics were back in the limelight in November 2009 when approximately 1,000 purloined emails to and from scientists involved in preparing an influential report for the Intergovernmental Panel on Climate Change were leaked to the press. Although the embarrassing revelations did not undermine the integrity of the science in the report, they provided grist for the skeptics' allegations that the report was untrustworthy.[78]

President Obama made no effort to use his bully pulpit to refute the bogus charges and educate the public on how climate change legislation would prevent massive economic and social disruption in the future. By the time that Congress completed the health care bill in March 2010, the repeated refrains of "climategate" and "cap and tax" from the conservative media echo chamber had so soured the public on the proposed legislation that the 60-vote majority needed to stop a promised Republican filibuster was unattainable. After the 2010 elections returned the House to Republican control, the Obama Administration gave up entirely on a climate change bill, American consumers fell in love with SUVs once again, and greenhouse gas emissions increased by a larger amount than in any previous year.[79]

EPA Greenhouse Gas Initiatives. The climate change battlefield then shifted to EPA. First, EPA granted California's request for a waiver allowing it to regulate auto emissions of greenhouse gases. Thirteen other states then adopted the stringent California limitations.[80] Second, EPA made a formal finding that greenhouse gas emissions "endangered" the environment, thereby triggering EPA's own obligation to regulate motor vehicle emissions.[81] Third, in a joint rulemaking facilitated by behind-the-scenes negotiations with the recently bailed-out auto industry, EPA and NHTSA promulgated regulations that simultaneously limited greenhouse gas emissions and raised fuel economy standards for sedans, SUVs, and pickups.[82] Fourth, the agency withdrew a controversial Bush Administration memorandum concluding that greenhouse gas emissions did not trigger the new source review requirements for new and modified major emitting facilities, and it promulgated a "tailoring" rule that established new thresholds for "majorness" to ensure that only very large facilities were subject to the "best available technology" requirement for major sources.[83]

The affected industries and the Chamber of Commerce returned to the familiar divert and delay strategy, challenging all of the regulations in appeals that were consolidated in the D.C. Circuit.[84] Conservative think tanks argued that the regulations would force millions of farmers and other small emitters to obtain permits from EPA, force U.S. companies to relocate overseas, and have other devastating impacts on the nation's fragile economy.[85]

Mercury. EPA responded to the judicial remand of the Bush Administration's Mercury regulation in March 2011 by proposing to establish a hazardous emission standard under section 112 of the Clean Air Act reflecting the "maximum degree of reduction in emissions" that was "achievable" (MACT). EPA predicted that compliance with these standards would reduce mercury emissions from power plants by about 91 percent, and this would in turn prevent 17,000 premature deaths, 11,000 heart attacks, and 120,000 asthma attacks per year.[86]

The electric utility and coal industries, however, vehemently opposed the new proposal, arguing that it would cause electric rates to soar, lead to rolling brown-outs, and put thousands of workers out of jobs.[87] The industries spent almost $100 million on a massive lobbying blitz directed at EPA and the environmental committees in Congress. A "Ten-Point Plan to Create Jobs" circulated by the Competitive Enterprise Institute urged EPA to withdraw the proposal, and Grover Norquist's Americans for Tax Reform warned that compliance with the rules would cause a "shock to electricity prices in the United States." A coalition of coal and utility companies spent around $35 million on television advertising criticizing the EPA proposal.[88] In a speech to Congress in September 2011, however, President Obama rejected "the argument that says for the economy to grow, we have to roll back . . . rules that keep our kids from being exposed to mercury." The agency promulgated a final rule in late December 2011 that varied from the ambitious proposal in only minor regards.[89]

Wetlands. In April 2011, EPA and the Corps of Engineers drafted new guidelines for determining the extent to which wetlands came within the meaning of "navigable waters" for purposes of requiring a permit from the Corps. The new guidelines expanded the permit requirement from the previous administration's guidance to include wetlands adjacent to tributaries of navigable streams and other marginal waters. The agency further announced its intention to make the guidelines binding on future administrations through the rulemaking process. Soon thereafter, Republican members in the House and Senate introduced bills to invalidate the guidance and prohibit EPA from turning it into a rule. [90]

BOEMRE Initiatives. In early 2010, President Obama proudly announced that the Minerals Management Service (MMS) would be opening up previously protected areas in the Atlantic, the Gulf of Mexico, and Northern Alaska to offshore drilling.[91] The *Deepwater Horizon* disaster of April 2010, however, revealed that the sophisticated technologies for extracting oil and gas from far beneath the ocean floor had far outpaced MMS's very limited capacity to ensure that lessees behaved responsibly.[92] Interior Secretary Ken Salazar reacted to intense criticism of MMS following the blowout by placing a moratorium on new drilling leases in the Gulf of Mexico, renaming MMS the "Bureau of Ocean Energy Management, Regulation and Enforcement" (BOEMRE), and creating a separate "Office of Safety and Environmental Enforcement" within BOEMRE to house its regulatory oversight functions. This modest reshuffling, however, did little to reduce the institutional conflict of interest that had historically plagued the offshore leasing program.[93]

The new Bureau lifted the moratorium in October 2010 and promulgated two "patch-and-repair" rules in response to specific failures identified in the

Deepwater Horizon investigations. Instead of beefing up the agency's enforcement presence, the administration continued to rely heavily on private certification agencies.[94] Legislative efforts to address deepwater drilling died in the Senate after Republicans and oil patch Democrats opposed a provision subjecting oil companies to unlimited liability for spills. After the Republican Party assumed control of the House in 2011, the momentum shifted toward Republican bills aimed at opening more offshore locations to oil and gas leasing and expediting permitting. By September 2011, the crisis was apparently over, and drilling in the Gulf of Mexico had returned to near-normal levels.[95] BOEMRE reopened the Gulf of Mexico to renewed leasing and approved BP's application to drill four deepwater wells, and BP returned to profitability, earning $7.7 billion in the last quarter of 2011.[96]

Mountaintop Removal Mining Initiatives. In June 2009, OSM, EPA, and the Corps of Engineers entered into a formal Memorandum of Understanding under which the three agencies agreed to review existing regulations and procedures with the goal of reducing the environmental impact of mountaintop removal mining. OSM agreed to revisit the Bush Administration's recent revisions to the "buffer zone" rule. The Corps agreed to preclude future use of its lenient nationwide permit for mountaintop removal mining projects, and it promulgated a final rule to that effect a year later.[97] With the nationwide permit no longer available, EPA and the Corps agreed to review the expected large influx of individual dredge and fill permit applications more carefully. In September 2009, EPA announced that it had discovered serious environmental problems with all 79 of the new permits that it was currently reviewing. As EPA and the Corps worked through the applications, several were approved after the operators agreed to modifications and mitigation measures, and many more were withdrawn. Then EPA for the first time in its history revoked a previously issued permit on the ground that it would have an "unacceptable adverse effect" on the environment.[98] Any hope that these grand initiatives would bring about lasting change disappeared, however, as the coal industry successfully challenged both the EPA veto and the EPA-Corps agreement, the Corps reinstated the nationwide permit, and EPA lost enthusiasm for its promise to revisit the Bush Administration's rule defining permissible "fill" to include mountaintop removal waste.[99]

WORKPLACE SAFETY AND HEALTH

During the first three years of the Obama Administration, OSHA completed a single pending rulemaking (a safety standard protecting crane and derrick workers from falls and electrocutions) before the 2010 elections returned the House to the Republican Party, at which point OSHA once more became a poster child for Republican polemics against federal regulation.[100] A proposal to regulate silicon dust languished in OIRA for more than a year while OIRA met with industry representatives intent on killing it, and rulemaking initiatives to control worker exposure to a lung-deteriorating chemical called diacetyl and to prevent explosions due to accumulations of flammable dust were formally placed on the back burner.[101] OSHA head David Michaels's signature project, a rule that would make employers responsible for developing and implementing "injury and illness prevention programs" containing "best practices" for addressing all significant workplace hazards, became the target of congressional investigators and did not even reach the proposal stage.[102]

Largely because of a disastrous April 2010 explosion at Massey Energy Company's Upper Big Branch mine in Beckley, West Virginia, in which 29 miners were killed, the number of coal-mine fatalities in 2010 was the highest since 1992.[103] Both MSHA and an independent team appointed by the governor of West Virginia attributed the blast to the company's failure to suppress coal dust as required by MSHA regulations.[104] Critics argued that the disaster might have been prevented had MSHA promulgated regulations requiring mines to install real-time coal-dust monitors. And a panel assembled by the National Institute of Occupational Safety and Health concluded that if MSHA inspectors had "engaged in timely enforcement" of MSHA regulations, the explosion might have been prevented.[105] The explosion precipitated the resignation of Massey's CEO, Don L. Blankenship (who was soon back in business as McCoy Energy Co.), and the purchase of the company by Alpha Natural Resources. It also inspired MSHA to promulgate an emergency temporary standard requiring mine operators to take additional steps to prevent coal-dust accumulations.[106] The disaster, however, absorbed a great deal of the agency's energies, and other rulemaking projects suffered from lack of attention.[107]

DRUG AND DEVICE SAFETY

FDA quickly put the new revenues and authorities provided by the 2007 reauthorization act to good use. After hiring 79 additional staffers, the surveillance office launched a "Sentinel" initiative under which it mined the health records of millions of patients in the federal Medicare system for evidence of adverse effects of drugs and medical devices.[108] Unlike some of her predecessors, FDA Commissioner Hamburg welcomed dissent within the ranks, and she gave the Office of Drug Safety more authority to decide how to address previously approved drugs on the basis of scientific information that did not come up to the stringent criteria that governed approval of new drug applications.[109]

After publishing a scathing self-critique of its medical device office for yielding to political pressure in granting abbreviated approvals, the agency ordered manufacturers of devices that had never undergone the full approval process to submit safety and effectiveness data sufficient to justify full approval status within 120 days. A panel assembled by the National Institute of Medicine recommended that FDA urge Congress to scrap the abbreviated approval process altogether, but FDA declined to take that advice. The pace of full approvals for new devices slowed somewhat, but that was partially attributable to the fact that application fees supported less of the device program than the drug program.[110]

Following the 2010 elections, the agency once again had to respond to complaints from the drug industry and its allies in Congress that the United States was experiencing a "drug lag" because new drugs were being approved more rapidly in other countries. In fact, it looked as though another drug rush might be underway as new drug approvals increased in 2011 to a level that had been exceeded only once in the previous decade. For example, upper-level officials in late 2011 approved an anti-clotting drug over the objection of the staff reviewer who thought that the pivotal study underlying the application was flawed.[111]

FOOD SAFETY

Early in Commissioner Hamburg's tenure, FDA finalized a rulemaking initiative begun in 1999 to address *Salmonella* in eggs using a "farm-to-table" sanitation approach. The regulations, however, came too late to prevent a *Salmonella* outbreak in August 2010 that resulted in the recall of half a billion eggs.[112] USDA in August 2009 decided to test the meat at slaughterhouses for *E. coli* O157:H7 before it entered the grinding stage.[113] While this represented a significant shift in the agency's approach to the *E. coli* prohibition, its full impact remains to be seen. In the wake of a highly publicized European outbreak caused by sprouts contaminated with a strain of *E. coli* even more virulent than *E. coli* O157:H7, the Department in September 2011 promulgated a final rule extending the ban on *E. coli* O157:H7 to six other highly pathogenic strains of *E. coli*. Although the action infuriated the meat industry, it demonstrated that USDA was still capable of decisive action in response to a crisis.[114]

After a series of outbreaks of foodborne illness during 2008, several major food producers and large retailers joined food safety advocates in calling for legislative reforms. The Obama Administration jumped on the bandwagon.[115] Small farmers, FreedomWorks (another offshoot of Citizens for a Sound Economy), and Tea Party advocates weighed in against any reforms.[116] Although Congress briefly debated a comprehensive reform bill that would have created a single agency to implement all of the federal food safety protections, it quickly settled on modifications to the law's substantive requirements that left the existing institutional framework in place.[117]

The Food Safety Modernization Act of 2010 required most food processors to prepare and implement hazard analysis at critical control point (HACCP) programs like the ones that USDA had required of meat processors in the mid-1990s. In addition, FDA had to write "science-based" minimum sanitation standards for production and harvesting of fruits and vegetables. The statute for the first time empowered FDA to order mandatory recalls, and it expanded the agency's authority to quarantine food that might be adulterated. The new law also authorized FDA to bar imports from foreign facilities that refused to allow an FDA inspection and to write regulations requiring importers to certify that their products complied with FDA food safety requirements. On the enforcement front, the statute required FDA to conduct at least one inspection at every "high risk" domestic facility by 2016 and every three years thereafter. It also required the agency to conduct at least 600 inspections of foreign establishments before 2012 and to double that number every year for the next five years.

If properly implemented and enforced, the HACCP programs for food processors and risk-reduction programs for growers, packagers, and distributors of produce should greatly reduce the incidence of pathogens in the nation's food. But the manufacturers' incentive to cut corners will remain, and the programs themselves are largely under their control. Companies implementing HACCP programs can easily "game the system" if the implementing agency fails to provide effective verification and oversight. Likewise, the new import provisions leave testing and verification largely in the hands of importers. Their success will lie in the efficacy with which FDA inspectors can oversee the foreign facilities in actual operation.

These new responsibilities and the statute's ambitious mandates for inspections of high-risk and foreign facilities will require a substantial infusion of new resources. Recognizing this, a coalition of consumer groups and industry trade associations pressed the leadership of both parties in Congress to increase FDA's FY 2012 budget for its food programs by $39 million, despite an overall push by House Republicans to reduce federal spending. Their efforts were no doubt aided by another crisis in which 30 mostly elderly people were killed and 146 sickened in the fall of 2011 by *Listeria*-contaminated cantaloupes grown and processed at a Colorado farm and distributed by Del Monte in 17 states.[118]

Despite the infusion of resources, progress in implementing the statute's ambitious new programs was glacial. Sixteen months after enactment, FDA had already missed the statutory deadline for publishing proposals for "science-based" produce safety standards and an import certification program because the proposals were held up at OIRA for review. An Obama Administration proposal to enhance FDA's inspectorate by charging fees to regulatees was strongly opposed by the food industry and was therefore dead on arrival in the Republican-controlled House of Representatives. In the meantime, *Salmonella*-contaminated cantaloupes from an Indiana farm were responsible for an outbreak that sickened 178 people in 21 states, and a North Carolina farm recalled all of its cantaloupes and honeydew melons after finding that they were contaminated with Listeria.[119]

The statute did not address the controversial subject of non-therapeutic antibiotic use in animal feed, but a federal judge in March 2012 ordered FDA to initiate long-delayed hearings on its 1977 proposal to ban the non-therapeutic use of penicillin and tetracycline in farm animals. Soon thereafter, FDA promulgated a rule establishing a voluntary program under which animal drug manufacturers could agree to label changes prohibiting the use of their drugs without a veterinarian's prescription. Because it was not mandatory, consumer groups believed that it was "tragically flawed."[120]

The new law also did nothing to cure the institutional problems that have plagued food safety regulation since the early twentieth century. By failing to create a new food safety agency, Congress left regulatory authority for meat and poultry in USDA, a department whose primary mission is to promote, not regulate agribusiness. Likewise, FDA's food safety program will remain a weak sister to its drug and device programs. And unprocessed seafood will remain orphaned in the Department of Commerce. Consequently, the potential for conflict and overlap will continue into the indefinite future as multiple agencies struggle with increasingly complex food production, processing, and marketing practices.

TRANSPORTATION SAFETY

The most pressing transportation safety issue at the outset of the Obama Administration was the problem of drivers, pilots, and engineers becoming distracted by mobile and onboard electronic devices. Several academic studies indicated that drivers using cell phones were four times as likely to become involved in accidents as undistracted drivers and that hands-free devices did not reduce that risk.[121] An April 2009 collision in which a texting truck driver crashed into a school bus lent urgency to the issue. A Virginia Tech Transportation Institute study concluding that texting by truck drivers increased collision risks by 23 percent provided the additional scientific support that FMCSA needed to propose a ban on the use of all hand-held mobile telephones by commercial drivers.[122] A similar highly publicized head-on collision between a freight train and a Los Angeles Metrolink commuter train that failed to stop because the engineer was texting messages over his cell phone inspired FRA to promulgate regulations prohibiting all railroad crew members from using cell phones and other handheld electronic devices while on duty.[123] A year later, FMCSA promulgated a final rule banning the use of handheld cell phones by commercial truck and bus drivers.[124]

NHTSA's agenda was dominated by a crisis arising out of complaints that certain Toyota automobiles experienced "sudden acceleration" incidents that prevented the drivers from controlling the vehicles through braking. NHTSA had opened an investigation into the complaints in 2004, but two Toyota engineers (both of whom had previously worked for NHTSA) persuaded the NHTSA investigator to exclude 27 of the 37 reported incidents as probably attributable to drivers erroneously stepping on both the brake and acceleration pedals at the same time. Another investigation in March 2007 focusing on thick floor mats that could trap the accelerator pedal in a depressed position resulted in a voluntary recall of 55,000 vehicles to replace the mats.

After a highly publicized August 2009 crash of a Lexus ES350 driven by a California highway patrol officer, NHTSA persuaded Toyota to recall 3.8 million vehicles to replace or re-shape the accelerator pedals to reduce floor mat impingement risks. Later, Toyota executives stunned NHTSA officials with the news that the company had known for at least a year that "sticky" gas pedals it had purchased from CTS Corporation failed to return to the idle position as rapidly as drivers expected, thus leading to the sensation that the vehicle was unintentionally accelerating. CTS vigorously denied the allegation, noting that, at most, a sticky pedal would cause the vehicle to "experience near-idle levels," and not a sudden acceleration. Nevertheless, Toyota announced a recall of 2.3 million vehicles to replace the pedals with pedals of a different design. The Toyota incident inspired lengthy (and largely inconclusive) investigations, but no legislation. NHTSA did publish a proposal in April 2012 to require manufacturers of cars and light duty trucks to install brake-throttle override systems to allow drivers to stop the vehicle even if the accelerator pedal malfunctions.[125]

In July 2009, FRA proposed regulations to implement the Rail Safety Improvement Act of 2008 by requiring electronic positive train control systems on most trains and collision avoidance technologies on most tracks used for passenger and hazardous materials transportation. Arguing that it could ill afford to invest $7–24 billion over the next 20 years, the railroad industry lobbied the White House to exempt sections of track carrying little hazardous cargo or passenger traffic. The final rule dutifully created a broad *"de minimis* risk" exemption that had the potential to blossom into a gaping loophole. Following the 2010 elections, the agency announced that it was in the process of drafting a proposal to modify the rule to make it even less costly for the railroads.[126]

After abandoning the Bush Administration's hours of service rule, FMCSA invited public comment on a proposal to revise its driver fatigue rules to reduce the existing 11-hour daily driving limit to 10 hours and to add further restrictions to the 34 consecutive hour break that drivers had to take between 60- or 70-hour work weeks. Responding to strong opposition from the trucking industry, however, the final rule left both the 11-hour limit and 34-hour break provisions undisturbed and put into effect only minor changes that affected a small minority of drivers.[127] From a safety perspective, the rule did not improve greatly on the Bush Administration standard.

The February 2009 Continental Connections crash near Buffalo, New York, inspired Congress to write a narrow provision in FAA's 2010 reauthorization bill requiring it to promulgate revised pilot fatigue rules. In September 2010, the agency proposed regulations that would have tightened its hours of service requirements for pilots of commercial airlines, charter airlines, and cargo carriers (the last two of which were not subject to the existing rules) to give pilots at least nine hours between shifts and 30 consecutive off-duty hours per week. The airlines, the Chamber of Commerce, and some pilots opposed the regulation, and they took their case to OIRA. The final rule was somewhat less stringent than the proposal (e.g., giving pilots eight or nine hours between flights, depending on the time of day and other factors), and they allowed the exemption for cargo carriers to remain in effect.[128]

CONSUMER PROTECTION

The Federal Trade Commission. President Obama elevated Democratic Commissioner Jon Leibowitz, a former Senate aide with a pro-consumer record, to chair the FTC. Leibowitz appointed David C. Vladeck, a law professor and former head of the Public Citizen Litigation Group, to lead the agency's Bureau of Consumer Protection.[129] In October 2009, FTC gingerly tiptoed back into the messy world of consumer advertising when it amended its 1980 guidelines on product endorsements to require internet bloggers to disclose any payments or free products received from the manufacturers of products that they endorsed in their blogs. The guidelines also clarified that false or misleading claims for products on the internet were subject to FTC enforcement actions under the same authorities that prohibited deceptive advertising on television and in newspapers.[130]

One of Vladeck's early priorities was "behavioral targeting" on the internet, a practice through which individuals automatically allowed online publishers and advertisers to collect information on their web browsing behavior when they visited a commercial website and agreed to its privacy policies. A 2007 FTC survey found that the automatic "opt in" approach did not offer effective protections to consumers, and a detailed August 2009 critique of the industry's voluntary privacy guidelines concluded that they were "no longer sufficient." Joined by the Obama Administration's Commerce Department, the internet marketing industry complained that an "opt out" approach, under which individuals could place their names on a "do not track" list of persons whose browsing behavior could not be traced, would endanger the current system of free internet content.

In February 2012, President Obama endorsed a voluntary code of conduct prepared by the Department of Commerce to govern the collection and use of personal information gathered on the internet. At the same time that the president was encouraging companies to adopt the voluntary code, FTC Chairman Jon Leibowitz promised that it would aggressively penalize companies that declined to follow voluntary privacy programs. A month later, FTC published a report calling for companies to adopt the voluntary privacy policies, including a "do not track" program. Although the agency did not believe that it had the authority to mandate such a program, it promised to seek such authority from Congress if companies did not adopt and enforce voluntary programs. With the Republican Party in control of the House of Representatives, however, any such legislation was dead on arrival. And companies began to waffle on their commitments, arguing that do not track programs could still collect data for market research and product development purposes.[131]

The Consumer Product Safety Commission. After appointing Inez Tenenbaum, the former Superintendent of the South Carolina Education Department, to chair CPSC in early May 2009, President Obama quickly filled the remaining two positions on the recently expanded Commission with consumer advocates. The Commission's first task was to implement the Consumer Product Safety Improvement Act of 2008 (CPSIAct), which a Democrat-controlled Congress had enacted in response to the toy import crisis of 2007 and President Bush had reluctantly signed in August 2008 to forestall increased state regulation.[132]

The new statute drastically reduced the permissible concentrations of lead in children's products and in paint used on all consumer products, but it authorized CPSC to grant petitions to exclude individual items from the statutory limits. It further prohibited the sale of child care articles and toys containing more than 0.1 percent of three designated endocrine disrupting phthalates. The statute required CPSC to create an internet-searchable database containing incident reports that it received from consumers, notices of recalls, and voluntary corrective actions. It also enhanced the agency's recall authorities and gave the agency the power to file court actions to seize products it found to be "imminently hazardous." On the enforcement front, the CPSIAct increased maximum penalties and empowered state attorneys general to enforce the federal consumer product safety laws. An increase in CPSC's appropriation authorization from $66 million in FY 2007 to $122 million in FY 2010 allowed the refurbished Commission to implement the new law aggressively. Within a year, the agency had become the target of a predictable round of complaints from the business community.[133]

In December 2008, the National Association of Manufacturers urged CPSC to grant broad exemptions from the CPSIAct's testing and certification requirements to several classes of products that were either not intended for use by children or contained lead in places that would ordinarily be inaccessible to children. Recognizing that the rulemaking process could take years, the Commission effectively exempted *all* toys by formally staying its enforcement of the statutory ban for one year and then another.[134] A court holding that the statutory ban on sales of toys containing high levels of lead and phthalates was applicable to sales of *existing* toys as well as newly manufactured products caused considerable consternation in the retailing industry and even more distress among used product sellers like Goodwill Industries.[135]

In August 2011, Congress amended the statute to clarify that the statutory lead limits were not retrospective and to empower CPSC to prescribe a higher lead limit if it was not technologically feasible to manufacture a product that met the statutory limit or if lead at a higher level would have no measurable adverse effect on public health or safety. The revision also required CPSC to consider promulgating "special rules" for "small batch" manufacturers (typically producers of hand-made toys) that would take into account the limits on their ability to hire third-party certifiers for each new product and to exempt such manufacturers if economically practicable alternative testing procedures were unavailable.[136]

MORE VIGOROUS ENFORCEMENT

During the first two years of the Obama Administration, the federal government was a vigorous enforcer of protective laws and regulations. OSHA used its beefed-up resources to conduct more inspections at "high-risk" workplaces and to conduct more follow-up inspections at companies cited for "severe" violations. The effort produced a dramatic turnaround in the number of citations for serious risk during its first year. The agency also initiated a "regulation by shaming" program in which it publicly named violators and the hazards for which they were responsible. Occupational fatalities dropped during 2009, but mostly because of the lower employment rates brought on by an economic downturn.[137]

Following the 2006 Sago Mine disaster, Congress enacted an emergency supplemental appropriation allowing MSHA to hire an additional 170 inspectors. Once they were on board, citations increased by 7 percent, and assessed fines went up by 40 percent.[138] In the wake of the April 2010 Upper Big Branch explosion, President Obama ordered a five-day inspection blitz at 57 repeat violators that resulted in more than 1,000 citations and an unprecedented six withdrawal orders.[139] The agency then followed up with a series of "impact inspections" in which it issued hundreds of citations to several mines.[140] EPA's enforcement presence also increased substantially, but OSM's inspections continued to decline, from around 4,000 per year in the late 1990s to fewer than 1,500 in 2009.[141]

Agency-imposed fines also went up during the Obama Administration. In the wake of the Heparin disaster, FDA forced several manufacturers to pay fines in excess of $100 million apiece for violations of its good manufacturing standards.[142] In April 2010, Goldman Sachs paid a record $550 million fine to settle an SEC civil action alleging that it marketed a complex mortgage-backed security to unsuspecting customers so that a prominent client could reap a huge profit when the security predictably turned sour.[143] CPSC also entered into several multi-million-dollar settlements with major toy manufacturers for selling lead-contaminated toys.[144]

Occasionally, industry resistance overwhelmed the agencies. After MSHA chief Joseph Main eliminated the Bush Administration's informal settlement conferences (during which fines were invariably reduced or withdrawn), contested cases became the norm. In August 2009, MSHA concluded that 48 separate mines had exhibited patterns of violations warranting shutdown, but after all 48 contested their citations, the agency backed down. By early 2010, a backlog of 18,000 cases swamped MSHA's legal staff. Main concluded that the companies were "deliberately abusing the system and creating a backlog." The agency later proposed regulations empowering inspectors to issue "pattern of violations" orders while prior citations were under challenge.[145]

The Upper Big Branch mine explosion focused public attention on the extraordinarily high rate of safety violations at some mines. MSHA inspectors had assessed fines totaling $897,000 against that mine for 458 safety violations in 2009, only $168,000 of which had been collected by the time of the April 2010 explosion. During 2009 and the first quarter of 2010, the mine had received more than 60 orders to withdraw miners from various parts of the mine based upon its "unwarrantable failure" to comply with MSHA regulations. Prior to the explosion, Don Blankenship, Massey Energy's CEO, boasted that "we don't pay much attention to the violation count."[146] In December 2011, the Justice Department and MSHA entered into a settlement with the company's successor in which it agreed to pay $209 million in fines, penalties, and compensation to the victims and their families.[147]

In response to the Upper Big Branch explosion, the administration drafted a bill requiring mine operators to pay contested penalties into escrow accounts (to reduce the incentive to drag out the penalty assessment process) and increasing penalties for criminal violations. The House leadership combined the administration's bill with a pending bill that would have given OSHA similar powers. With the business community adamantly opposed to the OSHA bill, the combined bill did not have a chance in the Senate, where Republicans voted in lock-step against any bill strongly opposed by the business community and a few Democrats would dependably vote against cutting off a filibuster.[148]

The 2007 amendments to the FDA's statute authorized an increase in its inspectorate from 1,300 in 2007 to 1,800 in 2010. The number of inspections increased 5 percent in 2009. The agency cracked down on the growing practice of marketing combinations of drugs and dietary supplements without prior agency approval.[149] It also got more serious about citing device manufacturers for poor manufacturing practices, failing to report adverse events, and bribing doctors with lucrative consultancy arrangements.[150] In early 2010, FDA filed enforcement actions against 17 major food manufacturers, claiming that their front-of-package health claims were misleading. "Economic adulteration" of fish by pawning off meat from farm-raised fish and cheap species as meat from wild or desirable species also assumed a higher priority at FDA during the Obama Administration.[151]

Despite greater enforcement activity at the agency level, the Justice Department remained reluctant to pursue criminal prosecutions against corporations and their officers. By the end of 2010, the Justice Department had sought precious few indictments against the mortgage companies that generated millions of "liar loans," forged employment documents, and swindled elderly citizens out of their life savings. And it did not come close to pursuing the bankers who bundled worthless mortgages into securities or the credit rating agencies that gave them AAA ratings. As of the end of 2011, the only criminal action coming out of the Upper Big Branch disaster was the conviction of a security officer for lying to investigators and destroying evidence. The Justice Department did bring several criminal actions against prominent pharmaceutical companies for promoting their drugs for unapproved uses, and for the first time in a long while it sought indictments against drug company executives under the "responsible corporate officer" doctrine, which imposed liability without regard to personal knowledge of the criminal activity. The companies typically settled for very large fines, rather than risk felony convictions that would have barred their products from Medicare reimbursement.[152]

THE CIVIL JUSTICE SYSTEM

Consumer advocates and plaintiffs' attorneys were optimistic that the 2008 elections would give Congress an opportunity to reverse several recent preemption rulings in federal courts. Confident that President Obama would "understand these issues and their importance in a way a lot of politicians don't," they hoped that he would make preemption of state common law claims a high priority. They were sorely disappointed. Beyond issuing a memorandum to the agencies in May 2009 discouraging them from preempting state regulations and common law, President Obama took no action to expand the civil liability of corporations, and he expressed an openness to the possibility of "tort reform" legislation aimed at further restricting the rights of injured plaintiffs to sue in state courts.[153]

After the 2010 elections placed 16 additional governorships and 675 legislative seats in Republican hands, state legislatures began enacting tort reform statutes again, even in the absence of an insurance crisis. By mid-2011, at least 18 states had passed laws changing the civil justice system in ways that favored business defendants. Texas again led the pack by enacting a modified "loser pays" provision that allowed district judges to shift most of the defendant's litigation costs to the plaintiff if the court determined that the lawsuit was baseless or if the plaintiff rejected a settlement offer and subsequently obtained a jury verdict for less than 80 percent of the rejected offer.[154]

BUSINESS COMMUNITY RESPONSE

As the nation reacted to its worst financial crisis since the Great Depression, monthly recalls of adulterated food, frequent reports of lead-laced imported toys, and a massive oil spill, the "small government/balanced budget/family values" narrative of the conservative media's echo chamber continued to appeal to worried middle-class Americans. Blaming past failures on politicians who had strayed from that narrative, business-friendly think tanks urged a return to the "eternal verities" of free markets and limited government. Fox News resumed the heckler role that it had played so effectively during the Clinton Administration with the addition of a new talk show host named Glen Beck. After telling the Conservative Political Action Caucus that he wanted Barack Obama to fail, Fox host Rush Limbaugh for a time became the de facto spokesperson for the Republican Party.[155]

As revitalized agencies increased their regulatory output during the first two years of the Obama Administration, the business community struck up the familiar refrain that regulations were killing jobs and contributing to the recession. The Heritage Foundation published a frenetic "Backgrounder" entitled "Red Tape Rising: Obama's Torrent of New Regulation." The Chamber of Commerce hosted a "jobs summit" where the "tsunami of regulation" that the business community expected in the near future was the primary topic.[156] That the business community's influence infrastructure could credibly invoke a recession caused by lax regulation of financial institutions to support deregulation was a testament to its idea infrastructure's success in molding public perceptions about the proper role of government in the economy.

President Obama initially reacted to the inevitable push-back from the business community by aggressively defending the administration's positions.[157] As it became clear that the Republican Party was headed for a major victory in the 2010 off-year elections, however, the president dialed down his criticism and went to great lengths to make peace with business leaders. Rather than rebut unsupported claims that regulation was killing jobs, the White House accepted the premise and invited the business community to identify specific regulations that were discouraging companies from creating jobs. The Business Roundtable responded with a 54-page report providing a detailed list of regulations that it urged the administration to repeal or rewrite.[158]

CONCLUSION

Historically, fundamental change has come about not through the slow process of compromise and accommodation, but through massive public education and legislative campaigns designed to overwhelm the business community's opposition during periods of great crisis.[159] The last half of the first decade of the twenty-first century was just such a period, as the nation experienced a confluence of crises, most of which were directly attributable to a debilitated protective governmental infrastructure. It was therefore critical for advocates of robust institutions of responsibility and accountability to strike while the iron was hot when the 111th Congress convened in January 2009.

Convinced that he and a few well-meaning Republican senators could, through a process of rational deliberation, agree on reforms necessary to address the ongoing crises, President Obama declined to use the "bully pulpit" of the presidency to generate the overwhelming public support necessary to secure the enactment of comprehensive protective legislation.[160] The president underestimated the commitment of the Republican leadership to resisting any initiative that did not command substantial support in the business community and the power of business community lobbyists to persuade Democratic members of Congress to join the Republicans in opposing comprehensive change. The Chamber of Commerce alone spent an average of $3 million per week opposing the administration's major policy initiatives.[161] President Obama also underestimated the ability of the business community's influence infrastructure to reframe the action-forcing problem from one of irresponsible conduct on the part of unregulated corporations to one of repressive governmental limitations on economic freedom.

The failure of Congress to enact worker safety legislation in the wake of the Upper Big Branch tragedy demonstrated how far the business community's idea and influence infrastructures had come during the Laissez Faire Revival. A similar tragedy in 1968 had inspired Congress to enact both the Coal Mine Health and Safety Act of 1969 and the Occupational Safety and Health Act of 1970, both of which put comprehensive reforms into place. This time, a threatened Republican filibuster prevented Congress from enacting a patch-and-repair bill aimed at remedying specific problems. Congress also failed to enact legislation to address deepwater drilling and global warming in response to the *Deepwater Horizon* crisis and dire warnings from climate scientists.[162]

The two statutes that Congress did enact during the first two years of the Obama Administration—the Dodd-Frank Act and the Food Safety Modernization Act—have great potential, but neither law will change the underlying incentives that gave rise to the financial meltdown and the food safety crisis. Except for creating a new Consumer Financial Protection Bureau, the new laws left existing institutions in place. At the end of President Obama's first two years in office, the American public was, if anything, more dubious about the need for a protective governmental infrastructure than it was when the president was elected.[163] Further progress toward protecting workers, consumers, neighbors, and the environment may therefore have to wait until public trust in government has been restored and future crises stir even stronger public demands for governmental action.

Striking a new Bargain

The regulatory programs established during the Progressive, New Deal, and Public Interest Eras and the civil justice reforms of the Public Interest Era brought about many remarkable improvements in consumer welfare, public health and safety, and the environment. The nation's air is cleaner, its waters are less polluted, and its workplaces, highways, railways, and airways are much safer than at the beginning of the twentieth century. Victims of corporate malfeasance have better access to corrective justice.[1] The regulatory and civil justice systems that brought about these welcome changes, however, have been depleted by three vigorous assaults over the past thirty years. Consequently, private sector actors are much freer to harm their workers, consumers, neighbors, and the environment than they were at the outset of the Laissez Faire Revival.

The confluence of crises of the late 2000s could have precipitated a fundamental renegotiation of the social bargain to restore the balance among freedom, responsibility, and accountability. Instead, a Democrat-controlled Congress enacted patch-and-repair fixes to a few regulatory programs, and many of the regulatory agencies got somewhat more aggressive in implementing those laws. This chapter will highlight some features of the regulatory and civil justice systems that could wait at the end of the road not taken during the first three years of the Obama Administration. Some of the "reforms" outlined here consist of little more than reversing the changes of the last thirty years. Others will require fresh ideas about how government can work effectively in a modern global economy. Still others will focus less on empowering government than on empowering individuals to hold both government and private sector actors accountable. The overall goal of comprehensive reform must be to change the underlying incentives of private sector actors in ways that motivate them to take more precautions for the benefit of their workers, their consumers, their neighbors, and the environment.

RESTORING PUBLIC TRUST IN GOVERNMENT

Any attempt to bring about greater regulatory protections must first overcome a profound public distrust in government stemming from two powerful, if largely mistaken, public perceptions. First, thirty years of anecdote-laden messaging from the conservative echo chamber has convinced many Americans that government officials are by nature less competent and more corruptible than the their equivalents in the private sector and that many courts are judicial "hellholes" where juries dole out "jackpot justice" to undeserving plaintiffs. Second, the debilitating attacks on the protective governmental infrastructure have persuaded the public that government is incapable of delivering the protections that the public rightly expects. In large part, these misperceptions stem from the fact that progressive activists have channeled most of their limited resources into defending the institutions of responsibility and accountability in the ongoing "ground war" and have not engaged the business community's idea infrastructure in the ideological "air war" described in the previous pages.

THE MISSING NARRATIVE

Supporters of regulatory and common law protections have not attempted to overcome the business community's anti-government narrative with a compelling narrative of their own that is capable of restoring public trust in regulatory agencies and the civil justice system.[2] They have not, for example, attempted to rebut the "incompetent government" narrative with accounts of dedicated civil servants working long hours to draft regulations to protect real people from devastating hazards. Nor have they attempted to inspire public faith in common law juries with stories of conscientious jurors holding misbehaving companies accountable to real victims who have suffered real damages. Instead, they have often aimed their own missiles at government incompetence and corruption featuring accounts of captured agencies, revolving doors, and missed opportunities.

The person who was in the best position to develop and communicate the much-needed narrative was President Barack Obama, a gifted orator with a keen sense of timing. Early in his tenure, however, it became apparent that he was more interested in building bridges with Republicans than in rebuilding governmental institutions and launching bold new substantive initiatives.

As he pressed Congress to enact emergency bailout and economic stimulus legislation to address the financial meltdown, he failed to develop the powerful narrative of rogue financial institutions enriching themselves at the expense of hapless homeowners and helpless pensioners in clear view of regulatory institutions that failed to rein them in because they were so deeply steeped in laissez faire ideology that they could not see the approaching disaster.[3]

Rather than seizing on the *Deepwater Horizon* crisis as an opportunity to educate the nation about the consequences of lax government oversight and the need for stronger controls over another powerful industry, President Obama treated it as a technical problem that business and government experts, working together, could solve. And after the oil began to reach the shores of Gulf Coast states, he failed to seize on the damage suffered by innocent citizens as an opportunity to craft a narrative about the need for a robust common law tort system. The message that the public took away from the ongoing spill was crafted by BP's $5 million per week advertising campaign, and it resonated with the good deeds of a company that had been an unfortunate victim of a terrible accident and was moving heaven and earth to make things right.[4]

Confident in his persuasive powers, the president thought he could best heal the wounds of a deeply divided nation not by speaking directly to the people with an appeal to commonly shared values, but by negotiating with Republicans to arrive at bipartisan solutions to the nation's pressing problems.[5] Rather than pressuring the substantial Democratic majorities in both Houses of Congress to rebuild the protective governmental infrastructure, he observed from a distance while Congressional Democrats took the initiative. After Congress predictably deadlocked, he personally attempted to mediate, usually with little success. And when crises created strong public demands for solutions, he assembled bipartisan commissions composed of experts and wise elders to deliberate over the causes of the crises and propose moderate solutions.

There was historical precedent for the new president's approach to government in the post–Civil War "Mugwumps," a loosely affiliated coalition of professionals, East Coast businessmen, clergymen, and educators who were repelled by the government corruption and loose business ethics of the Gilded Age. Although it conveyed the image of a careful fence-sitter with his mug on one side and his "wump" on the other, the term "Mugwump" was an Algonquin Indian word meaning "great men." Strong believers in the sanctity of private property and the virtues of free markets, the Mugwumps argued that the solutions to society's problems could best be achieved through reasoned deliberation among educated elites. After unsuccessfully attempting to steer a principled middle path during the last quarter of the nineteenth century, they became a little-noticed casualty of the fierce war between the populists and the business community that culminated in William McKinley's definitive 1896 victory.[6]

Having attended private schools for most of his life and having served as the president of the *Harvard Law Review,* President Obama had an abiding faith in the American educational meritocracy. Fully one-quarter of his appointments were either faculty members or alumni of Harvard University, and nearly all of them had advanced degrees from elite universities. In Larry Summers and Timothy Geithner, for example, he thought he had chosen the best minds in the country with the most expertise in the issues surrounding the financial meltdown. As the oil flowed for weeks from the *Deepwater Horizon* well, President Obama reminded the nation that Energy Secretary Steven Chu was a Nobel laureate. Sarah Palin therefore struck an exposed nerve when she complained that the high-level officials in the Obama Administration "think that, if we were just smart enough, we'd be able to understand their policies."[7]

FOUR PROGRESSIVE NARRATIVES

The confluence of crises of the late 2000s left most citizens deeply concerned for the economic and physical security of their families and their country. The Great Recession spawned by the financial meltdown of 2007–08 put millions of Americans out of work, and millions more in fear of losing their jobs, their pensions, and their health benefits. At the same time, the *Deepwater Horizon* spill, the Upper Big Branch mining disaster, the recalls of millions of toxic toys, and the dire predictions of climate scientists made ordinary citizens fearful for their health, safety, and environment. These powerful demonstrations of the failure of laissez faire minimalism can provide the grist for an easily accessible and compelling narrative about the necessity of maintaining robust institutions of responsibility and accountability in a modern political economy.

Freedom and security are two widely shared human values. We understand that economic freedom allows corporations to develop innovative products, to match those products to our desires as consumers, and to provide useful services at the least cost. But we also know that corporations have only one lawful goal—to maximize the return to their shareholders. We therefore desire the security of knowing that companies will not use their economic freedom irresponsibly to harm our families. Since corporations cannot be motivated by concerns for others insofar as they do not contribute to the bottom line, government must play a large role in providing for the economic and physical security of its citizens. Progressive activists may therefore weave a narrative around the shared value of *economic and physical security* that is at least as compelling as the business community's highly successful narrative built on economic freedom.

The most salient narrative of the assaults on the civil justice system focuses on the personal responsibility of plaintiffs for the harms for which they seek compensation. The personal responsibility narrative has also played a prominent role in the attacks on federal regulation of pharmaceuticals, deceptive advertising, occupational safety and health, and automobiles. During the Public Interest Era consumer and environmental activists employed a similar narrative that focused on *corporate responsibility* for the harms caused by dangerous products and activities. The business community's influence infrastructure turned the corporate responsibility narrative into a story about how companies voluntarily adopt more responsible approaches out of concern for corporate image and the health of the economy. In the wake of the crises of the late 2000s, this perversion of the corporate responsibility narrative has lost its vitality, and progressive activists should be able to reinvigorate the original version in support of stronger governmental protections and expanded corporate liability.

A third progressive narrative could focus on *corporate accountability*. Much of the public anger from across the political spectrum generated by the 2008–09 bailout of the financial industry stemmed from the apparent unwillingness or inability of the federal government to hold the banks and their corporate officers accountable for their irresponsible conduct. Not a single corporate official was convicted of any crime, and only a few financial institutions paid large fines. A narrative based on corporate accountability could motivate outraged citizens to support more effective enforcement, stronger sanctions, and corporate officer liability for corporate malfeasance.

Finally, progressive activists could fashion a narrative that focuses on the *social costs* that irresponsible products and activities impose on all citizens. To the extent that companies harm others without compensating them for their losses, the rest of us pick up the tab in increased insurance premiums and in taxes invested in Medicare and Medicaid. A social costs narrative should resonate fairly robustly in a declining economy characterized by large budget deficits and few new taxes.

All four of these narratives—*security, corporate responsibility, corporate accountability,* and *social costs*—may be employed by a new progressive idea infrastructure in the air wars over the proper role of government in the political economy. They should be illustrated with stories from the ground wars highlighting the damage caused by irresponsible corporate behavior, the virtues of strong rules of responsibility, and the need for robust institutions of responsibility and accountability to articulate and enforce those rules.

REBUILDING THE INSTITUTIONS OF RESPONSIBILITY

After thirty years of abuse and neglect, the protective governmental infrastructure is in a woeful state of disrepair. At the same time, the competitive pressures of an integrated global economy have created strong incentives for companies to act irresponsibly. The resulting confluence of crises strongly suggests that the time has come to rebuild the institutions of responsibility and to reshape them to fit the demands of the twenty-first-century global economy.[8]

INCREASE AGENCY RESOURCES

The business community discovered long ago that the most effective way to obtain relief from regulatory burdens while maintaining the appearance of effective protection was to starve the regulatory agencies. Most of the federal agencies had far fewer resources in inflation-adjusted dollars at the end of the George W. Bush Administration than they did at the end of the Carter Administration, even though their responsibilities had increased, sometimes dramatically, with the enactment of patch-and-repair statutes in response to various crises. The first step in rebuilding the protective governmental infrastructure must therefore be to allocate sufficient funds for them to do their jobs.

The need to increase regulatory agency budgets, however, is not at all obvious to ordinary citizens who interact with agencies only rarely and are not well aware of the resources needed to provide the protections they expect. It will take forceful and persuasive leadership to persuade Congress to put more resources into institutions that have failed so miserably in the recent past. The ultimate solution may lie in alternative sources of funding. The PDUFAct of 1992 gave FDA the power to assess fees from applicants for new drug approvals. Had that money not come with strings attached, it would have provided a welcome infusion of resources for the underfunded staff of the agency's Office of Drug Safety. Congress could empower other regulatory agencies to charge regulatees fees for the regulatory services they provide without prescribing precisely how they must use those funds. For example, Congress could expand import enforcement resources by empowering the agencies to charge user fees to importers to help defray the cost of inspections in foreign countries.[9]

AVOIDING AGENCY CAPTURE

The possibility of capture will always plague single-industry agencies that must deal with the same regulatees day in and day out. But presidents can reduce the risk of capture by looking beyond the regulated industries for agency leadership.

Agency leaders can foster institutional cultures in which staffers maintain a professional distance from regulatees and are prepared to become fierce adversaries when necessary. Congress could enact legislation placing strict limits on agency employees' representing regulatees before their agencies for a substantial period. Congress could also empower agencies to defend themselves from attacks by generating and disseminating information on the social impacts of irresponsible conduct by regulatees. Finally, Congress could empower citizens to monitor the regulatory process as discussed in more detail below.[10]

LOWERING ANALYTICAL AND PROCEDURAL HURDLES

The president can easily withdraw the executive orders that place burdensome analytical requirements on agencies or amend them to reduce those burdens and enhance regulatory effectiveness. Likewise, Congress can speed up agency rulemaking by eliminating existing statutory analytical and procedural hurdles. It could also amend individual statutes to signal to the courts that it does not intend for them to demand extensive documentation and analysis from federal agencies when they review protective regulations.

REORIENTING OIRA

OIRA has traditionally operated on a single principle—the economy is best served when regulatory agencies are forced to demonstrate to skeptical economists that the benefits of their regulations outweigh the costs. This is true no matter how resistant the benefits are to quantitative assessment and no matter how susceptible the costs are to manipulation by the regulated industries. Skepticism of Public Interest Era regulatory programs has become so thoroughly ingrained in OIRA's culture that it probably cannot be purged at this late date. Hence, the best solution for the near term may be for Congress to abolish OIRA altogether.[11] Failing that, the president can change OIRA's regulatory review role at the stroke of a pen. He could attempt to change the culture of OIRA review by appointing leaders who are anxious for the agencies to implement their missions and willing to push them in that direction. A reoriented OIRA could become the institutional home for promoting agency initiatives and defending agencies from attack in the ground wars over regulation.[12]

CREATING NEW AGENCIES

The kind of fundamental changes that will allow the federal regulatory system to live up to its potential will include replacing some existing agencies with new ones. For example, numerous blue ribbon panels, task forces, and respected scholars have advocated legislation combining the federal government's food safety regulatory functions under a single agency with authority to address emerging food safety issues in a comprehensive fashion. But the politically powerful meat industry, which is happy being regulated by USDA, has always successfully opposed the idea. Congress could eliminate inefficient turf wars in the future by combining the regulatory functions of all of the food safety agencies into a new agency.[13] Congress could likewise create new agencies to assume the regulatory responsibilities of other agencies, like MMS, OPS, and FRA, that suffer from serious institutional conflicts of interest.

CHANGING THE RULES

Congress, the federal agencies, and the courts can enhance the modest protections of the Laissez Faire Revival by promulgating stronger rules of responsibility that reflect a better balance among freedom, responsibility, and accountability. In many cases, they can replace doctrines that were deliberately sabotaged by laissez faire minimalist agency leaders with proven rules that have worked well in the past like the Glass-Steagall Act's prohibition on commercial banks engaging in investment banking. In other cases they will need to craft different rules that contemplate modern technologies and are designed to meet modern economic conditions.

REVISITING VOLUNTARY APPROACHES

We have seen how companies abuse voluntary programs and how agencies use them as excuses for avoiding the hard work of regulating. The president could order agencies to revisit all voluntary programs with an eye toward replacing failed voluntary approaches with enforceable rules. Similarly, agencies could write rules that reflect the judgment of independent experts, rather than relying on industry-drafted standards.[14]

INCENTIVES TO ACT RESPONSIBLY

Throughout the Laissez Faire Era, corporate managers experienced powerful economic incentives to emphasize short-term profits over long-term risk. Most corporations rewarded their executives on the basis of quarterly and annual earnings and share prices. The executives therefore had an incentive to belittle low probability risks of catastrophic loss because such disasters were unlikely to happen in any given year and were therefore not likely to affect the company's share prices or earnings. We have seen how this short-term perspective led to workplace tragedies, massive product recalls, catastrophic highway, rail, and airline accidents, a massive financial meltdown, and a rise in global temperatures that will change the way our children live in unpredictable ways.

Tax Bad Conduct. The most efficient and effective way to affect incentives is to tax irresponsible conduct. For example, a hefty tax on pollution gives companies an economic incentive to reduce emissions. Similarly, the government could encourage financial institutions to avoid focusing exclusively on short-term profits by taxing them at a higher rate than profits resulting from long-term planning. This fee-based approach can work, however, only if the conduct to be discouraged is easily monitored. An "injury tax" on employers, for example, could provide an incentive to reduce workplace injuries, but it would also provide an equally strong incentive to avoid *reporting* those injuries. In addition, the fee-based approach is not easily adapted to reducing low-probability high-consequence outcomes, like airplane and train crashes, where the taxable unit consists of a catastrophe that occurs only rarely.[15]

Reduce Moral Hazard. There have been so many meltdowns and subsequent bailouts that large banks can rest assured that the government will not allow them to fail when risky investments go catastrophically bad. Observers from across the political spectrum agree that the best solution to the problem of too-big-to-fail banks is to break them up and to prevent them from growing too large in the future. This solution would also reduce the competitive advantage that the mega-banks currently have by virtue of their implicit bailout guarantee. Congress missed an important opportunity in the Dodd-Frank Act of 2010 when it failed to restrict the size of existing mega-banks.[16] Change of this magnitude may therefore have to await the next financial meltdown.

Reduce Incentives to Deceive. One important goal of consumer protection regulation should be to replace incentives to deceive with incentives to deal fairly and honestly with consumers. The best way to limit predatory lending incentives, for example, may be to hold the investment banks that provide the money for financing mortgages vicariously liable for conduct by mortgage companies and brokers that violates federal predatory lending laws.[17] The best way to prevent local banks from ignoring the ability of borrowers to repay subprime loans may be to require them to retain a significant proportion of the risk of default.[18] Congress could readjust the incentives of the credit rating agencies by subjecting them to liability to any investor who could demonstrate that it relied on a rating that was influenced by the client marketing the rated securities. Or it could simply prohibit rating agencies from having consulting relationships with companies for which they perform ratings services.

PROACTIVE PRECAUTIONARY PROTECTIONS

Most of the agencies studied here have ample authority to adopt "precautionary" approaches to regulation under which the government acts proactively to protect the public in the face of scientific uncertainties. Portal regulatory regimes adopt the precautionary approach by placing the burden of proof on the regulatee to demonstrate that the licensed product or activity meets the relevant statutory criteria. But most portal statutes shift the burden of proof to the agency once it has approved the product or activity. Congress could greatly enhance the effectiveness of portal programs by placing the burden at all times on the regulatees to demonstrate that their products or activities will *not* pose unacceptable risks. And it could make other regulatory regimes more protective by converting them to portal programs. For example, it could require manufacturers of certain classes of products (e.g., toys) to obtain affirmative CPSC approval before marketing them and manufacturers of foods to obtain FTC approval prior to airing advertisements targeted primarily at children.[19]

Responding to complaints from the regulated industries about delays in license approvals, Congress created a number of abbreviated approval processes for portal programs. These processes were routinely abused during the Laissez Faire Revival to approve products and permit activities after only the most cursory of reviews. Unless agencies receive much larger appropriations in the future, however, eliminating abbreviated review processes may not be a realistic option. The agencies should therefore tighten the criteria that they employ in granting abbreviated reviews with an eye toward steering the relevant products through the full approval process.

Agencies that do not administer portal statutes can implement risk-based statutes in a more precautionary way. For example, USDA could amend HACCP regulations to require meat processors to test both incoming and outgoing meat for pathogens. And FDA could write the implementing regulations under its new authority to regulate produce safety to require multiple testing for pathogens. The banking agencies could promulgate regulations establishing steep minimum capital requirements for all financial institutions, ensuring that they meet those requirements with real money and not illusory credit default swaps, and preventing them from moving risky assets into offshore structured investment vehicles where they remain off the books.[20]

BEST EFFORTS

The "best efforts" or "technology-based" approach to risk reduction is a reliable regulatory strategy for ensuring that regulated industries make progress toward protective statutory goals. Unlike risk-based or cost benefit–based standard setting, both of which require immense amounts of data and analysis, best efforts standard setting requires the agency to gather information from regulatees and vendors of protective technologies and to promulgate standards based on the performance of the best available technologies. Congress could greatly improve regulatory oversight of offshore oil and gas extraction activities, for example, by amending the offshore leasing statute to require lessees to employ the best available spill prevention and response technologies for new and existing drilling and recovery operations.

BETTER SURVEILLANCE OF POTENTIALLY RISKY PRODUCTS AND TECHNOLOGIES

Companies have the freedom to market and use most products and technologies without first testing them for safety. For the relatively few products, like drug and devices, for which portal statutes require premarket testing and approval, the tests are not capable of detecting all of the potential risks. Agencies therefore need a capacity to monitor regulated products and activities in actual operation to identify those that present unacceptable risks before they cause any more harm. Most federal regulators conduct some surveillance, but resource constraints usually limit that function to secondary status. Congress could ensure better surveillance by appropriating more funds expressly for that purpose. It could also enact legislation empowering agencies to require regulatees to employ proven surveillance technologies, like "black box" data-gathering devices in moving vehicles and computer identification devices in cattle.

EROSION-RESISTANT RULES

In the wake of crisis-driven reform legislation, the business community's tried and true strategy is to erode away the new protections through judicial appeals, requests for exceptions, and demands for greater flexibility. Congress can ensure against erosion by using clear statutory language that is not subject to debilitating interpretations by unsympathetic agency heads and courts and by carefully confining the agency's discretion to exempt products and activities. Exemptions granted early in the process to ease the initial burden of compliance have a way of becoming permanent entitlements. Agencies should therefore be especially parsimonious in granting exemptions in the early years, despite pressure to reduce the economic impact of new statutes. Since neither Congress nor the agencies will be able to anticipate all of the techniques that attorneys for regulatees will come up with for evading the rules, agencies must be prepared to amend regulations when they prove ineffective.

REBUILDING THE INSTITUTIONS OF ACCOUNTABILITY

A renegotiation of the social bargain must include rebuilding the institutions of accountability and enhancing their capacity to steer the conduct of large economic institutions in socially desirable directions. Enforcement and common law liability are the vehicles through which society holds companies accountable for violating the rules of responsibility. Both functions are in need of serious attention.

ENSURING ACCOUNTABILITY THROUGH EFFECTIVE ENFORCEMENT

Empirical evidence on environmental enforcement demonstrates a clear relationship between the decline in enforcement during the Laissez Faire Revival and an increase in the incidence of recurrent, and sometimes unfettered, noncompliance. Rational companies can discount potential fines by the probability that violations will be detected and prosecuted in deciding how much to invest in regulatory compliance. During the Laissez Faire Revival, they could factor in a very steep discount because there was little risk that debilitated agency inspectorates would detect violations and because many agency leaders were willing to forgo prosecution if violators promised to do better in the future.[21]

Investing in Enforcement. During the Laissez Faire Revival, agencies shifted resources from enforcement to "compliance assistance" programs that greatly reduced citation rates and fine amounts, but did not demonstrably increase compliance rates. Agencies could increase all three by shifting resources back to investigating, prosecuting, and punishing violators.[22] Some agencies have understandably been reluctant to issue stiff penalties out of fear that too many violators will contest citations and overwhelm their capacity to pursue cases through the hearings and appeals that contested cases require.[23] Yet the answer to industry recalcitrance cannot be to let scofflaws off the hook. The best solution to this dilemma may be to levy high fines in a few egregious cases and vigorously pursue them to completion to send a message to potential scofflaws that the agency will not be cowed by the threat of appeals.

Match the Penalty to the Offense. Agencies can send a strong signal to regulatees that noncompliance does not pay by setting penalties at a level higher than the amount of money saved through noncompliance multiplied by the inverse of the probability of detection. Surprisingly, not all of the agencies examined here even have the option of levying civil penalties. Some of the agencies that do have civil penalty authority either lack authority to base the fines on costs avoided or face statutory caps on fines that render that approach infeasible. Congress could ensure better enforcement by giving agencies full authority to levy civil penalties at levels sufficiently high that it is not cheaper for regulatees to write fines into the cost of doing business.[24]

Tougher Settlements. During the Laissez Faire Revival, agencies routinely settled cases for amounts substantially less than the assessed fines. Steeply discounted settlements are not only incapable of providing adequate incentives to noncompliant companies, but they are also deeply distressing to victims seeking some degree of retribution. At a broader level, settlements negotiated behind closed doors cast serious doubt on the integrity of the enforcement process and ultimately undermine public confidence in government. Either Congress or the agencies could make the settlement process more visible as well as more equitable by inviting representatives of the beneficiaries of the relevant programs to participate in settlement negotiations.

Collecting Fines. Several agencies have simply failed to collect assessed fines during the Laissez Faire Revival. Obviously, the deterrent effect of civil sanctions is lost to the extent that a company can avoid punishment by simply refusing to pay. This problem could be remedied by forcing companies to pay assessed penalties into an escrow account, where they would become available to the agency at the end of any appeal. Otherwise, Congress could provide an incentive to agencies to collect fines expeditiously through legislation allowing them to retain some portion of collected fines, rather than sending them directly to the U.S. Treasury.

Stronger Criminal Enforcement. The most powerful incentive that the government has at its disposal is the threat of criminal prosecution. Corporations cannot be incarcerated, but they can be shamed, and a criminal conviction will tarnish a company's reputation far more deeply than a civil fine. Prosecuting a large corporation with virtually unlimited legal resources at its disposal, however, requires a huge expenditure of government resources. It is even more difficult to prosecute a corporate executive for conduct engaged in by underlings. Yet, the public theater of a criminal prosecution offers a powerful inducement to regulatees to obey the law, and it is a potent vehicle for reducing public cynicism. The regulatory agencies and the Department of Justice could achieve a great deal of additional deterrence by stepping up criminal prosecutions against corporate criminals and their executives.

Empowering Activist State AGs. State attorneys general have always played an important protective role by enforcing state laws and by representing their citizens in public nuisance litigation. At the onset of the Laissez Faire Revival, several attorneys general joined forces in so-called multi-state litigation to take on national problems that the federal government was not adequately addressing, usually because the federal agencies were not actively enforcing federal laws. This extraordinarily effective strategy induced major corporations from General Motors to America Online to change their business practices and, on occasion, to compensate states and their consumers for their losses.[25] Congress could increase the likelihood that protective statutes will be enforced when federal agencies shirk their enforcement responsibilities by enacting legislation that specifically empowers state attorneys general to enforce federal regulatory requirements.

ENSURING ACCOUNTABILITY THROUGH THE CIVIL JUSTICE SYSTEM

The possibility that twelve randomly selected representatives of the community will hold companies liable for violating common law standards provides a powerful incentive to the business community to behave responsibly. In addition to discarding this powerful incentive, the states that enacted the business community's tort reform measures during the Laissez Faire Revival deprived their injured citizens of compensation for their injuries and a sense of retributive justice at seeing wrongdoers held accountable for their misconduct. While there can be little doubt that the business community has profited handily from the changes to the common law, there is little evidence that the changes have brought about the promised benefits to consumers in lower prices and greater availability of goods and services.

Reinvigorating Nuisance Law. The common law of nuisance offers a vehicle for plaintiffs' attorneys and state attorneys general to address a broad array of irresponsible conduct that can harm human health and damage the environment.[26] For example, when it became clear that the George W. Bush Administration was not going to protect the public from global warming, eight states sued six utility companies that operated 174 fossil fuel burning power plants in twenty states seeking an order abating the nuisance that was allegedly created by their carbon dioxide emissions.[27] Unsure of their capacity to manage nuisance actions involving multiple plaintiffs and defendants and of their competence to resolve complex scientific and public policy disputes, the courts have understandably been reluctant to entertain large-scale nuisance actions. When the legislative and administrative processes fail to address problems within the scope of traditional public nuisance doctrine, however, the common law courts should not abandon their traditional role of preventing irresponsible conduct through innovative injunctive relief.[28]

Making the Common Law More Protective. After 30 years of chipping away at the civil justice system with no discernable improvement in consumer welfare, it is time to consider reforms designed to enhance the capacity of the common law to protect consumers and provide corrective justice. It is, for example, time for the American Law Institute to revise the *Restatement (Third) of Products Liability* to reflect the principles that guided the courts' application of the highly successful section 402A of the *Restatement (Second) of Torts*.[29] Courts could also explore burden-shifting techniques to induce companies to evaluate the hazards posed by their products and activities before marketing them and to take protective action before they injure innocent victims.[30] Finally, courts could provide a powerful incentive to comply with the rules of responsibility by making corporate officers personally liable for the irresponsible conduct of their companies when they take no action after becoming aware of misdeeds by lower-level employees.[31]

Reviving Class Action Lawsuits. The protections offered by the common law are difficult to achieve in cases involving products or activities that injure thousands of people but only to such a small extent that compensatory damages alone would not justify individual lawsuits. The Class Action Fairness Act of 2005 has effectively channeled most state class action lawsuits into the federal courts, which have not been sympathetic to that form of action during the Laissez Faire Revival. Congress could increase the likelihood that companies will be held accountable when the regulatory system fails by either repealing that statute or limiting it to very large cases that are truly national in scope. In addition, Congress (and the states) could ensure that the defendants are not able to sidestep class action lawsuits by prohibiting provisions in the fine print of standard-form contracts waiving the purchaser's right to participate in class actions.[32]

Revisiting Past "Reforms." Most state legislatures periodically revisit regulatory statutes after assessing how well the regulatory agencies have been performing their duties in some form of "reauthorization" or "sunset" review. They should consider initiating a similar periodic reassessment of the impact of tort reform statutes under which they revise or repeal legislatively imposed changes in the common law that failed to accomplish the promised benefits to consumers. For example, they should consider restoring joint and several liability in litigation involving the financial sector to allow courts to hold all companies participating in the solicitation, negotiation, securitization, and marketing of mortgage-backed securities liable for negligence or fraud, thereby providing an incentive to all of the relevant actors to do what they can to eliminate fraud from the system.

Depoliticizing the Judiciary. The viability of the common law depends entirely on the integrity of the state courts. As the business community has poured hundreds of millions of dollars into judicial elections in the 39 states in which judges must stand for election, those contests have deteriorated into embarrassing political brawls where the candidate with access to the most money usually wins. Since that candidate is almost invariably the candidate favored by the business community, the high courts in several important states have become dominated by judges who lean heavily toward defendants in cases brought by victims of dangerous products, fraudulent business practices, and risky activities.[33] Even if campaign contributions do not have a direct impact on the votes of individual justices in deciding specific cases, the fact that 76 percent of the population believes that they do speaks very poorly of an institution that is essential to a just and honorable society. In early 2010, former U.S. Supreme Court Justice Sandra Day O'Connor and several state supreme court justices created the Judicial Selection Initiative to advocate a hybrid judicial selection system in which the governor appoints a justice from a short list of qualified candidates prepared by a bipartisan panel. The appointed justice then stands for reelection in an up or down plebiscite that does not feature a candidate on the other side. If a majority of the voters does not favor an additional term for the sitting justice, a replacement is appointed through the same process.[34] State legislatures should follow Justice O'Connor's lead and replace judicial elections with this simple process for ensuring the integrity of the state judiciary.

EMPOWERING CITIZENS

As agencies promulgate regulations in response to crises or new statutory requirements, they can rest assured that the affected industries will participate fully in the notice and comment process and any public hearings. Any other citizen is also welcome to participate, and most agencies have facilitated such participation by publishing rulemaking notices and supporting documentation on their websites and allowing electronic submission of comments. Empirical studies consistently demonstrate, however, that regulatees dominate every stage of the rulemaking process from pre-proposal negotiations with the agency over the content of the rule (to which the public is rarely invited), to submission of comments on the proposal, to judicial challenges to the final rule. Moreover, regulatee participation has a discernable impact on rulemaking outcomes. One recent study of EPA rules regulating hazardous air pollutants concluded that changes to the substance of rules in response to public comments favored industry by a 5 to 1 margin.[35] Congress could level the playing field by appropriating a modest pool of funds to support citizen group participation in rulemakings by allowing them to hire consultants to analyze data and to pay lawyers to present their arguments. Thus empowered, citizen interveners could provide a much-needed counterweight to extensive participation of the regulated industries.[36]

Government enforcement, by contrast, is not participatory in nature, nor is it especially transparent. Agency enforcers rarely invite regulatory beneficiaries to participate in their settlement negotiations with violators. Indeed, the public is unlikely to learn of such negotiations at all when the outcome is that the government decides to withdraw the enforcement action. Although a few of the

Public Interest Era environmental statutes allow individual citizens or groups of citizens to sue in federal court to enforce federal requirements if the relevant state and federal agencies fail to do so, most regulatory statutes do not allow for citizen enforcement.[37] Citizen suits accomplished a great deal of environmental improvement in the years during which EPA's leadership was reluctant to enforce the environmental laws.[38] Congress could further enhance accountability by allowing ordinary citizens to enforce all protective regulations when agencies are either unwilling or unable to take that step.

BUILDING A PROGRESSIVE IDEA INFRASTRUCTURE

The founding funders created and sustained a pro-business idea infrastructure to generate politically attractive ideas and policy prescriptions for use in the air war over the proper role of government in society. Sound progressive policy proposals also trickled out of academia during the Laissez Faire Revival, but academics with classes to teach, papers to grade, and committee meetings to attend could not package and disseminate their ideas with the same clarity and aggressiveness as the well-endowed conservative think tanks. If they are to compete effectively in the ongoing air war, proponents of strong regulatory and civil justice systems will need to establish an alternative idea infrastructure that is capable of bringing ideas to the public policy arena in easily digestible packages and marketing them to policymakers and the public.[39]

A few such institutions already exist. The Center for American Progress (CAP) is a progressive think tank with a $10 million budget and a large staff of media-savvy professionals. Headed by President Clinton's former chief-of-staff John Podesta, CAP's goal is to "bridge the gap between leading thinkers and national policymakers." The American Constitution Society (ACS) serves as a progressive counterweight to the Federalist Society. ACS adheres to the Federalist Society model of hosting speakers at law schools around the country, holding conferences on major issues of constitutional law and national policy, and serving as a progressive network for law students and progressive attorneys. The Center for Progressive Reform, a group of about 60 academic scholars (mostly law professors) who donate their services to the organization, generates ideas and analyses of issues relevant to federal regulation and the civil justice system. All three of these relatively new institutions have successfully inserted themselves into the web of Washington, D.C. policymaking, and all three served as conduits for mid-level appointments in the Obama Administration. But many more similar institutions will be needed to engage their business-friendly counterparts effectively in the air war.[40]

The first task for an alternative idea infrastructure should be to draw a clear connection between strong regulatory programs, a robust civil justice system, and the protections that citizens expect from their government. Most Americans assume that they can safely purchase food, take prescription medications, travel in public transportation, and deposit their paychecks in a bank, because they believe that they are being protected by a functioning governmental infrastructure. As the preceding chapters have demonstrated, that belief is inconsistent with the reality of federal regulation and the civil justice system. The new idea infrastructure should highlight the cause-effect relationship between the reduced governmental protection attributable to the rise of laissez faire minimalism and the crises that will continue to erupt until the debilitated institutions of responsibility and accountability are repaired.

Second, the new idea infrastructure must be capable of conceiving and promoting broad ideas for fundamental change consistent with a principled theory of the proper role of government in society. Progressive thinkers must, of course, be willing and able to contribute to the policy debates that arise in response to particular crises with ideas for incremental change aimed at fixing the problems that gave rise to the crises. But they should also be laying the foundation for fundamental change with broad prescriptions for how government can protect the public from the vicissitudes of a market-driven economy. Finally, the progressive idea infrastructure must help generate persuasive narratives supporting a greater role for government in protecting American citizens from powerful economic institutions that currently have too much freedom to harm.[41]

BUILDING A PROGRESSIVE INFLUENCE INFRASTRUCTURE

Grand ideas for rearranging governmental institutions and transforming protective laws will be of little practical utility without organizations capable of advancing those ideas in the ground war being fought in the halls of Congress, state legislatures, and the courts. The foundations that tend to fund progressive groups, however, have been very reluctant to create an echo chamber of progressive media outlets.[42]

PROGRESSIVE MEDIA

The mainstream media that played a prominent role in focusing public attention on the need for reform during the Public Interest Era is not likely to play such a prominent role in the future. It faced a crisis of its own in the late 2000s as competitive pressures from the internet and cable television forced newspapers and the television networks to cut costs and, in some cases, to close their doors. Sadly, many of the failed papers were profitable enterprises but for the enormous debt burdens they were forced to assume during a wave of mergers and buyouts. No longer owned by families with commitments to serious journalism, newspapers struggled to meet the profit-driven expectations of Wall Street. Not anxious to take on stories that might bring on the wrath of their new corporate owners, editors focused less on corporate malfeasance and more on issues with broad reader appeal. Under the constant threat of attack from right-wing "media cops" for liberal bias, journalists strived mightily to produce "balanced" reporting by seeking quotes from the business community and conservative think tanks.[43] The repeal of the Fairness Doctrine during the Reagan Administration freed radio and television stations to orient 100 percent of their content in a conservative direction. Rupert Murdoch's media empire thrived in this new environment as his news network, television affiliates, and newspapers provided a constant stream of business-friendly "content."[44]

The first task for proponents of a robust protective governmental infrastructure should be to restore balance to the conservative media's news coverage. Two watchdog institutions, Fairness and Accuracy in Reporting and Media Matters for America, have shed a great deal of light on the conservative echo chamber and have documented numerous instances of gross bias in reporting.[45] But more than exposure is necessary. Congress passed a statute that would have restored the fairness doctrine in the early 1990s, but President George H. W. Bush vetoed it. After the 2006 elections, Senate Democrats raised the idea again, but the Obama Administration declined to support the effort. It should nevertheless remain near the top of the list of progressive reforms.[46]

Another priority should be to facilitate the movement away from the current Wall Street–dominated model for financing news reporting. The *St. Petersburg Times* and a number of other local newspapers that provide high-quality in-depth investigative reporting along with local news coverage successfully operate as nonprofit institutions. A similar nonprofit model has worked for Pro Publica, an organization composed of reporters who prepare in-depth investigative reports that Pro Publica either offers to newspapers free of charge or publishes on its own website. Congress could encourage such moves and ensure against abuse by amending the tax laws to encourage nonprofit news organizations while at the same time conditioning an organization's tax-exempt status on its refraining from endorsing political candidates either directly or indirectly.[47]

NETROOTS ORGANIZATIONS

The 2008 elections provided a powerful demonstration of a new force in American politics—netroots activists. One of the most successful progressive bloggers, Markos Moulitsas, hosted a convention of activists dubbed "Netroots Nation" in Las Vegas in July 2006 that attracted more than 1,000 bloggers and 120 reporters from the mainstream media. When the group convened again in Austin, Texas, in the summer of 2008, more than 2,000 bloggers and 200 representatives of the mainstream media showed up to attend dozens of well-planned panel discussions, browse at a large display sponsored by the Progressive Book Club, and discuss politics over free beer offered by internet service providers.[48] The Huffington Post, a popular site for posting news and commentary launched by former socialite Arianna Huffington, was so successful that it merged with America Online in an attempt to save that flagging institution. Created as a vehicle for criticizing the Clinton impeachment, the political organization Move On.org evolved into a web-based voice for a "pragmatic progressivism" that appealed to people who were not happy with the direction in which the country was moving under the leadership of George W. Bush.[49]

The primary threat to the progressive netroots community is the possibility that corporate America will seize control of the internet and limit access to those who can afford to pay the entry fee that they extract or, worse, censor the content of the messages that users send over it. The ongoing campaign to preserve "net neutrality," a term that connotes the absence of corporate interference with access to the internet, will be crucial to the future of this source of countervailing power.[50]

IMPEDIMENTS

In the months after Barack Obama's dramatic victory, talk of "the fall of conservatism" was common among the political pundits.[51] That assessment proved premature, however, as the business community dug in, the founding funders sponsored a successful Tea Party movement, and the Obama Administration squandered a unique opportunity to advance a progressive agenda.

A SCLEROTIC IDEA INFRASTRUCTURE

By mid-2008, the business community's idea infrastructure had, in the opinion of many conservative observers, become "sclerotic." Confronted with powerful evidence that the theory that lay at the core of nearly all of their policy prescriptions had failed, the opulent citadels of laissez faire minimalism were reduced to what one senior Republican congressional aide called "a bunch of moribund blogging societies." In a wistful reference to the good old days, the Heritage Foundation even created a new window on its website entitled "What Would Reagan Do?"[52] At the same time, a number of young conservative thinkers were churning the waters with policy prescriptions that were disturbing to social conservatives, but generally compatible with the economic interests of the business community. Although sympathetic to business, they were not laissez faire minimalists intent on slashing government. The extent to which these more moderate voices will become influential in conservative circles over the long haul remains unclear.[53] For now, the business community seems content to focus its energies on the single idea (government regulation kills jobs) and the single policy prescription (shrink government by balancing the budget without raising taxes) that Grover Norquist has advanced for the past 30 years. It may be that the business community's successful air war has so completely softened the opposition that it can advance its deregulatory goals by relying exclusively on the ground war.[54]

A ROBUST INFLUENCE INFRASTRUCTURE

If its idea infrastructure has grown moribund, the business community's influence infrastructure is more robust than ever as an unrepentant financial services industry regains its strength and throws its considerable resources in that direction. The election of Barack Obama allowed a reinvigorated conservative media echo chamber to switch from defending discredited Bush Administration policies to attacking the new administration. Industry lobbyists were especially adept at preventing Congress from enacting legislation and at slowing down agency implementation of crisis-driven reforms.[55] The Supreme Court's holding in *Citizens United v. Federal Election Commission* that the First Amendment prevents the federal government from limiting the amount of money that corporations may contribute to advocacy organizations for political purposes has given the business community a huge advantage in the ground war. Having raised around $50 million to support conservative Republican candidates during the 2010 election season, Karl Rove's Crossroads GPS group began raising money in late 2010 to run attack ads against sitting Democrats to soften them up for the 2012 campaign. At the very least, *Citizens United* has had the *in terrorem* effect of making moderate Democrats extremely reluctant to endorse legislation designed to expand (or even rebuild) the protective governmental infrastructure.[56]

CONCLUSIONS

With considerable financial help from progressive funders, progressive scholars and activists have made impressive gains in creating narratives and carrying their message to the people. The 2008 elections demonstrated that the public is receptive to that message, at least during crisis periods when the failures of laissez faire minimalism are so painfully apparent that the conservative media cannot mask them with appeals to prejudice and patriotism. But the progressive idea and influence infrastructures are still no match for those of the business community. A great deal of institution building remains to be done before proponents of a strong protective government can expect to hold their own in the ongoing air and ground wars and begin the process of renegotiating the social bargain. If and when that happens, many ideas for more effective regulatory programs and a more responsive civil justice system are ready for the bargaining table.

CONCLUSIONS

At the outset of the 2010 election cycle, the modest regulatory reforms of the Obama Administration and the Democratic 111th Congress were having little positive impact on working-class Americans. Far from restoring faith in government, the Obama Administration had generated additional cynicism about the government's capacity to protect its citizens. That, in turn, reversed the political momentum for greater governmental protection that had been building in response to the confluence of crises of the late 2000s. In the aftermath of the Roosevelt Administration's aggressive responses to the market failures that brought on the Great Depression, the business community could not credibly have advocated a return to a laissez faire economy. In the aftermath of President Obama's measured response to the market failures that brought on the Great Recession of 2008, the business community lost little time in launching another powerful assault on the partially refurbished protective governmental infrastructure.[1]

In a June 2010 speech to the Economic Club of Washington, D.C., Business Roundtable chairman Ivan G. Seidenberg fired the first salvo in the fourth assault when he declared that "we have reached a point where the negative effects" of the administration's regulatory initiatives "are simply too significant to ignore." The day before the speech, the Roundtable had delivered to the White House a 54-page document, entitled "Policy Burdens Inhibiting Economic Growth," complaining about specific actions taken or contemplated by federal regulatory agencies. Later that month, oil billionaire Charles G. Koch hosted a 4-day seminar in Aspen, Colorado, for a select "network" of more than 150 of the nation's wealthiest conservative donors. The program featured a lecture on the importance of financing judicial elections by two Chamber of Commerce officials and presentations on "Winning the Fight Between Free Enterprise and

Government" by the American Enterprise Institute, "Opportunities in Higher Education" by the Mercatus Center, and "Mobilizing Citizens for November" by Americans for Prosperity. A keynote speech by Glenn Beck was entitled "Is America on the Road to Serfdom?"[2]

THE FOURTH ASSAULT

When CNBC business reporter Rick Santelli, an Ayn Rand libertarian, went on a five-minute tirade in February 2009 against President Obama's plan to help homeowners refinance underwater mortgages, he suggested that America needed another Boston Tea Party. Recognizing the grass-roots appeal of that powerful symbol of popular American resentment, two well-funded successors to Citizens for a Sound Economy called Americans for Prosperity and Freedom-Works decided to devote their considerable resources, many of which derived from grants from founding funders Richard Mellon Scaife and Charles and David Koch, to giving the idea political traction. Within hours of the Santelli "rant," FreedomWorks had set up a website called "I'm With Rick" with suggestions for organizing local tea parties. The website became the virtual headquarters for the rapidly growing Tea Party movement. Both organizations provided a degree of coherence to the unwieldy amalgam of local groups by supplying travel funds and technical support. The fledgling movement also received a heavy boost from Fox News commentators Glenn Beck, Sean Hannity, and Sarah Palin. The Fox network itself rarely missed an opportunity to cover Tea Party activities.[3]

The Tea Party successfully deflected widespread public outrage away from the role that financial elites had played in bringing about the economic downturn and toward the government's apparent inability to heal the broken economy. Tea Party activists dutifully channeled the business community's argument that the ongoing crises were attributable to government limitations on economic freedom and that the solution was less government, fewer taxes, and a balanced budget. The message resonated well with an American public that, after years of repetition by Republican politicians and conservative think tanks, believed that government was incapable of solving the nation's problems. Their efforts bore fruit when, to the Obama Administration's apparent surprise, the Tea Party movement seized the political stage during the 2010 off-year elections.[4]

The business community launched its own public relations initiative highlighting its undocumented claim that a "regulatory hurricane" from the Obama Administration threatened to undermine economic growth. The U.S. Chamber of Commerce (CoC) alone spent upwards of $75 million on the 2010 election, the vast bulk of which financed attack ads aimed at Democratic candidates. The Wall Street bailout became a Republican Party bonanza as rescued banks contributed generously to the Chamber's project and directly to Republican candidates. FreedomWorks flew 40 local Tea Party leaders to Washington, D.C., for a 3-day "boot camp" where they received training in how to persuade like-minded citizens to vote for Tea Party–supported candidates in the November elections. The Supreme Court's *Citizens United* opinion came just in time to fill the coffers of all these organizations with anonymous corporate cash.[5]

The Republican Party won the House handily and left the Democrats with the thinnest of majorities in the Senate. In addition, a Tea Party caucus in both houses of Congress ensured that legislation calling for additional government regulation would be enacted only in response to dire crises and would be limited to the least intervention necessary to fix the problems that caused those crises. Any regulatory action that the Obama Administration cared to take would have to rely upon existing statutory authorities and would be subject to strict congressional oversight. The radical regulatory reformers in the think tanks saw the election as an opportunity to resume the war against regulation. The Heritage Foundation issued a "Backgrounder" entitled "Rolling Back Red Tape: 20 Regulations to Eliminate," that urged Congress to abolish the newly created Consumer Financial Protection Bureau and to overturn all of EPA's global warming regulations. Speaking at an event sponsored by the CoC, David McIntosh urged Congress to enact legislation forcing agencies to pay the attorneys' fees of companies who successfully defended themselves in enforcement actions. By the first anniversary of the enactment of the Dodd-Frank Act, Republicans had introduced two dozen bills in the House to repeal or dismantle various aspects of the regulatory structure that it had created.[6]

Instead of replacing exiting officials like Larry Summers and Rahm Emanuel with strong advocates of protective programs to reinvigorate grass-roots progressives, the president attempted to mollify the business community. The new chief of staff, William Daley, had been overseeing the efforts of JPMorgan Chase, a major packager of subprime loans, to avoid federal legislation limiting the size of megabanks, and he had co-chaired a CoC commission that called for tort reform and a rollback of post-Enron financial protections.[7]

Acknowledging that the administration's relationship with the business community had not been "managed by me as well as it needed to be," President Obama promised on election day that he would attempt "to boost and encourage our business sector." He then hosted a five-hour closed-door "summit" with 20 CEOs of major corporations where he promised to work closely with the business community to repair the broken economy and create jobs. In mid-January 2011, President Obama appeared on the op-ed page of Rupert Murdoch's *Wall Street Journal* to announce that he had signed a new executive order on federal rulemaking. In language almost identical to President Clinton's 1995 reassurances to the business community, President Obama affirmed that the administration's goal was "to strike the right balance" between "freedom of commerce" and "protect[ing] the public against threats to our health and safety." Magnanimous in victory, the chairman of the Business Roundtable praised President Obama for showing "a willingness to learn," and the president of the CoC assured the president that the vicious attacks that it had sponsored during the 2010 campaign had "never been personal."[8]

Soon after the election, FreedomWorks hosted a 2-day retreat in Baltimore for newly elected Republicans in which its chairman, Dick Armey, exhorted the freshmen not to stray from the limited government principles they had espoused during the campaign.[9] The House leadership got the message. At a closed-door meeting, House majority leader John A. Boehner (R-Ohio) assured 80 members of the Business Roundtable that he would be working with them in pursuit of a deregulatory agenda in the 112th Congress. In early January 2011, the new chairman of the House Committee on Oversight and Government Reform, Darrell Issa (R-California), asked industry groups to help him assemble still another "hit list" of federal regulations to schedule for revision or repeal. It took NAM only two days to come up with a list that included OSHA's as yet inchoate idea for mandatory injury and illness prevention programs, FMCSA's hours of service rulemaking, CPSC's product safety database, and every major regulation that EPA had proposed during the previous year.[10]

EPA was a special target of the Tea Party during the election season, and EPA reform became a high priority for House deregulators. A new bill limiting its authority came to the House floor almost every week for the first six months of the 112th Congress. Tea Party Republicans in the House chastised EPA for destroying jobs as they introduced bills to prevent it from regulating greenhouse gases, and global warming skeptics were once again invited to House hearings to explain why EPA was imposing expensive technological requirements on utility companies for no good reason. These criticisms were undermined by falling natural gas prices, which made it easy to comply with the new regulations by simply converting to that fuel, something that market forces were encouraging most utilities to do in any event.[11]

Although the gridlocked 112th Congress enacted little legislation of any kind, the House passed deregulatory legislation that made the omnibus regulatory reform bills of the Gingrich Congress look tame by comparison. In early December 2011, the House passed three omnibus regulatory reform bills, two of which (requiring more extensive cost benefit analysis for major rules and extending to all agencies the obligation to allow small businesses an early opportunity to comment on proposed rules) were quite reminiscent of the Gingrich Congress. The third bill, which was strongly supported by the CoC, would have required an affirmative vote of approval by both houses of Congress before any major rule could be finalized. Although all of these bills died in the Senate in the wake of a presidential veto threat, they created an opportunity for the regulatory reformers to air recent claims that federal regulations were killing jobs.[12]

Despite numerous victories in dozens of states in the 2010 elections, the business community still complained that the threat of common law liability was causing companies to cut jobs and move their operations overseas. After the Republican Party regained control over several state legislatures in the 2010 elections (often with the help of business-financed Tea Party candidates), tort reform legislation flourished once again. For example, a Tea Party–dominated Texas legislature in 2011 enacted legislation making it easier for judges to dismiss lawsuits prior to the discovery stage and requiring judges to make the losing plaintiff pay the defendant's court costs and attorney fees. More important, the campaign to remake the state judiciaries by financing attack ads against disfavored candidates in judicial elections continued unabated.[13]

THE PROGRESSIVE RESPONSE

If the business community was heartened by President Obama's overtures following the 2010 elections, progressive activists were deeply disappointed. They believed that the president was naively pursuing a "platonic ideal of bipartisanship" that, in the context of a Republican Party that was determined to replace him in two years, amounted to "unilateral political disarmament." The White House had been too willing to compromise on the financial reform legislation, and it was "AWOL" at "critical times" during the debates over the failed climate change legislation. The president conceded that "we probably spent much more time trying to get the policy right than trying to get the politics right." The only effective response to those who for partisan or ideological reasons were unwilling to pursue the common goal of economic and physical security for all citizens was to vigorously contest them for the political high ground. This, the Obama Administration failed to do until late in 2011, when its efforts could be written off as election year politicking.[14]

THE ROAD FORWARD

The patch-and-repair reforms that Congress enacted in response to specific crises of the late 2000s have the potential to bring about substantial improvements, but they do not represent comprehensive change. Because they have not changed the underlying incentives of the targeted industries, the reforms will probably have an impact on business operations in the targeted areas, but only if they are properly implemented and adequately enforced. Their Achilles heel is the perennial problem of funding. Future Congresses can easily forestall significant change if they simply defund the agencies that are charged with putting the new laws into effect. The Republican-dominated House of Representatives has already pushed Congress a long way in that direction.

The solutions to the ongoing crises will not come Mugwump-style from bipartisan commissions of wise men.[15] Comprehensive change will come only when enough people have accepted a new vision of the American future to replace the failed laissez faire minimalist ideology and are persuaded that alternative institutional arrangements and fresh substantive approaches will adequately protect their health, safety, and pocketbooks. This book has offered four narratives — security, corporate responsibility, corporate accountability, and social costs — that are capable of advancing a vision of a future America in which citizens can feel secure in the promise that government will protect them from corporate malfeasance. It has also suggested many approaches to regulation and litigation that are available for giving practical effect to that vision.

Very little in the way of constructive reform is likely, however, so long as the Senate remains fairly evenly divided between Republicans and Democrats and both sides are prepared to threaten to filibuster any legislative initiative that does not command overwhelming public support. Historically, it took a two-thirds majority (67 votes) to break a filibuster, but a post-Watergate amendment to the rules in 1975 changed the number to 60. As filibusters became easier to break, senators were less reluctant to employ that strategy. During the 111th Congress, the Democratic leadership correctly assumed that Republican senators would vote in lock-step against any cloture motion. Since it was unwilling to hold up the legislative process by forcing a real filibuster, the leadership effectively acknowledged that 60 votes were needed to pass any significant legislation. The stalemates have continued in the 112th Congress, this time to prevent radical deregulatory legislation passed by the House from passing the Senate. Until the climate in Congress changes, this dysfunctional state of affairs is likely to continue.[16]

In the meantime, the legacy of the Laissez Faire Revival endures. The situation will continue to deteriorate and the crises will continue to mount until the social and political forces realign themselves and a new bargain is struck under which the business community's economic freedoms are once again constrained by a government that is willing to impose greater responsibilities on powerful economic actors and a legal system that is capable of holding them accountable for the harm that they cause.

EPILOGUE: THE 2012 ELECTIONS

The nation entered the 2012 election season with the fourth assault well underway. The conservative media echo chamber developed a highly implausible narrative of President Obama as a dangerous radical who was determined to expand the reach of government over the lives of everyday people.[17] Determined to refute that caricature, the president continued to move closer to the business community's position on regulatory and civil justice issues, signaling that he was prepared to compromise away some of the advances made in the Executive Branch. In part this was attributable to the president's unshakable yearning to be the reasonable person who ends the partisan warfare that has dominated Congress since the Gingrich years, but it also reflected a decision by Democratic Party strategists going back to Bill Clinton's 1992 presidential campaign to avoid alienating the business community, its Washington, D.C. lobbyists (many of whom were prominent party operatives), and its Wall Street bankers (many of whom had been large contributors to the party).[18]

Whatever the outcome of the 2012 election, the fourth assault on regulation and the civil justice system will continue unabated. The Republican Party has become so thoroughly dominated by uncompromising laissez faire minimalists that it will dependably pursue deregulation and tort reform without regard to the interests of the consumers, workers, and communities who are the beneficiaries of regulatory programs and the civil justice system. So long as regulatory reform and tort reform remain high on the Republican agenda, Congress will either remain deadlocked or will implement that agenda.[19]

NOTES

In addition to the normal conventions of legal citation form, the notes that follow will employ the following abbreviations:

BNA Environmental Reporter—BNA Env. Rept.
BNA Occupational Safety & Health Reporter—BNA OSHR
BNA Product Safety & Liability Reporter—BNA PSLR
Los Angeles Times—LAT
New York Times—NYT
Wall Street Journal—WSJ
Washington Post—WP

INTRODUCTION. TWO TRAGEDIES

1. Except where otherwise noted, the description of the Monongah events is taken from Daniel J. Curran, Dead Laws for Dead Men 61, 76, 191 (1993) and Davitt McAteer, Monongah: The Tragic Story of the 1907 Monongah Mine Disaster (2007).
2. McAteer, Monongah, 160 (quoting Clarence Hall).
3. McAteer, Monongah, 167 (quoting Ohio Monongah investigation report).
4. McAteer, Monongah, 211 (quoting letter of January 17, 1907 from Johnson Newlon Camden to Aretas Brooks Fleming).
5. McAteer, Monongah, 214–17, 221, 250.
6. Kirk Johnson, *Utah Coal Area, A Region Apart, Knows Well the Perils of Mining*, NYT, August 9, 2007, at A10 (deepest); Paul Foy, *Utah Mine Cave-In Traps Six*, WP, August 7, 2007, at A7.
7. *Mine Efforts Suspended Indefinitely*, WP, September 1, 2007, at A7; Karl Vick, *Mine Rescuer's Death Unites Those Who Loved Him*, WP, August 18, 2007, at A1 (Huntsman quote); Kirk Johnson, *Safety Issues Slow Mine Rescue Efforts*, NYT, August 8, 2007, at 15.
8. Susan Saulny & Carolyn Marshall, *Mine Owner Has History of Run-Ins on Work Issues*, NYT, August 24, 2007, at 14; Karl Vick & Sonya Geis, *Many Pressures Led to*

Cave-In, WP, August 20, 2007, at A1 (pure profit quote); Kirk Johnson, *Facing the Multiple Risks of Newer, Deeper Mines*, NYT, August 16, 2007, at 17; Robert Gehrke, *Critics Blast Feds' Approval of Controversial "Retreat" Mining at Crandall Canyon*, Salt Lake Tribune, August 14, 2007, at A1 (MSHA approval); Patty Henetz, *Mine Told Officials It Would Be "Pulling Pillars,"* Salt Lake Tribune, August 8, 2007, at A1 (cut and gut quote); Seth Borenstein, *Studies: Mining Method Used in Utah Collapse Often Turns Deadly*, USA Today, August 7, 2007, at A3 (hazardous activities quote).

9. *Examining Global Warming Issues in the Power Plant Sector, Hearings Before the Senate Committee on Environment & Public Works*, 110th Cong. 1st Sess. (2007) (testimony of Robert Murray) (extremely misguided quote); Joe Bauman, *A History of Safety Violations*, Deseret Morning News, August 7, 2007, at A1 (statistics); Deborah Yetter, *Mining Company, 4 Employees Convicted of Safety Violations*, Louisville Courier-Journal, May 22, 2003, at A1.

10. John Harmon, *Crisis PR in the Mines*, LAT, August 21, 2007, at A6 (PR expert quotes); Robert Gehrke & Paul Beebe, *Murray's Meltdown: Angry, Rambling Briefing Draws Rebuke*, Salt Lake City Tribune, August 8, 2007, at A1 (Murray being Murray quote).

11. Editorial, *Not Again: Stickler Bad for MSHA*, Charleston Gazette, February 15, 2006, at A4.

12. Cara Buckley & Dan Frosch, *Mine Safety Leader Loses Some Respect for Actions in Utah*, NYT, August 24, 2007, at 14; Vick & Geis, *Many Pressures*; Maeve Reston, *Mine Safety Nominee Under Fire*, Pittsburgh Post-Gazette, February 1, 2006, at A4 (quote).

PART I. THE EVOLVING SOCIAL BARGAIN

1. New Deal Art, Art Lex Art Directory, available at http://www.artlex.com/ArtLex/n/newdeal.html; Federal Trade Commission, Federal Trade Commission 90th Anniversary Symposium (September 22–23, 2004), at 10.

2. See Bruce A. Ackerman, *Essays on the Supreme Court Appointment Process: Transformative Appointments*, 101 Harv. L. Rev. 1164 (1988); Frank Michelman, *Law's Republic*, 97 Yale L. J. 1493 (1988).

CHAPTER 1. FREEDOM REIGNS: THE LAISSEZ FAIRE BENCHMARK

1. Jack Beatty, Age of Betrayal 13 (2007); Herbert Hovenkamp, *The Classical Corporation in American Legal Thought*, 76 Geo. L. J. 1594, 1634 (1988); Edward C. Kirkland, Dream and Thought in the Business Community, 1860–1900 27 (1956).

2. Beatty, Age of Betrayal, 296; Sidney Fine, Laissez Faire and the General-Welfare State: A Study of Conflict in American Thought, 1865–1901 46, 119 (1956); Ray Ginger, The Age of Excess 20 (1965).

3. Others have used similar terms to describe this ideology. Michael Hirsh, Capital Offense (2010) ("free-market absolutism"); Paul Krugman, The Conscience of a Liberal 115 (2007) ("free market fundamentalism").

4. Fine, Laissez Faire, ch. 1; Matthew Josephson, The Robber Barons 305 (Harvest ed. 1962); Robert G. McCloskey, American Conservatism in the Age of Enterprise 24

(1951); William E. Forbath, *The Ambiguities of Free Labor: Labor and the Law in the Gilded Age*, 1985 Wis. L. Rev. 767, 768–69, 793 (1985).

5. Powell v. Pennsylvania, 127 U.S. 678, 684 (1888); County of Santa Clara v. Southern Pacific Ry Co., 118 U.S. 394 (1886); Munn v. Illinois, 94 U.S. 113 (1876); Josephson, Robber Barons, 306; McCloskey, American Conservatism, 3; Hovenkamp, *Classical Corporation*, 1632–33, 1658–59; Liam Seamus O'Melinn, *Neither Contract Nor Concession: The Public Personality of the Corporation*, 74 Geo. Wash. L. Rev. 201, 201–02 (2006); Robert L. Rabin, *Federal Regulation in Historical Perspective*, 38 Stan. L. Rev. 1189, 1208–17 (1986); Sanford A. Schane, *The Corporation as a Person: The Language of a Legal Fiction*, 61 Tul. L. Rev. 563, 568 (1987).

6. Fine, Laissez Faire, 140–51; Josephson, Robber Barons, 305; McCloskey, American Conservatism, 61, 72; Forbath, *Ambiguities*, 768–69, 793; Hovenkamp, *Classical Corporation*, 1601–02.

7. Mark A. Geistfeld, Essentials of Tort Law 7, 18–21 (2008); Mark A. Geistfeld, Principles of Products Liability 9, 14, 20 (2006); William Prosser, Handbook of the Law of Torts 528 (1941); Mark M. Hager, *Civil Compensation and Its Discontents: A Response to Huber*, 42 Stan. L. Rev. 539 (1990); William J. Maakestad & Charles Helm, *Promoting Workplace Safety and Health in the Post-Regulatory Era: A Primer on Non-OSHA Legal Incentives that Influence Employer Decisions to Control Occupational Hazards*, N. Ken. L. Rev. 17 (1989); Wex Malone, *Ruminations on the Role of Fault in the History of the Common Law of Torts*, 31 La. L. Rev. 1 (1970).

8. Fine, Laissez Faire, 358; John B. Judis, The Paradox of American Democracy 35 (2001) (quote).

9. Fine, Laissez Faire, 358; Ginger, Age of Excess, 36 (economic growth).

10. Mark Aldrich, Death Rode the Rails 43, 45, table 2.1 (2006); Beatty, Age of Betrayal, 17; Daniel J. Curran, Dead Laws for Dead Men 27 (1993); Lawrence M. Friedman, A History of American Law 65 (1973) (mining disasters); Valerie P. Hans, Business on Trial 7 (2000) (statistics); Steven W. Usselman, Regulating Railroad Innovation 118 (2002).

11. David Stradling, Smokestacks and Progressives 7, 25, 34 (1999); Usselman, Regulating Railroad Innovation, 118.

12. Ginger, Age of Excess, 29–30; Philip J. Hilts, Protecting America's Health 21 (2003).

13. Hofstadter, Age of Reform, 143; Gerald W. McFarland, Mugwumps, Morals & Politics, 1884–1920 37 (1975); John G. Sproat, "The Best Men": Liberal Reformers in the Gilded Age 9–10 (1968); Forbath, *Ambiguities*, 790.

14. Lawrence Goodwyn, Democratic Promise: The Populist Movement in America 25–31, 310, 358 (1976).

15. Beatty, Age of Betrayal, 273 (railroads); Curran, Dead Laws, 60 (mining); Goodwyn, Democratic Promise, 42, 47, 110–13, 362 (quoting newspaper).

CHAPTER 2. FREEDOM REINED: THE PROGRESSIVE
ERA THROUGH THE PUBLIC INTEREST ERA

1. Sidney Fine, Laissez Faire and the General-Welfare State: A Study of Conflict in American Thought 1865–1901 389 (1956) (Roosevelt); Philip J. Hilts, Protecting

America's Health 33 (2003); Richard Hofstadter, The Age of Reform 5–6, 132–35 (1955); William Graebner, Coal-Mining Safety in the Progressive Period 3 (1976); John B. Judis, The Paradox of American Democracy 21 (2001) (press); J.M. Balkin, *Populism and Progressivism as Constitutional Categories*, 104 Yale L. J. 1935, 1947 (1995) (science); Arthur F. McEvoy, *The Triangle Shirtwaist Factory Fire of 1911: Social Change, Industrial Accidents, and the Evolution of Common-Sense Causality*, 20 L. & Social Inq. 621, 630 (1995).

2. Meat Inspection Act of 1906, chapter 3913, 34 Stat. 674 (1906); Pure Food and Drug Act of 1906, Pub. L. 59–384, 34 Stat. 768 (1906); Stephen J. Ceccoli, Pill Politics 62–64 (2004); Marion Nestle, Safe Food 50–54 (2003) (Sinclair).

3. Act of May 16, 1910, Public Law No. 61–179, 36 Stat. 369 (1910) (mine safety statute); Federal Employers' Liability Act of 1908, chapter 149, 35 Stat. 65 (1908); Daniel J. Curran, Dead Laws for Dead Men 66–67 (1993); William Graebner, Coal-Mining Safety in the Progressive Period 23, 33 (1976); McEvoy, *Triangle Shirtwaist*, 646.

4. Federal Reserve Act of 1913, chapter 6, 40 Stat. 251 (1913); Louis D. Brandeis, Other People's Money, and How the Bankers Use It (1914); Simon Johnson & James Kwak, 13 Bankers 29 (2010).

5. Federal Trade Commission Act of 1914, chapter 311, 38 Stat. 717 (1914); Marc Winerman, *The Origins of the FTC: Concentration, Cooperation, Control, and Competition*, 71 Antitrust L. J. 1, 5–6 (2003).

6. Daniel M. Berman, Death on the Job 19 (1978); Martha T. McCluskey, *Efficiency and Social Citizenship: Challenging the Neo-Liberal Attack on the Welfare State*, 78 Ind. L. J. 783, 848–49 (2003); Martha T. McCluskey, *The Illusion of Efficiency in Workers' Compensation "Reform,"* 50 Rutgers L. Rev. 657, 669–72 (1998); Department of Labor, Employment Standards Administration, Office of Workers Compensation Programs, *State Workers' Compensation Laws* Table 6 (Washington, 1990).

7. MacPherson v. Buick Motor Co., 111 N.E. 1050 (1916) (quote); Restatement (Second) of Torts § 283; Mark A. Geistfeld, Essentials of Tort Law 27–29 (2008).

8. Berman, Death on the Job, 24; Hilts, Protecting, 66, 73; Matthew Josephson, The Robber Barons 452 (1962).

9. Food, Drug and Cosmetic Act of 1938, Pub. L. 75–717, chapter 675, 52 Stat. 1040 (1938); Wheeler-Lea Act of 1938, Pub. L. 75–447, 52 Stat. 11 (1938); Banking Act of 1933, Pub. L. No. 73–66, 48 Stat. 162 (1933); Ceccoli, Pill Politics, 70–72; Curran, Dead Laws, 91–93; Charles R. Morris, The Trillion Dollar Meltdown 44 (2008).

10. Administrative Procedure Act of 1946, Pub. L. 79–104, 60 Stat. 237 (1946); Motor Vehicle Manufacturers' Ass'n v. State Farm Mutual Automobile Ins. Co., 463 U.S. 29, 43 (1983); Clyde P. Weed, The Nemesis of Reform; The Republican Party During the New Deal pt. 3 (1994).

11. Food Additives Amendment of 1958, Pub. L. 85–929, 72 Stat. 1784 (1958); Federal Coal Mine Safety Act of 1952, Pub. L. 82–522, 66 Stat. 692 (1952); Curran, Dead Laws, 67, 97, 100; Hilts, Protecting, 117; Judis, Paradox, 64 (return to normalcy); Richard A. Merrill, *FDA's Implementation of the Delaney Clause: Repudiation of Congressional Choice or Reasoned Adaptation to Scientific Progress?* 5 Yale J. on Reg. 1, 74–88 (1988).

12. The description of the World's Fair is from the author's personal recollections from visits during the summers of 1964 and 1965. For a photographic depiction of the many exhibits at the fair, see http://www.westland.net/ny64fair.

13. David Vogel, Fluctuating Fortunes 40, 53, 96 (1989) (quote).

14. Judis, Paradox, 101–02; Michael Pertschuk, Revolt Against Regulation 29–33 (1982); Richard J. Lazarus, The Making of Environmental Law 81 (2004); Simon Lazarus, The Genteel Populists (1974); Vogel, Fluctuating Fortunes, 53, 95, 104.

15. Mark K. Landy, Marc J. Roberts & Stephen R. Thomas, The Environmental Protection Agency 24–25 (1990); Lazarus, Environmental Law, 83; Pertschuk, Revolt, 23 33–36; John Quarles, Cleaning Up America 172 (1976).

16. Mine Safety and Health Act of 1977, Pub. L. 95–164, 91 Stat. 1290; Occupational Safety and Health Act of 1970, Pub. L. 91–596, 84 Stat. 1590 (1970); Daniel J. Curran, Dead Laws for Dead Men 109–13, 123, 140–41 (1993); Thomas O. McGarity & Sidney A. Shapiro, Workers at Risk 34–36 (1993).

17. National Commission on Product Safety, Final Report 72 (1970).

18. A New Progressive Agenda for Public Health and the Environment (Christopher Schroeder & Rena Steinzor, eds. 2005); Hilts, Protecting, 143, 164; Susan J. Tolchin & Martin Tolchin, Dismantling America 16–20 (1983).

19. J. Clarence Davies, III, The Politics of Pollution 18, 73 (1970); Jeannette L. Austin, *The Rise of Citizen-Suit Enforcement in Environmental Law: Reconciling Private and Public Attorneys General*, 81 Nw. U. L. Rev. 220, 227 n.47 (1987) (citing statutes).

20. Dan B. Dobbs, The Law of Torts 1033–34 (2000); James E. Krier & Edmund Ursin, Pollution and Policy 11–12 (1977); Vogel, Fluctuating Fortunes, 54.

CHAPTER 3. FREEDOM, RESPONSIBILITY, AND ACCOUNTABILITY

1. Sidney Fine, Laissez Faire and the General-Welfare State: A Study of Conflict in American Thought 1865–1901 390–91 (1956) (quote); Robert E. Lane, *The Politics of Consensus in an Age of Affluence*, 59 Am. Pol. Sci. Rev. 874 (1965).

2. M. Stanton Evans, The Liberal Establishment (1965); Robert G. McCloskey, American Conservatism in the Age of Enterprise 168 (1951); Alfred S. Regnery, Upstream 122 (2008).

3. See Reuel E. Schiller, Rulemaking's Promise: Administrative Law and Legal Culture in the 1960s and 1970s, 53 Ad. L. Rev. 1139 (2001).

4. Dan B. Dobbs, The Law of Torts 311–28 (2000); Carl T. Bogus, Why Lawsuits Are Good for America 5, 138 (2001); Thomas O. McGarity, The Preemption War 36–37 (2008); David G. Owen, Products Liability Law 93–94 (2005); Restatement (Second) of Torts §§ 283, 286, 288; Robert L. Rabin, *Poking Holes in the Fabric of Tort: A Comment*, 56 DePaul L. Rev. 293, 304 (2007).

5. Mark A. Geistfeld, Principles of Products Liability ch. 5 (2006); Restatement (Third) of Torts — Products Liability § 1, 2, 6; Alexandra B. Klass, *Pesticides, Children's Health Policy, and Common Law Tort Claims*, 7 Minn. J. of L., Sci., & Tech. 89, 128 (2005); David G. Owen, *Manufacturing Defects*, 53 S. Car. L. Rev. 851 (2002).

6. William Andreen, *Beyond Words of Exhortation: The Congressional Prescription for Vigorous Federal Enforcement of the Clean Water Act*, 55 Geo. Wash. L. Rev. 202 (1987); Jack B. Weinstein, *Compensation for Mass Private Delicts: Evolving Roles of Administrative, Criminal and Tort Law*, 2001 Ill. L. Rev. 947, 964–65 (2001).

7. Jeannette L. Austin, *The Rise of Citizen-Suit Enforcement in Environmental Law: Reconciling Private and Public Attorneys General*, 81 Nw. U. L. Rev. 220, 227, n.47 (1987) (listing citizen suit provisions of environmental statutes); Barry Boyer & Erol Meidinger, *Privatizing Regulatory Enforcement: A Preliminary Assessment of Citizen Suits Under Federal Environmental Laws*, 34 Buffalo L. Rev. 833, 838 (1986).

8. David C. Vladeck, *Defending Courts: A Brief Rejoinder to Professors Fried and Rosenberg*, 31 Seton Hall L. Rev. 631, 632 (2001); Wendy Wagner, *When All Else Fails: Regulating Risky Products Through Tort Litigation*, 95 Georgetown L. J. 693, 713–14 (2007).

9. Mark A. Geistfeld, Essentials of Tort Law ch. 10–11 (2008).

10. Deborah R. Hensler, et. al., Class Action Dilemmas 4–6, 50, 84, 89, 109 (2000); Charles A. Wright, Arthur R. Miller & Mary Kay Kane, Federal Practice & Procedure § 1751 (2005); Edward F. Sherman, *Consumer Class Actions: Who are the Real Winners?* 56 Maine L. Rev. 223, 223–24, 231–33 (2004).

11. Dobbs, Law of Torts § 381; Stephanie Mencimer, Blocking the Courthouse Door 223 (2006); Marshall S. Shapo, Basic Principles of Tort Law 358–61, 366 (1999); Thomas C. Galligan, Jr., *Augmented Awards: The Efficient Evolution of Punitive Damages*, 51 La. L. Rev. 3, 38 (1990); David G. Owen, *The Moral Foundations of Punitive Damages*, 40 Ala. L. Rev. 705, 730 (1989).

12. See, e.g., Richard A. Epstein, Overdose 110 (2006) (acknowledging that "government has a role to play against the use of force, fraud, and breach of contract").

13. Milton Friedman, Capitalism and Freedom 4 (1962); Friedrich A. Hayek, The Road to Serfdom xliii, 16 (Bruce Caldwell, ed. 2007).

14. Carolyn Raffensperger & Joel Tickner, Protecting Public Health and the Environment (1999); David Driesen, *The Societal Cost of Environmental Regulation: Beyond Administrative Cost-Benefit Analysis*, 24 Ecol. L. Q. 545 (1997); Wendy E. Wagner, *Innovations in Environmental Policy: The Triumph of Technology-Based Standards*, 2000 U. Ill. L. Rev. 1553 (2000).

15. Epstein, Overdose, 113, 189; Milton Friedman & Rose D. Friedman, Free to Choose 203 (1980); Robert Smith, The Occupational Safety and Health Act, Its Goals and Achievements (1976); W. Kip Viscusi, Risk By Choice (1983); Martha T. McCluskey, *Efficiency and Social Citizenship: Challenging the Neo-Liberal Attack on the Welfare State*, 78 Ind. L. J. 783, 807 (2003) (origins of the concept of moral hazard).

16. Graham K. Wilson, The Politics of Safety and Health 6–7 (1985); Jon Hanson & David Yosifon, *The Situation: An Introduction to the Situational Character, Critical Realism, Power Economics, and Deep Capture*, 152 U. Pa. L. Rev. 129, 136, 197 (2003) (exogenous influences); Stewart J. Schwab, *Life-Cycle Justice: Accommodating Just Cause and Employment at Will*, 92 Mich. L. Rev. 8, 29 (1993).

17. Epstein, Overdose 11, 225, 235, 239 (2006); Friedman & Friedman, Free to Choose, 32, 215–17; Hayek, Road to Serfdom, 43; John Mendeloff, The Dilemma of Toxic Sub-

stance Regulation 232 (1988); John D. Graham, *Saving Lives Through Administrative Law and Economics*, 157 U. Pa. L. Rev. 395 (2008).

18. Frank Ackerman & Lisa Heinzerling, Priceless (2005); Thomas O. McGarity, A Cost-Benefit State, 50 Ad. L. Rev. 7, 40–49 (1998); Amy Sinden, Douglas A. Kysar & David M. Driesen, *Cost-Benefit Analysis: New Foundations on Shifting Sand*, 3 Reg. & Governance 48 (2009).

19. Friedman & Friedman, Free to Choose, 206; Peter W. Huber, Liability: The Legal Revolution and Its Consequences 14–15 (1988); Irving Kristol, Two Cheers for Capitalism 56 (1978); Deborah J. LaFetra, *Freedom, Responsibility, and Risk· Fundamental Principles Supporting Tort Reform*, 36 Ind. L. Rev. 645, 645–48 (2003).

20. Melody Petersen, Our Daily Meds 143 (2008); Mark M. Hager, *Civil Compensation and Its Discontents: A Response to Huber*, 42 Stan. L. Rev. 539, 556 (1990); Teresa M. Schwartz, *Prescription Products and the Proposed Restatement (Third)*, 61 Tenn. L. Rev. 1357, 1399, 1404 (1994).

21. Bogus, Lawsuits, 111; Matthew D. Zinn, *Policing Environmental Regulatory Enforcement: Cooperation, Capture, and Citizen Suits*, 21 Stan. Envt'l L. J. 81, 82, 88, 96 (2002).

22. Eugene Bardach & Robert A. Kagan, Going by the Book 6–7 (1982); Epstein, Overdose, 171–72, 195; Philip Howard, The Death of Common Sense (1994); Huber, Liability, ch. 10.

23. John Braithwaite, To Punish or Persuade 100 (1985); Rena I. Steinzor, Mother Earth and Uncle Sam 89 (2008); David L. Markell, *The Role of Deterrent-Based Enforcement in a "Reinvented" State/Federal Relationship: The Divide Between Theory and Reality*, 24 Harv. Env. L. Rev. 1, 11 (2000).

24. Epstein, Overdose, 171–72, 195; Huber, Liability, ch. 10.

25. Clayton P. Gillette & James E. Krier, *Risk, Courts, and Agencies*, 138 U. Pa. L. Rev. 1027, 1050 (1990); Christopher H. Schroeder, *Corrective Justice and Liability for Increasing Risks*, 37 UCLA L. Rev. 439 (1990).

CHAPTER 4. THE INTELLECTUAL AND FINANCIAL FOUNDATIONS

1. Paul Krugman, The Conscience of a Liberal 4, 50–51, 115 (2007); Alfred S. Regnery, Upstream xiv (2008); Robert B. Reich, Supercapitalism, ch. 1 (2007).

2. Friedrich A. Hayek, *The Road to Serfdom* (Bruce Caldwell, ed. 2007). See Murray Friedman, The Neoconservative Revolution 44 (2005); Regnery, Upstream, 27.

3. Alan Ebenstein, Friedrich Hayek: A Biography 37, 40, 42 (2001); Friedrich A. Hayek, Law, Legislation, and Liberty Vol. I 107–08, 133, 144 (1973); Friedrich A. Hayek, Law, Legislation, and Liberty Vol. III 42, 49, 131–32 (1973).

4. Ebenstein, Hayek, 60–63, 129, 135–36; Sherryl Davis Kasper, The Revival of Laissez-Faire in American Macroeconomic Theory 64 (2002) (quoting Friedrich Hayek).

5. Donald T. Critchlow, The Conservative Ascendancy 15 (2007); Ebenstein, Hayek, 168, 173–78; Regnery, Upstream, 29, 177–78; Ronald H. Coase, *Law and Economics at Chicago*, 36 J. L. & Econ. 239, 245 (1993).

6. Critchlow, Conservative Ascendancy, 16–17; Herman Finer, The Road to Reaction 22, 49, 134, 138–39 (1945); Walton H. Hamilton, *Book Review,* 53 Yale L. J. 805, 806 (1944); Kenneth C. Davis, *Book Review: The Road to Serfdom,* 23 Tex. L. Rev. 205 (1945).

7. Critchlow, Conservative Ascendancy, 15–16; Ebenstein, Hayek, 143–44; Friedrich Hayek, *On Being an Economist,* in The Trend of Economic Thinking (W.W. Bartley III & S. Kresge, eds. 1991).

8. Critchlow, Conservative Ascendancy, 16 (quoting Statement of Aims); Ebenstein, Hayek, 145 (quoting Statement of Aims).

9. Critchlow, Conservative Ascendancy, 16; Ebenstein, Hayek, 145–46, 211–13; Regnery, Upstream, 31–33. See The Mont Pelerin Society Homepage, available at http://www .montpelerin.org/home.cfm.

10. David Brock, The Republican Noise Machine 41 (2004); John B. Judis, The Paradox of American Democracy 101 (2001) (quoting poll results); David M. Ricci, The Transformation of American Politics 154–55 (1993).

11. Regnery, Upstream, 183–84; Judis, Paradox, 101–02.

12. John Micklethwait & Adrian Wooldridge, The Right Nation 79 (2004); John J. Miller, A Gift of Freedom 11–18, 23–24, 26 (quote), 32, 37, 40, 304 (2006).

13. Murray Friedman, the Neoconservative Revolution 187 (2005); Irving Kristol, Neoconservatism: The Autobiography Of An Idea ix, 221 (1995); Irving Kristol, Reflections of a Neoconservative 212 (1983); Miller, Gift, 43–45, 53, 83, 115.

14. Sidney Blumenthal, The Rise of the Counter-Establishment 6, 68, 159 (1986); Miller, Gift, ch. 9.

15. Micklethwait & Wooldridge, Right Nation, 79; Miller, Gift, 133; Regnery, Upstream, 197–98.

16. Micklethwait & Wooldridge, Right Nation, 78; David Vogel, Fluctuating Fortunes 222 (1989) (contributions); Dan Fitzpatrick, *Mellon Family's Legacy Lives On,* Pittsburgh Post-Gazette, July 1, 2007, at C1; Robert G. Kaiser & Ira Chinoy, *Scaife: Founding Father of the Right,* WP, May 2, 1999, at A1.

17. Russ Bellant, The Coors Connection vi, 1, 85–93 (1988); Blumenthal, Counter-Establishment, 37, 56; Miller, Gift, 91

18. Lee Cokorinos, The Assault on Diversity 68–69 (2003); Micklethwait & Wooldridge, Right Nation, 78; Jane Mayer, *Covert Operations,* New Yorker, August 30, 2010, at 45; Shawn Zeller, *Conservative Crusaders,* 35 Nat. J. 1286 (2003).

19. Brock, Republican Noise Machine, 48–49; Paul Krugman, Conscience, 165; Miller, Gift, 7 (quote).

CHAPTER 5. THE IDEA INFRASTRUCTURE

1. John B. Judis, The Paradox of American Democracy 116 (2001). All quotes from the Powell Memorandum are from Lewis Powell, Memorandum to Eugene B. Sydnor, Jr., Chairman, Education Committee, U.S. Chamber of Commerce, dated August 23, 1971.

2. John Jeffries, Justice Lewis F. Powell: A Biography 228 (2001).

3. William E. Simon, A Time for Truth 34, 43, 200, 244–45, 247 (1978).

4. David M. Ricci, The Transformation of American Politics 142 (1993); James A. Smith, The Idea Brokers 22 (1991).

5. Alan Ebenstein, Friedrich Hayek: A Biography (2001); Melvin W. Reder, *Chicago Economics: Permanence and Change,* 20 J. Econ. Lit. 1 (1982).

6. James R. Hackney, Jr., Under Cover of Science 99–103 (2006); Sherryl Kasper, The Revival of Laissez-Faire in American Macroeconomic Theory 16–19, ch. 2 (2002); Frank H. Knight, Risk, Uncertainty and Profit 301, 358 (1921); Reder, *Chicago Economics,* 1, 6.

7. Kasper, Revival, 29, 35–36, 49; Henry Simons, A Positive Program for Laissez Faire (1931); Steven M. Teles, The Rise of the Conservative Legal Movement 91–92 (2008); Ronald H. Coase, *Law and Economics at Chicago,* 36 J. L. & Econ. 239, 240 (1993); Reder, *Chicago Economics,* 25, 29.

8. Milton and Rose Friedman, Two Lucky People 155, 391–93 (1998); John Micklethwait & Adrian Wooldridge, The Right Nation 49 (2004); Elton Rayack, Not So Free to Choose: The Political Economy of Milton Friedman and Ronald Reagan 2, 9–11, 172–73 (1987); Paul Krugman, *Who Was Milton Friedman?,* New York Review of Books, February 15, 2007, at 27; Reder, *Chicago Economics,* 25.

9. Sydney Blumenthal, The Rise of the Counter-Establishment 115 (1986); Milton Friedman & Rose Friedman, Free to Choose 3 (1979) (Gilded Age quote); Milton Friedman, Capitalism and Freedom 110 (1962); Kasper, Revival, 77; David Vogel, Fluctuating Fortunes 222 (1989) (Scaife Foundation funding); Krugman, *Friedman,* 29 (abolish FDA)

10. Reder, *Chicago Economics,* 11.

11. Michael Hirsh, Capital Offense ch. 5 (2010); Paul Krugman, The Conscience of a Liberal 115 (2007); Reder, *Chicago Economics,* 13, 16; Patricia Cohen, *In Economics Departments, A Growing Will to Debate Fundamental Assumptions,* NYT, July 11, 2007, at B6.

12. Teles, Conservative Legal Movement, 12–13. For a lengthier and more nuanced description of the law and economics movement, see Thomas O. McGarity, *A Movement, A Lawsuit, and the Integrity of Sponsored Law and Economics Research,* 21 Stanford L. & Pol. Rev. 51 (2010).

13. Teles, Conservative Legal Movement, 4, 11–12, 17, 90, 138; Adam Benforado, Jon Hanson & David Yosifon, *Broken Scales: Obesity and Justice in America,* 53 Emory L. J. 1645, 1731 (2004).

14. John J. Miller, A Gift of Freedom 71, 95, 114 (2006); Teles, Conservative Legal Movement, 174–75, 190, 218; Martha T. McCluskey, *Thinking with Wolves: Left Legal Theory After the Right's Rise,* 54 Buffalo L. Rev. 1191, 1213 (2007); Michael L. Rustad & Thomas H. Koenig, *Taming the Tort Monster: The American Civil Justice System as a Battleground of Social Theory,* 68 Brooklyn L. Rev. 1, 76 (2002); Ira Chinoy & Robert G. Kaiser, *Decades of Contributions to Conservatism,* WP, May 2, 1999, at A25.

15. Hackney, Cover of Science, 93, 109; Nicholas Mercuro & Steven G. Medema, Economics and the Law 18, 57, 66–74 (1997); Gregory S. Crespi, *Does the Chicago School Need to Expand its Curriculum?* 22 L. & Soc. Inquiry 149, 149–51 (1997); Richard A. Posner, *Values and Consequences: An Introduction to Economic Analysis of Law,* in

Chicago Lectures in Law and Economics 189, 191 (E. Posner, ed. 2000); Mark Tushnet, *What Consequences Do Ideas Have?* 87 Tex. L. Rev. 447, 449 (2008).

16. Hackney, Cover of Science, 99, 105; Mercuro & Medema, Economics, 53; Miller, Gift, 114; Coase, *Law and Economics*, 243, 246–48; Edmund Kitch, *The Fire of Truth: A Remembrance of Law and Economics at Chicago, 1932–70*, 26 J. L. & Econ. 163, 180–81 (1983).

17. Hackney, Cover of Science, 108; Richard A. Posner, Economic Analysis of Law (1972); Teles, Conservative Legal Movement, 96 (first rank quote); C.G. Veljanovski, The New Law-and-Economics 12 (1982); George A. Hay, *The Past, Present, and Future of Law and Economics*, 3 Agenda 71, 73 (1996) (pied piper quote); Larissa MacFarquhar, *The Bench Burner*, New Yorker, December 10, 2001, at 78.

18. Richard A. Epstein, Takings ch. 5 (1985); Richard J. Lazarus, The Making of Environmental Law 121 (2004); Miller, Gift, 72; Jeffrey Rosen, *The Unregulated Offensive*, NYT Magazine, April 17, 2005, at 42.

19. Miller, Gift, 77, 80 (defunded quote); Teles, Conservative Legal Movement, 118, 133, 186–87.

20. Carl T. Bogus, Why Lawsuits Are Good for America 58–59 (2001); Peter W. Huber, Liability 218 (1988); Richard Posner, Economic Analysis of Law § 6.12 (1977) (quote); Gillian Hadfield, *The Second Wave of Law and Economics: Learning to Surf*, in The Second Wave of Law and Economics 50, 51 (M. Richardson & G. Hadfield, eds., 1999); Morton J. Horwitz, *Law and Economics: Science or Politics?* 8 Hofstra L. Rev. 905, 909 (1980); MacFarquhar, *Bench Burner* (scales of justice); Jedediah S. Purdy, *The Chicago Acid Bath*, American Prospect, January/February, 1998, at 88, 88–89.

21. Richard A. Epstein, *Products Liability as an Insurance Market*, 14 J. Legal Studies 645 (1985); George L. Priest & Richard A. Epstein, *Introduction*, 14 J. Legal Studies 459 (1985); George L. Priest, *The Invention of Enterprise Liability: A Critical History of the Intellectual Foundations of Modern Tort Law*, 14 J. Legal Studies 461, 462–63 (1985); Alan Schwartz, *Products Liability, Corporate Structure, and Bankruptcy: Toxic Substances and the Remote Relationship*, 14 J. Legal Studies 689 (1985).

22. This is certainly the message that the author of this book, who participated in the conference, took away from it.

23. Miller, Gift, 66 (quote); Teles, Conservative Legal Movement, 90, 105, 109, 118; Henry G. Manne, An Intellectual History of the George Mason University School of Law (1993), available at http://www.law.gmu.edu/about/history.

24. Nina J. Easton, Gang of Five 52, 67–68 (2000); Teles, Conservative Legal Movement, 137, 141; Spencer Abraham, *A Founder's Retrospective: The Journal at 30 Years*, 31 Harv. J. L. & Public Policy 1 (2008); George W. Hicks, Jr., *The Conservative Influence of the Federalist Society on the Harvard Law School Student Body*, 29 Harv. J. L. & Public Policy 623, 643 (2006).

25. Easton, Gang of Five, 69, 188, 235; Jan Greenburg, Supreme Conflict 98 (2007); Jean Stefancic & Richard Delgado, No Mercy 111 (1996); Teles, Conservative Legal Movement, 142–45; Jerry Landay, *The Federalist Society*, Washington Monthly, March 2000, at 17 (Tripp tapes); *House Republicans Go to War on Regulation*, WP, January 20, 1995, at A19 (David McIntosh).

26. Lee Cokorinos, The Assault on Diversity 2, 81, 125 (2003) (anniversary party); Miller, Gift, 95; Herman Schwartz, Right Wing Justice 196–97 (2004); Teles, Conservative Legal Movement, 18, 136–37, 165; Martin Garbus, *A Hostile Takeover*, American Prospect, Spring, 2003, at 16 (budget).

27. Blumenthal, Counter-Establishment, 38; Donald T. Critchlow, The Conservative Ascendancy 117–18 (2007); Ricci, Transformation, vii, 17, 117, 152; Smith, Idea Brokers, 96, 194; Gregg Easterbrook, *Ideas Move Nations*, Atlantic Monthly, January, 1986, at 66; *Note: The Political Activity of Think-tanks: The Case for Mandatory Contributor Disclosure*, 115 Harv. L. Rev. 1502, 1503, 1511 (2002).

28. Blumenthal, Counter-Establishment, 32, 39; Critchlow, Conservative Ascendancy, 119; Friedman, Neoconservative Revolution 53 (Friedman); Micklethwait & Wooldridge, Right Nation, 49; Smith, Idea Brokers, 174–75; Easterbrook, Ideas, 70.

29. Blumenthal, Counter-Establishment, 37, 41–42, 194; Critchlow, Conservative Ascendancy, 120–21; Smith, Idea Brokers, 176–77, William J. Lanquette, The *"Shadow Cabinets"—Changing Themselves as They Try to Change Policy*, 10 Nat. J. 296 (1978) (statistics); *The Revolving Door at the Think Tanks*, 10 Nat. J. 298 (1977); William H. Jones, *A New Magazine*, WP, October 20, 1977, at B3.

30. Critchlow, Conservative Ascendancy, 121 (expansion); Micklethwait & Wooldridge, Right Nation, 116; Ricci, Transformation, 213–14 (Baroody resignation).

31. Restructuring Banking & Financial Services in America (William S. Haraf & Rose M. Kushmeider, eds. 1988); Peter J. Wallison & Arthur F. Burns, *Dissenting Statement*, in National Commission on the Causes of the Financial and Economic Crisis in the United States, The Financial Crisis Inquiry Report 441 (2011); Julie Kosterlitz, Together at Last, 31 Nat. J. 3128 (1999) (quoting Charles Calomiris); Benton Ives, Risk and Regulation, Congressional Quarterly, March 17, 2008, at 678 (quoting Peter J. Wallison).

32. Michael Abramowitz, *Conservative Think Tank AEI Names a New Leader*, WP, July 15, 2008, at A3; Christopher DeMuth, *Think-Tank Confidential*, WSJ, October 11, 2008, at A21.

33. American Enterprise Institute, Liability Project, available at http://www.aei.org/ research/projectID.23/project.asp (quote). See Henry N. Butler & Larry E. Ribstein, The Sarbanes-Oxley Debacle (2006); Charles Fried & David Rosenberg, Making Tort Law (2003); Michael S. Greve, Harm-Less Lawsuits (2005).

34. Russ Bellant, The Coors Connection 1 (1988); Blumenthal, Counter-Establishment, 37, 45; Critchlow, Conservative Ascendancy, 121–22; Micklethwait & Wooldridge, Right Nation, 77.

35. Smith, Idea Brokers, 19 (revolution quote); Thomas Gale Moore, *Transportation*, in Agenda for Progress 159, 167–68 (Eugene J. McAllister, ed. 1981) (replace NHTSA and FRA); Phillip Longman, *Reagan's Disappearing Bureaucrats*, NYT Magazine, Feb. 14, 1988, at 42 (internship program); Sydney Blumenthal, *Outside Foundation Recruited the Inside Troops*, WP, September 24, 1985, at A1 (resource academic bank).

36. Juliette Eilperin, Fight Club Politics 19 (2008); Trudy Lieberman, Slanting the Story 72 (2000).

37. Robert L. Borosage, *The Mighty Wurlitzer*, American Prospect, May 6, 2002, at 13 (endowment and budget); Stuart M. Butler, et al., Web Memo, How to Turn the President's Gulf Coast Pledge into Reality, September 16, 2005.

38. Micklethwait & Wooldridge, Right Nation, 77, 157; Smith, Idea Brokers, 220; Jane Mayer, *Covert Operations*, New Yorker, August 30, 2010, at 45 (greenhouse gas denial); Shawn Zeller, *Libertarian to the Core*, 34 Nat. J. 1318 (2002) (social conservatives, Friedman prize); Richard Morin, *Free Radical*, WP, May 9, 2002, at C1.

39. Haltom & McCann, Distorting, 4, 41–42 (gurus quote); Lieberman, Slanting, 20 (mingle quote); Stephanie Mencimer, Blocking the Courthouse Door 26 (2006); Miller, Gift, 124 (brilliant quote); Kenneth J. Cheseboro, *Galileo's Retort: Peter Huber's Junk Scholarship*, 42 Am. U. L. Rev. 1637, 1709 (1993) (journalist quote).

40. See, e.g., Robert W. Crandall, Controlling Industrial Pollution (1983); Peter W. Huber & Robert E. Litan, The Liability Maze (1991); Lester B. Lave, The Strategy of Social Regulation (1981).

41. Sam Peltzman, Regulation and the Natural Progress of Opulence (AEI-Brookings Joint Center for Regulatory Studies, 2005); Cindy Skrzycki, *Bringing Brainpower to the Commentary on Rules*, WP, October 9, 1998, at G1; Peter Passell, *A New Project Will Measure the Cost and Effect of Regulation*, NYT, July 30, 1998, at D2.

42. Public Citizen, The Mercatus Center: A Wholly Owned Subsidiary of Koch Industries and Other Corporate Interests 2, 5, 44 (January 2003); Shawn Zeller, *Conservative Crusaders*, 35 Nat. J. 1286 (2003); Bob Davis, *In Washington, Tiny Think Tank Wields Big Stick on Regulation*, WSJ, July 16, 2004, at A1.

43. David Brock, The Republican Noise Machine 46 (2004); Krugman, Conscience, 119; Sheldon Rampton & John Stauber, Trust Us, We're Experts! 306 (2001); Ricci, Transformation, 180; Stefancic & Delgado, No Mercy, x, 145.

44. DeMuth, *Think-Tank Confidential.*

45. Brock, Noise Machine, 52; Krugman, Conscience, 119; Lieberman, Slanting, 9; Rampton & Stauber, Trust Us, 306; Ricci, Transformation, 165; Stefancic & Delgado, No Mercy, 57, 59.

46. Joe Conason, Big Lies 1 (2003); Hackney, Cover of Science, xix; Lieberman, Slanting, 37; Miller, Gift, 62 ($68 million), 81 (shelter quote); Regnery, Upstream, 265; Stefancic & Delgado, No Mercy, 5; Teles, Conservative Legal Movement, 182.

CHAPTER 6. THE INFLUENCE INFRASTRUCTURE

1. John Cassidy, *The Ringleader*, New Yorker, August 1, 2005, at 42; Daniel Franklin & A.G. Newmyer III, *Is Grover Over?* Washington Monthly, March 1, 2005, at 15.

2. David Brock, The Republican Noise Machine 50 (2004); Elizabeth Drew, Whatever It Takes 5 (1997) (quote); Nina J. Easton, Gang of Five 17, 74–75, 161, 359, 365 (2000); Cassidy, *Ringleader.*

3. Brock, Noise Machine 60; Robert Parry, *What Wouldn't Bob Dole do for Koch Oil?* Nation, August 26, 1996, at 11; J.A. Savage, *Astroturf Lobbying Replaces Grassroots Organizing*, Bus. and Soc. Rev., September 22, 1995, at 8; Peter H. Stone, *Grass-Roots Goliath*, 28 Nat. J. 1529 (1996).

4. Jane Mayer, *Covert Operations*, New Yorker, August 30, 2010, at 45; Judy Sarasohn, *Forces Fuse into FreedomWorks*, WP, July 29, 2004, at A21; Dan Morgan, *Think Tanks: Corporations' Quiet Weapon*, WP, January 29, 2000, at A1.

5. American Legislative Exchange Council, Disorder in the Court: A Guide for State Legislators 5 (2001); Defenders of Wildlife & Natural Resources Defense Council, Corporate America's Trojan Horse in the States 4–6, 9, 39 (2002); David Callahan, *Clash in the States*, American Prospect, June 18, 2001, at 28; Nick Penniman, *Outing ALEC*, American Prospect, July 1, 2002, at 12.

6. William Greider, Who Will Tell the People 48 (1992); Alfred S. Regnery, Upstream 326 (2008); David M. Ricci, The Transformation of American Politics 156 (1993); Robert B. Reich, *Taking Care of Business*, American Prospect, April 9, 2001, at 48; Burt Solomon, *How Washington Works*, 18 Nat. J. 1427 (1986).

7. Michael Pertschuk, Revolt Against Regulation 58 (1982); Tom Hamburger, *Chamber of Commerce Vows to Punish Anti-Business Candidates*, LAT, January 8, 2008, at A1 (quote); Brody Mullins & Susan Davis, *Chamber in Big Push for GOP*, WSJ, October 24, 2004, at A4

8. Sydney Blumenthal, The Rise of the Counter-Establishment 76 (1986) (mother quote); Jill Varshay, *Manufacturers' Lobby Savors New Visibility*, Cong. Q. Weekly, February 28, 2005, at 496; National Association of Manufacturers, Mission Statement, available at http://www.nam.org/AboutUs/History.

9. Pertschuk, Revolt, 57; Vogel, Fluctuating Fortunes, 198 (impact quote); Business Roundtable, About Us, available at http://www.businessroundtable.org/print/book/export/html/1823.

10. Louis Jacobson, *A Full-Court Press by Small Business*, 32 Nat. J. 884 (2000); Juliet Eilperin, *Small Business Group Sticks to One Side of Political Fence*, WP, May 16, 2002, at A23; National Federation of Independent Business, About NFIB, available at http://www.nfib.com/page/aboutHome.

11. Kathleen Hall Jamieson & Joseph N. Cappella, Echo Chamber 45 (2008); Thomas G. Krattenmaker & Lucas A. Powe, Jr., Regulating Broadcast Programming 61 (1994); Carl G. Miller, Modern Journalism 9 (1962).

12. Brock, Noise Machine 10–12, 74, 299; Jacob S. Hacker & Paul Pierson, Off Center 177 (2005); Jamieson & Cappella, Echo Chamber, 176; Eric Klinenberg, Fighting for Air 12 (2007); Krattenmaker & Powe, Broadcast Programming, 65; Trudy Lieberman, Slanting the Story: The Forces that Shape the News 3 (2000).

13. Russ Bellant, The Coors Connection 93 (1988); Brock, Noise Machine, 75–78; Joe Conason, Big Lies 36 (2003); Jamieson & Cappella, Echo Chamber, 163, 176; Lieberman, Slanting, 24–25.

14. Brock, Noise Machine, 12, 74; Conason, Big Lies, 1, 33–34, 52; Greider, Who Will Tell, 297 (lack of empirical support); Lieberman, Slanting, 27.

15. Brock, Noise Machine 52–53, 61–62, 203; William Haltom & Michael McCann, Distorting the Law 156 (2004); Robert W. McChesney, The Political Economy of Media 41–42, 136 (2008).

16. Jamieson & Cappella, Echo Chamber, 52, 76 (quote), 79; Micklethwait & Wooldridge, Right Nation, 162; Jean Stefancic & Richard Delgado, No Mercy 143 (1996);

Robert L. Borosage, *The Mighty Wurlitzer*, American Prospect, May 6, 2002, at 14; David Carr, *Tilting Rightward at The Journal*, NYT, December 14, 2009, at A1.

17. Jamieson & Cappella, Echo Chamber, 43, 46; Micklethwait & Wooldridge, Right Nation, 112, 162; Zev Chafets, *Late-Period Limbaugh*, NYT Magazine, July 6, 2008, at 30; Brian Stelter, *Master of the Airwaves*, NYT, July 3, 2008, at A1.

18. Brock, Noise Machine, 171–74, 319–20; Jamieson & Cappella, Echo Chamber, 43; Micklethwait & Wooldridge, Right Nation, 162.

19. Brock, Noise Machine 52, 175, 178, 183; Conason, Big Lies, 51; Hacker & Pierson, Off Center, 179; Howard Kurtz, *Washington Times Cuts in Staff, Coverage Cue New Era*, WP, December 3, 2009, at B3.

20. Brock, Noise Machine, 53; Borosage, *Mighty Wurlitzer*; Patricia J. Williams, *The Disquieted American*, Nation, May 26, 2003, at 9.

CHAPTER 7. THE ASSAULTS ON REGULATION

1. National Environmental Policy Act of 1970, Pub. L. 91–190, 83 Stat. 854 (1970); Thomas O. McGarity, Reinventing Rationality ch. 2 (1991); Graham K. Wilson, The Politics of Safety and Health 73 (1985); Oliver Houck, *President X and the New (Approved) Decisionmaking*," 36 Am. U. L. Rev. 535 (1987); Thomas O. McGarity, *Some Thoughts on Deossifying the Rulemaking Process*, 41 Duke L. J. 1385 (1992); Alan Morrison, *OMB Interference with Agency Rulemaking: The Wrong Way to Write a Regulation*, 99 Harv. L. Rev. 1059 (1986).

2. Regulatory Reform (W.S. Moore, ed. 1976).

3. Philip J. Hilts, Protecting America's Health 202 (2003); David Vogel, Fluctuating Fortunes 149 (1989); Mark K. Landy, Marc J. Roberts, and Stephen R. Thomas, The Environmental Protection Agency 39 (1990); *Nader's Invaders Are Inside the Gates*, Fortune, October, 1977, at 252.

4. Donald T. Critchlow, The Conservative Ascendancy 105 (2007); Richard J. Lazarus, The Making of Environmental Law 96 (2004); Trudy Lieberman, Slanting the Story 37 (2000); Michael Pertschuk, Revolt Against Regulation 49, 65, 72 (1982); *Two "Think Tanks" with Growing Impact*, U.S. News & World Rept., September 25, 1978, at 47.

5. Larry Kramer, *The Decade of the Regulatory Boom*, WP, December 39, 1979, at B1; Walter Guzzard, Jr., *The Mindless Pursuit of Safety*, Fortune, April 9, 1979, at 54; David Pauly & Jane Whitmore, *The Regulation Mess*, Newsweek, June 12, 1978, at 86.

6. Pertschuk, Revolt, 57–58, 62; Vogel, Fluctuating Fortunes, 12–14, 205–16; James W. Singer, *Labor Lobbyists Go on the Defensive As Political Environment Turns Hostile*, 12 Nat. J. 441 (1980).

7. Executive Order 12044, 14 Weekly Comp. of Pres. Doc. 558 (1978); Pertschuk, Revolt, 50, 64; Graham K. Wilson, The Politics of Safety and Health 73–74 (1985); Vogel, Fluctuating Fortunes, 172; Timothy B. Clark, *It's Still No Bureaucratic Revolution, But Regulatory Reform Has a Foothold*, 11 Nat. J. 1596 (1979); Timothy B. Clark, *Carter's Assault on the Costs of Regulation*, 10 Nat. J. 1281 (1978); Susan Tolchin, *Presidential Power and the Politics of RARG*, Regulation, July/August, 1979, at 44, 48–49.

8. Martha Derthick & Paul J. Quirk, The Politics of Deregulation 14, 56 (1985); Robert B. Reich, Supercapitalism 69 (2007); Pertschuk, Revolt, 65, 99; Vogel, Fluctuating Fortunes, 11, 148–50, 169–71, 229, 237.

9. Regulatory Flexibility Act of 1980, Pub. L. 96–354, 94 Stat. 1164 (1980); Magnuson-Moss Warranty - Federal Trade Commission Improvement Act of 1975, Public Law 96–252, 94 Stat. 375 (1980); Clean Air Act Amendments of 1977, Pub. L. 95–95, 91 Stat. 685 (1977); Clean Water Act Amendments of 1977, Pub. L. 95–217, 91 Stat. 1609 (1977); Judy Sarasohn, *Consumers Count Few Victories in 1979*, Cong. Q. Weekly, January 12, 1980, at 108 (Nader quote).

10. Heritage Foundation, Agenda for Progress (Eugene J. McAllister, ed. 1981); Ronald Brownstein, *Making the Worker Safe for the Workplace*, Nation, June 6, 1981, at 692 (AEI breakfast); Phillip Longman, *Reagan's Disappearing Bureaucrats*, NYT Magazine, February 14, 1988, at 4; Sydney Blumenthal, *A Vanguard for the Right: Activists Promote a New Establishment*, WP, September 22, 1985, at A1.

11. William J. Lanouette, *Off the Hill and Off the Record, Lobbyist Clubs Dine on Gourmet Tips*, 14 Nat. J. 633 (1982); Timothy B. Clark, *OMB to Keep Its Regulatory Powers in Reserve in Case Agencies Lag*, 13 Nat. J. 424 (1981).

12. Critchlow, Conservative Ascendancy, 187 (present quote); George C. Eads & Michael Fix, Relief or Reform? Reagan's Regulatory Dilemma 1 (1984); Charles Kolb, White House Daze 2 (1994); Lazarus, Environmental Law, 99; Alfred S. Regnery, Upstream 296 (2008); Vogel, Fluctuating Fortunes, 240.

13. Critchlow, Conservative Ascendancy, 189; Martha Derthick & Paul J. Quirk, The Politics of Deregulation 216 (1985); Donald J. Devine, Reagan's Terrible Swift Sword 2 (1991); Eads & Fix, Relief or Reform, 2–3; Rena I. Steinzor, Mother Earth and Uncle Sam 38 (2008); Brownstein, *Making the Worker Safe* (Miller appointment).

14. Executive Order No. 12,291, 3 C. F. R. 127 (1982); Exec. Order No. 12,630, 53 Fed. Reg. 8859 (1988) (takings); Exec. Order No. 12,612, 52 Fed. Reg. 41,685 (1987) (federalism); Exec. Order No. 12,606, 52 Fed. Reg. 34,188 (1987) (family); Exec. Order No. 12,261, 46 Fed. Reg. 2023 (1981) (trade).

15. Eads & Fix, Relief or Reform, 191 206, 204; Vogel, Fluctuating Fortunes, 248–49; Rochelle L. Stanfield, *EPA Administrator Lee Thomas is More a Manager Than a Policy Maker*, 18 Nat. J. 391 (1986); Timothy B. Clark, *Regulatory Agencies Get Double Whammy in Reagan Budget Cuts*, 13 Nat. J. 475 (1981) (fewer regulators quote).

16. Anne M. Burford, Are You Tough Enough? 91 (1986); Devine, Swift Sword, 44; Eads & Fix, Relief or Reform, 4, 254; Harold H. Bruff, *Presidential Management of Agency Rulemaking*, 57 Geo. Wash. L. Rev. 533, 582–83 (1989); Hazel Bradford & Richard Fly, *Congress Tries to Take the Fire Out of Wendy Gramm*, Business Week, September 8, 1986, at 84; Stuart Auerbach, *Conservative Study Faults Reagan Deregulation Effort*, WP, January 16, 1983, at F1 (transitory quote).

17. Hazardous and Solid Waste Amendments of 1984, Pub. L. 98–616, 98 Stat. 3224 (1984); Superfund Amendments and Reauthorization Act of 1986, Pub. L. 99–499, 100 Stat. 1617 (1986); Lazarus, Environmental Law, 117; Murray L. Weidenbaum, *Regulatory Reform under the Reagan Administration*, in The Reagan Regulatory Strategy: An Assessment 15, 22 (George C. Eads & Michael Fix, eds. 1984); Joann S. Lublin &

Christopher Conte, *Federal Deregulation Runs into a Backlash, Even from Businesses*, WSJ, December 14, 1983, at 1; Peter W. Bernstein, et al., *A Farewell to Deregulation*, Fortune, September 19, 1983, at 49.

18. Regnery, Upstream, 343; Steinzor, Mother Earth, 39–40; Sydney Blumenthal, *Quest for Lasting Power: A New Generation Is Being Nurtured to Carry the Banner for the Right*, WP, September 25, 1985, at A1.

19. Kolb, Daze, 3; Keith Schneider, *Bush on the Environment: A Record of Contradictions*, NYT, July 4, 1992, at A1 (environmental president quote); Trip Gabriel, *Greening the White House*, NYT, August 13, 1989, at F25; David Hoffman, *Pragmatism Is Bush's Mainstay*, WP, April 30, 1989, at A7; Judith Havemann, *Bush to Get 2,500 Conservative Resumes*, WP, November 15, 1988, at A17.

20. W. John Moore, *The True Believers*, 23 Nat. J. 2018 (1991); Dan Morgan, *Think Tanks: Corporations' Quiet Weapon*, WP, January 29, 2000, at A1 (CSE chairman); Neil A. Lewis, *Turning Loyalty and Service to Bush Into Power as Presidential Counsel*, NYT, December 12, 1990, at B12.

21. Nina J. Easton, Gang of Five 235–36 (2000); Jim Sibbison, *Dan Quayle, Business's Backdoor Boy*, Nation, July 29, 1991, at 141; Kirk Victor, *Quayle's Quiet Coup*, 23 Nat. J. 1676 (July 6, 1991); Andrew Rosenthal, *Quayle's Moment*, NYT Magazine, July 5, 1992, at 33.

22. Clean Air Act Amendments of 1990, Pub, L. 101–549, 104 Stat. 2399 (1990); Jonathan S. Cohn, *Damaged Goods*, American Prospect, Spring, 1993, at 64 (budgets); David McIntosh, *Breaking the Iron Triangle*, Regulation, Fall, 1993, at 26.

23. Jonathan Rauch, *The Regulatory President*, 23 Nat. J. 2902 (1991) (National Journal quote); John H. Cushman, Jr., *Big Growth in Federal Regulation Despite Role of Quayle's Council*, NYT, December 24, 1991, at A1; William G. Laffer III, George Bush's Hidden Tax: The Explosion in Regulation, Heritage Foundation Backgrounder No. 905, July 10, 1992 (rebellion).

24. President George H.W. Bush, *State of the Union*, reprinted in NYT, January 29, 1992, at A16 (moratorium); McIntosh, *Iron Triangle*, 30 (leaders not cowed); Kirk Victor, *Tale of the Red Tape*, 24 Nat. J. 684 (1992); Bob Woodward & David S. Broder, *Quayle's Quest: Curb Rules, Leave "No Fingerprints,"* WP, January 9, 1992, at A1.

25. Viveca Novak, *The New Regulators*, 25 Nat. J. 1801 (1993); Stephen Barr, *Rewriting the Rules on Rule-making*, WP, May 20, 1993, at A21.

26. Executive Order 12866, 3 CFR 638 (1993); Robert Duffy, *Regulatory Oversight in the Clinton Administration*, 27 Presidential Studies Q. 71 (1997); Susan E. Dudley & Angela Antonelli, *Congress and the Clinton OMB*, Regulation, Fall, 1997, at 17; *Clinton Regulation Will be "Rational": Interview with Sally Katzen, the New OIRA Administrator*, Regulation, Fall, 1993, at 36, 42 (Katzen quote); *Clinton Administration Changing Fewer Proposed Rules During Regulatory Review*, 23 BNA OSHR 732 (1993) (OIRA changes statistics); Curtis W. Copeland, Federal Rulemaking: The Role of the Office of Information and Regulatory Affairs 10, Figure 1 (Congressional Research Service, June 9, 2009) (OIRA review statistics); National Performance Review, From Red Tape to Results: Creating a Government that Works Better & Costs Less: Improving Regu-

latory Systems (1993); Stephen Barr, *White House Shifts Role in Rule-making*, WP, October 1, 1993, at A1.

27. Contract with America: The Bold Plan by Rep. Newt Gingrich, Rep. Dick Armey, and the House Republicans to Change the Nation 7, 11 (1994); Matthew Continetti, The K Street Gang 2 (2006), Micklethwait & Wooldridge, Right Nation, 101

28. Dan Balz & Ronald Brownstein, Storming the Gates: Protest Politics and the Republican Revival 149 (1996) (Armey description); Continetti, K Street Gang, 21 (Delay description); Elizabeth Drew, Showdown 27, 56 (1996); Jill Zuckman, *Freshmen Keep House on a Course to the Right*; Boston Globe, February 26, 1995, at 16.

29. *Repeal Most Federal Environmental Laws, Conservatives Urge Congress*, Pesticide & Toxic Chemical News, February 15, 1995 (Cato quote); *Hill Republicans Promise A Regulatory Revolution*, WP, January 4, 1995, at A1 (AEI seminar); *New Heritage Emerges In Orientation*, WP, December 10, 1994, at A9.

30. Business Round Table, *Toward Smarter Regulation* (1995); James A. Barnes, *Privatizing Politics*, 27 Nat. J. 573 (1995) (combat message development); *New Industry Group Calls for Expansion of Risk Assessment, Cost-Benefit Analysis Bill*, 24 BNA OSHR 1808 (1995); Cindy Skrzycki, *In Regulatory Assault, GOP Has a Lot to Be Thankful For*, WP, December 2, 1994, at D1.

31. Lou Dubose & Jan Reid, The Hammer 171 (2004) (DeLay quote); Jeffrey H. Birnbaum, *The Thursday Regulars*, Time, March 27, 1995, at 30; Gareth Cook, *Laws for Sale*, Washington Monthly, July, 1995, at 44; Peter H. Stone, *Taking Care of Business*, 28 Nat. J. 462 (1996); David Maraniss & Michael Weisskopf, *Speaker and His Directors Make the Cash Flow Right*, WP, November 27, 1995, at A1.

32. William J. Clinton, *State of the Union Address*, January 23, 1996; *Clinton Says Review Suggests Eliminating 20 Percent of Rules, Modifying 35 Percent*, 19 BNA Chem. Reg. Rept. 295 (1995); *President Directs Agency Heads to Modify Penalties, Cut Reports for Small Businesses*, 25 BNA Env. Rept. 2535 (1995).

33. John B. Judis, The Paradox of American Democracy 222 (2001); David Maraniss & Michael Weisskopf, Tell Newt to Shut Up ch. 5 (1996); *Clinton Offers GOP Compromise, Vetoes*, WP, April 8, 1995, at A1; *Business Leaves the Lobby and Sits at Congress's Table*, NYT, March 31, 1995, at A1; 141 Cong Rec S10400 (July 20, 1995) (cloture vote).

34. Small Business Regulatory Enforcement Fairness Act, Pub. L. 104–121, tit. II, subtit. E, 104th Cong., 2d Sess. (1996); Unfunded Mandates Reform Act, Pub. L. 104–4 § 101, 202, 203 205, 208, 401, 104th Cong., 1st Sess. (1995)

35. Easton, Gang of Five, 308; *Clinton Signs Omnibus Appropriations Bill, Immediately Waives Environmental Provisions*, 27 BNA Env. Rept. 8 (1996); *Clinton Vetoes EPA, Interior Bills; Agencies Shut Down For Second Time*, 26 BNA Env. Rept. 1552 (1995); *White House: Alleged Gingrich Snub No Reason To Shut Down U.S.*, Atlanta J. & Const., November 16, 1995, at A3; *Clinton Lashes Out At Congress, Citing Pollution and Guns*, NYT, August 2, 1995, at A1 (polluter's protection act quote).

36. Cindy Skrzycki, *Slowing the Flow of Federal Rules*, WP, February 18, 1996, at A1; *Environment Edges Up In Budget Debate*, Dallas Morning News, November 25, 1995, at A1 (Gingrich quote).

37. Stone, *Taking Care*; John M. Broder, *Deregulation: Crusade Shifts to Compromise*, NYT, January 31, 1997, at D1.

38. Dubose & Reid, Hammer, 144, 161; Juliette Eilperin, Fight Club Politics 41 (2008).

39. Continetti, K Street Gang, 44–45; Dubose & Reid, Hammer, 170–71, 177–78 (Norquist brainchild).

40. People for the American Way, The Federalist Society: From Obscurity to Power 8 (2001); Pamela Najor, *Business Round Table Proposes "Blueprint" to Protect Environment by Using Technology*, 32 BNA Env. Rept. 319 (2001); *Heritage Foundation Urges EPA Budget Cuts, Dismantling Superfund*, Inside EPA, January 26, 2001, at 11.

41. Critchlow, Conservative Ascendancy, 1.

42. Tom Brune, *Many Agencies Headed by Industry Veterans Who Are Watering Down Regulation*, Newsday, October 10, 2004, at A1; Steven Labaton, *Bush is Putting Team in Place for a Full-Bore Assault on Regulation*, NYT, May 23, 2001, at C1; Dana Milbank & Ellen Hakashima, *Bush Team Has "Right" Credentials*, WP, March 25, 2001, at A1.

43. Robert F. Kennedy Jr., Crimes Against Nature 62 (2004); *Nominations of Angela B. Styles, Stephen A. Perry, and John D. Graham, Hearings Before the Senate Committee on Governmental Affairs*, 107th Cong., 1st Sess. 153 (2001) (testimony of John D. Graham); Rebecca Adams, *Graham Leaves OIRA With a Full Job Jar*, Cong. Q. Weekly Report, January 23, 2006, at 226; Henry Pulizzi, *Bush Will Bypass Senate to Fill Top Regulatory Post*, WSJ, April 4, 2007, at A6; *White House Appoints Conservative Scholar to Regulatory Post*, WSJ, August 1, 2006, at A6.

44. Robert S. Devine, Bush vs. The Environment 200 (2004); Copeland, Federal Rulemaking, 14–15, 19, 22, 29; David Baumann, *Deep in the Bowels of OMB*, 33 Nat. J. 618 (2001); *OMB Proposes Greater Use of Internet to Boost Transparency of Review Process*, 31 BNA OSHR 969 (2001); James L Gattuso, Regulating the Regulators: OIRA's Comeback, Heritage Foundation Executive Memorandum No. 813, May 6, 2002.

45. Devine, Bush vs. Environment, 200; Copeland, Federal Rulemaking, at 19 (rules returned); Jeremy Bernstein & Steve Gibb, *Rolling Back the Regulatory State*, Environmental Forum, July/August, 2002, at 19; Stephen Power & Jacob M. Schlesinger, *Bush's Rules Czar Brings Long Knife to New Regulations*, WSJ, June 2, 2002, at A1.

46. Government Accountability Office, Federal Rulemaking: Improvements Needed to Monitoring and Evaluation of Rules Development as Well as to the Transparency of OMB Regulatory Reviews (2009); General Accounting Office, Rulemaking: OMB's Role in Reviews of Agencies' Draft Rules and the Transparency of Those Reviews (2003).

47. Peter Strauss, *Centralized Oversight of the Regulatory State*, 106 Columbia L. Rev. 1260, 1279–80 (2006) (hit lists); Cindy Skrzycki, *Report Sheds Light on Changing Role of Regulation*, WP, January 25, 2005, at E1 (OIRA report, public interest group complaints); Cindy Skrzycki, *Charting Progress of Rule Reviews Proves Difficult*, WP, December 7, 2004, at E1 (industry complaints).

48. Treasury and General Government Appropriations Act for FY2001 § 515, Pub. L. 106–554, 114 Stat. 2763 (2000); Salt Institute v. Leavitt, 440 F.3d 156 (4th Cir. 2006); Office of Management and Budget, Guidelines for Ensuring and Maximizing the Quality,

Objectivity, Utility, and Integrity of Information Disseminated by Federal Agencies, 67 Fed. Reg. 8453 (2002); *Critics Petition EPA to Withdraw Climate Report under New Data Law*, Inside EPA, June 7, 2002, at 5; Rick Weiss, *"Data Quality" Law is Nemesis of Regulation*, WP, August 16, 2004, at A1.

49. Chris Mooney, The Republican War on Science (2005); Tom Brune, *Many Agencies Headed by Industry Veterans Who Are Watering Down Regulation*, Newsday, October 10, 2004, at A1 (voluntary approaches); Robin Toner, *Conservatives Savor Their Roles as Insiders at the White House*, NYT, March 19, 2001, at A1 (Weyrich quote).

50. Executive Order No. 13,422, 72 Fed. Reg. 2763 (2007); Curtis Copeland, Changes to the OMB Regulatory Review Process by Executive Order 13422 (Congressional Research Service, 2007).

51. Margaret Kriz, *Thumbing His Nose*, 39 Nat. J. 32 (2007); Gardiner Harris, *The Safety Gap*, NYT Magazine, November 2, 2008, at 44.

CHAPTER 8. WORKER SAFETY

1. Bureau of Labor Statistics, U.S. Department of Labor, Workplace Injuries and Illnesses - 2009, available at http://www.bls.gov/news.release/archives/osh_10212010.pdf; Bureau of Labor Statistics, U.S. Department of Labor, Revisions to the 2009 Census of Fatal Occupational Injuries (CFOI) Counts, available at http://www.bls.gov/iif/oshwc/cfoi/cfoi_revised09.pdf.

2. Mine Safety and Health Administration, Injury Experience in Coal Mining, 2009 Table 1 (2011), available at http://www.msha.gov/Stats/Part50/Yearly%20IR's/2009/Coal-2009-Annual-IR.pdf; Mine Safety and Health Administration, Mine Safety and Health At a Glance, available at http://www.msha.gov/MSHAINFO/FactSheets/MSHAFCT10.HTM.

3. Daniel J. Curran, Dead Laws for Dead Men 119, 123, 142 (1993); Shari Ben Moussa, *Note: Mining for Morality at Sago Mine: Big Business and Big Money Equal Modest Enforcement of Health and Safety Standards*, 18 U. Fla. J. Law & Public Policy 209 (2007); Reports of Declining Injury Rates Faulted as Inaccurate; Roots of Problem Under Study, 25 BNA Labor Relations Week 2199 (2011).

4. 29 U.S.C. §§ 651–55, 661, 671; Thomas O. McGarity & Sidney A. Shapiro, Workers at Risk 35–36 (1993).

5. Occupational Safety and Health Administration, Occupational Exposure to 1,3 Butadiene, 61 Fed. Reg. 56,746, 56,795 (1996). See McGarity & Shapiro, Workers at Risk, 80–83, 99–101, 129–32, 171–72.

6. Mine Safety & Health Administration, Emergency Mine Evacuation, Emergency Temporary Standard, 71 Fed. Reg. 12,252, 12,266 (2006) (requiring mine operators to train miners and providing statistics of lives saved); Mine Safety & Health Administration, Use of Filer-Type and Self-Contained Self-Rescuers in Underground Coal Mines, 43 Fed. Reg. 54,241 (1978); United States Mine Rescue Association, Mine Accidents and Disasters, RAG American Coal Holdings, Inc. Willow Creek Mine Explosion & Fire, July 31, 2000, available at http://www.usmra.com/saxsewell/willow creek.htm.

7. Mine Safety & Health Administration, Diesel Particulate Matter Exposure of Underground Metal and Nonmental Miners, 66 Fed. Reg. 5706, 5854 (2001).

8. Curran, Dead Laws, 121, 153; Ted Gup Logan, *The Curse of Coal*, Time, November 4, 1991, at 54; *Guilty Pleas Set in U.S. Coal Case*, NYT, October 22, 1991, at A20; Glenn Frankel, *Pilgrim Mine: A Legacy of Fear, Doubt*, WP, December 20, 1980, at A1.

9. Joan Claybrook, Retreat from Safety 7 (1984); McGarity & Shapiro, Workers at Risk, 47–48; De11a Bunis, *OSHA's Leader Walks Loudly, But Some Say He Needs A Bigger Stick*, Newsday, 18 Aug. 1991, at 86.

10. McGarity & Shapiro, Workers at Risk, 37; Graham K. Wilson, The Politics of Safety and Health 59–60 (1985).

11. McGarity & Shapiro, Workers at Risk, 50; David Vogel, Fluctuating Fortunes 158 (1989); Wilson, Politics, 63; Michael Levin, *Politics and Polarity*, Regulation, November/December, 1979, at 33 (criticism).

12. Occupational Safety and Health Administration, Identification, Classification and Regulation of Potential Occupational Carcinogens, 45 Fed. Reg. 5001 (1980); American Petroleum Institute v. Industrial Union, AFL-CIO, 448 U.S. 607 (1980); Thomas O. McGarity, *The Story of the Benzene Case: Judicially Imposed Regulatory Reform through Risk Assessment*, in Environmental Law Stories 141 (Richard Lazarus & Oliver Houck, eds. 2005).

13. Ward Sinclair, *Under Pressure, U.S. Delays Requirement for Miner Safety Devices*, WP, December 25, 1980; Curtis Seltzer, *Coal Miners: Energy War Casualties*, WP, May 27, 1979, at C1; Tom Alexander, *New Fears Surround the Shift to Coal*, Fortune, November 20, 1978, at 50.

14. Claybrook, Retreat From Safety, 72–73 (cooperative regulator quote); Curran, Dead Laws, 154–57, 162–67; McGarity & Shapiro, Workers at Risk, 61–74, 80–83, 92, 149–50; Michael Wines, *Auchter's Record at OSHA Leaves Labor Outraged, Business Satisfied*, 15 Nat. J. 15 (1983).

15. AFL-CIO v. OSHA, 965 F.2d 962 (11th Cir. 1992); Occupational Safety and Health Administration, Air Contaminants, 54 Fed. Reg. 2332 (1989); McGarity & Shapiro, Workers at Risk, 122–29.

16. Logan, *Curse of Coal*; Robert D. Hershey, Jr., *Cutting Cost, Budget Office Blocks Workplace Health Proposal*, NYT, March 16, 1992, A13.

17. John Hood, *OSHA's Trivial Pursuit*, Policy Review, Summer 1995, at 59, 60; *The Hill May Be A Health Hazard For Safety Agency*, WP, July 23, 1995, at A1; *OSHA Rules "By Far" Most Burdensome, National Chamber Of Commerce Survey Says*, 26 BNA OSHR 113 (July 3, 1996); *Dear Pledges "Revitalized OSHA," Greater Use of Egregious Case Penalties*, 23 BNA OSHR 763 (1993) (Dear quote).

18. J. Davitt McAteer, *The Federal Mine Safety and Health Act of 1977: Preserving a Law that Works*, 98 W. Va. L. Rev. 1105, 1107 (1996); *President Will Veto GOP Bills, Gore Tells Top Labor Union Officials*, 25 BNA OSHR 1292 (1996).

19. Bill Clinton & Al Gore, The New OSHA: Reinventing Worker Safety and Health 2 (National Performance Review May, 1995) (Clinton quote); *OSHA to Cut 32 Percent of CFR Pages; Another 39 Percent to be Modified, DOL Says*, 25 BNA OSHR 549 (1995).

20. Mine Safety & Health Administration, Diesel Particulate Matter Exposure of Underground Metal and Nonmental Miners, 66 Fed. Reg. 5706 (2001).

21. John B. Judis, *Sullied Heritage*, New Republic, April 23, 2001, at 19; Julie Kosterlitz, *All Lined up for Chao*, 33 Nat. J. 270 (2001); *Chao Creates Management Review Board to Coordinate OSHA, Other DOL Agencies*, 31 BNA OSHR 792 (2001)

22. Jeff Goodell, Big Coal 62 (2006); Dennis B Roddy, *Feds Long Saw Mine Problems*, Pittsburgh Post-Gazette, January 19, 2006, at A1 (quote); Alan Maimon, *Bush Picks Mine Consultant to Head MSHA*, Louisville Courier-Journal, March 28, 2001, at A1.

23. *Henshaw Proposes Reorganization to Shift Directorates, "Maximize" Efficiency*, 32 BNA OSHR 389 (2002); Jeffrey Smith, *Under Bush, OSHA Mired in Inaction*, WP, December 29, 2008, at A1; Cindy Skrzycki, *OSHA Withdraws More Rules Than it Makes, Reviews Find*, WP, October 5, 2004, at E1.

24. Kris Maher, *Miners' Fate Underscores Safety-Overhaul Failures*, WSJ, August 15, 2007, at A6; Steve Twedt, *Yesterday's Blast Offers Grim Reminder of Sago*, Pittsburgh Post-Gazette, May 21, 2006, at A13

25. Mine Improvement and New Emergency Response Act (MINER Act) of 2006, Pub. L. 109–236, 120 Stat. 493 (2006); *OSHA Standards Writers Asked to Volunteer to Help MSHA Meet Rulemaking Deadlines*, 38 BNA OSHR 44 (2008).

26. *Bill to Force OSHA Combustible Dust Rule Passes in House Vote; Bush Threatens Veto*, 38 BNA OSHR 331 (2008); *Citing Recent Deaths, Unions Petition OSHA for Emergency Combustible Dust Standard*, 38 BNA OSHR 161 (2008); Cindy Skrzycki, *Sugar Plant Blast Puts Heat on OSHA's Rulemaking*, WP, March 18, 2008, at D4.

27. Occupational Safety and Health Administration, Cranes and Derricks in Construction; Final Rule, 75 Fed. Reg. 47,906 (2010); Lindsay Wise, et al., *Crane Collapse Kills 4*, Houston Chronicle, July 19, 2008, at A1; David Brown, *Tower Cranes: Efficient, Versatile—but How Safe?* WP, June 16, 2008, at A6.

28. Sheldon Rampton & John Stauber, Trust Us, We're Experts! 82–84 (2001); Jim Morris, *Slow Motion*, 39 Nat. J. 32 (2007); *OSHA Agenda Shows Action on Health Rules: Hex Chromium, Crystalline Silica, Beryllium*, 34 BNA OSHR 678 (2004); Smith, *OSHA Mired in Inaction*.

29. Occupational Safety and Health Administration, Occupational Exposure to Hexavalent Chromium; Final Rule, 71 Fed. Reg. 10,099, 10,224 (2006); Public Citizen Health Research Group v. Chao, 314 F.3d 143 (3d Cir. 2002); David Michaels, Doubt is Their Product 98, 99 101, 108–09 (2008)

30. Occupational Safety and Health Administration, Ergonomics Program, 65 Fed. Reg. 68,262 (2000); Lou Dubose & Jan Reid, The Hammer 113–15 (2004) (DeLay Meetings); Stuart Shapiro, *The Role of Procedural Controls in OSHA's Ergonomics Rulemaking*, 67 Public Administration Review 688, 691–96 (2007); U.S. Government Accountability Office, Safety in the Meat and Poultry Industry, While Improving, Could be Further Strengthened (2005); Kerry Hall, Ames Alexander & Franco Ordonez, *The Cruelest Cuts*, Charlotte Observer, February 10, 2008, at A1; Steven Greenhouse, *House Joins Senate in Repealing Regulations Issued by Clinton on Workplace Injuries*, NYT, March 8, 2001, at A17; Cindy Skrzycki, *Protection Racket? Repetitive Stress Surrounds Ergonomics Rule*, WP, August 8, 2000, at E1; Centers for Disease Control &

Prevention, Worker Health eChartbook, available at http://wwwn.cdc.gov/niosh-survapps/echartbook/Category.aspx?id=563.

31. Curran, Dead Laws, 121–24, 127; McGarity & Shapiro, Workers at Risk, 38, 41, 47, 158; Wilson, Politics, 63

32. Claybrook, Retreat From Safety, 111; Curran, Dead Laws, 159–63; McGarity & Shapiro, Workers at Risk, ch. 10; Vogel, Fluctuating Fortunes, 249; Wilson, Politics, 64; Mark D. Cowan, *Regulatory Reform: An OSHA Case Study*, 33 Labor L. J. 763, 764 (1982).

33. Curran, Dead Laws, 165, 170; Vogel, Fluctuating Fortunes, 249; Michael Wines, *Listening to the Roof*, 14 Nat. J. 386 (1987); Ward Sinclair, *Budget Cuts Hit Safety Enforcement Like a Ton of Kentucky Coal*, WP, February 15, 1982, at A1.

34. McGarity & Shapiro, Workers at Risk, 151–52; Bunis, OSHA's *Leader Talks Loudly*.

35. Peter Stone, *Back Off!* 26 Nat. J. 2840 (1994); David Jackson & Geoff Dougherty, *Safety is Casualty as Firms Chase Profits in Coal Country*, Chicago Tribune, September 24, 2002, at A1; *OSHA Inspections, Citations Hit Record Low in Fiscal 1995*, 15 BNA OSHR 827 (1995).

36. *Is OSHA Working for Working People?, Hearings Before the Subcommittee on Employment and Workplace Safety of the Senate Committee on Health, Education, Labor and Pensions*, 110th Cong., 1st Sess. (April 26, 2007) (testimony of Peg Seminario, AFL-CIO); Skrzycki, *OSHA Withdraws More Rules*.

37. George Miller, Review of Federal Mine Safety and Health Administration's Performance from 2001 to 2005 Reveals Consistent Abdication of Regulatory and Enforcement Responsibilities 5–6 (House Committee on Education and the Workforce Democratic Staff, January 21, 2006); Ken Ward, Jr., *As Mining Increased, MSHA Cut Staff*, Charleston Gazette, December 2, 2007, at A1 (Bush veto); Steve Twedt, *Audit Slams Mine Safety Agency Over Its Handling of Complaints*, Pittsburgh Post-Gazette, October 4, 2006, at A1.

38. R.G. Dunlop, *Mine Scrutiny Minimal Despite Record*, Louisville Courier-Journal, June 3, 2007, at A1 (MSHA statistics); David Barstow, *U.S. Rarely Seeks Charges for Deaths in Workplace*, NYT, December 22, 2003, at A1 (OSHA statistics); Jackson & Dougherty, *Safety is Casualty* (Kentucky prosecutions).

39. *The BP Texas City Disaster and Worker Safety, Hearing before the House Committee on Education and Labor*, 110th Cong., 1st Sess. (2007) (Testimony of Carolyn W. Merritt, U.S. Chemical Safety Board) (quote); British Petroleum Corporation, Fatal Accident Investigation Report: Isomerization Unit Explosion Interim Report, Texas City, Texas 7, 15, 24 (May 12, 2005).

40. *Henshaw Describes "Multi-Faceted" Strategy to Deal with Reactive Chemicals*, 33 BNA OSHR 955 (2003); *OSHA's Withdrawal of Numerous Safety, Health Efforts Draws Wellstone's Criticism*, 32 BNA OSHR 687 (2002).

41. Working People Hearings (testimony of David Michaels, George Washington University) (15 fatalities per day); Bureau of Labor Statistics, Department of Labor, Fatal Occupational Injuries and Workers' Memorial Day, April 25, 2012, available at http://www.bls.gov/iif/oshwc/cfoi/worker_memorial.htm; *Mine Fatalities Fell to All-Time*

Low in 2009, MSHA Says, Restating Target of Zero Deaths, 40 OSHR 9 (2010); *Workplace Fatalities Lowest Since 1992; Weakened Economy Cited in BLS Survey*, 39 BNA OSHR 727 (2009).

CHAPTER 9. ENVIRONMENTAL PROTECTION

1. 2 Encyclopedia of American Industries 1602 (2011); U.S. Fish & Wildlife Service, Status and Trends of Wetlands in the Conterminous United States 1998 to 2004 16 (2005); Minerals Management Service, Deepwater Gulf of Mexico 2008: America's Offshore Energy Future 4 (2009); Environmental Protection Agency, Air Emission Sources (2005), available at http://www.epa.gov/air/emissions/index.htm.
2. Clean Air Act Amendments of 1970, Pub. L. 91–604, 84 Stat. 1676 (1970); Thomas Jorling, *The Federal Law of Air Pollution Control*, in Federal Environmental Law 1058 (Erica L. Dolgin & Thomas G.P. Guilbert, eds. 1974).
3. 33 U.S.C. § 1251(a) (goals); Federal Water Pollution Control Act of 1972, Pub. L. 92–500, 86 Stat. 896 (1972); Robert Zener, *The Federal Law of Water Pollution Control*, in Federal Environmental Law 682 (Erica L. Dolgin & Thomas G.P. Guilbert, eds. 1974).
4. Surface Mine Control and Reclamation Act of 1977, Pub. L. 95–87, 91 Stat. 445 (1977); Edward Shawn Grandis, *The Federal Strip Mining Act: Environmental Protection Comes to the Coalfields of Virginia*, 13 U. Richmond L. Rev. 455 (1979), at 463.
5. Outer Continental Shelf Lands Act of 1953 as amended in 1978, Public L. 95 372, 92 Stat. 629 (1978); Public L. 212, Ch. 345, 67 Stat. 462 (1953); National Commission on the BP Deepwater Horizon Oil Spill and Offshore Drilling, Deep Water 60–62 (2011).
6. Council on Environmental Quality, Environmental Quality 1983 4 (1983).
7. Robert L. Sansom, The New American Dream Machine (1976); John C. Whitaker, Striking a Balance (1976); Yanek Mieczkowski, Gerald Ford and the Challenges of the 1970s 201–03, 208 (2005).
8. Thomas O. McGarity, Reinventing Rationality ch. 3 (1991); George M. Gray, Laury Saligman & John Graham, *The Demise of Lead in Gasoline*, in The Greening of Industry ch. 1 (J.D. Graham & J.K. Hartwell, eds. 1997).
9. William D. Ruckelshaus, EPA History Program Oral History Interview-1, January 1993, at 18 (quote); Quarles, Cleaning Up America, 51; Joel A. Mintz, *Agencies, Congress and Regulatory Enforcement: A Review of EPA's Hazardous Waste Enforcement Effort, 1970–1987*, 18 Env. L. 683, 691 (1988); Joel A. Mintz, *Some Thoughts on the Interdisciplinary Aspects of Environment Enforcement*, 36 ELR 10,495, 10,500 (2006).
10. Mark K. Landy, Marc J. Roberts, and Stephen R. Thomas, The Environmental Protection Agency 206–08 (1990); R. Shep Melnick, Regulation and the Courts 41 (1983) (quote); Mintz, *Some Thoughts*, 10,500.
11. Clean Air Act Amendments of 1990, Pub, L. 101–549, 104 Stat. 2399 (1990); Mintz, *Some Thoughts*, 10,502; Michael Weiskopf, *Clean Air Power*; Michael Ross, *Bush Hails Arrival of New Era in Signing Clean Air Act*, LAT, November 16, 1990, at A1.

12. Environmental Protection Agency, National Ambient Air Quality Standards for Ozone, 62 Fed. Reg. 38,856, 38,857 (1997); *Record Number of Enforcement Actions Taken in Fiscal 1994, EPA Says in Report*, 26 BNA Env. Rept. 462 (1995); *Criminal Cases, Fine Collections Rise in 1993, EPA Says in Report on Enforcement*, 24 BNA Env. Rept. 1516 (1993).

13. 30 U.S.C. § 1265(b)(3); 30 C.F.R. §§ 715.14, 715.17; Office of Surface Mining, Surface Mining Reclamation and Enforcement Provisions; Final Rules, 42 Fed. Reg. 62,639 (1977).

14. Hodel v. Virginia Surface Mining & Reclamation Ass'n, 452 U.S. 264 (1981); Donald C. Menzel, *Redirecting the Implementation of a Law: The Reagan Administration and Coal Surface Mining Regulation*, 43 Pub. Ad. Rev. 411, 412 (1983); Milt Copulos, Coal Conversion: Costs and Conflicts 4 (Heritage Foundation Report No. 37, September 22, 1977) (quote).

15. Bruce Allen, How Offshore Oil and Gas Production Benefits the Economy and the Environment, Heritage Foundation Backgrounder No. 2341, November 30, 2009.

16. Chevron U.S.A., Inc. v. Natural Resources Defense Council, 467 U.S. 837 (1984); Richard A. Harris and Sidney M. Milkis, The Politics of Regulatory Change: A Tale of Two Agencies 250 (1989); Landy, Roberts & Thomas, EPA, 40.

17. Harris & Milkis, Two Agencies, 254 (dismissive of staff); Landy, Roberts & Thomas, EPA, 18, 247–248; Jonathan Lash, Katherine Gillman & David Sheridan, A Season of Spoils 18, 29, 47–49 (1984); Michael E. Kraft & Norman J. Vig, *Environmental Policy in the Reagan Presidency*, 90 Pol. Sci. Q. 415, 428 (1984); Mintz, *Regulatory Enforcement*, 725–726.

18. Mintz, *Regulatory Enforcement*, 715, 743 (Gorsuch resignation); Sydney Blumenthal, *Outside Foundation Recruited the Inside Troops*, WP, September 24, 1985, at A1.

19. Ruckelshaus, Oral History Interview-1, January 1993, at 24; Landy, Roberts & Thomas, EPA, 251–55; Rochelle L. Stanfield, *EPA Administrator Lee Thomas is More a Manager than a Policy Maker*, 18 Nat. J. 391 (1986).

20. Bob Cavnar, Disaster on the Horizon 16, 76 (2010); National Commission, Deep Water, 56 (quote), 64; Alyson Flournoy, et al., Regulatory Blowout: How Regulatory Failures made the BP Disaster Possible, and How the System Can Be Fixed to Avoid a Recurrence 25 (Center for Progressive Reform, 2010).

21. National Commission, Deep Water, at 68; Juliet Eilperin, *Seeking Answers in MMS's Flawed Culture*, WP, August 25, 2010, at A1; Jim Tankersley & Julie Cart, *Oil Drilling Outpaces Regulation*, LAT, May 9, 2010, at A1; Russell Gold & Stephen Power, *Oil Regulator Ceded Oversight to Drillers*, WSJ, May 7, 2010, at A1.

22. Heritage Foundation, Mandate for Leadership 344–37 (1981); Martin H. Belsky, *Environmental Policy Law in the 1980s: Shifting Back the Burden of Proof*, 12 Ecology L.Q. 1, 76 (1984) (greater state discretion); Uday Deasi, T*he Politics of Federal-State Relations: The Case of Surface Mining Regulations*, 31 Nat. Res. J. 785, 796 (1991); Menzel, *Redirecting*, 414 (reorganization); Cass Peterson, *Bulldozers Driving Through Holes in 1977 Strip Mining Law*, WP, May 30, 1987, at A13; Dale Russakoff, *Watt Submits Resignation as Interior Secretary*, WP, October 10, 1983, at A1; Dale Russakoff, *The Unforcer*, WP, June 6, 1982, at A1.

23. Oil Pollution Control Act of 1990, Pub. L. 101–380, 104 Stat. 484 (1990); David Hoffman, *Pragmatism Is Bush's Mainstay*, WP, April 30, 1989, at A7.

24. W. John Moore, *The True Believers* 23 Nat. J. 2018 (1991); Kirk Victor, *Quayle's Quiet Coup*, 23 Nat. J. 1676 (1991); Michael Weiskopf, *Clean Air Power: EPA's Man With a Mission*, WP, December 7, 1990, at A21.

25. Bureau of Ocean Energy Management, Regulation and Enforcement, Safety and Environmental Management Systems for Outer Continental Shelf Oil and Gas Operations, 74 Fed. Reg. 28,639 (2009); National Commission, Deep Water, 71–72.

26. Environmental Protection Agency, Negotiated Rulemaking and Consensus-based Rulemaking (Quick Reference Fact Sheet, September 1996); *Browner Calls Pollution Prevention Key to Protecting Environment, Sound Economy*, 24 BNA Env. Rept. 240 (1993); Keith Schneider, *New Breed of Ecologist to Lead E.P.A.*, NYT, December 17, 1992, at B20.

27. Lazarus, Environmental Law,129; Bill Clinton & Al Gore, Reinventing Environmental Regulation 2–3 (National Performance Review 1995); Environmental Protection Agency, Report to the President: Eliminating and Improving Regulations: Narrative Summary 3 (June 1, 1995).

28. Environmental Protection Agency, Regulatory Reinvention (XL) Pilot Projects, 60 Fed. Reg. 27,282 (1995); Joel A. Mintz, *Whither Environmental Reform?: Some Thoughts on a Recent AALS Debate*, 31 Env. L. Rept. 10,710, 10,720 (2001) (free for all quote); Rena I. Steinzor, *Regulatory Reinvention and Project XL: Does the Emperor Have Any Clothes?* 26 Env. L. Rept. 10,527 (1996).

29. Jedediah S. Purdy, *Rape of the Appalachians*, American Prospect, November/December, 1998, at 218.

30. Elizabeth Drew, Showdown 116, 226 (1996); Gareth Cook, *Laws for Sale*, Washington Monthly, July, 1995, at 44 (industry drafting); *Chafee Indicates Preference For Narrow Bill As Municipal Concerns Aired At Senate Hearing*, 26 BNA Env. Rept 1565 (1995).

31. Jeff Goodell, Big Coal xix (2006); Robert F. Kennedy Jr., Crimes Against Nature 129–31 (2004); John Mintz & Eric Pianin, *Symbol of a Shift at Interior*, WP, May 16, 2001, at A21.

32. Jeff Ruch, *EPA at Low Ebb*, Env. Forum, March/April, 2008, at 38, 41; Gregg Easterbrook, *Hostile Environment*, NYT Magazine, August 19, 2001, at 40; Zachary Coile, *Environmentalists Worry as EPA Chief Steps Down*, San Francisco Chronicle, May 22, 2003, at A1.

33. North Carolina v. EPA, 531 F.3d 896 (D.C. Cir. 2008); Stephen Power, *EPA Chief Makes Political Target*, WSJ, February 19, 2008, at A7; Margaret Kriz, *Vanishing Act*, Nat. J., April 12, 2008, at 18; Tom Hamburger, *EPA Chief Goes to Bat for Bush Policy*, LAT, April 2, 2004, at A19; *Often Isolated, Whitman Quits as E.P.A. Chief*, NYT, May 22, 2003, at A22.

34. Executive Order No. 13,212, 66 Fed. Reg. 28,367 (2001); Cavnar, Disaster, 81; National Commission, Deep Water, 73 (rapidly evolving technology); Flournoy, Regulatory Blowout, 24–26; Derek Kravitz & Mary Pat Flaherty, *Report Says Oil Agency Ran Amok*, WP, September 11, 2010, at A1; Juliet Eilperin, *Seeking Answers in MMS's Flawed Culture*, WP, August 25, 2010, at A1.

35. Ross Gelbspan, The Heat Is On 19, 31 (1997); Intergovernmental Panel on Climate Change, Climate Change: The IPCC Scientific Assessment (1990); Rudy Abramson, U.S. Flexes Its Muscles Before Earth Summit, LAT, May 30, 1992, at A19.

36. Gelbspan, Heat, 33, 64–70; Sandra Beth Zellmer, Sacrificing Legislative Integrity at the Altar of Appropriations Riders: A Constitutional Crisis, 21 Harv. Env. L. Rev. 457 (1997); Robert Wright, Some Like it Hot, New Republic, October 9, 1995, at 6; Richard L. Berke, Clinton Declares New U.S. Policies for Environment, NYT, April 22, 1993, at A1 (Gore quote).

37. Alice Kaswan, The Domestic Response to Global Climate Change: What Role for Federal, State, and Litigation Initiatives, 42 U. San Francisco L. Rev. 39, 42–43 (2007); Margaret Kriz, A Pro-Industry Tilt, 36 Nat. J. 1028 (2004); Andrew C. Revkin, Bush to Make Good on Promise to Cut Power Plant Emissions, NYT, March 10, 2001, at A1 (campaign promise).

38. Massachusetts v. EPA, 127 S.Ct. 1438, 1446–49 (2007); Environmental Protection Agency, Control of Emissions From New Highway Vehicles and Engines, 68 Fed. Reg. 52,922 (2003); Auto Fuel Economy Continues to Decline as Vehicles Become Heavier, EPA Report Says, 34 BNA Env. Rept. 1046 (2003); Juliet Eilperin, EPA Chief Denies Calif. Limit on Auto Emissions, WP, December 20, 2007, at A1.

39. Lisa Heinzerling & Rena Steinzor, A Perfect Storm: Mercury and the Bush Administration, 34 Env. Law Rept. 10,297, 10,298–99 (2004); Catherine A. O'Neill, Mercury, Risk and Justice 34 Env. L. Rept. 11,070, 11,072 (2004); Michael Janofsky, A Study Finds Mercury Levels in Fish Exceed U.S. Standards, NYT, August 4, 2004, at A15; Eight Percent of Women of Child-Bearing Age Have Unsafe Levels of Mercury, EPA Reports, 34 BNA Env. Rept. 480 (2003).

40. 42 U.S.C. § 7412(b),(c),(e); Environmental Protection Agency, Regulatory Finding on Emissions of Hazardous Air Pollutants from Electric Utility Steam-Generating Units, 65 Fed. Reg. 79,825 (2000); Environmental Protection Agency, Mercury Study Report to Congress (1997).

41. Heinzerling & Steinzor, Perfect Storm, 10,300–06; Margaret Kriz, Mercury Uprising, 36 Nat. J. 30 (2006); Bruce Barcott, Changing All the Rules, NYT Magazine, April 4, 2004, at 38.

42. New Jersey v. EPA, 517 F.3d 574, 582 (D.C. Cir. 2008) (quote); Environmental Protection Agency, Standards of Performance for New and Existing Stationary Sources: Electric Utility Steam Generating Units, 70 Fed. Reg. 28,606 (2005); Environmental Protection Agency, Revision of December 2000 Regulatory Finding, 70 Fed. Reg. 15,994 (2005); Juliet Eilperin, Mercury "Hot Spots" Identified in U.S. and Canada, WP, January 6, 2007, at A7; Michael Hawthorne, Coal Plants Spew More Mercury, Chicago Tribune, April 29, 2006, at A1; Felicity Barringer, E.P.A. Accused of a Predetermined Finding on Mercury, NYT, February 4, 2005, at A16; Juliet Eilperin, EPA Wording Found to Mirror Industry's, WP, September 22, 2004, at A29; Tom Hamburger & Alan C. Miller, Emissions Rule Geared to Benefit Industry, Staffers Say, LAT, March 16, 2004, at A1; Eric Pianin, EPA Led Mercury Policy Shift, WP, December 30, 2003, at A17.

43. Richard P. Novitzki, R. Daniel Smith & Judy D. Fretwell, *Wetland Functions, Values, and Assessment*, in National Water Summary on Wetland Resources 2 (U.S. Geological Survey Water Supply Paper 2425, 1996); Environmental Protection Agency, Functions and Values of Wetlands (EPA 843-F-01–002c, September 2001); U.S. Geological Survey, Executive Summary 2 (U.S. Geological Survey Water Supply Paper 2425, 1996).

44. Act of March 3, 1899, Ch. 425; 42 U.S.C. § 1344, United States v. Standard Oil Co., 384 U.S. 224 (1966); United States v. Republic Steel Corp., 362 U.S. 482 (1960).

45. United States v. Riverside Bayview Homes, Inc., 474 U.S.121 (1985); Margaret E. Kriz, *Swamp Fighting* 21 Nat. J. 1919 (1991).

46. Nina J. Easton, Gang of Five 236–37 (2000) (McIntosh); Joseph Alper, *War Over the Wetlands: Ecologists v. the White House*, 257 Science 1043 (1992); Kriz, *Swamp Fighting*, 1919; Stephen Barr, *Clinton to Revise Wetlands Policy*, WP, August 25, 1993, at A1; John H. Cushman, *Quayle, in Last Push for Landowners, Seeks to Relax Wetland Protections*, NYT, November 12, 1992, at A16; Philip J. Hilts, *U.S. Aides Retreat on Wetlands Rule*, NYT, November 23, 1991, at A1.

47. Solid Waste Agency of Northern Cook County v. Corps of Engineers, 531 U.S. 159 (2001); Dina Cappiello, *EPA Dropped Wetlands Cases after High Court Ruling*, Houston Chronicle July 8, 2008, at A5; John M. Broder, *After Lobbying, Rules Governing Protected Wetlands are Narrowed*, NYT, July 6, 2007, at A13; Eric Pianin, *Administration Establishes New Wetlands Guidelines*, WP, January 11, 2003, at A5.

48. Ohio Valley Environmental Coalition v. Aracoma Coal Co., 556 F.3d 177, 186–87 (4th Cir. 2009); Bragg v. West Virginia Coal Association, 248 F.3d 275, 286 (4th Cir. 2001); Kennedy, Crimes Against Nature, 114–15; Joby Warrick, *Appalachia is Paying Price for White House Rule Change*, WP, August 17, 2004, at A1.

49. Duffy, *How Filled Was My Valley: Continuing the Debate on Disposal Impacts*, 17 Nat. Res. & Env. 144, 145 (2003); Warrick, *Appalachia is Paying Price*.

50. Warrick, *Appalachia is Paying Price* (quoting a senior government scientist).

51. 30 USC §1265(c) (2006); Duffy, *Valley*, 145; Eric Reece, *Death of a Mountain: Radical Strip Mining and the Leveling of Appalachia*, Harpers, April 1, 2005, at 41; Purdy, *Rape*, at 218.

52. 33 U.S.C. §1342 (2006), Nationwide Permit Program, 33 CFR pt. 330; Michael Shnayerson, Coal River 14 (2008); Duffy, *Valley*, 145.

53. Bragg v. West Virginia Coal Association, 248 F.3d 275 (4th Cir. 2001); U.S. Army Corps of Engineers, Final Revisions to the Regulatory Definitions of "Fill Material" and "Discharge of Fill Material," 67 Fed. Reg. 31,129 (May 9, 2002); Kennedy, Crimes, 139; Shnayerson, Coal River, 103, 113–16; Duffy, *Valley*, 178.

54. Office of Surface Mining Reclamation and Enforcement, Excess Spoil, Coal Mine Waste, and Buffers for Perennial and Intermittent Streams, 73 Fed. Reg. 75,814 (2008); Duffy, *Valley*, 145, 177; *Interior Department Says Final Rule Clarifies Disposal of Coal Mining Waste Near Streams*, 39 BNA Env. Rept. 2451 (2008) (mining industry delighted); Elizabeth Shogren, *Mining Damage in Appalachia Extensive, U.S. Finds*, LAT, May 30, 2003, at A32.

55. Landy, Roberts & Thomas, EPA, 249; Andreen, *Motivating Enforcement*, 72 (statistics); Mintz, *Regulatory Enforcement*, 719, 731 (black mark quote), 746 (Ruckelshaus).

56. Deasi, *Politics*, 796; John D. Edgcomb, *Comment: Cooperative Federalism and Environmental Protection: The Surface Mining Control and Reclamation Act of 1977*, 58 Tulane L. Rev. 299, 317–18 (1983) (penalty cap regulations); Menzel, *Redirecting*, 415; Keith Schneider, *U.S. Mine Inspectors Charge Interference By Agency Director*, NYT, November 22, 1992, at A1; Russakoff, *Unforcer* (vetoes).

57. Andreen, *Motivating Enforcement*, 74; Mintz, *Some Thoughts*, 10,502; *Record Number of Enforcement Actions Taken in Fiscal 1994, EPA Says in Report*, 26 BNA Env. Rept. 462 (1995); *Criminal Cases, Fine Collections Rise in 1993, EPA Says in Report on Enforcement*, 24 BNA Env. Rept. 1516 (1993).

58. Purdy, *Rape*, 218.

59. John Sullivan & John Shiffman, *Green Club an EPA Charade*, Philadelphia Inquirer, December 9, 2008, at A1 (considerable noncompliance quote); *Pending IG Study Finds Few Facilities Meet EPA Performance Track Duties*, Inside EPA, March 9, 2007, at 1; Rebecca Adams, *Too Much Carrot, Not Enough Stick*, Cong. Q. Weekly, February 27, 2006, at 528.

60. Devine, Bush vs. The Environment, 91, 99–100; Ronald H. Rosenberg, *Doing More or Doing Less for the Environment: Shedding Light on EPA's Stealth Method of Environmental Enforcement*, 35 Env. Affairs 175, 178–79, 213–215 (2008); Environmental Integrity Project, Paying Less to Pollute: Environmental Enforcement Under the Bush Administration 1–2 (2008) (statistics); Sullivan & Shiffman, *Green Club* (quoting GAO study); *EPA Needs to Prod Compliance Efforts by Oil Refineries, Inspector General Says*, 35 BNA Env. Rept. 1406 (2004).

61. Eric Schaeffer, *A Fresh Start for EPA Enforcement*, 39 Env. L. Rept. 10,385 (2008); *ExxonMobil Agrees to $6.1 Million Penalty for Violating Consent Decree at Refineries*, 39 BNA Env. Rept. 2488 (2008); *AEP Settles Lawsuit Alleging Violations, Will Spend $4.6 Billion on Emissions Cuts*, 38 BNA Env. Rept. 2165 (2007); *CITGO Petroleum Refinery Found Guilty of Criminal Violations of Clean Air Act*, 38 BNA Env. Rept. 1424 (2007).

62. Cavnar, Disaster, ch. 1, 8, 36–42, 95–100; *New Flow Estimates Affirm Gulf Accident as Largest Spill, Geological Survey Chief Says*, 41 BNA Env. Rept. 1271 (2010); Ian Urbina, *Documents Show Earlier Worries About Safety of Rig*, NYT, May 30, 2010, at A1; Steven Mufson, *Costly Drilling Effort Might Have Rushed BP and Transocean on Safety Measures*, WP, May 28, 2010, at A8.

63. Steven Mufson, *Experts, Rivals Blast BP's Practices*, WP, November 10, 2010, at A4 (culture quote); Ian Urbina, *Workers on Doomed Rig Voiced Concern on Safety*, NYT, July 21, 2010, at A1 (drilling priorities quote); Sarah Lyall, *In BP's Record, A History of Boldness and Costly Blunders*, NYT, July 13, 2010, at A1 (chronically unable quote, equipment assessment); Abraham Lustgarten & Ryan Knutson, *Reports at BP Over the Years Find History of Problems*, WP, June 8, 2010, at A1; Barry Meier, *Gulf Rig Owner is Known for Testing the Rules*, NYT, July 9, 2010, at A2; Clifford Krauss & Tom Zeller, Jr., *A Behind-the-Scenes Firm is Caught in the Spotlight*, NYT, May 24, 2010, at B1 (push envelope quote).

64. Cavnar, Disaster, 108–10; Matthew Daly, *BP Ad Spending Since Spill: $5 Million a Week*, WP, September 2, 2010, at A21; Campbell Robertson, *Gulf of Mexico Has Long Been Dumping Site*, NYT, July 30, 2010, at A1 (4000 wells); Dan Eggan, *BP is Getting More Political, and That May Help Weather Oil-Spill Storm*, WP, May 6, 2010, at A17 (lobbying expenses).

CHAPTER 10. DRUG AND DEVICE SAFETY

1. Marcia Angell, The Truth About Drug Companies xii (2004); Philip J. Hilts, Protecting America's Health xiv (2003); Melody Petersen, Our Daily Meds 9 (2008); *FDA's Drug Approval Process: Up to the Challenge? Hearings Before the Senate Committee on Health, Education, Labor and Pensions*, 109th Cong., 1st Sess. (2005); *Risk and Responsibility: The Roles of FDA and Pharmaceutical Companies in Ensuring the Safety of Approved Drugs, Like Vioxx, Hearings Before the House Committee on Government Reform*, 109th Cong., 1st Sess. (2005); FDA Science Board, FDA Science and Mission at Risk 1 (Report of the Subcommittee on Science and Technology, November, 2007); Gardiner Harris, *The Safety Gap*, NYT Magazine, November 2, 2008, at 44.
2. Medtronic, Inc. v. Lohr, 518 U.S. 470, 478–79 (1996) (substantial equivalence); Peter B. Hutt & Richard A. Merrill, Food and Drug Law 477–478 (2 ed. 1991); Hilts, Protecting, 164.
3. Stephen J. Ceccoli, Pill Politics 76–77 (2004); Hilts, Protecting, 152–58.
4. Sam Peltzman, *An Evaluation of Consumer Protection Legislation: The 1962 Drug Amendments*, 81 J. Pol. Econ. 1049 (1973); William M. Wardell, *Introduction of New Therapeutic Drugs in the United States and Great Britain: An International Comparison*, 14 Clinical Pharmacology & Therapeutics 559 (1973).
5. See, e.g., Henry G. Grabowski, Drug Regulation and Innovation (AEI Evaluative Studies No. 28, 1976); William M. Wardell & Louis Lasagna, Regulation and Drug Development (AEI Evaluative Studies, 1975).
6. Department of Health, Education and Welfare, Final Report of the Review Panel on New Drug Regulation 28–30 (1977); *Competitive Problems in the Drug Industry, Part 23: Development and Marketing of Prescription Drugs, Hearings Before the Senate Committee on Small Business*, 93d Cong., 1st Sess. (1973) (testimony of Leonard G. Schifrin, Samuel H. Baker III); Mark Green, *The Faked Case Against Regulation*, WP, January 21, 1979, at C1.
7. Hilts, Protecting, 192, 207; Ceccoli, Pill Politics, 90; Marian Burros, *Kennedy's Kind Farewell to FDA a Fond Farewell*, WP, June 28, 1979, at E1; Gene I. Macroff, *New President of Stanford*, NYT, June 14, 1980, at A7; Warren Brown, *Biologist Appointed FDA Commissioner*, WP, March 4, 1977, at A2.
8. Hilts, Protecting, 216–18, 239; Julie Kosterlitz, *Reagan is Leaving His Mark on the Food and Drug Administration*, 15 Nat. J. 1568 (1985); Spencer Rich & Douglas B. Feaver, *Educator Chosen for FDA*, WP, May 9, 1984, at A29; Morton Mintz, *Administration Seeks to Speed Approval of New Drugs*, WP, October 12, 1982, at A2; Morton Mintz, *Reagan Backed Repeal of Drug Effectiveness Law*, WP, December 20, 1980, at A9.

9. Food and Drug Administration, Investigational New Drug, Antibiotic, and Biological Drug Product Regulations; Procedures for Drugs Intended to Treat Life-Threatening and Severely Debilitating Illnesses, 53 Fed. Reg. 41,516 (1988); Hilts, Protecting, 239–40, 249; Warren E. Leary, *F.D.A. Announces Changes to Speed Testing of Drugs*, NYT, October 20, 1988, at A1.

10. David Kessler, A Question of Intent 7 (2001) (demoralized quote); Marlene Cimons, *FDA Plans Safety Reviews of Several Medical Devices*, LAT, April 28, 1992, at A14; Marlene Cimons, *FDA to Restrict Cosmetic Silicon Breast Implants*, LAT, April 17, 1992, at A1; Marlene Cimons, *New Chief Makes FDA a Regulatory Tiger*, LAT, May 16, 1991, at A16; Philip J. Hilts, *U.S. Cracks Down on Health Devices Made Before 1976*, NYT, February 24, 1991, at A6.

11. Prescription Drug User Fee Act of 1992, Public Law No. 102–571, 106 Stat. 4491 (1992); Ceccoli, Pill Politics, 106–08; Hilts, Protecting, 276–79; Margaret Gilhooley, *Vioxx's History and the Need for Better Procedures and Better Testing*, 37 Seton Hall L. Rev. 941, 959 (2007); Richard A. Merrill, *The Architecture of Government Regulation of Medical Products*, 82 Va. L. Rev. 1753, 1795–96 (1996).

12. Ceccoli, Pill Politics, 41; Hilts, Protecting, 295–96, 309; Andrew Lawler, *FDA: Congress Mixes Harsh Medicine*, 269 Science 1038 (1995); Peter H. Stone, *Ganging Up on the FDA*, 27 Nat. J. 410 (1995); John Schwartz, *Conservative Foes of Government Regulation Focus on the FDA*, WP, January 21, 1995, at A7 (Gingrich quotes).

13. David Kessler, et. al, *Approval of New Drugs in the United States: Comparison with the United Kingdom, Germany, and Japan*, 276 JAMA 2409 (1996) (agency response).

14. Hilts, Protecting, 318; Marlene Cimons, *FDA Goes Up Against a Newly Revived GOP*, LAT, January 2, 1995, at A1; John Schwartz, *FDA Quickly Whittles Down Stack of Applications for Medical Devices*, WP, November 29, 1994, at A21 (backlog decline); Lawrence M. Fisher, *Frustration for Medical Innovators*, NYT, June 30, 1993, at D1; James M. Gomez, *Devices Languish in FDA Limbo*, LAT, April 30, 1993, at A1; Laura Jereski, *Block That Innovation*, Forbes, January 18, 1993, at 48.

15. Hilts, Protecting, 296, 328–29; Kessler, Question of Intent, 18, 286; Jeffrey Goldberg, *Next Target: Nicotine*, NYT, August 4, 1996, at M23 (bills pulled); Kathleen Day, *Drug, Biotech Industries Cautious on FDA Reform*, WP, May 20, 1995, at D1; Schwartz, Conservative Foes.

16. John Schwartz, *With Leadership in Transition, FDA to Face Many Challenges in New Congress*, WP, December 1, 1997, at A30; John Schwartz, *In Swan Song, Kessler Croons of FDA Progress*, WP, December 11, 1996, at A23 (quote).

17. FDA Modernization Act of 1997, Pub. L. 105–115, 111 Stat. 2296 (1997); Peter B. Hutt, Richard A. Merrill & Lewis A. Grossman, Food and Drug Law 736 (3d Ed. 2007); Henry I. Miller, *Failed FDA Reform*, Regulation, Fall, 199, at 24, 28 (profound disappointment quote); Robert Pear, *Congress Clears Measure to Speed Drugs to Market*, NYT, November 10, 1997, at A28 (industry pleased).

18. National Institute of Medicine, The Future of Drug Safety 1–6 (2006) (2002 renewal); Jennifer Washburn, *Undue Influence*, American Prospect, August 13, 2001, at 16 (drug lag complaints); Robert Langreth, *Crisis in the Cabinet*, Forbes, December 10, 2001, at 133 (drug lag complaints).

19. National Institute of Medicine, Future, 3–2 (poor FDA staff morale); Union of Concerned Scientists, Voices of Scientists at FDA: Protecting Public Health Depends on Independent Science 3 (July 2006); Eric J. Topol, *Failing the Public Health — Refocoxib, Merck, and the FDA*, 351 New Eng. J. Med. 1707 (2004) (Vioxx description); Marc Kaufman & Brooke A. Masters, *After Criticism, FDA Will Strengthen Drug Safety Checks*, WP, November 6, 2004, at A12; Robert Pear & Andrew Pollack, *Bush's Choice for F.D.A. to Keep Other Job*, NYT, September 25, 2005, at A24; Rebecca Adams, *A Low Dose of FDA Oversight*, Cong. Q. Weekly, April 11, 2005, at 886 (little effect); Marc Kaufman, *Many FDA Scientists Had Drug Concerns, 2002 Survey Shows*, WP, December 16, 2004, at A1 (Inspector General survey); Ricardo Alonso-Zaldivar, *Early Vioxx Alarms Alleged*, LAT, November 19, 2004, at A1; Mark Kaufman, *FDA Officer Suggests Strict Curbs on 5 Drugs*, WP, November 19, 2004, at A1 (Vioxx estimates).

20. Adams, *A Low Dose* (quoting Representative Joe Barton).

21. Gardiner Harris & David M. Halbfinger, *F.D.A. Reveals It Fell to a Push By Lawmakers*, NYT, September 25, 2009, at A1; Alicia Mundy, *Political Lobbying Drove FDA Process*, WSJ, March 6, 2009, at A8.

22. Petersen, Daily Meds, 331 (drug withdrawals); FDA, *Industry Reach Tentative Agreement on Fees for Product Safety, Reviewing Ads*, 35 BNA PLSR 37 (2007); Rebecca Adams, *Pharma Braces for Battle*, Cong. Q. Weekly, November 27, 2006, at 3176.

23. Food and Drug Administration Amendments Act of 2007, Public L. No. 110–85, 110 Stat. 823 (2007); Gilhooley, *Vioxx's History*, 960–61;

24. Angell, Truth, 35, 209; Hilts, Protecting, 335; National Institute of Medicine, Future, 2–9 (average time), 3–8; *How a New Policy Lead to Seven Deadly Drugs*, LAT, December 20, 2000, at A1; Stephen Pomper, *Drug Rush*, Washington Monthly, May 1, 2000, at 31.

25. Peter Barton Hutt, The State of Science At The Food and Drug Administration, Appendix B to FDA Science Board, FDA Science and Mission at Risk B-16–17 (Report of the Subcommittee on Science and Technology November, 2007) (one percent, officers left agency); Gardiner Harris, *F.D.A. is Lax on Oversight During Trials, Inquiry Finds*, NYT, January 12, 2009, at A10 (conflicts of interest); Diedtra Henderson & Christopher Rowland, *Once "Too Slow," FDA Approvals Called "Too Fast,"* Boston Globe, April 10, 2005, at A1 (reviewer complaints); Kaufman, *Many FDA Scientists* (survey results); *New Policy Lead to Seven Deadly Drugs* (sweatshop quote, inquiry shift).

26. Rena Steinzor & Margaret Clune, The Hidden Lesson of the Vioxx Fiasco: Reviving a Hollow FDA 17 (Center for Progressive Reform, October 2005).

27. David Willman, *Bitter Pill*, Washington Monthly, September 1, 1999, at 33; David Willman, *The Rise and Fall of the Killer Drug Rezulin*, LAT, June 4, 2000, at A1; Marc Kaufman, *Controversial Diabetes Drug is Withdrawn*, WP, March 22, 2000, at A1; David Willman, *"Fast-Track" Drug to Treat Diabetes Tied to 33 Deaths*, LAT, December 6, 1998, at A1 (quote).

28. National Institute of Medicine, Future, 2–6 through 7, 7–1; Government Accountability Office, Drug Safety: Improvement Needed in FDA's Postmarket Decision-making and Oversight Process 25 (March 2006); Hutt, State of Science, B-14; Office of the

Inspector General, Department of Health and Human Services, FDA's Review
Process for New Drug Applications: A Management Review ii (March 2003); *Sen-
ate Drug Approval Hearings* (testimony of Sandra L. Kweder, FDA); *House Vioxx
Hearings* (testimony of Steven Galston, Acting Director, Center for Drug Evalua-
tion and Research, FDA); *The Adequacy of FDA to Assure the Safety of the Nation's
Drug Supply, Hearings Before the Subcommittee on Oversight and Investigations of the
House Committee on Energy and Commerce,* 110th Cong., 1st Sess. (2007) (testimony
of Andrew C. von Eschenbach, David Graham); *Lack of Funds Hurts FDA's Safety
Efforts for Drugs Already on Market, Report Says,* 34 BNA PSLR 966 (2006); Ricardo
Allonzo-Zaldivar, *When New Drugs Go Wrong: Role of FDA Debated,* LAT, Novem-
ber 26, 2004, at A38.

29. National Institute of Medicine, Future, 3–10 though 3–11; Pomper, Drug Rush, 31;
    Gardiner Harris, *Potentially Incompatible Goals at F.D.A.,* NYT, June 11, 2007, at A14
    (five officers chastised); Gardiner Harris, *F.D.A. Issues Strictest Warning on Diabetes
    Drugs,* NYT, June 7, 2007, at A1.

30. Government Accountability Office, FDA Should Take Steps to Ensure that High-
    Risk Device Types are Approved through the Most Stringent Premarket Review Pro-
    cess 13–16 (2009) (98 percent); Reed Abelson, *Quickly Vetted, Treatment is Offered to
    Cancer Patients,* NYT, October 27, 2008, at A1; Kit R. Roane, *Replacement Parts,* U.S.
    News & World Report, July 29, 2002, at 54.

31. Matthew Herper & Robert Langreth, *Dangerous Devices,* Forbes, November 27, 2006,
    at 94 (2001–06 statistics); Roane, *Replacement Parts* (quoting letter).

32. Institute of Medicine, Safe Medical Devices for Children 86–87, 152, 163, 183, 190
    (2005); Michael D. Green & William B. Schultz, *Tort Law Deference to FDA Regula-
    tion of Medical Devices,* 88 Geo. L. J. 2119, 2142 (2000); Barry Meier, *History of Hernia
    Patch Raises Questions on Implant Recalls,* NYT, March 16, 2007, at A1 (benefit of the
    doubt); Barry Meier, *A Choice for the Heart,* NYT, June 23, 2005, at A1; Barry Meier,
    Implants With Flaws: Disclosure and Delay, NYT, June 14, 2005, at A1.

33. *Official Says FDA Seeks Authority, Resources to Address Pressing Safety Issues,* 38 BNA
    PSLR 246 (2010) (statistics); Harris, *Safety Gap;* Marc Kaufman, *FDA Scrutiny Scant
    in India, China as Drugs Pour Into U.S.,* WP, June 17, 2007, at A1.

34. Stuart O. Schweitzer, *Trying Times at the FDA—The Challenge of Ensuring the
    Safety of Imported Pharmaceuticals,* 358 New Eng. J. Med. 1773 (2008) (statistics);
    Harris, *Safety Gap;* Jennifer Corbett Dooren, *FDA Lacks Enough Funds for Foreign
    Drug Checking,* WSJ, April 23, 2008, at A14; Anna Wilde Mathews, *FDA Faulted
    for Scrutiny of Medical-Device Manufacturers,* WSJ, January 29, 2008, at A2; Walt
    Bogdanich, *As F.D.A. Tracked Poisoned Drugs, A Winding Trail Went Cold in China,*
    NYT, June 17, 2007, at A1.

35. Angell, Truth, 115, 136–38, 142–43; Kassirer, On the Take, 17, 68 (describing literature),
    91–93; Petersen, Daily Meds, 67–69; Eric G. Campbell, *Doctors and Drug Compa-
    nies—Scrutinizing Influential Relationships,* 357 New Eng. J. Med. 1796 (2007); Dan-
    iel Carlat, *Dr. Drug Rep,* NYT Magazine, November 25, 2007, at 64; Reed Abel-
    son, *Possible Conflicts for Doctors are Seen on Medical Devices,* NYT, September 22,
    2005, at A1.

36. Ceci Connolly, *With More Oversight on the Horizon, Drugmakers Work to Polish Image*, WP, January 8, 2009, at A1 (40 companies).

37. Ceccoli, Pill Politics, 154; Joseph Weber & John Carey, *Drug Ads: A Prescription for Controversy*, Business Week, January 18, 1993, at 58; Carla Lazzareschi, *Pitching Pharmaceuticals to the Public*, WP, May 15, 1988, at H7.

38. Stephanie Saul, *Medical Journal's Article Questions TV Ads for Stent*, NYT, May 15, 2008, at A3; Stephanie Saul, *For Jarvik Heart Pioneer, Drug Ads Raise Profile and Questions*, NYT, February 7, 2008, at A1 (statistics); *Study Faults TV Ads for Medications, Says Their Educational Value Limited*, 35 BNA PSLR 108 (2007); Julie Schmit, *FDA Races to Keep Up with Drug Ads that Go Too Far*, USA Today, May 30, 2005, at A1; John Schwartz, *FDA Releases Rules for On-Air Drug Ads*, WP, August 9, 1997, at A1.

39. Hilts, Protecting, 216; Robert Pear, *Panel Calls Federal Drug Agency Unable to Cope with Rising Tasks*, NYT, April 11, 1991, at A1.

40. Kessler, Question of Intent, 47; Julie Kosterlitz, *High-Wire Act*, 24 Nat. J. 1289 (1992); Gina Kolata, *Questions Raised on Ability of F.D.A. to Protect Public*, NYT, January 26, 1992, at A1; Philip J. Hilts, *New Chief Vows New Vitality at F.D.A.*, NYT, February 27, 1991, at B7.

41. Roane, *Replacement Parts* (deterioration); Alicia Mundy, *Congress Presses FDA on Investigations*, WSJ, June 11, 2008, at A19 (criminal statistics); Jared Favole, *FDA Warning Letters to Companies Decline Sharply*, WSJ, June 7, 2008, at A2 (warning letters); Mathews, *FDA Faulted*; Melody Petersen, *Who's Minding the Drugstore?* NYT, June 29, 2003, at C1.

42. Schweitzer, *Trying Times*; Gardiner Harris, *Problems in Blood Drug Lead to Halt by Factory*, NYT, February 12, 2009, at A15; Walt Bogdanich, *The Drug Scare That Exposed a World of Hurt*, NYT, March 30, 2008, at WK3; Walt Bogdanich & Jake Hooker, *China Didn't Check Drug Supplier, Files Show*, NYT, February 16, 2008, at A1.

43. Walt Bogdanich, *Chinese Chemicals Flow Unchecked to Market*, NYT, October 31, 2007, at A1; Emily Parker, *"Made in China,"* WSJ, July 12, 2007, at A15; David Barboza, *China Steps Up Its Safety Efforts*, NYT, July 7, 2007, at A1 (massive sweep, death sentence).

44. Alicia Mundy & Jared A. Favole, *FDA is Faulted for Oversight of Foreign Drugs*, WSJ, October 22, 2008, at A5 (office); Alicia Mundy, *Democrats, FDA Officials at Odds Over Inspection Plan*, WSJ, May 2, 2008, at A4; Alicia Mundy, *Congress, FDA Debate Foreign Inspections*, WSJ, April 26, 2008, at A5; *FDA Needs Additional Resources, Greater Regulatory Authority, Senators Say*, 36 BNA PSLR 456 (2008) (GAO report).

45. For a more detailed description of the Ketek story, see Thomas O. McGarity, *Corporate Accountability for Scientific Fraud: Ketek and the Perils of Aggressive Agency Preemption*, 58 Emory L. J. 287 (2008). See also David B. Ross, *The FDA and the Case of Ketek*, 356 New England J. Med. 1601 (2007); *The Adequacy of FDA to Assure the Safety of the Nation's Drug Supply, Hearings Before the Subcommittee on Oversight and Investigations of the House Committee on Energy and Commerce*, 110th Cong., 1st Sess. (2007); *Ketek Clinical Study Fraud: What Did Avenetis Know? Hearings*

Before the Subcommittee on Oversight and Investigations of the House Committee on Energy and Commerce, 110th Cong., 2d Sess. (2008).

46. Melody Petersen, Our Daily Meds 7 (2008); David C. Vladeck, *The FDA and Deference Lost: A Self-Inflicted Wound or the Product of a Wounded Agency? A Response to Professor O'Reilly,* 93 Cornell. L. Rev. 981, 997 (2008).

47. Alastair J.J. Wood, *Playing "Kick the FDA"—Risk-free to Players but Hazardous to Public Health,* 358 New Eng. J. Med. 1774 (2008); Hutt, State of Science, at B-7.

CHAPTER 11. FOOD SAFETY

1. Nicols Fox, Spoiled 147 (1997); Carole Sugarman, *On the Trail of Salmonella,* WP, October 17, 1999, at E1; Amanda Spake, *A Crackdown on Bad Eggs,* U.S. News & World Report, July 12, 1999, at 50; Daniel P. Puzo, *Food Bites Back: Issues of 1990,* LAT, January 3, 1991, at H2; Daniel P. Puzo, *3 of 5 Chickens in U.S. Test Found to Have Salmonella,* LAT, May 4, 1990, at A1.

2. Fox, Spoiled, 12, 51; Marion Nestle, Safe Food 27 (2003).

3. 1 Encyclopedia of American Industries 1 (2011) (slaughterhouses); 2 Encyclopedia of American Industries 1485 (2011) (poultry).

4. Institute of Medicine & National Research Council, Enhancing Food Safety 21 (2010).

5. Meat Inspection Act of 1906, Chapter 3913, 34 Stat. 674 (1906).

6. Food Additives Amendment of 1958, Pub. L. No. 85–929, 72 Stat. 1784 (1958); Pure Food and Drug Act of 1906, Pub. L. No. 59–384, 34 Stat. 768 (1906); Philip J. Hilts, Protecting America's Health 54 (2003); Nestle, Safe Food, 52–53; Lars Noah & Richard A. Merrill, *Starting From Scratch?: Reinventing The Food Additive Approval Process,* 78 B.U.L. Rev. 329, 338–40 (1998).

7. Food and Drug Administration, General Recognition of Safety and Prior Sanctions for Food Ingredients, 41 Fed. Reg. 53,600, 53,604 (1976)

8. Food and Drug Administration, Hazard Analysis and Critical Control Point (HAACP); Procedures for the Safe and Sanitary Processing and Importing of Juice; Final Rule, 66 Fed. Reg. 6138, 6183 (2001); Food Safety and Inspection Service, Pathogen Reduction; Hazard Analysis and Critical Control Point (HACCP) Systems, Final Rule, 61 Fed. Reg. 38,806, (1996); Food and Drug Administration, Procedures for the Safe and Sanitary Processing and Importing of Fish and Fishery Products, 60 Fed. Reg. 65,096, 65,185–86 (1995); J.D. Vojdani, L.R. Beuchat & R.V. Tauxe, Juice Associated Outbreaks of Human Illness in the United States, 1995 through 2005, 71 J. Food Protection 356 (2008).

9. Nutrition Labeling and Education Act of 1990, Pub. L. 101–535, 104 Stat. 2353 (1990); Hilts, Protecting, 265; Nestle, Food Politics 250 (2002); Cindy Skrzycki, *Walking on Eggshells,* WP, December 12, 2000, at E1; Carole Sugarman, *Labels About Safe Handling to be Required on Meat, Poultry Products,* WP, August 12, 1993, at A3 (quoting regulations); Malcolm Gladwell, *FDA Puts Squeeze on "Fresh" Juice,* WP, April 25, 1991, at A1.

10. Fox, Spoiled, 192, 262; Nestle, Safe Food, 28.

11. National Research Council, National Academy of Sciences, Ensuring Safe Food from Production to Consumption 2 (1998); Dennis G. Maki, *Coming to Grips with Foodborne Infection—Peanut Butter, Peppers, and Nationwide Salmonella Outbreaks*, 360 New Eng. J. Med. 949 (2009); Ben Worthen, *Weak Links in the Food (Supply) Chain*, WSJ, June 24, 2008, at B5.

12. Adam Benforado, Jon Hanson & David Yosifon, *Broken Scales: Obesity and Justice in America*, 53 Emory L. J. 1645, 1689, 1758–60 (2004); Kelly D. Brownell & Kenneth E. Warner, *The Perils of Ignoring History: Big Tobacco Played Dirty and Millions Died. How Similar is Big Food?* 87 Milbank Quarterly 259, 263, 280 (2009).

13. Food and Drug Administration, Saccharin and its Salts, Proposed Rule Making, 42 Fed. Reg. 19,996 (1977); Hilts, Protecting, 202–06; William R. Havender, *Ruminations on a Rat: Saccharin and Human Risk*, Regulation, March/April, 1979, at 17; Richard A. Merrill, *Saccharin: A Regulator's View*, in The Scientific Basis of Health and Safety Regulation 150, 159–60 (Robert W. Crandall & Lester B. Lave, eds. 1981).

14. Joan Claybrook, Retreat from Safety 32 (1984); Hilts, Protecting, 217, 261.

15. Hilts, Protecting, 261; John Schwartz, *FDA Clears Drug to Lift Milk Yields*, WP, November 6, 1993, at A1.

16. Fox, Spoiled, 244; Nestle, Safe Food, 73; Daniel P. Puzo, *Texas Professor to Head U.S. Food Inspection Agency*, LAT, February 11, 1992, at A19; *Crawford Leaves USDA Inspection Service Post*, LAT, August 22, 1991, at H1.

17. Agricultural Marketing Service, National Organic Program, 65 Fed. Reg. 80,548 (2000); Food and Drug Administration, Food Code; 1999 Revision; Availability, 64 Fed. Reg. 8576 (1999); Food and Drug Administration, Hazard Analysis and Critical Control Point (HAACP); Procedures for the Safe and Sanitary Processing and Importing of Juice; Final Rule, 66 Fed. Reg. 6138 (2001); Food Safety and Inspection Service, Pathogen Reduction; Hazard Analysis and Critical Control Point (HACCP) Systems, Final Rule, 61 Fed. Reg. 38,806 (1996).

18. Annys Shin, *Nation's Top Meat Safety Official is Leaving USDA Post*, WP, September 27, 2008, at D6.

19. Dave Michaels & Sherry Jacobson, *"You Get What You Pay For," In Strapped System, FDA Relies on States*, Dallas Morning News, February 15, 2009, at 1A (quoting William Hubbard).

20. Brownell & Warner, *Perils*, 266; Centers for Disease Control, CDC Estimates of Foodborne Illness in the United States, available at http://www.cdc.gov/foodborneburden.

21. Food Safety and Inspection Service, Enhanced Poultry Inspection, 59 Fed. Reg 35,639, 35,643 (1994) (zero tolerance proposal); Richard Behar & Michael Kramer, *Something Smells Fowl*, Time, October 17, 1994, at 42 (worst decision); Daniel P. Puzo, *Can USDA Bird Bath Clean Up Poultry Problems*, LAT, March 17, 1994. at H32; Good Housekeeping, Chicken Safety Strategies, available at http://www.goodhousekeeping.com/food/cooking/grilling-chicken-safety-tips (raw chicken contamination).

22. Food and Drug Administration, Prevention of Salmonella Enteritidis in Shell Eggs During Production; Proposed Rule, 69 Fed. Reg. 56,823 (2004); Fox, Spoiled, 147–57, 172; Alec MacGillis, *Before Salmonella Outbreak, Egg Firm Had Long Record of Violations*, WP, August 22, 2010, at A1; David Brown, *Salmonella-Tainted Eggs From*

Big Producer in Iowa Have Sickened at Least 1,200, WP, August 20, 2010, at A3; William Neuman, *Egg Recall Expanded After Salmonella Outbreak*, NYT, August 18, 2010, at A1.

23. Supreme Beef Processors, Inc. v. USDA, 275 F.3d 432 (5th Cir. 2001); Food Safety and Inspection Service, Pathogen Reduction; Nestle, Safe Food, 72; Daniel P. Puzo, *Is Congress Ready to Approve a New Food Inspection System?* LAT, February 23, 1995, at H2 (jousting); *Academy of Sciences Urges Changes in Meat Inspection*, NYT, September 18, 1990, at B7.

24. *Meat Plants Faulted on Safety Rules*, WP, February 5, 2003, at A24 (USDA audit); Joby Warrick, *An Outbreak Waiting to Happen*, WP, April 9, 2001, at A1 (gaming system).

25. Bud Hazelkorn, *Poultry Plant Slow to Report Sharp Increase in Bacteria*, NYT, December 21, 2002, at A14; *USDA Failed to Act Against Plant's Listeria, Inspector Says*, WP, December 12, 2002, at A10.

26. Food Safety and Inspection Service, E. coli O157:H7 Contamination of Beef Products, 67 Fed. Reg. 62,325 (October 7, 2002) (final zero-tolerance rule); Fox, Spoiled, 7, 42, 245, 249, 260; Carole Sugarman, *Sorry to See Esty Go? Some Are, Some Aren't*, WP, October 13, 1994, at A17 (FSIS announcement).

27. Nestle, Safe Food, 82; Michael Moss, *The Burger that Shattered Her Life*, NYT, October 4, 2009, at A1; Bill Tomson, *U.S. Beef Safety Plan Languishes Amid New Illnesses*, WSJ, July 10, 2009, at A5.

28. Institute of Medicine, Antimicrobial Resistance: Issues and Options 1 (Polly F. Harrison & Joshua Lederberg, eds., 1998) (resistance to human pathogens); Margaret Mellon, Charles Benbrook & Laren Lutz Benbrook, Hogging It: Estimates of Antimicrobial Abuse in Livestock (Union of Concerned Scientists, 2001) (statistics); Putting Meat on the Table: Industrial Farm Animal Production in America 5–7 (Pew Commission on Industrial Farm Animal Production, 2008); Dan Ferber, *WHO Advises Kicking the Livestock Antibiotic Habit*, 301 Science 1027 (2003); Michael Pollan, *Our Decrepit Food Factories*, NYT Magazine, December 16, 2007, at 25.

29. Food and Drug Administration, Animal Drugs, Feeds, and Related Products; Enrofloxacin for Poultry; Withdrawal of Approval of a New Animal Drug Application, 90 Fed. Reg. 44,048 (2005); Nestle, Safe Food, 46; World Health Organization, Overcoming Antimicrobial Resistance (2000) (mounting evidence); Alicia Mundy & Jared Favole, *FDA Calls Off Ban on Animal Antibiotics*, WSJ, December 10, 2008, at B3; Marian Burros, *F.D.A. Proposal on Meat Safety Draws Criticism*, NYT, June 8, 1983, at C1.

30. Government Accountability Office, Food Safety: Improvements Needed in FDA Oversight of Fresh Produce 10, 24 (2008); Jane Zhang, *FDA Stymied in Push to Boost Safety of Produce*, WSJ, May 16, 2007, at A1; Mary Engel & Rong Gong Lin II, *Processing May Spread E. Coli*, LAT, January 20, 2007, at A1; Libby Sander, *Nebraska Woman's Death Brings to 3 Those Attributed to Spinach*, NYT, October 7, 2006, at A16; Marla Cone, *E. Coli Pervades Harvest Area*, LAT, September 21, 2006, at B1.

31. Nestle, Safe Food, 114; Michael R. Taylor, The FDA Food Safety Modernization Act: A New Paradigm for Importers, Speech at the Global Food Safety Conference, Feb-

ruary 17, 2011 (statistics); Jeff Gerth & Tim Weiner, *Imports Swamp U.S. Food-Safety Efforts*, NYT, September 29, 1997, at A1.

32. Government Accountability Office, Food Safety: Agencies Need to Address Gaps in Enforcement and Collaboration to Enhance Safety of Food 14, 17 (2009); Joby Warrick, *Overseas Meat Processors Fail to Make Grade*, Austin American-Statesman, March 3, 2002, at A19.

33. Public Health Security and Bioterrorism Preparedness and Response Act of 2002, Pub. L. No. 107–188, 116 Stat. 631 (2002); Nestle, Safe Food, 114; National Academy of Sciences, Ensuring Safe Food, 89; Government Accountability Office, Improvements Needed, 8; Government Accountability Office, Gaps in Enforcement, 16, 31; General Accounting Office, Food Safety: FDA's Imported Seafood Safety Program Shows Some Progress, but Further Improvements Are Necessary 14, 17 (2004); General Accounting Office, Food Safety: Federal Oversight of Seafood Does Not Sufficiently Protect Consumers 28, 32 (2001).

34. Government Accountability Office, Food Safety: USDA and FDA Need to Better Ensure Prompt and Complete Recalls of Potentially Unsafe Food 15 (2004); Julie Schmit & Barbara Hansen, *Most Recalled Meat Isn't Recovered*, USA Today, December 3, 2007, at 1B (44 percent decline).

35. Peter Barton Hutt, The State of Science at the Food and Drug Administration, Appendix B to FDA Science Board, FDA Science and Mission at Risk B-20 (Report of the Subcommittee on Science and Technology November, 2007); Victoria Kim, *Cattle Inspections Thwarted*, LAT, February 20, 2008, at B1 (FSIS vacancies); Marian Burros, *F.D.A. Inspections Lax, Congress is Told*, NYT, July 18, 2007, at C3; OMB Watch, Federal Meat Inspectors Spread Thin as Recalls Rise, March 4, 2008, available at http://www.ombwatch.org/node/3624 (statistics).

36. Government Accountability Office, Improvements Needed, 36; Caroline Smith DeWall, *On the Trail of Tainted Foods*, Newsday, February 1, 2009, A15 (civil penalty authority).

37. Marian Burros, *F.D.A. to Ban Product Labels that Mislead on Fat Content*, NYT, June 5, 1991, at A1; Anthony Ramirez, *3 Companies Cited on Cholesterol Claims*, NYT, May 15, 1991, at D1; Malcolm Gladwell, *FDA Puts Squeeze on "Fresh" Juice*, WP, April 25, 1991, at A1 (Citrus Hill); Cristine Russell, *FDA Cut Termed a Threat to Public Health*, WP, August 12, 1982, at A21 (60 percent decline).

38. Hannah Thomas, *It's What's For Dinner*, Harper's, April 2003, at 22 (FSIS instructions); Elizabeth Becker, *Critics Take Aim at Guidelines on Standards for Food Safety*, NYT, November 2, 2002, at A14.

39. FDA Science Board, FDA Science and Mission at Risk 21 (Report of the Subcommittee on Science and Technology, November 2007) (1972 comparison); Lyndsey Layton, *FDA Inspections of Food Plants, Enforcement Down, Officials Say*, WP, April 7, 2010, at A6 (enforcement action decline); Seth Borenstein & Brett J. Blackledge, *US Relies on States for Food Safety Inspections*, San Francisco Chronicle, February 10, 2009, at A7 (400 inspector loss); Andrew Bridges & Seth Borenstein, *FDA Food-Safety Inspections Steadily Decreasing*, Seattle Times, February 27, 2007, at A9.

40. Melody Petersen & Christopher Drew, *As Inspectors, Some Meatpackers Fall Short*, NYT, October 10, 2003, at A1; Annys Shin & Ylan Q. Mui, *Whole Foods Recalls Beef Processed at Plant Long at Odds with USDA*, WP, August 10, 2008, at A1; Mark Kawar, *Plant Open as Rules "Restated,"* Omaha World-Herald, January 28, 2003, at D1; Elizabeth Becker, *Government in Showdown in Bid to Shut Beef Processor*, NYT, January 23, 2003, at A6.

41. Moni Basu & Michelle E. Shaw, *Anatomy of an Outbreak: How Salmonella Sleuths Solved a Deadly Mystery*, Atlanta Journal-Constitution, March 15, 2009, at 1A; Lyndsey Layton & Nick Miroff, *The Rise and Fall of a Peanut Empire*, WP, February 15, 2009, at A1; Michael Moss, *Peanut Case Shows Holes in Food Safety Net*, NYT, February 9, 2009, at A1 (19,000 estimate); Lyndsey Layton, *Every Peanut Product from Ga. Plant Recalled*, WP, January 29, 2009, at A1.

42. Michael Moss & Andrew Martin, *Food Safety Problems Elude Private Inspectors*, NYT, March 6, 2009, at A1; Kent Garber, *Food Safety's Dirty Little Secret*, U.S. News & World Report, September 15, 2008, at 27.

43. Fox, Spoiled 13, 19, 87 (1997); FDA, Food Protection Plan 9 (November 2007); Karen Ann Cullotta, *Researchers Put a Microscope on Food Allergies*, NYT, December 9, 2008, at D5; Sam Roe, *Children at Risk in Food Roulette*, Chicago Tribune, November 21, 2008, at C1; *Stronger Bacteria Threaten Nation's Food, Study Warns*, Houston Chronicle, February 20, 2002, at A7; Greg Winter, *Contaminated Food Makes Millions Ill Despite Advances*, NYT, March 18, 2001, at A1.

44. Trust for America's Health, Keeping America's Food Safe: A Blueprint for Fixing the Food Safety System at the U.S. Department of Health and Human Services 6 (2009).

45. FDA Science Board, Mission at Risk, 3.

CHAPTER 12. TRANSPORTATION SAFETY

1. Research and Innovative Technology Administration, Department of Transportation, Key Transportation Indicators 17, 20, 26 (2011); Department of Transportation, Press Release, March 2, 2011, available at http://www.dot.gov/affairs/2011/fhwa0311.html.

2. Alan Levin, No U.S. Airline Fatalities in 2010, USA Today, January 21, 2011, at T1; Federal Railroad Commission, Accident/Incident Overview (2010), available at http://safetydata.fra.dot.gov/OfficeofSafety/publicsite/Query/statsSas.aspx; United States Census Bureau, The 2011 Statistical Abstract, available at http://www.census.gov/compendia/statab/cats/transportation/motor_vehicle_accidents_and_fatalities.html; .

3. *Ensuring the Safety of Our Nation's Motorcoach Passengers, Hearings Before the Subcommittee on Surface Transportation and Merchant Marine Infrastructure, Safety, and Security of the Senate Committee on Commerce, Science and Transportation*, 112th Cong., 1st Sess. (2011) (Testimony of Deborah A.P. Hersman, Chairman, National Transportation Safety Board).

4. National Traffic and Motor Vehicle Safety Act of 1966, Pub. L. 89–563, 80 Stat. 718 (1966).

5. Robert Burkhardt, The Federal Aviation Administration (1967); Frank A. Burnham, Cleared to Land! The FAA Story (1977).

6. 49 U.S.C. § 20103; Congressional Research Service, Federal Railroad Safety Programs: Selected Issues in Proposed Reauthorization Legislation 3–4 (August 10, 2007).

7. *Traffic Deaths in 2010 Drop 3 Percent to Lowest Level Since 1949, Report Says*, 39 BNA PSLR 392 (2011); Gibson Vance, *Lawsuits Are Making Our Cars Safer*, WP, April 16, 2011, at A16.

8. Motor Vehicle Mfgs. Ass'n v. State Farm Mut. Auto. Ins. Co., 463 U.S. 29 (1983); National Highway Traffic Safety Administration, Federal Motor Vehicle Safety Standards; Occupant Crash Protection, 71 Fed. Reg. 51,768 (2006); Jerry L. Mashaw, *The Story of Motor Vehicle Mfrs Ass'n of the US v. State Farm Mutual Automobile Ins. Co.*, in Administrative Law Stories 334, 359–63 (Peter L. Strauss, ed., 2006); David Shepardson, *Air Bag Arms Race*, Detroit News, May 3, 2007, at C1; National Highway Traffic Safety Administration, Lives Saved in 2009 by Restraint Use and Minimum-Drinking-Age Laws, September 2010, available at http://www-nrd.nhtsa.dot.gov/pubs/811383.pdf.

9. Paccar v. NHTSA, 573 F.2d 632 (9th Cir. 1978); National Highway Traffic Safety Administration, Occupant Restraint Systems, 42 Fed. Reg. 34,289 (1977); *Claybrook Set to Head Highway Traffic Safety*, WP, February 15, 1977, at D7.

10. Joan Claybrook, Retreat from Safety 187, 199 (1984); Warren Brown, *Job Shifts Spark Charges of Agency Purge*, WP, March 4, 1985, at A9; Jeannye Thornton & Clemens P. Work, *Highway Safety Agency Hits a Rough Road*, U.S. News & World Report, May 2, 1983, at 68.

11. Commercial Motor Vehicle Safety Act of 1986, Pub. L. 99–570, 100 Stat. 3207 (1986); Richard Corrigan, *Squeeze on Safety*, 19 Nat. J. 356 (1987).

12. Rail Safety Improvement Act of 1988, Pub. L. 100–342, 102 Stat. 624 (1988); Reginald Stuart, *The Man on the Spot over Rail Safety*, NYT, January 20, 1987, at A18; *Train Ignored Signals, Crash Probers Allege*, LAT, January 8, 1987, at A27.

13. Donald E. Whitnah, U.S. Department of Transportation: A Reference History 177 (1998); Burt Solomon, *FAA Runs into Some Heavy Turbulence in Aviation's Worst Year for Fatalities*, 17 Nat. J. 2313 (1985).

14. Warren Brown, *Acceleration at Highway Safety Agency*, WP, February 25, 1991, at A7.

15. Penny Loeb, *Running Off the Rails*, U.S. News & World Report, May 27, 1996, at 40; Don Phillips, *FAA to Review How it Does its Job*, WP, July 13, 1995, at D9.

16. Myron Levin, *Upgrades on Auto Safety Standards Languish*, LAT, September 18, 2000, at A1 ($1 per vehicle); Tom Incantalupo, *Agency in Hot Seat*, Newsday, September 13, 2000, at A7 (Republican Congress).

17. Federal Motor Carrier Safety Amendments of 1999, Pub. L 106–159; 113 Stat. 1748 (1999); Cindy Skrzycki, *Trying to Move Truck Safety Forward*, WP, November 26, 1999, at E1; Cindy Scrzycki, *Critics Trying to Reengineer Bus, Truck Safety Office*, WP, May 21, 1999, at E1.

18. Keith Bradsher, High and Mighty ch. 3 (2002); Michael Posner, *Tough Tire-Safety Measure Rides Through Senate Panel*, 32 Nat. J. 39 (2000); Judy Pasternak, *Safety Agency Takes Heat Over Firestone Tire Recall*, LAT, August 19, 2000, at A1.

19. Transportation Recall Enhancement, Accountability and Documentation Act of 2000, Pub. L. 106–414, 114 Stat. 1800 (2000); Haroon H. Hamid, *The NHTSA's Evaluation of Automobile Safety Systems: Active or Passive*, 19 Loyola Consumer L. Rev. 227, 236 (2007); Cindy Skrzycki, *At NHTSA, Firestone Fallout*, WP, November 14, 2000, at E1.

20. Cindy Skrzycki, *Trauma Doctor from N.C. Likely to Head Up NHTSA*, WP, June 9, 2001, at E1.

21. Safe, Accountable, Flexible, Efficient Transportation Equity Act of 2006, Public Law No. 109–59, 119 Stat. 1144 (2005); Bradsher High & Mighty, 408–09; David Shepardson, *NHTSA Chief Submits Resignation*, Detroit News, July 16, 2008, at C1; Jeff Plungis, *Departing Auto Safety Chief Pushed for Major Reforms*, Detroit News, July 15, 2005, at D1; Jeff Plungis, *Money, Clout Key to Fixing NHTSA*, Detroit News, March 6, 2002, at A1.

22. Cindy Skrzycki, *Agency Heads Learned Safety as Executives*, WP, November 12, 2002, at E1.

23. Federal Motor Carrier Safety Administration, Hours of Service of Drivers, 73 Fed. Reg. 69,567 (2008); Cindy Skrzycki, *Agency Alliances With Industry Growing*, WP, August 30, 2005, at D1.

24. *Railroad Safety, Hearings Before the Subcommittee on Surface Transportation and Merchant Marine of the Senate Committee on Commerce, Science and Transportation*, 107th Cong., 2d Sess. (2002) (testimony of Allan Rutter, FAA); Frank Ahrens, *A Switch on the Tracks: Railroads Roar Ahead*, WP, April 21, 2008, at A1; Matthew L. Wald & Walt Bogdanich, *New York Official to Head U.S. Rail Agency*, NYT, March 18, 2005, at A15; Walt Bogdanich & Jenny Nordberg, *Head of Railroad Administration, Facing Two Inquiries, is Quitting in Two Weeks*, NYT, December 18, 2004, at A16; *Texan Allan Rutter Named to Head FRA*, Railway Age, May 1, 2001, at 6.

25. Andy Pasztor & Christopher Conkey, *Safety Pushes Stall at Embattled FAA*, WSJ, June 26, 2008, at A1; Matthew L. Wald, *Fatal Airplane Crashes Drop 65% Over 10 Years*, NYT, October 1. 2007, at A1; Aerospace Industries Association, Marion C. Blakey, available at http://www.aia-aerospace.org/assets/mcb_bio.pdf.

26. Myron Levin, *Upgrades on Auto Safety Standards Languish*, LAT, September 18, 2000, at A1.

27. Bradsher, High & Mighty, 23–30, ch. 3; Edward M. Ricci & Scott C. Murray, *Sport Utility Vehicles: Orphans of Auto Safety*, Trial, November 1, 1994, at 28 (no standards for multi-purpose vehicles); Michael deCourcy Hinds, *Minivans' Popularity Prompts Bid to End Safety Exemptions*, NYT, August 19, 1989, at A48 (3 million vehicles).

28. National Highway Traffic Safety Administration, Federal Motor Vehicle Safety Standards; Electronic Stability Control Systems, 72 Fed. Reg. 17,236 (2007); *ESC Effective at Cutting Likelihood of Fatal Crashes, NHTSA Report Says*, 39 BNA PSLR 898 (2011); *Insurance Study Credits Stability Control With Dramatic Drop in SUV Fatality Rate*, 39 BNA PSLR 616 (2011); Warren Brown, *Acceleration at Highway Safety Agency*, WP, February 25, 1991, at A7 (several regulations).

29. National Highway Traffic Safety Administration, Federal Motor Vehicle Safety Standards; Roof Crush Resistance; Phase-In Reporting Requirements; Final Rule, 74 Fed.

Reg. 22,347 (2009); Christopher Conkey, *U.S. Sets New Crush-Resistance Standards for Car Roofs*, WSJ, April 30, 2009, at A15 (auto industry comfortable); Jeff Plungis & Bill Vlasic, *European Vehicles Exceed Standard for U.S. Car Roofs*, Detroit News, April 12, 2004, at A9 (European subsidiaries); Christopher Jensen, *Regulators Considering Making Car Roofs Safer*, Cleveland Plain Dealer, November 8, 2001, at F1 (statistics); Myron Levin, *Upgrades* (static test).

30. Bradsher High & Mighty, 183 (industry dismissal); Eric R. Teoh & Adrian K. Lund, IIHS Side Crash Test Ratings and Occupant Death Risk in Real-world Crashes (Insurance Institute for Highway Safety, January 2011) (statistics); *Voluntary Effort to Lick "Mismatch" Risks in SUV-to-Car Crashes Works, Study Says*, 39 BNA PSLR 1092 (2011); Jayne O'Donnell, *Automakers Give Up on Safety Plan*, USA Today, July 30, 2008, at A7 (industry abandons voluntary initiative); David Shepardson, *Feds OK Tougher Side Air Bag Rule*, Detroit News, September 6, 2007, at A1 (airbags insufficient); Frank Swoboda, *Safety Experts, Carmakers Redesigning Behemoths, Small Vehicles to Improve Unequal Odds of Survival*, WP, June 25, 2000, at H1; Donald W. Nauss, *Detroit Circles the Trucks*, LAT, April 5, 1998, at D1 (Martinez quote).

31. Public Citizen v. FMCSA, 374 F.3d 1209, 1212 (D.C. Cir. 2004) (describing original regulations); Government Accountability Office, Motor Carrier Safety: A Statistical Approach Will Better Identify Commercial Carriers That Pose High Crash Risks Than Does the Current Federal Approach 6 (2007) (statistics); Ralph Vartabedian, *Big Rigs Put the Squeeze on Smaller Vehicles*, LAT, July 16, 2003, at A1; Peter T. Kilborn, *In a Nonstop Economy, Truckers Keep Rolling*, NYT, November 24, 1999, at A16.

32. Steven Labaton, *As Trucking Rules Are Eased, a Debate on Safety Intensifies*, NYT, December 3, 2006, at A1; Phillip J. Longman, *Sweatshops on Wheels*, U.S. News & World Report, September 11, 2000, at 60; Ricardo Alonso-Zaldivar, *Trucking Reforms Steer Straight into Backlash*, LAT, July 3, 2000, at A1 (industry opposition).

33. Public Citizen v. FMCSA, 374 F.3d 1209, 1213–17 (D.C. Cir. 2004) (describing proposed and final rules).

34. Federal Motor Carrier Safety Administration, Hours of Service of Drivers; Proposed Rule, 75 Fed. Reg. 82,170, 82,187 (2010); Federal Motor Carrier Safety Administration, Commercial Motor Vehicle Facts, December 2010, available at http://www.fmcsa.dot.gov/documents/facts-research/CMV-Facts.pdf (statistics).

35. Keith Schneider, *California Spill Exposes Gaps in Rail Safety Rules*, NYT, July 27, 1991, at A6; Richard C. Paddock & Jennifer Warren, *Lake Shasta Expected to be Hit by Toxic Flow Today*, LAT, July 17, 1991, at A1.

36. CSX Transportation v. Williams, 406 F.3d 667 (D.C. Cir. 2005) (local regulations preempted); Alexandra Marks, *Why Railroad Safety Debate Keeps Rolling*, Christian Science Monitor, January 24, 2005, at A1 (NTSB finding); Tim Doulin, *Rails Bring Danger to Town, But Threat Hard to Quantify*, Columbus Dispatch, January 20, 2005, at A1 (FRA refrained).

37. Hazardous Materials Transportation Safety and Security Reauthorization Act of 2005, Pub. L. 109–59, 119 Stat. 1891 (2005); David M. Meezan & Meaghan G. Boyd, *Federal Regulation of Hazardous Materials Transportation*, 12 Nat. Res. & Env. 22 (2006).

38. Pipeline and Hazardous Materials Safety Administration & Federal Railroad Administration, Hazardous Materials; Enhancing Rail Transportation Safety and Security for Hazardous Materials Shipments, 73 Fed. Reg. 20,752 (2008); Christopher Conkey, *U.S. Sets Hazardous Material Rules*, WSJ, June 17, 2008, at A15 (quoting Brent Blackwelder, Friends of the Earth).

39. Jerry L. Mashaw & David L. Harfst, *Regulation and Legal Culture: The Case of Motor Vehicle Safety*, 4 Yale J. Reg. 257, 263 (1987).

40. United States v. General Motors, 541 F.2d 400, 401–06 (1988) (botched recall); Warren Brown, *GM X-Car Brake Case Reveals Regulatory System Breakdown*, WP, September 5, 1983, at A1.

41. Warren Brown, *Government Ends Probe of GM Trucks*, WP, December 3, 1994, at A1; Warren Brown, *GM to Reject Recall of 4.7 Million Trucks*, WP, April 30, 1993, at A1.

42. Kevin M. McDonald, *Is It Time to End Vehicle Safety Recalls*, Detroit News, August 16, 2006, at A15 (vehicles not repaired); Lisa Zagaroli & Jeff Plungis, *Repairs Favored Over Recalls*, Detroit News, March 4, 2002, at A5; Caroline E. Mayer, *Highway Safety Agency Faulted on Probes*, WP, January 10, 2002, at E2 (Inspector General Report).

43. Matthew L. Wald, *Agency Faults Safety Reports Filed by F.A.A.*, NYT, March 31, 1998, at A17 (infrequent follow-ups); Matthew L. Wald, *Safety Board Faults Airline and F.A.A. in ValuJet Crash*, NYT, August 20 1996, at A16 (ValuJet); Stephen J. Hedges, Richard Newman & Peter Cary, *What's Wrong with FAA*, U.S. News & World Report, June 26, 1995, at 28; Martin Tolchin, *Near Collisions of Aircraft Among Sins of Safety Crisis, Many Experts Say*, NYT, May 17, 1987, at A28 (Reagan budget cuts); *Report Calls U.S. Airline Inspections Inadequate*, NYT, June 7, 1987, at A27; Ralph Blumenthal, *System of Assuring Air Travel Faces Growing Strain, Experts Say*, NYT, March 23, 1986, at A1.

44. Jim Morris, *Waiting to Happen*, Mother Jones, July/August, 2006, at 47; *Airlines Outsource Repairs at Greater Rate*, WP, October 5, 2008, at A4 (2008 percentage); Marla Dickerson, *U.S. Airlines Flock to Foreign Repair Shops*, LAT, April 30, 2008, at A1; Jeff Bailey, *Aging Jet Fleets an Added Strain on U.S. Airlines*, NYT, April 12, 2008, at A1 (little oversight); Don Phillips, *Report Urges Tighter Oversight of Airline Repairs*, WP, July 11, 2003, at A8 (1999 percentage, incomplete quote).

45. Memorandum to Members of the Committee on Transportation and Infrastructure from Majority Oversight and Investigations Staff re: Critical Lapses in FAA Safety Oversight of Airlines: Abuses of Regulatory "Partnership Programs," dated April 1, 2008, at 1–2, 4, 14; Christopher Conkey & Andy Pasztor, *Criticism of FAA Stacks Up*, WSJ, March 20, 2008, at A10 (reliance on private inspectors); Matthew L. Wald, *F.A.A. Fines Southwest Air in Inspections*, NYT, March 7, 2008, at A1.

46. Government Accountability Office, Rail Safety: The Federal Railroad Administration is Taking Steps to Better Target Its Oversight, but Assessment of Results is Needed to Determine Impact 12–13, 15 (2007) (400 inspectors, settlements); Memorandum to Members of the Subcommittee on Railroad, Pipelines, and Hazardous Materials from Subcommittee on Railroad, Pipelines, and Hazardous Materials Staff re: Hearing on Rail Safety Legislation, dated May 4, 2007, at 8 (few inspections, few fines); Nurith Aizenman, *The Case for More Regulation: Lax Federal Trucking and*

Railroad Safety Oversight, Washington Monthly, October, 1997, at 16 (reliance on railroads); Walt Bogdanich, *For Railroads and the Safety Overseer, Close Ties,* NYT, November 7, 2004, at A1; Michael Weiskopf, *Railroad Regulatory Agency Hampered by Ineffective Inspectors, GAO Finds,* WP, November 9, 1989, at A21.

47. Government Accountability Office, Statistical Approach, 8; Cindy Skrzycki, *Critics Trying to Reengineer Bus, Truck Safety Office,* WP, May 21, 1999, at E1 (few inspections).

48. *Toyota's Recall and the Government's Response, Hearings Before the Senate Committee on Science and Transportation,* 111th Cong., 2d Sess. (2010) (testimony of Clarence M. Ditlow); Cindy Skrzycki, *Using Criminal Penalties as a Deterrent,* WP, October 10, 2000, at F1.

49. National Transportation Safety Board, Loss of Control on Approach, Colgan Air, Inc., Operating as Continental Connection Flight 3407, Bombardier DHC-*-400, N200WQ, February 12, 2009 x, 8–9, 11–14 (2010); Sholnn Freeman, *Panel on Fatal Crash Looks at Pilots' Pay, Commutes,* WP, May 14, 2009, at A2; Sholnn Freeman, *Panel Finds Pilots Broke Rules Before Fatal Crash,* WP, May 13, 2009, at A5; Matthew L. Wald, *Pilot in Fatal Crash Near Buffalo Did Not Reveal 2 Past Test Failures,* NYT, May 12, 2009, at A21.

50. Sholnn Freeman, *A Crowded Hub Away from Home,* WP, August 4, 2009, at A10 (half of flights), David M. Halbfinger, Matthew L. Wald & Christopher Drew, *A Commuter Pilot's Life: Exhausted, Hungry and Poorly Paid,* NYT, May 17, 2009, at A1; Andy Pasztor & Susan Carey, *Commuter Airlines: Questions of Safety,* WSJ, December 1, 2009, at A1 (high accident rates).

51. Matthew L. Wald & Christine Negroni, *Errors Cited in '09 Crash Could Persist, F.A.A. Says,* NYT, February 1, 2010, at A14 (FAA rules); Matthew L. Wald, *Small Lines are Target of New Rules for Pilots,* NYT, June 16, 2009, at 17; Andy Pasztor & Susan Carey, *Pilot Fatigue Spurs Calls for New Safeguards,* WSJ, September 12, 2008, at A1; Andy Pasztor & Christopher Conkey, *Safety Pushes Stall at Embattled FAA,* WSJ, June 26, 2008, at A1 (FAA proposal).

52. Keith Bradsher, High and Mighty 169 (2002) (SUV statistics); Government Accountability Office, *Federal Railroad Administration is Taking Steps,* 7 (derailment statistics); *NHTSA Data: Traffic Deaths at Lowest Levels: Industry Presses for Softer Senate Safety Bill,* 39 PSLR 1347 (2011) (highway deaths); Memorandum to Members of the Subcommittee, 7 (grade crossing statistics); National Highway Traffic Safety Administration, Traffic Safety Facts (2009), available at http://www-nrd.nhtsa.dot.gov/Pubs/811392.pdf, at 9 (truck statistics).

CHAPTER 13. FINANCIAL PROTECTION

1. 15 *Michie on Banks and Banking* §6 (M.J. Divine, et al. eds., 1999); Stephen Pizzo, Mary Fricker & Paul Muolo, Inside Job 21–22 (1991); National Commission on the Causes of the Financial and Economic Crisis in the United States, The Financial Crisis Inquiry Report 29 (2011); National Commission on Financial Institution Reform, Recovery and Enforcement, Origins and Causes of the S & L Debacle:

A Blueprint for Reform 17–19 (1993); Federal Reserve Board, 97th Annual Report 76 (2010); Office of the Comptroller of the Currency, Annual Report: Fiscal Year 2010 31 (2011); Office of Thrift Supervision, Annual Report 3 (2009).

2. Patricia A. McCoy, Andrey D. Pavlov & Susan M. Wachter, *Systemic Risk Through Securitization: The Result of Deregulation and Regulatory Failure*, 41 Conn. L. Rev. 1327, 1355–56 (2009); Congressional Oversight Panel, Special Report on Regulatory Reform 2 (January 2009); National Commission, Recovery and Enforcement, 20–23.

3. Simon Johnson & James Kwak, 13 Bankers 133–34 (2010).

4. Elizabeth Renuart & Kathleen Keest, Truth in Lending 2, 5, 660 (6th ed. 2007); Gong-Soog Hong & Ramona K.Z. Heck, *Credit Regulation*, in Regulation and Consumer Protection 343, 350–51 (Kenneth J. Meier & E. Thomas Garman, eds. 1995); Timothy J. Muris, *Statutory Powers*, in The Federal Trade Commission Since 1970 1, 16 (Kenneth W. Clarkson & Timothy J. Muris, eds. 1981); HUD-Treasury Task Force on Predatory Lending, Curbing Predatory Home Mortgage Lending 1–3 (2000).

5. Robert Kuttner, Everything for Sale 173 (1996); Pizzo, Fricker & Muolo, Inside Job, 24; Renuart & Keest, Truth in Lending, 5.

6. Depository Institutions Deregulation and Monetary Control Act of 1980, Pub. L. 96–221, 94 Stat. 132 (1980); Truth in Lending Simplification Act of 1980, Pub. L. 96–221, 94 Stat. 168 (1980); Renuart & Keest, Truth in Lending, 5–7; National Commission, Recovery and Enforcement, 34; Cathy Lesser Mansfield, *The Road to Subprime "HEL" Was Paved With Good Congressional Intentions: Usury Deregulation and the Subprime Home Equity Market*, 51 S. Car. L. Rev. 473, 493 (2000).

7. Lisa Keyfetz, *The Homeownership and Equity Protection Act of 1994: Extending Liability for Predatory Subprime Loans to Secondary Mortgage Market Participants*, 18 Loyola Consumer L. Rev. 151, 152–53 (2005).

8. Renuart & Keest, Truth in Lending, 660; National Commission, Recovery and Enforcement, 34; Mansfield, *Subprime HEL*, 493, 523.

9. Keyfetz, HOEPA, 152–53; Mansfield, *Subprime HEL*, 511–12, 520, 526–29, 532–35; Edmund Sanders, *Banks Moving Into Subprime Lending Arena*, LAT, May 13, 1999, at C1.

10. Johnson & Kwak, 13 Bankers, 76–77; National Commission, Financial Crisis Inquiry Report, 129; Kathleen C. Engel & Patricia A. McCoy, *Turning a Blind Eye: Wall Street Finance of Predatory Lending*, 75 Fordham L. Rev. 2040, 2041 (2007); Mansfield, *Subprime HEL*, 532; HUD-Treasury Task Force, Curbing, 2, 661.

11. Keyfetz, HOEPA, 160–61, 163; Renuart & Keest, Truth in Lending, 8, 661; National Commission, Financial Crisis Inquiry Report, 13–14, 90; HUD-Treasury Task Force, Curbing, 2–3; Ruth Simon & James R. Hagerty, *The Middle Men*, WSJ, July 5, 2007, at A1.

12. Mansfield, *Subprime HEL*, 526; General Accounting Office, Consumer Protection: Federal and State Agencies Face Challenges in Combating Predatory Lending 21 (2004).

13. Home Ownership and Equity Protection Act, Pub. L. 103–325, 108 Stat. 2190 (1994); Renuart & Keest, Truth in Lending, 659–62; Keyfetz, HOEPA, 174, 177–79 185; Mansfield, *Subprime HEL*, 542, 562–63.

14. Renuart & Keest, Truth in Lending, 8.

15. Truth in Lending Amendments of 1995, Pub. L. 104–29, 109 Stat. 161 (1995); Michael Hirsh, Capital Offense 145 (2010); Renuart & Keest, Truth in Lending, 9.

16. Linda Singer, *When States are Shut Out*, Legal Times, January 5, 2009, at 36.

17. Charles R. Morris, The Trillion Dollar Meltdown 63, 69 (2008) (statistics); National Commission, Financial Crisis Inquiry Report, 5, 41; Jo Becker, Sheryl Gay Stolberg & Stephen Labaton, *White House Philosophy Stoked Mortgage Bonfire*, NYT, December 21, 2008, at A1.

18. National Commission, Financial Crisis Inquiry Report, 18; Federal Deposit Insurance Corporation, Managing the Crisis: The FDIC and RTC Experience 10–13, 26, 37, 40 (1994); National Commission, Recovery and Enforcement, 32–33; Robert A. Bennett, *Wide Effect of Bank Changes*, NYT, December 8, 1992, at D1.

19. Kenneth B. Noble, *Wider Washington Role*, NYT, July 27, 1984, at A1; Robert A. Bennett, *Chilling Specter at Continental*, NYT, May 20, 1984, at C1; Raymond Bonner, *U.S. Rule on Bank Fees Draws Fire*, NYT, December 19, 1983, at D1; Nancy L. Ross, *Bank Regulators "Panting to Catch Up,"* WP, April 5, 1983, at A1.

20. Garn-St. Germain Depository Institutions Act of 1982, Pub. L. 97–320, 96 Stat. 1469 (1982); Pizzo, Fricker & Muolo, Inside Job, 25–26; National Commission, Recovery and Enforcement, 29–30 (85 percent), 34, 40.

21. Morris, Meltdown, 30; Pizzo, Fricker & Muolo, Inside Job, 24, 37, 46, 48; National Commission, Recovery and Enforcement, 45–48; James O'Shea, *The Savings Industry Saved Too Little*, Chicago Tribune, September 28, 1988, at C1 (brokered deposits); Rich Thomas, *Who's Killing the Thrifts?* Newsweek, November 10, 1986, at 51 (mortgage-backed securities); Tom Furlong, *Columbia S&L Thrives on Taking Risks*, LAT, October 20, 1985, at E1 (looting).

22. National Commission, Recovery and Enforcement, 55–57, 89; Timothy Curry & Lynn Shibut, *The Cost of the Savings and Loan Crisis: Truth and Consequences*, FDIC Banking Review, December, 2000, at 26 (700 S&Ls); *Edwin Gray on the S&L Crisis*, WP, October 9, 1988, at H9 (quoting Edwin Gray); Peter W. Bernstein, *The New Revolving Door*, Fortune, October 17, 1983, at 58.

23. Financial Institutions Reform, Recovery, and Enforcement Act of 1989, Pub. L. 101–73, 103 Stat. 183 (1989); National Commission, Recovery and Enforcement, 61; Daniel B. Gail & Joseph J. Norton, *A Decade's Journey from "Deregulation" to "Supervisory Reregulation": The Financial Institutions Reform, Recovery, and Enforcement Act of 1989*, 45 Business Lawyer 1103, 1105, 1108–1110 (1990); FDIC, Managing the Crisis, 10.

24. Douglas Jehl, *Bush Eases Regulations on Banking*, LAT, April 25, 1992, at D1; Rudolph A. Pyatt, Jr., *It's Time for Congress and Regulators to Review the S&L Rescue Law*, WP, July 5, 1990, at D2; Robert A. Rosenblatt & James Bates, *New Standards Peril 800 S&Ls*, LAT, November 7, 1989, at A1.

25. *Banking & Finance*, LAT, December 23, 1995, at D2 (OTS rescinding regulations); Robert A. Rosenblatt & David W. Myers, *Clinton Moves to Ease Way for Business Loans*, LAT, March 11, 1993, at D1.

26. Financial Services Modernization Act of 1999, Pub. L. 106–102, title V, 113 Stat. 1445 (1999); Johnson & Kwak, 13 Bankers, 133–34; Morris, Meltdown, 44; David C. John,

Gramm-Leach-Bliley Act (S. 900): A Major Step Toward Financial Deregulation, Heritage Foundation Backgrounder No. 1338, October 28, 1999; Robert A. Rosenblatt, *Congress, White House, Forge Bank Reform Deal*, LAT, October 23, 1999, at A1.

27. Becker, Stolberg & Labaton, *Mortgage Bonfire*; Binyamin Appelbaum & Ellen Nakashima, *Banking Regulator Played Advocate over Enforcer*, WP, November 23, 2008, at B1; Nicole Duran, *GAO Sides with OCC in Equity Ownership Dispute*, American Banker, September 19, 2001, at 4 (reduce reserves).

28. Morris, Meltdown, 44, 74; Engel & McCoy, *Blind Eye* 2048; National Commission, Financial Crisis Inquiry Report, at 8, 46; Robert O'Harrow Jr. & Brady Dennis, *Downgrades and Downfall*, WP, December 31, 2008, at A1.

29. Johnson & Kwak, 13 Bankers, 123–24; Morris, Meltdown, 39–40, 44; National Commission, Financial Crisis Inquiry Report, 43–44, 118–22; Engel & McCoy, *Blind Eye*, 2046–49; Thomas J. Fitzpatrick & Chris Sagers, *Faith-Based Financial Regulation: A Primer on Oversight of Credit Rating Agencies*, 61 Ad. L. Rev. 557, 575 (2009); Amadou N.R. Sy, The Systemic Regulation of Credit Rating Agencies and Rated Markets 15 (IMF Working Paper WP/09/129, 2009); Jill Drew, *Frenzy*, WP, December 16, 2008, at A 1.

30. Johnson & Kwak, 13 Bankers, 75, 81–82, 124–26, 137–38; Morris, Meltdown, 37, 41, 75; Engel & McCoy, *Blind Eye* 2063; National Commission, Financial Crisis Inquiry Report, 8, 50; Gretchen Morgenson, *Time to Unravel a Financial Knot*, NYT, January 25, 2009, at B1.

31. Morris, Meltdown, 44, 54, 112; Houman B. Shadab, *The Challenge of Hedge Fund Regulation*, Regulation, March 22, 2007, at 36; Nicholas Varchaver & Katie Benner, *The $55 Trillion Question*, Fortune, October 13, 2008, at 134.

32. Hirsh, Capital Offense, 176; Wendy L. Gramm & Gerald D. Gay, *Leading a Regulatory Agency*, Regulation, Winter 1994, at 64; Jeff Gerth & Richard A. Oppel, Jr., *Senate Bill Showed Complexities of Power Couple's Ties to Enron*, NYT, January 18, 2002, at C1; Jerry Knight, *Gramm Moves to Keep "Swaps" Unregulated*, WP, January 13, 1993, at F1.

33. Hirsh, Capital Offense, 1–13; Johnson & Kwak, 13 Bankers, 7–9; National Commission, Financial Crisis Inquiry Report, at 47.

34. Commodities Futures Modernization Act of 2000, Pub. L. 106-554-Appendix E, 114 Stat. 2763A-365 (2000); Hirsh, Capital Offense 17–18; Morris, Meltdown, 49, 53; National Commission, Financial Crisis Inquiry Report, 48.

35. Jeff Madrick, *How We Were Ruined & What We Can Do*, N.Y. Rev. of Books, February 12, 2009, at 15.

36. Renuart & Keest, Truth in Lending, 661; GAO Mortgage Report, 31, Figure 1; Mansfield, *Subprime HEL*, 476; Edmund L. Andrews, *Fed and Regulators Shrugged as Subprime Crisis Spread*, NYT, December 18, 2007, A1.

37. Engel & McCoy, *Blind Eye*, 2043–44, 2059; Keyfetz, HOEPA, 155–59; Mansfield, *Subprime HEL*, 556–57; National Commission, Financial Crisis Inquiry Report, 6; HUD-Treasury Task Force, Curbing, 2; GAO Mortgage Report, 19; Louise Story, *Home Equity Frenzy Was a Bank Ad Come True*, NYT, August 15, 2008, at A1; Michelle

Singletary, *Some Mortgage Originators Skipped State Licensing,* WP, September 9, 2007, at F1.

38. National Commission, Financial Crisis Inquiry Report, 7; Congressional Oversight Panel, Special Report, 3; GAO Mortgage Report, 88; Ronald D. Utt, The Subprime Mortgage Market Collapse, A Primer on the Cause and Possible Solutions, Heritage Foundation Backgrounder No. 2127, April 22, 2008 (quote).

39. Cuomo v. Clearing House Association, 129 S.Ct. 2710 (2009) (preemption); Watters v. Wachovia Bank, 550 U.S. 1 (2007) (preemption); Hirsh, Capital Offense, 145; National Commission, Financial Crisis Inquiry Report, xxiii, 10–13, 76; Daniel Immergluck, *Private Risk, Public Risk: Public Policy, Market Development, and the Mortgage Crisis,* 36 Fordham Urban L. J. 447, 484–85 (2009); Binyamin Appelbaum, *As Subprime Lending Crisis Unfolded, Watchdog Fed Didn't Bother Barking,* WP, September 27, 2009, at A1.

40. Engel & McCoy, *Blind Eye* 2043, 2067, 2049; National Commission, Financial Crisis Inquiry Report, 4, 89, 91–92; Congressional Oversight Panel, Special Report, 9, 18; Benton Ives, *Risk and Regulation,* Cong. Q. Weekly, March 17, 2008, at 678; Rick Brooks & Constance Mitchell Ford, *The United States of Sub Prime,* WSJ, October 11, 2007, at A1 ($1.5 trillion).

41. Federal Reserve System, Bank Holding Companies and Change in Bank Control, 66 Fed. Reg. 8466 (2001); Joseph E. Stiglitz, Freefall 270 (2010); National Commission, Financial Crisis Inquiry Report, 54; McCoy, Pavlov & Wachter, *Systemic Risk,* 1351–57; Binyamin Appelbaum, *By Switching Their Charters, Banks Skirt Supervision,* WP, January 22, 2009, at A1; Applebaum & Nakashima, *Banking Regulator Played Advocate.*

42. Morris, Meltdown, 37–38, 41–42, 58; Joe Nocera, *Risk Mismanagement,* NYT Magazine, January 4, 2009, at 24; Drew, *Frenzy.*

43. Johnson & Kwak, 13 Bankers, 81, 108, 138; Morris, Meltdown, 60, 69, 74; Engel & McCoy, *Blind Eye,* 2065; Immergluck, *Private Risk,* 462; Congressional Oversight Panel, Special Report, 4; Schwartz & Creswell, *What Created This Monster?* (Buffet quote).

44. Securities and Exchange Commission, Alternative Net Capital Requirements for Broker-Dealers That Are Part of Consolidated Supervised Entities; Final Rule, 69 Fed. Red. 34,428 (2004); McCoy, Pavlov & Wachter, *Systemic Risk,* 1358–60; Joseph Stigletz, *Capitalist Fools,* Vanity Fair, January, 2009, at 50; Stephen Labaton, *Agency's '04 Rule Let Banks Pile up New Debt,* NYT, October 3, 2008, at A1.

45. Morris, Meltdown, 78; Fitzpatrick & Sagers, *Faith-Based Regulation,* 559, 568–69, 573, 586–88; National Commission, Financial Crisis Inquiry Report, 210; Roger Lowenstein, *Triple-A Failure,* NYT Magazine, April 27, 2008, at 10.

46. Credit Rating Agency Reform Act of 2006, Pub. L. 109–291, 120 Stat. 1329 (2006); Fitzpatrick & Sagers, *Faith-Based Regulation,* 562, 595–96; Sy, Systematic Regulation, 6–7; David Segal, *Debt Raters Avoid Overhaul After Crisis,* NYT, December 8, 2009, at A1.

47. Morris, Meltdown, 60–61; Congressional Oversight Panel, Special Report, 14; Varchaver & Benner, *$55 Trillion Question* (no disclosure requirement); Gretchen

Morgenson, *Behind Insurer's Crisis, Blind Eye to a Web of Risk*, NYT, September 28, 2008, at A1.

48. Stiglitz, Freefall, 46; Jo Becker & Gretchen Morgenson, *Member and Overseer of Finance Club*, NYT, April 27, 2009, at A1; Robert O'Harrow & Jeff Gerth, *As Crisis Loomed, Geithner Pressed But Fell Short*, WP, April 3, 2009, at A1.

49. 2004 GAO Mortgage Report, 38.

50. Anitha Reddy, *Lending Case to Cost Citigroup $215 Million*, WP, September 20, 2002, at F1; Diana B. Henriques, *A Home Lender in a Settlement for $60 Million*, NYT, March 22, 2002, at A1.

51. William Greider, *How Wall Street Crooks Get Out of Jail Free*, Nation, March 23, 2011, at 11; Carrie Johnson, *Prosecutors Expected to Spare Wall St. Firms*, WP, October 3, 2008, at D1; Carrie Johnson, *A Labyrinthine Path to Justice*, WP, February 14, 2008, at D1; Carrie Johnson, *Mortgage Probes Face Big Hurdles*, WP, December 27, 2007, at D1.

52. Mara Der Hovanesian, *Nightmare Mortgages*, Business Week, September 11, 2006, at 70.

53. Mansfield, *Subprime "HEL,"* 555; Charles Duhigg, *Tapping Into Homes Can Be Pitfall for the Elderly*, NYT, March 2, 2008, at A1; Floyd Norris, *In Parts of U.S., Foreclosures Top Sales*, NYT, March 1, 2008, at C1; Nelson D. Schwartz, *Can the Mortgage Crisis Swallow a Town?* NYT, September 2, 2007, at C1.

54. Richard A. Posner, A Failure of Capitalism 113 (2009); Hirsh, Capital Offense, 266 (quoting Christine Romer, Chairperson, Council of Economic Advisors).

55. Johnson & Kwak, 13 Bankers, 10 (4 percent, trillion dollar paper loss); Morris, Meltdown, 155; Aaron Luccheti & Peter Lattman, *Wall Street Shudders as Lawmakers Take Aim at the Industry's Pay System*, WSJ, March 19, 2009, at A1 (Goldman Sachs); Michael J. de la Merced & Sharon Otterman, *A.I.G. Takes Its Session in Hot Seat*, NYT, October 8, 2008, at A1.

56. Congressional Oversight Panel, Special Report, 2; Anthony Faiola, Ellen Nakashima & Jill Drew, *What Went Wrong*, WP, October 15, 2008, at A1 (Born warning); Andrews, *Fed and Regulators Shrugged* (Bair Warning).

57. Johnson & Kwak, 13 Bankers, 100; William Greider, Come Home, America 184 (2009).

58. Johnson & Kwak, 13 Bankers, 13, 180; Stiglitz, Freefall, 296; Bernie Becker & Ben White, *Lehman's Chief Defends His Actions as Prudent for the Time*, NYT, October 7, 2008, at B1 (Lehman CEO blames press); Steven Perlstein, *The Words Left Unspoken in the Bailout Debate*, WP, September 24, 2008, at D.

CHAPTER 14. CONSUMER PROTECTION

1. Consumer Product Safety Act of 1972, Pub. L. 92–573, 86 Stat. 1207 (1972).

2. 15 U.S.C. §§ 1191–1204; 1261–62, 1278(a)-(c), 1471–76.

3. Teresa M. Schwartz, *The Consumer Product Safety Commission: A Flawed Product of the Consumer Decade*, 51 Geo. Wash. L. Rev. 32, 43–44 (1982); *Playing It Safe*, Trial,

October 1, 1998, at 20 (baby walker standard); Terri Shaw, *New Safety Law for Garage Doors*, WP, December 31, 1992, at T5.

4. Magnuson-Moss Warranty—Federal Trade Commission Improvement Act of 1975, Pub. L. 93–637, 88 Stat. 2183 (1975); Michael Pertschuk, Revolt Against Regulation 24–25 (1982); Michael J. Wisdom, *Comment, An Empirical Study of the Magnuson-Moss Warranty Act*, 31 Stan. L. Rev. 1117, 1119–21 (1979).

5. Tanzina Vega, *Agency Seeks to Tighten Rules for "Green" Labeling*, NYT, October 7, 2010, at 4.

6. Consumers Union of U.S., Inc. v. FTC, 801 F.2d 417 (D.C. Cir. 1986) (used cars); Harry and Bryant Co. v. FTC, 726 F.2d 993 (4th Cir. 1984) (funeral homes); Katherine Gibbs School v. FTC, 612 F.2d 658 (2d Cir. 1979) (vocational schools); Thomas O. McGarity, *Some Thoughts on "Deossifying" the Rulemaking Process*, 41 Duke L. J. 1385, 1389–90, n. 22 (1992).

7. Pertschuk, Revolt, 53–54; Susan J. Tolchin & Martin Tolchin, Dismantling America 152 (1983).

8. Association of National Advertisers, Inc. v. FTC, 627 F.2d 1151, 1155, n.1 (D.C. Cir. 1979); Federal Trade Commission, Children's Advertising, 43 Fed. Reg. 17,967 (1978); Pertschuk, Revolt, 55 (sleeping giant quote), 71, 93; Tolchin & Tolchin, Dismantling America, 154–55, 160, 166; Linda E. Demkovich, *Pulling the Sweet Tooth of Children's T.V. Advertising*, 10 Nat. J. 24 (1978), Editorial, *The FTC as National Nanny*, WP, March 1, 1978, at A22.

9. Pertschuk, Revolt, 72; David Vogel, Fluctuating Fortunes 167 (1989); Tolchin & Tolchin, Dismantling America, 153; James W. Singer, *The Federal Trade Commission - Business's Government Enemy No. 1*, 11 Nat. J. 1676 (1979); Larry Kramer, *Trying to Work in the Trenches*, WP, November 18, 1979, at D7; Ward Sinclair, *A Corporate Army Wades Into Battle to Curb the FTC*, WP, June 24, 1979, at A3.

10. Federal Trade Commission Improvement Act of 1980, Pub. L. 96–254, 94 Stat. 374 (1980); Tolchin & Tolchin, Dismantling America, 164; Marc Allen Eisner, Antitrust and the Triumph of Economics 178 (1991).

11. Pertschuk, Revolt, 73, 115; James W. Singer, *Out Like a Lamb*, 12 Nat. J. 867 (1980); Peter Behr, *FTC Surfacing After Business' Attack*, WP, March 23, 1980, at F1; Larry Kramer, *Proposed Curbs on Funeral Industry Cut Back*, WP, March 10, 1979, at A10.

12. James C. Miller III, The Economist as Reformer 14 (1989); Michael Wines, *Regulation Writing in Washington—Making Days Stretch into Years*, 14 Nat. J. 1937 (1982); Caroline E. Mayer, *FTC's Critic Within*, WP, July 18, 1982, at L1 (Murris quote).

13. Miller, Reformer, 4; Timothy J. Muris, *Rules Without Reason: The Case of the FTC*, Regulation, September/October, 1982, at 20, 22–23; Barry Meier, *New Teeth at the F.T.C. (Fangs to Some)*, NYT, April 25, 1996, at D1; Jesus Sanchez, *FTC Moves to Overturn Eye-Care Industry Curbs*, LAT, February 11, 1988, at A1; *FTC Won't Require Dealers to Offer 30-Day Trial Period*, LAT, September 17, 1985, at D2; Stuart Auerbach, *FTC Rejects Regulation of Food Claims*, WP, December 18, 1982, at F1; Mayer, *Critic Within*; Merrill Brown, *FTC Retreats on Over-Counter Drug Ads*, WP, February 12, 1981, at A1.

14. John R. Wilke, _FTC Chairman Majoras to Resign_, WSJ, February 27, 2008, at A1; Jonathan Krim & Caroline E. Mayer, _FTC Chairman Muris Plans to Step Down_, WP, May 12, 2004, at E1; John R. Wilke, _Ardent Reaganite Plays a New Tune as Head of FTC_, WSJ, April 4, 2003, at A1; Caroline E. Mayer, _FTC Nominee Muris Commits to Mission, But Not to Legislation_, WP, May 17, 2001, at E3 (quote).

15. Southland Mower Co. v. CPSC, 619 F.2d 499 (5th Cir. 1980) (lawnmower standard); Aqua Slide 'N' Dive Corp. v. CPSC, 569 F. 2d 831 (5th Cir. 1978) (judicial roadblock); Schwartz, _CPSC_, 47 (200 petitions), 53, 93–94; _Consumer Product Safety Commission Oversight, Hearing before the Senate Committee on Government Operations_, 93d Cong., 2d Sess. (1974) (Testimony of Richard O. Simpson, Chairman, CPSC); John D. Morris, _Consumer Panel Charges Politics_, NYT, December 19, 1973, at 46.

16. Consumer Product Safety Commission Improvement Act of 1976, Pub. L. 94–284, 90 Stat. 503 (1976) § 7; _Consumer Product Safety Commission Oversight, Hearings Before the Senate Committee on Commerce_, 94th Cong., 1st Sess. (1975) (industry criticism).

17. Bill Curry, _Product Safety Commission: An Agency Tied Up in Knots_, WP, May 16, 1977, at A1; Larry Kramer, _Saw Industry, CPSC Move On Standards_, WP, December 9, 1977, at D5 (voluntary standards).

18. Schwartz, _CPSC_, 54; David T. McLaughlin, _Setting Standards for Product Safety: It's Time for a New Approach_, 10 Nat. J. 700 (1978) (industry complaints); Ward Sinclair, _Regulation Bogus Issue, CPSC Chairman Claims_, WP, March 14, 1979, at D10; Larry Kramer, _Consumer Movement Seen as 'Going Too Far, Too Fast,'_ WP, May 31, 1978, at E3 (Chamber of Commerce); Larry Kramer, _King Becomes First Democrat to Head CPSC_, WP, June 30, 1978, at F3.

19. Carolyn E. Mayer, _Lobbyists Fumble Try to Transform CPSC_, WP, November 5, 1981, at D12; _Stockman Moves to Kill Consumer Safety Panel_, NYT, May 9, 1981, at A9.

20. Consumer Product Safety Amendments of 1981, Pub. L. 97–35, 95 Stat. 703 (1981); Elliott Klayman, _Comment, Standard Setting Under the Consumer Product Safety Amendments of 1981—A Shift in Regulatory Philosophy_, 51 Geo. Wash. L. Rev. 96, 101–02, 104, n. 39 (1982); Teresa M. Schwartz, _The Role of Federal Safety Regulations in Products Liability Actions_, 41 Vand. L. Rev. 1121, 1159 (1988) (regulatory output, data collection).

21. Joan Claybrook, Retreat from Safety 62 (1984) (government experience); Molly Sinclair, _Safety Hinges Ordered by CPSC on Toy Chests_, WP, February 10, 1983, at B4; Molly Sinclair, _CPSC Facing Renewed Attack, Waxman Says_, WP, January 22, 1983, at D10; Molly Sinclair, _CPSC Votes Stiff Rule on Wood Stoves_, WP, January 20, 1983, at E4; Stuart Auerbach, _Conservative Study Faults Reagan Deregulation Effort_, WP, January 16, 1983, at F1; Michael DeCourcy Hinds, _Chief of Consumer Safety Presses Independence_, NYT, May 13, 1982, at B16.

22. Margaret E. Kriz, _Leashed Watchdog_, 19 Nat. J. 2663 (1987); Bill McAllister, _Terrence M. Scanlon: Ending the "Heavy-Handed" Approach to Product Safety_, WP, March 30, 1987, at A9; Irvin Molotsky, _A Case of Memorandums at 19 Paces_, NYT, March 30, 1985, at A8; Sari Horwitz, _Safety Agency Reaches a Turning Point_, WP, December 9, 1984, at F1.

23. Frank Donner & James Ledbetter, *Deregulation by Sleaze*, 246 Nation 163 (February 6, 1988) (no standards); Kriz, *Leashed Watchdog; Chairman Leaving Consumer Agency*, NYT, November 21, 1988, at A16; Bob Baker, *Congress Passes Legislation Banning the Sale of Dangerous Lawn Dart*, LAT, October 22, 1988, at A30.

24. Michael deCourcy Hinds, *Troubles of a Safety Agency*, NYT, March 18, 1989, at A52; Dale Russakoff, *The Little Agency that Can't*, WP, February 2, 1989, at A23 (quote).

25. Kirk Victor, *Clinton and Consumers*, 26 Nat. J. 145 (1994) (budget cut); Darlene Superville, *Consumer Chief Jump-Starts Agency*, LAT, May 2, 1995, at D6; Cindy Skrzycki, *OSHA Marches Out Its "Truth" Team to Take On Detractors*, WP, March 3, 1995, at F1 (horror stories).

26. *CPSC Lack of Quorum, "Brain Drain" Draws Attention of House Consumer Panel Leaders*, 35 BNA PLSR 169 (2007); Elizabeth Williams, *Industries Paid for Top Regulators' Travel*, WP, November 2, 2007, at A1; Larry Liebert, *Chairman of Safety Commission Heads to Law Firm*, WP, July 17, 2005, at A13; Jane Hadley, *Safety Commission May See a Big Change at the Top*, Seattle Post-Intelligencer, November 1, 2001, at A5.

27. Michael J. Gidding & Andrea S. Paterson, *Reliance on Voluntary Standards and the Consumer Product Safety Commission: A Concept that May Have Outlived Its Time (If it Ever Had One to Begin With)*, 34 BNA PSLR 1212 (2006); *CPSC Votes to Reform, Streamline In-House Voluntary Standards Practices*, 34 BNA PSLR 687 (2006) (statistics); Jane Hadley, *Voluntary Standards Rule the Industry*, Seattle Post-Intelligencer, October 25, 2001, at A14.

28. Pamela Gilbert, *Consumer Product Safety Commission: Safety First*, in Change For America: A Progressive Blueprint for the 44th President (Center for American Progress, 2008) (budget); Annys Shin, *CPSC Rebuilds After Years of Decay*, WP, April 5, 2008, at D1; Williams, *Industries Paid*; Stephen Labaton, *Senate Panel Approves Beefing Up Safety Agency*, NYT, October 31, 2007, at C2.

29. Government Accountability Office, Consumer Safety: Better Information and Planning Would Strengthen CPSC's Oversight of Imported Products (2009), at 7; Public Citizen, Santa's Sweatshop: "Made in D.C." With Bad Trade Policy (December 19, 2007), at 2–4; Jane Hadley, *Safety Agency Lacks Teeth, Some Say*, Seattle Post-Intelligencer, October 24, 2001, at 14.

30. Marion Nestle, Food Politics 186, 190 (2002) (educational books); Federal Trade Commission, Marketing Food to Children and Adolescents: A Report to Congress ES 4 (2008); Institute of Medicine, Food Marketing to Children and Youth 2–4, 8, 21–22 (2005); Cynthia Odgen & Margaret Carroll, Prevalence of Obesity Among Children and Adolescents: United States, Trends 1963–1965 Through 2007–2008 (Centers for Disease Control 2009) (obesity rates); Adam Benforado, Jon Hanson & David Yosifon, *Broken Scales: Obesity and Justice in America*, 53 Emory L. J. 1645, 1701 (2004) (citing studies); Susan Linn & Josh Golin, *Beyond Commercials: How Food Marketers Target Children*, 39 Loyola at Los Angeles L. Rev. 13, 14–16 (2006); Jennifer L. Pomeranz, et al., *Innovative Legal Approaches to Address Obesity*, 87 Milbank Quarterly 185, 189 (2009); Committee on Communications, American Academy of Pediatrics, *Children, Adolescents, and Advertising*, 118 Pediatrics 2563, 2563–64 (2006).

31. Kelly D. Brownell & Kenneth E. Warner, *The Perils of Ignoring History: Big Tobacco Played Dirty and Millions Died. How Similar is Big Food?* 87 Milbank Quarterly 259, 265, 277 (2009); Todd G. Buchholz, *Burgers, Fries, and Lawyers*, Policy Review, February, 2004, at 45 (conservative critique); Ronald Bailey, *Time for Tubby Bye Bye?* Reason.com, June 11, 2003, available at http://reason.com/archives/2003/06/11/time-for-tubby-bye-bye (Epstein quote).

32. Central Hudson Gas & Electric Corp. v. Public Services Commission of New York, 447 U.S. 557 (1980); Institute of Medicine, Food Marketing, 31; Benforado, Hanson & Yosifon, *Obesity and Justice*, 1770–71; Pomeranz, et al., Innovative Legal Approaches, 188; Sarah Taylor Roller, Theodore Voorhees, Jr. & Ashley K. Lunkenheimer, *Obesity, Food Marketing and Consumer Litigation: Threat or Opportunity*, 61 Food & Drug L. J. 419, 424 (2006); Susan Levine & Lori Aratani, *Inertia at the Top*, WP, May 19, 2008, at A1.

33. John Markoff, *Guidelines Don't End Debate on Internet Privacy*, NYT, December 18, 1997, at A24; David Segal, *FTC Backs Industry's Internet Privacy Rules*, WP, December 18, 1997, at E2.

34. Edmund Sanders, *FTC to Drop Push for More Privacy Laws*, LAT, October 2, 2001, at C1; John Schwartz, *Government is Wary of Tackling Online Privacy*, NYT, September 6, 2001, at C1 (AEI study); Stephen Labaton, *White House and Agency Split on Internet Privacy*, NYT, May 23, 2000, at C1 (Clinton position); Jeri Clausing, *Fate Unclear for F.T.C.'s Privacy Push*, NYT, May 22, 2000, at C1 (lobbying effort).

35. Annys Shin, *Fighting for Safety*, WP, January 26, 2008, at D1; *Long Delay in Issuing, Upholstered Furniture Standard Cited as Waste of Taxpayers' Money*, 34 BNA PSLR 856 (2006); Larry Kramer, *Tougher Fire Rules Sought on Furniture*, WP, November 21, 1978, at D7 ($10 per unit).

36. Consumer Product Safety Commission, Standard for the Flammability of Residential Upholstered Furniture, Proposed Rule, 73 Fed. Reg. 11,702 (2008); Directorate for Engineering Sciences, CPSC, Briefing Package, Standard for the Flammability of Clothing Textiles, ANPR to Amend and Update (2002).

37. Government Accountability Office, Better Information, 8, 12, 23–24, 27–28; Public Citizen, Santa's Sweatshop; *Senators Quiz CPSC's Nord on Toy Safety, Efforts With China, Agency Staffing Goals*, 36 BNA PSLR 452 (2008); Eric Lipton, *Safety Agency Faces Scrutiny Amid Changes*, NYT, September 2, 2007, at A1.

38. *Consumer Agency Unveils Plan to Monitor, Bar Entry of Unsafe Products at U.S. Ports*, 36 BNA PSLR 245 (2008); *CRS Report Cites Economic Implications of Chinese Goods' Safety, Quality Concerns*, 36 BNA PSLR 69 (2008); *CPSC Announces Recalls of Thousands More Toys Because of Lead Paint Hazards*, 35 BNA PSLR 972 (2007).

39. CPSC, *Chinese Agency Announce Agreement to Stop Use of Lead Paint in Children's Toys*, 35 BNA PSLR 970 (2007); *Nord Tells Senate Panel CPSC Taking Four-Pronged Approach on Import Safety*, 35 BNA PSLR 682 (2007); David Barboza, *China Suspends Exports from 750 Toy Makers*, NYT, November 2, 2007, at C3; Martha Mendoza, *Did Government Hide Lunch-Box Lead Levels?* Seattle Times, February 19, 2007, at D5.

40. Paul H. Rubin, *Why Regulate Consumer Safety?* Regulation, Fall, 1991, at 58, 59; *Playing it Safe*, 20 (quoting Commissioner Ann Brown); Julie Shop, *The New, Improved*

CPSC, Trial, September 1, 1994, at 22; *Protecting Consumers the Reagan Way*, U.S. News & World Report, August 8, 1983, at 50; Lipton, *Safety Agency Faces Scrutiny*; *Stuffed Birds are Recalled*, WP, April 17, 1983, at B5.

41. *CPSC Appropriations, Hearings Before the Subcommittee on Financial Services and General Government of the Senate Committee on Appropriations*, 110th Cong., 1st Sess (2007) (Testimony of Nancy A. Nord, Chairwoman, CPSC, Testimony of Lisa Madigan, Attorney General, Illinois); Annys Shin, *When Recalls Return*, WP, September 26, 2007, at D1; Hadley, *Safety Agency Lacks Teeth*.

42. Athione Industries, Inc. v. CPSC, 707 F.2d 1485 (D.C. Cir. 1983) (setback); Claybrook, Retreat, 60 (statistics); Bill McAllister, *CPSC Takes Cautious Stance on Voluntary Safety Standards*, WP, March 26, 1987, at E3 (cold shoulder).

43. Caroline E. Mayer, *Unsafe Products Reaching Retail Shelves, Consumer Reports Say*, WP, October 4, 2004, at E1; Barry Meier, *All-Terrain Vehicles: Still a Safety Hazard*, NYT, December 30, 1989, at A50; *Survey Says ATV Dealers Violating Pact*, LAT, December 6, 1989, at D4.

44. *Report of the American Bar Association Section of Antitrust Law Special Committee to Study the Role of the Federal Trade Commission*, 58 Antitrust L. J. 53, 65 (1989) (enforcement declined); Michael Wines, *Miller's Directive to the FTC—Quit Acting Like a "Consumer Cop,"* 13 Nat. J. 2149 (1981); Michael deCourcy Hinds, *The Rational Consumer May Be Just a Deregulator's Dream*, NYT, November 1, 1981, at D8.

45. Cindy Skrzycki, *Slowing the Flow of Federal Rules*, WP, February 18, 1996, at A1; Alex Pham, *It's Not Easy Being Green: FTC Issues Some Guidelines*, WP, July 29, 1992, at G3; Michael Specter, *Making Sense of Labeling on Products*, NYT, December 16, 1991, at B1.

46. Michael J. Sniffen, *Federal Probe of Telemarketing Fraud Nabs Nearly 1000*, WP, December 18, 1998, at A18; *66 Firms Accused of Telemarketing Fraud*, LAT, August 12, 1998, at A3; Jeff Leeds, *Telemarketing Probe Nets $35,000 Settlement, Little Else*, LAT, April 5, 1998, at B1.

47. Jennifer C. Kerr, *FTC, 6 Firms Settle Do Not Call Charges*, WP, November 8, 2007, at D2; *DirectTV Fined for Sales Calls*, NYT, December 14, 2005, at C2; *U.S. Accuses 8 Firms of Porn Spam*, LAT, July 21, 2005, at C10; *U.S. Making Arrests in Spam, Fraud Sweep*, LAT, August 26, 2004, at C9.

48. *CPSC Appropriations Hearings* (Testimony of Nancy A. Cowles, Kids in Danger, Lisa Madigan, Attorney General, Illinois, Kyran Quinlan, American Academy of Pediatrics); Patricia Callahan, *Inside the Botched Recall of a Dangerous Toy*, Chicago Tribune, May 7, 2007, at A1.

49. Marla Felcher, *You're Not the Regulator of Me: How the Bush Administration Made America Safe for Dangerous Toys*, Mother Jones, November/December, 2007, at 30 (statistics); OMB Watch, Product Safety Regulator Hobbled by Decades of Negligence, February 5, 2008, available at http://www.ombwatch.org/node/3599 (injury rates).

50. Annys Shin, *Recall of Toy With Dangerous Chemical Prompts Support for Mandatory Testing*, WP, November 9, 2007, at D1.

51. Christopher Conkey, *Rise in ATV-Accident Deaths Intensifies Debate Over Safety*, WSJ, February 15, 2008, at A12.

52. Benforado, Hanson & Yosifon, *Broken Scales*; William H. Dietz, Donald E. Menken, Alicia S. Hunter, *Public Health Law and the Prevention and Control of Obesity*, 87 Milbank Quarterly 215, 216, 220 (2009); Karen Weisse, *Remedies for Internet Fraud: Consumers Need All the Help They Can Get*, 14 Loyola Consumer L. Rev. 205 (2002); Frances E. Zollers, Peter Shears & Sandra N. Hurd, *Fighting Internet Fraud: Old Scams, Old Laws, New Context*, 20 Temple Envtl. L. & Tech. J. 169 (2002); Federal Trade Commission, Marketing Food to Children and Adolescents: A Report to Congress ES-2 (2008); Institute of Medicine, Food Marketing to Children and Youth 1, 4, 18 (2005).

CHAPTER 15. CIVIL JUSTICE

1. Michael D. Axline, *The Limits of Statutory Law and the Wisdom of Common Law*, 18 Env. L. Rept. 10,268 (2008); Anthony J. Sebok, *Dispatches from the Tort Wars*, 85 Tex. L. Rev. 1465, 1512 (2007); Jon S. Vernick, et al., *Role of Litigation in Preventing Product-Related Injuries*, 25 Epidemiol. Rev. 90 (2003).

2. Restatement (Second) of Torts § 402A; Mark A. Geistfeld, Principles of Products Liability 10–19, 31–32 (2006); Robert L. Rabin, Perspectives on Tort Law 68 (2d Ed. 1983); John P. Frank, *The American Law Institute, 1923–1998*, 26 Hofstra L. Rev. 615, 625 (1998); Report of the National Commission on State Workmen's Compensation Laws (1972).

3. Charles A. Wright, Arthur R. Miller & Mary Kay Kane, Federal Practice & Procedure (2005) §§ 1752, 1756, 1805; Deborah R. Hensler, et al., Class Action Dilemmas 105 (2000); Edward F. Sherman, *Consumer Class Actions: Who are the Real Winners?* 56 Maine L. Rev. 223, 225–26 (2004).

4. Carl T. Bogus, Why Lawsuits Are Good for America 34 (2001); Thomas F. Burke, Lawyers, Lawsuits, and Legal Rights 6 (2002); William Haltom & Michael McCann, Distorting the Law 38 (2004); F. Patrick Hubbard, *The Nature and Impact of the "Tort Reform" Movement*, 35 Hofstra L. Rev. 437, 438 (2006).

5. Valerie P. Hans, Business on Trial 15 (2000); Stephen Daniels & Joanne Martin, *Texas Plaintiffs' Practice in the Age of Tort Reform: Survival of the Fittest - It's Even More True Now*, 51 N.Y.L. School L. Rev. 285, 289, 294–95 (2007); Haltom & McCann, Distorting, 151–53; Hubbard, *Nature and Impact*, 472, 524–25.

6. Burke, Lawyers, 2–3; Haltom & McCann, Distorting, 62–63 (analysis of tort tales); Stephanie Mencimer, Blocking the Courthouse Door 11–12 (2006); Mark Galanter, *Real World Torts: An Antidote to Anecdote*, 55 Md. L. Rev. 1093, 1098 (1996).

7. Except where otherwise noted, the description of the Liebeck case is taken from the following sources: Haltom & McCann, Distorting, 183–96; Mencimer, Courthouse Door, 18–21.

8. Hans, Business on Trial, 77; Haltom & McCann, Distorting, 19–20; Sebok, *Dispatches*, 1504.

9. Burke, Lawyers, 2; Bogus, Lawsuits, 4–5; Haltom & McCann, Distorting, 50, 63–64; Max Boot, Out of Order: Arrogance, Corruption and Incompetence on the Bench (1998); Phillip K. Howard, The Death of Common Sense (1996).

10. Peter W. Huber, Liability 16, 54, 182–85 (1988); Deborah J. LaFetra, *Freedom, Responsibility, and Risk: Fundamental Principles Supporting Tort Reform*, 36 Ind. L. Rev. 645, 645–46, 659 (2003).

11. Huber, Liability, 182–85; Richard A. Epstein, *Products Liability As An Insurance Market*, 14 J. Legal Studies 645, 653 (1985); LaFetra, *Freedom*, 669; Martha T. McCluskey, *Efficiency and Social Citizenship: Challenging the Neo-Liberal Attack on the Welfare State*, 78 Ind. L. J. 783, 807 (2003) (insurance industry origins).

12. Robert S. Peck & John Vail, *Blame It On The Bee Gees: The Attack on Trial Lawyers and Civil Justice*, 51 N.Y.L. School L. Rev. 323, 328 (2007) (describing attacks).

13. Mencimer, Courthouse Door, 113 (describing attacks); Michael L. Rustad & Thomas H. Koenig, *Taming the Tort Monster: The American Civil Justice System as a Battleground of Social Theory*, 68 Brooklyn L. Rev. 1, 2, 4, 50 (2002) (describing attacks).

14. Haltom & McCann, Distorting, 56 (describing attacks); Mark Galanter, *Predators and Parasites: Lawyer-Bashing and Civil Justice*, 28 Ga. L. Rev. 633, 647–48 (1994) (describing attacks).

15. Richard A. Epstein, Overdose 196 (2006); Peter Huber, *Safety and the Second Best: The Hazards of Public Risk Management in the Courts*, 85 Colum. L. Rev. 277, 285 (1985); Stephen D. Sugarman, *Taking Advantage of the Torts Crisis*, 48 Ohio St. L. J. 329, 338 (1987) (describing attacks).

16. Burke, Lawyers, 3; Haltom & McCann, Distorting, 55; Hans, Business on Trial, 52–53; Rustad & Koenig, Taming, 4, 90.

17. Burke, Lawyers, 25 (few lawsuits); Haltom & McCann, Distorting, 83 (few lawsuits); Sebok, *Dispatches*, 1489–90, 1513 (same compensation).

18. Hans, Business on Trial, 23, 58, 175–76; Steven Daniels & Joanne Martin, *Myth and Reality in Punitive Damages*, 75 Minn. L. Rev. 1 (1990); Theodore Eisenberg, *Damage Awards in Perspective: Behind the Headline-Grabbing Awards in Exxon Valdez and Engle*, 36 Wake Forest L. Rev. 1129, 1130–31 (2001); Deborah Hensler, *Jurors in the Material World: Putting Tort Verdicts in Their Social Context*, 13 Roger Williams U. L. Rev. 8, 28 (2008).

19. Burke, Lawyers, 45; Haltom & McCann, Distorting, 76, 100–06; Mencimer, Courthouse Door, 6; Sebok, *Dispatches*, 1501–02.

20. Burke, Lawyers, at 47, 52; Haltom & McCann, Distorting, at 75, 106, 112–18; 124–26, 131; Mencimer, Courthouse Door, at 102–03; Hubbard, *Nature and Impact*, at 480.

21. Burke, Lawyers, 27; Haltom & McCann, Distorting, 51; Terry M. Dworkin, *Federal Reform of Product Liability Law*, 57 Tul. L. Rev. 602, 619 (1983) (laissez faire benchmark); Hubbard, *Nature and Impact*, 448–49, 467, 475; Rustad & Koenig, Taming, 67.

22. James R. Chelius, Workplace Safety and Health: The Role of Workers' Compensation 63–65 (1977); Dworkin, *Federal Reform*, 618; Walter Guzzard, Jr., *The Mindless Pursuit of Safety*, Fortune, April 9, 1979, at 54; Department of Commerce, Model Uniform Product Liability Act, 44 Fed. Reg. 62,714 (1979).

23. Burke, Lawyers, 31–32; Dworkin, *Federal Reform*, 605; Robert L. Rabin, *Poking Holes in the Fabric of Tort: A Comment*, 56 DePaul L. Rev. 293, 293–94 (2007); Martha T. McCluskey, *The Illusion of Efficiency in Workers' Compensation "Reform,"* 50 Rutgers

L. Rev. 657, 705 (1998); *The Devils in the Product Liability Laws*, Business Week, February 12, 1979, at 72 (statistics, extreme laws).

24. Eliot M. Blake, *Comment: Rumors of Crisis: Considering the Insurance Crisis and Tort Reform in an Information Vacuum*, 37 Emory L. J. 401, 402–05, 411 (1988) (ad campaign); Nancy L. Manzer, *Note: 1986 Tort Reform Legislation: A Systematic Evaluation of Caps on Damages and Limitations on Joint and Several Liability*, 73 Cornell L. Rev. 628, 632 (1988); Robert Sherrill, *One Paper that Wouldn't Shut Up*, 242 Nation 688 (1986) (credulous media); Maxwell Glen, *Congress Joins the Hue and Cry Over Liability Crisis*, 18 Nat. J. 380 (1986).

25. Burke, Lawyers, 29; Philip Hilts, Smokescreen 200–01 (1996); Mencimer, Courthouse Door, 17; Rustad & Koenig, *Taming*, 84 (Schwartz description); Margaret E. Kriz, *Liability Lobbying*, 20 Nat. J. 191 (1988).

26. Ronald Reagan, Remarks to Members of the American Tort Reform Association, May 30, 1986; Sugarman, *Taking Advantage*, 340; Kriz, *Liability Lobbying*.

27. Haltom & McCann, Distorting, at 42–43 (describing conference); Peter W. Huber, Galileo's Revenge (1991); Huber, Liability; Walter K. Olson, The Litigation Explosion (1991); Jean Stefancic & Richard Delgado, No Mercy 106 (1996) (copies sent).

28. Richard Kluger, Ashes to Ashes 686–87 (1996); Mencimer, Courthouse Door, 38–39; Blake, *Rumors*, 410; Alexandra B. Klass, *Tort Experiments in the Laboratories of Democracy*, 50 William & Mary L. Rev. 1501, 1513–14 (2009); Nancy L. Ross, *Insurance Firms Profit from Crisis*, WP, December 21, 1986, at K7.

29. McCluskey, *Illusion of Efficiency*, 679–81, 705, 769, 774–75, 779, 788.

30. Charles Kolb, White House Daze 41–42 (1994); Dan Quayle, *Civil Justice Reform*, 41 Am. U. L. Rev. 559, 560–61 (1992); *Product Liability Bill Dies in Senate After Supporters Fail to End Filibuster*, 20 BNA PSLR 995 (1992); Saundra Terry & Mark Stencel, *Bush, Quayle Put Lawyers in Election-Year Docket*, WP, August 28, 1992, at A16.

31. Bogus, Lawsuits, 6–7; Mencimer, Courthouse Door, 5, 97; Grover Norquist, *A Winning Drive*, American Spectator, March, 1994, at 5; Saundra Torry, *Trial Lawyers vs. Tort Reformers*, WP, November 21, 1994, at F7.

32. Stefancic & Delgado, No Mercy, 106; Dan Morgan, *Think Tanks: Corporation's Quiet Weapon*, WP, January 29, 2000, at A1; Peter H. Stone, *Grass-Roots Group Rakes in the Green*, 27 Nat. J. 621 (1995).

33. Carl Tobias, *Common Sense and Other Legal Reforms*, 48 Vand. L. Rev. 699, 707, 729–33 (1995); John M. Broder, *Clinton Vetoes Bill to Limit Product-Liability Lawsuits*, LAT, May 3, 1996, at A1; Neil A. Lewis, *House Passes New Standards Limiting Awards in Civil Suits*, NYT, March 11, 1995, at A1.

34. John Anderson, Follow the Money 15 (2007) (Rove view); Mencimer, Courthouse Door, 55, 95; Robert Dreyfuss, *George W.'s Compassion*, American Prospect, September 1, 1999, at 36 (Rove's income); Louis Jacobson, *Trying Times*, 30 Nat. J. 863 (1998); Martha Middleton, *A Changing Landscape*, 81 ABA J. 56 (1995).

35. Anderson, Follow, 61 (TLR); Nate Blakeslee, *Naked Emperors and Wet Rats*, Texas Observer, February 15, 2002, at 4 (TLR); Jennifer L. Reichert, *Big Business Backs "Grassroots" Tort "Reform" Efforts, Report Says*, Trial, October 1, 2000, at 86 (CALA);

Mimi Swartz, *Hurt? Injured? Need a Lawyer? Too Bad*, Texas Monthly, November, 2005, at 164 (TLR); Dan Zegart, *The Right Wing's Drive for "Tort Reform*," Nation, October 25, 2004, at 13 (CALA).

36. Mencimer, Courthouse Door, 57 (statistics); David A. Anderson, *Judicial Tort Reform in Texas*, 26 Rev. of Litigation 1, 3 (2007); George Lardner, Jr., *"Tort Reform": Mixed Verdict*, WP, February 10, 2000, at A6; William Glaberson, *Some Plaintiffs Losing Out in Texas' War on Lawsuits*, NYT, June 7, 1999, at A1; Sue Anne Pressley, *Texans Draw Line in Sand on Lawsuits*, WP, February 23, 1995, at A3.

37. Klass, *Tort Experiments*, 1514 (30 states); Hubbard, *Nature and Impact*, at 523; David Frum, *Unreformed*, Forbes, February 1, 1993, at 82; William Glaberson, *State Courts Sweeping Away Laws Curbing Suits for Injury*, NYT, July 16, 1999, at A1; Michael Quint, *Crackdown on Job-Injury Costs*, NYT, March 16, 1995, at D1.

38. Bogus, Lawsuits, 38; Mencimer, Courthouse Door, 71; Anderson, *Judicial Tort Reform*, at 3; Lawrence M. Friedman, *Benchmarks: Judges on Trial, Judicial Selection and Elections*, 58 DePaul L. Rev. 451 (2009); Texans for Public Justice, Pay to Play 3 (2001).

39. Anderson, Follow, 61; Mencimer, Courthouse Door, 71; Herman Schwartz, Right Wing Justice 224 (2004).

40. George W. Conk, *Is There a Design Defect in the Restatement (Third) of Torts: Products Liability?*, 109 Yale L. J. 1087, 1103 (2000) (statement); Teresa M. Schwartz, *Prescription Products and the Proposed Restatement (Third)*, 61 Tenn. L. Rev. 1357, 1357–58 (1994). See, e.g., James A. Henderson & Aaron D. Twerski, *A Proposed Revision of Section 402A of the Restatement (Second) of Torts*, 77 Cornell L. Rev. 1512 (1992); James A. Henderson, Jr., *The Efficacy of Organic Tort Reform*, 77 Cornell L. Rev. 596, 611 (1992) (admitting that the author is "taking the side of piecemeal, eclectic, grab-bag, politically-oriented, scruffy tort reform").

41. Marshall S. Shapo, *Private Organization, Public Responsibility*, 23 Law & Social Inquiry 651, 653–54 (1998); John F. Vargo, *The Emperor's New Clothes: The American Law Institute Adorns a "New Cloth" for Section 402A Products Liability Design Defect—A Survey of the States Reveals a Different Weave*, 26 Memphis L. Rev. 493, 517–18 (1996).

42. Geistfeld, Principles, 26–27; Owen, Products Liability, 33; Conk, *Design Defect*, at 1088; Rustad & Koenig, *Taming*, at 90.

43. Restatement (Third) of Torts—Products Liability §§ 4(a), (b), 6(c), (d); Teresa M. Schwartz, *Regulatory Standards and Products Liability: Striking the Right Balance Between the Two*, 30 Mich. J. L. Ref. 431, 433–34 (1997); Victor E. Schwartz, *The Restatement (Third) of Torts: Products Liability—The American Law Institute's Process of Democracy and Deliberation*, 26 Hofstra L. Rev. 743 (1998) (business community thrilled).

44. Walter Olsen, The Rule of Lawyers: How the New Litigation Elite Threatens America's Rule of Law (2003); LaFetra, *Freedom*, 645, 659; John Cochran, *A Simple Case of Complexity*, Cong. Q. Weekly, January 31, 2005, at 230 ($120 million); Rick Casey, *Incredible Lawsuit Tales*, Houston Chronicle, November 25, 2007, at B1.

45. Mencimer, Courthouse Door, 6–7; *DOJ Reports Huge Decline in Tort Case Resolved Through U.S. District Court Trial,* 33 BNA PSLR 861 (2005); Jonathan Weisman, *Lawsuit Reform a Bush Priority,* WP, December 16, 2004, at A6 (quote); David G. Savage, *A Trial Lawyer on Ticket Has Corporate U.S. Seeing Red,* LAT, September 13, 2004, at A1.

46. Class Action Fairness Act of 2005, Pub. L. 109–2, 119 Stat. 4 (2005); Sherman, *Consumer Class Actions,* 230; Seth Stern, *Lawsuits, Lagging Economy Linked in Tort Reform Push,* Cong. Q. Weekly, May 29, 2004, at 1270.

47. Wyeth v. Levine, 555 U.S. 6 (2009); Thomas O. McGarity, The Preemption War ch. 6 (2008); Cindy Skrzycki, *Agencies' Rules Quietly Enable Tort Reform,* WP, September 27, 2005, at A15.

48. Hubbard, *Nature and Impact,* 536 ($100 million); Peter Lattman, *Tort-Reform Supporters Buy In to Power of the Press,* WSJ, April 25, 2007, at B2; Ryan Myers, *Newspaper Publisher Says Claims of Jury Tampering "Ridiculous,"* Beaumont Enterprise, April 14, 2007, at A1; Jeffrey H. Birnbaum, *Advocacy Groups Blur Media Lines,* WP, December 6, 2004, at A1 (academic critics).

49. Anderson, *Judicial Tort Reform,* at 3–4; Daniel & Martin, *Texas Plaintiffs,* at 316; Terry Carter, *Tort Reform Texas Style,* ABA J., October, 2006, at 30; Swartz, *Hurt?,* at 164 (owners' box); *Texas Governor Signs Reform Measure Creating Repose Law, Warning Presumption,* 31 BNA PSLR 625 (2003).

50. American Tort Reform Foundation, Defrocking Tort Deform (2008) (unfamiliar position); Jonathan D. Glater, *To the Trenches: The Tort War is Raging On,* NYT, June 22, 2008, at B1; *"Cheeseburger Lawsuits" Restricted in Illinois Under Recent Legislation Signed by Governor,* 32 BNA PSLR 754 (2004).

51. Mencimer, Courthouse Door, 63–67; Public Citizen, Tom Donohue 11 (February 2005) (23 of 24 races); Peck & Vail, *Attack,* 326–27; Chuck Lindell, *Republicans Maintain Tight Grip on State Judicial Races,* Austin American-Statesman, November 5, 2008, at A15; Tom Hamburger, *Chamber of Commerce Vows to Punish Anti-Business Candidates,* LAT, January 8, 2008, at A1.

52. Caperton v. A.T. Massey Coal Co., 129 S.Ct. 2252 (2009); Adam Liptak, *Case May Alter Judge Elections Across Country,* NYT, February 15, 2009, at A29; Adam Liptak, *Motion Ties W. Virginia Justice to Coal Executive,* NYT, January 14, 2008, at A15; Deborah Solomon, *A Coal CEO's Unusual Pastime: Firing Up West Virginia Politics,* WSJ, February 13, 2006, at A1.

53. Terry Carter, *Boosting the Bench,* ABA J., October, 2002, at 29 (coalition); Barbara Vaida, *Judging Politics,* 39 Nat. J. 36 (2007).

54. Mencimer, Courthouse Door, 24 (jury trials); Glater, *To the Trenches* (large verdicts).

55. Emery G. Lee, III, & Thomas E. Willging, The Impact of the Class Action Fairness Act of 2005 on the Federal Courts: Fourth Interim Report to the Judicial Conference Advisory Committee on Civil Rules 1 (April 2008).

56. George Lardner, Jr., *"Tort Reform": Mixed Verdict,* WP, February 10, 2000, at A6.

57. Congressional Budget Office, The Effects of Tort Reform: Evidence from the States viii (2004).

58. Hubbard, *Nature and Impact*, 536; Congressional Budget Office, Effects of Tort Reform, viii.
59. McCluskey, *Illusion of Efficiency*, 705, 711, 713, 788.
60. Herbert M. Kritzer, *Law is the Mere Continuation of Politics By Different Means: American Judicial Selection in the Twenty-First Century*, 56 DePaul L. Rev. 423, 461 (2007); Vaida, *Judging Politics*, (Ohio); Texans for Public Justice, Pay to Play 1 (2001) (Texas study); Mike France & Lorraine Woellert, *The Battle Over the Courts*, Business Week, September 27, 2004, at 36 (2002 poll).
61. Bogus, Lawsuits, 35; Burke, Lawyers, 30–31; Haltom & McCann, Distorting, 119; Rustad & Koenig, *Taming*, 71; *How Business Trounced the Trial Lawyers*, Business Week, January 7, 2007, at cover; Glater, *To the Trenches* (quoting Thomas J. Donohue).
62. Bogus, Lawsuits, 36–37; Blake, *Rumors*, 406; Daniel & Martin, *Texas Plaintiffs*, 291–92; Hubbard, *Nature and Impact*, 483, 487. 490, 497, 510–14; Sebok, *Dispatches*, 1512.

CHAPTER 16. DISABLED GOVERNMENT

1. William Greider, Come Home, America 173 (2009); Rena Steinzor & Sidney Shapiro, The People's Agents 4 (2010).
2. Patricia A. McCoy, Andrey D. Pavlov & Susan M. Wachter, *Systemic Risk Through Securitization: The Result of Deregulation and Regulatory Failure*, 41 Conn. L. Rev. 1327, 1355–56 (2009); Edmund L. Andrews, *Fed Shrugged as Subprime Crisis Spread*, NYT, December 18, 2007, at A1.
3. James Lardner, *Watching the Watchers*, American Prospect, June 2010, at A10; Edmund L. Andrews, *Bernanke Says Fed "Should Have Done More,"* NYT, December 4, 2009, at A1; Arthur Levitt, Jr., *Regulatory Underkill*, WSJ, March 21, 2008, at A13.
4. *Report of the American Bar Association Section of Antitrust Law Special Committee to Study the Role of the Federal Trade Commission*, 58 Antitrust L. J. 53, 141–43 (1989); CPSC Appropriations, Hearings Before the Subcommittee on Financial Services and General Government of the Senate Committee on Appropriations, 110th Cong., 1st Sess. (2007) (Testimony of Rachel Weintraub, Consumer Federation of America); Federal Trade Commission, Fiscal Year 2009 Congressional Budget Justification, available at http://www.ftc.gov/ftc/oed/fmo/budgetsummary09.pdf.
5. Sholnn Freeman, *Toyota's Woes Raise Questions About NHTSA Resources*, WP, February 10, 2010, at A15.
6. Steinzor & Shapiro, People's Agents, ch. 3; Paul C. Light, *A Government Ill-Executed: The Depletion of the Federal Service*, 68 Pub. Admin. Rev. 413 (2008).
7. Simon Johnson & James Kwak, 13 Bankers 92–97 (2010); Robert Kuttner, A Presidency in Peril 4, 7 (2010); Thomas O. McGarity, The Preemption War ch. 7 (2008); Paul J. Quirk, Industry Influence in Federal Regulatory Agencies 4–21 (1981); Rachel E. Barkow, *Insulating Agencies: Avoiding Capture Through Institutional Design*, 89 Tex. L. Rev. 15, 19–23 (2010).
8. Marion Nestle, Food Politics 368 (2002); National Commission on the BP Deepwater Horizon Oil Spill and Offshore Drilling, Deep Water 56 (2011), (quote); Gareth Cook,

Uncle Sam's Not-So-Friendly Skies, Washington Monthly, January 1, 1996, at 9; Juliet Eilperin, *Seeking Answers in MMS's Flawed Culture*, WP, August 25, 2010, at A1.

9. Thomas O. McGarity, Reinventing Rationality ch. 10 (1991); Lisa Bressman & Michael P. Vandenbergh, *Inside the Administrative State: A Critical Look at the Practice of Presidential Control*, 105 Mich. L. Rev. 47 (2006).

10. Mark Seidenfeld, *A Table of Requirements for Federal Administrative Rulemaking*, 27 Fla. St. L. Rev. 533, 536 (2000).

11. Charles R. Morris, The Trillion Dollar Meltdown 54 (2008); Joseph E. Stiglitz, Freefall 163 (2010).

12. Lyndsey Layton, *Healthy Foods Carry Hidden Dangers, New Study Finds*, WP, October 6, 2009, at A5.

13. David C. Vladeck, *The Failed Promise of Workplace Health Regulation*, 111 W. Va. L. Rev. 15, 18 (2008); *After Rising Black Lung Rates Reported, Mine Union Calls for Stronger Dust Controls*, 37 BNA OSHR 823 (2007).

14. Haroon H. Hamid, *The NHTSA's Evaluation of Automobile Safety Systems: Active or Passive*, 19 Loyola Consumer L. Rev. 227–28 (2007); Myron Levin, *Upgrades on Auto Safety Standards Languish*, LAT, September 18, 2000, at A1.

15. Executive Order No. 13212, 68 Fed. Reg. 27,429 (2001); National Commission, Deep Water, 55, 73, 80; Steven Mufson & Juliet Eilperin, *Lawmakers Attack Plans Oil Companies Had in Place to Deal With a Spill*, WP, June 16, 2010, at A1; Ian Urbina, *U.S. Said to Allow Drilling Without Needed Permits*, NYT, May 14, 2010, at A1; Juliet Eilperin, *U.S. Exempted BP's Gulf of Mexico Drilling from Environmental Study*, WP, May 5, 2010, at A4.

16. Chenglin Liu, *The Obstacles of Outsourcing Imported Food Safety to China*, 43 Cornell Int'l L. J. 249, 269, 283–84 (2010); Government Accountability Office, Consumer Safety: Better Information and Planning Would Strengthen CPSC's Oversight of Imported Products 8, 23–24 (2009); Michael R. Taylor, The FDA Food Safety Modernization Act: A New Paradigm for Importers, Speech at the Global Food Safety Conference (Feb. 17, 2011) (statistics); Joaquin Sapien & Aaron Kessler, *China Plays Tug-of-War with U.S. Inspectors Over Drywall*, Sarasota Herald-Tribune, October 25, 2010, at A1; Joby Warrick, *Overseas Meat Processors Fail to Make Grade*, Austin American-Statesman, March 3, 2002, at A19.

17. James W. Singer, *Out Like a Lamb*, 12 Nat. J. 867 (1980); Matthew L. Wald, *Change Often Comes Slowly After Crashes*, NYT, February 23, 2009, at A19; Eric Lipton, *Safety Agency Faces Scrutiny Amid Changes*, NYT, September 2, 2007, at A1; *To Avoid Cumbersome Rulemaking, More Resources to be Put Into Guidance*, 32 BNA OSHR 604 (2002).

18. Jerry L. Mashaw & David L. Harfst, *Regulation and Legal Culture: The Case of Motor Vehicle Safety*, 4 Yale J. Reg. 257, 273 (1987); Lyndsey Layton, *Officials Worry About Consumers Lost Among the Recalls*, WP, July 2, 2010, at A1; Barry Meier, *A Life or Death Decision*, NYT, April 7, 2009, at B1; Mitch Lipka, *A System Destined to Fail*, Florida Sun-Sentinel, November 29, 1999, at A1; Richard Witkin, *Inquiry Set on Plane's Cargo Door Locks*, NYT, April 25, 1989, at A16.

19. National Institute of Medicine, The Future of Drug Safety 7–1 (2006); National Institute of Medicine, Safe Medical Devices for Children 152, 163, 183, 190 (2005); National Research Council/Institute of Medicine, Enhancing Food Safety 5 (2010); Kimberly Kindy, *Analysis Finds Uneasy Mix in Auto Industry and Regulation*, WP, March 9, 2010, at A1; Annys Shin, *Goodbye to Bob*, WP, January 5, 2008, at D1 (CPSC).

20. Hilts, Protecting America's Health, 252–54 (FDA); Joel A. Mintz, *Agencies, Congress and Regulatory Enforcement: A Review of EPA's Hazardous Waste Enforcement Effort, 1970–1987*, 18 Envtl. L. 683, 715 (1988) (EPA); Elizabeth Williams, *Industries Paid for Top Regulators' Travel*, WP, November 2, 2007, at A1.

21. Stiglitz, Freefall, 92–93; Agricultural Marketing Service, National Organic Program; Final Rule, 65 Fed. Reg. 80, 548 (2000).

22. Stiglitz, Freefall, 92; Congressional Oversight Panel, Special Report on Regulatory Reform 4 (January 2009); Michael Booth, *"It's a System that Doesn't Appreciate Truthtelling, Even When Human Lives Are at Stake,"* Denver Post, October 30, 2011, at A1; Andrew Martin, *Food Safety Problems Elude Private Inspectors*, NYT, March 6, 2009, at A1 (quote).

23. Government Accountability Office, OSHA's Voluntary Protection Programs: Improved Oversight and Controls Would Better Ensure Program Quality (2009); Stephen Labaton, *S.E.C. Concedes Oversight Flaws Fueled Collapse*, NYT, September 27, 2008, at A1 (quote); *Pending IG Study Finds Few Facilities Meet EPA Performance Track Duties*, Inside EPA, March 9, 2007, at 1.

24. Johnson & Kwak, 13 Bankers, 12, 86; Stiglitz, Freefall, 7, 114, 296; John Maggs, *Mine Fields of Moral Hazards*, Nat. J., October 6, 2007, at 57.

25. Thomas McGarity, et al., Workers at Risk: Regulatory Dysfunction at OSHA 6–7 (Center for Progressive Reform, 2010).

26. Gardiner Harris, *President Plans Team to Overhaul Food Safety*, NYT, March 15, 2009, at A24.

27. OMB Watch, Federal Meat Inspectors Spread Thin as Recalls Rise, March 4, 2008, available at http://www.ombwatch.org/nodc/3624.

28. *Toyota's Recall and the Government's Response, Hearings Before the Senate Committee on Science and Transportation*, 111th Cong., 2d Sess. (2010) (testimony of Clarence M. Ditlow).

29. National Commission, Deep Water, 68, 78.

30. Jeff Bailey, *Aging Jet Fleets an Added Strain on U.S. Airlines*, NYT, April 12, 2008, at C1 (quoting DOT Inspector General).

31. Uday Deasi, *The Politics of Federal-State Relations: The Case of Surface Mining Regulations*, 31 Nat. Res. J. 785, 796 (1991) (OSM); Anne P. Fortney, *Consumer Credit Compliance and the Federal Trade Commission: Continuing the Process of Education and Enforcement*, 41 Business Lawyer 1013 (1986) (FTC); Joel A. Mintz, *Some Thoughts on the Interdisciplinary Aspects of Environment Enforcement*, 36 ELR 10,495, 10,502–03 (2006) (EPA); Shari Ben Moussa, *Note, Mining for Morality at Sago Mine: Big Business and Big Money Equal Modest Enforcement of Health and Safety Standards*, 18 U. Fla. J. L. & Pub. Pol'y 209, 239 (2007) (MSHA); Government Accountability

Office, Rail Safety: The Federal Railroad Administration is Taking Steps to Better Target Its Oversight, but Assessment of Results is Needed to Determine Impact 12 (2007) (FRA).

32. Office of Inspector General, Department of Labor, OSHA Needs to Evaluate the Impact and Use of Hundreds of Millions of Dollars in Penalty Reductions as Incentives for Employers to Improve Workplace Safety and Health 1–3 (September 30, 2010).

33. *Toyota's Recall Hearings* (Testimony of Clarence M. Ditlow).

34. Melody Petersen & Christopher Drew, *As Inspectors, Some Meatpackers Fall Short*, NYT, October 10, 2003, at A1.

35. Majority Staff of the Senate Committee on Health, Education, Labor and Pensions, Discounting Death: OSHA's Failure to Punish Safety Violations that Kill Workers 5 (2009).

36. Keith Schneider, *U.S. Mine Inspectors Charge Interference By Agency Director*, NYT, November 22, 1992, at A1.

37. Jared Favole, *FDA Warning Letters to Companies Decline Sharply*, WSJ, June 7, 2008, at A2.

38. Matthew L. Wald, *Agency Faults Safety Reports Filed by F.A.A.*, NYT, March 31, 1998, at A17.

39. David Barstow & Lowell Bergman, *Deaths on Job, Slaps on Wrist*, NYT, January 10, 2003, at A1.

40. Majority Staff, OSHA Report, 5.

41. Michael Cooper, Gardiner Harris & Eric Lipton, *In Mine Safety, A Meek Watchdog*, NYT, April 10, 2010, at A1.

42. Frank Rich, *The Bipartisanship Racket*, NYT, December 18, 2010, at Wk10; Michael Hiltzik, *Law Little Threat to Rogues of Finance*, LAT, January 12, 2009, at C1.

43. Amanda Bronstad, *Going After the Little Guy, So Far*, Nat. L. J., April 28, 2008, at 1; AFL-CIO Safety and Health Dept., Death on the Job: The Toll of Neglect (April 2011), at 16 (statistics).

44. Stephanie Mencimer, Blocking the Courthouse Door 3 (2006); Carl T. Bogus, *Introduction: Genuine Tort Reform*, 13 Roger Williams L. Rev. 1, 4 (2008) (45 states); Anthony J. Sebok, *Dispatches from the Tort Wars*, 85 Tex. L. Rev. 1465 (2007).

45. Michael L. Rustad & Thomas H. Koenig, *Taming the Tort Monster: The American Civil Justice System as a Battleground of Social Theory*, 68 Brooklyn L. Rev. 1, 92 (2002); Larry S. Stewart, *Strict Liability for Defective Product Design: The Quest for a Well-Ordered Regime*, 74 Brooklyn L. Rev. 1039, 1040–45 (2009).

46. Credit Rating Agency Reform Act of 2006, Pub. L. No. 109–291, 120 Stat. 1329 (2006); David Segal, *Suddenly, the Rating Agencies Don't Look Untouchable*, NYT, May 23, 2010, at B1 (perfect litigation record).

47. Mencimer, Courthouse Door, 138.

48. Dawn Wotapke, Homeowners Win Settlement on Chinese Drywall, WSJ, December 16, 2011, at B1 (settlement reached with Chinese subsidiary of German corporation); Rebecca Mowbray, *Revised La. Law Could Hamper Plaintiffs to Drywall Cases*, New Orleans Times-Picayune, September 24, 2009, at A1.

49. Allan Kanner & M. Ryan Casey, *Consumer Class Actions after CAFA*, 56 Drake L. Rev. 303, 313–15 (2008); *Court Refuses to Certify Two Classes in Suits Over Salmonella in Peanut Butter*, 36 BNA PSLR 732 (2007).

50. Richard A. Epstein, Overdose 230 (2006); Dan Quayle, *Civil Justice Reform*, 41 Am. U. L. Rev. 559 (1992).

51. Mencimer, Courthouse Door, 193–94; F. Patrick Hubbard, *The Nature and Impact of the "Tort Reform" Movement*, 35 Hofstra L. Rev. 437, 452 (2006); Rustad & Koenig, *Taming*, 6, 103.

52. Thomas O. McGarity & Sidney A. Shapiro, Workers at Risk ch. 2 (1992); Martha T. McCluskey, *The Illusion of Efficiency in Workers' Compensation "Reform,"* 50 Rutgers L. Rev. 657, 681, 769, 779 (1998); N.R. Kleinfield & Steven Greenhouse, *For Injured Workers, a Costly Legal Swamp*, NYT, March 31, 2009, at A1.

53. Reigel v. Medtronic, Inc., 127 S.Ct. 1000, 1008 (2007); Robert S. Adler & Richard A. Mann, *Preemption and Medical Devices. The Courts Run Amok*, 59 Mo. L. Rev. 895, 916 (1995).

54. Cuomo v. Clearing House Association, 129 S.Ct. 2710 (2009); Watters v. Wachovia Bank, 550 U.S. 1 (2007).

55. Morris, Meltdown, 56; Richard A. Posner, A Failure of Capitalism 98 (2009); Stiglitz, Freefall, 79.

56. *The BP Texas City Disaster and Worker Safety, Hearing before the House Committee on Education and Labor*, 110th Cong., 1st Sess. (2007) (Testimony of Carolyn W. Merritt, U.S. Chemical Safety Board).

CHAPTER 17. PATCH-AND-REPAIR

1. Justin Fox, The Myth of the Rational Market xiii (2009); Simon Johnson & James Kwak, 13 Bankers 68–70, 102–04 (2010); George Soros, *The Crisis & What To Do About It*, N.Y. Rev. of Books, December 4, 2008, at 63; Edmund L. Andrews, *Greenspan Concedes Error on Regulation*, NYT, October 24, 2008, at B1 (Greenspan quote).

2. Charles R. Morris, The Trillion Dollar Meltdown 33 (2008); Greg Ip, James R. Hagerty & Jonathan Karp, *Housing Bust Fuels Blame Game*, WSJ, February 27, 2008, at A1.

3. Richard A. Posner, A Failure of Capitalism ii (2009).

4. Congressional Oversight Panel, Special Report on Regulatory Reform 19 (January 2009).

5. Johnson & Kwak, 13 Bankers, 5.

6. John W. Kingdon, Agendas, Alternatives and Public Policies (1997); David Vogel, Fluctuating Fortunes 38 (1989); National Research Council, National Academy of Sciences, Ensuring Safe Food from Production to Consumption 8 (1998).

7. Daniel J. Curran, Dead Laws for Dead Men 4, 10 (1993); Michael Pertschuk, Revolt Against Regulation 121 (1982).

8. Rena Steinzor & Sidney Shapiro, The People's Agents 220–21 (2010); John Cranford, *The Renegotiation*, Cong. Q. Weekly, January 19, 2009, at 119.

9. John B. Judis, *The Quiet Revolution*, The New Republic, February 18, 2010, at 15.

10. Jonathan Alter, The Promise ch. 10 (2010); Michael Hirsh, Capital Offense 275 (2010); Robert Kuttner, A Presidency in Peril 4, 28–29 (2010); Dana Milbank, *The Clinton Administration, Brought to You by Barack Obama*, WP, July 15, 2010, at A2.

11. Jerry Markon, *Union Official Turned U.S. Mine Safety Chief Shoulders a Burden*, WP, April 14, 2010, at A17; OSHA Biography, *David Michaels*, available at http://www.osha .gov/as/opa/michaels_bio.html.

12. Rob Stein & Lyndsey Layton, *FDA Pick Was NYC Health Chief*, WP, March 12, 2009, at A2; EPA, *Administrator Lisa P. Jackson*, available at http://www.epa.gov/aboutepa/ administrator.html.

13. Andy Pasztor & Susan Carey, *FAA Administrator Nominee Gets Strong Airline Support*, WSJ, March 27, 2009, at A10; United Transportation Union, *Obama Taps UTU's Szabo for FRA*, UTU News, April, 2009, available at http://www.utu.org/worksite/ newspdfs/2009/UTU0904.pdf.

14. *Obama Names Bernanke for 2nd Term*, WP, August 26. 2009, at A9; Randall Smith, Tom McGinty & Kara Scannell, *Obama's Pick to Head SEC Has Record of Being a Regulator with a Light Touch*, WSJ, January 15, 2009, at B1; Edmund L. Andrews, *Obama Names Insider to Commodities Post*, NYT, December 19, 2008, at B3.

15. White House, Revocation of Certain Executive Orders Concerning Planning and Review, 74 Fed. Reg. 6113 (2009); Memorandum from Barack Obama to Heads of Executive Departments and Agencies, re: Preemption, dated May 20, 2009; Jonathan Weisman & Alex P. Kellogg, *Obama Defends Government Action in Michigan Speech*, WSJ, May 1, 2010, at A1; Dan Balz, *Obama Goes Populist as Democrats Lick Their Wounds*, WP, January 24, 2010, at A2.

16. Steinzor & Shapiro, People's Agents, 221; *OIRA's Sunstein Seen as Able to Implement Regulatory Changes Without New Order*, 38 BNA PSLR 481 (2010).

17. Rena Steinzor, Michael Patoka & James Goodwin, Behind Closed Doors at the White House 7–10 (Center for Progressive Reform, November, 2011) (OIRA changes); OMB Watch, The Obama Approach to Public Protection: Rulemaking (September 2010), at 5; *EPA Critic's Move to OMB Spurs Activist Fears Over Opposing Strict Rules*, Inside EPA, December 4, 2009, at 1; *Clinton Administration Changing Fewer Proposed Rules During Regulatory Review*, 23 BNA OSHR 732 (1993) (OIRA changes statistics).

18. Juliet Eilperin, *Official Questions Pollution Proposal*, WP, December 4, 2009, at A15.

19. Improving Regulation and Regulatory Review, Executive Order 13,563, 76 Fed. Reg. 3821 (2011). The executive order also required agencies to factor "human dignity" into the cost-benefit calculus for regulations. See Alan Charles Ruhl, *Obama Review of Regulatory Burden to Be Weighed in Cost-Benefit Analysis*, 39 BNA PSLR 171 (2011).

20. Barack Obama, *Toward a 21st Century Regulatory System*, WSJ, January 18, 2011, at A19.

21. Ruhl, *Obama Review* ("President Obama has . . . placed himself squarely in the camp of those who believe that federal regulations must be rigorously justified"); Dan Froomkin, *Cass Sunstein: The Obama Administration's Ambivalent Regulator*, Huffington Post, June 13, 2011, available at http://www.huffingtonpost.com/2011/06/13/cass-sunstein-obama-ambivalent-regulator-czar_n_874530.html (quoting Peg Seminario,

AFL-CIO); *Obama Orders Repeal, Modification of All Outdated Federal Regulations*, 39 BNA PSLR 85 (2011) (quoting Rena Steinzor, Center for Progressive Reform) (hook, line and sinker quote); *Facing GOP Attack, White House Steps Up Review of Key EPA Policies*, Inside EPA, December 10, 2010, at 1.

22. Laura Meckler & Carol E. Lee, *White House Regulation Shift is a Political Bet*, WSJ, September 12, 2011, at A1.

23. *OMB Asks Independent Agencies to Comply with Regulatory Review*, 39 BNA PSLR 141 (2011); Froomkin, *Cass Sunstein* (Sunstein blog).

24. *Sunstein Says Agencies Cutting Burdens; Republicans Seek More Aggressive Effort*, 42 BNA Env. L. Rept. 1299 (2011) ($1 billion); *White House Has Agencies' Review Plans; Questions About Impact of Process Remain*, 41 BNA OSHR 462 (2011); Binyamin Appelbaum, *Federal Review Finds Rules to Live Without*, NYT, May 26, 2011, at B1 (quoting William L. Kovacs, U.S. Chamber of Commerce); Cass Sunstein, *21st-Century Regulation: An Update on the President's Reforms*, WSJ, May 25, 2011, at A17.

25. John McArdle & Emily Yehle, *Obama Admin Outlines 500 Reforms It Says Will Save Businesses Billions*, Greenwire, August 23, 2011, available at http://www.nytimes.com/ gwire/2011/08/23/23greenwire-obama-admin-outlines-500-reforms-it-says-will-24456 .html?pagewanted=all; Laura Meckler, *White House to Scale Back Regulations on Businesses*, WSJ, August 23, 2001, at A1 (quoting Bill Kovacs, U.S. Chamber of Commerce); David Nakamura, *Obama Plan Would Drop Hundreds of Regulations*, WP, August 24, 2011, at A4 (quoting Rena Steinzor, Center for Progressive Reform).

26. Letter to Lisa Jackson from Cass R. Sunstein, dated September 2, 2011, available at http://www.whitehouse.gov/sites/default/files/ozone_national_ambient_air_qual ity_standards_letter.pdf. See also John M. Broder, *Obama Abandons Tougher Ozone Standard*, Boston Globe, September 3, 2011, at A2.

27. John M. Broder, *Re-election Strategy is Tied to a Shift on Smog*, NYT, November 16, 2011, at A1. Sunstein and Daley met later in the day with representatives of environmental groups, where Mr. Daley asked about the health impacts of unemployment. Id.

28. *Industry Makes Blocking EPA's Ozone Revision a Key Test for Obama*, Inside EPA, July 22, 2011, at 6.

29. Broder, *Re-election Strategy*.

30. Id.

31. Letter to Lisa Jackson from Cass R. Sunstein, dated September 2, 2011, available at http://www.whitehouse.gov/sites/default/files/ozone_national_ambient_air_quality_ standards_letter.pdf. See Broder, *Obama Abandons*.

32. Froomkin, *Cass Sunstein* (quoting Robert Weissman, Public Citizen) ("the overall picture is disappointing at best").

33. *Congress Approves Appropriations Bill With $10.3 Billion for EPA in Fiscal 2010*, 40 BNA Env. Rept. 2526 (2009); *Obama Proposes $573 Million for OSHA in 2011, With Cut for Voluntary Program*, 40 BNA OSHR 87 (2010); Elizabeth Williamson & Melanie Trottman, *Regulators See Big Funding Boost*, WSJ, March 2, 2009, at A10.

34. OMB Watch, Obama Approach, 5, Appendix.

35. *Obama Requests Less Money for EPA But More to Address Climate Change*, 41 BNA Env. Rept. 297 (2010).
36. Alter, Promise, 129–30; Kutner, Presidency in Peril, xvii; Mark J. Drajern & Catherine Dodge, *Obama Wrote 5% Fewer Rules Than Bush While Costing Business*, Bloomberg, October 25, 2011, available at http://mobile.bloomberg.com/news/2011–10–25/obama-wrote-5-fewer-rules-than-bush-while-costing-business?category=; Cass Sunstein, *The Smart Approach to Reforming Regulations*, WP, July 1, 2011, at A17; Carl Hulse & Adam Nagourney, *Senate Republican Leader Finds Weapon in Unity*, NYT, March 18, 2010, at A13; Editorial, *The Corporate House*, NYT, January 6, 2011, at A26 (job killing strategy).
37. Alter, Promise, 29, 50–53; Johnson & Kwak, 13 Bankers, 186; Kutner, Presidency in Peril, 21; Joseph E. Stiglitz, Freefall 47 (2010); Sarah Wheaton & Jackie Calmes, *Former Treasury Secretary to Lead Economic Council*, NYT, Nov. 23, 2008, at A26; Peter S. Goodman, *A Fresh Look at the Apostle of Free Markets*, NYT, April 13, 2008, at WK3 (Friedman quote).
38. Stephen Labaton, *Obama Plans Fast Action to Tighten Financial Rules*, NYT, January 25, 2009, at A1; Jeff Zeleny, *Obama Reviewing Bush's Use of Executive Power*, NYT, November 10, 2008, at A19 (quoting Rahm Emanuel).
39. Johnson & Kwak, 13 Bankers, 206–07, 209 (quoting Paul Volcker), 210–11 (quoting Alan Greenspan); Stiglitz, Freefall, 114.
40. Alter, Promise, 200–01; Kutner, Presidency in Peril, xviii; David M. Mason, Credit Derivatives: Market Solutions to the Market Crisis (Heritage Foundation Backgrounder No. 2262, April 23, 2009).
41. William Greider, Come Home, America 44 (2009); Congressional Oversight Panel, Special Report, 12.
42. Johnson & Kwak, 13 Bankers, 209 (Volcker position); Elizabeth Warren, *Unsafe at any Rate*, Democracy, Summer, 2007, at 8; *The Future of Financial Services Regulation, Hearing before the House Committee on Financial Services*, 110 Cong., 2d Sess. (2008) (Testimony of Joseph Stiglitz).
43. Alter, Promise, ch. 15 (back seat); Johnson & Kwak, 13 Bankers, 191, 198, 208–09; David Skeel, The New Financial Deal 3 (2011); Eric Dash, *Overhaul Leaves Rating Agencies Largely Untouched*, NYT, June 18, 2009, at B7; Joe Nocera, *A Financial Overhaul Plan, But Only a Hint of Roosevelt*, NYT, June 18, 2009, at A1.
44. Johnson & Kwak, 13 Bankers, 179; Peter H. Stone, *The Financial Guns of August*, Nat. J., August 1, 2009, at 48; Stephen Labaton, *Lobbyists Mass to Try to Shape Financial Reform*, NYT, October 15, 2009, at B1.
45. Brady Dennis, *Financial Industry Is in Group's Sights*, WP, August 23, 2009, at A10.
46. Dodd-Frank Wall Street Reform and Consumer Protection Act, Pub. L. 111–203, 124 Stat. 1376 (2010). Johnson & Kwak, 13 Bankers, 177, 181–85, 192; Skeel, New Financial Deal, 3–4; Brady Dennis, *Obama Signs Financial Overhaul Into Law*, WP, July 22, 2010, at A13; Damian Paletta, *Finance Overhaul Falters as '08 Shock Fades*, WSJ, September 10, 2009, at A10.
47. The description is drawn from the following sources: Skeel, New Financial Deal, 4–8; Financial Stability Oversight Council, 2011 Annual Report ch. 6 (2011); Skad-

den, Arps, Slate, Meagher & Flom, Summary of Dodd-Frank Wall Street Reform and Consumer Protection Act, July, 2010.

48. Rachel E. Barkow, *Insulating Agencies: Avoiding Capture Through Institutional Design*, 89 Tex. L. Rev. 15, 75, 78 (2010).

49. Robert Johnson, *Reform and its Obstacles*, American Prospect, June, 2010, at A2; Damian Paletta & Aaron Lucchetti, *Law Remakes U.S. Financial Landscape*, WSJ, July 16, 2010, at A1; Joe Nocera, *A Dubious Way to Prevent Fiscal Crisis*, NYT, June 4, 2010, at B1; Eric Dash & Nelson D. Schwartz, *As Reform Takes Shape, Some Relief on Wall St.*, NYT, May 23, 2010, at B1; David Segal, *Debt-Rating Agencies Avoid Overhaul After Crisis*, NYT, December 8, 2009, at A1.

50. Skeel, New Financial Deal, 4–7; Saule T. Omarova, *The Dodd-Frank Act: A New Deal for a New Age?* 15 N. Car. Banking Inst. 83 (2011).

51. Press Release, U.S. Chamber Highlights Regulatory Tsunami to Follow Financial Reform Bill, June 28, 2010, available at http://www.uschamber.com/press/releases/2010/june/us-chamber-highlights-regulatory-tsunami-follow-financial-reform-bill (regulatory tsunami); John Gapper, *The Wall Street Mind: Anxious . . .*, New York Magazine, April 18, 2011, at 36.

52. Nathaniel Popper, *New Rules for Banks Haven't Curtailed Profits*, LAT, July 20, 2011, at A1; Wyatt, *Dodd-Frank Under Fire*; Jim Puzzanghera, *Goldman Boosts D.C. Lobby Force*, LAT, July 5, 2011, at B1.

53. Jenna Greene, *Agenda Unknown*, Nat. L. J., February 7, 2011, at 1 (staff); Joe Nocera, *The Travails of Ms. Warren*, NYT, July 22, 2011, at A19 (vicious attacks); Ben Protess, *Community Banks Fret Over Rules*, NYT, May 24, 2011, at B1 (meetings); Edward Wyatt, *Elizabeth Warren Tells Chamber of Commerce They Share Some Ideals*, NYT, March 31, 2011, at B9; Ben Protess, *Consumer Bureau Official Debates G.O.P. Critics on Hill*, NYT, March 17, 2011, at B10 (vicious attacks); Victoria McGrane & Maya Jackson Randall, *Banking's Scourge on Charm Offensive*, WSJ, March 15, 2011, at B1; Sewell Chan, *Warren to Lead Watchdog Agency as Assistant to Obama*, NYT, September 16, 2010, at B3; Michael Kranish, *Push On to Have Professor Head Consumer Agency*, Boston Globe, July 22, 2010, at A7.

54. Laura Meckler & Victoria McGrane, *Parties Seek Edge as Pick is Blocked*, WSJ, December 9, 2011, at A5; Suzanna Andrews, *The Woman Who Knew Too Much*, Vanity Fair, November 2011, at 36, Kate Davidson & Cheyenne Hopkins, *GOP Move Likely to Force CFPB Recess Appt*, American Banker, May 6, 2011, at 1; Richard Shelby, *The Danger of an Unaccountable "Consumer-Protection" Czar*, WSJ, July 21, 2011, at A19 (continued Republican opposition); Edward Wyatt, *Dodd-Frank Under Fire a Year Later*, NYT, July 18, 2011, at B1 (business community support); Binyamin Appelbaum, *Former Ohio Attorney General to Head New Consumer Agency*, NYT, July 17, 2011, at B1.

55. Suzy Khimm, *Cordray Proceeds Despite Appointment Challenges*, WP, January 6, 2012, at A2; Victoria McGrane & Evan Perez, *Obama Recess Pick Riles GOP, Firms*, WSJ, January 6, 2012, at A6.

56. Sewell Chan, *Limits Emerge for a New Bureau Without a Director*, NYT, September 30, 2010, at B4 (no authority). The agency did have the authority that was

transferred from other agencies to implement and enforce pre-existing consumer financial protection laws.

57. Binyamin Appelbaum, *On Finance Bill, Lobbying Shifts to Regulations*, NYT, June 26, 2010, at A1; Tomoeh Murakami Tse, *Financial Overhaul Measure Elicits Cheers and Concern*, WP, June 27, 2010, at A1 (quoting Douglas Heller, Consumer Watchdog).

58. Skeel, New Financial Deal, 88.

59. Skeel, New Financial Deal, 88; Robert Kuttner, *Too Big To Be Governed?* American Prospect, December, 2010 at 30 (quoting anonymous banker); Jesse Eisinger, *In Trading Scandal, a Reason to Enforce the Volcker Rule*, NYT, September 29, 2011, at B5.

60. James B. Stewart, *Volcker Rule, Once Simple, Now Boggles*, NYT, October 22, 2011, at B1; Ben Protess, *Volcker Rule Divides Regulators*, NYT, October 17, 2011, at B1; Scott Patterson & Alan Zibel, *Putting the Clamps on Banks*, WSJ, October 13, 2011, at A1.

61. Suzy Khimm, *Volcker in the Spotlight*, WP, May 12, 2012, at A12; Jesse Eisinger, *The Volcker Rule, Made Bloated and Weak*, NYT, February 23, 2012, at B4; Ben Protess & Peter Eavis, *At Volcker Rule Deadline, a Strong Pushback From Wall St.*, NYT, February 14, 2012, at B4; Gretchen Morgenson, *How Mr. Volcker Would Fix It*, NYT, October 23, 2011, at B1; Stewart, *Volcker Rule Boggles*; Patterson & Zibel, *Putting the Clamps on Banks* (quoting Tim Ryan, Securities Industry and Financial Markets Association).

62. Andrew Ross Sorkin, *At JPMorgan, Too Much Icing on the Cake*, NYT, May 15, 2012, at B1; Jean Eaglesham & Victoria McGrane, *Behind the Scenes, Battle for Face Time As Regulators Craft Rule's Wording*, WSJ, October 12, 2011, at B5; Scott Patterson & Victoria McGrane, *The Multibillion-Dollar Leak*, WSJ, October 7, 2011, at A1; Scott Patterson & Victoria McGrane, *Volcker Rule May Lose Its Bite*, WSJ, September 22, 2011, at B1.

63. Ben Protess & Edward Wyatt, In Washington, Mixed Messages Over Tighter Rules for Wall Street, NYT, May 15, 2012, at B1; Edward Wyatt, *Bank's Lobbyists Sought Loophole on Risky Trading*, NYT, May 12, 2012, at A1; Nelson D. Schwartz, *A Shock from JPMorgan Is New Fodder for Reformers*, NYT, May 11, 2012, at B1; Jessica Silver-Greenberg & Peter Eavis, *JPMorgan Chase Loses $2 Billion From Its Trades*, NYT, May 11, 2012, at A1.

64. *Defining the Market: Entity and Product Classifications under Title VII of the Dodd-Frank Wall Street Reform and Consumer Protection Act, Hearing before the House Committee on Agriculture*, 112th Cong., 1st Sess. 28 (2011) (testimony of Gary Gensler, Chairman, CFTC).

65. Skeel, New Financial Deal, 5; Gapper, *Wall Street Mind*.

66. Defining the Market Hearings (Gensler Testimony).

67. Keybridge Research, An Analysis of the Coalition for Derivatives End-Users' Survey on Over-the-Counter Derivatives (February 11, 2011); *Assessing the Regulatory, Economic, and Market Implications of the Dodd-Frank Derivatives Title, Hearing Before the House Committee on Financial Services*, 112th Cong., 1st Sess. 5 (2011) (opening statement of Patrick T. McHenry (R- North Carolina) (citing report), testimony of Gary Gensler, Chairman, CFTC); *Hearing to Review Implementation of Title VII*

of the Dodd-Frank Wall Street Reform and Consumer Protection Act, Hearings Before the Committee on Agriculture and the Subcommittee on General Farm Commodities and Risk Management of the House Committee on Agriculture, 112th Cong., 1st Sess. 7 (2011) (testimony of Gary Gensler, Chairman, CFTC); *Legislative Proposals to Promote Job Creation, Capital Formation, and Market Certainty, Hearing Before the Subcommittee on Capital Markets and Government Sponsored Enterprises of the House Committee on Financial Services,* 112th Cong., 1st Sess. 14 (2011) (testimony of Luke Zubrod, Coalition for Derivatives End-Users); Ben Protess, *Regulators to Ease a Rule on Derivatives Dealers,* NYT, April 18, 2012, at B6; Andrew Ross Sorkin, *A Firm's Vanishing Advisors,* NYT, February 14, 2011, at B1.

68. Jamila Trindle, *CFTC Tightens Swaps Reins,* WSJ, January 12, 2012, at C3; David S. Hilzenrath & Peter Whoriskey, *Gensler, a Colleague Turned Regulator,* WP, November 5, 2011, at A10; Azam Ahmed, Ben Protess & Susanne Craig, *A Romance With Risk That Brought On a Panic,* NYT, December 12, 2011, at A1.

69. Financial Stability Oversight Council, Authority to Designate Financial Market Utilities as Systemically Important, 76 Fed. Reg. 44,763 (2012); Financial Stability Oversight Council, Authority to Require Supervision and Regulation of Certain Nonbank Financial Companies, 76 Fed. Reg. 64,264 (2011); Edward Wyatt, *Fed Oversight of Nonbanks is Weighed,* NYT, October 12, 2011, at B1; Eric Dash & Julie Creswell, *Too Big to Fail, or Too Trifling for Oversight,* NYT, June 12, 2011, at A1; Victoria McGrane, *'Systemically Important' Label Divides U.S. Regulators,* WSJ May 6, 2011, at A1; Damian Paletta, *Infighting Besets Financial-Oversight Council,* WSJ, September 29, 2010, at A1.

70. Federal Reserve Board, Enhanced Prudential Standards and Early Remediation Requirements for Covered Companies, 77 Fed. Reg. 594 (2012); Letter to Board of Governors of the Federal Reserve System from Brian Leach, Chief Risk Officer, Citibank, dated April 30, 2012; Dave Clarke, *Big Is Not Bad, Banks Tell Fed,* WP, April 28, 2012, at A12; Victoria McGrane, *Banks Push Fed on Rule,* WSJ, April 28, 2012, at B2; Edward Wyatt, *Fed Unveils Plan to Limit Chance of a Banking Crisis,* NYT, December 21, 2011, at B1.

71. *Does the Dodd-Frank Act End Too Big To Fail? Hearing Before the Subcommittee on Financial Institutions and Consumer Credit of the House Committee on Financial Services,* 112th Cong., 1st Sess. (2011) (testimony of Christy Romero, Acting Special Inspector General, Office of the Special Inspector General for the Troubled Asset Relief Program); *Has Dodd-Frank Ended Too Big To Fail? Hearing Before the Subcommittee on TARP, Financial Services, and Bailouts of the Public and Private Programs of the House Committee on Oversight and Government Reform,* 112th Cong., 1st Sess. (2011) (testimony of Neil Barofsky, Special Inspector General for the Troubled Asset Relief Program); Zachary A. Goldfarb, *In Obama's Tenure, A Resurgent Wall Street,* WP, November 7, 2011, at A1; Stewart, *Volcker Rule Boggles.*

72. *Stronger Air Rules Predicted as EPA Drops Defense of Regulations from Bush Years,* 40 BNA Env. Rept. 2632 (2009); *EPA "Back on the Job," Jackson Says, in "Arduous Process of Reexamining Rules,"* 40 BNA Env. Rept. 641 (2009); *Activists Eye Greater EPA*

Influence After Key Policy Office Appointments, Inside EPA, December 4, 2009, at 6; Juliet Eilperin, *Nominee Signals Big Changes for EPA*, WP, January 15, 2009, at A8.

73. Environmental Protection Agency, Notice to Terminate the National Environmental Performance Track Program, 74 Fed. Reg. 22,741 (2009); John Sullivan & John Shiffman, *Green Club an EPA Charade*, Philadelphia Inquirer, December 9, 2008, at A01 (quote).

74. Alter, Promise, 60; Margaret Kriz, *Changed Climate*, Nat. J., February 7, 2009, at 40; Steven Mufson, *Coalition Agrees on Emissions Cuts*, WP, January 15, 2009, at D1.

75. *Obama Plan Uses 2005 Emissions Baseline; Reductions in Line With Recent Legislation*, 40 BNA Env. Rept. 474 (2009).

76. Steven Mufson, David A. Fahrenthold & Paul Kane, *In Close Vote, House Passes Climate Bill*, WP, June 27, 2009, at A1.

77. Julie Kosterlitz, *The Chamber's Summer Offensive*, Nat. J., July 4, 2009, at 46; Ben Lieberman, Proposed Global Warming Bills and Regulations Will Do More Harm than Good, Heritage Foundation WebMemo No. 2665, October 23, 2009; Fred L. Smith, Jr. & William Teatman, *Cap and Traitors*, Washington Times, July 9, 2009, at A15 (Competitive Enterprise Institute).

78. Eli Kintisch, *Stolen E-Mails Turn Up Heat on Climate Change Rhetoric*, 326 Science 1329 (2009); Eli Kintisch, *Panel Faults IPCC Leadership But Praises its Conclusions*, 329 Science 1135 (2010); Juliet Eilperin & David A. Fahrenthold, *Series of Missteps by Climate Scientists Threatens Climate-Change Agenda*, WP, February 15, 2010, at A1.

79. Mike Ramsey & Sharon Terlep, *Americans Embrace SUVs Again*, WSJ, December 2, 2011, at A1; Justin Gillis, *Global Carbon Dioxide Emissions in 2010 Show the Biggest Jump Ever Recorded*, NYT, December 2, 2011, at A4; Ryan Lizza, *As the World Burns*, New Yorker, October 11, 2010, at 70; Juliet Eilperin & Steven Mufson, *Obama Shifting Climate Strategy After GOP Gains*, WP, November 5, 2010, at A3.

80. David A. Fahrenthold, *EPA to Let Calif. Set Own Auto Emissions Limits*, WP, July 1, 2009, at A2.

81. Environmental Protection Agency, Endangerment and Cause or Contribute Findings for Greenhouse Gases Under Section 202(a) of the Clean Air Act, 74 Fed. Reg. 66,496 (2009).

82. Environmental Protection Agency, National Highway Traffic Safety Administration, Light-Duty Vehicle Greenhouse Gas Emission Standards and Corporate Average Fuel Economy Standards; Final Rule, 75 Fed. Reg. 25,324 (2010).

83. Environmental Protection Agency, Prevention of Significant Deterioration and Title V Greenhouse Gas Tailoring Rule, 74 Fed. Reg. 55,292 (2009); *EPA Begins to Phase in Requirements to Control Stationary Source Emissions*, 41 BNA Env. Rept. 727 (2010).

84. *Challenge to EPA Greenhouse Gas Regime May Turn on Tailoring Rule, Attorneys Say*, 43 BNA Env. L. Rept. 493 (2012).

85. Ben Lieberman & Nicholas D. Loris, Five Reasons the EPA Should Not Attempt to Deal with Global Warming, Heritage Foundation Web Memo No. 2407, April 23, 2009; *Assessing the Impact of Greenhouse Gas Regulations on Small Business, Hearing Before the Subcommittee on Regulatory Affairs, Stimulus Oversight and Government*

Spending of the House Committee on Oversight and Government Reform, 112th Cong., 1st Sess. 20 (2011) (Testimony of David W. Kreutzer, Heritage Foundation) (millions of permits).

86. 42 U.S.C. § 7412(d); Environmental Protection Agency, Reducing Toxic Pollution from Power Plants, at 7, 13, available at http://www.epa.gov/airquality/powerplanttox ics/pdfs/presentation.pdf.

87. *Out of Thin Air: EPA's Cross-State Air Pollution Rule, Hearing Before the House Committee on Science, Space, and Technology*, 112th Cong., 1st Sess. (2011) (Testimony of Wayne E. Penrod, Sunflower Electric Power Corp.) (grid reliability and brownouts); Sandy Bauers, *EPA Looks at Crackdown on Smokestack Emissions*, Philadelphia Inquirer, July 8, 2011, at A1 (quoting Steve Miller, president of the American Coalition for Clean Coal Electricity) (job losses).

88. Competitive Enterprise Institute, CEI Presents Alternative to American Jobs Act, States News Service, September 9, 2011; Manuel Quinones, *Coal Industry Deploys Donations, Lobbying as Its Issues Gain Prominence*, NYT, October 13, 2011, available at http:// www.nytimes.com/gwire/2011/10/13/13greenwire-coal-industry-deploys-donations -lobbying-as-it-45582.html?pagewanted=all (lobbying campaign); Americans for Tax Reform Center for Fiscal Accountability, Environmental Protection Agency, available at http://www.fiscalaccountability.org/?content=COGD1113 (quote); Daniel J. Weiss, *Poor Little Big Coal Says EPA Smog Standards Too Expensive*, Grist, November 17, 2011, available at http://www.grist.org/coal/2011-11-17-poor-little-big-coal-says -epa-smog-standards-too-expensive (lobbying expenditures).

89. Environmental Protection Agency, National Emission Standards for Hazardous Air Pollutants, From Coal- and Oil-Fired Electric Utility Steam Generating Units and Standards of Performance for Fossil-Fuel-Fired Electric Utility, Industrial-Commercial-Institutional, and Small Industrial-Commercial-Institutional Steam Generating Units, 76 Fed. Reg. 23,399 (2011); *EPA Finalizes Rule to Reduce Mercury, Air Toxics Emissions From Power Plants*, 42 BNA Env. Rept. 2877 (2011); Amy Harder, *Mercurial*, National Journal, September 17, 2011, at 54 (Obama Speech).

90. *House Bill Would Invalidate Clean Water Guidance*, 43 Env. L. Rept. 897 (2012); *EPA Advances Controversial Rulemaking on Clean Water Act's Scope*, Inside EPA, October 21, 2011, at 1.

91. Kevin McGill & Noaki Schwartz, *Oil Drilling Accidents Prompting New Safety Rules*, Mobile Register, April 24, 2010, at A2.

92. Jeremy P. Jacobs, *Federal Oil Spill Probe Finds U.S. Regulations Lacking*, NYT, September 29, 2011, at B5; Russell Gold & Angel Gonzalez, *Final Oil-Spill Report Chastises BP, Others*, WSJ, September 15, 2011, at A1; Jad Mouawad & Barry Meier, *Risk-Taking Rises to New Levels as Oil Rigs in Gulf Drill Deeper*, NYT, August 29, 2010, at A1; Jim Tankersley & Julie Cart, *Oil Drilling Outpaces Regulation*, LAT, May 9, 2010, at A1.

93. National Commission on the BP Deepwater Horizon Oil Spill and Offshore Drilling, Deep Water 55 (2011); Margaret Kriz Hobson, *A Year After Oil Spill, Urgency Turns to Impasse*, Congressional Quarterly, April 18, 2011, at 852; Alyson Flournoy, et al.,

Regulatory Blowout: How Regulatory Failures Made the BP Disaster Possible, and How the System Can Be Fixed to Avoid a Recurrence, 26–27 (Center for Progressive Reform, 2010); Peter J. Honigsberg, *Conflict of Interest that Led to the Gulf Oil Disaster*, 41 ELR 10414 (2011); Siobhan Hughes, *Salazar Details Plans to Break Up Oil Regulator*, WSJ, May 19, 2010, at A2.

94. Siobhan Hughes & Tennile Tracy, *Safety Rules Steeled on Offshore Drilling*, WSJ, September 30, 2010, at A1 (blowout preventer proposal); Department of Interior, Press Release, Salazar Announces Regulations to Strengthen Drilling Safety, Reduce Risk of Human Error on Offshore Oil and Gas Operations, September 30, 2010 (emergency rule); David S. Hilzenrath, *Oil Rigs' Safety Net Questioned as Governments Rely on Private Inspections*, WP, August 15, 2010, at G1 (patch and repair).

95. Hobson, *Year After Oil Spill*; Russell Gold, *Oil Drilling Rebounds in Gulf After Spill*, WSJ, September 15, 2011, at B1; *House Approves Measures to Expand Offshore Drilling, Expedite Permitting*, 42 BNA Env. Rept. 1066 (2011); *Reid Cancels Votes on Oil Spill Bills After Some Democrats Break Ranks*, 41 BNA Env. Rept. 1777 (2010).

96. *Interior Bureau Approves BP Permit for Deepwater Drilling in Gulf of Mexico*, 42 BNA Env. Rept. 2424 (2011); Clifford Krauss & Julia Werdigier, *Two Years After Spill, BP Profits and Plans*, NYT, February 8, 2012, at B1; Tom Fowler, *Return to Gulf: Big Oil Grabs Leases*, WSJ, December 15, 2011, at B10.

97. Corps of Engineers, Suspension and Modification of Nationwide Permit 21, 75 Fed. Reg. 34,711 (2010); Office of Surface Mining Reclamation and Enforcement, Stream Buffer Zone and Related Rules, 74 Fed. Reg 62,664 (2009); *Army Corps Plan Would Ban Permit for Mountaintop Mining in Appalachia*, 40 BNA Env. Rept. 1444 (2009).

98. *Administration Details, Defends Its Actions of Appalachian Surface Coal Mining Permits*, 42 BNA Env. Rept. 1649 (2011); *EPA Says 79 Surface Coal Mining Proposals Need More Review on Environmental Impacts*, 40 BNA Env. Rept. 2193 (2009); *Army Corps Plan Would Ban Permit for Mountaintop Mining in Appalachia*, 40 BNA Env. Rept. 1444 (2009); John M. Broder, *U.S. Revokes Permit for West Virginia Mining Plan*, NYT, January 14, 2011, at A14.

99. *Administration Violated Law When It Revised Surface Coal Mining Regulations, Court Rules*, 42 BNA Env. Rept. 2303 (2011). Ken Ward, Jr., *Obama Brings Back Streamlined Coal Mine Permits*, Charleston Gazette, February 16, 2012, at A1; John M. Broder, *Court Reverses E.P.A. on Big Mining Project*, NYT, March 24, 2012, at A10; Paul Quinlan, *EPA Loses Enthusiasm for Swift Rollback of Bush "Fill Rule,"* NYT, February 26, 2011, available at http://www.nytimes.com/gwire/2011/02/25/25greenwire-epa-loses-enthusiasm-for-swift-rollback-of-bus-27352.html.

100. Occupational Safety and Health Administration, Cranes and Derricks in Construction; Final Rule, 75 Fed. Reg. 47,905 (2010).

101. *Exposure Limits, Program Rule Top OSHA Spring Agenda; Others Labeled "Long Term,"* 42 BNA OSHR 69 (2012); *Safety Engineers Group Urges White House to Complete Review of OSHA Silica Proposal*, 41 BNA OSHR 831 (2011).

102. *Think Tank Says Time Running Short for Injury, Illness Prevention Program Rule*, 41 OSHR 400 (2011); *Michaels, Barab Seek to Allay Industry Fears About Upcoming*

Prevention Program Rule, 41 OSHR 249 (2011); *Injury Prevention Rule, Consultation Program Draw Scrutiny of House Oversight Committee,* 41 BNA OSHR 138 (2011).

103. *Number of Coal Mine Deaths in 2010 at 48: Worst Since 1992,* WSJ, December 30, 2010, at B12.

104. Sabrina Tavernise, *Mine Company's Ex-Chief Rejects Finding in Fatal Blast,* NYT, June 4, 2011, at A14; Sabrina Tavernise, *Report Faults Mine Owner for Explosion that Killed 29,* NYT, May 20, 2011, at A11.

105. Steven Mufson, *Report Criticizes Mine Regulators,* WP, March 24, 2012, at A9; Ken Ward, Jr., *Internal Review Outlines Missed Inspections, Weak Enforcement at UBB,* Charleston Gazette, March 6, 2012, at A1; Ken Ward, Jr., *Industry, Regulators Ignored Coal-Dust Meters,* Charleston Gazette, September 25, 2010, at A1.

106. James R. Carroll & Tom Loftus, *Ex-Massey Chief Has Started Mining Company in Kentucky, Records Show,* Louisville Courier-Journal, December 7, 2011, at A1; Ken Ward, Jr., *MSHA Increases Rock Dust Standard,* Charleston Gazette, September 21, 2011, at A3; Kris Maher, *Post Massey Merger, Alpha CEO Makes Safety Priority No. 1,* WSJ, August 9, 2011, at B7; Clifford Krauss, *Massey Energy's Chief is Quitting, Renewing Talk of a Takeover,* NYT, December 4, 2010, at B7.

107. OMB Watch, *Obama Approach,* 19–20; Ken Ward, Jr., *In Wake of Disaster, Main Tries to Keep MSHA Focused,* Charleston Gazette, December 19, 2010, at B1.

108. Governmental Accountability Office, Drug Safety: FDA Has Begun Efforts to Enhance Postmarket Safety, But Additional Actions are Needed (2009); Jared A. Favole & Alicia Mundy, *Data System to Help FDA Spot Dangerous Products,* WSJ, May 23, 2008, at B8.

109. General Accountability Office, Drug Safety; Andrew Zajac, *Under Obama, A Renewed FDA,* LAT, October 9, 2010, at 11.

110. Harris, *Increased Drug Approvals;* Editorial, *How Safe Are Medical Devices,* NYT, August 5, 2011, at A22; David Brown & N.C. Aizenman, *Panel Calls FDA Device Approvals,* WP, July 30, 2011, at A2.

111. Thomas M. Burton, *FDA Overrules Staff Analysis in Approving Anticlotting Drug,* WSJ, November 5, 2011, at B1; Gardiner Harris, *F.D.A. Officials, Hoping to Stave Off Critics, Point to Increased Drug Approvals,* NYT, November 4, 2011, at A18; Jonathan D. Rockoff & Ron Winslow, *Drug Makers Refill Parched Pipelines,* WSJ, July 11, 2011, at B1; Avery Johnson & Ron Winslow, *Drug Makers Say FDA Safety Focus is Slowing New-Medicine Pipeline,* WSJ, June 30, 2008, at A1.

112. Food and Drug Administration, Prevention of Salmonella Enteritidis in Shell Eggs During Production, Storage, and Transportation, 74 Fed. Reg. 33,029 (2009); Andrew Martin, *Egg Recall Exposes Flaws in Nation's Food Safety System,* NYT, August 24, 2010, at B1.

113. William Neuman, *2 Agencies Take Steps to Improve Food Safety,* NYT, August 1, 2009, at B3.

114. William Neuman, *Ban on E. Coli in Ground Beef Is to Extend to 6 More Strains,* NYT, September 13, 2001, at B1; Judy Dempsey & James Kanter, *In Germany, Answers Are Elusive as E. Coli Outbreak Rages,* NYT, June 1, 2001, at A12..

115. Gardiner Harris, *President Plans Team to Overhaul Food Safety*, NYT, March 15, 2009, at 24; Matthew Hay Brown, *Food Safety Reforms Favored*, Baltimore Sun, February 15, 2009, at A1.

116. Jane Zhang, *Small Farms Challenge Expansion of FDA's Authority*, WSJ, July 27, 2009, at A15.

117. Alicia Mundy, *Food-Safety Bill Inches Forward but Still Faces Senate Obstacles*, WSJ, September 21, 2010, at A12.

118. Michael Booth, *One Death Added as CDC Says Listeria Outbreak Over*, Denver Post, December 9, 2011, at B2.

119. Food and Drug Administration, News Release, Chamberlain Farms Recall, August 28, 2012, available at http://www.fda.gov/NewsEvents/Newsroom/PressAnnouncements/ucm316665.htm; Food and Drug Administration, News Release, Burch Equipment LLC Recall, August 13, 2012, available at http://www.fda.gov/NewsEvents/Newsroom/PressAnnouncements/ucm313743.htm. Dina ElBoghdady, *Food-Safety Rules in Limbo at Office of Management and Budget*, WP, May 3, 2012, at A1.

120. Dina ElBoghdady, *FDA Plan Calls for Voluntary Limits on Drugs in Animal Feed*, WP, April 12, 2012, at A12; Gardiner Harris, *New Prescription Requirement Will Cut Use of Antibiotics in Livestock, F.D.A. Says*, NYT, April 12, 2012, at A19.

121. Matt Richtel, *Promoting the Car Phone, Despite Risks*, NYT, December 7, 2009, at A1.

122. Federal Motor Carrier Safety Administration, Drivers of CMVs: Restricting the Use of Cellular Phones, 75 Fed. Reg. 80,014 (2010); Sholnn Freeman, *Texting and Driving Don't Mix*, WP, July 29, 2009, at A7.

123. Federal Railroad Administration, Restrictions on Railroad Operating Employees' Use of Cellular Telephones and Other Electronic Devices, 75 Fed. Reg. 59,580 (2010).

124. Federal Motor Carrier Safety Administration, Drivers of CMVs: Restricting the Use of Cellular Phones, 76 Fed. Reg. 75,470 (November 23, 2011).

125. *Toyota's Recall and the Government's Response, Hearings Before the Senate Committee on Science and Transportation*, 111th Cong., 2d Sess. (2010) (testimony of Ray LaHood, testimony of Clarence M. Ditlow); Letter to Ray LaHood, from Henry A. Waxman & Bart Stupak, dated February 22, 2010, at 1, 4–7 (quoting internal NHTSA emails and memos); *NHTSA Chief Asks Panel for More Muscle, Higher Penalties in Reauthorization Bill*, 39 BNA PSLR 829 (2011); Nick Bunkley, *A Proposed Rule Seeks to Stop Runaway Cars*, NYT, April 13, 2012, at B7; Nick Bunkley, *Toyota Concedes 2 Flaws Caused Loss of Control*, NYT, July 15, 2010, at B1; Peter Whoriskey, *Toyota Used its "Game Plan" to Escape a Major Early Recall*, WP, March 19, 2010, at A1; Kate Linebaugh & Matthew Dolan, *Pedal Maker Says It's Not to Blame*, WSJ, February 9, 2010, at A3; Jayne O'Donnell & David Kiley, *Technology Puts Unintended Acceleration Back in Spotlight*, USA Today, April 18, 2004, at B1.

126. Federal Railroad Administration, Positive Train Control Systems, 75 Fed. Reg. 2598 (2010); *DOT to Revisit Train Control Systems, NEPA Rules in Broad Regulatory Review*, 42 BNA Env. Rept. 1241 (2011); Christopher Conkey, *Safety Costs Chafe Railroads*, WSJ, October 26, 2009, at A4.

127. Federal Motor Carrier Safety Administration, Hours of Service of Drivers, 76 Fed. Reg. 81,134 (2011).

128. Airline Safety and Federal Aviation Administration Extension Act of 2010, Pub. L.

111–216, 124 Stat. 2348 (2010); Federal Aviation Administration, Flightcrew Member Duty and Rest Requirements, 77 Fed. Reg. 330 (2012) (final rule); Federal Aviation Administration, Flightcrew Member Duty and Rest Requirements, 75 Fed. Reg. 55,852 (2010) (proposed rule); Andy Pasztor, *Regulators Delay New Rules on Pilot Fatigue*, WSJ, August 3, 2011, at B1; Rachel Leven, *Business Group: Scrap Pilot Rest Mandate*, The Hill, July 14, 2011, at 11; Kathryn A. Wolfe, *Rest Rules Pose FAA Stress Test*, Congressional Quarterly, November 29, 2010, at 2741.

129. Brent Kendall, *Leibowitz Tapped as FTC Chairman*, WSJ, February 27, 2009, at A1; Federal Trade Commission, *FTC Chairman Jon Leibowitz Appoints Senior Staff*, available at http://www.ftc.gov/opa/2009/04/seniorstaff.shtm.

130. Cecilia Kang, *FTC Sets Endorsement Rules for Blogs*, WP, October 6, 2009, at A18.

131. *FTC Report on Consumer Privacy Urges Congress to Pass Legislation*, 102 BNA Antitrust & Trade Reg. Rept. 393 (2012); Julia Angwin, *Regulators Urge Web Privacy Rules*, WSJ March 27, 2012, at B3; Cecilia Kang, *Voluntary Plan for Internet Privacy*, WP, February 23, 2012, at A12; Edward Wyatt, *White House, Consumers in Mind, Offers Online Privacy Guidelines*, NYT, February 23, 2011, at B1; Edward Wyatt & Tanzina Vega, *Stage Set for Showdown on Online Privacy*, NYT, November 10, 2010, at B1; Stephanie Clifford, *Fresh Views at Agency Overseeing Online Ads*, NYT, August 5, 2009, at B1 (survey results).

132. *Senate Confirms Tenenbaum As CPSC Chair; Commerce Hearing Pointed to Favorable Vote*, 37 BNA PSLR 698 (2009); *Bush Signs Landmark CPSC Reform Act; Law Strengthens Funding, Agency Authority*, 36 BNA PSLR 784 (2008); Annys Shin, *Toymakers Frustrated by Patchwork of Safety Rules*, WP, June 25, 2008, at D1 .

133. The Consumer Product Safety Improvement Act of 2008, Pub. L. 110–314, 122 Stat. 3016 (2008); Government Accountability Office, Consumer Safety: Better Information and Planning Would Strengthen CPSC's Oversight of Imported Products 13 (2009).

134. *Lead Enforcement Stayed Additional Year, Parts Testing OK; CPSC Votes Other Stays*, 37 BNA PSLR 1285 (2009); *NAM Coalition Petitions CPSC for Interim Final Rule on Exclusions to New Lead Limits*, 36 BNA PSLR 1271 (2008).

135. *CPSIA Effects Will be Long-Lasting, Result in Job Loss, Bankruptcy, Manufacturers Say*, 37 BNA PSLR 194 (2009); Melanie Trotman, *New Lead Rules May Crimp Those Thrift-Shop Bargains*, WSJ, January 8, 2009, at A10.

136. Pub. L. 112–28, 125 Stat. 273 (2011); Mark Duvall, Felix Yeung & Erica Zilioli, *Fixing the Consumer Product Safety Improvement Act: Are We There Yet?* 39 BNA PSLR 1121 (2011).

137. *Michaels Gives Guidance on Rulemakings, Welcomes More Congressional Oversight*, 40 OSHR 1031 (2010); *Report Cites "Dramatic" Change in Course for OSHA Enforcement Under Obama*, 39 BNA OSHR 1020 (2010); *OSHA Plans to Inspect Up to 4,500 Sites Over Next Year Based on Highest Injury Risk*, 39 BNA OSHR 472 (2009).

138. Emergency Supplemental Appropriations Act of 2006, Pub. L. 109–234, 120 Stat. 418 (2006); Goodell, Big Coal, 64, 71 (meager Sago fine); *Evaluating the Effectiveness of MSHA's Mine Safety and Health Program, Hearings Before the House Committee on Education and Labor*, 110th Cong., 1st Sess. (2007) (testimony of Richard E. Stickler); *As Mining Safety Continues to Improve, MSHA Emphasizes Health Issues*, 40 BNA OSHR S-18 (2010); *MSHA Sues Kentucky Darby for Failure to Pay Fines Assessed After Fatal Explosion*, 39 OSHR 1234 (2009).

139. *Obama Tells Solis, MSHA to Strengthen Enforcement, Inspect Troubled Mines,* 40 BNA OSHR 330 (2010); Kris Maher, *Mine Safety Sweep Yields Citations, Closures,* WSJ, May 6, 2010, at A9.

140. Ken Ward, Jr., *MSHA Issues More than 300 Violations in Inspection Sweep,* Charleston Gazette, October 19, 2011, at A1.

141. OMB Watch, The Obama Approach to Public Protection: Enforcement 25, 28 (2010).

142. See, e.g., Gardiner Harris & Duff Wilson, *$750 Million for Drug Maker of Tainted Goods,* NYT, October 27, 2010, at A1.

143. Zachary A. Goldfarb, *Goldman Sachs to Pay Record Settlement in Fraud Suit, Change Business Practices,* WP, July 16, 2010, at A1.

144. See, e.g., *Importer to Pay $2 Million Civil Penalty; CPSC Hails Accord as Important Precedent,* 38 BNA PSLR 224 (2010).

145. *MSHA Has Improved Enforcement But Needs Stronger Law, Agency Chief Tells Committee,* 41 BNA OSHR 297 (2011); *Inspections Without Warning for Pattern of Violations Would Increase Under Proposal,* 41 BNA OSHR 95 (2011); *Backlog at Mine Commission Could Lead to Lower Fines, Safety Lapses, Speakers Say,* 40 OSHR 160 (2010) (quoting Joseph A. Main); Kimberly Kindy, *Longtime Tug of War on Mine Safety,* WP, January 4, 2011, at A1; Kris Maher, Stephen Power & Siobhan Hughes, *Appeals by Mines Delayed Sanctions,* WSJ, April 15, 2010, at A1.

146. Bernard Condon, *Not King Coal,* Forbes, May 26, 2003, at 80 (quote); Ken Ward, Jr., *Mine Received 64 Closure Orders Prior to Disaster,* Charleston Gazette, April 8, 2010, at A1; Steven Mufson, Jarry Markon & Ed O'Keefe, *West Virginia Mine Has Been Cited for Myriad Safety Violations,* WP, April 7, 2010, at A1.

147. David Fahrenthold & Kimberly Kindy, *Owner of W. Va. Coal Mine Agrees to Pay $209 Million Penalty for Fatal Explosion,* WP, December 7, 2011, at A3; Sabrina Tavernise, *Mine Owner Will Pay $209 Million in Blast That Killed 29 Workers,* NYT, December 7, 2011, at A14.

148. Kris Maher, *Employer Groups Criticize Mine-Safety Bill,* WSJ, July 13, 2010, at A3; *Michaels Tells House Subcommittee He Supports OSHA Reform Measures,* 40 BNA OSHR 223 (2010).

149. Eric Lipton, *With Obama, Regulations Are Back in Fashion,* NYT, May 12, 2010, at 15; Jared A. Favole, *FDA Warns Bayer on 2 Aspirin Products,* WSJ, October 29, 2008, at D4 (combination crackdown); *FDA Says Viagra Ad Left Out Risks,* WSJ, April 22, 2008, at A22 (more vigorous enforcement); Julie Schmit, *Drug Ads to Get More FDA Scrutiny,* USA Today, February 25, 2008, at A18 (increased budget); Stephanie Saul, *Committee Investigates Ad Tactics for Lipitor,* NYT, February 7, 2008, at C3 (congressional investigations).

150. Natasha Singer, *F.D.A. Again Warns a Generic Maker Apotex About Conditions at Its Plants,* NYT, April 15, 2010, at B6; Gardiner Harris, *Prosecutors Plan Crackdown on Doctors Who Accept Kickbacks,* NYT, March 4, 2009, at A14; Jon Kamp, *Medtronic Unit Cited by FDA for New Lapses,* WSJ, April 29, 2008, at D2.

151. Lyndsey Layton, *FDA Pressured to Combat Rising "Food Fraud,"* WP, March 30, 2010, at A1; Lyndsey Layton, *FDA Warns 17 Food Companies of Misleading Claims on Labels,* WP, March 4, 2010, at A8.

152. Jean Eaglesham, *Financial Crimes Bedevil Prosecutors*, WSJ, December 8, 2011, at B1; Ken Ward Jr., *Ex-Upper Big Branch Security Director Found Guilty*, Charleston Gazette, October 26, 2011, at A1; Vanessa O'Connell & Michael Rothfeld, *U.S. Targets Drug Executives*, WSJ, September 13, 2011, at A1; David Evans, *When Drug Makers' Profits Outweigh Penalties*, WP, March 21, 2010, at G1.

153. Memorandum from Barack Obama to Heads of Executive Departments and Agencies, re: Preemption, dated May 20, 2009; Sheryl Gay Stolberg & Robert Pear, *Obama Open to Reining in Medical Suits*, NYT, June 15, 2009, at A1; Nick Timiraos, *Groups Aim to Roll Back Curbs on Lawsuits*, WSJ, November 3, 2008, at A5.

154. David Hendricks, *Some Notable Wins for Business*, San Antonio Express-News, June 1, 2011, at C1; Angela Morris, *Senate Passes New Version of Loser Pays*, Texas Lawyer, May 24, 2011, at 6; *States Reform Civil Justice*, UPI, June 22, 2011, available at http://www.upi.com/Top_News/US/2011/06/22/States-reform-civil-justice/UPI-80931308759354/; Editorial, *Loser Pays, Everyone Wins*, WSJ, December 15, 2010, at A17 (election results).

155. Kutner, Presidency in Peril, 219–20; Patricia Cohen, *Conservative Magazines: Their Vision Isn't G.O.P.'s*, NYT, June 13, 2009, at C1; Howard Kurtz, *White House Lets Limbaugh Be Voice of GOP Opposition*, WP, March 3, 209, at A4.

156. James L. Gattuso, Diane Katz & Stephen A. Keen, Red Tape Rising: Obama's Torrent of New Regulation (Heritage Foundation Backgrounder No. 2482, October 26, 2010); Elizabeth Williamson, *U.S. Business Groups Air Policy Concerns*, WSJ, July 14, 2010, at A1 (jobs summit); Lipton, *With Obama* (quoting Erin Streeter, National Association of Manufacturers).

157. Peter Baker & David M. Herszenhorn, *Obama Chastises Wall St. In Call to Stiffen Rules*, NYT, April 22, 2010, at A1; Henry J. Pulizzi, *Obama Urges CEOs to Rally Behind Business Agenda*, WSJ, February 24, 2010, at A1.

158. Elizabeth Williamson, *Revisiting the Regulations Affecting Business*, WSJ, July 12, 2010, at A4.

159. Jean Stefancic & Richard Delgado, No Mercy 152 (1996); Rick Perlstein, *A Liberal Shock Doctrine*, American Prospect, September, 2008, at 22.

160. Kutner, Presidency in Peril, 161.

161. Dan Eggen & Michael D. Shear, *Chamber of Commerce Losing Battles Against Obama*, WP, July 22, 2010, at A3.

162. Editorial, *An Insult to Their Memory*, NYT, December 10, 2010, at A20; David A. Farenthold & Juliet Eilperin, *Historic Oil Spill Fails to Produce Gains for U.S. Environmentalists*, WP, July 12, 2010, at A1.

163. Peter Baker, *What Does He Do Now*, NYT Magazine, October 17, 2010, at 40, 45 (quoting Ken Duberstein); Matthew Dowd, *Votes of Passion*, Nat. J., September 25, 2010, at 74.

CHAPTER 18. STRIKING A NEW BARGAIN

1. Rena Steinzor & Sidney Shapiro, The People's Agents viii (2010); Debra S. Knopman & Richard A. Smith, *20 Years of the Clean Water Act*, 35 Env't 16, 34 (1993); David C. Vladeck, *The Failed Promise of Workplace Health Regulation*, 111 W. Va. L. Rev. 15, 16 (2008).

2. Jerome Armstrong & Markos Moulitsas, Crashing the Gate 38, 51 (2006); Paul Starobin, *The New Leftist Narrative*, 41 Nat. J. 16 (2009).

3. Robert Kuttner, A Presidency in Peril xiii-xiv (2010); Joseph E. Stiglitz, Freefall 35–37 (2010); Frank Rich, *Why Has He Fallen Short*, N.Y. Rev. of Books, August 19, 2010, at 8.

4. Matthew Daly, *BP Ad Spending Since Spill: $5 Million a Week*, WP, September 2, 2010, at A21.

5. Peter Baker, *What Does He Do Now*, NYT Magazine, October 17, 2010, at 40, 44.

6. Eric F. Goldman, Rendezvous with Destiny 17–18 (1955); Gerald W. McFarland, Mugwumps, Morals & Politics, 1884–1920 1, 18–22, 50 (1975); John G. Sproat, "The Best Men": Liberal Reformers in the Gilded Age 8–10 (1968).

7. Jonathan Alter, The Promise 64 (2010); William Greider, *Obama Without Tears*, Nation, November 10, 2010, at 15; Michael Joseph Gross, *Sarah Palin: The Sound and the Fury*, Vanity Fair, October, 2010, at 250 (quote); Rich, *Why Has He Fallen Short*.

8. Rena I. Steinzor, Mother Earth and Uncle Sam 4 (2008); Robert B. Reich, Supercapitalism 126 (2007).

9. Stuart O. Schweitzer, *Trying Times at the FDA—The Challenge of Ensuring the Safety of Imported Pharmaceuticals*, 358 New Eng. J. Med. 1773 (2008); Lisa Reinand & Ed O'Keefe, *A Negative Poll for Federal Workers*, WP, October 18, 2010, at A1.

10. Rachel E. Barkow, *Insulating Agencies: Avoiding Capture Through Institutional Design*, 89 Tex. L. Rev. 15, 45–50, 59–60 (2010).

11. Rena Steinzor, *The Case for Abolishing Centralized White House Review*, 1 Mich. J. Env. & Ad. L. 209 (2012).

12. See Steinzor & Shapiro, People's Agents, 215; Rena Steinzor, Michael Patoka & James Goodwin, Behind Closed Doors at the White House 63–64 (Center for Progressive Reform 2011).

13. National Research Council/Institute of Medicine, Enhancing Food Safety 17 (2010); Trust for America's Health, Keeping America's Food Safe: A Blueprint for Fixing the Food Safety System at the U.S. Department of Health and Human Services 15 (2009).

14. Christopher Schroeder & Rena Steinzor, A New Progressive Agenda for Public Health and the Environment 170 (2005); National Commission on the BP Deepwater Horizon Oil Spill and Offshore Drilling, Deep Water ch. 3 (2011).

15. James R. Hackney, Jr., Under Cover of Science: American Legal-Economic Theory and the Quest for Objectivity 99, 105 (2006); Schroeder & Steinzor, New Progressive Agenda, 42–44; Robert Solow, *The Economist's Approach to Pollution and Its Control*, 123 Science 498 (1971).

16. Simon Johnson & James Kwak, 13 Bankers, 173, 206–08, 211–12 (2010); Stiglitz, Freefall, 165; James B. Stewart, *Volcker Rule, Once Simple, Now Boggles*, NYT, October 22, 2011, at B1 (quoting Henry Kaufman, former managing director of Salomon Brothers).

17. Kathleen C. Engel & Patricia A. McCoy, *Turning a Blind Eye: Wall Street Finance of Predatory Lending*, 75 Fordham L. Rev. 2040, 2042 (2007).

18. Stiglitz, Freefall, 86; Karl S. Okamoto, *Skin in the Game*, Legal Times, September 29, 2008, at 53.

19. Schroeder & Steinzor, New Progressive Agenda, 94–97.

20. Charles R. Morris, The Trillion Dollar Meltdown 157, 161–62 (2008); Stiglitz, Freefall, 163, 174; Congressional Oversight Panel, Special Report on Regulatory Reform 4 (January 2009).

21. James R. May, *Now More Than Ever: Trends and Environmental Citizen Suits at 30*, 10 Widener L. Rev. 1, 46 (2003).

22. Sidney A. Shapiro & Randy Rabinowitz, *Punishment Versus Cooperation in Regulatory Enforcement: A Case Study of OSHA*, 49 Ad. L. Rev. 713, 716 (1997).

23. Office of Inspector General, Department of Labor, OSHA Needs to Evaluate the Impact and Use of Hundreds of Millions of Dollars in Penalty Reductions as Incentives for Employers to Improve Workplace Safety and Health 10 (September 30, 2010).

24. John Braithwaite, To Punish or Persuade 91 (1985); Majority Staff of the Senate Committee on Health, Education, Labor and Pensions, Discounting Death: OSHA's Failure to Punish Safety Violations that Kill Workers 5 (2009) (damage caps).

25. Johnson & Kwak, 13 Bankers, 141–42; Jason Lynch, *Comment, Federalism, Separation of Powers, and the Role of State Attorneys General in Multistate Litigation*, 101 Colum. L. Rev. 1998 (2001); Peggy A. Lautenschlager & Daniel P. Bach, The Citizen's Advocate: A Perspective on the Historical and Continuing Role of State Attorneys General 2, 5 (American Constitution Society, October, 2007); Caroline Mayer, *Attorneys General Crusade Against Corporate Misdeeds*, WP, February 19, 2003, at E1.

26. See Daniel A. Farber, *Tort Law in the Era of Climate Change, Katrina, and 9/11: Exploring Liability for Extraordinary Risks*, 43 Valparaiso U. L. Rev. 1075 (2009); Steven Batrick, *Tort Claims Under Common Law a Key Tactic for Attorneys Litigating Environmental Cases*, 40 BNA Env. Rept. 2789 (2009).

27. Connecticut v. American Electric Power Co., Inc., 582 F.3d 309 (2d Cir. 2009). After EPA made a finding that it could regulate greenhouse gas emissions under the Clean Air Act, the Supreme Court held that the nuisance action was preempted by that statute. American Electric Power Co. v. Connecticut, 131 S.Ct. 2527 (2011).

28. Farber, *Tort Law*, 1126–28.

29. Mark A. Geistfeld, *The Value of Consumer Choice in Product's Liability*, 74 Brooklyn L. Rev. 781, 804 (2009); Larry S. Stewart, *Strict Liability for Defective Product Design: The Quest for a Well-Ordered Regime*, 74 Brooklyn L. Rev. 1039, 1048–49 (2009).

30. Alexandra B. Klass, *Pesticides, Children's Health Policy, and Common Law Tort Claims*, 7 Minnesota J. of Law, Science, & Technology 89, 92 (2005).

31. Steinzor & Shapiro, People's Agents, 201.

32. Stephen B. Burbank, *The Class Action Fairness Act of 2005 in Historical Context: A Preliminary View*, 156 U. Pa. L. Rev. 1439 (2008); Elizabeth J. Cabraser, *The Class Action Counter Reformation*, 57 Stan. L. Rev. 1475, 1483–84 (2005); Myriam Gilles, *Opting Out of Liability: The Forthcoming, Near-Total Demise of the Modern Class Action*, 104 Mich. L. Rev. 373, 379 (2005).

33. Terry Carter, *Boosting the Bench*, ABA J., October, 2002, at 29 (76 percent); Lawrence M. Friedman, *Benchmarks: Judges on Trial, Judicial Selection and Elections*, 58 DePaul L. Rev. 451, 462 (2009); Sandra Day O'Connor, *Justice for Sale*, WSJ, November 15, 2007, at A25; Texans for Public Justice, Pay to Play 3 (2001).

34. Institute for the Advancement of the American Legal System, O'Connor Judicial Selection Initiative, available at http://www.du.edu/legalinstitute/judicial_selection .html.

35. Marissa M. Golden, *Interest Groups in the Rulemaking Process: Who Participates? Whose Votes Get Heard?* 8 J. Pub. Admin. Research & Theory 245 (1998); Wendy Wagner, Katherine Barnes & Lisa Peters, *Rulemaking in the Shade: An Empirical Study of EPA's Air Toxic Regulations*, 63 Ad. L. Rev. 99 (2011) (5 to 1 margin).

36. Schroeder & Steinzor, New Progressive Agenda, 178; Marc B. Mihaly, *Citizen Participation in the Making of Environmental Decisions: Evolving Obstacles and Potential Solutions through Partnership with Experts and Agents*, 27 Pace Env. L. Rev. 151, 213–16 (2009–10).

37. William L. Andreen, *Motivating Enforcement: Institutional Culture and the Clean Water Act*, 24 Pace Env. L. Rev. 67, 71 (2007); Matthew D. Zinn, *Policing Environmental Regulatory Enforcement: Cooperation, Capture, and Citizen Suits*, 21 Stan. Envt'l L. J. 81, 127–31 (2002).

38. Jeannette L. Austin, *The Rise of Citizen-Suit Enforcement in Environmental Law: Reconciling Private and Public Attorneys General*, 81 Nw. U. L. Rev. 220, 221 (1987); May, *Now More Than Ever*, 3–4.

39. Robert Kuttner, *The Death and Life of American Liberalism*, American Prospect, June 2005, at 16; Andrew Rich, *Think Tanks and the War of Ideas in American Politics*, in In Search of Progressive America 72 (Michael Kazin, ed. 2008); Martha T. McCluskey, *Thinking with Wolves: Left Legal Theory After the Right's Rise*, 54 Buffalo L. Rev. 1191, 1233 (2007).

40. Alter, Promise, 47; Center for American Progress, Mission Statement 4 (2003) (quote); Michael A. Fletcher, *Legal Organization May Become Influential Beyond its Dreams*, WP, December 7, 2008, at A5; Jeff Jeffrey, *Critical Moment for Liberal Law Group*, Legal Times, November 17, 2008, at 14; Katherine Q. Seelye, *Democrats, Seeing Conservative Media Dominance, Form New Group to Fight It*, NYT, June 5, 2003, at A25.

41. Matt Bai, The Argument 111–12, 200–01 (2007); Rich, *Think Tanks*, 83; David D. Kallick, Progressive Think Tanks: What Exists, What's Missing 28 (Open Society Institute, 2002).

42. Joe Conason, Big Lies 36 (2003); Ronald Brownstein, *Ready to Rumble*, American Prospect, September, 2007, at 40.

43. Leonard Downie, Jr. & Robert G. Kaiser, The News About the News 12, 25–26, 78–79, 133–34, 137, 177, 231 (2002); Eric Klinenberg, Fighting for Air 126 (2007); Robert W. McChesney, The Political Economy of Media 41–46 (2008); Michael Massing, *The Press: The Enemy Within*, N.Y. Rev. of Books, December 15, 2005, at 15.

44. David Brock, The Republican Noise Machine 171–74, 314 (2004); Kathleen Hall Jamieson & Joseph N. Cappella, Echo Chamber 47 (2008).

45. Conason, Big Lies, 37; Elizabeth Newlin Carney, *Extreme Makeover*, 37 Nat. J. 598, 603 (2005).

46. Brock, Noise Machine, 382; Jacob S. Hacker & Paul Pierson, Off Center 218 (2005) (Bush veto); Jamieson & Capella, Echo Chamber, 46; Robert F. Kennedy Jr., Crimes Against Nature 176 (2004).

47. Pro Publica, About Us, available at http://www.propublica.org/about/; Julie Kosterlitz, *Nonprofit News?* 40 Nat. J. 44 (2008); Clifford Krauss, *Balancing Bottom Lines and Headlines*, NYT, September 30, 2007, at C1.

48. Bai, Argument, 227–32; Downie & Kaiser, News About News, ch. 7; Patrick Beach, *Netroots Gets a Lift from Unexpected Visit by Gore*, Austin American-Statesman, July 20, 2008, at A1; Noam Cohen, *Blogger, Sans Pajamas, Rakes Muck and a Prize*, NYT, February 25, 2008, at C1.

49. Armstrong & Moulitsas, Crashing the Gate; Bai, Argument, 67; Christopher Hayes, *MoveOn@Ten*, Nation, April 11, 2008, at 11; Paul Farhi, *In HuffPo Merger, Arianna Wins Big*, WP, February 8, 2011, at C1.

50. Al Gore, The Assault on Reason 267–68 (2007); Klinenberg, Fighting, 173 (quoting Barry Diller); McChesney, Political Economy, 19, 144.

51. George Packer, *The Fall of Conservatism*, New Yorker, May 26, 2008, at 47.

52. Packer, *Fall of Conservatism* (sclerotic quote); Matt Bai, *Newt, Again*, NYT Magazine, March 1, 2009, at 28 (moribund quote); Patricia Cohen, *Conservative Thinkers Think Again*, NYT, July 20, 2008, at Wk3 (website quote).

53. Ross Douthat & Reinan Salam, Grand New Party (2008); David Frum, Comeback Conservatism (2008). See David Brooks, *The Sam's Club Agenda*, NYT, June 27, 2008, at A19.

54. William Greider, Come Home, America 175 (2009); Mark Schmitt, *Can Identity Politics Save the Right*, American Prospect, June, 2008, at 12.

55. David Carr, *Cable News Stokes Political Fever*, NYT, March 30, 3009, at B1; Brian Stelter, *For Conservative Radio, It's a New Dawn, Too*, NYT, December 22, 2008, at B1.

56. Citizens United v. Federal Election Commission, 130 S.Ct. 876 (2010); Jim Rutenberg, *For Donor Groups Vote Lays the Groundwork for 2012*, NYT, October 31, 2010, at A1; Brody Mullins, *Big Donors Plan Boost in Campaign Spending*, WSJ, January 22, 2010, at A6.

CHAPTER 19. CONCLUSIONS

1. Jonathan Alter, The Promise xiii (2010); Robert Kuttner, A Presidency in Peril 225 (2010); Matthew Dowd, *Votes of Passion*, Nat. J., September 25, 2010, at 74; Ross Douthat, *The Great Bailout Backlash*, NYT, October 25, 2010, at A27.

2. Policy Burdens Inhibiting Economic Growth (Business Roundtable & The Business Council, June 21, 2010); Kate Zernike, *Secretive Republican Donors Are Planning Ahead*, NYT, October 19, 2010, at A18; Lori Montgomery, *Business Leaders Say Obama's Economic Policies Stifle Growth*, WP, June 23, 2010, at A12 (Seidenberg quote); Understanding and Addressing Threats to American Free Enterprise and Prosperity, Program for Seminar held at Aspen, Colorado, June 27–28, 2010.

3. Alter, Promise, 264; Kate Zernike, Boiling Mad (2010); Jane Mayer, *Covert Operations*, New Yorker, August 30, 2010, at 45; Kate Zernike, *Shaping Tea Party Passion Into Campaign Force*, NYT, August 26, 2010, at A1; Brian Stelter, *Pundit Stakes Out a More Activist Role in Politics*, NYT, November 22, 2009, at A25; Michael M. Phillips,

FreedomWorks Harnesses Growing Activism on the Right, WSJ, October 6, 2009, at A4; Brian Stelter, *CNBC Replays Its Reporter's Tirade*, NYT, February 23, 2009, at B7.

4. Amy Gardner, *A Movement Without a Compass*, WP, October 24, 2010, at A1.

5. Dan Eggen & T.W. Farnam, *In Preview of 2012, Interest Groups Drive Spending Through Roof*, WP, November 3, 2010, at A24; T.W. Farnam, *Firms Helped by Bailout Now Give Generously to Candidates*, WP, October 24, 2010, at A3; Jim Rutenberg, Don van Natta, Jr. & Mike McIntire, *Offering Donors Secrecy, and Going on Attack*, NYT, October 11, 2010, at A1 ($75 million); Zernike, *Shaping Tea Party Passion* (boot camp).

6. Diane Katz, Rolling Back Red Tape: 20 Regulations to Eliminate (Heritage Foundation, January 26, 2011); *Chamber of Commerce Panel Urges Limits on Agencies' Regulatory Authority*, 41 BNA OSHR 252 (2011); Edward Wyatt, *Dodd-Frank Under Fire A Year Later*, NYT, July 19, 2011, at B1 (two dozen bills); Dan Balz, *Election Results Are Open to (Careful) Interpretation*, WP, November 4, 2010, at A31; Scott Wilson, *Obama May Be On His Own If He Wants Big Changes*, WP, October 17, 2010, at A1.

7. Eric Lipton, *In Daley, A Businessman's Voice in Oval Office*, NYT, January 7, 2011, at A1; Dan Balz, *Obama Signals Continuity, For Now, With Staff Changes*, WP, October 3, 2010, at A2; Michael Hudson, Obama's New Chief of Staff Sought to Loosen Post-Enron Corporate Reforms (Center for Public Integrity, January 6, 2011), available at http://www.publicintegrity.org/articles/entry/2808/.

8. Barack Obama, *Toward a 21st-Century Regulatory System*, WSJ, January 18, 2011, at A17 (Obama quote); Jia Lynn Yang, *U.S. Chamber, White House Mending Rift*, WP, January 11, 2011, at A12 (willingness quote); Perry Bacon, Jr. & Jia Lynn Yang, *Obama, Business Leaders Seek Detente*, WP, December 16, 2010, at A16 (summit); Michael D. Shear, *After Months of Feuding, Obama Makes Overture to Business Group*, NYT, November 4, 2010, at B4 (Obama quote)

9. Amy Gardner, *FreedomWorks Gathers GOP Lawmakers to Refocus on Tea Party Goals*, WP, November 12, 2010, at A1; Jennifer Steinhauer, *Focusing on Next Step, Tea Party Rallies Congressional Freshmen*, NYT, November 12, 2010, at A10.

10. Jim Puzzanghera, *Rep. Darrell Issa Targets Business Burdens*, LAT, January 5, 2011, at B1 (hit list); Bacon & Yang, *Obama, Business Leaders Seek Detente* (Boehner assurance); Letter to Darrell Issa from Jay Timmons, dated January 7, 2011 (NAM response); Avery Johnson & Ron Winslow, *Drug Makers Say FDA Safety Focus is Slowing New-Medicine Pipeline*, WSJ, June 30, 2008, at A1. See Thomas O. McGarity, Deregulatory Riders Redux, 1 Michigan J. Env. & Ad. L. 33 (2012).

11. *Climate Science and EPA's Greenhouse Gas Regulations, Hearing Before the Subcommittee on Energy and Power of the House Committee on Energy and Commerce*, 112th Cong., 1st Sess. (2011) (Testimony of John R. Christy, University of Alabama, Huntsville); *Barrasso Bill Would Eliminate EPA Authority to Regulate Greenhouse Gas Emissions*, 42 BNA Env. Rept. 217 (2011); Margaret Kriz Hobson, *Political Tidal Wave Turns EPA Strategy*, Cong. Quarterly Weekly, February 14, 2011, at 335; Coral Davenport, *Power Forward*, Nat. J., February 4, 2012, at 37.

12. *House Clears Bill Requiring Cost Study, Delays in Key Air Pollution Regulations*, 42 BNA Env. Rept. 2173 (2011); *White House Threatens TRAIN Act Veto, Warns EPA*

Rules Delay Would Harm Health, 42 BNA Env. Rept. 2139 (2011); *House Approves Bill to Require Congressional Approval of Major Rules*, 39 PSLR 1342 (2011); *House Passes Two Anti-Regulatory Bills, Sparking Concern Among Safety Advocates*, 41 OSHR 1046 (2011); *House Approves Legislation to Assess Broader Array of Costs of Regulation*, 39 PSLR 1316 (2011); *Senate Votes Down Reform Bills That Sought to Limit Regulatory Agencies*, 41 BNA OSHR 981 (2011).

13. Stephanie Mencimer, Blocking the Courthouse Door 254 (2006); *Perry Signs Tort Reform Bill Into Law*, Houston Chronicle, July 28, 2011, at B3; John Gramlich, *Judges' Battles Signal a New Era for Retention Elections*, WP, December 3, 2010, at A8.

14. Kuttner, Presidency in Peril, xvii; Alan Brinkley, *The Philosopher President*, Democracy J., Winter 2011, at 80, 86; David Nather, *A Liberal Dose of Disappointment*, Cong. Q. Weekly, September 7, 2009, at 1947 (AWOL quote); Peter Baker, *What Does He Do Now*, NYT Magazine, October 17, 2010, at 40, 42 (Obama quote); Frank Rich, *Why Has He Fallen Short*, N.Y. Rev. of Books, August 19, 2010, at 8 (platonic ideal quote); John M. Broder, *Environmentalists Cooling on Obama*, NYT, February 18, 2010, at A18.

15. William Greider, Come Home, America 24 (2009).

16. Juliette Eilperin, Fight Club Politics 35 (2008); Nather, *Liberal Dose*.

17. Alter, Promise, xiii-xiv.

18. Paul Krugman, The Conscience of a Liberal 5 (2007).

19. Thomas E. Mann & Norman J. Ornstein, *Let's Just Say It: The Republicans Are the Problem*, WP, April 29, 2012, at E1.

INDEX